MARKETING
A Managerial Approach

WILLIAM H. CUNNINGHAM

Professor of Marketing and Associate Dean
Graduate School of Business Administration
University of Texas at Austin

ISABELLA C. M. CUNNINGHAM

Professor of Advertising and Chairman
Department of Advertising
University of Texas at Austin

Published by

S10   **SOUTH-WESTERN PUBLISHING CO.**

CINCINNATI   WEST CHICAGO, ILL.   DALLAS   PELHAM MANOR, N.Y.   PALO ALTO, CALIF.

ISBN: 0-538-19100-7

Library of Congress Catalog Card Number: 80-53818

2 3 4 5 6 7 8 9 D 9 8 7 6 5 4 3 2 1

Printed in the United States of America

PREFACE

Marketing is essential to the operation of any business firm or public service organization. The successful enterprise in today's changing and competitive world is increasingly characterized by its understanding of the many facets of marketing and by its ability to deliver goods and services to the market more efficiently than its competitors.

As a principles book, this text is designed to introduce college students to the basic concepts, practices, and analytic techniques of marketing. The book is comprehensive in scope, contemporary in outlook, and managerial in orientation. Many of the students who will use this book will take up careers in marketing management. Other students will pursue careers in nonbusiness-related fields. It is our hope that this book will help all its readers, regardless of career path, become more informed consumers and more knowledgeable participants in the great drama of economics, politics, and history shaping the world today.

Because of our concern for clarity, we have made this book as concise and readable as possible. We have included many examples and illustrations to show students how abstract theory and principle relate to marketing as it is actually practiced. The text contains a large amount of tabular and graphic material that is designed to present summary data about an industry or topic, or to depict key relationships or otherwise difficult concepts.

Each of the 21 chapters concludes with a list of summary points and a set of questions for discussion and review; each of the eight parts is concluded with at least two cases based on real business problems. Finally, a study guide is available for the student. The study guide, with questions and answers keyed to pages in the text, reinforces the major ideas in each chapter and gives the student an opportunity to apply these ideas in exercises and problems.

Another primary concern in developing the book was to arrange the topics in a straightforward, logical manner. All too often, unfortunately, texts suffer from an almost random sequencing of chapters. Accordingly, this book begins with a discussion of foundation concepts, the marketing environment, and strategic planning. The second part looks at buyer behavior and two important marketing tools — marketing research and market segmentation. The next four parts address, in turn, the basic elements of the marketing mix — product, communication, price, and distribution. Two special topics, international marketing and the marketing of services, are examined in the seventh part. The last part discusses alternative forms of organizing the marketing department, marketing information systems, and the integrating role of the marketing control function. The text concludes with a look at the extension of the marketing concept to nonprofit organizations and the future of marketing.

The authors are grateful to the following individuals for permitting us to use their cases in this book: Terry L. Allen, Kenneth L. Bernhardt, Roger D. Blackwell, Charles G. Burck, Richard H. Buskirk, C. Merle Crawford, William P. Dommermuth, Dan Dorfman, James F. Engel, Norman A. P. Govoni, Thomas V. Greer, Marye Hilger, Jean-Pierre Jeannet, Roger A. Kerin, Thomas C. Kinnear, David T. Kollat, John H. Murphy, Charles H. Patti, Robert A. Peterson, Joel Saegert, William J. Schnick, Jr., James H. Sood, William J. Stanton, Elliot Wendt, and Peter Yates.

In addition, we would like to thank our colleagues and former students at The University of Texas at Austin and St. Edwards University for their assistance on this project. Special thanks must go to Dean George Kozmetsky, Dean Robert Jeffries, Robert A. Peterson, Gaylord Jentz, Robert E. Witt, Brother Cornelius Corcoran, Meryl Klein, and Tricia Reid for their encouragement and valuable insights. Finally, Christopher Swift and Carla Williams provided invaluable assistance. Their effort will always be deeply appreciated.

William H. Cunningham
Isabella C. M. Cunningham

Table of Contents

v

PART 2   Market Identification

PART 3   Product

PART 4   Communication

PART 5   Pricing

PART 6   Distribution

PART 7   Marketing Specialties

1

The Environments of Marketing

Marketing decisions cannot be made in a vacuum. Instead, marketing, in its broadest sense, operates in many environments. These environments can be categorized as either societal or organizational in nature.

In Part 1, you will discover: ways in which marketing decisions affect society; how marketing planning takes place within a firm and how it relates to other business activities; how marketing decisions are constrained by social and legal considerations.

3

Topics discussed in Chapter 1:

1. The place of marketing in the distribution of products from manufacturers to consumers.
2. The role and importance of marketing within the firm.
3. The historical development of marketing as a discipline.
4. The production and marketing concepts.
5. The interactive variables involved in marketing problems, as well as the fact that such problems do not automatically yield correct, absolute solutions.
6. The application of marketing to the nonprofit sectors of the economy.
7. The importance of studying marketing.

This first chapter provides a framework for our study of marketing. You will soon realize that marketing is much more of an art than a science, unlike some disciplines in which each problem, if clearly defined, has a definite answer. However, the study of marketing still requires a rigorous exploration of the important issues in the discipline. This text helps you explore these issues. We begin by looking at the role of marketing in a capitalistic society.

THE ROLE OF MARKETING IN SOCIETY

Some people think of marketing as an evil, wasteful practice and of marketers as manipulators who enjoy taking advantage of innocent consumers in the marketplace. According to this view, the objective of marketing is to induce consumers, by whatever means available, to buy low-quality merchandise at unjustifiably high prices. Some people view marketing, one of the major functions of the firm, as generally divorced from the production function. For some mystical reason, the men and women who manufacture or grow products are often considered more valuable in our society than the merchants who distribute them even though both groups are involved in providing the goods and services we desire. These merchants are thought to add little or no value to the goods they handle; instead they simply tack on their own markups and reap large profits for themselves. Finally, marketing is said to foster materialism, often through advertising, by "making" us purchase products that we don't even want.

Unfortunately, some marketers do use hard-sell tactics to sell inferior goods at high prices. Although this is no defense of such marketers, it is also true that we have a few fast-buck physicians, dishonest politicians, lazy bureaucrats, faithless ministers, and ignorant teachers. The point is that the unscrupulous behavior of a few practitioners does not characterize all those involved in the field, nor should those practitioners be allowed to represent to the public the image of the discipline as a whole. Therefore, let's begin by examining the vital functions that marketing performs for society, as well as for the individual firm, i.e., macromarketing and micromarketing.

Macromarketing

Macromarketing refers to the role of the total marketing system in distributing goods and services to buyers. In a primitive society, most goods used within a household are produced by members of the household. People soon realize that some of their family needs can be met better by exchange than by production. For example, one family may be good at making clothing whereas another is skillful in making baskets. The clothing family may be able to produce two units of clothing and the basket family two baskets faster than either family could make one unit of clothing and one basket. Therefore, if both families produce a surplus of goods beyond their immediate needs, they can exchange merchandise and obtain more total goods with less effort.

This same basic value of exchange exists in our modern world. To make the exchange process more efficient, marketing performs three essential functions.

Information Function. First, when the marketing system operates effectively, it provides an information network that links together producers and consumers. This information is vital if the productive sector of society is to meet the changing needs of the consumer in a cost-efficient manner. For example, cattle ranchers need to know what the market will pay for beef as well as the expected cost of feed before they determine the size of their herds. The more timely and accurate the information flowing through the market, the closer the market comes to being perfectly efficient.

Equalizing and Distributing Function. Second, goods do not flow in a perfectly even pattern from producers to consumers. Nor do consumers purchase an amount of merchandise exactly equal to that which is produced. The function of equating supply and demand falls on the marketing system. Therefore, the marketplace must create ways of storing goods until buyers are willing to accept them. The trade-off is always between the expected increase in the price of the merchandise and the added cost of warehousing the product. As an example, if the entire U.S. corn crop were sold immediately after the fall harvest, the price of corn would fall so low because of the preponderance of supply over demand that the farmer could not earn a living. As a result, much of the crop is withheld from the market for several months through storage in order to prevent the price of corn from dropping. In this case, the added storage costs are more than offset by the price stability obtained.

Centralized Exchange Function. Third, the marketing system provides a centralized exchange through which merchandise is distributed to members of society in return for some form of payment. To illustrate the efficiency of such

FIGURE 1-1   Exchanges in Decentralized and Centralized Markets

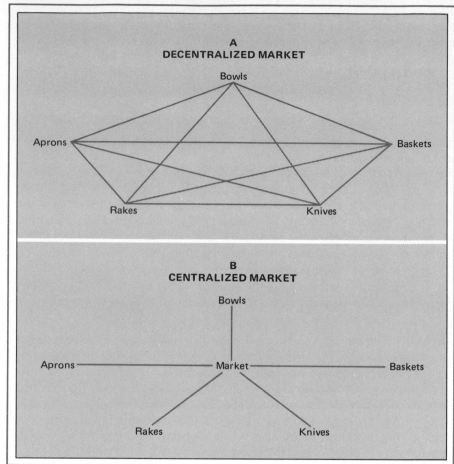

an exchange mechanism, let's look at an economy consisting of five households. Each of these households produces a surplus of a given product needed
by the other families. As shown in Figure 1-1A, ten separate exchanges are
required if there is no central market. However, as illustrated in Figure 1-1B,
only five exchanges are required if this decentralized pattern of exchange is
replaced by a centralized market.

Micromarketing

Whereas the focus of macromarketing is society, the focus of micromarketing is the firm. **Micromarketing** is the process of formulating and implementing a product development, distribution, pricing, and communication strategy
that enables the firm to earn a profit in the marketplace. This process begins
with marketing research, that is, a determination of the needs of potential
buyers. After an appropriate product is developed to satisfy these needs, it is
priced, its virtues are made known through a mix of advertising and personal
selling, and the product is sold to the consumer.

FIGURE 1-2 Basic Marketing Tasks

Demand State	Marketing Task	Formal Name
No Demand	Create Demand	Stimulational Marketing
Latent Demand	Develop Demand	Developmental Marketing
Faltering Demand	Revitalize Demand	Remarketing
Full Demand	Maintain Demand	Maintenance Marketing
Overfull Demand	Reduce Demand	Demarketing

Source: Adapted from Philip Kotler, "The Major Tasks of Marketing Management," *Journal of Marketing* (October, 1973), pp. 42–49, by permission of the American Marketing Association.

The actual role of marketing within the organization is a function of several factors, of which the state of demand for the product is probably the most critical.[1] Figure 1-2 presents five states of demand along with the principal marketing task required by each.

No Demand. The situation of no demand is self-explanatory: no demand whatsoever exists for the item in question. This situation occurs under three conditions: (1) the item is common and has no value, such as empty beer cans or old barbed wire; (2) the item has value but not in the place where it is located, such as burglar alarms in a low crime area or boats in a desert; or (3) the item is unfamiliar and has no value because the market is not aware of its existence or its value, such as any *totally* new product.

The no-demand situation poses an extremely difficult challenge to the marketing executive. The task of converting no demand to positive demand is called **stimulational marketing**. It is usually accomplished by connecting the valueless object with some existing need in society. Empty beer cans, for example, could be given value by promoting their collection and recycling as a partial solution to the national problems of waste disposal and energy consumption. A second approach is to modify the environment to make the product more acceptable — an artificial lake, for example, might be created to stimulate interest in boating. Finally, the marketing executive can make more information available about the product in the hope that the lack of demand is simply the result of a lack of information.

When marketing people practice stimulational marketing, they are often criticized for inducing or coercing people into purchasing unwanted products. However, the real need is not manufactured by the organization; it is merely stimulated or activated. If consumers did not perceive any benefits in the product, they would not buy it. Stimulational marketing has been responsible for the adoption by society of many new life-improving products, practices, and services. Examples include new vaccines to eliminate disease, new child-rearing practices, and better farming machinery. Although marketing may have

---

[1]The following sections on demand are adapted from Philip Kotler, "The Major Tasks of Marketing Management," *Journal of Marketing* (October, 1973), pp. 42–49. Adapted by permission of the American Marketing Association.

little to do with the actual development of these innovations, it has very much to do with moving them out of the research laboratory and into the hands of the ultimate beneficiary, the consumer. Disseminating these technologies, products, or services throughout society — that is, generating demand — is essentially the task of marketing.

Latent Demand. Latent demand exists when there is a significant, unmet need. Here, a large number of people share a need for some sort of product or service that has not yet been developed and made available by the business sector. Over the years, many products have developed in response to latent demand. For example, until a few years ago, there were no low-calorie beers generally available; however, when such beers finally appeared on store shelves, they immediately captured a substantial percentage of the beer market. Apparently, low-calorie beers represented a solution to the problem faced by many a beer drinker: "I enjoy drinking beer but I don't like all the calories."

Latent demand has occasionally been described as a supply problem rather than as a marketing problem. However, it is not simply a supply problem. Rather, latent demand must first be recognized, and then the right product must be produced, priced, promoted, and distributed. If these four vital marketing functions are not performed properly, the product will not be as successful as it might otherwise have been. The process of converting latent demand into actual demand is called **developmental marketing**.

Relatively little social criticism has been directed at developmental marketing, because it is not a process of creating demand, but of finding the demand and then providing the necessary product or service. In this sense, the buyer and seller are in perfect harmony.

Faltering Demand. The term faltering demand describes the situation in which the demand for a product has fallen off. An example is rail passenger service in the United States. In the case of faltering demand, the challenge is to remarket the product or service. **Remarketing** usually involves a complete reexamination of the market to be served, the product's distinguishing features, and its marketing strategy.

In remarketing a product, the product itself should be examined and any problems should be identified and corrected before the firm attempts to launch a new promotional campaign. For instance, it would have been a mistake for Amtrak to promote rail travel without first replacing old equipment and repairing worn rail beds. If a promotional campaign had been undertaken without a corresponding program of equipment modernization, some people might have been lured to an Amtrak train once, but not a second time. The important point is that cosmetic marketing involves a new image for an old product, whereas remarketing involves a reconsideration of all aspects of the product prior to any promotional effort.

Full Demand. In many ways, full demand is the ideal state — current demand is equal to the firm's ability to supply the desired product. Many products have achieved full demand at one time or another. Unfortunately, full demand is subject to two forces that can knock the firm out of an equilibrium position. First, the needs and preferences of the market may change. A few years ago, the public wanted large automobiles, which were not particularly fuel efficient; today, these cars are difficult, if not impossible, to sell. In the same manner, slide rules became obsolete when electronic calculators were developed. Second, in a free enterprise economy, successful products typically attract competition. Therefore, a firm marketing a successful new product can expect to find its competitors introducing a similar product.

When full demand exists, the job of the marketing executive is appropriately called **maintenance marketing**. The marketing executive must ensure that the product's marketing strategy is carried out as efficiently as possible. In addition, the market is monitored continually to detect any changes in buyer preferences or the presence of any new competitors.

Overfull Demand. When demand is significantly greater than supply, the product is said to suffer from overfull demand. If the firm does not want to increase its productive capacity to meet this demand, it must reduce demand by **demarketing** the product. Demarketing can either be general or selective. In the case of **general demarketing**, the firm attempts to reduce overall demand for the product. In the wake of the 1973 oil embargo, the oil companies faced an excess demand situation. They attempted to reduce demand for petroleum fuel products, especially gasoline, by changing the theme of their advertisements. Rather than promoting unnecessary driving, the new advertisements attempted to enhance corporate image and to encourage fuel efficiency and automobile safety.

In contrast to general demarketing, the task of **selective demarketing** is to limit the demand of only certain segments (portions) of the market. Selective demarketing is typically implemented when one particular market segment is not profitable. A mail-order wholesaler imposing a handling surcharge to discourage small orders is an example of a firm practicing selective demarketing.

Lastly, chronic overpopularity on the part of the seller can result in overfull demand. Examples include the John F. Kennedy Center for Performing Arts in Washington, D.C., which has larger crowds than it can handle, and the tourist resorts in Hawaii, which sometimes attract so many people that it is difficult to see the beach!

Demarketing is really marketing in reverse. It usually involves a combination of price hikes, quality or service reductions, and promotional changes. The consumers who are the targets of the demarketing campaign may feel they are being discriminated against — demarketing may be necessary but it generally is not popular.

IMPORTANCE OF MARKETING TO THE FIRM

The firm is a classic example of a system. As shown in Figure 1-3, the firm is made up of a set of interconnected parts. If any of these parts, or functions, fails to perform effectively, the business will not be able to accomplish its objectives. If the finance department cannot raise money for new product development, the organization will not remain competitive in the future. Similarly, if the personnel department does not recruit the best talent available, the firm will suffer as its executives retire and are replaced by less capable individuals.

FIGURE 1-3   The Firm as a System

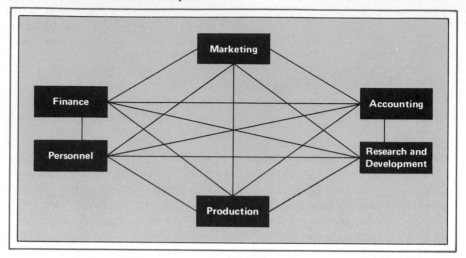

Is marketing any more important than the other components of the system? The answer would seem to be a very guarded yes. Obviously, all parts of the system are important in that they must all work together if the total system is to function smoothly. However, if the business is not able to sell or service its products, it will face immediate financial problems that could lead to bankruptcy. Very few organizations can survive more than a few months if sales stop altogether. In this sense, all other components of the enterprise serve as facilitating activities to the marketing department. If the organization has an excellent accounting department but cannot sell its products, it will simply "know" that it is bankrupt — small consolation for its shareholders. In the same way, if the business produces a large quantity of products that do not sell, it will have to build more warehouses to hold the excess stock.

There are two reasons why we give a guarded "yes" to the question above. First, as we stated above, each component is important — if any one component fails, the firm suffers. Second, some businesses require more marketing expertise than others. In retailing, executives spend most of their time dealing with marketing problems. The same situation exists for consumer-product firms such as General Foods and Procter & Gamble. In contrast, executives for a firm such as the Electric Boat Company, which builds nuclear submarines, spend most of their time on research and construction. The chief executive officer is most likely to be an engineer or a research scientist. However, it is still true that if the Electric Boat Company fails to obtain a sufficient number of contracts, which is the function of the marketing department, its great technical expertise will not likely prevent it from going out of business.

THE HISTORICAL DEVELOPMENT OF MARKETING THOUGHT

Marketing is a very old profession. Even before the Middle Ages, men and women were involved in purchasing products for eventual resale. These traders were well aware that if they did not procure the right merchandise, price it properly, and promote it effectively through word-of-mouth communication, they would not be able to make a profit. However, while marketing has been practiced for many years, the systematic study of marketing began only in the early 1900s. Numerous approaches to the study of marketing have developed over the years. Among the more popular are the commodity, institutional, and functional approaches.

Commodity Approach

The **commodity approach** to marketing involves the study of a vertical chain of distribution beginning with the producer and ending with the final consumer. Specifically, the movement of a product in the distribution channel is traced in order to locate points where costs can be reduced and efficiency increased. This technique was first employed in the mid-1910s in the apple, cotton, and wood industries.

The severe economic depression that gripped agriculture in the U.S. for most of the period from 1870 to 1928 was the primary impetus behind the development of the commodity approach. As Figure 1-4 indicates, in only five years during the period 1910 to 1927 did U.S. farmers receive more for the products they produced than they paid for the goods they purchased. A great many farmers reacted to their economic plight by leaving agriculture.

The farmers who remained in agriculture were forced to find new ways to cut costs and increase revenues. Many believed that their financial difficulties stemmed from inefficient marketing practices. In particular, if the distribution channel could be made more efficient and the profits earned by the rest of the channel returned to the farmers, then, they believed, their economic problems would be solved. As a result, farm cooperatives sprang up across the country and grew rapidly during the early 1900s. These cooperatives sponsored numerous commodity studies in order to find out how they could distribute their

FIGURE 1-4   Ratio of Prices Received to Prices Paid

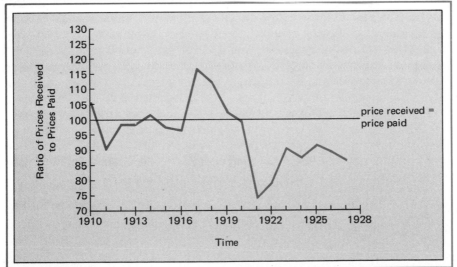

Source: Herbert Hoover, *Report of the Committee on Recent Economic Changes* (New York: McGraw-Hill Book Company, 1929).

members' products more efficiently. In addition, the newly created United States Department of Agriculture undertook a large number of commodity studies in order to determine how to end the farm depression. Although commodities studies are still performed in the United States, they are limited to agricultural marketing because their results cannot be generalized.

Institutional Approach

The **institutional approach** is concerned with the study of specific marketing institutions. Whereas the commodity approach investigates an entire vertical channel, the institutional approach examines various types of organizations, such as retailers and wholesalers. Most of the texts in this area describe the functions of the institutions and how they can be performed most efficiently.

The institutional approach evolved in response to the many new types of marketing institutions that appeared during the late 1800s and early 1900s. Marketing practitioners wanted to know more about the efficient operation of their businesses; marketing educators realized the importance of examining these new institutions in order to provide the business community with a body of knowledge applicable to a changing world.

The primary reason for the development of these new marketing institutions was the rapid urbanization of the U.S. When the country was primarily an agrarian society, most products were either grown on the farm or purchased from general stores. However, as people left the farm and moved to the city, they became a part of a new industrial world. Their factory jobs frequently enabled them to earn more money than they had been able to make on the farm. The new city residents were able to purchase products at a variety of retail institutions depending on their tastes and preferences. This influx of urban residents with excess income made it possible for new retail outlets to prosper.

A second force behind the institutional approach was the tremendous proliferation of new products during the early 1900s. Automobiles, radios, electrical appliances, and many other items appeared on the market for the first time during this period, and their sales skyrocketed. For example, sales of electrical appliances jumped from $178,250,000 in 1922 to $361,404,000 in 1927; sales of automobiles also nearly doubled during the same five-year period.[2] It is unclear whether the growth in the sales of these new items caused habits to change or whether such sales merely reflected a change in the values of society. However, at the least, it can be said that many of these products required new marketing institutions to sell them. The automobile industry, for example, was one of the first businesses to employ a nationwide franchising network to sell its products.[3]

The institutional approach to the study of marketing is still in use today. However, it tends to suffer from the same limitation as the commodity approach — that is, the results of institutional research cannot be generalized. Although institutional research can teach us a great deal about supermarket

[2]Herbert Hoover, *Report of the Committee on Recent Economic Changes* (New York: McGraw-Hill Book Company, 1929), p. 593.
[3]See Chapter 15 for a discussion of franchising.

management, the same research is not very useful to the manager of a department store. As a result, the discipline of marketing has largely moved away from the institutional approach.

Functional Approach

The functional approach to marketing evolved in at least two stages — classical and managerial. Both resulted from the failure of previous approaches.

Classical Functionalism. Classical functionalism was based on the realization that the marketplace had become so complex, with its myriad products and institutions, that a new approach to marketing was necessary in order to formulate general principles applicable to all marketing systems. The functionalists generally recognized eight functions of marketing, i.e., eight "major activities that must be performed in the marketing of all products."[4] These functions are: buying, selling, transporting, storing, standardizing and grading, financing, risk bearing, and collecting and disseminating marketing information.

The major shortcoming of classical functionalism is its failure to integrate the various marketing functions; each function is treated as if it is independent of the others. In this sense, texts embracing this approach appear to be collections of individual monographs, each dealing with a separate activity. In *Modern Sales Management*, George Frederick made an early attempt to deal with this problem.[5] The first 23 chapters of his 1919 text discussed the functions of the sales manager. The last chapter was a 12-page case which attempted to draw the descriptive generalizations into a managerial context. Although a noble effort, the text fell short of providing an integrated approach to sales management.

Managerial Marketing. Fundamental to managerial marketing is the notion that a successful marketing program consists of a set of well-integrated components. Although each component must be studied individually, they must also be coordinated if the firm is to achieve its objectives. In the first managerial marketing text, *Planned Marketing*, published in 1929, Virgil Reed describes five major components of the marketing plan: the company, the product, the market, distribution, and advertising. According to Reed, each element of the plan should be thought of as a gear in a machine:

> . . .each of the gears may be perfect as a separate unit, the machine may remain entirely useless or ineffective if they are not carefully and accurately enmeshed, synchronized and lubricated, with the proper driving force applied. This meshing, timing, lubrication and application of force makes the successful marketing plan.[6]

Over the years, Reed's approach has been modified and updated to fit the modern world. However, the notion that the marketing plan integrates the many sub-plans, or functions, remains essential to the managerial marketing approach. As a historical aside, Reed's text was not immediately recognized as

---

[4]Theodore N. Beckman and William R. Davidson, *Marketing* (8th ed.; New York: The Ronald Press Company, 1967), p. 423.

[5]J. George Frederick, *Modern Sales Management* (New York: D. Appleton and Company, 1919).

[6]Virgil D. Reed, *Planned Marketing* (New York: The Ronald Press Company, 1929), p. 43.

an important new effort, perhaps as a result of two factors. First, many people in the press blamed marketing for the Great Depression of 1930. The effect of this criticism was to make the study of marketing rather unpopular. Second, from the late 1930s through 1945, most of the U.S.'s attention was directed to World War II. By the time the war was over, Reed's text was 15 years old. Delayed, too, was the development of the marketing concept, the business philosophy basis of Reed's text.

THE MARKETING CONCEPT

The **marketing concept** is a philosophy of management for the entire enterprise. It was developed by Ralph Coordiner, the president of General Electric, in the early 1950s. Coordiner, a noted management scientist, had become convinced that a new philosophy of business was needed to propel General Electric into the second half of the century. The marketing concept has since been adopted by both large and small companies, but many firms still do not fully appreciate the importance of the idea. Before we examine the marketing concept, we will look at its predecessor — production orientation.

Production Orientation

The distinguishing feature of the **production orientation** is its overriding concern with production efficiency. The emphasis on maximizing output from a given level of input is largely a result of the work of Frederick W. Taylor. Taylor's original work was quite practical — for example, determining the optimum size for a coal shovel or how much a load of pig iron should weigh in order to avoid exhausting a laborer before the ten-hour workday was finished. Out of this work emerged a number of studies about the best way to perform many different production tasks and processes.[7]

The Role of the Sales Department. During the early days of the production orientation (1900–1930), selling the product was not considered an important problem. The economies of mass production along with the increasing affluence of the urban population made it quite easy for many firms to sell almost anything they produced. As a result, sales departments tended to be relatively small and unimportant in the overall structure of the organization. Generally speaking, business firms undertook very little research to determine what products the customer wanted or how satisfied the customer was with the products already available.

The Great Depression provided the right conditions for a reexamination of the value of the production orientation. The combination of excess production capacity and a lack of consumer and investor confidence caused many firms to adopt aggressive sales tactics in order to sell their products. An executive for Pillsbury summed up the sales strategy of the firm during this period as follows:

---

[7]William L. Dejon, *Principles of Management: Text and Cases* (Menlo Park, Calif.: The Benjamin/Cummings Publishing Company, Inc., 1978), p. 6.

We are a flour-milling company, manufacturing a number of products for the consumer market. We must have a first-rate sales organization which can dispose of all the products we can make at a favorable price. We must back up this sales force with consumer advertising and market intelligence. We want our salesmen and our dealers to have all the tools they need for moving the output of our plants to the consumer.[8]

Note the emphasis on selling and the customer. The statement, however, represents not so much a change of philosophy as it does a concern with simply giving more resources to the sales department so that it will be more successful in "unloading" the firm's products. Here, the customer is of interest primarily from the perspective of determining what sales tools will be most effective in convincing him or her to purchase a Pillsbury product. The real needs of the customer are left totally unattended.

The Chelsea Example.[9] Even well-managed businesses that have long ago adopted the marketing concept can slip occasionally into a product orientation and lose track of market conditions. In 1978 Anheuser-Busch, one of the best-managed firms in the United States, test marketed a new soft drink called Chelsea. The product was a blend of lemon, lime, apple, ginger, and other natural ingredients. As a result of chemical interaction among the ingredients, the product also contained a small amount of alcohol, less than one half of one percent. It resembled beer because of its yellow color, foam head, and packaging. Anheuser-Busch targeted the product at the adult soft-drink beverage market.

Initial sales of the product were encouraging. Unfortunately for Anheuser-Busch, many people felt that the firm's real objective in marketing Chelsea was to introduce young people to beer. Such groups as the Virginia Nurses Association, the Sacramento Parents-Teachers Association, and the *Washington Star* criticized Anheuser-Busch in this regard. In addition, a member of the Senate subcommittee on alcoholism threatened to press for action to ban the product, while Secretary of Health, Education, and Welfare Joseph Califano summed up many people's feelings when he said:

> There must be better things the alcohol industry can do with its money than directing advertising campaigns at the teen and subteen in this country.[10]

It appears that Anheuser-Busch did adequately research the needs of the intended consumer — a market did exist for an adult soft drink and Chelsea apparently met that need. However, the firm did not anticipate the negative reaction of the public at large, specifically the allegation that Chelsea was a not-so-subtle way of developing the future beer-drinking market. After all, the product looked like beer, was developed and distributed by a major brewer, contained alcohol, and was being purchased by children. As a result of the controversy, Anheuser-Busch suspended test marketing of Chelsea. The com-

---

[8]Robert J. Keith, "The Marketing Revolution," *Journal of Marketing* (January, 1960), p. 37.

[9]This example is adapted from "Nurses Foaming Over Chelsea," *Advertising Age* (October 23, 1978), p. 8; "A-B Withdraws Chelsea Ads," *Advertising Age* (October 30, 1978), p. 2; and "Uproar Over Chelsea: Concern Over Advertising," *Beverage Industry* (December 8, 1978), p. 5.

[10]"Nurses Foaming Over Chelsea," *Advertising Age* (October 23, 1978), p. 8.

pany's chances of initially marketing the product successfully would have been improved if it had been slightly less concerned with the product and more concerned with the potential reaction of the public.

The New Concept

The marketing concept is more complex than the production orientation. As Figure 1-5 shows, the production orientation can be broken down into three steps — raise money, produce a product, sell the product. By contrast, under the marketing concept the firm begins with market needs and then raises money, produces a product to meet the needs, and markets it. Note that we said *markets* the product rather than *sells* the product. The difference between the two is that marketing entails an integrated plan encompassing distribution and communications, as well as sales. Finally, a firm practicing the marketing concept continually monitors the market to determine not only how well the product is selling but also whether it is really what the consumer wants. This effort enables the firm to estimate the long-term success of the product and to forecast and be ready to produce the products that will be needed in the future.

In addition to its complexity, the marketing concept demands more of management's time. As a result, it usually involves greater expense than the production orientation. However, if the firm is to adapt to future consumer needs and thereby generate long-term profits, the marketing concept is a virtual necessity, despite slightly higher costs.

Several major principles are involved in the marketing concept.

FIGURE 1-5 Comparison of the Production and Marketing Concepts

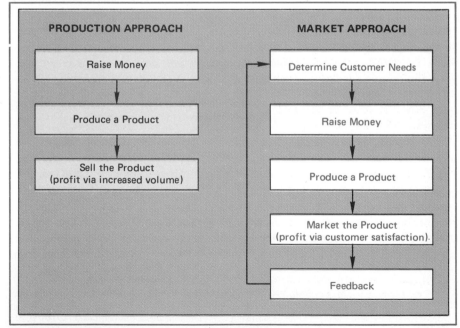

Source: Adapted from Philip Kotler, *Marketing Management: Analysis, Planning, and Control* (3d ed.; Englewood Cliffs, N.J.: Prentice-Hall, Inc., 1976), p. 15.

Customer Satisfaction. The firm must be dedicated to satisfying customer needs. If it is interested only in maximizing profit, it will not prosper in the long run. A statement by Henry Ford illustrates the importance of satisfying customer needs:

> Our policy is to reduce the price, extend the operations, and improve the article. You will notice that the reduction of price comes first. We have never considered any costs as fixed. Therefore, we first reduce the price to the point where we believe more sales will result. Then we go ahead and try to make the prices. We do not bother about the costs. The new price forces the costs down. The more usual way is to take the costs and then determine the price; and although that method may be scientific in the narrow sense, it is not scientific in the broad sense, because what earthly use is it to know the cost if it tells you that you cannot manufacture at a price at which the article can be sold? But more to the point is the fact that, although one may calculate what a cost is, and of course all of our costs are carefully calculated, no one knows what a cost ought to be.[11]

Although Henry Ford was known as a great production genius, he was also a very sound marketing executive. Ford realized that what the U.S. wanted in the early 1900s was inexpensive automobile transportation. His procedure was first to determine the price that the market was willing to pay for a car and then to design a car that could be manufactured and sold at that price. The result was a standard, mass-produced automobile with few, if any, options. From 1909 to 1926 the Ford Motor Company sold more than half of all cars produced in the United States. During this period the price of the Model-T fell from $850 to $263.

Broad Corporate Definition. The implementation of the marketing concept usually is based on a broad definition of the firm's mission. This definition is critical if the firm is to adjust to the changing needs of society. Charles Revson, past-president of Revlon, Inc., expressed the Revlon mission when he was asked what his firm produced. He responded, "In the factory we make cosmetics, in the drugstore we sell hope."[12]

Figure 1-6 lists four U.S. companies that modified their mission from a rather narrow orientation to a broad market orientation. As an illustration, a few years ago most of the major oil companies were only in the petroleum business. Recently, however, as it has become apparent that the world supply of oil is rapidly declining, they have moved into the energy business. Accordingly, most major oil companies now are also heavily invested in coal, atomic energy, and solar energy. As other new ways of generating energy become available, the "energy" companies can be expected to move into these areas as well. This emphasis on energy rather than simply on oil will enable the oil companies to change as society changes, to prevent overreliance on a single type of energy source, and to remain in business even after the last well has run dry.

---

[11]Henry Ford, *My Life and Work* (New York: Doubleday, Page & Company, 1923), pp. 146–147.

[12]Philip Kotler, *Marketing Management: Analysis, Planning, and Control* (3d ed.; Englewood Cliffs, N.J.: Prentice-Hall, Inc., 1976), p. 183.

FIGURE 1-6 Comparison of Product and Market Definitions

Company	Product Definition	Market Definition
Exxon Corporation	Oil	Energy
American Telephone & Telegraph Co. (AT&T)	Telephones	Communications
International Business Machines Corp. (IBM)	Computers	Problem Solving
Boeing Co.	Airplanes	High-Speed Transportation

Belief in Competitive Substitutes. The firm adopting the marketing concept understands that even its most successful product will some day be obsolete. Unfortunately, many firms with products generating substantial profits year after year are lulled into the belief that their products will never become obsolete. These firms eventually face a rude awakening when their products are displaced from the market.

Figure 1-7 lists six items that became obsolete virtually overnight. Many thousands of products, such as black-and-white televisions, have disappeared more slowly from the market. The firm with a marketing orientation anticipates this problem; the constant monitoring of changing consumer needs means that it, not one of its competitors, will be the firm to develop the new product making the old product obsolete. In this way, the firm will be able to generate profits into the future.

Buyer Research. Embracing the marketing concept usually means investing a significant amount of money to determine what types of products the market really wants. At times, the opinions of a few prominent experts may be useful, but usually it will also be necessary to survey the final users of the product. In this way, the firm can learn not only what type of products are demanded, but also what forms of promotion will be most effective in communicating the

FIGURE 1-7 Examples of Obsolete Products and Their Replacements

Market	Old Product	New Product
Railroad	Steam Locomotives	Locomotives
Cities	Trolley Cars	Buses
Education and Engineering	Slide Rules	Slide Rule Calculators
Accounting	Adding Machines	Printing Calculators
Data Processing	Punch Card Systems	Computers
Private Homes	Wood Stoves	Electric Stoves

product's message to the public. Part 2 examines the problems and techniques of diagnosing and predicting consumer behavior.

Top Management Acceptance. The chief executive officer (CEO) of the firm does not have to be a marketing person, but he or she must understand the importance of marketing to the organization. Regardless of the size of a business, the CEO is responsible for setting the tone of its operations; if this person does not understand the importance of customer needs and instead simply focuses on the product, it will be very difficult to implement the marketing concept.

Profit, Not Sales. If a firm cannot make a profit, the question of whether it is satisfying a customer or societal need is immaterial since the firm will not be in business for long. In this sense, profit is not so much an objective as it is a constraint. In short, the firm must first survive. Also, in evaluating a business, it is not how many sales a product generates but how much profit it contributes to the enterprise (i.e., increased sales do not assure increased profits). As a result, the firm may be forced to abandon a product that contributes to overall sales but not to profits.

A few years ago, Reginald Jones, the president of General Electric, announced that GE would no longer consider any of its traditional businesses as sacred; each would be examined to determine whether it contributed to company profits. As a result, General Electric is currently studying the possibility of leaving the nuclear power business. General Electric claims that the complex governmental licensing and regulatory procedures have become so costly that the company is having a difficult time making any profit at all on its nuclear equipment.

CHARACTERISTICS OF MARKETING PROBLEMS

The job of the marketing executive is difficult because so many variables must be considered in any marketing decision. Moreover, there is never an absolutely correct solution to a marketing problem.

Large Number of Variables

The complexity of marketing decisions is very difficult for many people to understand. Figure 1-8 illustrates the major forces influencing the development of the firm's marketing strategy. The uncontrollable environmental variables include, among others, economic factors, demographic shifts, legal and political considerations, and the environmental movement. They are uncontrollable in the sense that the marketing executive, although influenced by these variables, has no control over them. To illustrate, an economic recession has an effect on how the firm sells its product and on how many it sells, but the marketing executive, alone, cannot modify the state of the economy. Uncontrollable variables are analyzed in some detail in Chapter 2.

The second ring in Figure 1-8 denotes the people with whom the marketing executive must work. Marketing plans rest on predictions of how customers

FIGURE 1-8   Forces Influencing a Firm's Marketing Strategy

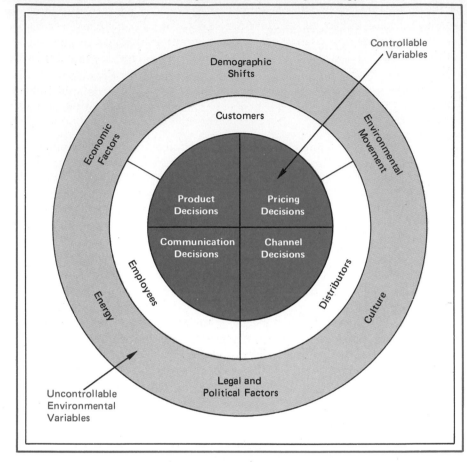

will behave. However, the buying public in general and the firm's customers in particular are very fickle; the more we study human behavior, the less we really understand it. A few years ago, a friend ordered a Chevrolet Corvette. Owing to factory backlogs, the car could not be delivered for four months. After waiting three months, the buyer became disenchanted and purchased a Vega, a product radically different from the Corvette in terms of price, power, image, fuel efficiency, and design. Why the change? There are many plausible explanations. The intent of the example, however, is simply to illustrate the notorious inconsistency, unpredictability, and thus the uncontrollability of consumer behavior.

The marketing executive must also work with distributors. Distributors are independent business people who cooperate with the manufacturer as long as it is in their best interests to do so. For example, a retailer, deciding that a product is not being marketed properly by the supplier, may stop selling the product altogether or create a "local" promotion strategy for the product.

Finally, the marketing executive must deal with the employees of the marketing department. These individuals, especially those involved in advertising and personal selling, tend to be more outgoing, self-confident, aggressive, and resilient than others in the organization. Good salespeople, for example, view themselves as independent business people, and not really as employees of the firm. This independent attitude makes salespeople slightly more difficult to manage. These employee variables are said to be uncontrollable not in the sense that the people themselves are uncontrollable or that they cannot be fired, but rather in the sense that marketing employees tend to share a number of personality traits.

With an understanding of the two outside circles in Figure 1-8, the marketing executive is ready to design a marketing strategy and to make decisions concerning product, price, communications, and channels of distribution. The following statement by two marketing analysts reflects the complexity of the process:

> . . .imagine that the decision maker's strategy includes five possible product designs, five prices, five patterns of distribution, and five ways of communicating with the customer. This is a total of 625 strategies. If there are four competitors, it is not unreasonable to assume that each of the competitors had 625 strategies available. Presuming that there are five states of nature, then the number of different conditions that can prevail is 476,837,158,203,125. Ironically, the only ludicrous thing about this number is that it is far too small to describe the actual situation.[13]

No Right Answer

One of the most frustrating things about marketing problems is that they usually do not have one and only one solution. Two equally capable individuals may analyze a problem and arrive at significantly different solutions. Both solutions might generate profits for the firm or both might prove to be disasters.

Edwin Land, the holder of 524 U.S. patents and founder of the Polaroid Corporation, resigned as the firm's chief executive officer in 1980 largely as a result of the failure of his prized invention, Polavision instant home movies.[14] The corporation was forced to take a $68 million write-down on its Polavision inventory in late 1979. While several of Polaroid's key executives had opposed Polavision, Land insisted that it be brought to market. According to Land, new inventions create their own success and market research is a waste of money. This philosophy had worked well for Land and Polaroid on such previous inventions as the SX-70 pocket-sized automatic camera. Unfortunately, in the case of Polavision, the picture quality was often poor and the product itself was quite expensive — $675 for the camera and viewer, plus $9.95 for the two-minute, 40-second film. In addition, while almost all families have a snapshot camera, only one in four have a movie camera. Finally, many people who might have purchased Polavision decided that they would prefer to purchase a videotape system that could be used with their television sets.

There is no single reason why Polavision failed. Land had many other products become successful even though his executives had believed that there were no markets for them. However, in this case the market was not willing to accept the great inventor's product. The message of Polavision is clear — marketing problems are extremely complex and not easily solved.

---

[13]David W. Miller and Martin K. Starr, *Executive Decisions and Operations Research* (Englewood Cliffs, N.J.: Prentice-Hall, Inc., 1960), p. 172, in Harper W. Boyd and William Massy, *Marketing Management* (New York: Harcourt Brace Jovanovich, Inc., 1972), pp. 8–9.

[14]"Polaroid's Land Steps Down," *Time* (March 17, 1980), p. 68.

EXTENDING THE MARKETING CONCEPT

Although marketing is most frequently viewed as a business activity, non-profit organizations must also sell a product or service if they are to survive. Does marketing have anything to offer them?

Marketing and the Nonprofit Organization

Marketing clearly has moved beyond simply selling toothpaste, vacuum cleaners, and reinforced steel. The first step in this new direction may have taken place in the 1960 presidential campaign when John F. Kennedy used marketing research (polling) extensively. As a result, when Kennedy traveled from state to state, he was able to address the issues that were most important to each group of citizens. Marketing research is now a standard practice of all political candidates running for major offices. Nonprofit organizations using marketing extensively now include museums and art galleries, libraries, police departments, public and private universities, and churches.[15]

Simply having the capability to do something "good" or "beautiful" for society is not enough. The product or service of the organization must also be made readily available. It must be professional and of appropriate quality, and it must satisfy a societal need. Otherwise the product will simply be ignored. Once the director of a nonprofit organization realizes and accepts these facts, a marketing plan for the product or service can then be developed. Such a plan may call for modification of the product, or the manner in which it is delivered, in order to increase public demand for it. Alternatively, the market for the product may need to be reexamined to determine whether it consists of homogeneous consumers or a set of submarkets, each characterized by a different type of consumer. In the case of submarkets, the director of the nonprofit organization may have to consider marketing several products or services rather than just one. In addition, a separate communications strategy for each submarket may be necessary. In this respect, the director, realizing that the public must be made aware of the offerings of the organization, may even be required to use contests, discount coupons, and other promotional gimmicks. In short, a nonprofit organization, just like a commercial firm, must market its product in order to survive. Let's look at an example of a nonprofit organization involved in marketing a product.

The Brooklyn Academy of Music

The Brooklyn Academy of Music (BAM) was founded in 1859 as a cultural center for the performance of ballet and theatre.[16] BAM has four theatres ranging in seating capacity from 200 to 2,200. Although it prospered in the 19th and early 20th centuries, BAM fell on hard times until it began to actively market its performances. BAM now recognizes that if it is to survive, it must

---

[15]For more information see Philip Kotler and Sidney J. Levy, "Broadening the Concept of Marketing," *Journal of Marketing* (January, 1969), pp. 10–15, and Philip Kotler, "A Generic Concept of Marketing," *Journal of Marketing* (April, 1972), pp. 46–54.

[16]This section is based on Robert Ricklefs, "A Cultural Institution Succeeds by Marketing Its Wares Aggressively," *The Wall Street Journal*, January 23, 1979, pp. 1, 18.

Unfortunately, most colleges and universities have not been good marketers. Like most nonprofit institutions, they do not understand marketing. Many college administrators equate marketing with hard-sell, high-pressure techniques. To further complicate matters, many of them lack a management background and tend to believe that it is "against the rules" to evaluate a college in the same way that one would evaluate a business.

Why Is This Problem Important to You? Hopefully you feel a sense of loyalty to your college or university. For your college to provide a high-quality education in years to come, it must be in a position to attract good students and sufficient financial resources to pay the ever-increasing costs of higher education. Bear in mind that the value of your degree depends on the continued reputation of your school. If your school prospers, your degree will be held in high esteem; if the reputation of your school falters, people will quickly forget that when you attended the school it really was a good college.

What Can Be Done? When you have finished reading this text, you should be able to answer this question yourself. For now, however, we will respond by saying that colleges and universitities should adopt the marketing concept. An educational institution exists to serve the needs of society, not merely to perpetuate itself. Thus, the school may have to take unpopular actions such as eliminating low enrollment courses or programs. Also, college administrators should carefully determine what market or markets their institution serves, and the differing needs of each market. Continuing education programs for skilled workers, for example, are much different than advanced management programs for top executives. Programs for undergraduate students differ significantly from those for graduate-level students. In the long run, the school may not be able to serve all of the groups that it formerly did.

Finally, college administrators should develop marketing plans utilizing mass communication — such as brochures and radio commercials — as well as personal selling by students, alumni, faculty, and administrators. The purpose of the plan should be to convince talented students to attend the school and to persuade society to support the school financially. Although it will not be easy to market colleges and universities, administrators must begin working on this problem now!

Marketing & You

divide its market and actively promote to each submarket. Some of BAM's most recent promotional activities include:

- BAM theatre fans received a "Theatre-Lovers $10 Dance Sale" brochure. The promotion described BAM drama subscribers as "among the most adventuresome people in town." A similar promotion for the "Music-Lovers $10 Dance Sale" was mailed shortly afterward. Both promotions were successful.
- BAM schedules events of direct interest to minorities. These events are promoted by an individual whose full-time job is to deal with black and Hispanic social and church groups.
- In bad weather, ticket holders are permitted to reschedule their playgoing. The unused seats are sold to students at reduced prices.
- A computer file is maintained on all ticket purchasers so that promotional material can be sent directly to individuals who enjoy specific types of events.
- To promote its African dance series, BAM held a street fair with African crafts and elephant rides for children.
- To promote ballet sales, BAM held a "dance-lovers" sweepstakes with a trip to London as first prize.

BAM is just one example of the effective use of marketing by nonprofit organizations. While such organizations have long recognized the importance of personnel management, accounting, and other business functions, marketing has somehow been ignored. These organizations are now beginning to recognize the benefits of understanding the marketing function.

THE NEED TO STUDY MARKETING

Marketing is worthy of study for a variety of reasons. First, marketing adds value to the products offered by the economic system. Second, many people spend much of their professional life in marketing careers. Third, as consumers, we all spend a great deal of time interacting with the marketplace.

Value Added by Marketing

The value added by marketing to the products that we purchase is almost staggering. In addition to the contribution by such distribution industries as wholesaling, retailing, and advertising, many nondistribution industries such as agriculture and mining must perform the marketing activities of buying, promoting, transporting, and storing merchandise or raw materials. The classic study by Reavis Cox indicates that 45.3 percent of the cost of consumer products goes to distribution.[17] With the recent growth in the service industry, it is likely that this percentage has risen. As Table 1-1 shows, the value added by distribution varies significantly depending on the specific industry. If in any way we can make our distribution system more efficient, millions and even billions of dollars would be made available for other uses.

---

[17]Reavis Cox, Charles Goodman, and Thomas C. Fichandler, *Distribution in a High-Level Economy* (Englewood Cliffs, N.J.: Prentice-Hall, Inc., 1965), p. 155.

TABLE 1-1 Market Value Added by Distribution and Nondistribution Activities

				Market Value Added by:		
	Total (Millions)	Nondistribution Activities (Millions)	Distribution Activities (Millions)	Total (Percent)	Nondistribution Activities (Percent)	Distribution Activities (Percent)
Total	$95,682	$54,941	$40,741	100.0	57.4	42.6
Nondistribution industries	65,899	54,941	10,958	100.0	83.4	16.6
Agriculture, forestry, fisheries	16,564	14,759	1,805	100.0	89.1	10.9
Mining	3,409	3,133	276	100.0	91.9	8.1
Manufacturing	38,573	30,431	8,142	100.0	78.9	21.1
Public utilities	1,456					
Services	5,744	6,618	735	100.0	90.0	10.0
Miscellaneous	153					
Distribution industries	29,783	—	29,783	100.0	—	100.0
Transportation and storage:						
Railroads	2,706	—	2,706	100.0	—	100.0
Trucking	1,395	—	1,395	100.0	—	100.0
Overseas transportation	223	—	223	100.0	—	100.0
Other water transportation	256	—	256	100.0	—	100.0
Air transportation	26	—	26	100.0	—	100.0
Pipeline transportation	153	—	153	100.0	—	100.0
Warehousing and storage	145	—	145	100.0	—	100.0
Wholesale trade	6,782	—	6,782	100.0	—	100.0
Retail trade	16,581	—	16,581	100.0	—	100.0
Advertising	1,516	—	1,516	100.0	—	100.0
Total, excluding public utilities, services, and miscellaneous	88,329	48,323	40,006	100.0	54.7	45.3

Source: Reavis Cox, Charles Goodman, and Thomas C. Fichandler, *Distribution in a High-Level Economy* (Englewood Cliffs, N.J.: Prentice-Hall, Inc., 1965), p. 145.

Careers in Marketing

Although it is difficult to estimate, roughly 25 percent of the people in the United States make a living performing marketing activities. This figure represents more than a three-fold increase since 1870. Many people begin their marketing career in sales-related positions; others start in product planning, marketing research, advertising, or distribution. Each of these subfunctions of marketing has career paths to marketing management positions as well as to top corporate management positions. There is a good chance that you already have some marketing-related experience — perhaps behind a fast-food counter, on a newspaper route, or as a sales clerk. In addition, you may very well be interviewing for a marketing career position within the next two or three years.

Daily Interaction

Because as consumers we interact daily with the marketplace, it is important to understand both the market system and what individual firms are trying to accomplish. For example, once a new product has been introduced to the market, is its price likely to go up, down, or stay the same over its life? Are products that are heavily promoted more or less expensive than those that receive little or no advertising? If you buy a product and change your mind about it, do you have any recourse? By exploring these and many other questions in the chapters to come, it is hoped that you will become a more informed and intelligent consumer.

A PREVIEW OF THE TEXT

The remaining chapters in Part 1 look at the types of planning that are essential to the success of the marketing organization and at the environmental factors beyond the control of the marketing manager, as well as at the variables that can be manipulated in order to market a product profitably. Part 2 looks at how marketers identify their markets and why buyers behave the way they do. The next four parts examine the key marketing ingredients: product, mass and personal selling, pricing, and distribution. Part 7 investigates specialty areas of marketing, including marketing of services and international marketing. Part 8 summarizes by discussing the need for marketing planning, both short and long term.

summary points

1. Macromarketing refers to the role of the marketing system in distributing goods and services to buyers throughout society.

2. Marketing performs three basic functions in order to make the exchange of goods and services more efficient: (a) it provides information to the producer about consumer preferences and to the consumer about the availability of goods and services; (b) it serves as a pricing mechanism to equate supply and demand; and (c) it provides a network for the centralized distribution of goods and services.

3. Micromarketing is the process of formulating and implementing product development, distribution, pricing,

and promotion strategies that enable the firm to earn a profit in the market-place.

4. The five states of demand are no demand, latent demand, faltering demand, full demand, and overfull demand.

5. The commodity approach to marketing involves the study of product movement in the distribution channel in order to identify points where costs can be reduced and efficiency increased.

6. The institutional approach to marketing is concerned with the study of specific marketing organizations such as wholesalers and retailers.

7. The functional approach to marketing emphasizes the study of specific marketing functions. It developed in two stages: classical functionalism and managerial marketing.

8. The philosophy of management based on the production orientation is concerned with production efficiency, that is, with maximizing output from a given level of input.

9. Under the marketing concept, the primary aim of the firm is to satisfy consumer needs. Implementation of the concept requires a commitment to consumer satisfaction, a broad definition of the firm's mission, a willingness to develop new products to ensure long-term profitability, extensive consumer research, and the active support of top management.

10. Marketing problems are characterized by a large number of variables and by the fact that they do not necessarily yield a single best solution.

11. In recent years many nonprofit organizations have begun to adopt the marketing concept and to show a growing concern for customer satisfaction.

12. Marketing is studied because of the value it adds to goods and services, because of the high percentage of the work force employed in marketing activities, and because of the amount of time that we, as consumers, spend interacting with the marketplace.

---

questions for discussion

1. What role does marketing play in the U.S. economy? Is there any reason to believe that marketing will play a less important role in the mid-1980s than it does today?
2. How does micromarketing differ from macromarketing?
3. If a firm had its choice, would it want its product to be in a state of latent demand, faltering demand, or overfull demand? Why?
4. Why do marketing executives feel that their activities are more important to the enterprise than any of the other activities of the firm? Are they correct?
5. Compare and contrast the commodity, institutional, and functional approaches to marketing.
6. What factors led many firms to adopt the production orientation? Are any of these factors still important today?
7. What is the marketing concept?
8. Have most U.S. companies embraced the marketing concept? Can you give any examples?
9. Why do marketing executives feel that frequently there is no one best answer to their problems?
10. Why should nonprofit organizations adopt the marketing concept?

Topics discussed in Chapter 2:

1. Strategy as a set of objectives and purposes designed to direct the firm's efforts in the future.
2. The characteristics of effective marketing strategy.
3. Three critical stages in the strategy development process.
4. Strategic positioning.
5. Marketing mix decisions involving product, price, distribution, and communication.
6. The impact of uncontrollable environmental factors on marketing decisions.

Developing marketing strategy is of key importance to marketing executives. Marketing strategy must mesh with overall corporate strategy, and thus the marketing executive must understand how an effective corporate strategy is designed. While the process of developing strategy for the firm is not easy, once it is completed and agreed upon by top management, the firm is in a position to pursue its corporate objectives. Marketing executives can then develop a marketing strategy, taking into consideration the impact of uncontrollable environmental variables on their marketing decisions.

THE ROLE OF BUSINESS STRATEGY[1]

Strategy is the set of plans, programs, and policies that guide managers in achieving their objectives. It is not merely a ringing statement of purpose or objective, but rather the means by which the organization develops cohesiveness. In addition, strategy brings the members of the firm together by fostering a shared belief in the logic of the firm's mission as well as a shared commitment to execute that strategy successfully.[2] Let's begin our discussion of strategy by examining its meaning more precisely, as well as considering its temporal dimensions.

The Meaning of Strategy

The strategy of an organization is a long-term plan consisting of a prescribed set of objectives and policies that are designed to direct the firm's efforts in the future. Formulating corporate strategy is the work of the chief executive officer. Although many executives may influence this process through their suggestions, it is the chief executive officer who determines the final course of action for the enterprise. In the same manner, a firm with a divisional

---

[1]This section is adapted, by permission of the *Harvard Business Review*, from "How to Design a Strategic Planning System" by Richard F. Vancil and Peter Lorange (September-October, 1976). Copyright © 1976 by the President and Fellows of Harvard College; all rights reserved.

[2]Richard F. Vancil, "Strategy Formulation in Complex Organizations," *Sloan Management Review* (Winter, 1976), pp. 1–2.

structure usually has a separate strategy for each division. Formulating divisional strategy is the responsibility of the division manager. The divisional strategy must be consistent with the overall corporate strategy; its purpose is to direct the division's future operating efforts.

A strategy includes several ingredients other than the objectives and purposes of the organization. It must include the *constraints*, such as financial limitations, and *policies* that restrict the organization's activities. In a publicly held firm, the responsibility for formulating these constraints and policies is given to the chief executive officer by the board of directors. In a privately owned firm, constraints and policies are established by the owner-president after a careful analysis of the environment. Corporate strategy also contains a *set of plans* for the achievement of the firm's long-term objectives. Finally, the strategy has an implied or expressed *temporal dimension*. The strategist realizes that factors such as new products, new customers, or new or existing competitors may force the business to modify its plans and possibly even its objectives in order to stay competitive in a dynamic world.[3] Figure 2-1 further clarifies the terms discussed in this section by illustrating a power boat manufacturer forced to change strategies by the energy crisis.

FIGURE 2-1   Strategic Terms Illustrated for a Powerboat Manufacturer

Strategy	Shift the firm's product line from primarily powerboats to sailboats.
Objectives	1. Introduce two new large sailboats (24 and 28 foot). 2. Introduce three small sailboats (12, 14, and 16 foot). 3. Phase out poor-selling powerboats.
Constraints	1. Limited risk capital — $13,000,000. 2. Few research and development personnel.
Policies	1. Sell only for cash. 2. Hire only experienced personnel. 3. New products must be projected to break even in two years.
Plans	1. Do marketing research on the need for precise types of sailboats. 2. Hire sailboat designer. 3. Meet with dealers to explain the new program.
Temporal Dimensions	1. The sailboats must be ready for dealer shows in 22 months. 2. Poor-selling powerboats should be phased out as quickly as present stock can be sold.

[3]*Ibid.*

Situation Specific

The procedures used to develop corporate strategy, as well as the strategy itself, must fit the specific situation of an enterprise. The organizational structure and management style of the firm, for example, are too important not to be considered in the strategy development process. Therefore, although generalized principles of planning and strategy development do exist, we recognize that they must be tailored to fit each specific business organization.

CHARACTERISTICS OF EFFECTIVE STRATEGY[4]

Conceptually, the process of developing a business strategy is very simple: managers at all levels of the firm's hierarchy must agree on a plan of action for the coming year. This process typically begins with the establishment of corporate objectives or plans and ends with a one-year profit program. However, reaching such agreement and formulating a specific action plan — who does what, for whom, and when — can be quite difficult. There are three guidelines for effective strategy development from the perspectives of both large and small companies:

1. There must be communication of corporate plans.
2. There must be continuous scanning of the environment.
3. The role of the corporate planning officer must be clearly defined.

Communication of Corporate Plans

In a small company the president of the firm initiates the strategy development process by setting company objectives for the coming year and then sharing them with subordinates. Typically, the president does not formulate explicit profit goals. Rather, functional managers develop a set of action plans for achieving the president's stated objectives for the company.

The process of strategy development in a small firm, therefore, is directed much more toward the analysis of alternative plans than toward the establishment of corporate goals. Company strategists, such as the production manager or the marketing manager, tend to have a more narrow perspective than the president, as well as a shorter time horizon. Functional managers do not need to know the president's exact performance goals; rather, their job is simply to recommend alternative plans of action. The president then selects the best possible overall plan or strategy for the firm from among these recommendations.

Strategy development is much more complex in a large firm where top management finds it impossible to be familiar with each of the organization's activities. Although the division managers must pay attention to any directives from top management with regard to corporate objectives, it is a well-recognized fact that the division managers typically are in better positions to assess

---

[4]This section is adapted by permission of the *Harvard Business Review*, from "How to Design a Strategic Planning System" by Richard F. Vancil and Peter Lorange (September-October, 1976). Copyright © 1976 by the President and Fellows of Harvard College; all rights reserved.

the potential of their markets if not biased by corporate expectations. There-fore, divisional managers usually are held responsible by top management for developing their own business objectives. If these objectives are not acceptable to top management, the division managers may be asked to modify them.

Environmental Scanning

A strategic planning system must include a long-term plan of action for the firm and it must help the firm adapt to a changing environment. In small com-panies the president and an immediate staff assistant evaluate the operational environment. For example, a firm with a product market consisting of middle- and upper-income teenagers might devote a substantial amount of time to the study of demographic trends and changes in per capita income. An objective, well-reasoned forecast of the size of the market three, five, and ten years into the future will help the firm understand its growth potential.

In the case of large firms, the job of scanning the market is too involved to be performed by top management alone. Instead, division management per-sonnel monitor the segments of the environment that directly affect their oper-ations, while top management provides studies dealing with more aggregate issues, such as forecasts of real economic growth, expected changes in the rate of inflation, and market modifications caused by various social changes.

The Role of the Corporate Planning Officer

Strategic planning is a line management function; it should not be per-formed by staff personnel and then simply issued to line managers. However, most firms have found it necessary to designate one staff member, called a corporate planning officer, to be in charge of ensuring that the firm develops effective strategies. In a small firm the corporate planning officer often is an assistant to the president. While coordinating the planning activities of the man-agers of marketing, production, finance, and accounting, the chief planner fo-cuses on the president's problem of selecting the best set of plans.

In a large company the chief planning officer is primarily responsible for ensuring that the various divisional managers engage in strategic planning. In a sense, the chief planning officer acts as a catalyst to encourage division person-nel to adopt a strategic orientation. Although the chief planner for a large com-pany can train people in strategic planning, he or she should not become in-volved in developing strategic plans for each of the company's divisions. The chief planner has neither the time nor a sufficiently precise understanding of each division's markets and products to design its strategic plans. How, then, is a strategy developed?

THE PROCESS OF DEVELOPING STRATEGY

There are three critical stages in the strategy development process: (1) formulation of the overall plan, (2) analysis of the market, and (3) develop-ment of the product's marketing mix.

The Overall Plan

The overall plan, or strategy, is a set of directives indicating how the firm expects to take advantage of opportunities that exist in the firm's environment by utilizing its available resources in a manner consistent with its goals and values. The overall plan is usually a rather general statement about the markets that the firm will attempt to develop over the next three to five years. The plan serves as a guide for the rest of the enterprise. Examples include the plan of an oil company to begin mining coal and uranium, or the decision of an airline manufacturer to produce rapid transit systems for urban areas. The inputs to the overall plan — the environment, resources, and goals and values — are shown in Figure 2-2.

The Environment. The environment refers to those external variables over which the firm is not able to exercise control. These variables are relevant to the firm's overall strategic plan because of their influence on the types of products that the consumer is willing, or eager, to purchase. For example, as the dollar depreciated relative to the Japanese yen during the mid-1970s, Japanese automobiles became more expensive in the United States, which in turn affected how U.S. automobile manufacturers priced and promoted their vehicles. Besides economic factors, other external variables include the political, social, and technological changes taking place in society. These factors will be discussed in greater detail later in this chapter.

FIGURE 2-2 The Development of the Overall Plan

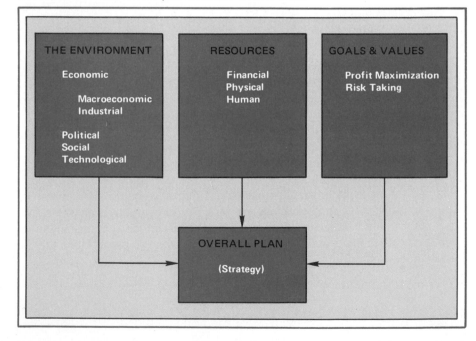

Source: Richard D. Rippe, "The Integration of Corporate Forecasting and Planning," *Columbia Journal of World Business* (Winter, 1976), p. 57.

Resources. Resources are the productive inputs used by the firm to manufacture its products. **Financial resources** are all the firm's assets except for physical plant and inventories, and represent the purchasing power available to the firm to carry out its business. **Physical resources** are items such as plant, equipment, building, and mineral resources. In evaluating physical resources, it is important to analyze their location, age, state of repair, and market value. **Human resources** refer to the management and labor force employed by the firm. Important human resource variables include the experience, formal and informal training, and general abilities of the work force. The firm's overall plan is significantly affected by the quantity and quality of the resources that it has available to achieve its objectives.

Goals and Values. Key ingredients in the development of any overall business plan are the goals and values of management, the board of directors, and the stockholders. In addition to specific goals, such as whether the firm should enter a particular market, other more general goals, attitudes, and concerns affect the business plan. These include the willingness of the firm to undertake risky investment, the issue of immediate profit versus future potential profit, the working environment of employees, and the firm's sense of responsibility to its customers and to society.

Market Analysis

Once the overall plan has been approved, the firm next examines the market position of each of its products. This type of market analysis, known as **strategic positioning**, can best be accomplished by looking at the long-term *product-market attractiveness* and *competitive position* of each market. Long-term product-market attractiveness is measured by the anticipated growth rate for the product in question. Attractive products tend to be in the development stage, whereas less attractive products have typically reached their sales peak and may actually be declining. Frequently, planners define a growth market as one which can be expected to expand at the same rate as or faster than the economy as a whole.

The simplest way to measure competitive position is to evaluate the firm's market share relative to its competition. This technique rests on the assumption that as output increases up to some point, the per unit production, marketing, and distribution costs decrease. This cost reduction results from larger, more efficient production runs, the substitution of lower cost factor inputs, the use of new technology, and a generally increased level of experience in dealing with the product. Therefore, the larger the firm's market share, the more likely it is to be profitable.

Long-term product-market attractiveness and competitive position are displayed in matrix form in Figure 2-3. Each cell in the matrix describes an alternative strategic position.[5]

Low Potential/Low Position. A product in the low potential/low position category is an unattractive member of the firm's portfolio of products. It is

---

[5]The following sections are adapted with permission from William K. Hall, "SBUs: Hot, New Topic in the Management of Diversification," *Business Horizons* (February, 1978), pp. 19–21.

FIGURE 2-3   Strategic Positions

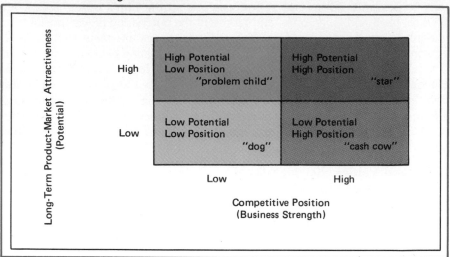

Source: Adapted from William K. Hall, "SBUs: Hot, New Topic in the Management of Diversification," *Business Horizons* (February, 1978), p. 19. © 1978 by the Foundation for
the School of Business at Indiana University. Used with permission.

frequently referred to as a "dog," a "mortgage," or a "cash trap." The strategy in dealing with such items is to maximize short-term cash flow, which can
be accomplished by stopping production or by selling the production rights.
Other ways of dealing with these products include ruthless cost cutting, drasti-
cally modifying short-term pricing policies, or relinquishing market share.

Low Potential/High Position. A low potential/high position product serves
a low growth market from a position of strength. Such products are often
called "cash cows." Here, the strategy of the firm is to milk the product for as
much as possible, though not as aggressively as with a "dog" product. Instead,
the marketing executive aims to maintain the product's relative market share so
that it will be profitable for some intermediate period of time. In so doing, the
executive must be careful to select the right target market for the product. It is
also customary to follow a policy of selected cost reductions and limited capital
investment in order to maintain a stabilized price structure.

High Potential/Low Position. A product in the high potential/low position
category is often thought of as a "question mark" or "problem child." In this
case, the strategy of the firm is to determine why its product, which is located
in a growth market, has not done well. If after such an analysis, the firm is still
not able to increase the product's market share, it will have to accept the fact
that the product, in all likelihood, will not be profitable. A good example is
General Electric's computer business. For more than a decade, GE manufactured mainframe computers. During this period the computer industry was
clearly a growth business; GE, however, was never able to achieve more than
a 3 to 4 percent share of the total market. After a thorough review, the company decided that its chances of increasing its market share were not good

enough to warrant additional investment and effort. As a result, General Electric sold its computer-related businesses to Honeywell.

High Potential/High Position. The high potential/high position category is the firm's ideal product position. A product in this category enjoys a significant share of the market in a growing industry. Typically, it is given enough resources and corporate support to ensure its long-term growth and profitability. Such products are often called "stars" and, if well managed, they usually generate the vast majority of the firm's profits and sales.

Having formulated an overall plan, and analyzed its market(s), the firm is now ready for the third stage of the planning process — i.e., development of the marketing mix.

Marketing Mix Decision Variables

Marketing mix decisions revolve around four basic questions. What constitutes the product? For how much will it be sold? How will it be distributed? How will it be promoted to the customers? While the questions seem simple enough, the answers may be difficult and complex.

Product. Although it might seem self-evident that the product or service is the physical object being sold, in reality it is much more than that. Specifically, a **product** consists of all the factors that the customer considers when making a purchase. How is the item serviced? Does it have a warranty? What is its reputation? The answers to these questions also constitute the product.

Price. The pricing decision is rather simple if the product in question is very much like others currently on the market. In this situation, the firm sets the selling price roughly equal to the market price of competitive products. However, if the product has features that differentiate it from similar products, or if it is a truly new product, then the firm must make a series of pricing decisions. Should the item be priced to generate immediate or long-term profits? Should demand or cost factors be utilized in setting price? These are just two of the questions that must be considered in pricing the product.

Distribution. Many times, the most important factor in determining the success of a product is not the product itself, but rather how it is sold. Firms such as Gillette, Procter & Gamble, and General Foods are much more likely to successfully introduce new products than are small local companies simply because of their large, already established national retail networks. Some of the more important decisions affecting distribution are determined by the following questions: Who should distribute the product? Should the distribution structure be owned by the manufacturer or should independent wholesalers be utilized? What levels of inventories should be maintained at each level in the distribution organization?

Communication. It is somewhat naive to think that a good product *always* finds a market. Buyers must be made aware of the product before they can purchase it. In most cases, personal selling and mass media promotional campaigns must be employed to acquaint potential buyers with the product and to convince them of its merits.

Interaction of the Marketing Mix Variables

The four marketing mix decision variables — product, price, distribution, and communication — are interactive. That is, a decision with respect to one variable will have an impact on the others. Figure 2-4 depicts this interaction.

FIGURE 2-4   Marketing Variables — An Interactive Process

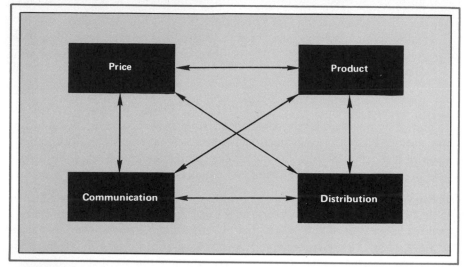

Many products have failed because the firm has not recognized the need to coordinate its marketing mix decisions. For example, a major consumer-products firm introduced a women's hair curler in California. The product had several minor advantages over competitive products, and it was roughly 10 percent less expensive. The firm made higher-than-average advertising expenditures in order to introduce the product to the public. Unfortunately retail stores ran out of the item almost immediately because the firm did not have the distribution capabilities to meet the large number of rush orders. Consequently, most of the promotional dollars were wasted, and many potential customers were upset because they were unable to buy the product.

This type of mistake could have been avoided if the firm had considered the interactive nature of the decision variables. In the above example, the positive impact of a heavily promoted, low-price, high-quality product was just too much for the distribution capabilities. The firm should have considered some combination of higher price and less promotion in order to control demand until its distribution capabilities were upgraded.

UNCONTROLLABLE ENVIRONMENTAL VARIABLES

Most of today's upper level business executives learned their management skills during the 1960s — a time of unprecedented economic stability. Managers were able to concentrate their efforts on resource allocation without worrying about economic, social, and political uncertainties. As a result, management skills developed from World War II until the mid-1970s focused on corporate resource allocation rather than on planning skills.

In today's business environment, however, executives must learn to cope with a wide range of uncertainties created by environmental variables that are external to the firm. Typically, the firm is able to exercise little or no control over these variables, and hence they constrain the firm's activities. But environmental variables can also be sources of opportunity. The marketing executive must establish an information system to monitor these variables closely and be ready to modify the marketing plan in response to changes in the environment. Inflation, slow economic growth, the energy crisis, the environmental movement, demographic shifts, consumer confidence, the changing role of women, consumerism, and legal constraints are some of the variables marketing executives must consider today.

Inflation

During the last decade the United States experienced a new and difficult problem — double-digit inflation. Historically, prices increase sharply during periods of war and then level off or even decline during the ensuing periods of peace and stability. However, as Figure 2-5 indicates, the consumer price index has been rising rapidly in the United States since 1969. (The **consumer price index** compares the change in prices of a group of commodities over a given time period.) It is important for the marketing executive to understand the causes of such high inflation and the implications of inflation for a business.

Causes of Inflation. Although it is impossible to identify exactly the cause of rising prices, it is tied to the acceptance of wage increases that exceed productivity gains. **Productivity** is defined here as the amount of output generated (products produced) by a given amount of input (wages). This situation began in the 1960s and has continued throughout the 1970s. Each percentage point of compensation in excess of productivity has been accompanied by a corresponding percentage point increase in the consumer price index.[6]

A lack of productivity gains is not the only cause of inflation. Wage increases in one sector of the economy generate demand for wage increases in other sectors, and hence upward pressure on prices. Also, the widespread belief that inflation will continue indefinitely causes managers to increase prices in order to cover future cost increases.[7] The shortage of some major natural resources (especially petroleum), the evolution of easy credit through bank credit cards, the floating of the exchange rates for the U.S. dollar, as well as some monetary policies of the federal government have all tended to push up wholesale and retail price levels.

Implications of High Inflation. The nonconsumer sectors of our economy have tried to deal with inflation by purchasing more expensive but more durable and reliable goods in order to minimize replacement and servicing costs. Therefore, when selling products to the industrial and service sectors, marketing executives must show the relationship between price and quality. A product that is more expensive than competitive brands will probably have to perform significantly better.

---

[6]George H. Brown, "Bicentennial Trends in the Business Environment," *The Conference Board Record* (July, 1976), pp. 9–10.

[7]James Earl Carter, *Economic Report of the President* (Washington, D.C.: U.S. Government Printing Office, 1978). p. 142.

FIGURE 2-5 U.S. Consumer Price Index, 1960–1979

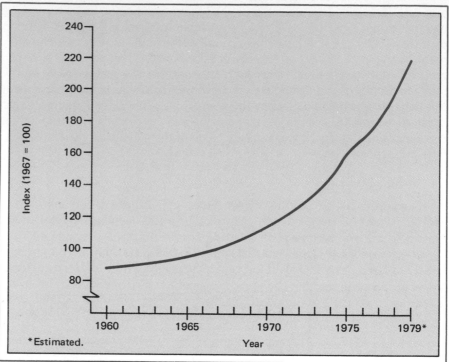

*Estimated.

Source: U.S. Department of Labor, Bureau of Labor Statistics.

In the consumer sector the concern about inflation is very real. In one recent study 72 percent of the respondents stated that inflation was a more important problem than unemployment. Consumers seem to cope with inflation in four ways. First, many people simply buy less merchandise than they have in the past. Second, they substitute low-cost items for more expensive products. Examples include the substitution of poultry for beef and non-branded items for branded items. Third, many families use their savings to maintain their quality of life. Fourth, in many families both the husband and the wife take jobs so that family purchasing power keeps pace with inflation.[8]

Inflation in the consumer sector has important implications for marketing executives. Figure 2-6 shows that some products have suffered much more from inflation than have others. Food products and energy-related goods appear to have the most dramatic price increases. Consumers, growing increasingly concerned about inflation, are buying more often on the basis of price alone. The next time you're in a supermarket, watch how people shop. You will probably notice that shoppers are spending a great deal of time examining products to determine which one represents the best buy. Many shoppers use a calculator to compute relative price-per-ounce or price-per-pound ratios. Also, you'll see some shoppers choose nonbranded items rather than nationally branded items. Although the quality of branded items is sometimes better, consumers apparently are willing to sacrifice quality for a lower price. Accord-

[8]Fabian Linden, "Double-Digit Inflation Again," *Across the Board* (October, 1978), pp. 74–76.

FIGURE 2-6   A Profile of Price Changes (August, 1972 = 100)

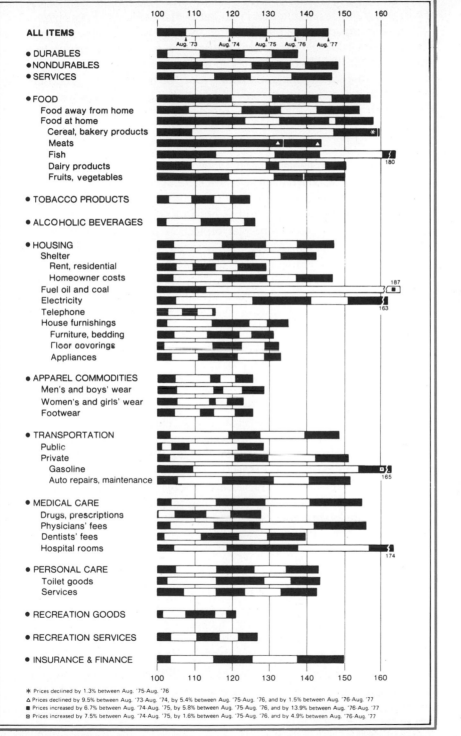

Source: U.S. Department of Labor and The Conference Board, as printed in Fabian Linden,
"Inflation of Price. Price Inflation," *Across the Board* (December, 1977), p. 67.

ingly, firms, like their customers, should become price conscious: they must be aware of changing consumer buying habits, and they should monitor the prices of competing goods and attempt to undercut them whenever possible.

Another implication of inflation, and also of changing work patterns, is that the market for relatively expensive convenience goods will continue to expand (see Chapter 8). Families in which both the husband and wife work often don't have much time for shopping, preparing food, or housecleaning; consequently, they tend to be major purchasers of labor-saving and time-saving products. Marketers should direct their efforts accordingly.

Slow Economic Growth[9]

Another uncontrollable environmental variable with which marketers must contend is slow economic growth. Most economists agree that economic growth in the United States will slow during the 1980s. One reason is simply that the rate of population growth has begun to decline. Also, as recent events have already shown, environmental protection and clean-up as well as the development of new domestic energy sources require a major redirection of capital resources, leaving less capital available for production and production-related technological research. Already, since 1968, the amount of real dollars invested by industry and government on new research has declined by more than 6 percent.

In the long run, what slower economic growth means is that a firm will no longer have the easy option of increasing sales by taking advantage of growth in the overall market. Rather, it will have to grow by increasing its market share, that is, by taking sales away from its competitors. Thus price, product, and cost decisions will become increasingly important. In this regard, the firm must be careful to maintain acceptable profit margins on its products, which may mean pricing ahead of anticipated cost changes as well as eliminating products that cannot be sold at a profit. In addition, new products must be subjected to rigorous analysis to ensure that they have a reasonable chance of meeting the firm's profit goals. Finally, the company may wish to adopt stringent cost control measures to increase profitability. Some firms have gone as far as adopting zero-based budgeting, which forces every unit within the organization to justify all future funding requests.

The Energy Crisis

The United States currently faces an energy crisis. Lines of cars at gas stations and drastic price increases seem to indicate that the United States must make major changes in the amount and the types of energy that it consumes. There is no question that this country's traditionally high standard of living has been predicated on the existence of cheap and abundant energy. Although the United States has less than 6 percent of the world's population, it consumes more than 30 percent of the world's energy supplies.[10] In contrast, West Ger-

---

[9]This section is based on Donald K. Clifford, Jr., "Thriving in a Recession," *Harvard Business Review* (July-August, 1977), pp. 57–68.

[10]The Executive Office of the President, *The National Energy Plan* (Washington, D.C.: U.S. Government Printing Office, April, 1977), p. 13.

many, with a standard of living similar to that of the United States, uses half as much energy per capita.

Figure 2-7 shows that the United States has gone through at least three distinct energy-use stages. Up until the mid-1880s, wood was the primary source of fuel. It was abundant and very inexpensive. By 1900 coal had become the dominant source of energy. It produced far more heat per dollar than did wood. However, by 1950 coal had been displaced by cleaner, easier-to-burn, and cheaper oil and natural gas. Such reliance on petroleum can be expected to continue through the 1980s.

An Energy Crisis or an Oil Crisis? Although the United States does face an energy crisis, it would be more accurate to say that it faces an *oil* crisis. During the last two decades, domestic oil consumption has outpaced new oil discoveries. The dependence of the United States on oil imports was made even more serious in 1973 when the Organization of Petroleum Exporting Countries (OPEC) raised the price of oil *three-fold* and again in 1979 when it raised the price 60 percent in less than six months. The increased cost of imported oil has led directly to major deficits in our balance of payments, which in turn has forced the dollar to decline in value on overseas markets. As a result, all im-

FIGURE 2-7   Fuel Use Patterns in the United States

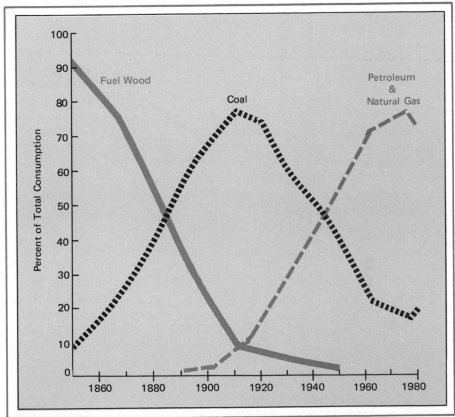

Source: U.S. Bureau of Mines and the Federal Energy Administration, as printed in The Executive Office of the President, *The National Energy Plan* (Washington, D.C.: U.S. Government Printing Office, April, 1977), p. 11.

ported goods have become more expensive. This situation is not expected to improve. As displayed in Figure 2-8, federal government projections show that even with mandatory fuel efficiency standards for automobiles, the gap between oil consumption and total domestic production will increase substantially during the 1980s.

New Fuels. Since it is clear that the U.S. cannot rely on inexpensive oil to solve energy problems, what alternatives are there? Answers to this question, of course, raise new questions and problems. The use of coal certainly is an alternative, but resultant higher levels of air pollution are prohibited by clean air legislation. Nuclear energy may play a larger role in energy production than in the past, but the waste storage safety problem associated with nuclear reactor plants has prohibited their growth. Solar energy holds great potential, but currently it is not economical for most purposes. Other potential sources of energy are available, such as hydroelectric power and geothermal power. However, all sources have problems associated with them. A supplementary

FIGURE 2-8 U.S. Oil Production and Consumption

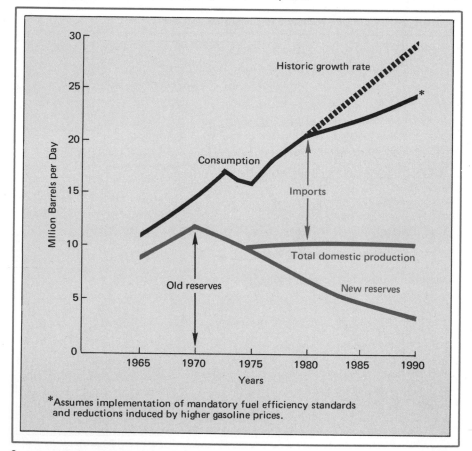

Source: U.S. Bureau of Mines and the Federal Energy Administration, as printed in The Executive Office of the President, *The National Energy Plan* (Washington, D.C.: U.S. Government Printing Office, April, 1977), p. 13.

solution to the energy problem is to conserve what sources are currently available.[11]

Conservation. Every unit of energy not consumed means one less unit of energy imported. But will conservation slow economic growth? Many economists have argued that the growth rate of an economy is directly related to the amount of energy consumed. However, this simply may not be the case, at least for private organizations if not for the economy as a whole. Many firms — such as General Motors, Exxon, Dow, DuPont and American Telephone & Telegraph — have undertaken major energy conservation programs without sacrificing productive capacity or growth in their product lines. Most firms have found that it takes three or four years for investments in energy-saving equipment to pay for themselves.

As one illustration of the potential for energy conservation at the corporate level, American Telephone & Telegraph recently cut its total energy consumption by 8.7 percent and reduced energy consumption per newly installed telephone by 20 percent. AT&T found that these energy cuts could be made by managing its resources more efficiently. The company expects to complete the ten-year period following the 1974 oil embargo without increasing its overall level of energy consumption, despite the fact that its business will have grown by almost 50 percent.[12]

Implications of the Energy Crisis. The energy crisis in the United States will cause major shifts in the way people live and work. For example, as gasoline continues to become more expensive, more and more people will move closer to where they work. In this sense, U.S. urban centers will begin to resemble those of Europe, where even in small towns most people live in apartments close to their place of employment. Responding to these demographic shifts, shopping centers and independent retail stores can be expected to relocate just as they did 30 years ago when they followed the middle class out to the suburbs.

A second implication of the energy crisis is that many products will be redesigned to be more energy efficient. Even today, automobiles are smaller, lighter, and more efficient than they were ten years ago. In the same way, houses are being built with insulated windows, more efficient heating and cooling systems, and as much as five times the amount of insulation that went into homes built just a few years ago.

A third implication of the energy crisis for marketing is that executives will have to learn to effectively sell the idea that "less is better." For many years, marketing managers trained their staffs to assume just the opposite. Now, marketing people will have to learn to sell the energy efficiency of their products in the same way that they sell other features, such as warranties and service. Similarly, advertising agencies will be challenged to design creative campaigns emphasizing energy-efficient features.

---

[11]For two good sources on energy see Alexander McRae and Janice L. Dudas, *The Energy Source Book* (Aspen: The Center for Compliance Information, 1978), and Carroll L. Wilson, *Energy: Global Prospects 1985–2000* (New York: McGraw-Hill Book Company, 1977).

[12]"Will Energy Conservation Throttle Economic Growth?" *Business Week* (April 25, 1977), pp. 69–70.

Finally, marketing practices will be examined in the light of the new higher energy costs. Some salespeople who once spent many hours traveling in a car will be required to spend more time selling via the telephone. At the very least, salespeople will drive less powerful company cars and will make more of an effort to plan efficient sales routes.

The Environmental Movement

Yet another uncontrollable variable confronting marketers is the increased concern by the people of the United States about the quality of the environment. This concern has been primarily the result of small groups of politically active people who brought to society's attention the appalling rate at which natural resources were being depleted, air quality in urban areas was being destroyed, the nation's river system was being turned into an open sewer, and the countryside was giving way to urban sprawl. The environmental movement culminated in 1968 with the creation of the Environmental Protection Agency (EPA), which is charged by Congress with the establishment and enforcement of air and water quality standards. Many programs have also been initiated at the state and local level to clean up the environment. The best known may be Oregon's law prohibiting the sale of no-deposit, no-return bottles and cans.[13]

The impact of environmental concerns on industry has been substantial. According to the Council on Environmental Quality, by 1982 the United States will have spent $274 billion to install and operate pollution-abatement equipment. Of this amount, approximately $106 billion will have been spent on air pollution control, $121 billion on water treatment facilities, and $42 billion on solid waste management. In addition to the vast amount of capital redirected to environmental protection, other substantial dislocations will occur in the economy. For example, the price of steel will probably increase by almost one third, and 16,000 jobs may be lost in the pulp and paper industries as old plants which cannot be economically retrofitted with pollution-abatement equipment are closed.[14] Regardless of these "economic" concerns, the democratic process has spoken and environmental concerns are here to stay.

Energy vs. the Environment. A major conflict has arisen between the U.S.'s need for energy and its concern for a clean and safe environment. Almost all sources of energy cause one type of environmental problem or another. For example, an accident at an off-shore oil drilling platform can leave hundreds of miles of beaches spoiled for many years. Other energy hazards include:

1. Acid mine drainage from underground coal mining.
2. Destruction of the landscape as a result of strip mining.
3. Marine pollution in the transportation of oil.
4. Salt water disposal from oil wells.
5. Air pollution from oil refining when volatile hydrocarbons are not controlled.
6. Air pollution from burning fossil fuels for heat and electricity.

---

[13]For an excellent discussion of the impact of Oregon's bottle law see Pat Murphy, "A Cost/Benefit Analysis of the Oregon 'Bottle Bill'," *1974 Combined Proceedings* (Chicago: American Marketing Association, 1974), pp. 347–352.

[14]Robert W. Fri, "Facing Up to Pollution Controls," *Harvard Business Review* (March-April, 1974), pp. 26–27.

7. Air pollution from automobile emissions.
8. Thermal pollution from electrical generation plants.
9. Environmental contamination resulting from nuclear electrical generation.[15]

This inherent conflict between energy and the environment has been exacerbated by the recent emphasis on environmental protection and conservation. The automobile industry provides a good case study of this problem. The federal government has required that automobiles produce less air pollution. The simplest way to solve this problem is to add pollution control devices to the car. However, such devices significantly reduce fuel efficiency. Fewer miles per gallon, in turn, mean that the car will burn more gasoline and thus may not meet federally mandated gasoline economy standards. Another example of energy-environment conflicts is found in the increased use of the U.S.'s abundant coal supplies. Greater reliance on domestic coal results in less reliance on imported oil. Unfortunately, however, coal has a high sulphur content and thus is a potential source of increased air pollution.

Environmentally Concerned Consumers. Several studies indicate the existence of a large group of ecologically concerned consumers. One study attempted to contrast environmentally concerned individuals with people not particularly concerned about protecting the environment. Figure 2-9 shows that, demographically, ecologically concerned consumers tend to be young, have a high level of education, possess high status jobs, be members of the higher social classes, and be from families in the early stages of the family life cycle.[16] Psychologically, they may be described as follows:

> . . .ecologically responsible consumers seem quite alienated, yet personally competent. Thus, it seems that ecologically responsible consumers are self-actualizing individuals and probably largely insulated from the need for social sanction. Alienated from the conventions of society, the ecologically responsible consumer may well view the conventional wisdom in most of its manifestations with skepticism, including conventional business practice, products, and appeals. Ecologically responsible consumers are less dogmatic, less conservative, less status conscious, more cosmopolitan, better educated, of higher socio-economic status, and younger than the typical household resident. These factors are suggestive of a general receptivity to innovation or change, a higher exposure level to information from diversified sources, and a preference for logical, factual appeals in lieu of status motives or other essentially emotional appeals.[17]

This type of information is useful in telling the marketing executive what approaches work best in selling products to ecologically concerned consumers. Although the exact size of the market for environmentally oriented consumer goods is unclear, one study showed that 59.8 percent of the subjects tested would be willing to pay "something extra" for a product if that product did not have a negative impact on the environment.[18] Dr. Karl Henion, a recognized

[15]Bruce C. Netschert, "Energy vs. Environment," *Harvard Business Review* (January-February, 1973), p. 26.
[16]W. Thomas Anderson, Jr., Karl E. Henion, II, and Eli P. Cox, III, "Socially vs. Ecologically Responsible Consumers," *1974 Combined Proceedings* (Chicago: American Marketing Association, 1974), p. 308.
[17]*Ibid.*, p. 310.
[18]Richard C. Reizenstein, Gerald E. Hills, and John W. Philpot, "Willingness to Pay for Control of Air Pollution: A Demographic Analysis," *1974 Combined Proceedings* (Chicago: American Marketing Association, 1974), p. 325.

FIGURE 2-9 Comparison of Ecologically and Nonecologically Concerned
Consumers

	Ecologically Concerned Individual	Average Individual*
Demographic Variables		
Age of head of household	30 years old	35 or older
Education of head of household	College educated	High school or some college
Occupation of head of household	Manager, official, or proprietor	Clerical or sales position
Socioeconomic status	Upper middle class	Lower-middle or middle class
Stage in family life cycle	Oldest child is 4–5 years of age	Teenage or post-teenage children
Psychographic Variables		
Alienation	More	Less
Conservatism	Less	More
Cosmopolitanism	More	Less
Dogmatism	Less	More
Personal Competency	More	Less
Status Consciousness	Less	More

*The average individual is defined as someone who has no strong feeling either positive or negative toward ecological issues.

Source: W. Thomas Anderson, Jr., Karl E. Henion, II, and Eli P. Cox, III, "Socially vs. Ecologically Responsible Consumers," *1974 Combined Proceedings* (Chicago: American Marketing Association, 1974), p. 308.

expert in ecological marketing, however, thinks that the actual figure may be as low as 30 percent.

Implications of Growing Environmental Concern. As a result of the dramatic increase in environmental awareness in the United States, the market for environmentally benign products will probably continue to expand. This new market, whatever its actual size, is as much a result of growing public interest in these products as it is a result of new federally legislated standards. Those firms that recognize the need for environmental products and that promote their merchandise accordingly will be able to capture important new markets.

Another implication for marketing executives is that the environmental movement, in many ways, translates into a new morality for business. If the organization does not attempt, on its own, to minimize its negative impact on the environment, it may find federal, state, and local authorities mandating excessively rigorous or conflicting standards. As an example, if a number of states pass bottle return laws with different specifications and provisions, major beverage producers will face dramatically increased costs as they are forced to provide unique containers for each state. Therefore, these companies should seriously consider alternatives to the disposal problem — for example, creating more recycling centers, as Pearl Beer has done in Texas, or voluntarily eliminating no-deposit, no-return bottles altogether.

Demographic Shifts

Marketers must also contend with various shifts in the population. During the next five years, two out of every five U.S. families will move to a new residence. Twenty percent of these residential moves will be to a new state. Although families change residences for a variety of reasons, certainly one of the most important is the desire to find or accept a better job. Recent population and employment shifts from the older, high density, slow-growth areas of the North to the so-called Sunbelt are worthy of special attention.

Shifts in U.S. Employment. Although employment in the northeastern and north central states increased 21.7 percent and 36.2 percent, respectively, from 1960 to 1975, the southern and western states averaged more than a 69 percent increase. Between 1970 and 1975, the number of new job positions in the Northeast actually declined by 0.6 percent, while employment in the South increased by 55.8 percent. In terms of population, the nation as a whole grew 18.8 percent from 1960 to 1975; the population of the Northeast grew by 10.7 percent during this period, that of the Midwest grew by 11.7 percent, while the population in the South and West grew by 23.9 percent and 35.0 percent, respectively.

Why have these dramatic shifts in population taken place? No single reason can account for these changes, but several factors do seem relevant:

1. The industrial infrastructure of the nation's older regions has become old and is no longer competitive.
2. Aging regions have developed a variety of entrenched special interest groups that inhibit change and make it difficult for the area to adapt to new industrial demands.
3. New transportation technologies, such as dry bulk cargo and jumbo freight aircraft, no longer give the older port cities locational advantages.
4. Many towns in the South and West have been very receptive to new industry. A variety of tax incentives has been liberally used to entice industry.
5. Labor costs are significantly less in the South and West than in the older sections of the country, partially as a result of the poor organizing record of labor unions in the Sunbelt.
6. The cost of living is lower in the Sunbelt than in the older areas of the country.[19]

Urban Migration. Two distinct patterns seem to be occurring with respect to urban migration. First, the 16 urban areas in the United States with populations of more than two million are expected to grow by only 0.3 percent yearly from 1970 to 1990, considerably slower than their 3.7 percent historical annual growth rate. It is also interesting to note that cities with populations in the 500,000 to 1,999,999 range will grow more slowly than in the past but still more than five times faster than the larger cities. Finally, nonmetropolitan areas, which actually experienced a decline in population from 1950 to 1970, along with the minor metropolitan areas will grow more than twice as fast as the major urban areas.

[19]George Sternlieb and James W. Hughes, "New Regional and Metropolitan Realities of America," *Journal of American Institute of Planners* (July, 1977), pp. 237–241.

The figures describing the movement away from the nation's largest cities would be even more spectacular if Miami, which is expected to experience significant growth through 1990, were not included in the data. This migration away from the large cities is the result of several factors, one of which is the Sunbelt and its many commercial and residential attractions. Most southern cities are smaller than the older northern cities, many of which have grown so large that they can now grow only by increasing their population densities. In many cases, natural barriers make it difficult for these cities to spread out geographically. Many people apparently do not want to be any more crowded in the future than they are now; therefore, they are willing to move out of the large northern cities.

At least two other factors are responsible for these demographic shifts. First, the chief industrial advantage of large cities is abundant labor. However, economic studies have shown that this advantage does not increase greatly as the population of an area rises above 500,000.[20] Older cities, as a result, have not been able to compete with newer, smaller, Sunbelt cities in attracting industry. Second, many people have decided that the quality of life is better in smaller cities than in the larger industrial centers. Whether they will actually be happier once they escape the noise and air pollution of the big city is not the issue — what is important is that they think they will be.

The second distinct urban migration pattern is occurring within the city itself. Many of the larger cities, from which the middle class fled to the suburbs during the last 20 years, are beginning to experience a rebirth of their downtown areas. One result is that land occupied by slums has become valuable because of its location, and the current inhabitants are too weak politically and economically to prevent slum clearance and urban redevelopment. Urban property is being purchased by developers, old buildings are being razed, and high-rise office and apartment buildings are being constructed in their place.[21]

Although this pattern exists to some extent in most urban areas, it is more pronounced in cities dominated by white-collar workers who must commute long distances to reach the suburbs. In contrast, cities with industrial cores and relatively nearby suburbs, such as Cleveland, are not as likely to experience a return of the middle class to the inner city.

Population Growth Patterns. Population growth trends in the Western nations are dramatically different than those of other parts of the world. Figure 2-10 shows the projected growth in world population, assuming a 1 percent growth rate in the developed nations and a 2.4 percent growth rate in the less-developed nations. In particular, based on these assumptions, the population of Latin America is expected to double in 24 years, that of Africa in 27 years, that of Asia in 31 years, that of the United States and the Soviet Union in 70 years, and that of Europe in 88 years.[22]

The composition of this growing population is also important. Marketers must stay well informed on the age make-up of the various markets they serve,

[20]Juan de Torres, "The New Pattern of Urban Migration," *The Conference Board Record* (May, 1976), pp. 28–34.

[21]David L. Birch, "Toward a Stage Theory of Urban Growth," *Journal of the American Institute of Planners* (March, 1971), p. 80.

[22]John Hein, "World Population Growth and People's Well-Being," *The Conference Board Record* (September, 1973), p. 7.

FIGURE 2-10   Trends in World Population

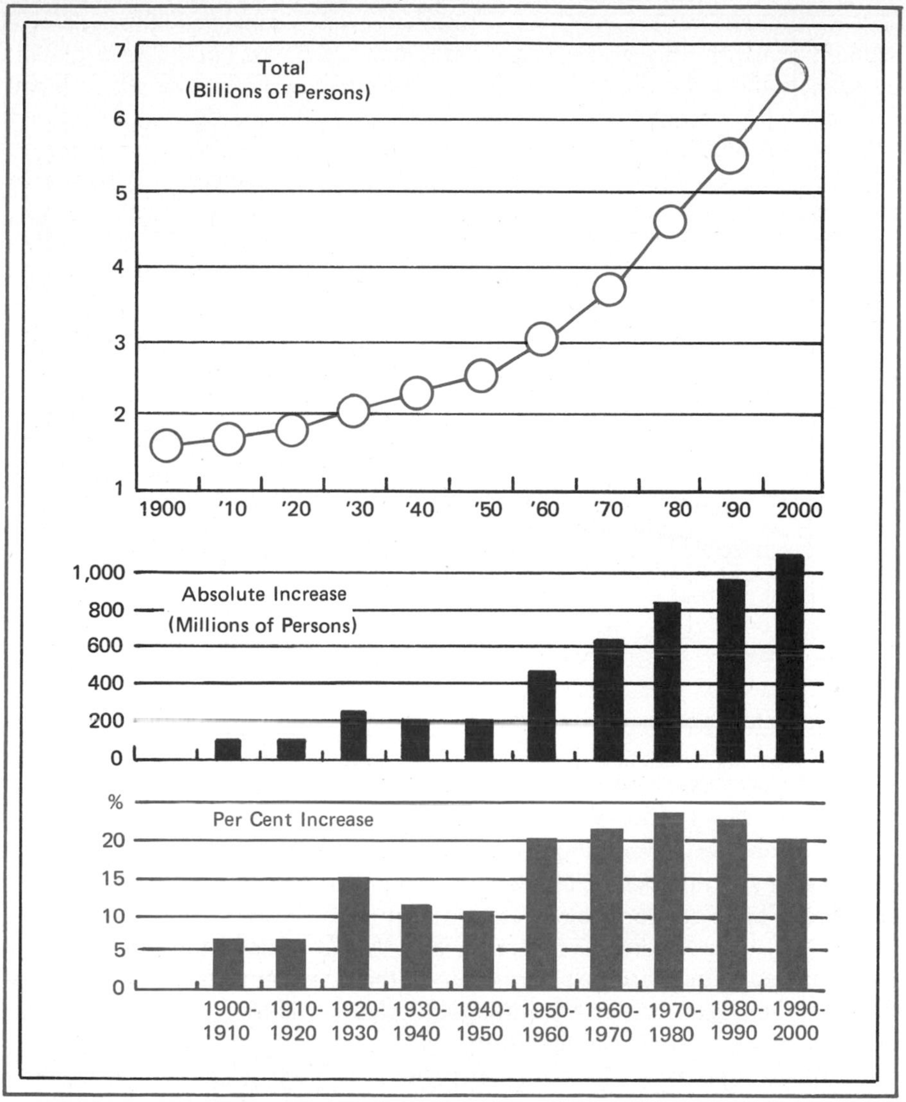

Source: John Hein, "World Population Growth and People's Well-Being," *The Conference Board Record* (September, 1973), p. 7.

or wish to serve. The United States has always had a romance with youth. It is a young nation and it prides itself on thinking young. But demographically, its citizens are getting older, not younger. In 1975, 35 percent of all U.S. citizens were under 20 years of age. By 1985, the under-20 age group will have declined by 4 percent. Conversely, as Figure 2-11 shows, the 25–34 age group will have risen by 29 percent, while the over-55 age group will have grown by almost 14 percent.[23] Rapidly changing population growth rates account, in part, for these dramatic shifts. These shifts in population present both problems and opportunities for the marketing executive.

_____

[23]"Metamorphosis in the Marketplace," *Dun's Review* (February, 1977), pp. 65–67.

FIGURE 2-11   Population Patterns in the United States

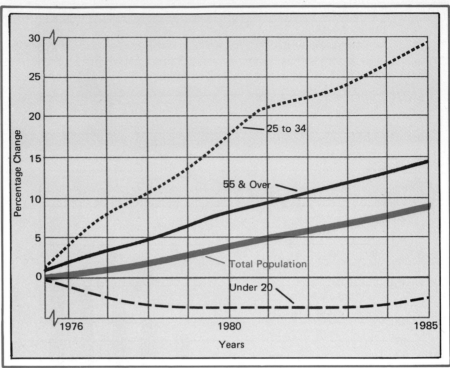

Source: Reprinted with special permission of *Dun's Review* (February, 1977). © 1977, Dun
& Bradstreet Publications.

Implications of Demographic Shifts. Regionally, the implication of the
increase in the number of employment opportunities for the South is quite
obvious. For example, major retail chains such as Federated Department
Stores, Inc., Allied Stores Corporation, and May Department Stores will invest
more money in their Sunbelt stores than in their northern stores. Other service
trades — from plumbers to advertising agencies — will also find expanding opportunities in the South and the West.

The changes in urban migration patterns will also affect marketing decisions. The fact that smaller cities are expected to grow much faster than larger
cities will force retail firms to open new stores. Many of the major chains have
already begun to expand. Federated's Foley's department store, which traditionally has been located only in Houston, recently opened two new stores in
Austin, Texas, which is almost 200 miles from their nearest branch store.
Sanger-Harris, a large Dallas-based department store, is opening up stores in
several medium-sized cities in Oklahoma.

As the 20-and-under age group declines in size, there will probably be
smaller markets for such items as blue jeans and record albums. Again, this will
present new problems and opportunities for marketing people. Finally, the
number of people in the 55–64 age group, one of the wealthiest segments of
society, will increase significantly. The test for marketing people will be to find
new products for this growing segment.

Consumer Confidence

A truly uncontrollable and unpredictable variable marketers encounter is consumer confidence. The more confident consumers are about the economy and their financial future, the more likely they are to make major purchases. Though the marketing executive can do very little, if anything, to affect consumer confidence, it can be measured and the results used to modify the firm's sales forecast.

The best-known measure of consumer confidence is published monthly by the University of Michigan's Survey Research Center. Each month, the center surveys a large number of consumers to determine how likely they are to purchase a set of products. These results are then combined into an overall index of consumer confidence, as illustrated in Figure 2-12. It is interesting to note that the nation's consumer confidence level, which averaged more than 95 from the end of 1959 until the second quarter of 1969, has not reached that level since 1969. Also, consumer confidence has been in a slow decline since the second half of 1976.[24]

FIGURE 2-12   Index of Consumer Sentiment (February, 1966 = 100)

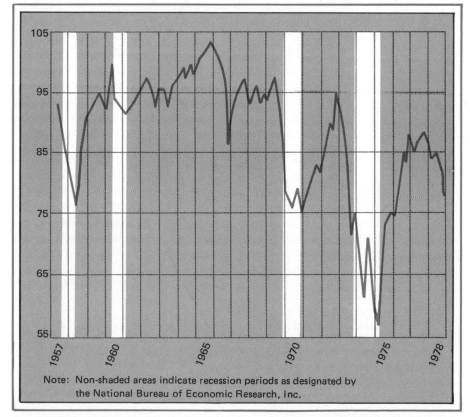

Note: Non-shaded areas indicate recession periods as designated by the National Bureau of Economic Research, Inc.

Source: Richard T. Curtin, "Continued Slow Decline in Confidence, *Economic Outlook USA* (Autumn 1978), p. 70.

[24]Richard T. Curtin, "Continued Slow Decline in Confidence," *Economic Outlook USA* (Autumn, 1978), pp. 69–71.

Consumer confidence is especially important to firms selling expensive items such as automobiles, major appliances, and houses, the purchase of which can be postponed almost indefinitely. Typically, these items are purchased when consumers feel secure about their future. In contrast, when people feel they may lose their jobs, they are not as willing to purchase an expensive item that they could do without. Moreover, since in many cases these items would be financed out of future income, consumers are even more cautious in times of financial insecurity.

The Changing Role of Women

Each year more women seek employment. At the turn of the century, only 20 percent of women in the U.S. were employed outside the home; by 1975 the figure had risen to 46 percent. The U.S. Bureau of Labor Statistics now estimates that by 1985 more than 51 percent of the nation's women will be part of the work force.[25]

Perhaps the increase in educational achievement best tells the story of the increase in female employment: today, more than 15 million women have some college education — twice as many as only two decades ago. Although over the years men have also increased their level of educational attainment, the educational gap between men and women has narrowed. In 1960, for example, women constituted only 36 percent of college graduates; [26] by 1976 they accounted for just over 46 percent; and today women account for almost 48 percent of those individuals graduating from college.[27] In many large, nationally recognized Masters in Business Administration programs, women make up more than 30 percent of the incoming classes. Only a decade ago, this figure was less than 10 percent.

Why Do Women Work? Like their male counterparts, most women work for economic reasons. One study of working mothers indicated that 89 percent of the clerical, sales, and blue-collar workers and 71 percent of mothers holding professional jobs worked for economic reasons.[28] The increases in cost of living have simply forced many women into the work force in order to help pay the monthly bills. Other reasons for the increase in the number of working women include the following:

1. The number of jobs traditionally held by women has increased significantly. Today, there is a greater need for teachers, clerks, office machine operators, and medical technicians than ever before.
2. High-paying, high-status jobs that traditionally have not been open to women are now available in large numbers. In many cases, employers are spending a great deal of effort trying to locate well-qualified women for middle- and top-management positions.

---

[25]Rena Bartos, "The Moving Target: The Impact of Women's Employment on Consumer Behavior," *Journal of Marketing* (July, 1977), p. 31.

[26]Fabian Linden, *Women: A Demographic, Social, and Economic Presentation* (New York: The Conference Board, 1973), p. 19.

[27]*Standard Educational Almanac, 1979–80* (Chicago, Ill.: Marquis Academic Media, 1979), p. 333.

[28]William Lazer and John E. Smallwood, "The Changing Demographics of Women," *Journal of Marketing* (July, 1977), p. 19.

3. Modern birth control methods permit women to decide if they want children and, if they do, to choose the size of their families. Many women are attempting to time the birth of children in order to minimize time lost from their jobs.

4. The large number of household labor-saving devices available today make life much easier for women who must both work and take care of domestic duties. Other services, such as child-care centers, have made it easier for mothers to hold down jobs.

5. The concept of "working woman" has become socially acceptable. She is no longer thought of as an "economic unfortunate" whose husband does not have a good enough job to support the family.[29]

These reasons explain, in part, why women work, but there are still some very important attitudinal questions that must be considered.

Attitudinal Issues. One major question today for working women is whether or not to have children. Most women want to have children, but many feel that doing so will require them to give up their jobs or, at least, to take extended leaves of absence. Although child-care facilities are available to most families, many child psychologists believe that children should not be separated from their mothers for extended periods of time until at least the age of three.[30]

Another attitudinal issue is how women will be treated in a "man's" world. Top management of most large companies realize that they have both a legal and ethical responsibility to hire and promote women, but this feeling is not always transmitted down the line. The study illustrated in Figure 2-13 shows some of the problems involved. Only three terms — flexible, intelligent, and decisive — used to describe a "good manager" by a panel of men were also

FIGURE 2-13   Characteristics of the Ideal Woman vs. a Good Manager

The Ideal Woman	A Good Manager
Attractive	Intelligent
Wealthy	Aggressive
Educated	Objective
Supportive	Decisive
Flexible	Reliable
Intelligent	Flexible
Mature	Motivated
Tolerant	Pressurized
Decisive	Sensitive
Open-minded	Responsible
Frugal	Trustworthy
Loving	Considerate
Gentle	Imaginative
Soft-spoken	Goal-oriented
Good Conversationalist	

Source: Daniel A. Polk, "Women in the Corporation: One Man's View," *NABW Journal* (September/October, 1977). Reprinted by permission of the *NABW Journal*, official publication of the National Association of Bank Women, Inc.

[29]Suzanne H. McCall, "Meet the Workwife," *Journal of Marketing* (July, 1977), p. 56.
[30]Selma Fraiberg, "What's a Working Mother To Do?" *Across the Board* (September, 1978), pp. 14–18.

used to describe the "ideal woman." Unfortunately, as with other forms of discrimination, it will take years to eradicate sex discrimination in business.

Implications of the Changing Role of Women. One of the most subtle, yet important, results of the changing role of married women is that their added income frequently catapults the family from a low-income to middle-income status, or from middle-income to upper-income status. As an example, in 1978, of those families in the $20,000–$25,000 income category, 62 percent were two-income families. This same pattern holds true for both the $15,000–$20,000 category and the $25,000–$50,000 income category. The only exception to this pattern was the over $50,000 category where one-income families slightly exceed the two-income families in number.[31]

An implication of the multiple-earner family is that upper-income status is not quite as elite as may have once been assumed. Today, the upper-income family is no longer necessarily characterized by a professional male who commutes to work and a wife who stays at home. Rather, such families, as often as not, are made up of two moderately educated, skilled workers. As a result, upper-income families should not be thought of as constituting a homogeneous group that wants and needs the same types of products. The composition of the upper-income group is diverse, and its membership is highly volatile as married women move in and out of the labor force.[32]

There are also several other implications of the changing role of women for marketing. One study shows that the purchase decision process varies somewhat with the age and income of women. In general, the younger and wealthier the women, the more likely they are to assume an active role in the purchase decision process.[33]

What women will buy and where they will buy it will reflect their increased role in the work force. For example, there will continue to be a very strong interest in labor-saving appliances and convenience foods despite their high price and/or high energy requirements. Also, stores — not only supermarkets but also general merchandise outlets carrying such items as clothing, appliances, and furniture — that remain open longer hours will best meet the needs of the working family.

Consumerism

Consumerism, another uncontrollable variable, is a social movement the objective of which is to increase the power of consumers relative to that of sellers. The seller has traditionally had the right to introduce virtually any product to the market as long as the product was not known to be hazardous to the user. The seller also has been free to formulate the promotional messages for products, to spend as much money on promotion as necessary, and to price the products according to the firm's sales and profit objectives.

The buyer's rights, in contrast, are not as significant. Principally, the buyer has the right to refuse to buy the product. The buyer also has the right to

---

[31]"The Big Clout of Two Incomes," *Dun's Review* (April, 1979), p. 44.

[32]See Fabian Linden, "The Two (and Three) Earner Family," *Across the Board* (May, 1977), pp. 50–51; "The Big Clout of Two Incomes," *Dun's Review* (April, 1979), pp. 43–48.

[33]Robert T. Green and Isabella C. M. Cunningham, "Feminine Role Perception and Family Purchasing Decisions," *Journal of Marketing Research* (August, 1975), pp. 325–332.

A great deal of time has been devoted to evaluating how environmental forces will affect market practices in the future. Now, let's look at how these forces are likely to affect **you**.

Inflation. The high rate of inflation is making a college education increasingly more expensive. You and many of your college friends may be living at home while attending college, or attending two-year rather than four-year colleges because of the high costs of a college education. Even parents of upper-middle income families are finding it difficult to support more than one or two children in college at the same time. Inflation is forcing more students to seek part-time employment and to finance their education through borrowing.

Slow Economic Growth. The expected slow economic growth during much of the 1980s means that many college graduates will not be able to find white-collar, managerial positions. In short, the supply of managerial talent will be greater than the demand for it. If you have special technical skills or if you can contribute quickly to a firm's profitability, you will likely be among the first to be hired. Graduates of business administration and engineering programs will probably remain in demand.

The Energy Crisis. Continuing energy problems in the U.S. will mean many new career opportunities for you in the fields of energy conservation, exploration, and development. Energy-related products should provide one of the real growth opportunities in the United States economy during the 1980s.

Demographic Shifts. The United States will continue to be a mobile society. As in the past, advancement in managerial careers will depend on your willingness to be transferred from one area of the country to another. Although new job opportunities will appear in the South and Southwest, many natives of these areas will be required to move to other regions of the country during their careers. Many leading U.S. corporations are headquartered in the Midwest or the Northeast.

The Changing Role of Women. In the years ahead, young women will be in much greater demand to fill executive positions than they were in the 1970s. Vigorous recruiting of talented women will be the result of government pressure as well as enlightened self-interest on the part of private enterprise. Men are likely to face even stiffer competition for executive positions in private industry.

Are you preparing now to meet the challenges and take advantage of the opportunities of the 1980s?

Marketing & You

expect the product to be safe if used according to directions and to be essentially what the seller represents it to be.

Consumer advocates feel very strongly that the seller has had the upper hand in dealing with the consumer and that this situation should not be permitted to continue. In examining the consumer movement, we will look at such issues as why consumerism developed and what implications it has for business.

What Stimulated the Consumer Movement? In retrospect, the consumer movement seems to have been caused by a number of factors rather than just one. Noted author Philip Kotler has speculated that the structural strains of the 1960s — inflation, the war in Vietnam, racial strife, and environmental pollution — all led to public discontent and frustration.[34] This societal dissatisfaction eventually emerged as a general belief that consumers were being abused. Social critics such as John Kenneth Galbraith[35] and Vance Packard[36] helped encourage this attitude. President Kennedy's message to Congress in which he called for a consumer bill of rights giving consumers the rights to safety, to be informed, to be heard, and to choose perhaps laid the basis for consumerism. In any case, it certainly gave the ensuing movement a high degree of legitimacy.

In addition to the social causes of consumerism, consumer dissatisfaction with defective products, hazardous or unsafe products, and defective repair work or service were cited in a study of more than 3,400 executives as major contributing factors. Data from this study are highlighted in Table 2-1. Other research has indicated that 20 percent of all consumer purchases result in dissatisfaction, that in less than half of these cases do consumers complain, and that only two thirds of their complaints are ever resolved to their satisfaction.[37]

Implications of Consumerism. Consumerism is definitely here to stay. Consumer advocates are no longer thought of as radicals. Rather, they are seen as established members of society who believe that consumers must be better served and protected. Also, most business executives now realize that consumer advocates do not want to destroy the capitalistic system but simply to get better products to a more informed public.

One firm that has clearly recognized and responded to the consumerism movement is Eastman Kodak. Included in Kodak's response are:

1. A product design philosophy that anticipates and eliminates consumer mistakes before they occur.
2. A free photo advice service for consumers that handles more than 150,000 inquiries per year.
3. Thirty-nine consumer service centers located across the United States that provide free advice and minor equipment repairs.

[34]Philip Kotler, "What Consumerism Means for Marketers," *Harvard Business Review* (May-June, 1972), p. 49.

[35]John Kenneth Galbraith, *The Affluent Society* (3d ed.; Boston: Houghton-Mifflin, 1976), and *The New Industrial State* (3d ed.; Boston: Houghton-Mifflin, 1978).

[36]Vance Packard, *The Hidden Persuaders* (New York: D. McKay Co., 1960), and *The Waste Makers* (New York: D. McKay Co., 1960).

[37]Alan R. Andreasen and Arthur Best, "Consumers Complain — Does Business Respond?" *Harvard Business Review* (July-August, 1977), p. 93.

TABLE 2-1   Causes of Consumer Dissatisfaction

Economic and Social Factors	Importance Rating*	Business and Marketing Practices	Importance Rating*
Consumer concern over rising prices	4.2	Defective products	4.5
Consumers feeling a growing gap between product performance and marketing claims	4.1	Hazardous or unsafe products	4.3
Increased consumer expectations for product quality	3.8	Defective repair work or service	4.1
Deterioration in product quality	3.8	Misleading advertising	3.9
Political appeal of consumer protection	3.8	Poor complaint-handling procedures by retailers	3.9
Failure of normal marketplace operations to satisfy consumers	3.6	Advertising which claims too much	3.9
A feeling that business should assume greater social responsibilities	3.6	Deceptive packaging and labeling	3.8
Impersonal nature of the marketplace	3.5	Poor complaint-handling procedures by manufacturers	3.8
Greater public concern over social problems generally	3.5	Failure to deliver merchandise which has been paid for	3.6
Consumers demanding more product information	3.5	Inadequate guarantees and warranties	3.5

*The importance rating is based on a 5-point scale ranging from "very important" (5) to "very unimportant" (1).

Source: Reprinted by permission of the *Harvard Business Review.* Exhibit from "Business Is Adapting to Consumerism" by Stephen A. Greyser and Steven L. Diamond (September–October, 1974). Copyright © 1974 by the President and Fellows of Harvard College; all rights reserved.

4. A nonprofit publication program that distributes 100 different pamphlets and 25 books on photography.
5. An assistant vice-president whose primary responsibility is customer service for all divisions.
6. High standards of product quality control and an easily read and understood warranty.

Other major firms, including General Electric, Whirlpool, Quaker Oats, and Federated Department Stores, have established strong consumer programs. As businesses continue to adopt consumer programs that appeal to the public and that thereby generate extra revenue and profits, other firms will be forced to do the same. In short, competition will force the marketplace to become more consumer oriented.

Legal Constraints

The capitalistic system operates on the assumption that each firm within an industry competes as vigorously as possible with its competitors. However, history has shown that many firms, for one reason or another, have concluded that they could earn more profit by "working together" rather than by competing with one another. As a result, Congress has passed a series of laws, including the Sherman Act, the Clayton Act, and the Federal Trade Commission Act, in an attempt to ensure that all firms behave competitively in the marketplace. The role and impact of these and other marketing-related legislation will be discussed in detail in the next chapter.

summary points

1. A strategy is a long-term plan consisting of a set of objectives and policies that are designed to direct the firm's efforts in the future.

2. In a small firm the president initiates the strategic development process by establishing company goals. In a large firm strategy development lies mainly with divisional managers.

3. The three critical stages in the development of corporate strategy are formulating the overall plan, analyzing the market, and developing the product's marketing mix.

4. After developing the overall strategic plan, the firm examines the market position of each of its products. Referred to as strategic positioning, this process involves analyzing each market's long-term, product-market attractiveness and competitive position.

5. Marketing mix decisions involve determining the product or products the firm will produce and sell, the way they will be priced and distributed, and the promotional tactics that will be used to communicate the product message to potential buyers.

6. Inflation has forced many consumers to buy fewer products and to pay more for them. Others have been forced to substitute less expensive items for high-priced products. In the future, buyers will be more sensitive to price-quality relationships than they have in the past.

7. The slower economic growth expected for the United States in the coming years means that firms will grow primarily by increasing market share, not by taking advantage of growth in the overall market.

8. The high price of petroleum-based products will cause major shifts in the types and designs of products. The oil crisis will also affect the way marketing people sell their merchandise.

9.The growing concern in this country for protecting the environment will cause the market for environmentally benign products to expand.

10. In response to population and other demographic changes in the United States, retail firms are beginning to relocate their facilities in the South and in medium-sized cities. Also, the movement of people back to downtown areas of some large cities will create opportunities for the development of new high-rise shopping centers.

11. Consumer confidence is an especially critical concern of a manufacturer of expensive, durable consumer goods. Typically, the purchase of these items is postponed when consumers feel financially insecure or pessimistic about the economy.

12. The increasing number of women entering the job market will mean that many families will have more disposable income. As a result, sales of labor-saving and time-saving products will continue to grow.

13. Consumerism is here to stay. Firms will have to provide better products to the market or face the prospect of unhappy and vocal consumers.

questions
for
discussion

1. Differentiate between the following terms: strategies, objectives, policies, constraints, plans, and temporal dimensions. Using an organization to which you currently belong, illustrate the application of these terms.
2. Describe the strategic planning process in your own words.
3. Compare and contrast the strategic planning process of a small firm with that of a large firm.
4. Under what circumstances should the corporate planning officer act as more than a catalyst to the organization?
5. When creating the overall plan for an organization, why is it necessary to integrate the environment, the firm's resources, and the goal and values of the organization?
6. Evaluate the concept of strategic positioning. Does it make sense to analyze products in terms of their long-term product-market attractiveness and the firm's relative competitive position? Why or why not?
7. When should a firm integrate its marketing mix decisions?
8. Do you expect inflation to continue at its current level for the next several years? What do you think will be the long-term impact of excessive inflation on the U.S. economy?
9. Do you believe that marketing executives, in order to conserve energy, will be successful at selling the idea that "less is better"? How would you sell such a concept?
10. If you were the chief marketing executive for the Chevrolet Division of General Motors, how would you respond to the energy situation?
11. Do you think that people will purchase more environmentally safe products five years from now than they do today? Will they be ready to pay 10 percent more for environmentally safe products?
12. As a marketing executive for the Coca-Cola Company, how would you respond to the demographic shifts taking place in the world today?
13. Can measures of consumer sentiment be useful to a business selling relatively inexpensive products? Explain your answer.
14. Do you feel that women will continue to work for the same reasons in the 1980s that they did during the 1970s? Support your answer.
15. What product and shopping behavior changes can be expected if even more women work in the 1980s?
16. Is the consumerism movement healthy for the economy?

Topics discussed in Chapter 3:

1. The U.S. antitrust framework, including specific legislation and court decisions.
2. Price fixing and price discrimination.
3. Laws pertaining to channels of distribution.
4. The regulation of promotion.
5. Consumer protection legislation.
6. The marketing executive and social responsibility.

Today, marketing executives must not only be concerned with ethical standards of behavior but also with the legal implications of their actions. Unfortunately, all too often even attorneys have a difficult time forecasting how the courts will interpret the law.

THE ANTITRUST FRAMEWORK

One of the basic tenets of the capitalist system of the United States is that businesses should compete with one another in a free and open manner. While most firms have chosen to do this, some have decided that collusion is more profitable than competition. In an attempt to discourage collusion, the U.S. Congress has passed a series of laws. Four major laws which make up this antitrust framework include the Sherman Act, the Clayton Act, the Federal Trade Commission Act, and the Celler-Kefauver Act.

The Sherman Act

The Sherman Act, passed in 1890, was a reaction against the wave of mergers and other conduct and agreements which created monopolies during the 1870s and 1880s. Although agreements between two or more businesses not to compete were illegal under common law at that time, the government had not been able to control certain practices by interests such as the then-powerful railroad and banking trusts.[1]

Provisions of the Sherman Act. The two primary provisions of the Sherman Act are based on the notion that pure competition is good for the economic health of the nation, and conspiracies or monopolies are not:

- Section 1. Every contract, combination . . . or conspiracy, in restraint of trade or commerce among the several States, or with foreign nations, is hereby declared

---

[1]For an excellent discussion of early trusts see Matthew Josephson, *The Robber Barons* (New York: Harcourt, Brace and Company, 1934), and Stewart H. Holbrook, *The Age of the Moguls* (Garden City, N.Y.: Doubleday and Company, 1953).

to be illegal. Every person who shall make any such contract or engage in any such combination or conspiracy, shall be deemed guilty of a felony. . . .

- Section 2. Every person who shall monopolize, or attempt to monopolize, or combine or conspire with any other person or persons, to monopolize any part of the trade or commerce among the several States, or with foreign nations, shall be deemed guilty of a felony. . . .

These two provisions were written into law before modern economic theory had fully developed. As a result, there was a marked reluctance on the part of the federal government to enforce the Sherman Act. The Attorney General of the United States in 1895 stated that he had taken the "responsibility of not prosecuting under a law (Sherman Act) believed to be no good." Today, most economists still believe that it is impossible and probably even undesirable to eliminate all restraints of trade or monopolistic practices. Most business executives attempt to escape the rigors of pure competition by differentiating their products from those of their competitors. Although, strictly speaking, this might be viewed as a monopolistic practice, it surely would not be in society's best interest for all firms in an industry to produce exactly the same products.

Supreme Court Decisions. The U.S. Supreme Court realized that it was not possible to eliminate all restraints of trade. Therefore, in the Standard Oil of New Jersey case (1911), the court held that Standard Oil should be broken up because it constituted an "unreasonable" monopoly.[2] According to the court, only those combinations in restraint of trade that were unreasonable were subject to the antitrust laws. The court held that the conduct of the firm, not market structure, was the controlling factor in determining whether a firm had acted illegally.

The Supreme Court reaffirmed its position on the legality of restraints of trade in the Chicago Board of Trade case (1918). The court stated:

Every agreement covering trade, every regulation of trade, restrains. To bind, to restrain, is of their very essence. The true test of legality is whether the restraint imposed is such as merely regulates and perhaps thereby promotes competition or whether it is such as may suppress or even destroy competition. To determine that question the court must ordinarily consider the facts peculiar to the business to which the restraint is applied: its condition before and after the restraint was imposed; the nature of the restraint and its effect, actual or probable. The history of the restraint, the evil believed to exist, the reason for adopting the particular remedy, the purpose or end sought to be attained, are all relevant facts.[3]

In these cases, the Supreme Court was not saying that monopolies or monopolistic practices were acceptable business behavior, but rather that such practices were not necessarily or always bad. In particular, according to the court, a firm was not guilty of antitrust behavior merely because it had a large share of the market. The court placed the burden of proof on the government

---

[2]Standard Oil Co. of New Jersey v. United States, *U.S. Supreme Court Reports*, Vol. 221, p. 62 (1911).

[3]Chicago Board of Trade v. United States, *U.S. Supreme Court Reports*, Vol. 246, p. 231 (1918).

to show that a particular firm had intended to monopolize a market. This interpretation of the Sherman Act by the Supreme Court has made it difficult for the antitrust division of the Department of Justice to obtain antitrust convictions.[4]

The Clayton Act

The Clayton Act and the Federal Trade Commission Act both were passed in 1914 in an attempt to give the federal government more authority to deal with monopolies. While the Sherman Act said that "every contract, combination . . . or conspiracy, in restraint of trade" was illegal, the Clayton Act stated that certain practices were illegal "where the effects may be to substantially lessen competition or tend to create a monopoly." Through this wording Congress made antitrust convictions easier to obtain.

Provisions of the Clayton Act. Three sections of the Clayton Act deserve special attention; each prohibits a specific marketing activity:

1. **Section 3** prohibits tying agreements and exclusive agreements. A **tying agreement** is an agreement whereby a seller agrees to sell or lease a product or service to a customer on the condition that the customer also purchases other, often unwanted, merchandise from the seller. An **exclusive agreement** is an arrangement whereby the seller, as a condition of the sale, forbids the buyer to purchase for resale the products of competitive sellers.
2. **Section 7** prohibits corporations from purchasing the stock of competing firms. This section, amended by the Celler-Kefauver Act (1950), is particularly relevant to firms considering the acquisition of other businesses as a means of diversifying or expanding into new product lines.
3. **Section 8** prohibits a person from sitting on the board of directors of two or more competing companies that have sales in excess of one million dollars. The aim of this section of the Clayton Act is to discourage monopoly practices such as price fixing and dividing sales territories and customers between competing companies.

It must be remembered that the prohibited actions described above are not in and of themselves illegal; rather, they are in violation of the law only when "the effects may be to substantially lessen competition or tend to create a monopoly." For example, the government would not bring action against a firm that had just purchased the stock of one of its competitors if it were apparent that the purchase would not materially lessen competition in the industry.

Supreme Court Decisions. Over the years, the U.S. Supreme Court has handed down many important decisions involving the Clayton Act. The two cases discussed here show not only how the court has interpreted the Clayton Act but also that it sometimes makes some rather unusual decisions.

In the famous FTC v. Procter & Gamble decision in 1967, the Supreme Court ruled that Procter & Gamble's purchase of the Clorox Company was in violation of Section 7 of the Clayton Act.[5] At the time of the attempted merger,

---

[4]Louis W. Stern and John R. Grabner, *Competition in the Marketplace* (Glenview, Ill.: Scott, Foresman and Company, 1970), p. 81.

[5]FTC v. Procter and Gamble, *Supreme Court Reporter*, Vol. 87, p. 1224 (1967).

P&G was the dominant firm in the home cleaning products area even though it did not produce or sell a liquid chlorine bleach. Clorox, a much smaller firm, was the leading seller of liquid chlorine bleaches in the United States. The court prohibited the merger of P&G and Clorox on the grounds that it would reduce *potential* competition by deterring other firms from entering the chlorine bleach market. The court also reasoned that if P&G did not purchase Clorox, it might introduce its own chlorine bleach, thereby increasing competition in the industry. This decision led one well-known analyst to state:

> In virtually no instance will a major producer be secure in acquiring a firm in a related industry. In almost every case the replacement of a firm by a powerful oligopolist will render the field less attractive for potential entrants. In short, virtually every case involving a conglomerate merger will be vulnerable to the Court's logic: the movement toward concentration must be condemned.[6]

Another case involving the Clayton Act centered on the 1955 attempted purchase of the G. R. Kinney Company by the Brown Shoe Company. The Supreme Court again ruled that the proposed merger violated Section 7 because it would tend to substantially lessen competition in the shoe industry. What puzzled legal and marketing analysts about the decision was the fact that the shoe industry historically has been fragmented. At the time of the proposed merger, Brown had only 4 percent of the shoe market. The court stated that in fragmented industries, such as the shoe industry, rank not market share was the critical variable in determining the legality of a merger. Brown was the fourth largest shoe company and Kinney was the twelfth; the merger of the two, the court felt, would represent an unjustifiable concentration of power. The court chose not to consider any economic efficiencies, and subsequent lower prices, that may have resulted from the merger. In the majority opinion written by Chief Justice Earl Warren, the Supreme Court stated:

> We cannot fail to recognize Congress' desire to promote competition through the protection of viable, small, locally owned businesses. Congress appreciated that occasional higher costs and prices might result from the maintenance of fragmented industries and markets. It resolved these competing considerations in favor of decentralization. We must give effect to that decision.[7]

The Federal Trade Commission Act

The Federal Trade Commission Act was passed in 1914 as companion legislation to the Clayton Act. This act had two primary objectives. First, it established the Federal Trade Commission (FTC) to enforce the Clayton Act. In this capacity the FTC was empowered to investigate violations and either to serve as a resource to the antitrust division of the Attorney General's Office or to prosecute its own cases in the federal courts. The second objective of the FTC act was to eliminate monopoly in its initial stages. To do so, the FTC was given the broad authority to define and prohibit "unfair methods of competition" and to issue cease and desist orders. A **cease and desist order** is a

---

[6]Ray W. Werner, "Marketing and the United States Supreme Court, 1965–1968," *Journal of Marketing* (January, 1969), p. 21.

[7]Brown Shoe Company v. FTC, *U.S. Supreme Court Reports*, Vol. 384, p. 316 (1966).

ruling by the FTC requesting a company to stop a specific business practice that the FTC feels is illegal. If the firm accepts the FTC consent order, it usually will not hear from the FTC again about the matter. However, if the firm does not stop the practice in question, the FTC may attempt to prosecute the company in a federal court for violation of one of the antitrust laws.

The FTC Improvement Act. The FTC Improvement Act of 1975 increased the FTC's antitrust power significantly by giving additional clout to cease and desist orders and by broadening the power of the FTC to redress damages in the marketplace. In the past, a cease and desist order affected only the firm to which it was directed; the FTC Improvement Act, on the other hand, permits the commission to seek fines against individuals or businesses that were not a party to the order. As an illustration, if a cease and desist order is issued against Mobil Oil Company for a specific action, Shell Oil is also subject to the prohibitions if it has received notice of the order. If Shell knowingly commits the proscribed act, it is subject to a $10,000 per day fine for each violation.[8] For this reason, the FTC sends copies of its cease and desist orders to all firms that might be affected within the industry.

As stated above, the FTC Improvement Act gave the FTC additional power to restore competitive balance in markets where "unfairness and deception" had created monopolistic positions. The ReaLemon case illustrates how far the FTC can go to correct past practices. In 1976, the FTC found that the Borden Company, through its product ReaLemon, had created and maintained a monopoly position in the processed lemon juice industry by discriminatory and predatory pricing. The FTC was not willing to settle for a mere cease and desist order; instead, it required Borden for a period of ten years to grant licenses to manufacturers to sell lemon juice with the ReaLemon label. Borden was permitted to obtain a royalty of not more than one half of 1 percent of the licensee's selling price. In addition, Borden had to advertise the availability of these licenses in three major magazines four times per year. In reality, the FTC rewrote Borden's ReaLemon licensing contracts.[9]

Criticisms of the FTC. For many years, the FTC was criticized for being too involved with industry and for spending too much time investigating trivial matters. Many social critics felt that the FTC was little more than a pawn of industry. However, in the last few years the situation has changed significantly. The agency has initiated many massive investigations of important industries that have led to prosecutions. Its appropriations from Congress have been rising at nearly 15 percent annually, and it has 570 staff attorneys working on more than 700 independent investigations.

Many business people believe that the FTC has violated its charter in its drive to test new legal theories that go beyond the power granted to it by Congress. This criticism is stated by William E. LaMothe, president of Kellogg Co.:

---

[8]Gerald G. Udell and Philip J. Fischer, "The FTC Improvement Act," *Journal of Marketing* (April, 1977), p. 83.
[9]*Ibid.*, pp. 84–85.

The FTC is seeking to redefine the term "monopoly" without benefit of Congress. It accuses the major manufacturers of breakfast cereals of being what the commission calls a "shared monopoly." It seeks to break us up, strip away our plants, force us to help set up new companies to which we would have to give exclusive rights to our most successful products.[10]

In this particular case, the FTC has charged Kellogg, General Foods, General Mills, and Quaker Oats with monopolizing the cereal market. The FTC has stated that these firms tacitly agreed not to reduce price but to compete for shelf space in supermarkets on the basis of advertising. The FTC further claims that the large advertising expenditures involved, in excess of $95 million per year, serve as a barrier to the entry of new competitors.[11] This landmark case of "shared monopoly" may not be resolved until the early 1980s.

The FTC is also criticized by business executives because its investigations are so costly to industry and because it sometimes appears just to be on a "fishing trip." For example, the FTC is currently investigating why people smoke. As part of its investigation, the FTC has subpoenaed much of Brown & Williamson Tobacco Corporation's marketing research data. Charles I. McCarty, chairman and chief executive officer of Brown & Williamson, has stated that answering the FTC subpoena could cost his firm more than $500,000.[12] The FTC claims that all its investigations have specific goals even though some may not appear to. Also, for the FTC to collect the data it really needs, it must often camouflage its real objectives.

The Celler-Kefauver Act

The Celler-Kefauver Act of 1950 is the most recent major piece of legislation in the government's antitrust arsenal. The law, an amendment to the Clayton Act, has been called the antimerger act. Like the Clayton Act and the Federal Trade Commission Act, it is aimed at mergers the effect of which "might be to substantially lessen competition or tend to create a monopoly." The act is designed to deal with monopoly in its initial stages.

During the debates leading to passage of the Celler-Kefauver Act, Congress recognized a need for additional antitrust legislation since the Sherman Act deals with only a few obvious monopolistic practices. The restrictions of Section 7 of the Clayton Act apply only to stock acquisitions, not asset acquisitions. Therefore, the Celler-Kefauver Act was passed making it illegal for one firm to purchase the assets of another firm if this action would "substantially lessen competition or tend to create a monopoly." In addition, while the Clayton Act prohibits only mergers involving direct competitors, the Celler-Kefauver Act permits the FTC to investigate mergers between manufacturers and distrib-

---

[10]"The Escalating Struggle Between the FTC and Business," *Business Week* (December 13, 1976), p. 53.

[11]G. David Hughes, "Antitrust Caveats for the Marketing Planner," *Harvard Business Review* (March-April, 1978), p. 54.

[12]"The Escalating Struggle Between the FTC and Business," *Business Week* (December 13, 1976), p. 59.

utors that might lead to a lessening of competition. Thus, not only horizontal mergers come under the scrutiny of the FTC but now also vertical mergers.[13]

REGULATION OF PRICING

Two central pricing concerns that affect marketing executives are price fixing and illegal price discrimination. **Horizontal price fixing** refers to price fixing between directly competing companies such as two manufacturers or two retailers. In contrast, **vertical price fixing** involves price fixing between members of a channel of distribution, such as would occur if a manufacturer required that a retailer sell the manufacturer's products at a specific price. This section begins with a discussion of horizontal price fixing.

Horizontal Price Fixing

When two or more business executives from competing firms get together to decide how much to charge for their products or which of them will bid the lowest on a certain contract, they are in violation of the Sherman Act and the Federal Trade Commission Act. It is wise for executives who participate in such practices to understand the risks involved. First, the company that employs the executive can be fined up to $1 million for each act of price fixing. In addition, any buyer that can prove in civil court that it was damaged by a price-fixing agreement between two or more sellers can receive triple damages from the price-fixing companies.

Second, price fixing is a criminal offense. The executive begins making calls from telephone booths so that they cannot be traced, or registering under assumed names when meeting with accomplices. Most executives are not comfortable playing the role of a criminal.[14] In addition, the executive who is convicted of conspiracy to fix prices may be fined up to $100,000 and/or spend as much as three years in prison. Most executives find that prison has a less pleasant atmosphere than their country clubs. Third, exposure of the price-fixing activity will probably mean the dismissal of the people involved. Although the executives may claim participation in the price-fixing scheme was for the good of the firm, top management will have no choice but to fire them. Figure 3-1 describes the action taken against executives in the folding-carton industry who participated in a price-fixing scheme.

So why do firms still engage in price fixing? There seem to be three major reasons: chronic overcapacity in the industry, undifferentiated products, and/or lack of top management surveillance.

Chronic Overcapacity. When production capacity in an industry exceeds buyer demand, there is a tendency for competing firms to engage in price wars in order to get a higher percentage of the available business. Price wars lead to lower profit margins as competing firms reduce their prices to win even a modest share of industry sales. One tempting but illegal way around this problem is

---

[13]Stern and Grabner, *op. cit.*, pp. 91–92.
[14]For an interesting article on how to effectively fix prices, see John Q. Lawyer, "How to Conspire to Fix Prices," *Harvard Business Review* (March-April, 1963), pp. 95–103.

FIGURE 3-1   Costs of Price Fixing

In late 1976, a federal judge imposed fines, probation, or jail terms on 47 executives in 22 companies charged with and found guilty of price-fixing violations in the folding-carton industry. In terms of the numbers of defendants, this case was the largest price-fixing one since 1964.

Of those convicted, 15, including chief executive officers, were sentenced to brief prison terms, from 5 to 60 days, and were individually fined as much as $35,000. Of the remaining executives, 17 were fined from $500 to $30,000, and placed on probation. The remaining 15 executives were fined between $100 and $2,500. The 22 companies were initially fined $50,000 each, the maximum fine for a misdemeanor violation. The maximum fine now for a felony violation of antitrust law is $1 million for each violating company.

Following these criminal convictions, the companies faced 45 civil suits filed by customers seeking damages for alleged overcharges. Over the past two years, many of these same companies have been inundated with charges of criminal price fixing involving felony and misdemeanor violations in virtually every one of the converting ends of the business. One chief executive officer reported that his folding-carton division's past five years' earnings had been surpassed by just the legal fees involved in this case. The cost to image and company morale is incalculable.

Source: Jeffrey Sonnenfeld and Paul R. Lawrence, "Why Do Companies Succumb to Price Fixing?" *Harvard Business Review* (July-August, 1978), p. 155. Copyright © 1978 by the President and Fellows of Harvard College; all rights reserved.

for the managers of competing firms to agree not to reduce their price below a specified level. In this way, even reduced sales will generate some profits.

Undifferentiated Products. In some industries, all competing products are basically the same, i.e., undifferentiated. For firms in such industries, price reductions may be the only way to stay competitive. As one firm in the industry after another begins to lower its prices, profits throughout the industry decline. Again, the answer given by some industries to this problem is to control the price by deciding in advance which firm will bid lowest on each sale.

As an example, three automobile dealers in a small town competing for sales of vehicles to the city could meet and decide that dealer A would bid lowest on police cars, dealer B on sanitation trucks, and dealer C on utility trucks. This would insure that each dealer sold some vehicles to the city at a healthy profit. Profitable perhaps, but illegal!

Lack of Top Management Surveillance. In almost all price-fixing conspiracies broken up by the federal government, the chief executive officers of the firms involved stated that they spent a great deal of time trying to ensure that their companies did not participate in such activities. It is clear, however, that it takes more than one memo a year from top management to prevent a price conspiracy from developing. Top management, through direct discussion with middle management, should make it absolutely clear that no one in the firm is to participate in a price-fixing conspiracy, and that those who do will be severely punished.

Vertical Price Fixing

Vertical price fixing exists when two or more firms in a channel of distribution conspire to establish the price for a product. In 1937 Congress passed the Miller-Tydings Act, which exempted vertical price-fixing contracts from the antitrust laws if the state in which the transaction occurred also recognized the legality of such contracts. This action led to the passage of so-called fair trade laws by a majority of the states. Such laws permitted a manufacturer to set the price that each of its retail outlets would charge for its products.

The push for fair trade laws came from small merchants who feared that large discount retail stores would be able to sell products cheaper than they could. The major problem with fair trade laws was that their enforcement was always left to the manufacturer. Therefore, a manufacturer who decided to "fair trade" its products was constantly having to sue its large retail customers for violation of the fair trade law when the retailer discounted the price of the manufacturer's products. Most manufacturers found that it was not in their best interest to continually fight with their large distributors and therefore discontinued fair trading their products. In 1977 Congress repealed the Miller-Tydings Act, and as a result vertical price fixing is now once again a violation of both the Sherman Act and the Federal Trade Commission Act.[15]

The Robinson-Patman Act

The Robinson-Patman Act of 1936 prohibits any seller engaged in commerce from selling to two or more different purchasers, within a reasonably close period of time, commodities (not services) of like *grade and quality* at different prices where the result would be to substantially lessen competition or create an injury to competition. The Robinson-Patman Act also made it illegal for a seller to discriminate between two buyers in terms of supplementary services provided to them. This provision of the Robinson-Patman Act will be discussed in greater detail in the section of the chapter dealing with the legal aspects of advertising. Finally, the Robinson-Patman Act made it illegal for buyers to use their purchasing power to force sellers into granting discriminatory prices or services.

Defenses to Charges of Price Discrimination. The Robinson-Patman Act provides three defenses for the seller charged with price discrimination. In each case, the burden is on the defendant to prove the defense.

1. **Cost Justification.** The law reads that nothing "shall prevent (price) differentials which make only due allowance for differentials in the cost of manufacture, sale or delivery." Thus, a firm can charge different prices to different customers if the price differentials represent manufacturing or quantity discount savings. In terms of manufacturing, however, the courts have been willing to accept only price differentials resulting from transportation efficiencies, which can easily be verified from bills of lading. The courts generally have not viewed manufacturing efficiencies as a legitimate justification for price differentials because of the

---

[15]Discussion of fair trade laws adapted from L. Louise Luchsinger and Patrick M. Dunne, "Fair Trade Laws — How Fair?" *Journal of Marketing* (January, 1978), pp. 50–53.

difficulty in determining exactly the cost of specified units of a mass-produced product.

2. **Changing Market Conditions.** The second defense against price discrimination permitted by the Robinson-Patman Act was designed to meet fluid product or market conditions, such as the deterioration of perishable goods, the obsolescence of seasonal products, a distress sale under court order, or a legitimate going-out-of-business sale. For example, a fresh produce warehouse may change its prices from one day to the next, or even from one customer to the next, depending upon the freshness of its fruits and vegetables. A shoe warehouse engaging in similar price-changing behavior might be viewed as practicing price discrimination. The court has been rather liberal in accepting such a defense so as not to limit the flexibility of a firm in responding to changing product or market conditions.

3. **Meeting Competition.** The final defense of price discrimination is that a reduction in price is necessary in order to stay even with competition. Specifically, if the price quoted by a seller to a buyer is undercut by a competitor, the law gives the seller the right to lower the price charged to the buyer for the product in question. Since the seller may elect not to reduce the price for all customers in a competitive area, price discrimination is being practiced. The courts have been willing to accept this defense as long as the seller reduces the price to that of the competition, not below it. Undercutting the competitor, on the other hand, has been interpreted as illegal price discrimination.[16]

Court Decisions. Two landmark cases illustrate the application of the Robinson-Patman Act. The first, the Perkins case,[17] involved the sale of products by Standard Oil of California to the Clyde A. Perkins Company and Signal Oil Company. As claimed by Perkins, Standard Oil of California had been selling its products to Signal at a much lower price than to Perkins. Perkins stated that this cost differential made it difficult for its retail outlets to compete with Signal's retail outlets which passed on their savings to their customers.

Standard's defense of the price differential was that Signal sold its products to an independent secondary wholesaler, who in turn sold them to Regal, a retail distributor (see Figure 3-2). Standard argued that Regal was "so far removed from Standard in the chain of distribution" that any price discrimination that may have taken place was beyond the coverage of the Robinson-Patman Act. The court ruled that Standard's price discrimination injured Perkins because Perkins' retail outlets were not able to compete with Regal's retail outlets. The fact that Signal sold its products to an independent wholesaler, who in turn sold them to Regal, did not eliminate Standard Oil of California's responsibility for illegal price discrimination.[18]

The second case involved the sale by Borden, Inc., of chemically identical evaporated milk at two different prices. Borden sold the milk distributed under its own name at a higher price than the milk packaged under a private label.

---

[16]Robert N. Corley, Robert L. Black, and O. Lee Reed, *The Legal Environment of Business* (New York: McGraw-Hill Book Company, 1977), pp. 298–299.

[17]Clyde A. Perkins v. Standard Oil of California, *U.S. Supreme Court Reports*, Vol. 395, p. 642 (1969).

[18]Ray O. Werner, "Marketing and the U.S. Supreme Court, 1968–1974," *Journal of Marketing* (January, 1977), pp. 36–37.

FIGURE 3-2   Sales of Gasoline by Standard Oil of California

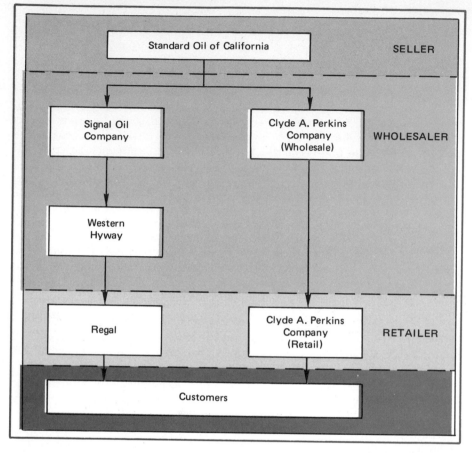

Borden argued that the products were different because they had different brand names and because they were perceived to be different by consumers in the marketplace. The court held that "the economic factors inherent in brand names and national advertising should not be considered in the jurisdictional inquiry under the 'like grade and quality' test."[19] In essence, physically identical products must be sold at the same price no matter what the marketing tactics involved (including branding strategy).

REGULATING THE CHANNELS OF DISTRIBUTION

The law also regulates much of the behavior among members of a distribution channel. The pattern in the United States and Canada has been the expansion of regulation into more areas of distribution each time Congress or Parliament meets. Three areas of distribution law directly affect marketing and include refusals to deal, franchising, and territorial restrictions.

---

[19]FTC v. the Borden Co., *U.S. Supreme Court Reports*, Vol. 383, p. 367 (1966).

Most of us have ethical standards founded in our religions and in the teachings and actions of our parents, teachers, and friends. These standards are often put to the test in the marketplace. While sitting in a marketing class, it is easy to say that **you** would never participate in an illegal price conspiracy; it is quite another thing to resist such a temptation in practice.

You and Your Company. As a management trainee, you will gradually be given increased responsibility, and you will likely begin to internalize the values, goals, and style of your firm. "It is *our* policy. . . ." "*We* believe that. . . ." Such statements become commonplace as you move up the corporate ladder, especially when you are singled out from other trainees and informally designated as a "comer" with top management potential.

The Rationalization. Once you develop a feeling of loyalty and identify your own welfare with that of your firm, the possibility of an ethical conflict becomes very real. Imagine that you are a junior executive on the "fast track." You've been singled out for great things. One day you're asked to attend an important policy meeting. You're flattered. In the meeting, you hear the vice-president say that *it's time for the industry to get its prices in line*. It sounds a little "funny" to you, but should you say something? The fact that you're in the meeting shows how highly regarded you are by top management. Would you want to jeopardize that? Might not some of the following rationalizations sound tempting?

1. The proposed action may be a little unusual but it *probably* isn't illegal. After all, I'm not a lawyer.

2. It's in the best interest of the company and its hourly workers whose jobs may be in jeopardy if profits fall.

3. It's in the best interest of the nation. Foreign competition is beating us to death by dumping cheap, poorly made products on the U.S. market.

4. It's an industry tradition that executives from competing firms occasionally meet to discuss common problems. How can I know when casual conversation about prices becomes a price conspiracy? In any case, these meetings have been going on for years so how can they be illegal?

Test of Ethical Behavior. Is a proposed action within the bounds of ethical behavior? Here are a few questions to ask yourself: If you followed through on the action, could you tell your family about it? Must you fill out phony statements or hide something from internal auditors? Would you be willing to describe your actions to the firm's legal staff?

In the end, only your own values can protect you.

Marketing & You

Refusals to Deal

As early as 1919, in the so-called Colgate doctrine, the Supreme Court recognized the right of sellers to choose their dealers. This right, however, is not absolute. For example, businesses that sell to the public may not refuse to deal with a buyer because of race, color, or creed. The court has also forbidden sellers or dealers from acting jointly to eliminate other dealers from the market. A classic example of such action involved the General Motors Corporation. In the early 1960s, this automobile company sold its Chevrolets in California through 85 independent auto dealers. Twelve of the dealers had made arrangements to sell through discount operators. GM cooperated with three California automobile dealer associations to obtain written agreements from all 85 Chevrolet dealers to the effect that they would refrain from selling to discounters in the future. GM then worked with several dealers to catch "cheaters" who continued to sell to discounters. In each case GM retaliated by restricting the number and types of new cars shipped to the cheaters. The Supreme Court held that this action was a "classic conspiracy in the restraint of trade: joint, collaborative action by dealers, the defendant associations, and General Motors to eliminate a class of competitors [in this case, the discounters] by terminating business dealing with them and to deprive franchised dealers of their freedom to deal through discounters. . . ."[20] This type of conspiracy is an obvious violation of the Sherman Act; the protection of free and open competition overrides the right of an individual firm to select the dealers with whom it will do business.

Franchising

A **franchise** is a contractual relationship under which the franchisor permits the franchisee to sell its products under a strict set of rules, to display the franchisor's sign, and to call upon the marketing and operating assistance of the franchisor, if required. In return, the franchisee pays the franchisor a fee or royalty payments in order to be a member of the franchise system and to derive the benefits therefrom. Earlier in the chapter we mentioned that an agreement binding a buyer to a specific seller is called an exclusive agreement and is in violation of Section 3 of the Clayton Act. Therefore, it would seem that a distributor (franchisor) cannot make a buyer (franchisee) enter into a contract whereby the franchisee agrees to make all purchases from the franchisor, thereby creating an exclusive agreement.

The Supreme Court, however, has interpreted the issue of exclusive agreements rather liberally. When a distributor (franchisor) would be damaged if the buyer (franchisee) did not make purchases exclusively from that distributor, the court has let such exclusive contracts stand. In making such a determination, the court has reviewed the distributor's method of operation, public image, uniformity of the product offering, and the volume of commerce that would be affected if the exclusive agreement were not permitted to stand.[21] For example,

---

[20]United States v. General Motors Corporation, *U.S. Supreme Court Reports*, Vol. 384, p. 127 (1966).

[21]David Fromson, "Manufacturer's Rights and Limitations," *Industrial Distribution* (November, 1977), p. 66.

McDonald's Corp., the fast-food franchisor, could suffer severe financial injury if it had no control over where the franchisee purchased meat, produce, and other food products. As a result, the court has permitted McDonald's and other similar operations to use exclusive agreements.

Two other areas of the law relate directly to the problems of franchising: (1) the termination of franchisees and (2) full disclosure laws, which have been passed by many states in the U.S. and by several provinces in Canada.

Termination of Franchisees. Most franchise agreements have a clause giving either party the right periodically — usually once a year — to terminate the franchise agreement. However, the law clearly indicates that a franchisor, regardless of the wording of the franchise agreement, cannot terminate the agreement without showing good cause if the parties involved have done business for a number of years and if the franchisee has a significant investment in the continuation of the franchise relationship.

A case illustrating the termination issue involved the Marinello family and the Shell Oil Company.[22] The Marinellos had operated a Shell Oil dealership for more than 15 years. The lease had been renewed periodically until Shell decided to terminate it in 1972. The New Jersey Supreme Court held unanimously that there was an "implied covenant" between Shell and the Marinellos that their lease would be renewed. As a result of such court decisions, several states have passed laws requiring franchisors to renew franchise agreements unless good cause can be shown not to renew.[23]

Full Disclosure Laws.[24] One of the biggest problem areas in franchising has been the purchase of worthless franchises by unsuspecting people. Many people have lost their entire life savings as a result of such purchases. Most of the abuses can be categorized as one or more of the following:

1. Misleading information concerning profitability of the franchise.
2. Refusal to show actual profit-and-loss statements for the franchise.
3. Hidden charges to the franchisee.
4. Use of celebrities' names to promote the franchise.
5. Misleading promises concerning aid to the franchisee.
6. Use of high-pressure sales techniques.

In 1971 the state of California passed a law designed to eliminate such practices and to protect the prospective franchisee from misrepresentation. The essential provisions of this law are summarized in Figure 3-3. Eleven more states have passed similar legislation in recent years. In each case the law requires the franchisor to register with the state securities administration and to provide each prospective franchisee with a set of documents describing the investment accurately and objectively. In California, the franchise investor must see an investment prospectus at least 48 hours prior to signing any agreement.

Although these laws are expensive to administer, it is clear that they have substantially reduced the incidence of fraudulent practices. It is reasonable to

[22]Shell Oil Co. vs. Marinello, *New Jersey Superior Court Reports*, Vol. 120, p. 357; *Atlantic Reporter*, 2d Series, Vol. 294, p. 253 (1972).

[23]Fromson, *op. cit.*, p. 67.

[24]Shelby D. Hunt and John R. Niven, "Full Disclosure Laws in Franchising: An Empirical Investigation," *Journal of Marketing* (April, 1976), pp. 53–62.

FIGURE 3-3   Summary of California's Full Disclosure Law

1. Regulation of full disclosure for franchising is carried out by the State Commissioner of Securities.

2. Franchisors must register a prospectus with the Office of Securities. Exempted from the registration requirement are large franchisors (net worth greater than $5 million) who have had a minimum of 25 franchises at all times during the preceding five years.

3. Some of the items that must be included in the prospectus are:
   a. Disclosure of the background of the principals involved with the franchisor (especially any felonies committed by the principals).
   b. Recent financial statement.
   c. Sample franchise contract.
   d. Policy of the franchisor concerning franchise fees, royalties, and supplies.
   e. Contract termination provisions.
   f. Terms and conditions of any financial arrangements.
   g. Substantiation of any profit projections in pro forma statements.
   h. Disclosures relating to using the name of public figures.
   i. Number of franchises presently operating and proposed to be sold.
   j. Territorial protection given to the franchisee.

4. All franchisors must show the prospectus to all potential franchisees at least 48 hours before signing the agreement (or receiving any consideration).

5. All advertisements for franchisees must be registered with the commissioner at least three business days prior to publication of the advertisement.

Source: Shelby D. Hunt and John R. Nevin, "Full Disclosure Laws in Franchising: An Empirical Investigation," *Journal of Marketing* (April, 1976), pp. 54–55.

expect that before long the federal government will also pass legislation protecting potential franchisees.

Territorial Restrictions

Does a manufacturer have the right to restrict the sales territories of its dealers or distributors? This question was answered, at least temporarily, by the Schwinn Bicycle Co. case of 1967.[25] Schwinn had been selling its bicycles to independent Schwinn wholesalers. The Schwinn distributor contract made it clear that the wholesalers were permitted to sell Schwinn products only to the franchised Schwinn retail outlets in their territory. The court held that once "risk, dominion and title" had passed to the buyer, the seller had no control over to whom the product was eventually sold. The court also said that any attempt to exercise such control was a per se offense, which requires no investigation into the impact of the act in question on competition. That is, even if the territorial restriction did not injure competition, it was still illegal.[26]

[25]United States v. Arnold Schwinn and Company, *U.S. Supreme Court Reports*, Vol. 388, p. 365 (1967).

[26]For further information on the Schwinn case see James R. Burley, "Territorial Restrictions in Distribution Systems: Current Legal Developments," *Journal of Marketing* (October, 1975), pp. 52–56.

The court, however, reversed itself in 1977 in the GTE-Sylvania, Inc., case.[27]. Sylvania's contract with its dealers was similar to Schwinn's original territorial agreement. Sylvania gave each dealer an "exclusive" right to a territory; the dealer in turn agreed not to establish other sales outlets outside its territory. Sylvania believed that by reducing intrabrand competition (one Sylvania dealer against another), it could strengthen its own position and thereby increase interbrand competition (Sylvania dealers against other television dealers).[28] The court held that ". . .there has been no showing in this case [Sylvania] either generally or with respect to [the] agreements, that vertical restrictions have or are likely to have a 'pernicious effect on competition' or that they 'lack . . . any redeeming value.' "[29] In effect, the court overruled the per se rule, reversing the position it had taken in the Schwinn case. According to the Sylvania decision, all future territorial restrictions must be judged on the basis of their impact on competition. "Reasonable" restrictions that do not have a negative impact on competition, such as those in the Sylvania case, will be permitted.

THE REGULATION OF PROMOTION

The U.S. Supreme Court in 1931 ruled that the authority of the Federal Trade Commission extended only to the injury of competition. The FTC, as a consequence, had no authority over fraudulent advertising because it injured only consumers without creating a competitive injury. To deal with this problem, Congress passed the Wheeler-Lea Act in 1938. This law amended Section 5 of the Federal Trade Commission Act to read:

> Unfair methods of competition in commerce and unfair or deceptive acts or practices in commerce are hereby declared unlawful.

This amendment enlarged the responsibilities of the Federal Trade Commission to include the protection of consumers against unfair trade practices, regardless of whether they involved competitive injury. The Wheeler-Lea Act also explicitly prohibited the fraudulent advertising of "foods, drugs, devices, (and) or cosmetics." This clause was tantamount to making the protection of public health a primary objective of the commission.

Keeping the Wheeler-Lea Act in mind, let's look at the FTC's role in the regulation of personal selling and advertising. Then we'll examine a current controversy surrounding advertising directed to children and what role the FTC has played in that controversy.

The Regulation of Personal Selling

One of the major complaints against personal selling is that some salespeople use high-pressure tactics, that is, they trick or persuade customers into buying a product that they really do not want. A high-pressure salesperson may try to impress the buyer with the urgency of the purchase: "If you do not buy

---

[27]Continental T.V. Inc., et al. v. GTE-Sylvania Inc., Trade Reg. Rep. (CCH), ¶ 61,488 (S. Ct., June, 1977).

[28]Ray W. Werner, "The 'New' Supreme Court and the Marketing Environment, 1975–1977," Journal of Marketing (April, 1978), pp. 60–61.

[29]Continental T.V. Inc., et. al. v. GTE-Sylvania Inc., loc. cit., as quoted in Ibid., p. 61.

now, we may be sold out for a month!'' Other appeals are based on fear: "There have been burglars in this area. You cannot be safe without this alarm for your home.'' Or flattery may be used: "Everyone in your social position owns one of these.'' Emotional sales pitches may also get results: "If you do not buy a subscription to this magazine, I may not be able to go back to college next year.''

Confused by the fast-talking salesperson, the customer may buy an unnecessary product or service or one that may cause future financial strain. In an attempt to protect the credulous, insecure, gullible, or unsuspecting consumer, the Federal Trade Commission promulgated the Cooling-Off Rule and Congress passed the truth-in-lending act.

The Cooling-Off Rule. The Cooling-Off Rule says that anyone purchasing a product or service for $25 or more from a door-to-door salesperson has the right to cancel the purchase within 72 hours of the transaction and to receive a full refund. This cooling-off period allows the consumer to reconsider what might have been a hasty and ill-advised purchase. The rule also requires the salesperson to inform the buyer of this right of cancellation, as well as to provide instructions for cancelling the purchase. In addition, the seller must furnish the buyer with a written sales report, receipt, or contract.[30]

Several states have passed their own cooling-off laws. These state regulations must be at least as restrictive as the FTC rule, and some impose even tougher restrictions on certain types of door-to-door sales.

So far, the results of cooling-off regulations have been beneficial. Research results made available by a large direct-sales firm show that the FTC Cooling-Off Rule does help the consumer even though it does not eliminate all door-to-door selling abuses.[31]

The Truth-in-Lending Act. Credit has become a way of life in the United States. Consumers, however, often do not understand how much they must pay in order to finance their purchases. Table 3-1 illustrates this problem by showing how real interest rates vary depending upon the repayment provisions of the loan contract. The truth-in-lending act authorized the Federal Reserve Board to adopt regulations "to assure a meaningful disclosure of credit terms so that the consumer will be able to compare more readily the various credit terms available to him to avoid the uninformed use of credit.''

The Federal Reserve Board requires full credit disclosure for all consumer transactions where the debtor is a person, as distinguished from a business entity, and where the credit obtained is primarily for personal, family, household, or agricultural purposes. Full disclosure means that all finance charges that are paid directly or indirectly by the debtor must be shown to the debtor. These include among others interest, service charges, loan fees, points, finder's fees, and appraisal fees. In addition, the law requires that the lender disclose

---

[30]*Cooling-Off Period for Door-to-Door Sales*, Federal Trade Commission Trade Regulation Rule, promulgated October 18, 1972, effective June 7, 1974.

[31]William L. Shauklin and Herbert G. King, "Evaluating the FTC Cooling-Off Rule,'' *The Journal of Consumer Affairs* (Winter, 1977), pp. 101–106.

TABLE 3-1 Differences in True Interest as a Function of Payment Schedules

	Payment at End of One Year*	Principal & Interest Paid in 12 Equal Monthly Payments**	Interest Deducted at Time of Loan***
Loan	$1,000	$1,000	$1,000
Interest Charges	$100	$100	$100
Real Interest	10%	18%	11.1%

*Assumes that principal and interest are paid back together at the end of the year.
**Assumes that principal and interest are paid back in equal monthly payments over 12 months.
***Assumes that interest is deducted from the principal at the time the money is borrowed and that the loan is repaid at the end of the year. In this case, the loan is effectively $900.

the finance charge expressed as a percentage and specifies that the method for calculating the annual percentage interest rate treat each payment as first being applied to the finance charge and then to the principal.

While the main impact of the truth-in-lending law has been to help consumers make comparisons among financing alternatives, it also gives debtors the right to cancel transactions in which they have given their homes as security if they cancel within three days. It also limits the liability of the holder of a lost or stolen credit card to $50 in the event it is used by an unauthorized individual.[32]

The Regulation of Advertising

The FTC has concerned itself with the regulation of advertising for many years. As early as 1922, the FTC issued a cease and desist order against an underwear manufacturer that had labeled its largely cotton products as "natural merino," "natural wool," and "natural worsted."[33]

Today the Federal Trade Commission uses rather flexible standards in determining whether any given advertisement is deceptive. Generally speaking, an advertisement is considered deceptive if the overall impression or meaning is misleading, irrespective of whether the specific claims are literally true, or if it has two meanings, one of which is misleading.[34]

These principles have not stopped advertisers from using so-called puffery. **Puffery** refers to the sometimes innocent exaggerations often used to sell a product. For example, a local jewelry store might advertise that it "offers the best deal in town," or that "no firm can beat our financing." In the beginning of the 20th century, puffery often became rather flagrant — the claims made for patent medicines and mineral water are excellent examples. Today, the

---

[32]Robert N. Corley, Robert L. Black, and O. Lee Reed,*The Legal Environment of Business* (New York: McGraw-Hill Book Company, 1977), pp. 532–536.

[33]FTC v. Winstead Hosiery Co., *U.S. Supreme Court Reports*, Vol. 258, p. 483 (1922).

[34]Lee Loevinger, "The Attack on Advertising and the Goals of Regulation," *The Conference Board Record* (January, 1973), p. 25.

FIGURE 3-4   An Ad from a Weekly New York Newspaper of the 1880s.

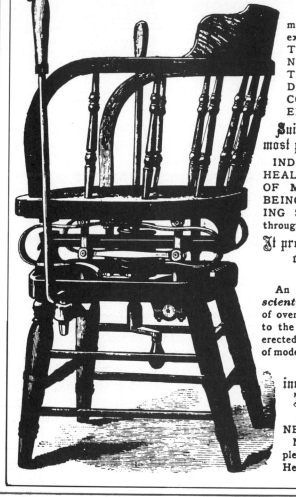

The Health Jolting Chair

COPYRIGHT.

The most important Health Mechanism ever produced

A Practical Household Substitute for the Saddle-Horse.

It affords a PERFECT means of giving EFFICIENT exercise to the ESSENTIALLY IMPORTANT NUTRITIVE ORGANS OF THE BODY in the most DIRECT, CONVENIENT, COMFORTABLE, and INEXPENSIVE manner.

Suitable for all ages and for most physical conditions.

INDISPENSABLE TO THE HEALTH AND HAPPINESS OF MILLIONS OF HUMAN BEINGS WHO MAY BE LIVING SEDENTARY LIVES through choice or necessity.

It preserves Health, cures Disease, and prolongs Life.

An *ingenious, rational, scientific, mechanical* means of overcoming those impediments to the taking of proper exercise, erected by the artificial methods of modern society.

For certain classes of invalids a veritable Treasure-Trove.

A CONSERVATOR of NERVOUS ENERGY.

No dwelling-house is completely furnished without The Health Jolting Chair.

Source: Dick Sutphen, *The Mad Old Ads* (New York: McGraw-Hill Book Company, 1966) p. 37.

example shown in Figure 3-4 would clearly be in violation of FTC-enforced rules and regulations.

One of the more far-reaching FTC activities is its advertising substantiation program. Begun in 1971, this program requires advertisers to submit data to the commission proving that their advertising claims are true. It is essential, therefore, that advertisers have data and research results backing their claims. These tests must be run on the product before the advertisement is shown to the public. For example, an automobile company may not claim that one of its cars traveling 50 miles an hour can stop within 150 feet unless it has already run tests demonstrating this to be true. If the company made the claim without these tests, it would be in violation of FTC regulations even if it later proved that the car could stop within 150 feet.

When the FTC finds that an advertisement is deceptive, it may require the firm involved either to make an affirmative disclosure or to run corrective advertising. In an **affirmative disclosure**, the firm provides additional information about the product, frequently about a deficiency or limitation. In one case, the manufacturer of a swimming aid was ordered to state in its advertising that the product was not a life preserver and was to be used in shallow water only.[35]

With **corrective advertising**, on the other hand, the firm attempts to remedy, or correct, an impression that may have arisen from false, deceptive, or misleading advertising in the past. The FTC's first corrective advertising order was issued in 1971 against ITT Continental Baking Company.[36] The firm, maker of Profile Bread, for many years had promoted Profile bread as a diet product. Profile bread did have a few less calories per slice than other breads. The problem, however, was that the lower calorie count resulted primarily because Profile bread was sliced thinner than most other breads. In addition, the FTC felt that the reduction in the number of calories per slice was not sufficient to make any meaningful difference between Profile and other breads in terms of an individual's caloric intake. As a result, the FTC ordered Continental to spend 25 percent of its media budget for one year on FTC-approved corrective advertising.

Advertising and Children

In the past ten years, parents and educators alike have shown a growing concern about the effects of television and, in particular, television advertising on children.

The Proposed FTC Regulation. Throughout the late 1970s, a group known as Action for Children's Television (ACT), made up of parents and teachers, applied nearly continuous pressure on Congress and the FTC to take more positive steps to regulate advertisements directed to children. In 1977, ACT petitioned the FTC to prevent candy manufacturers from using television to advertise their products to children. After an investigation of the issue, the FTC proposed a trade regulation rule on children's advertising.[37] The set of rules proposed is as follows:

(a) Ban all televised advertising for any product which is directed to, or seen by, audiences composed of a significant proportion of children who are too young to understand the selling purpose of or otherwise comprehend or evaluate the advertising;

---

[35]Kemec Sports, Inc., *et al.*, Trade Reg. Rep., Vol. 2, ¶19,971 (1972).

[36]ITT Continental Baking Co., *et al., Trade Reg. Rep.,* Vol. 3, ¶19,539 (1971).

[37]Federal Trade Commission, "Children's Advertising — Proposed Trade Regulation Rule Making and Public Hearing," *Federal Register*, Vol. 43, No. 82 (April 27, 1978), pp. 17967–17972.

(b) Ban televised advertising for sugared food products directed to, or seen by, audiences composed of a significant proportion of older children, the consumption of which products poses the most serious dental health risks;

(c) Require televised advertising for sugared food products not included in Paragraph (b), which is directed to, or seen by, audiences composed of a significant proportion of older children, to be balanced by nutritional and/or health disclosures funded by advertisers.[38]

Besides ACT, several other associations back the FTC in its proposed regulations — the American Academy of Pediatrics, American Parents' Committee, the Dental Health Section of the American Public Health Association, and many others. This *proposed* ruling constitutes a significant step toward establishing standards of performance for advertisers.

Voluntary Compliance. The Federal Trade Commission has also been able to work out several types of voluntary compliance with the advertising industry. In 1974, for example, the commission asked television advertisers to stop using premiums in commercials directed to children. As discussed in Chapter 10, **premiums** are nonmerchandise-related objects sometimes included in products' packages. A toy soldier in a cereal box would be a premium. The FTC took this action for three reasons: (1) the main purpose of the premium is to distract the attention of the viewer from criteria that should guide product choice; (2) the actual effect of a premium offer is to encourage the child viewer to want a product in order to obtain the premium; and (3) premium advertising makes it more difficult for the child to make a purchase decision. Television advertisers have honored the FTC request and no longer use advertising of premiums during children's programming.

In addition, several independent associations have begun to develop their own regulations regarding children's advertising. Although such codes are not legally binding, they do help control abuse and prevent deceptive advertising. An example of such an association is the National Advertising Review Board (NARB), established in 1974 to deal with the issue of truth and accuracy in national advertising. Its children's unit initiated a high-priority program to regulate children's television advertising. By 1976 the council had a list of significant accomplishments: monitoring procedures for children's ads; the selection of a group of consultants on matters relating to guideline development, specific investigations, and broad issues; and finally, the establishment of the Revised Children's Advertising Guidelines of the National Advertising Division.[39]

CONSUMER PROTECTION LEGISLATION

Consumer protection means more than just protecting the public from deceptive advertising. What are some other objectives of consumer protection laws? Why have existing laws not been as effective as they might have been?

---

[38]*Ibid.*, p. 17968.

[39]National Advertising Division, Children's Advertising Review Unit, *Advertising to Children: Report of a Seminar Conducted by the CARU* (June, 1976), p. 3.

Consumer Protection Laws

In addition to the Federal Trade Commission Act and the Wheeler-Lea Act, a number of other major consumer protection laws have been passed since the early 1900s. Figure 3-5 presents an abbreviated history of consumer

FIGURE 3-5 Selected Consumer Protection Laws

Act	Description
Food and Drug Act (1906)	Established the Food and Drug Administration and prohibited unsafe and adulterated food and drug products from being sold in interstate commerce.
Federal Trade Commission Act (1914)	Established the Federal Trade Commission to guard against "unfair methods of competition."
Food, Drug, and Cosmetic Act (1938)	Amended Food and Drug Act (1906) to include cosmetics and therapeutic devices.
Wheeler-Lea Act (1938)	Amended the Federal Trade Commission Act; expanded the consumer protection activities of the FTC to include "unfair or deceptive acts or practices."
Flammable Fabrics Act (1953)	Made it illegal to sell or manufacture clothing that is flammable enough to be dangerous.
Hazardous Substance Labeling Act (1960)	Controls the labeling of packages of hazardous products that are sold to final consumers.
Kefauver-Harris Amendment (1962)	Amended Food, Drug, and Cosmetic Act of 1938 to require all manufacturers of drugs to test their products for safety and efficacy before they can be sold.
Fair Packaging and Labeling Act (1966)	Regulated packaging and labeling of consumer goods; provided for the voluntary adoption, by industry, of uniform packaging standards.
Cigarette Labeling Act (1966)	Required health warning labels on cigarette packaging.
Consumer Credit Protection Act (1968) (Truth in Lending)	Required full disclosure of terms and conditions of finance charges in consumer credit transactions.
Child Protection and Toy Safety Act of 1969	Amended Hazardous Substance Labeling Act (1960) to ban toys and other articles used by children that pose electrical, mechanical, or thermal hazards.

CONTINUED

FIGURE 3-5   Selected Consumer Protection Laws (Continued)

Act	Description
Consumer Product Safety Act (1972)	Established Consumer Product Safety Commission which assumed many FDA product safety standards for a broad range of consumer products with the ability to levy penalties for failure to meet the standards.
Magnuson-Moss Warranty/Federal Trade Commission Improvement Act (1975)	Permitted the FTC to make rules with respect to consumer product warranties. Also provided consumer redress, including class action. Increased FTC jurisdiction to matters "affecting commerce" and its general rule-making powers with respect to unfair or deceptive acts or practices.
Consumer Goods Pricing Act (1975)	Repealed federal antitrust exemptions which permitted states to enact fair trade (resale price maintenance) laws. These state laws had legalized price fixing at the retail level.
Consumer Leasing Act (1976)	Amended Consumer Credit Protection Act to require meaningful disclosure of lease terms and ultimate liability in connection with leased products.
Consumer Education Act (1978)	Established the Office of Consumer Education. It is responsible for supporting research projects which are designed to provide consumer education to the public.

protection legislation. We will look specifically at the Food and Drug Act, the Magnuson-Moss Warranty Act, and the Consumer Product Safety Act.

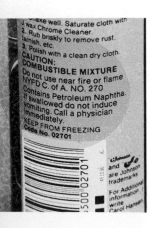

The Food and Drug Act. The Food and Drug Act of 1906 created the Food and Drug Administration (FDA), currently housed in the Department of Health, Education, and Welfare. The FDA regulates a larger percentage of U.S. industry than any other regulatory agency with the exception of the FTC. Traditionally, it has been responsible for protecting the nation's health. Subsequent legislation — including the Food, Drug, and Cosmetic Act of 1938 — expanded the scope of FDA activities to include:

> . . .insuring that foods are safe, pure and wholesome; drugs are safe and effective; cosmetics are harmless; therapeutic devices are safe and effective; products are honestly and informatively labeled and packaged; . . . counterfeiting of drugs is stopped; and interstate travelers are afforded adequate levels of sanitation and control of health hazards.[40]

The FDA does an admirable job with relatively little funding. It spends approximately 38 to 40 percent of its budget regulating prescription and non-

[40]Office of the Federal Register, *United States Government Organization Manual, 1971/72* (Washington, D.C.: U.S. Government Printing Office, July 1, 1971), p. 332.

prescription drugs. On a routine basis, the FDA conducts extensive clinical studies on more than 400 new drugs each year. The FDA must certify that each of these products is safe and effective. In addition, the FDA is responsible for ensuring that the nation's 70,000 food processing and warehousing establishments produce and store high quality food under sanitary conditions. The FDA makes some 22,000 on-site inspections of food establishments each year. Finally, the FDA has the authority to remove from the market any cosmetic that it finds harmful to users.[41]

The Magnuson-Moss Warranty Act. This important piece of federal consumer protection legislation was passed in 1975. It applies only to purchases made by final consumers for personal, family, or household purposes. This act, which is normally enforced by the FTC, is designed to prevent deceptive warranty practices, to make consumer warranties easier to understand, and to provide *effective* ways of enforcing warranty obligations.

The act therefore applies only to those firms that voluntarily decide to provide a warranty for a product they have sold. The law does require that with a *full warranty* the seller must assume a set of minimum duties and obligations for products costing ten dollars or more. For example, the seller must agree to *repair or replace* any defective product within a *reasonable* time without charge. If the seller is unable to repair the product the purchaser can select either a *cash refund* or *replacement* without charge. Consequential damages such as for personal or property damage resulting from the defective product can be disclaimed only if the product limitation is conspicuous. A written warranty that does not meet each of these standards is called a *limited warranty*.[42]

The Consumer Product Safety Act. The Consumer Product Safety Act, passed by Congress in 1972, created the Consumer Product Safety Commission (CPSC) and gave it broad authority to propose safety standards for all consumer products. At the time of passage, the law made mandatory the voluntary safety standards of many industries. Since that time, the commission, where appropriate, has also developed new standards for other industries.

Once a product safety rule has been adopted, the federal courts have the authority to remove from the market any product not meeting prescribed standards. The manufacturer is subject to a $2,000/day fine for each violation. In addition, the Consumer Product Safety Act permits a consumer to sue for injuries in federal court if a manufacturer knowingly violates a product safety rule.

While it is still too early to determine the effect of the Consumer Product Safety Act, supporters say that the law has been successful in disseminating information about hazardous products and injuries caused by these products. In addition, they argue that since the passage of the act the actual number of consumer product-related injuries and deaths has declined.[43] The degree of success of other consumer protection laws is not quite so clear.

---

[41]Laurence P. Feldman, *Consumer Protection: Problems and Prospects* (St. Paul, Minn.: West Publishing Co., 1976), pp. 54–64.

[42]Corley, *et al.*, *op. cit.*, pp. 528–529.

[43]*Ibid.*, pp. 545–546.

Are Consumer Protection Laws Effective?

While consumer protection laws have not really failed, they simply have not proven as effective as they might have. The principal reason is that consumers do not really understand their rights, as illustrated in a study conducted in 1975.[44] The objective of the research was to find out what percentage of consumers and lawyers really understand ten different areas of consumer law, ranging from false or deceptive advertising to deceptive retail practices.

As Table 3-2 shows, the public knows relatively little about most areas of consumer protection law, and lawyers do not know much more. For example, 33.5 percent of the consumers and only 46.5 percent of the lawyers responded correctly to the questions about false or deceptive advertising. Excluding credit card regulations, the spread between the correct answers for the two groups averaged 12.2 percent.

The implications of the research are quite clear — the U.S. may not need additional consumer protection legislation as badly as it needs a better way of informing consumers about their rights under existing legislation. Local bar associations can play a major role in providing information to the public — assuming that bar members take the time to read up on consumer law! Also, legal experts on consumer protection could speak to church groups, PTAs, and

TABLE 3-2   Responses of Consumers and Lawyers on Consumer Protection Laws

	Total Consumer Sample	Total Lawyer Sample
	Percentage of Correct Responses	Percentage of Correct Responses
False or deceptive advertising	33.5%	46.5%
False or deceptive retail advertising	35.1	51.5
Credit regulations	63.7	75.2
Credit reporting	60.6	80.0
Door-to-door selling	29.4	38.8
Auto sales	77.5	85.5
Credit cards	44.5	77.0
Labels	64.5	52.5
Truth in lending	83.5	94.5
Deceptive retail practices	37.8	50.6
Total number of respondents	(607)	(175)

Source: William H. Cunningham and Isabella C. M. Cunningham, "Consumer Protection: More Information or More Regulation?" *Journal of Marketing* (April, 1976), p. 66.

[44]William H. Cunningham and Isabella C. M. Cunningham, "Consumer Protection: More Information or More Regulation?" *Journal of Marketing* (April, 1976), pp. 63–68.

similar organizations. High schools and even junior high schools could begin to offer consumer protection programs. Although 35 states and the District of Columbia have endorsed consumer education in policy statements, most states still do not offer broad consumer education programs in their school systems.[45]

SOCIAL RESPONSIBILITY

The social responsibilities of a corporation and its marketing executives are difficult to assess, first, because it is hard to define "correct" behavior in a normative sense and, second, because marketing executives must operate and make decisions in a dynamic society involving changing ethical considerations. Although the executive may be free to make short-run decisions within market-imposed constraints, in the long run those decisions must be consistent with the norms of society. Two important questions arise. What are the attitudes of consumers and business executives toward the subject of ethical business practices? What is marketing's responsibility to the low-income sector of society?

Attitudes Toward Business Ethics

Consumers and executives alike are troubled by the ethical implications of many business practices. Whether or not their perceptions are correct, all too often they feel that the primary objective of most business people is to benefit themselves and their companies irrespective of any harm done to society as a whole.

Consumer Attitudes. Table 3-3 presents the partial findings of a study involving a national sample of consumers.[46] Less than 25 percent of the sample felt that business operates on the assumption that the consumer is always correct; more than 37 percent thought that "let the buyer beware" is the guiding philosophy of most manufacturers. In the area of product quality, it was encouraging to see that 78.6 percent of the sample thought that manufacturers make an effort to design products to fit consumer needs. Unfortunately, a large percentage of consumers also felt that manufacturers design products to wear out as quickly as possible and that manufacturers often withhold good products from the market. Finally, the results of the study suggest that most consumers simply do not believe the claims of advertisers.

A second study examined 34 consumer products.[47] The key questions concerned whether consumers were satisfied with their purchases of these products and, if not, whether they did anything about their dissatisfaction. Once again, the results were not encouraging. Overall, approximately 20 percent of all consumer purchases resulted in at least some buyer dissatisfaction. Considerably more than half of those dissatisfied did nothing to alleviate the

---

[45]Louis Cook, "Classroom Consumerism," *Austin American Statesman*, July 21, 1979, p. A2.

[46]Hiram C. Barksdale and William R. Darden, "Consumer Attitudes Toward Marketing and Consumerism," *Journal of Marketing* (October, 1972), pp. 28–35.

[47]Alan R. Andreason and Arthur Best, "Consumers Complain — Does Business Respond?" *Harvard Business Review* (July-August, 1977), pp. 93–101.

TABLE 3-3   Consumer Attitudes on the Operating Philosophies of Business

Statements	Level of Agreement				
	Strongly Agree	Agree	Uncertain	Disagree	Strongly Disagree
1. Most manufacturers operate on the philosophy that the consumer is always right.	2.0%	21.5%	15.8%	47.2%	13.6%
2. Despite what is frequently said, "let the buyer beware" is the guiding philosophy of most manufacturers.	5.6	32.5	24.6	34.2	3.1
3. In general, manufacturers make an effort to design products to fit the needs of consumers.	5.4	73.2	8.8	11.9	0.8
4. Manufacturers often withhold important product improvements from the market in order to protect their own interests.	11.3	37.9	34.7	15.5	0.6
5. Manufacturers do not deliberately design products which will wear out as quickly as possible.	4.0	31.6	22.6	31.9	9.9
6. Most product advertising is believable.	0.6	30.2	13.8	42.4	13.0

Source: Hiram C. Barksdale and William R. Darden, "Consumer Attitudes Toward Marketing and Consumerism," *Journal of Marketing* (October, 1972), pp. 29–30.

situation. Of those individuals who did complain, only 56.5 percent felt that their complaints were resolved to their satisfaction.

Executive Attitudes. Many executives grow quite cynical when they compare their behavior with that of the "average executive." The magnitude of this cynicism can be seen from a study of *Harvard Business Review* readers.[48] The participants were asked about illegal payments to foreign nationals as a means to help obtain international contracts. Forty-two percent of the subjects stated that they would refuse to pay a bribe regardless of the situation; whereas only 9 percent of the subjects indicated that the average executive would refuse to pay the bribe in the same situation. Even more disturbing was the fact that more than 85 percent of those who said that the average executive would view such payments as unethical indicated that they would personally be willing to make the payments.

The same study also dealt with the issue of whether ethical standards had changed significantly from 1961 to 1977. The study split quite evenly — 32 percent said that standards were lower, 11 percent said they were about the same, and 27 percent felt that standards had actually risen.

The subjects were then asked why ethical standards had either risen or fallen from 1961 to 1977. The results are shown in Table 3-4. Note that of the six factors said to be responsible for higher standards, only two were subject to a significant measure of business influence — the education and professionalism of management and a growing sense of awareness and responsiveness on the part of management. Similarly, of the six major factors said to be responsible for a lowering of business ethics, only pressure for profits was under the control of management. Three major generalizations can be drawn from this study:

1. Public disclosure and concern are the strongest forces for improving ethical standards.
2. Individual greed and some general feeling of decay in the nation's moral fiber are the strongest pressures leading to unethical behavior.
3. Factors which influence shifts in ethical patterns are beyond the control of management.[49]

What Can Be Done? Considering the attitudes of consumers and executives, it is not surprising that there has been such a strong consumer movement in the United States. Many people feel that their interests are not being served by the market system. The only long-term solution to this problem is for top management of all firms to state clearly and unequivocally that they will no longer tolerate business practices that are not in the best interests of their customers.

Secondly, marketing executives must ensure that their products are of high quality. This may mean the withdrawal of some of the firm's products from the market. Substitute products will have to be more than just "new and improved"; they will have to meet higher performance standards.

---

[48]Steven N. Brenner and Earl A. Molander, "Is the Ethics of Business Changing?" *Harvard Business Review* (January-February, 1977), pp. 57–71.
[49]*Ibid.*, p. 63.

TABLE 3-4 Factors Influencing Ethical Standards

	Percentage of Respondents Listing
Factors Causing Higher Standards:	
• Public disclosure; publicity; media coverage; better communication.	31%
• Increased public concern; public awareness, consciousness, and scrutiny; better informed public; societal pressures.	20
• Government regulation, legislation, and intervention; federal courts.	10
• Education of business managers; increase in manager professionalism and education.	9
• New social expectations for the role business is to play in society; young adults' attitudes; consumerism.	5
• Business's greater sense of social responsibility and greater awareness of the implications of its acts; business responsiveness; corporate policy changes; top management emphasis on ethical action.	5
• Other factors.	20
Factors Causing Lower Standards:	
• Society's standards are lower; social decay; more permissive society; materialism and hedonism have grown; loss of church and home influence; less quality, more quantity desires.	34
• Competition; pace of life; stress to succeed; current economic conditions; costs of doing business; more businesses compete for less.	13
• Political corruption; loss of confidence in government; Watergate; politics; political ethics and climate.	9
• People more aware of unethical acts; constant media coverage; TV; communications create atmosphere for crime.	9
• Greed; desire for gain; worship of the dollar as measure of success; selfishness of the individual; lack of personal integrity and moral fiber.	8
• Pressure for profit within the organization from superiors or from stockholders; corporate influences on managers; corporate policies.	7
• Other factors.	21

Source: Reprinted by permission of the *Harvard Business Review*. Exhibit is from "Is Ethics of Business Changing?" by Steven N. Brenner and Earl A. Molander (January-February, 1977). Copyright © 1976 by the President and Fellows of Harvard College; all rights reserved.

A third remedial action is for firms to invest more money in buyer research — that is, they should implement the marketing concept. Both the firm and the buyer will benefit if new products meet a real societal need. Advertising practices must also be improved; less time should be spent on trivial appeals and more time on telling the customer what the product really can do.

Many other activities can be undertaken, such as mailing follow-up cards after product purchases for consumer feedback, developing more readable warranties and product manuals, and making consumer relations personnel available to the public so that customers can present their complaints to the manufacturers. The important point is that once a firm decides to make its market practices more ethical, it will have little difficulty finding ways to do so.

Marketing to the Poor

Unfortunately, the market system has not functioned well in serving the poorest members of society. Concern has been centered in two areas — the marketing of food products and the marketing of consumer durables.

Marketing Food Products. Several studies clearly indicate that there is little, if any, discrimination in the selling of food products to minorities.[50] However, the poor *do pay more* for food products. The well-stocked and efficiently managed supermarkets of suburban areas are rarely found in the urban ghetto. As a result, poor people, frequently members of a minority group and without an automobile, are forced to purchase groceries from small, inefficient "mom-and-pop" stores. In many ways, this atomistic distribution structure is more akin to that of underdeveloped countries than to the sophisticated retail networks dominating food sales in most of the United States.[51]

Although it is difficult to compare prices charged in ghetto and nonghetto stores because of different product assortments, ghetto stores do seem to charge between 7 and 21 percent more than suburban supermarkets for their merchandise. The higher prices may be more than offset by higher pilferage and insurance costs and less efficient management, but the poor person still pays more. In addition, ghetto and other low-income consumers typically must shop in dirty and run-down food markets. The resulting feeling of frustration was expressed well by one black shopper in a ghetto store:

> The manager of that grocery store must think we are a bunch of animals. The floors are filthy, there are flies all over the place, they handle our food with dirty hands and never say thank you or nothing else that nice.[52]

Marketing Consumer Durables. The situation for consumer durables, such as furniture and appliances, is even worse than for food products. First, ghetto residents have little choice but to buy their consumer durables from relatively small, inefficient stores. These stores typically incur higher operating costs, forcing the retailer to charge higher prices. Second, many ghetto retailers take advantage of the low-income consumer in ways that food retailers do not.[53] Four of these practices are outlined below:

1. **Consumer Credit.** Poor people buy up to 93 percent of all their purchases of consumer durables on credit. The interest rate is often more than 50 percent, apparently with little regard for federal truth-in-lending or state usury laws.

[50]Donald E. Sexton, "Comparing the Cost of Food to Blacks and Whites," *Journal of Marketing* (July, 1971), pp. 40–46.

[51]Frederick D. Sturdivant, "Better Deal for Ghetto Shopper," *Harvard Business Review* (March-April, 1968), p. 132.

[52]*Ibid.*, p. 133.

[53]Leonard L. Berry, "The Low-Income Marketing System: An Overview," *Journal of Retailing* (Summer, 1972), pp. 50–55.

2. **Markups.** Many consumer durables sold in low-income areas are priced significantly higher than they would be if sold in suburban stores. One study in this regard found that the markups on televisions ranged from 121 percent to 160 percent in the low-income areas of Los Angeles. This markup was twice as high as that found in other areas of the city.

3. **High-Pressure Salespeople.** Retailers in low-income areas often employ high-pressure salespeople who are good at closing a sale before the consumer has had an opportunity to think through the purchase. One technique often used is called *TO*, or *turnover*. The technique works as follows: if a salesperson feels the sale is being lost, the customer is turned over to a salesperson with an impressive title, such as store manager, who then finishes off the sale.

4. **Bait-and-Switch Advertising.** When a customer, coming into a store to buy a product advertised at a low price, is informed that the store just ran out of the item and that the item wasn't very good anyway, that customer is ripe for bait and switch. If the salesperson then proceeds to trade the prospect up to a better and much more expensive item, the customer has become a victim of this illegal technique.

What Can Be Done? There are no simple solutions to the problems of the ghetto marketplace. Certainly one of the first steps that must be taken is to provide more and better consumer education opportunities to poor people. They need to be familiar with the real cost of credit, the price differences between products sold in the ghetto and those sold outside, and techniques for resisting the hard-sell approach. This type of information can be made available through regular high school classes or through special adult night classes. Responsible businesses should take the lead and provide material and instructors for such courses.

A second step is to convince responsible large retailers to move back to the ghetto; poor people must have an alternative to mom-and-pop stores. The government can help by making special tax incentive plans and insurance programs available to convince large retailers that moving back to the ghetto makes economic sense.

A third helpful step is to provide management assistance to the small stores selling in the ghetto. In many cases these outlets are run by honest people who simply are not aware of efficient retail management practices. This assistance could be made available from a variety of sources, including local retail merchants' associations, the Small Business Administration, and local universities.

CONSTRAINTS OF MARKETING DECISIONS

Having reviewed some of the social and legal aspects of marketing, you should now have some appreciation of the constraints affecting marketing decisions. Marketing executives are not free to make decisions just to maximize their personal or corporate well-being. Instead, they are limited by environmental, legal, and ethical and moral considerations. These limitations will become even more evident as you read Parts 3 through 6. The impact of the limitations on designing and implementing a marketing program can, indeed, be profound.

summary
points

1. The purpose of the antitrust framework in the United States is to guarantee that businesses compete with one another in a free and open manner. This assumes that commercial competition is generally good for the economic health of the nation.

2. The major legislation comprising the antitrust framework are the Sherman Act (1890), the Clayton Act (1914), the Federal Trade Commission Act (1914), the FTC Improvement Act (1975), and the Celler-Kefauver Act (1950).

3. Horizontal price fixing is the practice whereby business executives from competing firms jointly determine how much to charge in the marketplace for their products, or which one of them will bid the lowest on a certain contract.

4. Firms fall into price-fixing schemes either because of chronic overcapacity within the industry, undifferentiated products, historical precedents within the industry, or because of a lack of top management surveillance.

5. Vertical price fixing exists when two or more firms in a channel of distribution conspire to establish the price of the product.

6. The Robinson-Patman Act (1936) prohibits the selling of a product at different prices to different customers "where the effects of such discrimination may be to substantially lessen competition or tend to create a monopoly or injure, destroy or prevent competition."

7. Sellers charged with price discrimination under the Robinson-Patman Act are permitted to defend themselves on the basis of product cost considerations, changing market conditions, or competitive considerations.

8. The three areas of distribution law relevant to marketing deal with refusals to deal, franchising, and territorial restrictions.

9. The law pertaining to franchise arrangements regulates exclusive agreements between the franchisor and franchisee, the conditions under which a party may terminate the agreement, and the full disclosure of information about franchise opportunities.

10. Territorial restrictions no longer appear to be illegal per se; rather, they are judged by the court on the basis of their overall competitive impact.

11. Currently, the authority of the Federal Trade Commission extends not only to business practices injurious to competition but also to deceptive trade practices and fraudulent advertising.

12. The Cooling-Off Rule allows anyone purchasing a product from a door-to-door salesperson for $25 or more to cancel the purchase within 72 hours of the transaction and to receive a full refund.

13. The Truth-in-Lending Act requires the seller to list the finance charges involved in a consumer credit transaction and to explain the computation of the annual percentage rate on the unpaid balance.

14. A firm found guilty of fraudulent advertising may be required to make an affirmative disclosure or to run corrective advertising.

15. The FTC plays a major role in the regulation of advertising directed specifically to children.

16. The Consumer Product Safety Act (1972) established the Consumer Product Safety Commission and gave it the authority to impose safety standards for all consumer products.

17. Ethically, in the long run, business decisions and actions must be consistent with the norms of society.

18. Research has shown that many consumers and business executives feel that corporations are not meeting their social responsibilities.

19. In general, it appears that the marketing system has not been very effective in serving the poor.

questions for discussion

1. Explain the provisions of Sections 1 and 2 of the Sherman Act. How did the Supreme Court's decision in the Standard Oil of New Jersey case (1911) affect the Sherman Act?
2. What is a tying agreement? What is an exclusive agreement?
3. Did the Clayton Act and the Federal Trade Commission Act materially aid the government in its fight against monopolies? If so, how?
4. What is the function of cease and desist orders?
5. How does the Celler-Kefauver Act strengthen the Clayton Act?
6. Differentiate between horizontal and vertical price fixing. What forces have tended to encourage each type of price fixing?
7. Do you feel the court ruled correctly in the Perkins v. Standard Oil of California and the FTC v. the Borden Co. cases? Explain your position.
8. What is the Colgate doctrine?
9. Do you think that the federal government has passed enough laws to protect the franchisee from an unscrupulous franchisor?
10. Analyze the impact of the Sylvania case (1977) on the issue of territorial restrictions.
11. Evaluate the impact of the Cooling-Off Rule and the Truth-in-Lending Act on the consumer.
12. Examine your local newspapers to determine whether they include any advertisements that the FTC might find misleading.
13. What options are available to the FTC when it determines that an advertisement is deceptive?
14. Should television commercials aimed at preschool children be permitted? Explain your position.
15. What steps do you think should be taken to better protect the consumer against fraudulent market practices?
16. What do you feel should be done to make the marketplace more responsive to the needs of consumers?
17. Should large chain retail organizations be responsible for ensuring that low-income consumers are treated fairly in the marketplace? If yes, what are their responsibilities in this area?

cases part 1
case 1
south west electronics

South West Electronics designs and produces electronic circuitry for use in computers. Its primary customers include IBM, Texas Instruments, and Motorola. The firm was founded in 1964 by Dr. Williams, a professor at The University of Texas in the electrical engineering department.

South West's sales approached $3.8 million in 1975, after rising almost 20 percent each year since 1968. However, from 1976 until 1980 the firm's sales began to plateau and increased an average of only 7.5 percent per year during that period. As a result, Williams felt that South West Electronics should begin to move into other types of businesses. Several of the firm's engineers were assigned the task of developing products that would permit the company to expand its sales.

South West engineers were working on a new circuitry system to be used in telephone switchgear equipment. The new circuitry system, which was named Apex, would permit preprogramming a telephone with up to 80 telephone numbers which could then be dialed automatically by simply pushing a button located next to the name of the individual being called. The competition for such a product included established corporations such as American Telephone & Telegraph (AT&T) and General Telephone, as well as such specialty communication houses as Swift Electronics and Custom Communications.

Automatic-dialing telephones were designed for executives who do not want to dial telephone numbers themselves. As a result, their office telephone consoles often have up to 30 preprogrammed numbers of customers, colleagues, or even family and friends.

The Secretary

Williams was so impressed with the Apex system that he decided to go into the personal office telephone business. He hired a designer to create a contemporary-looking telephone console and an applications engineer to build the rest of the telephone. The resulting product not only had the capability of automatically dialing 80 numbers, but it also had an electronic calculator, digital clock, and a cassette tape recorder built into it. The equipment was designed so that it could be plugged directly into the regular telephone company's lines. South West's automatic-dialing system was named the Secretary.

Distribution of the Secretary presented South West with a real challenge. Williams knew that AT&T and General Telephone had established sales forces as well as maintenance people who were constantly in touch with potential users. In addition, most electronic communication specialty houses had been in business for several years and sold a variety of products including self-dialing telephone systems. He felt that he could counter this competition by hiring specialists in communications as salespeople and paying them on a commission basis. A commission fee structure was designed so that a salesperson meeting the sales quota would earn $30,000 per year, which was at least 30 percent higher than the earnings of most salaried salespeople in the industry.

Williams was also concerned about providing service for the Secretary once it was installed. AT&T and General Telephone maintained their own products, as did most of the specialty houses. Williams was convinced that the only way to service the Secretary was to train independent local service specialists who also serviced other products such as television sets, CBs, and radios. Faulty telephone equipment would be picked up by the salesperson who sold the product and taken to the local service repair shop. Service would not be a major problem. The secretary had an unconditional 90-day warranty.

It was very difficult to determine a selling price for the Secretary. There appeared to be almost no price competition within the market for self-dialing telephone systems. Williams thought that the advanced technology of the Secretary would permit South West to sell it for 25 percent less than what the major telephone companies presently charged for their products. Williams finally decided on a price of $260, which was almost $90 less than competition.

Introduction of the Product

Because of the concentration of industry in the eastern U.S., Williams planned to introduce the Secretary first on the East Coast and then sell it nationwide. Williams expected to sell at least 100 units per month in the greater New York area alone in the first year. He expected to double that figure as the product began to be marketed in the rest of the eastern sector of the United States.

Williams hired two salespeople who had impeccable records and experience in the telephone communication industry. Their salary was to be $30,000 for their first year's efforts, regardless of how many units they sold.

During their first four months on the job, the two salespeople were able to sell only six units. Williams had a difficult time explaining this phenomenon, and he felt that the sales resistance resulted from the fact that potential customers were concerned about the reliability of the Secretary. While Williams expected price to be a major factor, he discovered that most executives did not seem to be very concerned about price. They looked at the Secretary, carefully considered it, and then almost inevitably bought comparable equipment either from one of the major telephone companies or from one of the established communication specialty houses. Finally, a number of individuals had suggested to him that while they liked the Secretary, they had no need for the ability to dial 80 telephone numbers.

1. Why did South West Electronics run into difficulty?
2. Develop a marketing strategy that would help South West to succeed.

case 2
chrysler
corporation

Chrysler Corporation is the third largest U.S. automobile company. While it has traditionally had 15 to 16 percent of the U.S. automobile market, Chrysler has recently had to struggle to retain 10 percent of the market. Although Chrysler has always been a "feast or famine" organization, it had not seriously been considered a candidate for bankruptcy. In 1978 Chrysler Corporation lost $204.6 million, and in 1979 it lost over $1 billion.

Lee A. Iacocca was hired in late 1978 as president of Chrysler after spending 32 years with the Ford Motor Company. Iacocca was known as a marketing genius at Ford and was responsible for the development of the highly successful Mustang.

Uncontrollable Environmental Variables

Iacocca's new position was made even more challenging by the uncontrollable variables listed below.

1. **Fuel Economy.** The U.S. government has established corporate fuel average economy standards for automobile manufacturers. Beginning in 1981, the fuel economy standard rises at two miles per gallon — twice the increase of the previous three years. By 1985 automobile manufacturers' fleet averages must be 27.5 miles per gallon. The automobile companies have argued unsuccessfully that these standards cannot be met in a cost-effective manner.

2. **Auto Emission Standards.** The Environmental Protection Agency is forcing the automobile industry to produce cars that do not damage the environment. Unfortunately, the needed technology is expensive and often state-of-the-art in nature. Chrysler's plan was to purchase much of this technology from General Motors.

3. **Auto Safety Standards.** By 1983 passive seat belt or air bag systems must be fitted on all cars. While the National Highway Traffic Safety Administration estimates the cost to be $119 per vehicle, industry experts estimate that the cost will be closer to $375 per car. Chrysler felt that the federal government's safety regulations have already added $600 to the cost of each car and that many of the improvements have not been cost effective.

Chrysler Corporation case material based on Peter Yates, "Is Chrysler the Prototype?" *Business Week* (August 20, 1979), pp. 102–110, and Helen Kahn, "Chrysler Explores All Angles in Quest for Break on Taxes," *Automotive News* (July 2, 1979), pp. 1, 44. Government loan guarantee figures from Dan Dorfman, "Chrysler a Risk Even with Bailout," *The Cincinnati Enquirer*, March 30, 1980, p. D-5.

4. **The Iranian Oil Crisis.** When the Shah of Iran was overthrown in 1978, a worldwide crude oil shortage developed. This shortage resulted in gas lines in the U.S. during the spring and summer of 1979 and in dramatically higher prices for crude oil products. As a result, the demand for small, fuel-efficient cars by U.S. car buyers surged. Unfortunately, the majority of cars that Chrysler had to sell were large "gas guzzlers."

5. **Economic Recession.** During a recession people frequently postpone purchasing expensive products such as automobiles. Except in the case where a car is "totaled" in an accident, the automobile can usually be repaired and used one more year. The United States was slipping into a recession during 1979–1980. This was bad news for the automakers.

6. **Inflation.** The record-breaking, double-digit inflation of 1979–1980 was especially hard on Chrysler for two reasons. First, the firm tried to live within the government guidelines of 7 percent price increases. Second, the high inflation forced the Federal Reserve Board to raise the prime interest rate in excess of 15 percent, making it very expensive for consumers to finance automobiles.

Other Considerations

Chrysler was still being plagued by a series of management mistakes that occurred in the mid- and late-1960s and early 1970s. Chrysler made several poor overseas acquisitions such as Rootes Motors in England. The firm also failed to introduce in 1971 a subcompact to compete with the Ford Pinto and the Chevrolet Vega. Rather, Chrysler chose to redesign its standard-sized cars. The 1973 oil embargo, however, destroyed the market for these cars only two months after they were introduced. Chrysler then introduced the Volare and Aspen compact models in 1976, just as the market softened for compact cars.

Chrysler has also had a series of quality control problems which have been partially a result of antiquated production facilities and partially a result of Chrysler being forced to react quickly to changes in a market that it did not forecast.

Impact of a Chrysler Failure

The impact on the economy of a Chrysler failure would be very significant. The U.S. Department of Transportation estimated that 100,000 Chrysler production employees, 50,000 Chrysler salaried employees, 180,000 employees of suppliers, 100,000 dealer-employed people, and 12,000 transportation-related workers would be out of work if Chrysler were to fold.

Chrysler's Immediate Plans

As of August 1, 1979, Chrysler had 80,000 cars in Detroit waiting to be sent to dealers. This figure represented a 95-day supply at then current sales rates. Iacocca developed a $400 rebate plan and a massive advertising blitz designed to convince the public that this was the best time ever to purchase a Chrysler product. Although the plan cost almost $90 million, it brought $400 million into the company and reduced Chrysler's inventory by 55,000 units.

The efforts of Chrysler's top management to secure enough working capital from the federal government to survive until the firm can begin making profits resulted in government loan guarantees of up to $1.5 billion with the stipulation that Chrysler first assemble a package of at least $1.43 billion of nonfederally guaranteed loans. Iacocca is now concerned that, because of the Federal Reserve Board's policy of high interest rates to control inflation, the amount Chrysler will have to pay for borrowed funds will be prohibitive.

1. Do you feel that Chrysler was really suffering from problems that were beyond its control? Was there anything that Chrysler could have done to control its environment better?
2. How would you advise Chrysler's management?
3. Evaluate the action taken by the federal government to help Chrysler.

case 3
fair way
department
stores

Fair Way Department Stores is a national chain with centralized purchasing in New York City. Each store is under the control of a general manager to whom the various merchandise division heads report. Department managers, who work for the division heads, are judged on both sales volume and margin.

The Fair Way policy of customer satisfaction is a critical ingredient in its promotional strategy. The original policy of unconditional refunds to any dissatisfied customers has been strictly adhered to over the years as an important part of Fair Way's promotional strategy. Many customers expressed the belief that you could never really get a "bargain" at Fair Way stores, but at least you could always buy with absolute confidence.

The vacuum cleaner department in one of the larger Fair Way stores was being harassed by what the department manager thought was unfair and unethical competition. Fair Way carries several price ranges of cannister and upright vacuum models, but the Fair Way Sweep Clean cannister model is its best seller, with a retail price of just under $60 plus attachments. It also is the lowest priced model in its vacuum cleaner line.

Several local retail firms were engaging in a bait-and-switch promotional strategy. They were advertising heavily that they would sell a like-new, reconditioned vacuum for $29.95, and customers were being asked to telephone their requests for a free home demonstration. Mr. Osker, the manager of the vacuum cleaner department at Fair Way, believes that this competition is hurting his department. He personally has answered several of the advertisements for a free home demonstration of the competition's $29.95 vacuum cleaner. In each instance, he discovered that a sales representative would arrive at his home, demonstrate an obsolete and inferior vacuum, and then attempt to trade-up the customer with a demonstration of a new, more expensive machine.

Mr. James, Mr. Osker's division head, has been reluctant to advise Mr. Osker to cut the price on the Sweep Clean since they both know it already represents a quality product at a reasonable price, in the best tradition of the Fair Way reputation. Mr. Osker and Mr. James decide to seek approval from the store manager, Mr. Martin Stern, for a bold counter-strategy. The following conversation takes place among Mr. Stern, Mr. Osker, and Mr. James:

Mr. Osker: Well, the lower-price cleaner we would like to sell must have some physical similarity to our Sweep Clean — that is, it should look like it belongs in our line. Then, it must be in sufficiently good condition to look new once it has been reconditioned and repainted.

Mr. Stern: I think I know what you're leading up to. . . .

Mr. James: We figured you would. The vacuum cleaner must not work *too* well. I'm sure Mr. Osker's used machine will fit the bill perfectly. It can almost be guaranteed not to pick up anything. In fact, this is even more dramatic because it sounds like it's working hard — it even shows a few sparks for an added effect! Then, we simply put on the Fair Way decal plate, and we've got ourselves a fighting brand! We advertise the phantom machine as a special at $29.95 — not often, mind you, but only when competitive strategy necessitates it. The customers come to the store to see the bargain, and, of course, we demonstrate it and our Sweep Clean.

Mr. Osker: And, of course, the Sweep Clean will appear to be the marvel of the century compared to the phantom vacuum.

Mr. Stern: How do you explain this strategy to your sales clerks? Would they cooperate, and how would they react?

Mr. Osker: I'm sure that will be no problem — they're good old boys, all of them, and they are just as concerned as we are about the position we're being forced into.

Mr. Stern: Fred, what do you think? After all, aren't we above bait-and-switch tactics?

Mr. James: I hate this kind of thing as much as you do, but I honestly think we've got to retaliate in this competitive situation. In fact, under the circumstances, we are really acting in the customer's best interest.

Mr. Stern: How's that, Fred? And is this in Fair Way's best interest in the long run? We've got a reputation to protect!

Mr. Osker: Mr. Stern, I personally guarantee that no one is going to be cheated. The Sweep Clean is an excellent product, and this temporary tactic will permit us to steer our customers to it. The alternative is that we do nothing and the Fair Way customer ends up buying from someone else, and probably buys an inferior product.

Mr. Stern: There is some truth in that, but how are you going to handle any complications? I mean, suppose someone really wants the phantom? Suppose someone demands it?

Mr. Osker: Well, first we don't permit mail or phone orders. Thus, we are sure every prospect gets a demonstration. This alone will deter most customers from seriously wishing to buy the phantom.

Mr. Stern: And for those who don't discourage so easily?

Mr. Osker: Well, we certainly won't actually sell the phantom in any event. As a last resort, we explain that the model is out of stock and simply back-order the cleaner. If need be, we can offer an inducement to substitute the Sweep Clean, after some reasonable amount of time. In addition, I would like to make it clear that I am serving two interests — first, Fair Way's, and second, my customers'. I will guarantee that I will improve my margin *and* my record for satisfied customers. If, indeed, any customers are really dissatisfied, I am quite willing to reduce the price of the Sweep Clean to $29.95 to satisfy them.

Mr. Stern: You always had the opportunity to reduce price, if Mr. James agreed — it's your department.

Mr. Osker: I don't want to cut price across-the-board to counter false competition. The Sweep Clean already is one of the best values we offer. I prefer to reduce price selectively to fulfill our obligations to satisfied customers. Massive sales and bargains are not, in my judgment, indicated here.

1. Could Fair Way take legal action against the local retail chains that are using bait-and-switch tactics?
2. Can the action that Fair Way is contemplating be justified on the basis that customers will get a better product if they purchase from Fair Way?
3. Is there a problem with how Fair Way pays its department managers?
4. What action should Mr. Stern take?

2

Market Identification

A crucial element in developing any marketing program is the identification of the market or markets to be served. Will the firm be meeting the needs of final consumers, such as yourself, or will it be serving other firms and organizations in the industrial sector of the economy?

Only when the target market is clearly identified and quantified can its buying and consumption behavior be studied and understood. In Part 2 you will examine the market identification process, the role of marketing research, and the development of marketing programs for specific customer groups.

Topics discussed in Chapter 4:

1. The purchase decision process.
2. The importance of culture and subculture in consumer behavior.
3. Social class as a factor in consumer behavior.
4. Reference groups and their influences on both product and brand decisions.
5. Family decision making.
6. Personal motivation from the perspective of physiological and learned drives.
7. Stimulus-response and cognitive learning models and factors affecting perception.
8. Consumer behavior and the economic perspective.
9. The role of post-purchase dissonance in buyer behavior.

This chapter presents a model of consumer behavior (i.e., how consumers act in the marketplace). The model is based on the assumption that no single behavioral science is capable of explaining buyer behavior. Therefore, the marketing analyst must be able to integrate several social sciences in order to understand why consumers behave as they do.

Social critics such as Vance Packard and Ralph Nader have suggested that U.S. industry is somehow able to persuade people to purchase products that they really don't want.[1] We are given the impression that somewhere there exists a cadre of bright social scientists who fully understand consumer behavior. These individuals, apparently, have sold out to industry and are using their powers to manipulate the marketplace.

Manufacturers do spend a significant amount of money to study the behavior of buyers as well as to try to convince them of the merits of their merchandise. However, keep in mind that consumers are very unpredictable and complex. An experiment performed by scientists at Purdue University demonstrates this unpredictability.[2] Two hundred and sixty-four subjects were asked to rank order their favorite soft drinks. A few days later the same subjects were given an opportunity to have a free soft drink. Only 50.8 percent of the subjects selected the product that three days earlier they had stated was their favorite soft drink.

---

[1]See Vance Packard, *The Hidden Persuaders* (New York: David McKay Company, Inc., 1957), and *The Waste Makers* (New York: David McKay Company, Inc., 1960); and Ralph Nader, Mark Green, and Joel Seligman, *Taming the Giant Corporations* (New York: W. W. Norton & Co., Inc., 1976).

[2]Frank M. Bass, Edgar A. Pessemier, and Donald R. Lehmann, "An Experimental Study of Relationships Between Attitudes, Brand Preference, and Choice," *Behavioral Science* (November, 1972), pp. 532–541.

Considering the 50 percent failure rate of new products, it is a little difficult to believe that marketing people understand the human psyche so well that they can consistently make people purchase unwanted products. In reality, the study of consumer behavior is a new and inexact science. At its base is the purchase decision process.

THE PURCHASE DECISION PROCESS

The act of buying is a significant part of nearly everyone's life. It has become such a routine activity that we rarely stop to analyze in detail the process that we go through when making a purchase. Just what steps are involved in the purchase decision process?

How Decisions Are Made

Generally speaking, consumers go through a five-stage process when they buy something:[3]

1. **Problem Recognition.** The individual recognizes some need, desire, or problem. Marketers must determine what needs, desires, and/or problems stimulate an individual to begin the purchase process.
2. **Information Search.** The consumer begins to collect information about purchase alternatives. The successful marketer must know the sources of information and their relative importance to the consumer.
3. **Alternative Evaluation.** Each consumer evaluates the various purchase alternatives in light of certain criteria. The marketer must determine which criteria the consumer will use in making a particular purchase decision.
4. **Choice.** The consumer makes a selection from among the purchase alternatives. Up to this point the marketer has done everything possible to influence the decision.
5. **Outcome.** The consumer will experience some degree of satisfaction/dissatisfaction with the purchase decision. Knowledge of this satisfaction (or lack of it) is crucial feedback for the marketer.

Only when the purchase decision process is thoroughly understood can an effective marketing program be developed to serve a firm's customers.

The Purchase Decision Process Illustrated

To illustrate the consumer's purchase decision process, consider the stages of a new car purchase. The decision process begins when the consumer experiences a need or desire for a new car. This *problem recognition* phase may be initiated for any one of several reasons — because recent repair bills have been high, because the present car needs a new set of tires, because the present car has been in an accident, or because the neighbor across the street just bought a shiny new sports car. Whatever the stimulus, the individual perceives a dif-

---

[3]For a more complete discussion of the consumer purchase decision process see James F. Engel, Roger D. Blackwell, and David T. Kollat, *Consumer Behavior* (3d ed.; Hinsdale, Ill.: The Dryden Press, 1978), pp. 17–39.

ference, or conflict, between the ideal and the actual state of affairs. The consumer begins to resolve the conflict by collecting the information that will serve as the basis for an eventual purchase decision. In this *information search* phase, the consumer may peruse such automobile enthusiast magazines as *Car & Driver* or *Road & Track*, or pick up a copy of *Consumer Reports*. Other sources of information include friends, family members, business associates, and promotion materials distributed by the automobile companies.

Once the consumer sifts through the available information and establishes the relative credibility of each source, the third phase — *alternative evaluation* — begins. At this point, the consumer must decide on the criteria that will govern the selection of the automobile. These criteria may include price, miles per gallon, options available, place of manufacture (foreign or domestic), what the experts say about the various products, and finally, the opinions of family and friends.

During the *choice* stage the consumer actually makes the purchase decision — whether to buy or not to buy. If the consumer decides to buy the car, then additional decisions must be made regarding type or model of car, when and from whom the car should be purchased, and how the car should be paid for. Hopefully the *outcome* is positive and the consumer feels that the right decisions have been made. A satisfied customer is more likely to talk about the joys of a new car purchase. On the other hand, problems may develop or the consumer may begin to feel a wrong decision has been made. Unfortunately, an unhappy customer will probably attempt to dissuade friends and associates from buying a new car, or at least will caution them against making the same mistake. Figure 4-1 illustrates the basic steps in the car purchase decision process.

Factors Influencing Purchase Decisions — A Model of Consumer Behavior

The act of purchasing a product can be very complex. The consumer not only must collect information and determine the selection criteria, but also must make many decisions concerning style, size, color, retail agent, and the like. If you were to ask a group of behavioral scientists to describe the key variables in the purchase decision process, you would probably be given several different answers. For instance, an economist might argue that the buyer looks primarily at cost and value. A psychologist might suggest that emotional reasons, which are buried very deep in the subconscious, actually determine the choice. A sociologist might argue that the pressure of social groups and family habits are the most important factors in purchasing a product. Finally, an anthropologist might trace the reasons for the choice of a particular product or brand back to the consumer's cultural background and ethnic group.

Although these explanations are based on extensive study and experimentation, no single theory — economic, psychological, social, or anthropological — has yet been developed to fully explain consumer behavior. Rather, the consumer can only be considered as an individual who behaves within a broad social and cultural environment. As shown in the model presented in Figure 4-2, there are several dominant forces that influence the consumer during the

FIGURE 4-1 Automobile Purchase Decision Process Activities

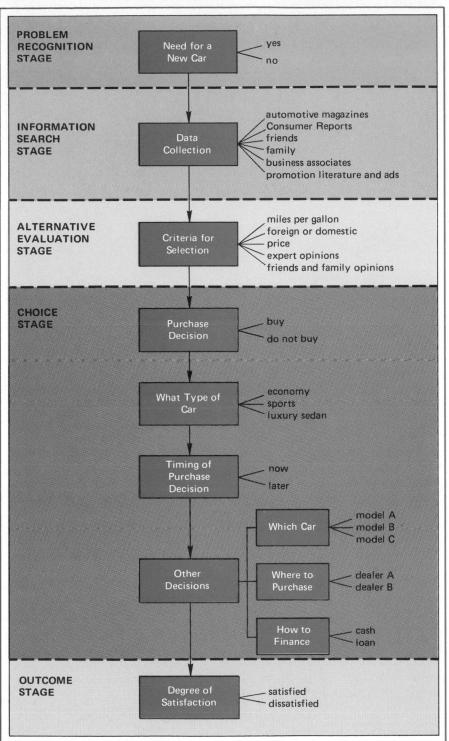

FIGURE 4-2 A Model of Consumer Behavior

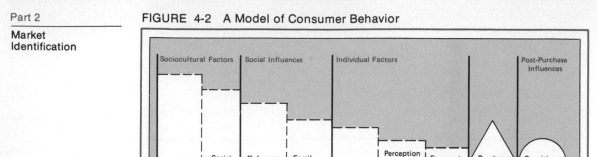

Source: Modified from Harold H. Kassarjian and Thomas S. Robertson (eds.), *Perspectives in Consumer Behavior* (Chicago: Scott, Foresman and Company, 1968). p. 4.

purchase decision. The model suggests that the sociocultural forces act as the basis for much of consumer behavior. These forces shape the way consumers respond to the various reference group and family influences, which in turn affect individual motivation, perception, learning, and economic constraints. Figure 4-2, in effect, shows that social, symbolic, and psychological factors, in addition to rational, optimizing considerations, act upon the individual during the purchase process.

These factors affecting buyer behavior will be examined in the next sections. We begin by looking at culture, the most general factor affecting consumer behavior.

THE INFLUENCE OF CULTURE

Culture is that set of values, ideas, attitudes, and other symbols and objects created by people which shape human behavior. Culture does not refer to an individual's instinctive response, nor does it include one-time solutions to unique problems. Rather, culture enables society to transmit from one generation to the next the material and abstract elements of its collective, problem-solving wisdom.[4] To understand culture more fully, we will analyze its general characteristics, the United States culture in particular, and the importance of subcultures in the U.S.

[4]*Ibid.*, p. 65.

Characteristics of Culture

Culture has two main characteristics: (1) it must satisfy a need within society and (2) it is a learned response.[5]

Culture Satisfies Needs. Culture exists to satisfy needs within society. Whenever a specific aspect of culture fails to do so, it is eliminated from the culture. Thus culture is dynamic, changing, and adaptive. The implication for business is that the cultural environment must be monitored closely to ensure that products and services are consistent with the changing values and needs of society.

Culture Is Learned. Although human beings are born with a certain genetic makeup, they are not inherently predisposed to learn one culture as opposed to another. A child learns its culture from many sources, including the family, teachers, peers, and even sports and television heroes. Interestingly enough, television commercials reinforce cultural learning. For example, when Benson and Hedges promotes its Virginia Slims cigarettes with the theme "You've come a long way, baby," it is reinforcing, and at the same time taking advantage of, the recent widespread belief that women should be free to control their own lives.

The United States Culture

It is difficult to identify the main ingredients of the U.S. culture since it is a land of such great diversity. There are many ethnic, religious, regional, racial, and economic groups, each of which has its own cultural values. Nonetheless, noted sociologist Seymour Lipset has described the U.S. culture as mechanistically concerned, where the individual is the master and people are predictable and equal. According to Lipset, this type of cultural foundation is responsible for the U.S.'s unique emphasis on material well-being, work, and conformity.[6]

Perhaps this character profile partially explains why U.S. consumers seek out products that not only function well but also save time. They seem to respond well to promotions that say "you deserve it" and that have a youth orientation. They also desire a wide choice of products, yet frequently purchase those that provide some identification with a particular social group. Although it is difficult to reconcile these contradictions, their existence demonstrates the complexity of the U.S. social system. Figure 4-3 lists core values held by people in the United States and the relevance of these values to marketing.

Subcultures

A **subculture** is a distinct cultural group existing as an identifiable segment within a larger culture. The members of a subculture tend to adhere to

---

[5]Leon G. Schiffman and Leslie Lazar Kanuk, *Consumer Behavior* (Englewood Cliffs, N.J.: Prentice-Hall, Inc., 1978), pp. 331–336.

[6]See Seymour M. Lipset, "A Changing American Character," in *Culture and Social Character*, edited by Seymour M. Lipset and Leo Lowenthal (New York: Doubleday & Co., 1971), pp. 136–171.

FIGURE 4-3 Summary of United States Core Values

Value	General Features	Relevance to Consumer Behavior
Achievement and success	Hard work is good; success flows from hard work.	Acts as a justification for acquisition of goods ("You deserve it").
Activity	Keeping busy is healthy and natural.	Stimulates interest in products that save time and enhance leisure-time activities.
Efficiency and practicality	Admiration of things that solve problems (e.g., save time and effort).	Stimulates purchase of products that function well and save time.
Progress	People can improve themselves; tomorrow should be better.	Stimulates desire for new products that fulfill unsatisfied needs; acceptance of products that claim to be "new" or "improved."
Material comfort	"The good life"	Foster acceptance of convenience and luxury products that make life more enjoyable.
Individualism	Being one's self (e.g., self-reliance, self-interest, and self-esteem).	Stimulates acceptance of customized or unique products that enable a person to "express his own personality."
Freedom	Freedom of choice.	Fosters interest in wide product lines and differentiated products.
External conformity	Uniformity of observable behavior; desire to be accepted.	Stimulates interest in products that are used or owned by others in the same social group.
Humanitarianism	Caring for others, particularly the underdog.	Stimulates patronage of firms that compete with market leaders.
Youthfulness	A state of mind that stresses being young-at-heart or appearing young.	Stimulates acceptance of products that provide the illusion of maintaining or fostering youth.

Source: Leon G. Schiffman and Leslie Lazar Kanuk, *Consumer Behavior*, © 1978, p. 359. Reprinted by permission of Prentice-Hall, Inc., Englewood Cliffs, N.J.

many of the cultural mores of the overall society, yet they also profess beliefs, values, and customs which set them apart. An understanding of subculture is important to marketing managers because the members of each subculture tend to show different purchase behavior patterns.

To illustrate, *nationality* may provide a basis for a subculture. Although Hispanic-Americans represent several different countries, as a group they have a strong preference for major brand-name products.[7] In the same way, one's *religious* affiliation may influence one's market behavior. Jewish consumers are the primary purchasers of kosher foods, while Mormons do not purchase tobacco or liquor and Christian Scientists avoid medical doctors and medicines. In addition, one study of *geographic* subcultures in the United States found that Southern men were more likely to use mouthwash or deodorants than Eastern men, and that Western men consumed more cottage cheese and regular coffee than Easterners or Southerners.[8]

Race can also delineate a subculture. Black Americans, for example, constitute a substantial subculture in U.S. society. As a subculture, blacks seem to have made significant social and economic progress in the United States in the last two decades. This progress can be measured in terms of increased family income, the doubling of the college graduation rate for young blacks, and the election of more than 3,000 black to political office, a tenfold increase during the last ten years.[9] Yet blacks also represent a subculture with some distinct consumer behavior practices. Although a few of these practices may result from the disparity between black and white family income levels (see Figure 4-1), some also are based on more complex cultural factors. Some of the recent research findings on black buyer behavior in the areas of store shopping, product selection, and communications are presented below.[10]

Store Shopping Behavior

1. The most important factors for black homemakers in deciding where to shop are convenience of location and friendliness of atmosphere.[11]
2. Black consumers shop more at discount stores than do white consumers.[12]
3. Black consumers "shop around" less than white consumers.[13]

---

[7]"Spanish Speaking Are $20 Billion U.S. Market," *Advertising Age* (November 21, 1973), p. 56.

[8]Subhash C. Jain, "Life Cycle Revisited: Applications in Consumer Research," in *Advances in Consumer Research*, edited by Mary Schlinger (Association for Consumer Research, 1975), p. 42.

[9]Juan Cameron, "Black America: Still Waiting for Full Membership," *Fortune* (April, 1975), pp. 163–164.

[10]For a detailed discussion of black consumer behavior see Raymond A. Bauer and Scott M. Cunningham, *Studies in the Negro Market* (Cambridge, Mass.: Marketing Science Institute, 1970); Marcus Alexis and Clyde M. Smith, "Marketing and the Inner-City Consumer," *Journal of Contemporary Business* (Autumn, 1973), pp. 45–80; David Caplovitz, *The Poor Pay More* (New York: The Free Press, 1967); and Donald E. Sexton, Jr., "Black Buyer Behavior," *Journal of Marketing* (October, 1972), pp. 36–39.

[11]"Consumer Dynamics in the Supermarket," *Progressive Grocer* (February, 1969), p. 196.

[12]Lawrence P. Feldman and Alvin D. Star, "Racial Factors in Shopping Behavior," in *A New Measure of Responsibility for Marketing*, edited by Keith Cox and Ben M. Enis (Chicago: American Marketing Association, June, 1968), pp. 216–226.

[13]Donald E. Sexton, Jr., "Differences in Food Shopping Habits by Area of Residence, Race, and Income," *Journal of Retailing* (Spring, 1974), pp. 37–48.

FIGURE 4-4   Black vs. White Income Distribution

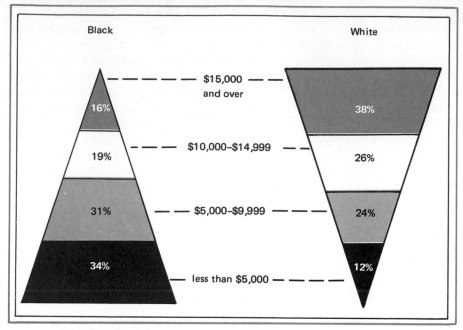

Source: U.S. Department of Commerce, in Juan Cameron, "Black America: Still Waiting for
Full Membership," *Fortune* (April, 1975), p. 165.

Product Selection

1. When income is held constant, blacks spend proportionately more than whites
   on clothing, personal care, home furnishings, alcohol, and tobacco, and proportionately less on medical care, food, transportation, education, and utilities.[14]
2. Black consumers respond no more favorably to packages designed specifically
   for blacks than they do to neutral packaging.[15]
3. Blacks are more innovative with respect to clothing than are whites.[16]

Communications

1. Black consumers respond more favorably to advertisements with black models
   or with black and white models than to advertisements with white models
   only.[17]
2. Blacks listen to radio more than whites although blacks are less likely to listen to
   FM radio.[18]
3. In recall and attitude shift tests, blacks respond more positively to advertisements than white consumers.[19]

---

[14]Raymond A. Bauer and Scott M. Cunningham, "The Negro Market," *Journal of Advertising
Research* (April, 1970), p. 6.
   [15]Herbert E. Krugman, "White and Negro Responses to Package Design," *Journal of Marketing Research* (May, 1966), pp. 199–200.
   [16]Thomas S. Robertson, Douglas J. Dalrymple, and Michael Y. Yoshino, "Cultural Compatibility in New Product Adoption," in *Marketing Involvement in Society and Economy*, edited by
Philip R. McDonald (Chicago: American Marketing Association, Fall, 1969), p. 72.
   [17]Arnold M. Barban, "The Dilemma of 'Integrated' Advertising," *Journal of Business* (October, 1969), pp. 477–496.
   [18]Gerald J. Glasser and Gale D. Metzger, "Radio Usage by Blacks," *Journal of Advertising
Research* (October, 1975), pp. 39–45.
   [19]John V. Petrof, "Reaching the Negro Market: A Segregated vs. a General Newspaper,"
Journal of Advertising Research (June, 1968), p. 42.

THE IMPACT OF SOCIAL CLASS

Social class is the second of the two sociocultural factors affecting consumer behavior. A **social class** may be thought of as a rather permanent and homogeneous group of individuals who have similar behavior, interests, and life-styles. Since people normally choose their friends and associates on the basis of commonality of interests, social classes have a tendency to restrict interaction, especially with regard to social functions. In addition, social classes are hierarchical in nature; thus people usually position their social group as either above or below other groups.[20]

Only a few years ago, it was felt that economic factors alone were sufficient to predict an individual's social class; however, recent research has shown clearly that social class is multidimensional. For example, the amount of money one has does not guarantee acceptance by members of the upper class; it must first be translated into socially approved behavior and the right manners. To illustrate, noted sociologist W. Lloyd Warner tells the true story of a Mr. John Smith, who wanted to become a member of an upper class social club. The following conversation took place between Mr. Smith and Mr. Grey:

> "Why the hell, Abner, am I being kept out of the X club?"
>
> Mr. Grey politely evaded the question. He asked Mr. Smith to be seated. He inquired after Mr. Smith's health, about the health of his wife, and inquired about other matters of simple convention.
>
> Finally, Mr. Smith said, "Ab, why the hell am I being kept out of the club?"
>
> "But, John, you're not. Everyone in the X club thinks you're a fine fellow."
>
> "Well, what's wrong?"
>
> "Well, John, we don't think you've got the kind of money necessary for being a good member of the X club. We don't think you'd be happy in the X club."
>
> "Like hell I haven't. I could buy and sell a half dozen of your board members."
>
> "I know that, John, but that isn't what I said. I did not say the amount of money. I said the kind of money."
>
> "What do you mean?"
>
> "Well, John, my coworkers on the charity drive tell me you only gave a few dollars to our campaign, and we had you down for a few thousand."
>
> For a moment Mr. Smith was silent. Then he grinned. So did Mr. Grey. Mr. Smith took out his fountain pen and checkbook. "How much?"[21]

The point is that while Mr. Smith had sufficient funds to be accepted into the club, he was not spending it in a manner that was consistent with the beliefs of the members of the club.

Six social classes have been identified in the United States. Let's take a look at their characteristics, as well as the impact of social class on consumer behavior.

Social Classes in the United States

Social classes in the U.S. are dynamic, i.e., there is mobility within the class structure. Individuals and families move up or down the social class hierarchy

---

[20]Engel, Blackwell, and Kollat, *op. cit.*, p. 294.

[21]W. Lloyd Warner, *et al.*, *Social Class in America* (Chicago: Science Research Associates, 1949), p. 21.

over long periods of time. John Smith, referred to earlier, who made his money in plumbing, may never become a member of the upper class, but his son, who attends a private Eastern school, may become sufficiently respectable to be offered membership in the city's finest clubs. What determines this acceptability?

Determinants of Social Class. Although it is impossible to define precisely what determines a person's social class, occupation is certainly one of the key determinants. The importance of occupation is evident whenever people meet and ask, "What do you do for a living?" In fact, people tend to identify themselves and others by their occupations. Table 4-1 presents a partial listing of occupations ranked according to perceived prestige. Other important determi-

TABLE 4-1 Prestige of Various Occupations in the United States

Occupation	Rating*	Occupation	Rating*
U.S. Supreme Court Justice	94	Trained machinist	75
Physician	92	Police officer	72
Cabinet member	90	Carpenter	68
College professor	90	Traveling salesperson	66
Lawyer	89	Plumber	65
Banker	85	Truck driver	59
Instructor in public schools	82	Singer in nightclub	54
Accountant	81	Dock worker	50
Building contractor	80	Taxi driver	49
Electrician	76	Bartender	48
		Garbage collector	39
		Shoe shiner	34

*The effective scale ranges from 94 to 34.

Source: Adapted from Robert W. Hodges, Paul M. Siegel, and Peter H. Rossi, "Occupational Prestige in the United States, 1925–1963," *American Journal of Sociology* (November, 1974), pp. 290–292.

nants of social class which often correlate closely with occupation include personal achievements, social interaction, possessions, and value orientations. These are analyzed briefly in Figure 4-5.

Six Social Classes. Although U.S. citizens often do not want to admit the existence of social classes in the United States, research has clearly documented the existence of six distinct classes:[22]

1. **Upper-upper, 1.4 percent of population.** This group, representing the old family elite, is sufficiently wealthy to maintain large houses in the best neighborhoods. Typically, the family wealth can be traced back more than one generation. These people provide leadership in many cultural and civic activities,

---

[22]Joseph A. Kahl, *The American Class Structures* (New York: Holt, Rinehart and Winston, 1967), p. 26.

FIGURE 4-5   Determinants of Social Class

Occupation	What kind of work does the individual do?
Personal performance	How successful is the individual in his or her occupation? "Best young lawyer in town."
Interactions	Who invites whom to dinner? People associate socially with members of their same class.
Possessions	Possessions act as symbols of class membership, not simply the amount but also the types of possessions.
Value orientations	People within a class have the same attitudes towards a number of specific values — capitalism, child-rearing, and achievement, for example.

Source: Adapted from *Consumer Behavior*, 3d ed., by James F. Engel, Roger D. Blackwell, and David T. Kollat. Copyright © 1978 by The Dryden Press, a division of Holt, Rinehart and Winston, Publishers. Adapted by permission of Holt, Rinehart and Winston, p. 110 and p. 113.

and they tend to belong to the most exclusive clubs in town. Members of the upper-upper class tend to own established businesses or are important members of the town's professional community.

2. **Lower-upper, 1.6 percent of population.** This group may be slightly wealthier than the upper-upper class but its wealth is "newer." Members also tend to display their wealth more openly than the upper-upper class since conspicuous consumption tells the world of their success. Lower-upper class members tend to be business executives who have started successful firms.

3. **Upper-middle, 10 percent of population.** Typical members of the upper-middle class are successful business executives and professional people. Although they are less affluent than members of the upper class, they often enjoy the same type of cultural events and consumer products. They tend to live in reasonably expensive modern homes. While a college education is usually necessary for membership, lineage is not.

4. **Lower-middle, 29 percent of population.** The lower-middle class is made up of small business people, teachers, and factory supervisors. This group tends to have high morals and be patriotic; the members are active church goers and lodge joiners. They tend to live in modest homes and avoid extravagant furnishings. The lower-middle class is usually a good market for do-it-yourself home products.

5. **Upper-lower, 33 percent of population.** Upper-lower class people are respectable blue-collar workers. Their homes are well kept and they generally experience little trouble with the law. These people look at work as the means to purchase enjoyment. They often earn reasonably high union wages and look to their union for job security. The men in upper-lower class families tend to be sports enthusiasts.

6. **Lower-lower, 25 percent of population.** This class represents the most poorly educated and least skilled segment of U.S. society. These people are frequently out of work and seek public assistance. Often the woman in the house is "forced" to work to be able to keep the family together. These people frequently find life frustrating.

Now that we have some idea of how people are classified according to social class, we must question what aspects, if any, of consumer behavior are a function of social class.

Social Class and Consumption Behavior

Several recent studies have pointed out that many differences in consumer behavior are largely a function of social class. These behaviors can be classified as communication skills, shopping behavior, leisure activities, and saving and spending habits.

Communication Skills. Members of the higher social classes are more likely to read magazines and newspapers stressing current events, whereas lower class people tend to read publications dramatizing romance. Also, the type of sophisticated humor and advertising that appears in magazines such as *The New Yorker* and *Esquire* is primarily aimed at members of the upper classes. Regarding television programming, members of the higher social classes tend to watch drama and current events programs; lower class people are usually more interested in soap operas, quiz shows, and situation comedies. Finally, some evidence suggests that television advertisements featuring self-made business people are best received by the lower class.[23]

Shopping Patterns. People are very realistic when it comes to deciding where they should shop; generally speaking, they try to match their values and expectations with the status of the store. Consumers ask themselves, "What kind of people shop here? How will the clerks treat me?" In many ways, the most important aspect of retail advertising is to identify clearly the social class of the store's clientele. In Chicago, the two largest grocery chains, A&P and Jewell, appeal to different types of consumers — A&P does well with the mass market, Jewell with the middle class.[24]

Leisure Activities. While members of the six social classes devote about the same amount of time to leisure activities, they do tend to choose different types of activities.[25] The most frequent users of public leisure facilities such as parks, museums, and swimming pools are members of the middle class. The upper classes tend to have their own leisure facilities, such as private tennis clubs, whereas the lower classes frequently do not have easy access to any recreational facilities at all. In addition, while sports such as football, baseball, and basketball are enjoyed by all social classes, other games seem to have a definite class appeal. For example, polo, tennis, bridge, and golf tend to appeal to the upper classes, while bowling, bingo, roller derby, and boxing appeal to the lower classes.

---

[23]Sidney J. Levy, "Social Class and Consumer Behavior," in *On Knowing the Consumer*, edited by Joseph W. Newman (New York: John Wiley & Sons, Inc., 1966), p. 155.

[24]Pierre Martineau, "Social Classes and Spending Behavior," in *Classics in Consumer Behavior*, edited by Louis E. Boone (Tulsa, Oklahoma: The Petroleum Publishing Company, 1977), pp. 310–311.

[25]James M. Carman, *The Application of Social Class in Market Segmentation* (Berkeley, Calif.: Institute of Business and Economic Research, University of California Graduate School of Business Administration, 1965), p. 31.

Are **you** a "real person"? The evidence is quite clear! Students are not real people. Can this be true? Yes, students are not real people — at least in terms of their attitudes and behavior in the marketplace.

As consumers, college students are systematically different from other people. This finding is of interest to companies that manufacture and sell products in student markets as well as to scholars of market behavior. One study contrasted student and nonstudent consumers on the following four factors.

1. Sociopsychological Variables. Students were found to be more alienated, less dogmatic, less conservative, more cosmopolitan, and substantially more responsible than their nonstudent counterparts.

2. Sources of Market Information. The two groups of consumers rely on different sources of market information. The subjects were asked about their sources of product information on major appliances, grocery products, furniture, and TV and stereo equipment. Generally nonstudents view comparative shopping and newspaper as relatively more important; students place greater reliance on television and other people as sources of product information. Neither group thought that radio was an important source of information, but both said that conversations with friends were.

3. Decision Factors. Which decision factors most influence product selection? Nonstudents chose brand name as the most significant factor in the purchase of major appliances, whereas students placed nearly equal emphasis on brand name and service and warranty. Nonstudent subjects also placed more importance on credit. Both groups named price, store location, and parking as the most important decision factors in the purchase of grocery products. For furniture purchases, both groups identified price as the critical factor. Nonstudents also emphasized store location and parking, while students mentioned personal recommendations as also important. Finally, TV and stereo purchases were made almost exclusively by both groups on the basis of brand name. Again, credit was an important factor to nonstudents.

4. Store Image. Mentioned as important factors in a store's image were physical characteristics of the store, ease of access, products offered, prices charged, store personnel, advertising by the store, and general characteristics of the company that owns the store. In almost all cases, the nonstudents assumed a more extreme position than did the student subjects in the perception of what the ideal store should be like. Once again, students were shown not to be "real people" in terms of their attitudes toward the marketplace.

Marketing & You

Saving and Spending Habits. The higher the individual's social class, the more that individual is likely to save money. Moreover, higher status individuals are more likely to invest in common stock and life insurance policies; lower status people tend to put their money in savings accounts and land.[26] Finally, a study relating social class to bank credit card usage indicates that members of lower social classes tend to use their cards primarily to purchase expensive durable goods such as appliances and furniture. They see their cards as providing instant installment credit. In contrast, members of the upper classes use their cards for convenience purposes.[27]

REFERENCE GROUPS

Reference groups are the most pervasive and important of the two social influences depicted in our model of consumer behavior, Figure 4-2 (page 104). A **reference group** is any set of individuals that influence another individual when he or she makes a decision. A person can belong to a group, such as the Rotary Club, but if it does not affect or shape that person's behavior it is not a reference group. In addition, the reference group is situation-specific — for example, the Democratic Party may act as a reference group during the November elections but then have no effect whatsoever on a party member purchasing a new car in January. Reference groups are important to marketing managers because they influence the product and brand decisions made by consumers and, therefore, the relative effectiveness of promotion strategies.

Types of Reference Groups

There are four distinct types of reference groups: membership groups, automatic groups, anticipatory groups, and negative groups.[28]

Membership Groups. Membership reference groups are those in which the consumer participates. They may be as small as the immediate family or as large as the American Medical Association. Even large organizations, in which the individual's role is minor, may influence personal attitudes as well as the product purchase decisions of their members.

Automatic Groups. Consumers are automatically members of groups based on age, marital status, sex, citizenship, and economic classification. Membership in such groups is often loose, and identification among members quite low. However, to prove to yourself the power of automatic reference groups, observe your fellow students during your next class session. You will find that many of them dress alike. The dominating influence in automatic reference groups comes from consumers' perceptions of what society expects them to do in certain circumstances, which obviously affects the types of products that people purchase.

---

[26]Martineau, *op. cit.*, pp. 312–313.
[27]H. Lee Mathews and John W. Slocum, Jr., "Social Class and Commercial Bank Credit Card Usage," *Journal of Marketing* (January, 1969), pp. 71–78.
[28]C. Glenn Walters, *Consumer Behavior, Theory and Practice* (3d ed.; Homewood, Ill.: Richard D. Irwin, 1978), pp. 411–413.

Anticipatory Groups. The anticipatory reference group is one to which the individual aspires to belong. As an example, this group influences the behavior of individuals who wish to belong to country clubs or to climb the social ladder within the community. The purchase decisions of an anticipatory group aspirant tend to be influenced by the consumption patterns of the group. Anticipatory groups usually affect purchases involving clothes, cars, and entertainment.

Negative Groups. The negative reference group, just the opposite of an anticipatory group, is one to which the individual has no desire to belong. Individuals, in fact, may take deliberate steps to dissociate themselves from such groups. The Ku Klux Klan, the nouveau riche, and politicians are all examples of negative reference groups for large numbers of individuals.

Reference Groups and Consumer Behavior

Many researchers have studied the relationship between reference groups and consumer behavior. In a widely quoted study, Stafford found that informal reference groups strongly influence the brand of product purchased by their members.[29] Another study confirmed that for beer and after-shave lotion, the more cohesive the group, the greater the brand choice conformity.[30]

Product and Brand Influence. The conspicuousness of a product is one of the key determinants in its susceptibility to reference group influence. To be conspicuous, a product must be seen and identified by friends and associates of the buyer, and it must not be owned by all members of society. As Figure 4-6 illustrates, reference group influence may operate with respect to brand alone (Brand +, Product −), brand and product (Brand +, Product +), or product alone (Brand −, Product +).[31]

Brand +, Product −. These are the kind of items owned by most people even though there are apt to be brand differences. Clothing is an excellent example. While everyone in our society wears clothing, the brand or type of clothing that people wear will be influenced by reference groups. To illustrate, male students wear blue jeans, male professors wear sport jackets, and male IBM executives wear three-piece suits.

Brand +, Product +. Cigarettes and beer are examples of items for which product and brand are socially conspicuous. Consumption of these items is influenced strongly by reference groups. Therefore, they have a positive product score. In addition, the type or brand that is consumed is also influenced by reference groups. Since there are often few real differences in these products, manufacturers often invest large sums of money to create images of the type of people who use their products. A good illustration is the "Marlboro Man."

---

[29]James E. Stafford, "Effects of Group Influence on Consumer Brand Preferences," *Journal of Marketing Research* (February, 1966), pp. 68–74.

[30]Robert E. Witt, "Informal Social Group Influence on Consumer Brand Choice," *Journal of Marketing Research* (November, 1966), pp. 473–476.

[31]Francis S. Bourne, "Group Influence in Marketing," in *Classics in Consumer Behavior*, edited by Louis E. Boone (Tulsa, Oklahoma: The Petroleum Publishing Company, 1977), pp. 211–225.

FIGURE 4-6   Reference Group Impact on Product and Brand Choice

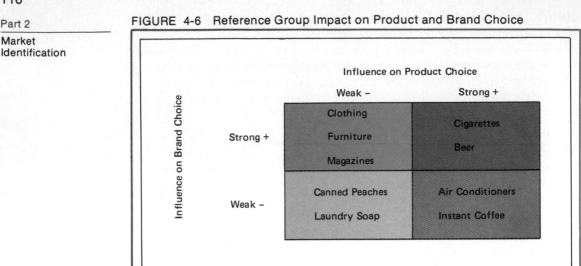

Source: Bureau of Applied Social Research, Columbia University.

Brand −, Product +. An air conditioner is the type of item to which little brand prestige is attached. However, here, reference group influence relates to the purchase of the product itself. People tend to recognize the existence of air conditioning in a home. Yet, it apparently makes little difference as to what brand of air conditioner is actually cooling the house. Several studies have shown that when window air conditioners were introduced, they spread rapidly within clusters of buildings. Immediate neighbors apparently served as powerful reference groups. Today, with the widespread use of air conditioners, particularly in the South, they have lost some of their product reference group appeal.

Brand −, Product −. The items in this category have little social conspicuousness. People tend to purchase them because of their product attributes. Examples include canned peaches and laundry soap.

Reference Groups and Advertising. A product having little or no reference group appeal should be promoted primarily on the basis of its attributes, namely, price, quality, and advantages over competing products. Where reference groups are operative, the advertiser should describe the type of person who uses the product rather than emphasize the qualities of the product itself. Often, what is said about a product is not as important as who says it. Note how well Volkswagen fits its product attributes to the reference group it's trying to reach through the ad displayed in Figure 4-7.

Sports celebrities are used a great deal to promote a large number of products. One study identified the relationship between the star's "familiarity," "talent," and "likeability" with his or her credibility.[32] The study found that credibility in product endorsements was most highly correlated with likeability. It is

---

[32]Alan R. Nelson, "Can the Glamour and Excitment of Sports Really Carry the Ball for Your Product?" *Marketing Review* (February, 1974), pp. 21–25.

FIGURE 4-7 An Advertisement for the Volkswagen Rabbit Aimed
at a Particular Reference Group

Courtesy: Volkswagen of America, Inc.

interesting to note that celebrities such as Joe Namath, Muhammad Ali, and Howard Cossell, who are among the most familiar sports figures, all have low scores on the credibility test. On the other hand, ex-baseball player Stan Musial, who ranks first in credibility, ranks only 25th in familiarity. The study also found that the *effectiveness* of sports figures in advertisements varied with the types of products promoted. Sporting goods, athlete's foot remedies, sportswear, and electric shavers lend themselves well to endorsement by sports celebrities, but pet foods, home furnishings, wine, and house paint generally do not.

Although more research is needed in this area, it is clear from past studies and advertising practices that celebrities often can be more effective than personal friends in promoting products. It may even be possible to divide markets into specific groups based on an individual's attraction to various sports or movie celebrities as well as to so-called experts such as TV repairers or plumbers who also promote products on television.[33]

So far, we have talked mainly about individual consumption behavior. What about the consumption behavior of a family?

FAMILY DECISION MAKING

The family has a substantial impact on many purchase and consumption decisions. While the nation's divorce rate continues to increase, there is still reason to believe that the vast majority of U.S. residents believes in marriage. Two trends, however, are important to the marketing executive: first, people are postponing marriages longer than ever before, and second, the average number of children per family is declining. Although the number of childless families remains relatively small at 9.5 percent, the average number of children per family has declined from 3.0 in the mid-1960s to just over 2.1 today.[34]

The female in the family has traditionally been assigned the role of family purchasing agent. Although the role of women in society has changed a great deal during the past few years, women still seem to do most of the day-to-day purchasing in the United States. A recent study of family purchasing behavior found that of 13 common household items, ranging from cold cereal to mouthwash, 12 were more likely to be purchased by the woman of the family than by the man.[35]

In addition to knowing who in the family makes the purchase, it is important to know who actually decides what products to buy. In a study of five product categories, data comparing husband and wife decision-making roles vary significantly depending on the product. As Table 4-2 illustrates, respondents in the 1973 study stated that women make grocery product purchase decisions; men make life insurance decisions; and husband and wives together make housing and vacation decisions.

It is also important to note the differences that have taken place since the 1955 study was undertaken. First, with regard to products such as groceries and life insurance, the decision-making responsibility in the family has become more specialized. This may be due to the increasing complexities of modern life. The second trend involves more joint decision making. This willingness to share decision making may indicate a greater sense of equality between husband and wife. Finally, that husbands no longer dominate automobile purchases can be explained by the fact that women participate more in activities outside the home than ever before. As a result, the family automobile is also an important item to her.

These findings clearly indicate that not all product decisions are affected in the same way by the changes taking place in society. Marketing executives must realize that product-specific information is required when trying to deter-

---

[33]A. Benton Cocanougher and Grady D. Bruce, "Socially Distant Reference Groups and Consumer Aspirations," *Journal of Marketing Research* (August, 1971), p. 381.

[34]William Lazer and John E. Smallwood, "The Changing Demographics of Women," *Journal of Marketing* (July, 1977), pp. 14–22.

[35]"Buying Study Called Good Support Data," *Advertising Age* (March 17, 1975), p. 52.

TABLE 4-2   Husband-Wife Decision-Making Roles, 1955 and 1973

Decision Area	1955 (%)	1973 (%)
Food and Groceries		
Husband usually	13	10
Both husband and wife	33	15
Wife usually	54	75
Number of cases	(727)	(248)
Life Insurance		
Husband usually	43	66
Both husband and wife	42	30
Wife usually	15	4
Number of cases	(727)	(247)
Vacation		
Husband usually	18	7
Both husband and wife	70	84
Wife usually	12	9
Number of cases	(727)	(247)
House or Apartment		
Husband usually	18	12
Both husband and wife	58	77
Wife usually	24	11
Number of cases	(727)	(247)
Automobile		
Husband usually	70	52
Both husband and wife	25	45
Wife usually	5	3
Number of cases	(727)	(248)

Source: Isabella C. M. Cunningham and Robert T. Green, "Purchasing Roles in the U.S. Family, 1955 and 1973," *Journal of Marketing* (October, 1974), p. 63.

mine who makes the product purchase decisions. In addition, more research is needed in the area of *how* families make decisions rather than simply on *who* makes the decisions.

MOTIVATIONAL THEORY

Our model of consumer behavior (page 104) illustrates that three individual factors affect consumer behavior: motivation, perception and learning, and economic influences. **Motivation** is the "why" of behavior. According to one writer, "motivation refers to the drives, urges, wishes or desires which *initiate* the sequence of events known as behavior."[36] Human motives sometimes originate with biological needs. When our physical or emotional balance, or

[36]Marguerite C. Burk, "Survey of Interpretations of Consumer Behavior by Social Scientists in the Postwar Period," *Journal of Farm Economics* (February, 1967), p. 2.

homeostasis, is disturbed, we feel a deprivation or **need** of some kind. The awareness of such a need is also called a **want**. When individuals attempt to satisfy a want or a need, they are experiencing some kind of motivation. Human needs, however, are many and include more than those of just a physiological nature. In fact, if the task of a firm were merely to satisfy the hunger or thirst of its consumers, it would be concerned primarily with the distribution of its products, and not market research, new product development, or changing consumer behavior.

A number of questions can be asked about motivation. Why do people drink alcoholic beverages? Certainly not just to satisfy thirst. Why do people wear fur coats? Certainly not just to protect themselves from the environment. It appears that other variables also motivate people to buy certain types of products. Our look at motivational theory begins by examining Abraham Maslow's hierarchy of needs.

The Hierarchy of Needs

Abraham Maslow and Sigmund Freud did much of the classic work on motivation theory. Maslow felt that motivation must be analyzed in terms of five sets of goals or needs.[37] As Figure 4-8 illustrates, these needs are ranked in a hierarchy of importance. The most important goal monopolizes the individual's attention while all other goals are either minimized or forgotten. However, once this goal is satisfied, the individual moves to the next higher goal, which now serves as the center of attention.

In reality, there is no sharp distinction between each level of need; almost all consumer purchases involve the satisfaction of needs at several levels. In a booming and affluent economy, it is doubtful that very many purchase decisions are based on biological need alone. Even in the supermarket, we observe

FIGURE 4-8   Maslow's Hierarchy of Needs

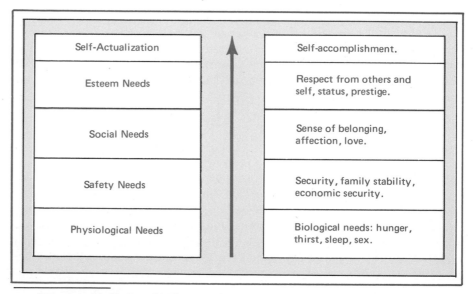

Self-Actualization	Self-accomplishment.
Esteem Needs	Respect from others and self, status, prestige.
Social Needs	Sense of belonging, affection, love.
Safety Needs	Security, family stability, economic security.
Physiological Needs	Biological needs: hunger, thirst, sleep, sex.

[37]Abraham H. Maslow, "A Theory of Human Motivation," *Psychological Review*, Vol. 60 (1943), pp. 370–396.

FIGURE 4-9 Promotional Appeals and Hierarchy of Needs

Need	Product	Promotional Appeal
Physiological	Small home	Inexpensive housing for the family; small but well-built.
Safety	Smoke alarm	Could save your family's lives; think of your children and your spouse.
Social	Gold bracelet	Show your sweetheart you care on Valentine's Day.
Esteem	Expensive luxury car	Picture car in front of "gracious" home or club.
Self-actualization	Graphite golf clubs	For the three-day-a-week golfer; for the golfer who is looking for only two strokes.

people purchasing at a premium price food that can be quickly served or that is sure to contain little or no nourishment, such as low-calorie soft drinks.

Maslow's hierarchy of needs is relevant to the firm because it can assist the marketing manager in positioning products so that they will be most appealing to prospective customers. As an illustration, most U.S.-made luxury cars use the appeal to status ("Impress your friends"). However, when Mercedes-Benz introduced its new Turbo Diesel, it stressed that the car is "luxurious and high-powered" as well as economical to operate. This appeal would seem to be aimed at self-actualization. Look at Figure 4-9 for other examples of Maslow's hierarchy of needs in relation to product and promotional appeals.

The Freudian Psychoanalytic Model

Taking a different perspective on motivation, Sigmund Freud believed that human beings are born with instinctive needs which they quickly realize they cannot satisfy without the help of others. Children, for example, attempt to satisfy their needs through intimidation and begging. As children mature, they develop more subtle mechanisms for getting what they want.

Freud divided the personality into three parts. The id is the source of biological instincts and basic drives. The super ego, the police officer of the mind, represents the internalized mores and ethical precepts of society at large. The job of the ego, then, is to reconcile the demands of the id with those of the super ego.

The most important implication of the Freudian model for marketing is that human beings are motivated by symbolic as well as by economic and functional concerns. At times, the marketing analyst must look beyond the apparent reason why an individual purchased a product in order to find the real reason. Five theories that Freudian researchers have developed from their studies about different products are presented below:

1. Prunes arouse feelings of old age and insecurity.
2. Men feel their cigars must have a strong odor to prove their masculinity.

3. When a woman bakes a cake, she is unconsciously going through the symbolic act of birth.
4. A man purchases a sports convertible as a substitute for a mistress.
5. Men who wear suspenders suffer from an unresolved castration complex.[38]

Although these findings are subject to debate, they do indicate that in designing promotion and sales strategies the marketing manager must determine the real reason why consumers purchase a particular product.

PERCEPTION AND LEARNING

The second set of the individual factors affecting consumer behavior includes perception and learning. Like motivation, the study of perception and learning deals with human beings as unique individuals.

Learning Theory

Learning may be defined as the process by which a pattern of behavior is established or modified by means of a stimulus-response or cognition mechanism. Learning does not include native response tendencies or temporary states such as fatigue. Beyond this definition of learning, there is little agreement among psychologists as to the nature of learning, how it occurs, and what stimulates or hinders it.[39] Learning is best studied from the perspectives of stimulus-response theory and cognitive theory.

Stimulus-Response Theory. Stimulus-response theory had its beginning with the Russian psychologist Pavlov. In his famous experiment, Pavlov rang a bell immediately before feeding a dog. Eventually, the dog, associating the sound of the bell with the arrival of dinner, learned to salivate when the bell was rung regardless of whether food was supplied. As a result, Pavlov concluded that learning was largely an associative process. Although this theory has been developed further by modern psychologists, it still rests on four basic principles:

1. **Drive.** Drive is a strong internal stimulus impelling action. It may be innate such as hunger, thirst, or sex, or it may be learned such as a need for status.
2. **Cue.** The cue is a weak stimulus in the environment determining how the individual responds to the drive. Advertisements frequently serve as cues. If a person is thirsty (basic drive), a soft drink advertisement may encourage the viewer to reduce that drive by visiting the refrigerator or a local convenience store.
3. **Response.** The reaction to the cue is the response. Individuals react differently to cues based on how rewarding their past responses have been.
4. **Reinforcement.** If the response is rewarding and positive, the individual is likely to react in the same manner to the cue every time it appears. The strength of the ensuing habit is a function of the number of situations in which the particular response has been reinforced. Therefore, a consumer having had good luck with a

[38]Philip Kotler, "Behavioral Models for Analyzing Buyers," *Journal of Marketing* (October, 1965), pp. 41–42.

[39]Harold H. Kassarjian and Thomas S. Robertson (eds.), *Perspectives in Consumer Behavior* (Glenview, Ill.: Scott, Foresman and Company, 1968), p. 59.

particular brand will likely continue purchasing that brand as long as the cue pattern remains the same. The habit diminishes when the response is not reinforced.[40]

The stimulus-response model has two important implications for marketing. First, when a new product is introduced, the firm should realize that it may have to extinguish existing brand habits and preferences before attempting to form new buying habits. In this light, the firm will wish to seriously consider the strength of its cues. For example, a one-time, 60-second television commercial is a relatively weak cue, whereas free samples delivered to potential customers' doors tend to be quite strong. With a television commercial cue, the individual still must leave the house to purchase the product before it can be tried. However, when the product is brought to the home, the cue is stronger because it requires less effort on the part of the consumer.

The second implication for marketing is that because people are conditioned through repetition and reinforcement, a single cue, such as a television advertisement, may not be sufficient to penetrate an individual's consciousness. Therefore, it often is necessary to repeat an advertisement a number of times.

Cognitive Theory. The second major learning theory rejects the idea that all learning is of a stimulus-response nature. Rather, cognitive theorists believe that habits are acquired by insight, thinking, and problem solving as well as through a stimulus-response mechanism. From this perspective, the central nervous system and the brain become very important intermediaries in the learning process.

Cognitive theory has several implications for marketing. For example, when the firm is designing a sales strategy, it cannot assume that the consumer is going to buy the product simply because of previous satisfaction with the firm. If the consumer has had successful transactions in the past, this will help the seller, but the buyer can also be expected to evaluate the firm's product with respect to its merits as well as compare it to competitors' offerings. Therefore, in situations where cognitive learning is likely to take place, the seller must develop logical presentations which help the potential buyer to evaluate the product in a favorable light.

Perception

Perception is the process by which individuals become aware of (through any of the five senses) and give meaning to their environment.[41] If buyers do not perceive or have not heard of the product, everything the firm has done to promote the product has been wasted. Thus, it is vital to look closely at the factors affecting perception as well as at the characteristics of perception.

Factors Affecting Perception. Several *technical factors* affect the way an object is perceived. These factors do not refer to the product's technology

---

[40]John A. Howard, "Learning and Consumer Behavior," in *Perspectives in Consumer Behavior, Revised,* edited by Harold H. Kassarjian and Thomas S. Robertson (Glenview, Ill.: Scott, Foresman and Company, 1973), pp. 75–86.

[41]Adapted from Paul Thomas Young, *Motivation and Emotion: A Survey of the Determinants of Human and Animal Activity* (New York: John Wiley & Sons, Inc., 1961), pp. 289–299.

FIGURE 4-10   Technical Factors Affecting Perception

Size	Large objects attract more attention. Large advertisements and large stores are perceived more quickly and more positively.
Color	Color attracts more than black and white. Color advertisements and colored objects are perceived quicker and remembered longer.
Intensity	Greater intensity attracts attention and affects memory and learning. Bright colors and colorful words are important for advertisements.
Movement	More movement attracts more attention. This factor is critical in television commercials and store signs.
Position	Where an object is located is important. Objects located shoulder-high are purchased most often.

Source: Adapted from C. Glenn Walters, *Consumer Behavior, Theory and Practice* (3d ed.; Homewood, Ill.: Richard D. Irwin, 1978), pp. 249–250.

itself, but rather to how the individual *sees* the object. Research studies, for example, have indicated that a large and multicolored advertisement is perceived more quickly and remembered longer than a small black-and-white advertisement. Figure 4-10 describes five technical aspects of perception: size, color, intensity, movement, and position.

A second important factor is the individual's *mental readiness* to perceive a product. Research has shown that buyers tend to become "fixed" on a mental image. For example, a consumer may continue to purchase a particular brand even after that consumer knows that a better product can be bought at a lower price. Mental readiness is also affected by the buyer's *level of attention*. Generally speaking, people have a limited attention span. That is, human beings only comprehend a limited number of objects or messages in a given amount of time. Also, people's attention tends to shift quickly from one object to another. These aspects of perception suggest the importance of keeping commercials simple and brief.

Social and cultural factors also shape perception. As already mentioned, culture and social class have a significant effect on how and what consumers purchase. As an illustration, consumers differ as to how important "upward mobility" is to them. Persons interested in climbing the social ladder will perceive certain products as inferior if they feel that members of the upper class do not purchase those products.

Past experience is a fourth factor influencing perception. To illustrate, a person may perceive a brand of canned peaches as being of high quality simply because of past favorable experiences with the product. Finally, the *mood* of the individual is an important determinant of perception; a person who is unhappy or depressed may find it difficult to see the positive side of a product.

Characteristics of Perception. Perception has three basic characteristics: it is subjective, selective, and summative.[42] It is *subjective* because no two individuals perceive the same object in the same way. People tend to see what they want to see and to hear what they want to hear. If former-President Ford gives a speech on national defense, a Republican is likely to find it "creative and far-reaching," whereas a Democrat may view it as "limited, political propaganda."

Perception is *selective* in that only a few of the signals that people receive each day are converted into messages. We receive between 1,500 and 2,000 advertising signals per day through exposure to billboards, store signs, and other forms of mass media. Since it is not possible to deal mentally with so many messages, our minds eliminate most of them from conscious awareness. Because of selective perception, advertising managers must carefully choose their media and the timing and placement of advertisements in order to maximize exposure. In addition, if the advertisement is cluttered with many messages, prospective buyers will probably not be able to remember any of them.

Perception is *summative* in the sense that the reception and recognition of a signal is frequently a function of the cumulative effect of multiple signals. The more often a signal is received, the greater the chance that it will be understood. Also, the probability that a receiver will correctly interpret a signal is enhanced if the signal is sent through two or more channels. These two points suggest why television advertisers repeat their commercials frequently. Also, the salesperson who wants to ensure that a message is understood may send the customer a direct-mail promotion and then visit the customer personally to demonstrate the product.

THE ECONOMIC PERSPECTIVE

The final *individual* factor influencing buyer behavior is the economic perspective of rational choice. Alfred Marshall, who first consolidated the various economic theories, is the major proponent of modern economic thought. Two principles of Marshallian economics relate directly to buyer behavior: the economic man concept and the law of diminishing returns.

Marshall's Economic Man

Marshall defines **economic man** as a rational decision maker who evaluates the consequences of each variable in the purchase decision process, one at a time, in a stepwise manner. Typically, the less desirable alternatives are progressively eliminated until finally that alternative providing the highest utility or satisfaction per dollar spent is selected. Marshall characterizes buyers following the economic man model as:

1. Continually attempting to maximize their economic well-being.
2. Possessing complete information about the market.
3. Being mobile in that they can reach any market offer at any time.

[42]W. J. E. Crissy, William H. Cunningham, and Isabella C. M. Cunningham, *Selling: The Personal Force in Marketing* (New York: Wiley/Hamilton, 1977), pp. 57–58.

Because the economic man is concerned with the economic consequences of successive purchases, the concept of marginal utility is especially important. **Marginal utility** is defined as the added satisfaction obtained from purchasing another unit of a given product. Closely akin to the concept of marginal utility is the law of diminishing returns.

The Law of Diminishing Returns

According to the **law of diminishing returns**, the utility of each additional unit of the same product decreases as more units are consumed. To illustrate, the first television in your home brings you a great deal of satisfaction or utility — it permits you to watch programs that otherwise would not be available to you. The second television set may be a worthwhile addition also — it gives you more convenience but it clearly is not as valuable as the first. The additional satisfaction, or marginal utility, derived from purchases of additional television sets decreases with each purchase.

According to the Marshallian model, people seek to achieve an economic state of balance. This is accomplished when the utility/price ratios (marginal utility divided by price per unit) of all the products that might be purchased are equal. Figure 4-11 illustrates the dilemma of an individual considering purchasing one of two products. Product A yields 10 units of utility per dollar while Product B yields 12.5 units of utility per dollar. Therefore, the person purchases Product B. When the need for Product A or B arises again, necessitating a second purchase, the marginal utility of Product B will fall as a result of the law of diminishing returns (i.e., the ownership of a second unit of Product B brings less satisfaction than the ownership of the first unit). In our illustration, Product B's marginal utility has declined to 1200. As a result, the utility/price

FIGURE 4-11   Illustration of the Law of Diminishing Returns

		Product A	Product B
Time 1	$\dfrac{\text{marginal utility}}{\text{price per unit}} =$	$\dfrac{1000}{100} = 10$	$\dfrac{1500}{120} = 12.5$
Time 2	$\dfrac{\text{marginal utility}}{\text{price per unit}} =$	$\dfrac{1000}{100} = 10$	$\dfrac{1200}{120} = 10$

ratios of the two products are now the same, and the individual has reached a state of equilibrium in regard to these two products. The purchase of either product would yield the same amount of satisfaction.

Economic Theory and Buyer Behavior

The application of economic theory to buyer behavior depends to some extent on whether buyers are individual consumers or industrial purchasing agents. Consumers are generally believed to behave less rationally than industrial purchasing agents. Since most consumer products are relatively inexpensive when compared to consumer incomes, consumers are not very likely to compare utility/price ratios for several alternative products. The time required would be prohibitive. However, the situation may be different when the consumer is considering the purchase of an expensive item such as a new car or a new home.

On the other hand, a purchasing agent, evaluating the quality of a product with respect to its price, is more likely to act in a rational and economic manner. However, purchasing agents usually do not have complete information with respect to all possible product alternatives; nor are they completely free to buy from any seller they choose. In addition, a purchasing agent may have established a long-term personal relationship with a particular supplier and may be more likely to buy from this supplier even if its products offer no real advantage in terms of service or price. The point here is that many purchasing agents do not mind paying more for a particular product if it gives them substantially more value or utility than the other available alternatives. The firm, therefore, must remember that it is not just selling a product; it is selling a product with a comparative value/cost ratio. The higher this ratio, the better the chance of completing a profitable sale. Purchasing by industrial buyers will be discussed in more detail in the next chapter.

POST-PURCHASE DISSONANCE

Post-purchase dissonance is another *individual factor* influencing consumer behavior. It has been separated from the other individual factors in Figure 4-2 to emphasize that it acts on the consumer after the purchase decision has been made.

Leon Festinger suggests that whenever people make decisions they experience some kind of post-purchase cognitive dissonance or discomfort.[43] No decision is perfect since it can always be argued that another choice or course of action would have been better and that buyers are cognitive, or aware, of this fact. Consumers strive to eliminate post-purchase dissonance by emphasizing the positive aspects of the purchase or the product chosen and by minimizing the drawbacks or negative aspects.

The Existence of Post-Purchase Dissonance

Post-purchase dissonance is likely to be strongest, and therefore of more interest to the manufacturer or seller, when the product is expensive relative to the purchaser's income. The purchase of a $100 gold pen may be very important to a person with a $20,000 income but much less so to a person earning $180,000. The extent of post-purchase dissonance is also influenced by the *range of reasonable alternatives* open to the purchaser. For example, a person buying an automobile may have to choose from among as many as 20 acceptable models. In this case, there is great potential for post-purchase cognitive dissonance since any of the 19 other models may have represented a better buy than the model actually chosen. In contrast, the purchase of electricity

---

[43]See Leon Festinger, *A Theory of Cognitive Dissonance* (Stanford, Calif.: Stanford University Press, 1957).

does not stimulate much dissonance since normally there is no alternative to the local monopoly power company.

A third item that influences dissonance is the visibility of the purchase decision. When a product is displayed repeatedly by the purchaser, it represents that person's judgment. Consumers are much more likely to worry about their selection of products when they feel that other people are evaluating them based on their decisions. Therefore, the purchase of a home is likely to cause dissonance because it tells the world about the purchaser's tastes and preferences. Because of its impact on buyer behavior, cognitive dissonance has been the focus of much research.

Research on Post-Purchase Dissonance

One of the many studies on post-purchase dissonance involved car buyers and the kind of automobile advertisements they read. The investigators hypothesized, first, that consumers typically feel dissonance after a new car purchase, and second, that they attempt to reduce this feeling by selectively reading automobile advertisements. The study found that recent car buyers are more likely to read advertisements about the car brand just purchased than about cars considered but not purchased.[44] This tendency was shown to be related to *decision making* and not simply to automobile *ownership*; people who had not purchased a new car recently were no more likely to read advertisements about their make of car than about any other type of car.[45]

Another study analyzed the effectiveness of telephone and mail communication in reducing post-purchase dissonance among recent buyers of refrigerators.[46] The findings were quite surprising. The buyers who received a letter from the seller congratulating them on their purchase experienced less post-purchase dissonance, had a more favorable attitude toward the store, and were more likely to shop again at the store than those who did not receive such a letter. The experiment suggests that a post-purchase letter can be an effective merchandising technique.

On the other hand, buyers receiving a post-purchase telephone call, rather than a letter, tended to be more dissonant, less positive toward the store, and less likely to return to the store. In this instance, the post-purchase communication was not only ineffective in reducing dissonance but also counter-productive. According to the researcher, these buyers may have perceived the telephone call as a nuisance or may have felt that the store had an ulterior motive for calling them.

Implications of Post-Purchase Dissonance

Not all customers experience dissonance after making a purchase. As we have indicated, the degree of post-purchase dissonance depends upon the im-

---

[44]Gerald D. Bell, "The Automobile Buyer After the Purchase," *Journal of Marketing* (July, 1967), p. 13.

[45]Danuta Ehrlich, Isaiah Guttman, and Peter Schonbach, "Post-Decision Exposure to Relevant Information," *Journal of Abnormal and Social Psychology*, Vol. 54 (1953), pp. 98–102.

[46]Shelby D. Hunt, "Post-Transaction Communications and Dissonance Reduction," *Journal of Marketing* (July, 1970), pp. 46–51.

portance of the purchase to the individual. Dissonance also depends upon the buyer's personality and the groups with which the buyer associates. Nonetheless, post-purchase dissonance is important to the seller or store owner because an unsatisfied customer may decide to return the offending product and demand a refund, to shop elsewhere in the future, or to tell friends and neighbors of the bad experience. In contrast, a satisfied customer often acts as an unpaid goodwill agent.

There are several ways for the firm to *minimize* dissonance. First, as suggested by the automobile advertising study, the firm can target a percentage of its promotional expenditures at customers who have recently purchased one of its products. Advertising can help to reinforce the customer's purchase decision. Second, a firm can communicate directly with recent buyers. However, it is clear from Hunt's study that the firm must exercise caution to ensure that the message reduces, not stimulates, dissonance. Finally, salespeople must be careful not to *oversell* products. Overselling tends to raise the consumer's expectations, thereby increasing the likelihood and intensity of dissonant reaction. In this regard, it may be better to let the product outperform the salesperson's claims.

summary points

1. Consumers go through a five-stage decision process when they purchase an item — problem recognition, information search, alternative evaluation, choice, and outcome.

2. Culture is a set of values, ideas, attitudes, and symbols created by people which shape behavior. For an element of culture to be passed from one generation to the next, it must satisfy a real need.

3. Subcultures are distinct cultural groups within society. Members often purchase different types of products for reasons different from the rest of society.

4. One of the most critical elements in determining social class is an individual's occupation. Other factors include personal performance, social interactions, possessions, and value orientations.

5. Social class influences people's communication skills, their choice of where to shop, their leisure activities and their saving and spending habits.

6. A reference group is any group within society that influences the behavior of an individual. There are membership, automatic, anticipatory, and negative reference groups. Reference groups have been shown to influence both product and brand decisions.

7. Studies of family decision making show who purchases products and who decides which products are to be purchased.

8. Maslow's hierarchy-of-needs motivation model ranks human needs according to the order in which they must be satisfied — from biological and instinctive on the primary level to the social and spiritual on the highest levels.

9. The Freudian psychoanalytic model implies that human beings are motivated by symbolic as well as by economic and functional concerns.

10. The stimulus-response learning model has four basic principles — drive, cue, response, and reinforcement.

11. Cognitive theory suggests that habits are acquired by insight, thinking, and problem solving as well as by a stimulus-response mechanism.

12. Technical considerations, mental readiness, social and cultural factors, and past experiences all affect perception.

13. Perception is subjective, selective, and summative.

14. The economic approach to buyer behavior assumes that human beings are perfectly rational.

15. Post-purchase dissonance exists whenever an individual is uncertain about the merits of a recently purchased product.

questions for discussion

1. Describe the decision process that you went through when you chose to attend this university or college. Is this the same process that you go through when you purchase a product?
2. Do you believe that behavioral scientists are close to developing one model that will explain all consumer behavior?
3. Are you a member of any subcultures? What are they? How does your membership in these subcultures influence the products you buy or the services you use?
4. Describe in your own words what is meant by social class. Is social class more important or less important in the United States than it was 20 years ago?
5. How do reference groups differ from subcultures?
6. How do the four types of reference groups differ from one another?
7. How much reference group appeal would men's shaving cream have? How would you advertise men's shaving cream?
8. What changes do you expect in the family purchase decision process in the next 20 years?
9. Why do you think people smoke cigarettes? What role might peer group pressure play in a person's decision to smoke?
10. Analyze the differences between Maslow's hierarchy-of-needs model and Freud's psychoanalytic approach to motivation.
11. Which theory is more useful to the marketing executive in explaining how people learn — stimulus-response theory or cognitive theory?
12. Why are the concepts of subjective, selective, and summative perception so important to marketing executives?
13. Discuss how the law of diminishing returns forces the individual into a state of equilibrium.
14. Do you think that purchasing agents are likely to behave in a more rational economic manner than consumers? What other forces influence purchasing agents besides economic factors?
15. Have you ever experienced post-purchase dissonance? How did you act to reduce the dissonance?

Topics discussed in Chapter 5:

1. The differences between consumers and organizational buyers.
2. The six-stage industrial purchasing process.
3. Legal implications of reciprocity.
4. The buying plan used by most retailers.
5. Buying methods such as cooperative buying, centralized vs. decentralized buying, buying committees, and resident buying offices.
6. Government procurement practices.

5

Intermediate Buyer Behavior

Unfortunately, relatively little has been written about organizational buying behavior. Considering that products are often sold three or more times before they ever reach the final consumer, a very significant portion of market behavior has been left uninvestigated. Included as organizational buyers are industrial buyers, retailers, and government purchasing agencies. We begin our study of organizational buying behavior by comparing some of the important differences between organizational buyers and consumers.

CONSUMER VS. ORGANIZATIONAL BUYERS

Certainly one of the most important comparisons between the consumer and organizational sectors of the economy is the number of buying units there are per sector. While there are roughly 60–65 million households and more than 200 million people in the United States, there are only slightly more than 3.5 million businesses. As Table 5-1 indicates, 38 percent of these businesses are classified as retailing and wholesaling, 28.1 percent as service-oriented, and 7.5 percent as manufacturing. Other differences between consumers and organizational buyers are as follows:[1]

1. Professional buyers in the organizational market are usually more technically qualified than consumers.
2. Organizational buyers are usually more rational.
3. Multiple buying influences are involved in virtually all organizational purchases.
4. Committee buying often exists in organizations.

---

[1]Robert Hass, *Industrial Marketing Management* (New York: Petrocelli Books, Ltd., 1976), pp. 13–14.

TABLE 5-1   Categories of Industrial Business, 1976

Industry Category	Number of Reporting Units	Percentage
Agriculture, forestry, and fisheries	42,699	1.0
Contract construction	394,963	9.5
Finance, insurance, and real estate	392,819	9.5
Manufacturing	310,633	7.5
Mining	25,436	0.6
Retailing	1,215,634	29.4
Wholesaling	357,653	8.6
Services	1,164,782	28.1
Transportation and other public utilities	155,219	3.8
Nonclassified establishments*	82,951	2.0
Total	4,142,789	100.0

*Includes reporting units that could not be classified in any major industry group because of insufficient information, as well as all institutions not included in other categories but covered by the Federal Insurance Contribution Act.

Source: U.S. Bureau of the Census, *County Business Patterns: United States Summary* (Washington, D.C.: U.S. Government Printing Office, 1976), pp. 1–2.

5. Organizational buyers frequently select several sources of supply to protect against possible shortages.
6. Reciprocity frequently exists in organizations.

Let's look at some of these factors as they relate to the industrial buying process.

THE INDUSTRIAL BUYING PROCESS

Figure 5-1 presents a model of the industrial buying process.[2] Although the buying process in an actual firm is more specific, this generalized model does include most of the key steps in the buying process.

The industrial buying process begins when someone in the organization realizes that a *need* exists for more merchandise, supplies, or production inputs. As Figure 5-1 indicates, at this point the firm determines *specifications* for the item in question so that it can collect *information* about potential suppliers. Before making a decision, however, the business consciously or unconsciously analyzes a series of *environmental variables* that may influence the choice of product and supplier. After making the final *purchase decision*, the firm monitors the performance of the product to see whether it lives up to expectations. This *product evaluation*, or feedback, determines whether or not

[2]For a description of other models of the industrial buying process see Jagdish N. Sheth, "A Model of Industrial Buyer Behavior," *Journal of Marketing* (October, 1973), pp. 50–56; and Frederick E. Webster, Jr., and Yoram Wind, "A General Model for Understanding Organizational Buying Behavior," *Journal of Marketing* (April, 1972), pp. 12—19.

FIGURE 5-1 Industrial Buying Process

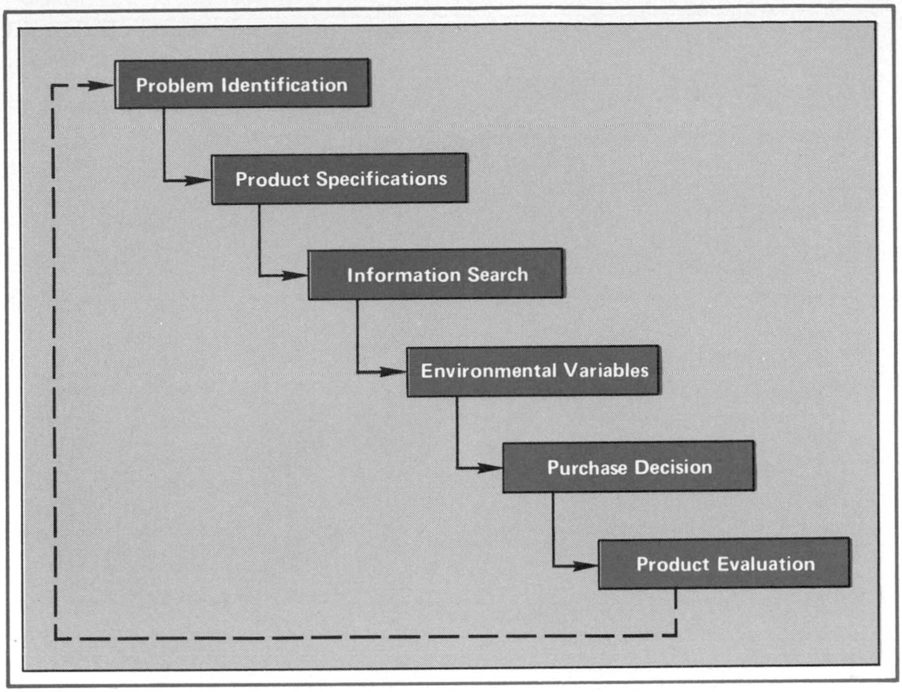

Source: Modified from Frederick E, Webster, Jr., and Yoram Wind, *Organizational Buying Behavior* (Englewood Cliffs, N.J.: Prentice-Hall, Inc., 1972), p. 31. Used by permission.

the firm repurchases the product. Each of these steps merits discussion in greater detail.

Problem (Need) Identification

A firm must first recognize that a *need* for a product or materials exists. In some poorly managed firms, for example, production personnel simply run out of a required raw material or an inventory manager exhausts the supply of a particular type of good. At this point a panic situation develops as the firm tries to obtain enough material quickly so that production or resale operations are not curtailed.

In well-managed firms, a variety of sources of information are available to the purchasing department concerning the need for additional merchandise. As Figure 5-2 indicates, salespeople can play an important role in this process. The buyer or purchasing agent may request that the vendor's salesperson monitor the firm's inventory levels to ensure that supplies are adequate. In addition, when a supplier has developed a new product, it is the salesperson's responsibility to learn how it can be most effectively utilized by the firm's customers. The salesperson is then in a position to design a strategy to present the new product to the buyer.

A supply need can also be recognized in advance of inventory exhaustion by means of advertisements and promotional materials. In the consumer mar-

FIGURE 5-2 Sources for Identifying New Purchase Needs

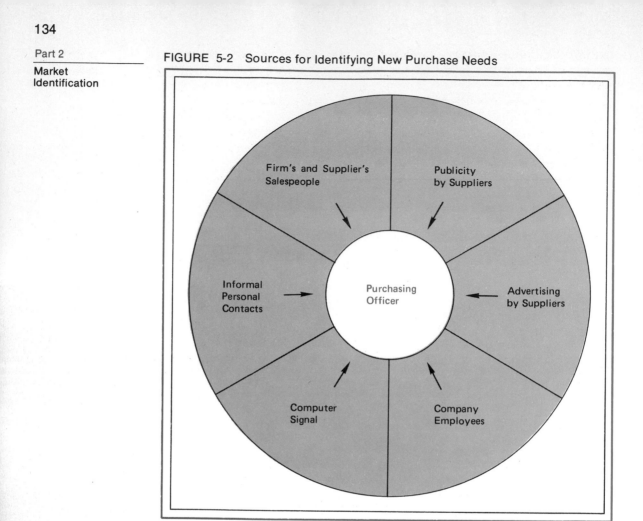

ket, advertisements are designed primarily to stimulate a product purchase, whereas in the industrial market they are designed to encourage the prospective customer to contact the supplier for more information. At this point, arrangements can be made for a salesperson to call on the prospective customer.

Company employees are normally involved in monitoring stock levels. However, their role goes beyond simple monitoring activities when they make a suggestion as to how the firm can manufacture its product more efficiently. These suggestions often lead to the purchase of new supplies or inputs and the elimination of others. Sophisticated computerized inventory control systems can be an invaluable aid to the inventory manager in monitoring inventory needs. Finally, informal contacts with people inside and outside the firm often lead to the discovery of new ways to solve old production, inventory, and distribution problems. Purchasing agents often discuss among themselves the effectiveness of new products as well as the reliability of individual vendors. Other people in the firm maintain similar contacts.

Product Specifications

Before the actual purchase process can begin, the firm must establish objectives and detailed specifications for the needed product. These objectives and specifications are usually established by the engineering department. However, depending on the exact nature of the product, the research and development department and the production department may also become involved. The purchasing department must ensure that the specifications have not been written so tightly that only a single supplier is able to bid on the product. When specifications are unrealistic or designed to satisfy rigorous theoretical criteria only, thereby excluding potential suppliers from the bidding process, the firm usually ends up paying a higher price for the product.

Information Search

Once the firm has written specifications, it must decide whether to purchase the same product from the same supplier, the same product from a new supplier, or an entirely new product. This decision is important because it will direct the organization's data collection activities. For example, if the firm is involved in routine stock replenishment, it will usually contact its current supplier. On the other hand, if it has had a problem with either the quality of the product or the purchase terms, it may choose to find a new supplier. In the extreme case, if the firm feels it needs an entirely new product to solve its supply problem, it will probably have to undertake an extensive information search in order to locate the right supplier.

The firm can obtain information on suppliers directly from potential suppliers or from exhibitions and trade shows, journal articles and advertising, professional and technical conferences, and trade publications. Despite the variety of sources, purchasing agents usually receive a disproportionately large amount of information directly from commercial supply sources. This information tends to be biased in favor of the organization providing it. Although purchasing agents are supposedly trained to deal with biased information, production and engineering personnel usually are not. As a result, many organizations do not permit vendor salespeople to meet privately with anyone except the firm's purchasing agents. When this policy exists, the engineering and production personnel must obtain their information from professional meetings or secondary publications.

Environmental Variables

The industrial buying process is influenced by factors external to the firm. As mentioned in Chapter 2, environmental variables cannot be controlled by the firm but they frequently play an important role in decision making. The following is a list of a few of the more important environmental variables affecting the industrial purchasing process. Several of these were discussed in more detail in Chapter 2.

1. *Physical Variables.* Such variables as climate and geographic location determine the availability of many raw materials and dictate the need for others, such as heating fuel and transportation services.
2. *Technological Variables.* New technology has a powerful influence on the buying process. For example, the computer has made automatic recording and accurate inventory control available to even small companies, and it is now used routinely to evaluate complex buying alternatives.
3. *Economic Variables.* The general economic health of the U.S. affects all facets of life. It is particularly important to the industrial purchasing process because

price and wage conditions, availability of money and credit, consumer demand, and interest rates largely determine how much output an industrial firm can expect to sell and thus how much input and supplies it should buy.

4. *Political Variables.* The government has vast powers to influence the industrial purchasing process. When the President of the United States speaks out against a specific company for raising its prices, a very strong political force is exerted on that company. Other illustrations of political influences include tariff and trade regulations, military spending, and government funding of particular social programs.

5. *Suppliers.* Providing sample merchandise and quick delivery of inventory, transporting merchandise, establishing terms of sale, financing the transaction, as well as many other supplier services are all vital to the industrial purchasing process. Vendor selection is often based on the services offered to customers, rather than on the products offered by the vendor.

6. *Labor Unions.* Labor unions influence the industrial buying process in several ways. For instance, if the safety of union employees will be affected by a particular product or production input, the union will have a strong voice in the purchase decision. Unions also frequently try to influence the purchase process by making sure that all products purchased are made in union shops. Finally, the threat of a union strike by the supplier's employees often persuades the buyer to find a new source of supply.

Purchase Decision

The purchase decision is an effort to satisfy the need that initiated the purchase process. The actual decision is a function of the *specifications* written for the product, the *information* gathered on potential suppliers, and the constraints imposed by *environmental variables.* Four important topics must be analyzed in relation to the actual purchase decision: (1) the behavioral characteristics of the buyer, (2) the use of multiple decision makers, (3) the evaluation of a product's performance relative to its price, and (4) vendor analysis.

Behavioral Considerations. The buyer is subject to the same social and behavioral considerations analyzed in Chapter 4. For instance, the purchasing agent comes from a specific subculture and social class. As we have seen, these affect the buyer's attitudes and influence buying decisions. In addition, the buyer may be influenced by the activities of people within a particular reference group or may be motivated by the need for status and recognition within the organization.

It is also important to analyze how industrial buyers handle risk. The buyer experiences risk when purchasing a new type of product or selecting a new supplier. If a problem develops as a result of one of these decisions, the "innovative" purchasing agent may have to accept some of the blame. The purchasing executive experiences risk even when a potential supplier's sales representative is allowed to meet with high-level production and engineering personnel. If these people feel that the salesperson has wasted their time, the purchasing agent's credibility within the organization will be damaged.

Purchasing agents deal with risk in different ways. One technique is to involve other individuals in making the decision. "Spreading" the risk seems to make agents feel more comfortable, but it often prolongs the process to such an extent that the final joint decision is no better than if an individual agent had acted alone. Another common response to the prospect of risk is for the individual to become more cautious and less willing to accept risk. Unfortunately, this attitude may eventually damage the buying firm by shutting it off from new products and new sources of supply.

Multiple Decision Makers. A study of 603 purchasing executives in the chemical industry found that only 13 percent of product supply source decisions were made by purchasing agents acting alone, and that only 10 percent were made by nonpurchasing department personnel acting alone. The remaining 77 percent were made jointly by personnel from the purchasing department and other departments.[3] Table 5-2, showing the results of a study of 106 industrial firms, indicates that in only 2.5 percent of the decisions did a single individual determine the supplier of a product.

TABLE 5-2   Number of Persons Influencing
Buying Decisions

Number	Percentage
7+	4.3
6	5.7
5	9.8
4	18.7
3	39.3
2	19.7
1	2.5

Source: Albert W. Frey, *Marketing Handbook* (2d ed.; New York: The Ronald Press Co., 1965), Section 27, p. 18.

Multiple decision making takes place in industrial firms when decisions involve large expenditures of money and require the evaluative skills of more than one individual. The individual purchasing agent, or buyer, is still important, however. The buyer often has the actual line authority to buy goods and services. In other situations, the buyer has the right to choose the supplier after someone else has decided that the product should be purchased. In either case, the purchasing agent is a critical influence in the buying process. Sometimes, the buyer plays the more limited, but still important, roles of making recommendations as to the selection of supplier, or acting as a "gatekeeper" for the organization. As a gatekeeper, the purchasing agent decides who the sales representative should see within the organization.

Value Analysis. The objective of **value analysis** is to measure the performance of a product relative to its price. This process begins by reviewing the product's specifications in relation to how it will be used. Figure 5-3 presents ten "tests for value" questions, originated at General Electric, that are now used by many firms when performing value analysis.

Value analysis often results in modification of a product's design, changes in specifications, elimination of unnecessary features, or other adjustments to reduce the product's cost without affecting its performance. It is not unusual,

[3]Robert Hass, *op. cit.*, p. 62.

FIGURE 5-3 Tests for Value

1. Does the use of the item contribute value?
2. Is its cost proportionate to its usefulness?
3. Does it need all its features?
4. Is there anything better for its intended use?
5. Can a usable part be made by a lower cost method?
6. Can a standard product be found that will be usable?
7. Is the product made on proper tooling, considering the quantities that are used?
8. Do material, labor, overhead, and profit total its cost?
9. Will another dependable supplier provide it for less?
10. Is anyone buying it for less?

Source: Albert W. Frey, *Marketing Handbook* (2d ed.; New York: The Ronald Press Co., 1965), Section 27, p. 21.

for example, for a firm to find that several product components are designed to last much longer than the product itself. These more durable components tend to drive up production costs. As an illustration, a foreign electronics producer found that by purchasing a slightly less expensive transistor for its radios, it was able to save $125,000 per year and not affect the quality of its radios.

Vendor Analysis. Related to value analysis is **vendor analysis**, the method used by the firm to determine the vendors with which it will do business. The following five elements are normally analyzed in evaluating vendors:[4]

1. *Technical and Production Capability.* What are the vendor's design, research testing, and production capabilities? Does the vendor initiate product development or simply copy the products of competitors? Analysis of articles appearing in trade journals and visits to the various plants will help the buyer evaluate the capabilities of each vendor.

2. *Financial Strength.* How strong is the vendor financially? If unable to obtain the necessary working capital, the vendor might have to stop production just when the buyer wants to make a purchase, leading to unwanted production delays for the buyer. Data necessary for a financial audit of a potential vendor frequently can be obtained by examining the firm's income statement and balance sheet as well as by talking with local bankers.

3. *Product Reliability.* Does the vendor consistently produce high quality products that are rarely defective and that require minimal maintenance? The simplest way to evaluate product reliability is to estimate the percentage of the vendor's products that must be returned or serviced before use. This data can be obtained from the buyer's own records of past transactions with the vendor or from other firms with which the vendor has done business.

4. *Delivery Reliability.* Does the vendor consistently meet delivery schedules? Are deliveries to the buyer on short notice, in cases of unexpected demand, possible? Like product reliability information, these data can best be obtained from

---

[4]Richard Hill, Ralph Alexander, and James Cross, *Industrial Marketing* (4th ed.; Homewood, Ill.: Richard D. Irwin, 1975), pp. 101–104. © 1975 by Richard D. Irwin.

company records if the two firms have done business in the past, as well as from other firms that have purchased products from the vendor.

5. *Service Capability.* Does the vendor have experienced service technicians located close to the buyer? For some products, such as industrial lubricants, there are virtually no service requirements. However, for items such as computers, service capability may be the most important criterion influencing the selection of a supplier. The buyer may even wish to have separate interviews with the vendor's service technicians to evaluate their competence.

Once the firm has considered the five vendor characteristics, it may wish to combine them into a composite score. A simple checklist, similar to the one shown in Table 5-3, permits the analyst to rate each variable from "excellent" to "unacceptable." The scores are then added together and averaged. The buyer normally selects the vendor with the highest average score. If the analyst

TABLE 5-3   Sample Composite Vendor Analysis

	Rating Scale				
	Excellent (4)	Good (3)	Fair (2)	Poor (1)	Unacceptable (0)
Technical and production capabilities	X				
Financial strength		X			
Product reliability	X				
Delivery reliability			X		
Service capability		X			
Total score: 4 + 3 + 4 + 2 + 3 = 16					
Average score: 16/5 = 3.2					

weighs some factors more heavily than others, the result is a *weighted mean* rather than an *arithmetic mean*. In addition, if a single factor receives a score of "unacceptable," the buyer should not purchase the product from that vendor regardless of the vendor's total score. A score of "unacceptable" implies that the particular deficiency outweighs whatever other merits the vendor may have.

Product Evaluation

Product evaluation, the last stage in the industrial buying process modeled in Figure 5-1, occurs after the product has been purchased. At this point the firm asks itself if the product satisfied the need that initiated the purchasing process. Was the product delivered on time? Did the seller show an interest in the problems of the buyer after the sale was completed? Has the product lived up to expectations? Have service needs been within the standards set for the product? When service was required, did the seller respond quickly? The answers to such questions not only indicate how good a job the buyer did in selecting a vendor, but they also serve as a guide when the time comes to make another purchase decision.

Reciprocity — A Special Problem[5]

A rather unique problem facing purchasing executives is reciprocity. **Reciprocity**, a common practice in industry, consists of "the use of purchasing power to obtain sales and the practice of preferring one's customers in purchasing."[6] The first half of the definition implies the use of coercion or market power in obtaining sales, whereas the second half merely indicates the favoring of one customer or supplier over all others. In either case, each party functions as both buyer and seller. Reciprocity would exist if a dry cleaning store that cleans all of the mechanics' work clothes from a nearby Chevrolet dealership feels it should buy its new delivery trucks from the Chevrolet dealer because that dealer is an important account.

Not all situations in which two firms buy and sell from each other involve reciprocity. In our example of the dry cleaning store, reciprocity would not exist if the dry cleaning store purchased Chevrolet trucks simply because they were the best vans available at the best prices. That is, reciprocity occurs only when one of the important reasons for purchasing a firm's products is because it purchases your company's products. Since most businesses do engage in reciprocity, let's examine the conditions that stimulate reciprocity, as well as the reactions of businesses to reciprocal pressures.

Conditions Favoring Reciprocity. Reciprocity seems to flourish when *standardized products*, such as coal and steel, are involved. In a reciprocal arrangement, a purchasing agent is asked to buy from a supplier who may not be the agent's first choice. Normally, the purchasing agent would be told to purchase the item as long as it is at least competitively priced with the offerings of other suppliers. Analyzing values for standardized products is relatively simple for the purchasing agent. Reciprocity, furthermore, is more common when there is relatively *little price competition*. When prices are volatile, however, the purchasing agent will seek firms that offer the best bargains rather than look to the company's best customers as potential suppliers. Finally, reciprocity is more likely to occur when at least one of the firms is a *major supplier* of the other. When one of the trading partners does most of the selling, the stage is set for **coercive reciprocity**, i.e., one firm pressures another to buy from it. The primary seller will feel tremendous pressure to buy from its customer for fear of losing a major account. On the other hand, when both firms sell a large amount of merchandise to each other, *mutual patronage* rather than coercive reciprocity is more likely to result.

Management's Response to Reciprocity. The Federal Trade Commission and the federal courts recently have been taking a tougher stance toward reciprocity than in the past. Coercive reciprocity is now defined as an unfair trade practice by Section 5 of the Federal Trade Commission Act. Many court cases, moreover, have been settled on the basis of whether the seller notified its sales

---

[5]A significant portion of this section is drawn from Reed Moyer, "Reciprocity: Retrospect and Prospect," *Journal of Marketing* (October, 1970), pp. 47–54.

[6]Robert M. Hausman, "Reciprocal Dealing and the Antitrust Laws," *Harvard Law Review* (March, 1964), p. 873.

department of its purchasing department's activities. When there has been an exchange of purchasing and marketing information, the courts have tended to rule that the reciprocity in question was illegal.[7]

However, neither the courts, the Federal Trade Commission, nor the Justice Department have attempted to eliminate so-called **innocent reciprocity**, which exists because "people like to do business with their friends." When no organized coercive efforts are evident, it is difficult to argue that the firm should not buy from its major customers especially when product quality, service, and price are equal to those offered by competitors. Under these circumstances, reciprocity costs the buyer nothing and helps maintain a positive relationship between the organizations. Yet when there is a discrepancy between the goods offered by the major customer and those offered by competing firms, the purchasing agent must resist reciprocity pressures. Otherwise, the firm will purchase materials that are either inferior or more expensive than those of the competition. In either case, the firm's ability to compete will be damaged in the long run.

Leaving industrial buying, we now turn attention to another intermediate buyer, the retailer. We will examine the problems, methods, and opportunities unique to retail buying.

RETAIL BUYING

Retail buying has many similarities to industrial purchasing. Well-managed retail organizations, like industrial firms, devote a great deal of attention to the types and quantities of merchandise they purchase. The key to success in retailing is understanding the market so that the right quantity of the right products is available when the consumer wants it. Buying mistakes lead to markdowns and losses. The sources of supply available to the retailer, retail buying plans, methods of buying, and the role of the retailer's buyer all influence the retailer's success.

Sources of Supply

While a few retailers do manufacture some of the products that they sell, most have abandoned this strategy because they realize that financial resources could be better invested in modernizing plant and equipment or in building new stores. The common sources of supply for the retailer are presented in Figure 5-4.

Manufacturers. Large manufacturers and retailers are frequently able to do business without going through any other intermediary. Retailers enjoy buying merchandise directly from the manufacturer because the manufacturer's salespeople are usually well trained and extremely knowledgeable about the firm's products. They have up-to-the minute information on how the manufacturer's products are selling at the consumer level in the region and around the

---

[7]F. Robert Finney, "Reciprocity: Gone But Not Forgotten," *Journal of Marketing* (January, 1978), pp. 54–59.

FIGURE 5-4 Sources of Supply for Retailers

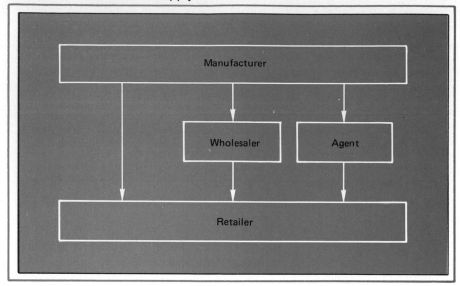

country. In addition, they are able to help the retailer design advertising and promotion strategies and monitor inventory levels.

A second advantage for large retailers in dealing directly with manufacturers is that they can specify the quality and style of the merchandise ordered. More than 80 percent of the merchandise sold by Sears, Roebuck and Co. is made to its exact specifications. In this way, Sears is able to guarantee the quality and consistency of its products. Many retailers also feel that dealing directly with the manufacturer enables them to obtain quicker delivery on critical out-of-stock merchandise at a lower price. Although this last point is probably true, there is no hard evidence to show that prices are necessarily lower when dealing directly with manufacturers. This issue will be explored in greater detail in Chapter 14, which examines channels of distribution.

Wholesalers. Wholesalers are intermediaries who perform certain marketing functions for their customers (usually retailers) and their suppliers (usually manufacturers). (See Chapter 16.) Wholesalers primarily serve small retailers that purchase a variety of merchandise at frequent intervals. These small retail organizations do not have the buying power to purchase a large quantity of any single item and, therefore, do not have direct access to manufacturers.

Wholesalers are also important to large retailers in at least two situations. First, even high-volume department stores sell some merchandise that they purchase in limited quantities because of a narrow market. Examples include Japanese tea sets or oriental rugs, which are usually sold only through wholesalers and, in some situations, through importers. Second, a department store may be able to obtain quicker delivery on an out-of-stock item from a local wholesaler's warehouse than from the manufacturer. In the case of high fashion or "fad" merchandise, the department store may decide that it cannot afford to wait for the manufacturer to produce more of the merchandise, and as a result, it may buy from a wholesaler.

Agents. Agents are intermediaries who do not take title to the products they ship, resell, or distribute. Depending on the industry, agents are called brokers, manufacturers' agents, sales agents, or commission agents. The primary responsibility of the agent is to bring two parties together so that a sale will take place. Consumers deal with agents when they purchase common stock (stockbroker) or when they buy or sell a home (real estate agent). In retailing, agents operate primarily in the food brokerage business. Supermarket chains often employ food brokers for volume purchases of staple products such as coffee. In this situation, the agent is paid to locate large quantities of coffee at the lowest possible price. At times, food brokers also assist supermarket chains in obtaining temporary financing for major purchases.

Knowing from whom to buy is not sufficient to be a successful retailer. The retailer must also have a well thought-out buying plan.

The Buying Plan[8]

Even if the retailer had unlimited financial resources, it could not stock every line of merchandise or product brand currently available. A bookstore typically does not stock every book currently in print; a clothing store does not carry the merchandise of every manufacturer in the industry; and a camera store usually carries only a few of the many camera brands on the market. Stocking every product available would require vast storage areas and would result in a great deal of unwanted merchandise. Accordingly, retailers must be selective in their inventory planning. Above all, they should keep an eye on the market for their merchandise. A retailer should repeatedly ask: How much merchandise can I expect to sell? How much new merchandise should I order? What assortment of merchandise will sell the best?

Expected Sales. Sales vary considerably from one month or season to the next. A logical basis for estimating sales for any one month, therefore, is to look at sales for that same month during each of the last two years. By using the figures for two years, the retailer's forecast will not be affected as much by any unusual circumstances that occurred during the previous year. In arriving at the final estimate, the retailer also needs to consider such factors as store expansion, local and national sales trends, changing levels of employment within the local market, and competitive conditions in the market area.

Inventory turnover is another way of estimating sales. In general, the average value of inventory should not exceed a certain fraction of sales. This fraction, varying from one department of a store to the next, is a function of how rapidly the inventory is sold or turned over. As an illustration, in the fine jewelry department of a department store, the inventory may turnover only twice each year. Therefore, average inventory should be one half of the total sales expected for the year. Although this approach provides a general guide for inventory planning, it does not guarantee that the retailer will have enough

---

[8]This section is partially adapted from Peter G. Thomas, *Modern Retailing Techniques* (3d ed.; Plymouth, England: Macdonald & Evans Ltd., 1972), pp. 49–52.

inventory on hand to offer an adequate assortment within each product group at any given time. The customer who does not have an opportunity to compare several products when making a purchase may go to another store with more variety. Also, inventory levels must be adjusted to cover planned selling events, a storewide founder's day sale, or the start of a fashion season. In short, the retailer may find it necessary to carry slightly more inventory than the amount dictated by turnover alone.

Once the retailer has determined expected sales for the period, the amount of inventory that should be purchased is determined based on two estimates: the planned purchases estimate and the open-to-buy estimate.

The Planned Purchase Estimate. The following formula can be used to estimate planned purchases:

$$\text{Planned purchases} = \text{planned EOM stock} + \text{planned sales} +$$
$$\text{planned reductions} - \text{planned BOM stock}$$

where EOM represents end-of-the-month stock and BOM represents beginning-of-the-month stock. EOM stock for one month is the same as BOM stock for the next month. For example, the February EOM inventory level and the March BOM inventory level are identical. Planned reductions consist primarily of merchandise that the store expects cannot be sold because of either damage or theft.

Assume that planned sales for March are $100,000, planned BOM stock for March 1 is $120,000, planned reductions for the month are $5,000, and planned EOM stock for March 30 is $90,000. The retailer will need to buy $75,000 worth of merchandise for March. The calculations are as follows:

Planned EOM stock (March 30)	$ 90,000	
Planned March sales	100,000	
Planned March reductions	5,000	
Total merchandise requirements — March		$195,000
Planned BOM stock (March 1)		120,000
Planned purchases — March		$ 75,000

Since all of the above calculations are based on retail prices, the store will spend something less than $75,000 for the purchases. If the markup is 40 percent, which represents the difference between cost of merchandise and retail price, then the retailer will spend only $45,000 (0.60 times $75,000) for the merchandise.

The Open-to-Buy Estimate. The planned purchase figure tells the retailer how much inventory should be purchased for the entire month, but it does not indicate how much should be purchased at any particular time in the month. The figure that does give this estimate is called **open to buy**. The open-to-buy estimating formula is similar to the planned purchase formula except that current inventory levels and unfilled orders to be delievered during the month, rather than planned BOM, are subtracted from total required purchases for the month. The open-to-buy formula is as follows:

Open to buy = planned EOM stock + planned sales + planned reductions
− current inventory − merchandise on order.

Using the data from our earlier example, open to buy is calculated as follows:

Planned EOM stock	$ 90,000	
Planned sales	100,000	
Planned reductions	5,000	
Total merchandise requirements		$195,000
Current inventory level	$130,000	
Merchandise on order	40,000	
Total merchandise available		170,000
Open to Buy — At retail prices		$ 25,000
Open to Buy — At cost (60% of retail)		$ 15,000

In this example, if the store has $130,000 worth of inventory on hand at the midpoint of the month and $40,000 of inventory on order, it would still be able to purchase $25,000 in inventory (at retail prices) at a total cost of $15,000 assuming a 40 percent markup.

Note that the retailer must purchase $25,000 of merchandise (at retail) if the buying plan is to be maintained. It is important to realize, however, that while the buying plan is essential to good retail management, the retailer should not purchase merchandise just to meet the buying plan. If acceptable merchandise is not available at a competitive price, the retailer should not take any action. In the same way, if an opportunity presents itself, the store may want to purchase additional merchandise even if sufficient open-to-buy dollars are not available according to the plan.

The Right Assortment. For every product on the market today, the consumer can choose from among many products having a wide variety of prices and quality. The clientele of a store, to a large extent, is determined by the price and quality of the merchandise carried, and vice versa. However, even within a given price range, it usually is not possible to stock every brand available due to space and financial limitations. Therefore, the successful retailer will reach a compromise between carrying incomplete lines of many suppliers and a large, comprehensive stock of only a few suppliers. In the first extreme, the many brands tend to compete with one another, and frequently demanded sizes and styles may not be stocked. In the second, sales are lost when leading brands are not carried at all.

Methods of Buying

The buying method of a retailer is often a function of an overall operating philosophy. Five methods of retail buying are generally recognized: cooperative, centralized, decentralized, committee, and resident office. While each buying technique has its own advantages, no one approach is best in all circumstances for all retailers.

Cooperative Buying. Under this buying arrangement, independent noncompeting retailers join together for the purpose of buying merchandise. The primary advantage of cooperative buying is that it gives small retailers an opportunity to participate in quantity discounts normally available only to large stores buying in large quantities.

Generally speaking, there are two types of cooperative buying units — voluntary chains and cooperative chains. A **voluntary chain** is organized by a wholesaler in order to combat large integrated retailers (retailers who also function as wholesalers). The retailers buying from the wholesaler often use similar store fronts and promotional aids, and the consulting services of the wholesaler. Independent Grocers Alliance (IGA), True Value Hardware, and Western Auto Stores are examples of voluntary chains.

Cooperative chains are organized by the retailers themselves. The objective, however, is the same — to obtain a buying advantage through aggregated purchases that will permit the retailers to offer lower prices to the consumer. As with voluntary chains, the participants often utilize the same store fronts. Statistical data indicate that cooperative chains have lower margins than either regular wholesalers or voluntary chains, primarily because they do not offer as many marketing services to their members as do voluntary chains.[9]

Centralized vs. Decentralized Buying. Large multi-store retailers face a very difficult problem, namely, whether to purchase inventory on a centralized, company-wide basis or to permit each store to make its own purchase decisions. The most significant advantage of **centralized buying** is the quantity discount obtained from high-volume purchases. A second advantage of centralized buying is that a full-time buying specialist can be employed to monitor narrow product groups, to keep current with fashion trends, as well as to help ensure that the store buys the best merchandise available at the lowest prices.

A good example of a centralized buying operation is the nation's largest retailer — Sears, Roebuck and Co. Sears has 430 buyers purchasing 1,290 lines of merchandise for all Sears stores. In addition to placing orders, many Sears buyers see their most important role as product development. In this regard, they are expected to work closely with Sears' suppliers so that new products are continually developed that meet the needs of Sears' customers. Although the individual store manager is permitted to "adjust stocks" to meet local competitive conditions, most of the important buying decisions are made at Sears' headquarters in Chicago.[10]

Under a **decentralized buying** arrangement, on the other hand, each store or group of stores makes its own purchase decisions. Retailers usually adopt this buying strategy when they feel that important local needs would be overlooked under a centralized buying arrangement. The more the retailer deals in fashion merchandise, which changes quickly, the more important local buying becomes. For many years, Federated Department Stores has allowed its 17 major department stores, located across the country, to make their buying decisions independently. The attitude of management is that the needs of consumers vary significantly from city to city. What customers want in San

[9]Carl M. Larson, Robert E. Weigand, and John S. Wright, *Basic Retailing* (Englewood Cliffs, N.J.: Prentice-Hall, Inc., 1976), pp. 249–250.

[10]"Why Sears Stays the No. 1 Retailer," *Business Week* (January 20, 1968), pp. 65–73.

Francisco may be quite different from the needs of consumers in Atlanta or in New York. Federated is fortunate in that each of its stores is large enough to take advantage of the quantity discounts usually available only to centralized buyers.

Buying Committee. A buying committee is an attempt to achieve the economies of centralized buying without having just one person responsible for purchase decisions. Buying committees are often used by hardware store chains, supermarket chains, and other retailers selling staple goods. One study indicated that three out of four supermarket chains use buying committees when purchasing a new product.[11]

The buying committee is usually made up of a buyer or purchasing executive, a merchandise manager, a sales promotion manager, and a store manager. The buyer makes a recommendation to the committee as to a given product's merits in relation to those of products already carried by the retailer. Many committees also require that the buyer suggest which product or products should be dropped from the line in order to make room for new ones. The value of this control procedure is that it prevents the store from stocking more alternative product lines than it can profitably handle. Also, since each store in the chain carries the same products, the chain can purchase in large quantities and at lower prices and can distribute the products itself to the individual stores. This process permits member stores to procure merchandise cheaper than if they had to purchase their products individually.

Resident Buying Offices. Certain cities in the United States, such as New York, San Francisco, Dallas, and Atlanta, serve as central markets for many types of retail goods. Accordingly, a number of **resident buying offices** have been established in these cities in order to facilitate the purchase and inventory planning decisions of retailers located in distant communities. These resident buying offices may be owned by one retail organization, or they may operate as independent entities providing services to many retailers. Regardless of who owns them, their primary function is to provide retailers with enough information so that they can make intelligent purchase decisions. To this end, the resident buying office continually sends the retailer reports concerning fashion and price trends. When the retail buyer comes to town, the resident buying office arranges special showings of various suppliers' merchandise and offers advice as to which merchandise is the best buy. Once an order has been placed, the resident buying office monitors, delivers, and processes adjustments for the retailer.

One of the most significant resident buying offices is Associated Merchandising Corporation (AMC), located in New York City, with buying offices in virtually every major trading center in the world. Noncompeting retailers such as Federated Department Stores, Dayton-Hudson Corp., and Carson Pirie Scott & Co. all utilize AMC services. AMC's major function is to monitor each trading area to determine what new products will be available. AMC representatives continually update reports that deal with the strengths and weaknesses of new items. They also develop entire purchasing programs for specific products, such as men's sport shirts.

[11]Delbert J. Duncan, Charles F. Phillips, and Stanley C. Hollander, *Modern Retailing Management: Basic Concepts and Principles* (Homewood, Ill.: Richard D. Irwin, 1977), p. 247.

Most executives complain that they spend far too much time in useless meetings. Many meetings don't seem to have a specific purpose, or the chairperson does not know how to run a meeting efficiently. No doubt, you too have experienced such problems in committee meetings. The following rules may help **you** be a better chairperson.

Set Objectives. Committee members should have a clear idea of the objectives of their meeting. The objectives may be handed down "from on high," or the committee may be forced to define its own objectives, which can become a major source of contention itself.

Select Members Carefully. As chairperson, you may be permitted to select committee members. It is important that diverse points of view be represented on the committee and that members be viewed as influential people in the organization.

Set Up Subcommittees. Any group of more than three people has only a limited chance of establishing objectives, evaluating alternative courses of action, or writing a report. If your committee has more than three people, you should consider appointing a subcommittee to accomplish specific tasks. The subcommittee will report back to the full committee, which can then plan its proper role of evaluation and criticism.

Make Compromises. Sometimes it is worthwhile to talk to prominent members of the committee before you actually submit formal recommendations to the committee. In this way, you can discover problems in the recommendations beforehand. It also gives you an opportunity to arrange compromises prior to the full committee meeting and thus avoid lengthy debates.

Keep It Short. A well-run meeting should rarely last more than one and a half hours. People get restless, impatient, and bored when a meeting lasts much longer. You can make a meeting more efficient by providing an agenda and any discussion materials several days in advance.

Keep the Meeting Focused. As chairperson, you must continually focus the discussion on the topics listed in the agenda. Although you do not want to be perceived as "heavy handed," you don't want to waste time either.

Take Minutes. Lastly, you are responsible for keeping a set of minutes of what is discussed at each meeting.

Why worry about running a meeting? Many firms use buying committees to make their purchase decisions. Time spent by these committees discussing buying decisions and relationships with vendors and dealers can and should be time well spent, not time wasted.

Marketing & You

The Role of the Buyer

The buyer, often the most important person in a retail organization, is responsible for the movement of merchandise from the manufacturer to the consumer. If the buyer is unable to secure the type of merchandise demanded by the store's customers, the store will find it difficult to survive. Buyers generally serve three specific functions — they determine merchandise assortment, they maintain relationships with resources, and they participate in promotion and sales activities.[12]

Determining Merchandise Assortment. In a small store the owner-buyer or manager-buyer is responsible for obtaining all the merchandise sold by the store. In contrast, the buying function in a large department or chain store is carefully divided among many buyers so that each individual buyer becomes an expert on limited lines of merchandise. For example, Foley's department store in Houston has more than 120 buyers who each specialize in purchasing for one of its many departments; Macy's in New York has more than 150 buyers. Regardless of the number of buyers in the store, the needs of the market must be understood if the store is to be profitable.

Buyers can obtain market information from a variety of sources. Trade publications, such as *Women's Wear Daily*, provide up-to-date articles on new fashion and sales trends. Stores also commission market research studies that help buyers understand the purchase motives of customers. A survey of consumer intentions can also be very useful in forecasting sales of major durable goods, such as washing machines. Buyers can also ascertain customer attitudes toward the store by actually getting out "on the floor" and selling. Finally, buyers hold regular meetings with the store's sales staff to obtain individual reactions as to why certain products are selling and why others are not.

Once the buyer understands the market, the actual buying can begin. Purchasing may involve listening to a vendor at the retailer's own office, traveling to a regional trade show, or spending three weeks in Europe looking for merchandise. At the moment of purchase, the buyer's judgment is very important: if the buyer does not purchase enough of a "hot" item, the store will lose potential profits; conversely, if the buyer loads up on unsalable merchandise, the store can lose a great deal of money in markdowns and sales. A few years ago, Van Heusen introduced a colored polyester men's dress shirt called the Hampshire House. The buyer for Foley's department store in Houston purchased more than 12,000 colored shirts, which represented about four times the size of the usual purchase of white dress shirts. Fortunately for Foley's and the buyer, the shirt was a tremendous success. It was also a bit of a gamble since men in Houston traditionally had worn white dress shirts. This is the type of decision that buyers are forced to make regularly.

Maintaining Resource Relationships. Typically, a supplier has a great many services and inducements that it can make available to retailers. It is the buyer's responsibility to see that a store obtains as much selling help as possible from the supplier. As an example, housewares and cosmetics vendors often

---

[12]For an excellent discussion of the activities and responsibilities of the buyer, see Maryanne Smith Bohlinger, *Merchandise Buying Principles and Applications* (Dubuque, Iowa: William C. Brown Company, 1977).

demonstrate their products to the store's salespeople as well as to the store's customers. Also, if urged or required by the store, the vendor may agree to extend the credit period, provide rapid delivery on rush orders, or accept returns on goods that have not been sold after a specified period of time.

The most common forms of assistance offered by vendors to retailers are cooperative advertising allowances and preticketed merchandise. **Cooperative advertising** is an arrangement between the vendor and the retailer whereby the vendor agrees to pay a portion of the retailer's advertising costs for the vendor's product. Perhaps as much as $2 billion are spent in cooperative advertising allowances each year in the United States.[13] **Preticketing** means that the vendor places a tag on each product listing its price, manufacturer, size, identification number, and color. Preticketing saves the retailer a great deal of time and money. Figure 5-5 provides a list of the varied vendor services available to the retailer.

Participating in Promotion Activities. The buyer has no specific authority to make advertising and sales promotion decisions. These decisions are usually made by store management personnel. However, the buyer takes a very active role in making sure that enough advertising dollars are allocated to specific products to ensure that they are well exposed to the market. In addition, many buyers advise the store's advertising department and its advertising agency as to what promotional material will be most successful.

In small specialty shops the sales personnel may actually work for the buyer. However, in department or chain stores, the buyer has only the power

FIGURE 5-5   Services Available from Merchandise Sources

- Cash discounts at least equal to those prevailing in the trade.
- Payment by the seller of some or all transportation costs.
- Cooperative advertising arrangements.
- Advertising aids, such as glossy photos (from which the store can have cuts made), copy suggestions, broadcast scripts.
- Special prices for store promotion.

- Exclusive distribution.
- Return and exchange privileges.
- Allowance for markdowns on the merchandise.
- Participation in store fashion events by sending trunk shows, visiting fashion experts, other consumer attractions.
- Materials or personnel to inform and stimulate the salespeople.

- Assistance in stock counts and stock control.
- Preticketing.
- Advance information on planned national advertising and possibility of mention of store name.
- Back-up stock.
- Precise information on fiber content, fur origin, and other requirements specified by government regulations.

Source: Adapted from Beatrice Judelle, *The Fashion Buyer's Job* (New York: National Retail Merchant's Association, 1971), pp. 81–82.

[13]Duncan, Phillips, and Hollander, *op. cit.*, p. 451.

of persuasion when dealing with the store's sales staff. As a result, good buyers often spend more than half of their time visiting store branches to keep in contact with sales personnel. Because everyone in the store recognizes the buyer as critical to the store's success, the buyer does have a significant amount of informal influence and power in sales and advertising decisions.

GOVERNMENT PROCUREMENT

The final organizational buyer to examine is the U.S. government. For many years business executives have talked about government as if it were nothing but a large regulating body performing a few inefficient services for society at a very high price. However, if one takes a less narrow point of view, it is evident that business and government have formed a complex and deep alliance — so deep, in fact, that many view it as a threat to society.[14] Our discussion of the government buying process begins by looking at the magnitude of U.S. government procurement.

The Government Market

Local, state, and federal governments in the United States purchase vast quantities of diverse products. In 1980 the federal government's budget alone was $564 billion, of which 60 percent represented purchases of goods and services from the private sector.[15] Although it is difficult to measure, spending by local and state governments probably exceeds federal expenditures.

These vast expenditures of funds affect various sectors of the economy differently. While it is commonly acknowledged that the aerospace industry is dependent on government, it is not so widely recognized that industries such as communications equipment, machine shop products, nonferrous metals, and electronic components also depend heavily on government purchases. In addition, virtually the entire construction industry depends on government contracts. On the other hand, the automobile repair industry and the drug, food, and apparel industries receive less than 10 percent of their revenues from government sales. Table 5-4 lists major industries and their relative dependence on government procurement.

Government Procurement of Goods and Services

The primary federal government procurement agency is the General Services Administration (GSA), created in 1949 to coordinate and centralize the procurement of merchandise for the various federal agencies. The major purchasing arm of the GSA is the Bureau of Federal Supply. Federal agencies usually obtain their supplies from the Bureau of Federal Supply, but they may also buy from private vendors, using contracts developed by the GSA. Departments or agencies, such as NASA, the Department of Energy, and the National

---

[14]For example, see Dwight D. Eisenhower's *Farewell Address to the Nation*, 1960.

[15]*1980 Economic Report of the President* (Washington, D.C.: U.S. Government Printing Office, 1980), p. 6.

TABLE 5-4 Degree of Dependence of Industry on Federal, State, and Local Governments

Major Industry	Percentage of Output Sold to Government
Research and development	98
Ordnance	88
Aircraft	82
Communications equipment	44
Machine shop products	42
Nonferrous metals	41
Electronics components	38
Scientific instruments	37
Maintenance construction	32
New construction	30
Transportation equipment	27
Electric lighting and wiring	25
Paint	24
Engines and turbines	22
Electronic industrial equipment	20
Iron ores	20
Chemical products	19
Coal mining	15
Radio and TV broadcasting	14
Crude petroleum	13
Printing and publishing	12
Plastics	11
Construction machinery	10
Automobile repairing	7
Finance and insurance	5
Drugs	5
Food	2
Apparel	2

Source: U.S. Department of Commerce in Blair A. Simon, "Analyzing Government Markets," *Handbook of Modern Marketing*, edited by Victor A. Buell (New York: McGraw-Hill Book Co., 1970), p. 55.

Bureau of Standards, that require nonroutine or high-technology products are authorized to buy directly from qualified vendors on a competitive bid basis.

The procurement operations for state and local governments vary a great deal. For a small town or school district, the mayor or school superintendent may do all the necessary purchasing. In contrast, large cities often have sophisticated buying procedures rivaling those of the federal government. Most states now have specialized purchasing offices resembling the federal government's GSA.

Regardless of the government buying entity, the actual purchase process for most goods and services is similar to that of the private sector. In general, most purchase decisions are made rationally on the basis of price and value. The few major differences between public and private buying are discussed below.[16]

Annual Budgets. Until recently, most government entities operated on annual budgets; many still do. Therefore, in making sales to the government, an important first step often is to meet with agency decision makers before they send their budget recommendations to the legislature. Annual budgeting complicates sales particularly for those selling capital equipment because long-term financing cannot be arranged.

Recently, in order to facilitate procurement, the Department of Defense instituted a five-year budgeting cycle, called the Five-Year Force Structure and Financial Plan. This plan is now part of the total federal five-year plan. With this trend toward five-year budget planning, the difficulty of selling to the government has been lessened somewhat. For example, most defense-related companies now prepare their own five-year marketing and sales plans based on the Department of Defense's five-year planning cycle.

Decision Makers. In dealing with government agencies, the salesperson is confronted almost invariably with many decision makers. For instance, in marketing to the military, the sales representative must influence more than commissioned officers and civil service employees in order to win a contract award. Given the tight controls on military and federal procurements, the salesperson is confronted with a multitude of decision points during this selling process. For example, in selling to the Army, it is usually necessary for the salesperson to be in contact with (1) the user command, that is, the branch or unit of the Army that will use the equipment in question; (2) the Army personnel involved in the proposal evaluation and approval cycles; (3) the personnel involved in the procurement and procurement practice cycle; and (4) those in the Army engineering branches involved in the development of the equipment. In addition, other units within the Department of Defense, such as the Department of Defense Research and Engineering, play a major role in procurement and contract approval. In total, the supplier selling to the military is often confronted with as many as 100 different contact points in any one sale. Perhaps only 20 percent of these contacts are with formal decision makers, but all are important to the buying/selling process. Also, many of the entities referred to in this example are located in different parts of the country, thus adding to the challenge of selling to the government.

Precise Specifications. The volume purchases of many commodities by local, state, and federal governments make it possible for their purchasing agencies to formulate product standards covering size, materials, inspection, and testing. The purchasing groups make an effort to ensure that the standards are not overly restrictive, so that each award is open to several potential suppliers. Some government agencies even require that products under consideration be tested before bids are entertained and contract decisions are made.

---

[16]The following four sections are largely taken from W. J. E. Crissy, William H. Cunningham, and Isabella C. M. Cunningham, *Selling: The Personal Force in Marketing*, (New York: John Wiley & Sons, Inc., 1977), pp. 366–367. Reprinted by permission of John Wiley & Sons, Inc.

Competitive Bids. Nearly all government agencies require competitive bidding. Although competitive bids are often utilized in private industry, they are much more common in government procurement. Only vendors on the qualified bidder's list, which is a compilation of qualified vendors, can receive a government contract. Getting on a competitive bidder's list may involve nothing more than completing a short form, or it may require fabricating a product mock-up which will then be tested by a government laboratory.

A distinction is often made between an invited bid and a competitive bid. An **invited bid** is simply a bid made by a single supplier or small group of suppliers at the request of the procuring agency. Bids are invited when a state or local government is making a reasonably small purchase — for example, less than $3,000. It is unlikely that any cost saving resulting from the extra competition afforded by additional bidders is sufficient to offset the cost of the bidding process itself. A **competitive bid**, on the other hand, is made in response to a public solicitation or notice issued by a government agency. Chapter 13 discusses the mechanics of competitive bidding.

Research and Development Procurement

The federal government is the largest purchaser of research and development (R&D) in the United States. Although the procurement process for R&D is similar to other federal purchasing practices, it differs somewhat in that R&D is not readily definable and government needs are one of a kind.

The federal government's research and development programs are funded by money appropriated by Congress. For example, when Congress began to make money available for research in solar energy, companies such as General Electric and Westinghouse began to monitor the activities of the scientists and engineers in the Department of Energy in order to determine how this money would be spent. Once the federal agency decides how it wants to spend its budget appropriations, it will issue a *request for proposal* (RFP). This document may be five or more pages long. If the research in question deals with a specific problem, such as how to make solar energy more efficient for heating older homes, the RFP will be very detailed. In contrast, RFPs may be quite brief, calling for the respondent to define the problem as well as to describe at length the research procedure.

Evaluating R&D proposals is very difficult. When the government is purchasing standard goods and services, it simply accepts the lowest qualified bid. R&D projects, on the other hand, must also be evaluated on the basis of what the supplier expects to do as well as how much money is required. Usually, the government asks a panel of nonbidding experts in the research area in question to recommend projects which the agency should fund. Finally, the contract officer chooses the winning R&D bid. Although attempts have been made to make this review process as unbiased as possible, by its very nature it cannot be as objective as the much simpler procedure used in the purchase of standard items.

1. Organizational buyers tend to be more technically qualified and more rational than final consumers. They also utilize committees to make their decisions and tend to select several supply sources for products they need.

2. In an industrial situation the buying process begins with the determination of a need for the product. Other steps include determining specifications, collecting information, analyzing environmental variables, making a purchase decision, and evaluating the purchased product.

3. The objective of value analysis is to measure product performance relative to its price. Vendor analysis determines with which suppliers the firm should do business.

4. Reciprocity tends to flourish when standardized products that have relatively little price competition are being purchased.

5. In creating a buying plan, the retailer must estimate its expected sales, calculate its planned purchases and open-to-buy figures, and select the correct assortment of merchandise.

6. The primary advantage of cooperative buying is that it gives small retailers a chance to participate in quantity discounts that are otherwise only available to large retailers. Centralized buying and buying committees provide the same advantage to a retailer that has a number of stores.

7. The primary objective of a resident buying office is to provide buyers with enough information so that they will be able to make intelligent purchase decisions.

8. The buyer is the most important person in the retail organization and is responsible for selecting the proper assortment of merchandise, maintaining good contacts with suppliers, and insuring that enough advertising dollars are spent to adequately expose the merchandise to the public.

9. The General Service Administration (GSA) is responsible for coordinating the procurement of merchandise for the U.S. government.

10. Problems faced by sellers to the U.S. government include the fact that most government procurement agencies operate with annual budgets, and that the seller will have to deal with multiple decision makers and competitive bids.

1. Distinguish between consumers and industrial buyers.
2. Describe in your own words the industrial buying process. How does it differ from the consumer purchase process for an expensive product?
3. How can the firm ensure that its purchasing agents act objectively?
4. What are the differences between value analysis and vendor analysis?
5. Should all reciprocity be eliminated from business transactions?
6. From the perspective of the retailer, what are the primary advantages to obtaining supplies from manufacturers? From wholesalers? From agents? What are the disadvantages of each supply source?
7. Assume a retailer has EOM stock of $50,000, planned sales of $80,000, planned reductions of $10,000, and planned BOM stock of $60,000. How much would the planned purchases be? Can this information be used to calculate "open to buy"?
8. Why do such firms as Sears find that centralized buying works best for them? In contrast, many department stores owned by large holding companies feel that decentralized buying works best. Why?
9. Analyze the role of the buyer in a modern retail store. Is this buyer's role likely to become more or less important in the future?
10. How do government procurement policies differ from procurement policies used in private industry?

6

Marketing Research

Marketing research is one of the most important but least understood aspects of marketing. It is especially critical to the implementation of the marketing concept. In order to serve its customers, a firm must know a great deal about the market. Through marketing research, the firm can determine the product features most demanded by the public, the total size of the market, whether the market can be broken down into distinct market segments, the responsiveness of the market to pricing and promotional decisions, the demographic and psychographic composition of the market, and the sales potential of particular products. Such information is vital to the development of effective marketing strategies.

ROLE OF MARKETING RESEARCH

To understand the role of marketing research in the firm's marketing program, it is first necessary to define marketing research and then to examine its major objective.

Definition of Marketing Research

The American Marketing Association (AMA) defines **marketing research** as the "systematic gathering, recording and analyzing of data about problems relating to the marketing of goods and services."[1] Accordingly, it is the responsibility of a firm's research department to provide objective analysis concerning the market for the firm's products and services. Marketing researchers must not become emotionally involved with a particular product or problem, as product managers sometimes do when they develop a new product.

The AMA's definition of marketing research is adequate for most of what is done in the field today, but it overlooks one important function: not only do

---

[1]"Report of the Definitions Committee of the American Marketing Association" (Chicago, Ill.: American Marketing Association, 1961).

marketing researchers analyze and solve problems, but they identify and define them as well. For example, several years ago, General Foods found itself spending a significant amount of money promoting Maxwell House Coffee in order to defend its share of the market for coffee sold in the states east of the Mississippi River. Their marketing research department identified the problem as an influx of a competitor's darker, richer, Western-blend coffee into the Eastern market. The research analyst solved the problem by first segmenting the coffee market on the basis of taste preferences and then blending a new coffee designed to counteract the market inroads of the competitor's brand without, at the same time, taking sales away from General Foods' other coffee products.[2]

The Objective of Marketing Research

The primary objective of marketing research is to reduce decision risk by providing management with relevant, timely, and accurate information. Marketing research often falls into disfavor with management because it only *reduces* but does not *eliminate* such risk. That even the best information does not eliminate risk entirely is painfully obvious when one realizes that the new product failure rate for large companies is nearly 50 percent, and much higher for small companies.[3]

There are at least two reasons why marketing research cannot provide perfect answers or eliminate risk entirely. First, human beings are extremely complex, and even the most powerful psychological and sociological tools can help us understand only a small percentage of human behavior. As a result, all too often marketing researchers simply reach the wrong conclusion in predicting what consumers will do in a particular purchase situation. Second, a sudden change in the environment, whether economic, legal, political, social, or technological in nature, can mean that the results of a market study are no longer relevant.

Marketing Research Activities

The activities of the marketing research department cover many areas. The most recent comprehensive study grouped them under five major headings — advertising research, business economics and corporate research, corporate responsibility research, product research, and sales and market research. Table 6-1 further divides these five into 30 subcategories for both industrial and consumer goods manufacturers and retail and wholesale organizations.

It is apparent from Table 6-1 that industrial and consumer goods manufacturers do much the same type of research. Both devote considerable effort to business economics, product, and sales and market research, but little effort to corporate responsibility research, except for studies of legal constraints on ad-

---

[2]Milton P. Brown, *et al., Problems in Marketing* (4th ed.; New York: McGraw Hill, 1968), pp. 439–466.

[3]See "New Product Success Ratio," *The Nielsen Researcher*, Vol. 5 (1971); *Management of New Products* (4th ed.; New York: Booz-Allen and Hamilton, 1965); and John T. O'Mera, "Selecting Profitable Products," *Harvard Business Review* (January–February, 1961), p. 83.

TABLE 6-1 Percentages of Businesses Conducting Research

	Consumer Companies	Industrial Companies	Retail and Wholesale Organizations
Advertising Research			
Motivation research	53	24	24
Copy research	54	32	27
Media research	51	43	44
Studies of ad effectiveness	64	47	44
Business Economics and			
Corporate Research			
Forecasting			
Short-range (up to 1 year)	77	75	60
Long-range (over 1 year)	76	73	58
Studies of business trends	69	73	58
Pricing studies	70	68	40
Plant and warehouse location			
studies	66	63	53
Product mix studies	66	65	51
Acquisition studies	67	69	53
Export and international studies	53	64	22
Corporate Responsibility			
Research			
Consumers' "right to know"			
studies	30	14	26
Ecological impact studies	35	34	18
Studies of legal constraints on			
advertising and promotion	52	42	40
Social values and policies			
studies	29	24	20
Product Research			
New product acceptance and			
potential	79	73	47
Competitive product studies	79	73	49
Testing of existing products	77	68	46
Packaging research: design or			
physical characteristics	67	53	36
Sales and Market Research			
Measurement of market			
potentials	79	75	60
Market share analysis	80	75	56
Determination of market			
characteristics	78	74	58
Sales analysis	80	75	62
Establishment of sales quotas,			
territories	79	73	46
Distribution channel studies	71	67	40
Test markets, store audits	73	33	36
Consumer panel operations	59	24	35
Sales compensation studies	66	64	33
Promotional studies of			
premiums, coupons,			
sampling, deals, etc.	64	31	38

Source: Dik W. Twedt, *1973 Survey of Marketing Research* (Chicago, Ill.: American Marketing Association, 1973), pp. 41, 43.

vertising and promotion. These legal studies would seem to be a direct result of the Federal Trade Commission's recent interest in this area. The major differences between the two types of manufacturers concern advertising research — consumer goods firms conduct more motivation research and copy, media, and general advertising effectiveness studies than do industrial firms. They also test market products more frequently and conduct more consumer panel studies than do industrial firms.

In general, retail and wholesale firms expend less effort on marketing research than either consumer goods or industrial manufacturers. As shown in Table 6-1, in only four of the 30 subcategories did the percentage of retail and wholesale firms engaging in research exceed that for industrial firms; in no instance was the percentage greater than that for consumer goods manufacturers. Research performed by retail and wholesale firms generally focuses on forecasting, market potential, measurement analysis of market characteristics, market share analysis, sales analysis, location analysis, and product mix studies. Again, marketing researchers both identify problems and help to solve them.

The Relationship Between Management and Marketing Research

A survey by the American Marketing Association found that marketing research is an important business function for many organizations.[4] As Table 6-2 indicates, 59 percent of the firms responding to the survey stated that they had a formal marketing research department. Consumer products firms were the most likely to have marketing research departments, whereas advertising agencies were the least likely to have such departments. The study also found that 45 percent of marketing research managers report directly to top management; ten years earlier, only 30 percent did so.

TABLE 6-2 Organization for Marketing Research by Type of Company

	Percentage Having Formal Department	Percentage Having One Person	Percentage Having No One Assigned
Manufacturers of consumer goods	70	13	17
Publishing and broadcasting	66	11	23
Manufacturers of industrial goods	59	19	22
Retailing and wholesaling	54	11	35
Advertising agencies	53	22	25
All firms	59	18	23

Source: Dik W. Twedt, *1973 Survey of Marketing Research* (Chicago, Ill.: American Marketing Association, 1973), p. 11.

---

[4]Dik W. Twedt, *1973 Survey of Marketing Research* (Chicago, Ill.: American Marketing Association, 1973), p. 25.

In spite of the increasing importance of marketing research, conflicts can and frequently do arise between marketing research and management personnel. One critic of marketing researchers faulted them for their: (1) ivory tower approach to problem solving, (2) failure to understand management's perspective, (3) inability to produce timely information for decision making, (4) preoccupation with research tools, (5) concealment of results in technical jargon, and (6) lack of imagination and creativity.[5] These criticisms may be harsh but they are not without foundation.

How can the relationship between management and the marketing research department be improved? How can conflicts be reduced? The key action in this regard is to define explicitly the responsibilities of the marketing research department. Specifically, top management should explain in writing the department's functions, limitations, and priorities as well as the role of the director of marketing research. All too often, such direction is not supplied and the marketing research department simply concentrates on what it considers important, not on what top management deems important.

For their part, members of the marketing research department should keep in mind that they are a part of a staff organization, the sole purpose of which is to serve the research needs of the firm. Consequently, the research group should make every effort to understand the thinking of top management, i.e., research must relate to profit goals, not merely to interesting research topics. In the same manner, researchers should periodically remind themselves that their work must be timely, decision oriented, and written in such a manner that nontechnical people can understand it and have confidence in it. Finally, marketing research personnel must be careful not to oversell their research. As stated above, marketing research can only reduce decision risk, not eliminate it. It is essential that the researcher point out the limitations of a particular study as well as the risks involved in recommended decision options.

THE DATA COLLECTION PROCESS

One of the marketing researcher's principal functions is to collect market data relevant to the problem under consideration. Before collecting such data, however, the problem itself must be identified and clearly defined. This step is the responsibility of the director of marketing research in consultation with the firm's line marketing officers. Unless the problem is clearly defined, the marketing research department may design an excellent research investigation, but one that will be of absolutely no use to management. Failure to define the problem is probably responsible for more errors in marketing research than any other single factor.

Actual data collection begins with an examination of the available **secondary data**, which are defined as information collected at an earlier time and for reasons other than solving the problem currently under investigation. This step may be followed by exploratory or preliminary research prior to the collection of original or **primary data**, that is, data collected by the researcher specifically for the problem under investigation. The most common techniques for

---

[5]James R. Krum, "Perception and Evaluation of the Role of the Corporate Marketing Research Department," *Journal of Marketing Research* (November, 1969), p. 459.

FIGURE 6-1 The Data Collection Process

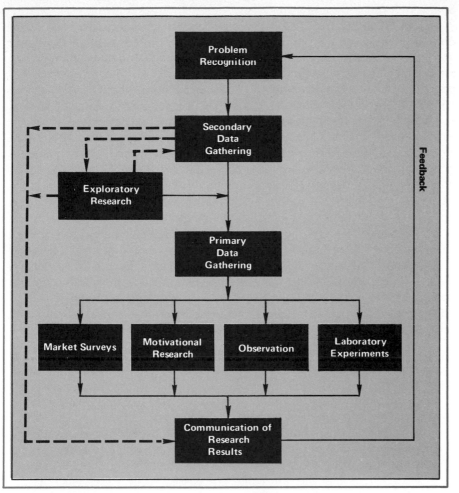

collecting primary data are market surveys, motivational research, observation, and laboratory experiments. The actual technique selected is a function of the research problem itself and of time, cost, and personnel constraints. Figure 6-1 depicts the data collection process. Each of the steps subsequent to problem definition is discussed below.

Gathering Secondary Data

Occasionally, secondary data is all the firm needs to answer its research questions (note in Figure 6-1 the dashed line which connects "secondary data" with "results"). More commonly, secondary data collection serves to prevent replication of previous work; such data enable the research to build on previous studies, i.e., to begin where others left off.

Secondary data can be classified as either internal or external. **Internal secondary data** are collected from within the firm; **external secondary data** originate from outside the firm. Examples of internal secondary data include previous studies conducted by the marketing research department, in-house accounting information, or sales analyses performed by sales management personnel. The type and quality of internal secondary data varies a great deal from company to company.

The U.S. government is one of the principal sources of external secondary data. The most famous and most useful body of information for consumer marketers is the *Census of Population*, which aggregates data at the national, state, county, and city levels (by census tract and block). This census provides population information according to sex, race, language, citizenship, education, family composition, employment status, place of work, and income. This data is invaluable to marketing researchers whenever the demographic characteristics of a market must be determined, such as when promotional appeals aimed at specific target markets or demographic groups are needed. Other U.S. government secondary data sources include the *Census of Retail Trade; Census of Wholesale Trade; Census of Selected Service Industries;* and *Census of Manufactures*. In addition, the government publishes many books, periodicals, and bulletins on a variety of topics of interest to the marketer.

Commercial firms, such as the A. C. Nielsen Company, also provide market-related information on such topics as who buys what in grocery stores and the amount of television watched by various income groups in the United States. A firm can also obtain valuable secondary data from its trade association, which often conducts research studies on problems common to the industry as a whole. Figure 6-2 lists some of the more important secondary data sources as well as the information they provide.

Advantages of Secondary Data. Secondary data have four distinct advantages over primary data. First, secondary data can be collected very quickly — often in a matter of hours or, at most, days. The time involved may be no greater than that required to go to a public library. Second, in most cases, secondary data is inexpensive, at least when compared to the cost of primary data. The original cost of collecting the data is borne by the sponsoring agency. Third, as mentioned above, careful examination of secondary sources can ensure that the firm does not replicate previous studies. Finally, some secondary data is of the type that the firm could not possibly collect itself, such as the nationwide population, demographic, and income information gathered by the Bureau of the Census. The Bureau of the Census requires retailers to provide sales, expenses, and profit information that would ordinarily not be given to a private researcher.[6]

Disadvantages of Secondary Data. There are two major drawbacks to secondary data. First, it is often difficult to locate such data in a form suited to the firm's particular research question. This problem is diminished, however, if the firm intends to build on secondary data rather than to use secondary data alone to solve its research problem. Second, some secondary data are of questionable validity. In particular, the researcher may not know whether the data were collected and analyzed in an objective, systematic, and unbiased manner. Although this problem is not usually common with government secondary data or with data from the more reliable commercial research sources, it is something with which most marketing researchers must deal at one time or another.

---

[6]Harper W. Boyd, Jr., Ralph Westfall, and Stanley F. Stasch, *Marketing Research: Text and Cases* (Homewood, Ill.: Richard D. Irwin, 1977), p. 146.

FIGURE 6-2   Some Sources of Secondary Data

Business Reference Sources: An Annotated Guide
Source: 1979 revised edition by Lorna M. Daniels, Baker Library, Graduate School of Business Administration, Harvard University, Boston, MA 02163.
Information Provided: A good reference for basic business information sources, including trade publications.

Business Intelligence & Strategic Planning
Source: 1978 edition by Lorna M. Daniels; available from source above.
Information Provided: Reference source on materials dealing with strategic planning.

Periodicals & Sources
Source: CIS, P.O. Box 30056, Washington, DC 20014.
Information Provided: A guide to 900 U.S. government statistical publications on business, finance, natural resources, demographics, and others.

Business Periodicals Index
Source: All public and university libraries.
Information Provided: Indexes over 150 business periodicals.

Sales & Marketing Management
Source: Available in most business school and public libraries.
Information Provided: Publishes four statistical issues per year: *Survey of Buying Power — Part I* (July), source of data on consumer purchases, population, income, and potential buying ability on a county basis; *Survey of Buying Power — Part II* (October), merchandise line sales and buying power information on a county basis; *Survey of Industrial Buying Power* (April), industrial market data on a county basis based on SIC codes; and *Survey of Selling Costs* (February), statistics on selling costs.

Dun & Bradstreet's Million Dollar Directory
Source: Most business school and public libraries.
Information Provided: Lists over 78,000 U.S. companies with their product-SIC code data, approximate sales, number of employees, and other data.

Standard & Poor's Corporation Industry Surveys
Source: Most business school and public libraries.
Information Provided: Current analyses of 34 major industries with comparison of leading companies within each industry.

Thomas Register of American Manufacturers
Source: Most business school libraries.
Information Provided: Manufacturers by product, including addresses.

Company Annual Reports and SEC 10K Reports
Source: Individual companies.
Information Provided: Financial and marketing information on individual companies; can be used in conjunction with *Moody's Investor Service* and *Standard & Poor's Corporation Stock Reports*.

U.S. Government Sources (Sample)
Source: Department of Commerce, Washington, D.C.
Information Provided: *Survey of Current Business* (monthly); *U.S. Industrial Outlook*; *Census of Manufactures*; *County Business Patterns*.

Conducting Exploratory Research

At the end of the secondary data phase, the researcher may still lack sufficient understanding of the problem to proceed with a full-scale research investigation. In this situation the researcher may decide to conduct **exploratory research**, the purpose of which is to provide a tentative explanation of the issue in question. Because so little knowledge is available at the beginning of the exploratory phase, this type of research is characterized by flexibility. In general, exploratory research provides the analyst with insights that can be tested later by more scientific research methods.[7]

Exploratory research also may occasionally provide the answer to the research question. Typically, this occurs not because the investigation has been completed but because a decision must be made and the firm cannot afford to wait for the results of more comprehensive research. The likely product of exploratory research is either additional secondary research or the development of a full-scale scientific research project. Let us now examine two types of exploratory research: the experience survey and the case study.

Experience Survey. The objective of an experience survey is to tap the knowledge of people who know something about the problem under investigation. The individuals questioned may range from company executives who have solved similar problems in the past, to people totally unassociated with the firm but who have some special understanding of the problem. The researcher should try to draw on many people, representing as many different backgrounds and philosophies as possible.

For example, exploratory research was conducted to determine the market potential of a skateboard park in Lubbock, Texas. Since the researchers did not know enough about skateboard parks to begin a full-scale research project, they conducted an exploratory experience survey. The investigators talked with skateboard retailers, junior high school counselors, and with people who sell plans for skateboard parks or who have opened skateboard parks in other cities. This particular study led to the conclusion that such a park was not feasible in Lubbock. Therefore, neither additional secondary data nor further research were deemed necessary.

Case Study. A second exploratory research technique involves the analysis of a group of cases, or situations, similar to the problem under study. The researcher seeks to understand what occurred in each particular situation, why it occurred, and how the various outcomes may relate to the research problem at hand.

A good illustration of case exploratory research is a study conducted by a firm to determine the factors differentiating effective salespeople from poor performers. In particular, the researcher studied two of the firm's best salespeople and two of its worst. After data had been collected on the background of the four subjects, the researcher spent two days with each salesperson in order to observe performance in the field. The result of this research was the tentative finding that effective salespeople were more likely to check the inventory levels of their customers and to point out items in need of restocking. As a result of this exploratory research, the firm was in a position to proceed with a more scientific study of sales force effectiveness.

After the firm has either conducted its exploratory research, or decided that such research is not necessary, the next step in the data collection process is to

---

[7]Gilbert A. Churchill, Jr., *Marketing Research* (Hinsdale, Ill.: The Dryden Press, 1976), pp. 62—67.

gather primary data through either a survey, motivational research, observation, or a laboratory experiment.

Gathering Primary Data: The Survey

All of us have been surveyed at least once in our lives. We have been asked about products, issues, presidential candidates, how we spend our leisure time, what kind of car we drive, or how we feel about abortion. Census workers ask us about the composition of our households, family income, age, and how much education we have. The telephone company asks us why we make long-distance telephone calls, or why we don't. Magazine publishers ask us whether we read *Sports Illustrated, Time*, or *Redbook*.

The survey is so frequently encountered in modern life that it hardly needs to be defined. But for those who have never been interviewed or who have never filled out a questionnaire, a **survey** is simply a systematic attempt to gather information by asking a group of people a series of questions. The research area of interest could be almost anything, as suggested above. As a formal research study, a survey must be designed and administered properly if it is to produce reliable information. The two most important concerns in this regard are sample selection and the data collection procedure employed.

Sample Selection. In conducting a survey, we must first determine the **population**, which is defined as all the individuals who are part of the group under study. For example, a population might be all homeowners in Seattle, Washington, or everyone in the United States who drives a 1981 Chevrolet. Questioning everyone in the population would constitute a census. Most of the time, it is simply too expensive, time consuming, and unnecessary to contact the entire population. Instead, a **sample** of the population is drawn. The objective in sample selection is to choose a group of people such that the results of the survey of that group can be accurately generalized to the entire population. An example of a sample is the Nielsen television survey mentioned earlier in the chapter. The population is all households with at least one television set; the sample is the 1,200 families whose television viewing habits are monitored by the company. Nielsen generalizes the results of its sample since, presumably, the viewing habits of these 1,200 families represent the viewing habits of the nation as a whole.

The procedure for selecting the sample is critical to the validity of the ensuing research. In a **random sample**, everyone in the population has an equal chance of being selected. In a **stratified random sample**, the population is broken down into strata or subunits, and then a random sample is selected from each stratum. This procedure ensures that a representative number of people is selected from each stratum, which enables generalizations to be drawn about the individual strata as well as about the population. To illustrate, a major research firm was hired by a Houston-based department store to evaluate the market for a new concept in small specialty stores that would sell only men's casual clothing. The *population* consisted of all male residents of Houston, Texas. Since a *census* of all Houston males would be too expensive, the firm decided to draw a stratified random sample based on race of the subjects.

This sampling method was chosen because the researchers wanted to ensure that the sample was *representative* of the male population of Houston. The researcher felt that unless a stratified random sample were selected there might not be sufficient numbers of Mexican-Americans and blacks in the sample.

Three Types of Surveys. The three most common ways to collect survey data are through mail questionnaires, telephone interviews, and personal interviews. *Mail questionnaires*, which are both sent and returned by mail, are relatively inexpensive since they eliminate the need for an interviewer. They also enable the subjects to participate in the survey at their leisure. A significant disadvantage of this technique is that it is difficult to exercise any control over who completes the questionnaire. Although a questionnaire is designed for and addressed to the head of the household, it may actually be completed by any member of the family. In addition, a mail questionnaire is often viewed by the recipient as a waste of time. For this reason, the response rate for mail questionnaires tends to be extremely low.

Telephone surveys have become popular during the last decade because most families now have telephones and because personal interviews have become disproportionately expensive. Although telephone surveys are more expensive than mail surveys, they are less expensive than personal interviews because there is less "dead" time spent traveling from one subject to the next. However, telephone surveys do have two major disadvantages. First, it is difficult to ask complex questions over the telephone. For example, imagine being asked over the telephone to rank order your preference for eight local shopping centers, or to indicate which of four advertising appeals you think is most effective in selling a new automobile. Second, the interviewer must be careful not to influence the respondent. Some people like to tell the interviewer what they think he or she wants to hear. When this happens, the results of the survey may not be very useful.

From the perspective of the quality of the information obtained, the *personal interview* is the preferred approach. Because the interviewer usually is able to identify the subject, the control problem of who is answering the survey does not exist. In addition, the interviewer can ask more complicated and thoughtful questions that may be difficult, if not impossible, to ask over the telephone or in a letter. Personal interviews, however, are expensive and, as with a telephone survey, there is always the danger that the subject will react to the interviewer and not to the interview instrument.

Advantages of Surveys. The two greatest advantages of surveys are their versatility and their relative low cost. In terms of versatility, surveys can be designed to generate many different kinds of information. It is amazing how much information can be obtained from people if the researcher approaches them on the basis that what they have to say is important. In addition, although surveys can be costly, they are considerably less expensive than motivational or laboratory experiments, especially considering the amount of data that can be generated.

Disadvantages of Surveys. The objective of survey research is to question a sample of people and generalize their responses to the population from which they were drawn. A characteristic problem of surveys is that anywhere from 40 to 90 percent of the sample refuses to participate. Mail surveys typically have

FIGURE 6-3   Letter from an Uncooperative Subject

TO WHOM THIS MAY CONCERN:

   I DONT' WANT YOU TO SEND ME ANY MORE OF YOUR SO CALLED
LITERATURE, IN THE FIRST PLACE.
I THINK ITS A DISGRACE TO OUR UNIVERSITY TO ALLOW SUCH
ABNOXIOUS PEOPLE TO BE ALLOWED IN OUR UNIVERSITY. I AM
ASHAMED FOR ALLOWING YOUR PEACE MARCHES AND ALLOWING THE
HIPPIES AND THE REST OF YOU PEOPLE, WITH YOUR SMALL MINDS
TO HAVE THE OPPORTUNITY THAT YOU HAVE IN OUR GREAT SCHOOL.
THE ONLY REASON THAT YOU PEOPLE WITH YOUR SMALL MINDS ARE
THERE IS TO KEEP FROM SERVING YOUR COUNTRY. YOU COWARDS
WITH YOUR YELLOW STREAKS DOWN YOUR BACKS HAVEN'T THE
SLIGHTEST OF COURAGE TO HELP IN ANY WAY TO LIGHTEN THE
BURDEN OF OUR SON'S WHO ARE SERVING THIS WONDERFUL LAND TO
SAVE YOUR CRUMBY NECKS THAT YOU MIGHT LIVE WITH YOUR DOPES
AND SEX LIVING FOR A USELESS CAUSE. YOU ALL SHOUD BE PLACED
IN FRONT OF A FIRING SQUAD. I WONDER HOW MUCH COURAGE YOU
WOULD HAVE THEN. EVEN ANIMALS HAVE MORE RESPECT FOR
HUMANITY THATN YOU COWARDS DO. KEEP YOUR LITERATURE YOU
RATS.

the lowest response rates, but telephone and personal interviewers often find that a substantial percentage of the people contacted refuse to be interviewed. Researchers must make the assumption that those individuals who do not participate in the research are similar to those who do, except, of course, for their attitude toward surveys. This assumption simply may not be valid, however, because respondents may be systematically different than nonrespondents. Consequently, some question arises as to the reliability of the results whenever the response rate is low.

Another problem with survey research is that we cannot know why people participate in a survey or whether they do so seriously. Respondent motivation is especially a problem with mail surveys. Figures 6-3 and 6-4 show two letters received by doctoral students while conducting market research studies for their dissertations. The first letter was written in response to a survey conducted during the time of the war in Vietnam. The writer of the letter was not in sympathy either with university life or with the quest for knowledge. The second letter was from an individual who not only had a delightful sense of humor but also probably spent a great deal of time thinking about the survey questions. The point is that it usually is impossible for the researcher to know whether the respondent is psychologically disturbed, is filling out the questionnaire in a random fashion, or is giving each question careful consideration.

Gathering Primary Data: Motivation Research

Many areas of personal behavior cannot be explored by direct questions, either because the respondents do not know why they behave as they do or because the researcher does not know what questions to ask. In these situations the researcher usually resorts to one of two types of motivation research: storytelling or focus group interviews.

FIGURE 6-4   Letter from a Cooperative Subject

Dear --

Since I am helping you toward a Ph.D. by filling in the questionnaire you sent to me (regardless of answers, either misunderstood, dumb, doubtful, etc.) I feel I can ask for your help toward my C.S. (Curiosity Satisfied). To make it easier for you I am enclosing a stamped self-addressed envelope. Your prompt reply will be greatly appreciated.

Please indicate with an X the correct answer. Your opinion means nothing; each question must have an answer.

1. Where did you get my name for one of your sample members?
   (a) From the telephone book?   Yes   No
   (b) From a friend?   Yes   No
   (c) From a mailing list?   Yes   No
   (d) Other (if other, please explain in detail)   Yes   No

2. Part three (3) of your questionnaire was loaded with 56 questions – some stupid, some intelligent, some dumb, some senseless, none funny. Would you say that this type of questioning actually has anything to do with marketing or:
   (a) You really have a secret ambition to be a
       psychologist?   Yes   No
   (b) You need so many pages to fill a thesis?   Yes   No
   (c) You wanted a good laugh at the people who
       filled in your questionnaire?   Yes   No
   (d) You really aren't too sure about this complex
       world so you are going to go along with the
       majority answers so you won't have to make
       your own decisions?   Yes   No

3. By now the kids should have the dinner dishes done, so would you say I was:
   (a) Smart to pretend I was doing an important
       research paper therefore getting out of
       helping with the dishes?   Yes   No
   (b) A fool for not having tv on to watch the
       baseball game?   Yes   No
   (c) An idiot for not reading my new Reader's
       Digest?   Yes   No
   (d) A dum-dum for not reading the newspaper
       completely?   Yes   No

Now that you have completed this form, may I tell you that it was a pleasure for me to help you by filling in your questionnaire, and that this idea of mine was to help put a little breather in your day. If you're working on a Ph.D. you probably don't ever stop working. There now, feel better?

Good luck to you now and in the future!

Storytelling. Under the storytelling approach, the researcher either shows the subject a picture, list, graph, or some other visual rendering, or describes an incident in words. The subject is then asked to respond to the visual or verbal

FIGURE 6-5 Shopping Lists

(A)	(B)
1½ lbs. hamburger	1½ lbs. hamburger
2 loaves Wonder Bread	2 loaves Wonder Bread
bunch of carrots	bunch of carrots
1 can Rumford baking powder	1 can Rumford baking powder
Nescafe instant coffee	Maxwell House coffee
2 cans Del Monte peaches	2 cans Del Monte peaches
5 lbs. potatoes	5 lbs. potatoes

Source: Mason Haire, "Projective Techniques in Marketing Research," *Journal of Marketing*
(April, 1950), p. 651.

stimulus. A classic example of storytelling involved Nescafe instant coffee.
Nescafe was one of the first instant food preparations when it was introduced
in the late 1940s. Although taste tests had indicated that most women, when
blindfolded, could not tell the difference between Nescafe and regular coffee,
people still did not purchase it. But when asked by a group of researchers what
they didn't like about the coffee, the subjects inevitably mentioned its taste.

The researchers surmised that the subjects' responses did not represent
their true feelings, so the researchers decided to use a storytelling approach. A
new sample of homemakers was selected and divided into two groups. The
first group was given the shopping list shown in Figure 6-5(A).

The other half of the sample was given the same list, shown in Figure
6-5(B), except that regular Maxwell House coffee, a drip grind, was substituted
for the Nescafe instant coffee. The members of each group were then asked to
examine their shopping lists and to describe the personality of the person who
had composed it.

As Table 6-3 indicates, the findings were dramatic: 48 percent of the subjects viewed the Nescafe shopper as "lazy," while only 4 percent chose this
term to characterize the Maxwell House shopper. Thus the reluctance to purchase the new instant product was apparently a function of prevailing social
attitudes rather than the actual flavor of the product. Yet, the answers to the
direct questions provided no indication of the underlying reason behind the

TABLE 6-3 Reported Differences in Shopping List Study

Characteristics	Nescafe Shopper	Maxwell House Shopper
Lazy	48%*	4%
Failed to plan household purchases	48	12
Thrifty	4	16
A spendthrift	12	0
A good wife	4	16

*To be read as: "of the subjects viewing the shopping list with the Nescafe item, 48% de-
scribed the shopper as lazy."
Source: Adapted from Mason Haire, "Projective Techniques in Marketing Research," *Journal
of Marketing* (April, 1950), p. 652.

poor sales of the coffee.[8] It is interesting to note that when this study was replicated 20 years later, no significant differences were found between the responses of the two samples, suggesting that social attitudes toward instant foods have changed considerably over the years.[9]

Focus Group Interview. A second type of study designed to uncover consumer motivation is the focus group interview, which involves bringing together a number of people and interviewing them as a group. The investigator's role is to keep the discussion lively and to explore any ideas that develop within the group. On many occasions, focus groups have led to the development of new product concepts that the research department previously had not considered.

The Ford Pinto is one product that has benefited from focus group interviews. Ford commissioned a series of such groups to determine public attitudes toward the Pinto. The subjects were brought together and given a chance to observe and drive the car. The researchers found that the Pinto was perceived as a *female* car — the perfect car for the young married homemaker or the young coed. Previously, no one in either the research group or the product department had thought of looking at cars from the perspective of gender.

The principal advantage of either type of motivation research is well illustrated by the Pinto example: both types encourage the generation of new questions, ideas, and perceptions, none of which may develop under the stimulus of direct questioning. The major disadvantage is cost, since the effective use of motivation techniques usually requires the presence of highly trained discussion leaders or group moderators. In addition, the results of motivation research are often difficult to interpret. With focus group interviews, for example, many hours must be spent listening to tape recordings of the group sessions. It is often hard to determine whether a group consensus emerged and, if so, the nature of the consensus. Also, a question usually arises as to whether the group's perceptions or ideas represent those of the population from which the group was drawn.[10] Finally, since the results must be evaluated subjectively by the researcher, they may suffer from a personal bias.

Gathering Primary Data: Direct Observation

Observing consumer behavior in the marketplace is another important way to collect market research information. Observation studies are frequently conducted to determine how shoppers behave in supermarkets. For example, a manufacturer of breakfast cereal might want to know whether the typical buyer is an adult accompanied by a child. Do the adult and child talk to each other about the cereal? Does either of them read the package? How much influence does the child have in the purchase decision? The answers to these questions

---

[8]Mason Haire, "Projective Techniques in Marketing Research," *Journal of Marketing* (April, 1950), pp. 649–652.

[9]Frederick E. Webster, Jr., and Frederick Von Peckmann, "A Replication of the Shopping List Study," *Journal of Marketing* (April, 1970), pp. 61–63.

[10]Bobby J. Calder, "Focus Groups and the Nature of Qualitative Marketing Research," *Journal of Marketing Research* (August, 1977), pp. 353–364.

can be very useful in designing media strategies and in making shelf location and packaging decisions.

When events are recorded as they actually occur, the researcher introduces virtually no bias into the study. If a hidden camera photographs the purchase behavior of shoppers, then the possibility of bias is limited to the data interpretation phase of the research. In this sense, observation is the most objective procedure for collecting marketing research data.

Observational research, however, tells the researcher little about consumer attitudes, motivations, or plans. The researcher knows *what* subjects are doing but not *why* they are doing it. In addition, observational research is usually conducted only at the time and place of purchase. In the purchase of a new car, for example, the researcher could record the behavior of the customer in the automobile showroom, but the observation data would tell the researcher nothing about what occurred before the customer walked through the showroom doors. Were there any family discussions about the merits of different cars? Had the customer already decided on the purchase before talking to the salespeson? Did the customer just come from a visit to the showroom of a competing dealer? Finally, direct observation tends to be expensive, often involving sophisticated camera and sound equipment plus a crew of technicians.

Gathering Primary Data: The Laboratory Experiment

The last primary data collection method, the laboratory experiment, is considerably different from the others. Rather than being questioned or observed, the subjects participate in a controlled experiment — that is, in an artificial setting, they are asked to perform some type of marketing activity. The investigator controls all aspects of the experiment except for the variable under study; the changes in this variable in response to controlled changes in another variable are measured. Over the years, a number of laboratory experiments have been conducted concerning pricing. In one study, women were exposed to simulated shopping trips.[11] In each trip the subject was shown an assortment of colas and coffee brands and then asked to choose the brand that she would purchase. The relative prices for the various brands were changed on each of the eight trips. In this manner, the analyst was able to determine the price level at which a shopper would shift from one brand to another.

The major advantage of laboratory experiments is that they permit the analyst to determine the impact of a change in one variable on another variable. Referring to our example of colas and coffees, a beverage manufacturer might want to know how much of a price increase would cause customers to begin to switch to another product.

Since a laboratory experiment is a controlled investigation in an artificial environment, it may not be possible to generalize the results of such an experiment to the marketplace. In many laboratory studies, the subjects seem to be reacting to the controlled environment as much as to the experiment itself. Such a reaction may invalidate the test results.

---

[11]Churchill, *op. cit.*, p. 88.

Right now, **you** are probably in the midst of making a career decision. Since this decision is among the most difficult and important in life, it tends to produce a considerable amount of anxiety. The first thing to realize is that you're not alone: nearly all of your fellow students are in the same situation. Bear in mind also that you need not make even a tentative career decision until you have completed the basic management, marketing, finance, and accounting courses. Use your time in school to pursue a variety of interests — keep an open mind.

After you have completed all your introductory courses, you'll have a general idea of the range of employment options available. Remember that you're not locked into your first career choice. Many executives, in fact, change careers several times during their professional lives.

Dr. Moak Rollins is a perfect example. After studying petroleum engineering in college, Rollins began a career in the petroleum equipment business, later founding a company in which he handled both finance and marketing operations. When his firm was acquired by Smith International, he returned to school, completed doctoral degree work in finance, and then joined the graduate finance faculty at The University of Texas at Austin. Rollins is currently on leave from the university and serves as one of three public utility commissioners in the state of Texas.

Besides your college coursework, other sources of career information are available from your college library or placement office. You'll find a wealth of published information including company annual reports, trade journals, government reports on job availability, and career decision guides.

Also, don't forget what probably is any university's greatest resource: its people! Faculty members and placement officers are more than willing to help you — it's their job. Most professors, for example, enjoy talking about their specialty (e.g., marketing or finance) and what career opportunities it has to offer. Placement officers usually have a very good feel for the job market. Your college may also have a psychological counseling service that can help you decide what career is best for you.

Finally, don't overlook local business executives. You may come into contact with them in your classroom when they serve as guest speakers or simply at different places in your community. You might be surprised how willing people are to talk about their jobs and about career prospects either with their company or in their industry.

Just as with any major business decision, your career decision should be based on the best information available. List all the appropriate alternatives, and research each one carefully and thoroughly. Good luck!

Marketing & You

Communicating Research Results

The last step in the data collection process depicted in Figure 6-1 is the communication of research results. Once the results of the data collection and analysis process have been compiled, they must be communicated to management in a timely and understandable manner. It is very easy for marketing research people to err in the final step by making their end product — the research report — too complex to be dealt with by management. The marketing research department must also make every effort to ensure that the study results are aimed at answering the original questions that stimulated the research.

The results of the research study may frequently stimulate other research studies on related problems. Hence, communicating the research results may result in feedback to the problem recognition step as depicted in Figure 6-1.

TEST MARKETING

A second major function of marketing research is **test marketing**, the process by which a firm makes a product available to the market in a limited geographical area in order to determine the product's commercial viability. Test marketing usually has two objectives: (1) to estimate how many units of the product will be purchased when it is made available to the entire market, and (2) to test the effectiveness of the product's promotion campaign. In many cases the firm is not as interested in how the product sells as it is in sharpening its promotional strategy. As a result, it may test market the same product in several different geographic markets, varying the promotional strategy slightly in each. In this way, it is possible to evaluate the relative effectiveness of the different strategies. Test marketing can also provide information about (1) market share, (2) the characteristics of consumers who purchase the product, (3) the characteristics of consumers who sample the product but who do not buy it again, (4) the frequency of purchase by different consumer groups, and (5) the ways in which the product is used by consumers.[12]

Where the firm should test market its products, some principles of test marketing, and how long the firm should conduct its test market are key topics for discussion.

Where to Test Market

In deciding where to test market a product, the most important step is to define as accurately as possible the overall market for the product. The test market area must be *representative* of the anticipated overall market area. For example, a fast-food chain interested in establishing a new line of Mexican food outlets nationwide should not test market the concept in the Southwest. People in the Southwest are more accustomed to and generally more favorably disposed to Mexican food than are people in other regions. Thus, the Southwest is not representative of the country as a whole for this product.

In determining whether a community is truly representative and would thus be a good test market, the firm should consider such consumer variables

---

[12]Boyd, Westfall, and Stasch, *op. cit.*, p. 599.

as age, culture, background, social class, and ethnic makeup, as well as factors relating to the product itself. Most firms considering national distribution for their products usually test market them in several locations to achieve a more representative national sample.

Principles of Test Marketing

There are four major principles to be followed in test marketing. First, the market area chosen should have representative, or normal, distribution and advertising media channels. For example, if the product is to be sold through department stores, discount stores, and convenience stores and is to be advertised on both television and radio, then the test market area must have these facilities available.

Second, the test market should be relatively self contained, so that little, if any, of the promotional effort is wasted outside the test market area. In addition, strong outside media influences should be kept to a minimum — such as widely read national newspapers or cable television, which makes many additional television stations available to consumers. When such influences are present, it is difficult to evaluate the impact of the promotional effort since it is competing with more than what is considered a normal amount of promotion.

Third, the firm should not overspend on introductory promotion. For test market results to be meaningful, the firm cannot spend more money per prospect in the test market area than it intends to spend in the market as a whole. Lastly, potential competitors will monitor the test market almost as closely as the firm itself. Since relatively few cities meet all the criteria for a good test market, most firms watch these cities closely to see whether new products are being tested. Some unscrupulous firms have been known to purchase large amounts of a product being tested in order to disrupt the research, but this is not a common practice.[13]

How Long to Test Market

There is no single answer to the question, "How long should a test market run?" The length of the test market depends on the goal established by the firm for the test marketing effort as well as on the product itself. If the goal is simply to get a feel for the market, the test market will not have to run as long as it would if the goal were to fine-tune the entire promotional package or to prepare for a major, nationwide product introduction.

Similarly, the length of time varies with the nature of the product. For nondurable package goods such as toothpaste or detergent, the test market must run, at a minimum, the length of the repurchase cycle. It is one thing for a clever promotional campaign to entice people to buy a product, but it is quite another for the product to perform well enough to bring about a second purchase. It is the second purchase that provides the critical data about whether the market accepts the product. However, for durable goods such as automobiles, washing machines, or machine tools, the extended length of the repurchase cycle, along with the high cost of manufacturing testable products, almost forces the firm to go ahead with full-scale introduction without the bene-

---

[13]*Ibid.*, p. 598.

fits of test marketing the products. Therefore, test marketing of durable goods usually involves only evaluating the potential effectiveness of various promotional campaigns, not the products themselves.

A Word of Caution

Researchers may make a major mistake when the results of the test market indicate that the product has a bright future. That is, they may forget that the product has been test marketed and evaluated without taking into account the impact of competition. A few years ago, when General Electric first test marketed the electric toothbrush, the company had no direct competitors for this product. By the time the product had been on the market one year, more than 50 competing products were being sold in the United States. In the U.S. economic system, success tends to attract competitors. Therefore, the results of a test market must be tempered with the understanding that if the product is successful, it will eventually have considerable competition.

SALES FORECASTING

Test marketing is one way to forecast the sales of a new product. Other techniques, however, must be used for existing products and for new products that are not amenable to test marketing. These techniques include opinion surveys and a variety of objective forecasting methods.

Opinion Surveys

An **opinion survey** involves the polling of either a group of executives or the sales representatives as to their expectations regarding future sales. Such an opinion survey usually is inexpensive and lends itself to rapid data collection; however, it is also quite subjective.

Jury of Executive Opinion. The jury of executive opinion, the oldest and simplest sales forecasting method, involves asking informed executives about their expectations for a product. The executives can be from within the firm or from outside the firm. For example, a researcher may ask members of top management who have a history of working with similar products how they feel a new product will sell. In responding, these managers will consider such factors as competition and the firm's production and distribution capabilities. Or the researcher could ask the firm's leading independent distributors and customers for their feelings about the product. Outside executives can add candor and objectivity to the analysis — qualities sometimes not easily obtained from within the organization.

The advantages of the jury of executive opinion are clear. First, it makes the experience of industry executives available to the researcher. And second, it is often the only feasible way of collecting data in a timely manner. The disadvantages are perhaps even more apparent. The data are nothing more than the opinions of individuals, however well-informed or experienced. In addition, the sales assessment represents the opinion of many people, with the result that no one person is responsible for the forecast. This approach is more reliable for aggregate forecasting than for breaking down the forecast by products, markets, or customer groups.[14]

Composite of Sales Force Opinions. Management often asks the firm's sales representatives to forecast the sales of the firm's products in their individual territories. The preferred approach is to forecast sales by product and by customer, which forces the salesperson to disaggregate, or break down, the data as much as possible. As a result, the forecasts are more objective and systematic, giving management an indication of how each salesperson arrived at the overall sales estimate for the product. The forecast of each salesperson should be reviewed by the sales manager to ensure that it is accurate. The forecasts are then compiled and analyzed to establish the overall sales forecast for the firm. It should also be noted that the composite forecast of the sales force may be modified by management.

The major advantage of this sales forecasting approach is that the people closest to the market actually make the estimates; they know best how products are selling and can be expected to sell in the future. Another advantage is that the people who make the forecasts are also the people who are largely responsible for making them come true. Meeting a forecast through a vigorous selling effort is certainly one way of making the forecast, in retrospect, seem reasonable, accurate, and informed.

There are also significant disadvantages to a forecast based on the opinions of the sales force. For example, the individual salesperson may not understand what is happening in the economy and in the industry as well as how developments in these areas might affect product sales. In addition, as the discerning reader may have guessed from the above, sales forecasts often serve as the basis for sales quotas. A sales representative who exceeds the quota usually receives a commission or a bonus. Consequently, some individuals may be tempted to play games with the forecast in order to discourage the firm from establishing too high a quota for the next year's performance. Finally, salespeople may not be particularly good forecasters simply because they don't have enough time to both make accurate forecasts and sell the firm's products.

Objective Methods

Two objective methods are commonly used to establish sales forecasts: the Buying Power Index and time-series analysis. Of course, each has its own advantages and disadvantages.

Buying Power Index. Each year, *Sales & Marketing Management* magazine publishes a special issue devoted to its annual survey of buying power. The magazine presents population, retail sales, and income data by region, state, Standard Metropolitan Statistical Area (SMSA), county, and city. It also presents an index of buying power for each area. The index is calculated by giving a weight of five to the area's percentage of U.S./Canadian effective buying income, a weight of three to its percentage of U.S./Canadian retail sales, and a weight of two to its percentage of U.S./Canadian population. The total of these

---

[14]Philip Kotler, *Marketing Management: Analysis, Planning, and Control* (3d ed.; Englewood Cliffs, N.J.: Prentice-Hall, Inc., 1976), p. 133.

TABLE 6-4 Data from *Sales & Marketing Management*

MICHIGAN

POPULATION—12/31/78 — RETAIL SALES BY STORE GROUP 1978

MICH. ESTIMATES

METRO AREA County / City	Total Population (Thousands)	% Of U.S.	Median Age of Pop.	18-24 Years	25-34 Years	35-49 Years	50 & Over	Households (Thousands)	Total Retail Sales ($000)	Food ($000)	Eating & Drinking Places ($000)	General Mtse. ($000)	Furniture/Furnish/Appliance ($000)	Auto-motive ($000)	Drug ($000)
ANN ARBOR	255.1	.1161	24.6	26.6	19.2	13.5	15.8	84.1	1,132,796	278,165	110,400	82,073	71,587	222,541	28,932
Washtenaw	255.1	.1161	24.6	26.6	19.2	13.5	15.8	84.1	1,132,796	278,165	110,400	82,073	71,587	222,541	28,932
• Ann Arbor	107.7	.0490	24.3	32.1	22.0	11.4	13.6	38.3	541,495	99,390	55,244	56,262	40,696	64,547	15,437
SUBURBAN TOTAL	147.4	.0671	24.9	22.6	17.2	15.0	17.5	45.8	591,301	178,775	55,156	25,811	30,891	157,994	13,495
BATTLE CREEK	182.6	.0831	30.1	12.5	15.8	16.9	25.4	63.9	593,540	136,387	63,500	62,401	23,720	149,846	20,578
Barry	42.5	.0193	30.2	11.5	16.1	16.5	25.7	14.3	64,364	19,103	5,286	2,238	2,196	17,505	2,020
Calhoun	140.1	.0638	30.1	13.5	15.6	17.0	25.4	49.6	529,176	117,284	58,214	60,163	21,524	132,341	18,558
• Battle Creek	37.0	.0168	31.8	13.7	13.8	14.5	31.1	14.8	279,430	58,856	23,070	45,838	12,485	73,633	7,683
SUBURBAN TOTAL	145.6	.0663	29.7	12.2	16.2	17.5	23.9	49.1	314,110	77,531	40,430	16,563	11,235	76,213	12,895
BAY CITY	119.9	.0545	28.6	12.3	15.9	15.9	24.0	39.2	489,192	104,907	40,910	57,071	24,455	140,778	18,079
Bay	119.9	.0545	28.6	12.2	15.9	15.9	24.0	39.2	489,192	104,907	40,910	57,071	24,455	140,778	18,079
• Bay City	48.6	.0221	30.7	13.2	13.9	14.4	29.6	17.2	234,180	46,364	17,938	27,382	12,299	67,281	10,500
SUBURBAN TOTAL	71.3	.0324	27.5	12.7	17.3	17.0	20.0	22.0	255,012	58,543	22,972	29,689	12,156	73,497	7,579

EFFECTIVE BUYING INCOME 1978

MICH. ESTIMATES

METRO AREA County / City	Total EBI ($000)	Median Hsld. EBI	(A) $8,000-$9,999	(B) $10,000-$14,999	(C) $15,000-$24,999	(D) $25,000 & Over	Buying Power Index
ANN ARBOR	2,066,319	21,077	4.2	12.4	29.8	38.7	.1367
Washtenaw	2,066,319	21,077	4.2	12.4	29.8	38.7	.1367
• Ann Arbor	945,467	20,056	4.7	13.7	27.2	37.8	.0625
SUBURBAN TOTAL	1,120,852	21,772	3.7	11.3	32.0	39.6	.0742
BATTLE CREEK	1,166,788	16,918	5.4	16.0	35.7	21.7	.0789
Barry	232,179	15,449	5.7	18.7	37.0	15.1	.0143
Calhoun	934,609	17,424	5.3	15.2	35.3	23.6	.0646
• Battle Creek	229,460	13,935	6.6	16.7	30.4	16.0	.0216
SUBURBAN TOTAL	937,328	17,663	5.0	15.7	37.4	23.4	.0573

ESTIMATES

METRO AREA County / City	Total EBI ($000)	Median Hsld. EBI	(A) $8,000-$9,999	(B) $10,000-$14,999	(C) $15,000-$24,999	(D) $25,000 & Over	Buying Power Index
BAY CITY	762,553	18,195	4.3	13.5	37.6	25.5	.0554
Bay	762,553	18,195	4.3	13.5	37.6	25.5	.0554
• Bay City	308,232	16,491	5.4	14.8	34.0	21.9	.0237
SUBURBAN TOTAL	454,321	19,407	3.4	12.4	40.5	28.3	.0317
△ BENTON HARBOR - ST. JOSEPH	1,166,947	14,285	6.4	21.1	34.2	12.6	.0872
Berrien	932,961	14,391	6.2	20.7	34.2	13.0	.0718
• Benton Harbor	67,855	11,179	6.9	20.7	26.9	7.0	.0105
• St. Joseph	83,240	15,401	6.2	18.0	31.3	20.2	.0063
Cass	233,986	13,890	7.3	22.4	34.0	10.8	.0154
SUBURBAN TOTAL	1,015,852	14,447	6.4	21.4	35.0	12.4	.0704

Source: "1979 Survey of Buying Power," *Sales & Marketing Management* (July 23, 1979), pp. C-102, C-108.

weights is then divided by ten to arrive at the Buying Power Index (BPI). Because the index is broad-based, it is primarily useful for estimating the potential for mass consumer products sold at popular prices.[15]

An example of *Sales & Marketing Management* data for selected cities in Michigan is presented in Table 6-4. Assume that you represent a firm selling toiletry products. By examining these data, you would be able to determine Ann Arbor's population (255,100) and the percentage of that population relative to the rest of the United States (0.116 percent). In addition, if your prod-

---

[15]"1979 Survey of Buying Power," *Sales & Marketing Management* (July 23, 1979), p. A-47.

ucts are sold primarily to young people, you could quickly determine that 26.6 percent of Ann Arbor's population is between 18 and 24 years of age. The data on retail sales indicates that $28,932,000 worth of drug-related products were sold in Ann Arbor in 1978. By looking at earlier issues of *Sales & Marketing Management*, you could also estimate the extent of past growth in this area. The median effective buying income (EBI) of $21,077 for Ann Arbor looks quite strong compared to Michigan's median EBI of $18,570.[16] It is interesting to note that the Buying Power Index for Ann Arbor (0.137) is higher than Ann Arbor's proportion of the nation's population, which indicates that this area represents an above-average market for your products.

The *Sales & Marketing Management* data enable the researcher to compare markets on the basis of key demographic and economic variables. In addition, the Buying Power Index indicates where sales are most likely to occur. Assume, for example, that the territory for a particular toiletry salesperson consisted of Ann Arbor, Battle Creek, and Bay City. According to Table 6-5, the salesperson could expect 50.4 percent of sales to be in Ann Arbor, 29.1 percent in Battle Creek, and 20.5 percent in Bay City. Such information is useful not only because it tells the salesperson how to apportion time, but also because it enables the salesperson to estimate the dollar sales potential of each market segment.

TABLE 6-5   Expected Percentage of Sales Based on Buying Power Index

Territory	Buying Power Index*	Expected Percentage of Sales
Ann Arbor	.1367	50.4
Battle Creek	.0789	29.1
Bay City	.0554	20.5
Total	.2710	100.0

*Taken from *Sales & Marketing Management* as shown in Table 6-4.

A word of caution is in order here: the Buying Power Index is a classic example of secondary data that are not applicable to all products. As stated above, it is best used with mass-distributed consumer products.

Time-Series Analysis. The time-series analysis method generates sales forecasts as a function of time rather than as a result of any particular market variables. *It cannot be used to forecast the sales of new products since they have no past sales history.* However, time-series analysis can be a very effective tool in forecasting the sales of existing products where the underlying demand factors are stable over time. Without these conditions, time-series analysis will produce erroneous sales forecasts. Trend, cycle, and seasonal fluctuations are three temporal components of time-series analysis. The interaction of these components may also provide more accurate forecasts for some items.

[16]*Ibid.*, p. C-110.

Trend Analysis. A trend is the result of long-term developments in basic economic factors that affect the sales of a product. When the trend is statistically significant,[17] it can become central to the sales forecast. An example would be the forecast for sales of refrigerators in the United States. Long-term trends affecting sales of refrigerators are a function of such factors as population, income, new housing starts, and the creation of families. If one assumes that these basic economic and demographic factors will continue to grow and to have the same type of impact on refrigerator sales, it is realistic to forecast sales by looking at how they relate to time. Figure 6-6(A) shows how a hypothetical trend line might look.

Cycle Analysis. The second component of time-series analysis, cycle, says that the sales of some products show a fairly constant wave-like pattern over time as shown in Figure 6-6(B). The cycle component of time-series analysis is more meaningful to many researchers when it is tied to the cyclical pattern of the economy. That is, the sales for a number of products, such as new houses, fluctuate directly with the general swing of the economy. Therefore, sales fluctuations that appear at first to be related to time may be affected more by changes in basic economic factors.

Seasonal Analysis. The sales of many products fluctuate with the seasons, as shown in Figure 6-6(C), which may be the result of temperature changes, holidays, or trade practices. For example, tennis clothes and bathing suits sell best in spring and summer; most gift items and many "luxury" items, such as small appliances, experience their greatest sales at Christmas. For many items, the time of year is a crucial component in forecasting short-run sales. Automobiles sell well in the late spring and summer when dealers make significant discounts available to customers to "make room" for new models.

Interaction of Time-Series Components. Trend, cycle, and seasonal factors interact for many items. It is the job of the marketing analyst to identify the factors and to determine their impact on the sales forecasts. To illustrate, it may be reasonable to assume in the long run that automobile sales in the United States are related to the nation's population and income growth. Therefore, if one assumes that there is no basic change either in the growth of these variables or in their relationship to automobile sales, it is possible to construct a long-term trend line from past sales data. In addition, most analysts think that automobile sales are directly related to cyclical changes in the economy. Therefore, if the economy is in a downswing, even though the sales trend is positive, the middle-term forecast might indicate that sales will begin to fall off. Finally, new car sales are related to the season of the year: they are higher in the fall and late spring than at any other time of the year. Therefore, even if the economy were sluggish, sales could be expected to rise in the spring.

---

[17]Statistically significant means that the relationship between two variables is strong enough to imply that random events probably do not explain what the researcher observes. This concept can be examined in more detail by looking at any of a number of good marketing research or statistics texts. See, for example, Eli P. Cox III, *Marketing Research Information for Decision Making* (New York: Harper & Row, Publishers, 1979).

FIGURE 6-6 Time-Series Analysis

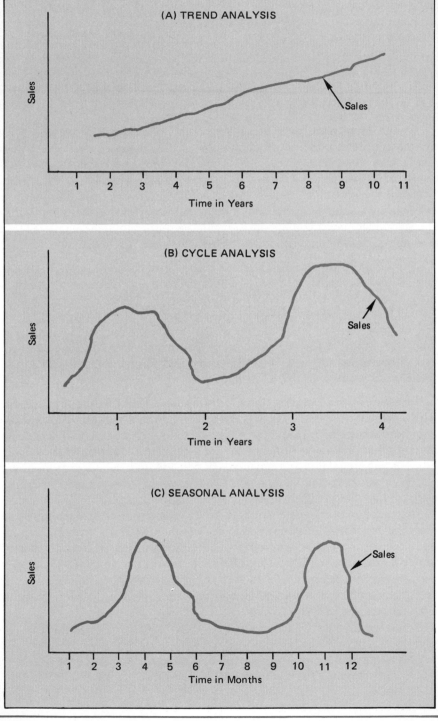

Forecasting Error

Are sales forecasts accurate? Can management depend on them? Are they useful in critical capital budgeting decisions and personnel allocations? Unfortunately, the answer to each question is only a qualified yes. The more *aggregate* the forecast, the more *accurate* the forecast. As a result, most professional economists are able to predict within one or two points the nation's gross national product (GNP) for the following year. GNP has enough components that when economists miss on the downside of one, they will probably miss on the upside of another. In other words, the errors are likely to be compensating in nature, and the overall forecast relatively accurate.

The same relationship also holds for an industry sales forecast. It is not as difficult to forecast automobile sales in general as it is to forecast how many cars Ford, in particular, will sell. Likewise, it is easier to forecast Ford's overall sales than to forecast sales of a particular model such as the Ford Thunderbird.

It is also more difficult to forecast accurately the sales of new products than to forecast the sales of established products. As we have seen, a high percentage of new products fail each year. We must remember that these are not only product failures but also forecasting failures. Before these products were introduced to the market, someone must have predicted that sales would be sufficient to justify introduction, or they would not have been introduced. Established products, on the other hand, have a history, and this history gives the analyst a much better feel for how these products will sell from one period to the next.

HOW MUCH RESEARCH?

How much research is enough? Again, there is no easy answer. It does seem apparent, however, that most successful firms today do make a consistent and substantial effort to keep themselves informed as to their customers' needs. Without this effort the commitment of the firm to the marketing concept becomes strictly a hit-or-miss proposition. Although in the short run, the firm may be lucky and sell a highly successful product, in the long run it will probably pay a heavy price for not monitoring the market.

Two factors must be considered in determining how much research the firm should undertake. These factors are time and risk. In terms of time, the marketing research department inevitably can provide better answers if it is given more time to work on a problem. The difficulty is that the longer the research effort, the greater the likelihood that competition will take advantage of the situation. This problem typically exists whenever new product market research is undertaken.

The second variable, risk, must be examined from two perspectives. The more risk the firm is undertaking, the greater the need for marketing research. However, marketing research sometimes involves significant expenditures of funds which may not be warranted. A Colorado-based electronics company is an illustration of a firm that avoided such expenditures. This company was interested in determining whether a market existed in Texas for its inexpensive calculators. Although the firm could have invested substantial time and money in a major market research effort on this problem, it chose instead to send its sales manager on a two-week "selling tour" of the state. Although the sales manager did sell a number of calculators to retailers, the firm decided that there was too much competitive pressure from Texas Instruments to warrant a major entry effort on its part.

In summary, marketing research presents a set of powerful tools which can be used in many situations to reduce decision risk. Marketing research, however, should be employed only when it can significantly reduce decision risk at a reasonable cost.

summary points

1. Marketing research is more than the "systematic gathering, recording, and analyzing of data." Marketing research personnel are also involved in identifying and defining problems as well as in solving them through research.

2. The major objective of marketing research is to reduce decision risk.

3. Marketing research activities cover numerous areas and frequently differ among consumer goods, industrial goods, and retail and wholesale firms.

4. A good working relationship must be maintained between top management and marketing research personnel.

5. The data collection process normally begins with the examination of all available secondary data.

6. Exploratory research is conducted when the researcher lacks sufficient understanding of the problem to proceed with a full-scale research project.

7. Surveys are the most flexible and, frequently, the most cost-efficient means for gathering primary market research data. In a survey, the researcher should devote considerable attention to sample selection and the type of survey instrument used.

8. Motivation research — storytelling and focus group interviews — is a useful primary data gathering technique when the research subjects are not aware of their motives or concerns in making product purchase decisions.

9. As a primary data collection technique, direct observation works well when the analyst needs to know what the research subjects do, not why they do it.

10. A controlled laboratory experiment is a primary data collection method that controls all aspects of the experiment except for the variable under study.

11. The research study results should be communicated to top management in a timely and understandable manner.

12. Test markets are used to estimate how many units of a new product the firm can expect to sell as well as to evaluate the effectiveness of a product's promotion campaign.

13. Sales forecasting techniques include opinion surveys and objective methods, such as the Buying Power Index and time-series analysis.

questions for discussion

1. In your own words, what is marketing research? Will marketing research departments be better able to meet their objectives in the future than they have been in the past? Explain.

2. Analyze the relationship that now exists between management and most marketing research departments. What can be done to improve this relationship?

3. If you were considering the construction of a shopping center, what types of available secondary data would assist you in evaluating your market?
4. What is the difference between an experience survey and a case study?
5. If you wanted to know why undergraduate students attend a college's football games, how would you go about selecting a sample?
6. In any given research study, how do you decide whether to use a mail, telephone, or personal interview survey in order to gather the necessary research data?
7. What role will laboratory experiments likely play in marketing research in the future? Explain.
8. What are the two objectives of test marketing? Is it difficult for the researcher to satisfy both of these objectives?
9. What are the key principles involved in good test marketing?
10. In terms of forecasting sales, what are the major differences between a jury of executive opinion and a composite of sales force opinions?
11. Explain how *Sales & Marketing Management's* Buying Power Index can be used to forecast sales. What are the limitations of this forecasting method?
12. Analyze the use of time-series analysis in sales forecasting. How do you combine the use of trend, cycle, and seasonal analysis into your sales forecast?
13. How should the firm determine whether it is spending enough money on marketing research?

7

Market Segmentation

All firms must formulate a strategy for approaching their markets. On the one hand, the firm may choose to provide one product to all of its customers; on the other hand, it may determine that the market is so heterogeneous that it has no choice but to divide or segment potential users into submarkets.

Segmentation is the key to the marketing strategy of many companies. **Segmentation** is a demand-oriented approach that involves modifying the firm's product and/or marketing strategies to fit the needs of individual market segments rather than those of the aggregate market. Members of each market segment are identified (1) by personal characteristics such as income, social class, and personality; (2) by product considerations such as usage rates and perceived benefits; or (3) by geographic location.[1] We begin our discussion of market segmentation by looking at the reasons for its development.

EMERGENCE OF MARKET SEGMENTATION

Only 15 to 20 years ago, relatively few firms used market segmentation. When they did, it was likely to be a rather haphazard effort rather than a scientific analysis of the market. During the last two decades, however, market segmentation has gained both respect and technical sophistication as an important marketing strategy.

Rationale for Market Segmentation

There are three reasons why firms use market segmentation: (1) because some markets are heterogeneous; (2) because market segments respond differently to different promotional appeals; and (3) because market segmentation is consistent with the marketing concept.

Heterogeneous Markets. Theoretically, a market can be subdivided into as many segments as there are people in the market who make purchase deci-

---

[1]The classic article dealing with market segmentation is Wendell R. Smith, "Product Differentiation and Market Segmentation as Alternative Marketing Strategies," *Journal of Marketing* (July, 1956), pp. 3–8.

sions. Although this extreme form of segmentation may work well when each product is made by hand on request from the purchaser, such as with custom-made clothes, it is not applicable when the item is mass-produced. Modern business managers realize, however, that under normal circumstances they cannot attract all of the firm's potential customers to one product — different buyers simply have different needs and wants. To accommodate this heterogeneity, the seller must provide different products. The seller's goal is to locate and cultivate those market segments that are large enough to be served profitably.

FIGURE 7-1   Products of the Coca-Cola Company

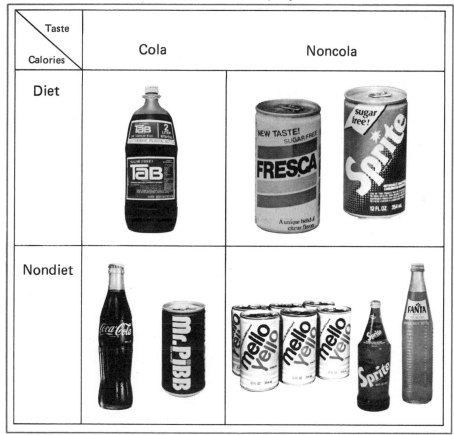

The Coca-Cola Company is an example of a firm that was forced to switch from selling only one product to the entire market to selling several products to distinct market segments. Until 1960, the Coca-Cola Company produced only one soft drink, Coke. As a result, the company had to convince the entire soft drink market, made up of people with a great variety of taste and calorie interests, that Coke was the best drink for everyone. Today, however, Coca-Cola has actively adopted market segmentation. As Figure 7-1 indicates, it produces a variety of products in addition to its traditional nondiet cola drink. These products can be described on two dimensions: flavor and number of calories.

Varied Promotional Appeals. A strategy of market segmentation does *not* necessarily mean that the firm must produce different products for each market segment. If certain promotional appeals are likely to affect each market segment differently, the firm may decide to build flexibility into its promotional strategy rather than to expand its product line. For example, many political candidates have tried to sell themselves to the electorate by emphasizing one message to labor, another to business, and a third to farmers.

As another example, the Sheraton Palace Hotel in San Francisco serves four distinct market segments: conventioneers, business people, tourists traveling with an organized tour, and tourists traveling by themselves. Each group has different reasons for using the hotel. Consequently, Sheraton uses different media and different messages to communicate with the various segments. The *Wall Street Journal, Forbes,* and *Business Week* reach the business traveler, but not the other segments. Similarly, the business traveler is interested in the proximity of the hotel to major business centers, whereas other segments are more concerned with cost, the number of rooms, or proximity to sightseeing activities. Although most rooms in the Sheraton are very much the same, the

FIGURE 7-2 Ads Illustrating the Market Segments for the Sheraton Palace Hotel

Purpose of Traveler	Vehicle	Message
Conventions	National Sheraton sales organization	Adequacy and price of meeting facilities, competitive room rates.
Business	*Wall Street Journal, Forbes,* and *Business Week*	Convenient location to centers, convenient on-premise restaurants.
Pleasure, tour	Travel agents, airline charters, fraternal organizations	Large number of rooms at reasonable prices, hotel located near sightseeing attractions.
Pleasure, nontour	Local newspapers, Sheraton reservation system, travel agents	Free parking, color television, convenient to sightseeing attractions.

hotel effectively practices market segmentation through its promotional campaign. Figure 7-2 illustrates four advertising messages, each one directed to one of Sheraton's markets.

Consistency with the Marketing Concept. A third reason for using market segmentation is that it is consistent with the marketing concept. Market segmentation recognizes the existence of distinct market groups, each with a distinct set of needs. Through segmentation, the firm directs its product and promotional efforts at those markets that will benefit most from or that will get the greatest enjoyment from its merchandise. This is the heart of the marketing concept.

Historical Forces Behind the Rise of Market Segmentation

Over the years, market segmentation has become an increasingly popular strategic technique as more and more firms have adopted the marketing concept. Other historical forces behind the rise of market segmentation include new economies of scale, increased education and affluence, greater competition, and the advent of new segmentation technology.[2]

Economies of Scale. The market for many products is so large that achieving production economies of scale is no longer considered a problem. As a result, many firms are able to tailor their products to several large market segments without losing production economies, i.e., they can still achieve a low unit cost. In addition, new production and scheduling technologies have enabled manufacturers to achieve economies of scale with fewer total units. For example, many automobile production facilities can now custom build cars economically by combining a large number of options.

Education and Affluence. Increased education and affluence in the United States have both encouraged product diversity and, therefore, market segmentation. As people become better educated, their interests broaden; as they become more affluent, they are able to buy more expensive goods designed specifically to fit their changing needs. This pattern is evidenced by the greater interest in labor-saving devices (e.g., microwave ovens, food processors, frost-free refrigerators), leisure-time products, and variety for its own sake.

Competition. Increased competition both at home and abroad have led many U.S. companies to adopt market segmentation strategies. When a firm faces little competition in a particular product class, it is almost in a position to ignore the needs of the buying public. However, as new firms enter the market with their own products, the original manufacturer must pay greater attention to the needs of prospective customers if it hopes to maintain dominance in the market. The result is often a redefinition of the market into subunits, each with a slightly different need for the product in question.

Segmentation Research. Two areas of social science research have also stimulated market segmentation. On the one hand, behavioral scientists have performed a remarkable amount of excellent research on the activities and attitudes of specific groups in society. This is exemplified by W. Lloyd Warner's classic, *Social Class in America*.[3] Warner segmented U.S. society into six social classes, each with unique communication and buying behavior. This type of research has proven invaluable for market segmentation. On the other hand, the advent of computers and related software packages have made it easier for the researcher to deal with large quantities of data. Although many of the algorithms used in today's research have been understood for years, it was

---

[2]Ronald E. Frank, William F. Massy, and Yoram Wind, *Market Segmentation* (Englewood Cliffs, N.J.: Prentice-Hall, Inc., 1972), pp. 4–5.

[3]W. Lloyd Warner, *et al., Social Class in America* (Chicago: Science Research Associates, 1949).

difficult to use them effectively in marketing prior to the development of the computer.[4]

Benefits of Market Segmentation

Market segmentation offers several benefits to the marketing manager. Since a segmentation strategy must be based on a thorough study of the market, it becomes a tool for appraising competitive strengths and vulnerabilities, for planning the firm's product line, for determining its advertising and sales strategies, and for setting specific marketing objectives against which performance can be measured. Specifically, segmentation analysis helps the marketing manager:

1. To design product lines that are consistent with the demands of the market and that do not ignore important segments.
2. To spot the first signs of major trends in rapidly changing markets.
3. To direct the appropriate promotional attention and funds to the most profitable market segments.
4. To determine the appeals that will be most effective with each market segment.
5. To select the advertising media that best matches the communication patterns of each market segment.
6. To modify the timing of advertising and other promotional efforts so that they coincide with the periods of greatest market response.[5]

Since these advantages hold for most commercial and industrial products as well as for consumer goods, market segmentation is clearly beneficial to most firms.

SEGMENTATION AND THE PLANNING PROCESS

The firm's segmentation strategy is a critical input to its overall marketing strategy. Unless the firm has identified the distinctive characteristics of its markets, the rest of its efforts will be wasted. To understand the role of segmentation in the planning process, we now look at the resources required for a successful segmentation strategy as well as at how a firm develops a segmentation strategy.

Resources Required for Market Segmentation

As mentioned above, a strategy of market segmentation offers a number of benefits, but like most marketing strategies, it also involves certain costs. At times, these costs outweigh the benefits, making segmentation impractical for the firm. Let us look at five of these costs from the perspective of what they really represent — the expenditure of the firm's limited capital and human resources.

---

[4]These are often referred to as "canned" computer programs. An excellent example of such packages can be found in Norman H. Nie, C. Hadlai Hull, Jean G. Jenkins, Karin Steinbrenner, and Dale H. Bent, *Statistical Package for the Social Sciences* (2d ed.; New York: McGraw-Hill Book Co., 1975).

[5]Daniel Yankelovich, "New Criteria for Market Segmentation," *Harvard Business Review* (March–April, 1964), pp. 83–84.

Product Costs. Often, the firm must design a specific product to accommodate each market segment. In some situations, the design effort may involve little more than a label change; in others, it may require a complete rethinking of the product for each market. When research and design personnel spend their time designing separate products for each market segment, they have less time available for developing the new products that are essential for the firm's long-term growth and success.

Production Costs. The firm must achieve sufficient sales volume in each market segment if it is to justify the costs involved in separate production runs. While technological breakthroughs have enabled firms to reduce the number of units needed to achieve economies of scale, production expenditures are still a problem for many companies. To illustrate, if total sales in each segment are not sufficient to keep production lines operating continuously, the firm may be forced to stop production periodically or to shift the line over to the production of products for other market segments. Either of these actions can be quite expensive.

Promotion Costs. In most instances, the organization develops a promotion strategy to fit each market segment. Multiple strategies often require large expenditures of both human and financial resources to prepare the different advertisements and to place them in the various media. In addition, since the firm must run several different advertisements rather than one basic ad for the entire market, it cannot take full advantage of quantity discounts. The result is much higher promotion costs. This problem will be discussed in more detail in Chapter 10.

Inventory Costs. The more market segments the firm attempts to serve, the larger its inventory costs will be. This pattern occurs for two reasons. First, with a larger selection of products, the firm must maintain more records concerning location and quantity of merchandise. Secondly, the company must maintain increased base stock for normal demand and increased safety stock for unpredicted levels of demand. The more products the firm carries, the more safety stock it must have in the system. With inventory costs around 20 to 30 percent of average annual inventory value, holding additional safety stock becomes very expensive. Base and safety stock will be discussed in greater detail in Chapter 17.

Marketing Management Costs. The last, and in some ways the most important cost, is the large amount of management time that a market segmentation strategy requires. For each of its markets, the firm must design a coordinated marketing strategy — that is, it must determine how much to charge for the product, how the product should be promoted, and where it should be sold. Many firms employ a "product" or "market" manager whose sole responsibility is to coordinate the organization's efforts for the various markets for each product. Regardless of the style of management involved, the more segments the firm tries to reach, the more its managerial resources must be devoted to developing and monitoring segmentation strategies.

Segmentation — The Strategic Input

Market segmentation is a key input in the firm's marketing planning process. The firm cannot decide how to market its products until it has clearly defined its respective market segments. Figure 7-3 illustrates this relationship. After the firm defines its strategy and identifies its resources, it performs seg-

FIGURE 7-3 Segmentation and the Planning Process

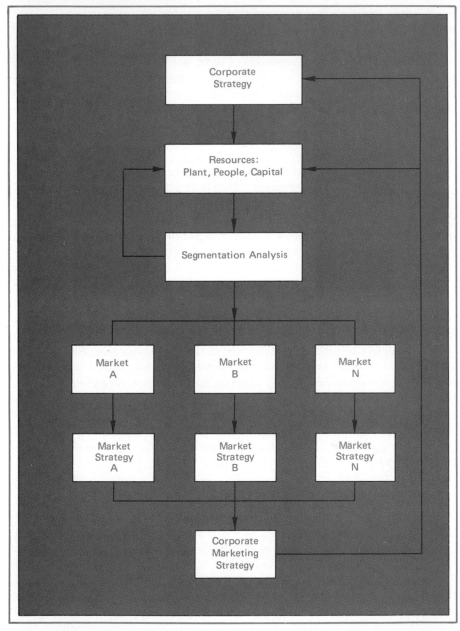

mentation analysis to determine the size and characteristics of the various customer market segments.[6] This step, in turn, leads to the development of a marketing strategy for each of the segments on which the organization chooses to focus. These strategies may include making adjustments in the physical nature of the product as well as in its price, distribution network, or promotional campaign.

As shown in Figure 7-3, the segmentation and planning process involves several feedback loops. Once the marketing strategy has been developed, it is checked for consistency with the firm's overall strategy as well as with its available resources. If the planning process follows the flow of events illustrated in Figure 7-3, there should be no major inconsistency at this point. The most important feedback loop is between "segmentation analysis" and "resources." In other words, the firm, on the basis of a market analysis, may decide that two or more distinct market segments do exist, but limited resources may prevent it from entering each individually.

Sunbeam Corporation's decision to enter the microwave oven market provides a good illustration of the planning process involving resources and segments. Sunbeam, the world's largest producer of small kitchen appliances, was a late entrant into the microwave oven market. Sunbeam delayed entry not because it did not have the technology to produce microwave ovens, but because more than 65 percent of microwave ovens are sold through television and furniture stores or through department stores that have major-appliance departments. Sunbeam did not have the sales force (i.e., people resources) to cover these outlets. When Sunbeam finally did make the decision to enter this market, it created a special sales force.[7]

BASES FOR MARKET SEGMENTATION

Unfortunately, there is no one best way to segment markets. This fact has caused a great deal of frustration for some marketing executives who insist that a segmentation variable that has proven effective in one market/product context should be equally effective in other situations. The truth is that a variable such as social class may describe the types of people who shop in particular stores, but prove useless in defining the market for a particular product. Therefore, in using a segmentation strategy, marketing managers should examine a variety of segmentation criteria in order to identify those that will be most effective in defining their markets.[8] Six important criteria for segmenting markets include: demographics, product benefits, psychological and attitudinal variables, life-style, geography, and usage rate.

---

[6]Strategy development was discussed in some detail in Chapter 2.

[7]*Sales & Marketing Management* (December 12, 1977), pp. 18–19.

[8]Three excellent articles that deal with the problems of selecting segmentation criteria are: Steven C. Brandt, "Dissecting the Segmentation Syndrome," *Journal of Marketing* (October, 1966), pp. 22–27; Robert D. Hisrich and Michael P. Peters, "Selecting the Superior Segmentation Correlate," *Journal of Marketing* (July, 1974), pp. 60–63; and Nariman K. Dhalla and Winston H. Mahatoo, "Expanding the Scope of Segmentation Research," *Journal of Marketing* (April, 1976), pp. 34–41.

Demographic Segmentation

Demographics is the most commonly used basis for market segmentation. Demographic variables are relatively easy to understand and measure, and they have proven to be excellent segmentation criteria for many markets. Information in several demographic categories is particularly useful to marketers.

Income. Average buyer income has long been considered a good variable for segmenting markets. Wealthy people, for example, are more likely to buy expensive clothes, to live in large houses, and to take expensive vacations. This trend was first formally recognized by Ernest Engel in 1857. Engel, a German statistician, compared the budgets of working class families. He found that as a family's income increased:

1. The percentage of its income spent on food decreased.
2. The percentage of its income spent on housing and household operations remained approximately constant.
3. The percentage of its income spent on other categories — such as clothing, transportation, and health products and services — increased.

More recent studies have found Engel's results to be applicable to the modern U.S. economy as well. In addition, income has been shown to be an excellent segmentation correlate for an even wider range of commonly purchased products, including household toiletries, paper and plastic items, frozen foods, pet foods, furniture, children's wear, and women's wear.[9]

Social Class. Proponents of social class as a segmentation variable believe that as the income of some blue-collar workers approaches or even exceeds the income of many middle-level white-collar workers, income becomes less effective in delineating markets. Some suggest that the life style of a plumber who earns $25,000 per year differs dramatically from that of an engineer earning the same amount.

A classic study on social class and consumption behavior was reported by Pierre Martineau in the late 1950s.[10] You will recall from Chapter 4 that Martineau found that the perceived social status of a store was the primary basis for its selection by the shopper. Similarly, in the area of communication skills, he found that the sophisticated advertisements appearing in such magazines as *The New Yorker* and *Esquire* were almost meaningless to lower-class people. This group, however, was very receptive to appeals by self-made business people who did their own commercials.

Martineau's work has been supported by two subsequent studies. The first study found that as social class rises, so does the importance of fashion as well as the frequency of shopping.[11] The second study showed that members of the

---

[9]See James H. Myers, Roger R. Stanton, and Arne F. Haug, "Correlates of Buying Behavior: Social Class vs. Income," *Journal of Marketing* (October, 1971), pp. 8–15; and James H. Myers and John F. Mount, "More on Social Class vs. Income as Correlates of Buying Behavior," *Journal of Marketing* (April, 1973), pp. 71–73.

[10]Pierre Martineau, "Social Class and Spending Behavior," *Journal of Marketing* (October, 1958), pp. 121–130.

[11]Stuart U. Rich and Subhash C. Jain, "Social Class and Life Cycle as Predictors of Shopping Behavior," *Journal of Marketing Research* (February, 1968), pp. 41–49.

different social classes vary dramatically in their use of bank credit cards. People in lower social classes tend to use bank credit cards as installment loans, while those in higher social classes use them for convenience purposes.[12] These differences in behavior can be significant when segmenting a market and developing a marketing program to serve each segment.

Ethnic and Racial Backgrounds. Ethnic and racial factors have been effectively used as a basis for segmenting markets. Although the U.S. is known as a great melting pot, certain groups have not been assimilated into society as quickly as others. In these situations, it has proven beneficial for firms to modify their product and promotion mix to fit the specific ethnic market. A good example is the Coke advertisement presented in Figure 7-4. The Coca-Cola Company advertises its products to young and old alike, as well as to specific ethnic groups. Another example is the HEB supermarket chain that operates throughout Texas. Many of HEB's stores in northern and central Texas have taken on a rather sophisticated appearance, as is evident in their selection of specialty foods as well as in the tone of their promotional efforts. In contrast, in south Texas where 20 counties are more than 90 percent Mexican-American, HEB stocks a wide variety of Mexican food products, including tamale wraps, chiles, jalapenos, tortillas, masa harina, and beans. In addition, many of its local television advertisements are in Spanish.

Ethnic segmentation is practiced in many other areas of the country as well. New York City, for example, has enough Hispanic residents to support several Spanish-language daily newspapers. New York also has more Jewish residents than Israel, while San Francisco has an almost independent colony of people of Chinese descent. Such groups offer very real opportunities to marketers who are aware of the differences in buyer behavior of various ethnic and racial groups.

Age. Market segments based on age are also important to many business people. Some aspects of age as a segmentation variable are quite obvious. For example, children constitute the primary market for toys, and people 65 years and older are major users of medical services and prescription drugs. Other aspects are not so apparent, however. In appealing to teenagers, for example, the marketing executive must continually monitor their *ever-changing* beliefs, mores, and political and social attitudes, as well as the entertainers and clothing that are most popular with young people at a particular time. Such factors are important in developing effective advertising copy and illustrations for a product directed to the youth market.

The marketing manager must also remember that age is a dynamic variable. Products that have been successfully marketed to one age group, for example, must be continually sold to people entering that age group. When Procter & Gamble introduced Head & Shoulders shampoo, it made a major effort to attract the teenage market. Because the product was initially very successful, P&G stopped its sample and trial-purchase programs, which led to sales decline. Why? Because the youth market is a perpetually new market; the stream of new consumers learned of the product primarily through Procter &

[12]H. Lee Mathews and John W. Slocum, Jr., "Social Class and Commercial Bank Credit Card Usage," *Journal of Marketing* (January, 1969), pp. 71–78.

FIGURE 7-4 An Advertisement for Coca-Cola

Courtesy: The Coca-Cola Company

Gamble's advertising program.[13] This same problem develops for any product designed to capture the attention of a particular age group.

Finally, the marketing manager must consider both the distribution and the location of age groups. Table 7-1 shows that the United States is characterized by an increasingly older population. In 1980, more than 16 percent of the population was between 25 and 34 years of age — an increase of more than 4

[13]George W. Schiele, "How to Reach the Young Consumer," *Harvard Business Review* (March–April, 1974), p. 82.

TABLE 7-1   Age Distribution of the U.S. Population, 1960–1990

Age Group	Percentage of Population in Each Age Group			
	1960	1970	1980*	1990*
Under 5 years	11.3%	8.4%	9.0%	8.3%
5–9	10.4	9.7	8.3	8.6
10–14	9.4	10.2	7.7	8.3
15–19	7.4	9.4	8.8	7.7
20–24	6.2	8.4	9.2	7.1
25–34	12.7	12.3	16.4	16.5
35–44	13.4	11.3	11.1	14.1
45–54	11.4	11.4	9.9	9.8
55–64	8.6	9.1	9.2	8.6
65 and over	9.2	9.8	10.4	11.0
Total	100.0%	100.0%	100.0%	100.0%
Total (thousands of people)	180,667	204,800	227,765	251,431

*Projected.

Source: U.S. Department of Commerce, Bureau of the Census, *Statistical Abstract of the United States* (Washington, D.C.: U.S. Government Printing Office, 1974), pp. 6–7.

percent from 1970. By 1990, projections suggest that 14.1 percent of the population will be between 35 and 44, with 11 percent over 65. The increasing average age is a result of the nation's declining birth rate and better medical care. In terms of the distribution of the population, Figure 7-5 shows that Alaska, Hawaii, and Virginia have relatively few older people, while Florida and Missouri have disproportionately large populations of older people. The extreme case is the city of Miami Beach, Florida, where almost half of the population is over the age of 65.

Stage in the Family Life Cycle. Although age has been shown to be an effective tool in segmenting markets, stage in the family life cycle — which combines the characteristics of age, marital status, presence and age of children, and survivor status of spouse — may be a richer variable for explaining family purchasing behavior. One reason is that changes in behavior may be associated less with the biological process of aging than with the individual's family situation.[14] For example, a 25-year-old bachelor will probably enjoy different activities and purchase different products than a married man of the same age. The purchase behavior of these two individuals will vary dramatically if the married man also has three children.

Although several schemes for describing the family life cycle have been developed, we recommend the one presented in Figure 7-6. Here the family life cycle classifications are illustrated along with the corresponding changes that take place over time both in the family's financial position and in its purchase decisions.

[14]John B. Lansing and Leslie Kish, "Family Life Cycle as an Indendent Variable," *American Sociological Review* (October, 1957), pp. 512–519.

FIGURE 7-5   Location, by State, of People Age 65 and Older

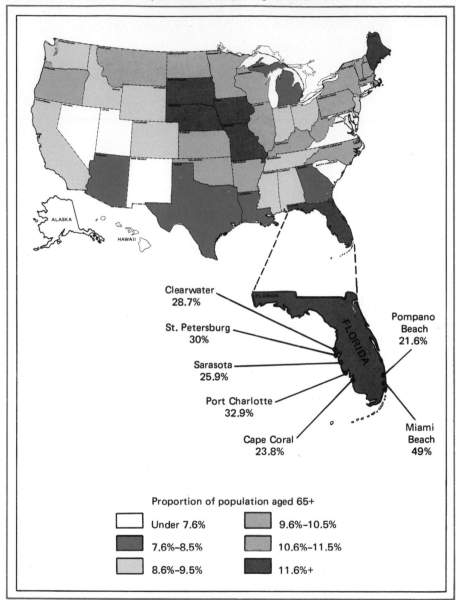

Source: Reproduced by permission from "The Power of the Aging in the Marketplace," *Business Week* (November 21, 1971), p. 57.

Benefit Segmentation

The assumption underlying **benefit segmentation** is that markets can be defined on the basis of the benefits that people seek from the product. Although research indicates that most people would like to receive as many benefits as possible from a product, it has also been shown that the relative

FIGURE 7-6 Stages in the Family Life Cycle

Bachelor Stage: Young, Single, Not Living at Home	Newly Married Couples: Young, No Children	Full Nest I: Youngest Child under 6	Full Nest II: Youngest Child 6 or over 6	Full Nest III: Older Married Couples with Dependent Children	Empty Nest I: Older Married Couples, No Children Living with Them, Head in Labor Force	Empty Nest II: Older Married Couples, No Children Living at Home, Head Retired	Solitary Survivor, in Labor Force	Solitary Survivor, Retired
Few financial burdens. Fashion opinion leaders. Recreation oriented. Buy: Basic kitchen equipment, basic furniture, cars, vacations	Better off financially than they will be in near future. Highest purchase rate and highest average purchase of durables. Buy: Cars, refrigerators, stoves, sensible and durable furniture, vacations	Home purchasing at peak. Liquid assets low. Dissatisfied with financial position and amount of money saved. Interested in new products. Like advertised products. Buy: Washers, dryers, TV, baby food, chest rubs and cough medicine, vitamins, dolls, wagons, sleds, skates	Financial position better. Some wives work. Less influenced by advertising. Buy larger-sized packages, multiple-unit deals. Buy: Many foods, cleaning materials, bicycles, music lessons, pianos	Financial position still better. More wives work. Some children get jobs. Hard to influence with advertising. High average purchase of durables. Buy: New, more tasteful furniture, auto travel, nonnecessary appliances, boats, dental services, magazines	Home ownership at peak. Most satisfied with financial position and money saved. Interested in travel, recreation, self-education. Make gifts and contributions. Not interested in new products. Buy: Vacations, luxuries, home improvements	Drastic cut in income. Keep home. Buy: Medical appliances, medical care, products that aid health, sleep, and digestion	Income still good but likely to sell home	Same medical and product needs as other retired group; drastic cut in income. Special need for attention, affection, and security

Source: William D. Wells and George Gubar, "The Life Cycle Concept in Marketing Research," *Journal of Marketing Research* (November, 1966), p. 362.

importance that people attach to particular benefits varies substantially.[15] These differences can then be used to segment markets.

Once the key benefits for a particular product/market situation are determined, the analyst must compare each benefit segment with the rest of the market to determine whether that segment has unique and identifiable demographic characteristics, consumption patterns, or media habits. Toothpaste provides an interesting example of benefit segmentation.

Illustration: The Toothpaste Market. The market for toothpaste can be segmented in terms of four distinct product benefits: flavor and product appearance, brightness of teeth, decay prevention, and price. As Figure 7-7 illustrates, it is also possible to identify four key variables that describe each segment. For example, people concerned about the brightness of their teeth tend to be young, usually in their teens. In addition, a large number of individuals in this segment are smokers concerned about cigarette stains. Members of this segment tend to be more "sociable" than consumers in other segments; they normally purchase products such as Gleem, Macleans, or Ultra Brite. This type of information is very useful in planning a marketing campaign. If we were to introduce a new product for the brightness market, our advertising should emphasize the social success bestowed on the user by the product. The media selected should attract teens and young people.

Advantages of Benefit Segmentation. The major advantage of benefit segmentation is that it is designed to fit the precise needs of the market. Rather than trying to create markets, the firm identifies the benefit or set of benefits that prospective customers want from their purchases and then designs products and promotional strategies to meet those needs. A second and related advantage is that benefit segmentation helps the firm avoid cannibalizing its existing products when it introduces new ones. When Procter & Gamble introduced Ivory Snow, it inadvertently reduced the share of the market held by Ivory Flakes. Both products, it turned out, were competing for the same basic market segment. This situation might have been avoided if Procter & Gamble had more carefully examined the benefits consumers derived from Ivory Flakes and the benefits they could expect to derive from Ivory Snow.[16]

Psychological and Attitudinal Segmentation

In the early 1970s, marketing practitioners began using psychological profiles to segment markets. It seemed only reasonable to assume that if one learned the attitudinal construct of a particular market segment, then identifying products and promotional strategies that would appeal to that segment would be relatively easy. If a particular group of customers could be described as "conservative," the company could promote its products to these individuals on the basis of the firm's "long-standing reputation." Likewise, a market segment that was "anti-big business" might be approached on the theme that the seller's relatively small size enabled it to pay greater attention to each customer's problems.

---

[15]Russell I. Haley, "Benefit Segmentation: A Decision-Oriented Research Tool," *Journal of Marketing* (July, 1968), pp. 30–35.

[16]Haley, *op. cit.*, p. 34.

FIGURE 7-7 Market Segments for Toothpaste

Segment Names	Principal Benefit Sought	Demographic Strengths	Special Behavioral Characteristics	Personality Characteristics	Brands Disproportionately Favored
The Sensory Segment	Flavor, product appearance	Children	Users of Spearmint-flavored toothpaste	High self-involvement	Colgate, Stripe
The Sociables	Brightness of teeth	Teens, young people	Smokers	High sociability	Gleem, Ultra Brite
The Worriers	Decay prevention	Large families	Heavy users	High hypochondriasis	Crest
The Independent Segment	Price	Men	Heavy users	High autonomy	Brands on sale

Source: Adapted from Russell I. Haley, "Benefit Segmentation: A Decision-Oriented Research Tool," *Journal of Marketing* (July, 1968), p. 33.

Mixed Results. Based on research evidence, psychological and attitudinal variables appear to have been only partially successful in defining markets. The most famous study in this area was conducted by Franklin B. Evans.[17] Evans used the Edwards Personal Preference Schedule, which consists of 11 psychological variables, to test for significant psychological differences between Chevrolet owners and Ford owners. Although these variables permitted him to correctly predict whether an individual would own a Ford or a Chevrolet in 61 percent of the cases, demographic data alone led to a 70 percent correct prediction rate. As a result, Evans concluded that personality variables were not a very powerful tool for predicting automobile ownership. In the same vein, Harold H. Kassarjian concluded, after reviewing more than 120 studies of personality and buying behavior, that "a few studies indicate a strong relationship between personality and consumer behavior, few indicate no relationship, and the great majority indicate that if correlations do exist they are so weak as to be questionable or perhaps meaningless."[18]

Possible Improvements. Why have personality and attitudinal variables failed to live up to their potential as segmentation correlates? The answer lies in the fact that the personality measures used in the tests were designed to measure generalized personality traits that may have little or no relationship to market behavior. To use this criterion effectively, therefore, marketers must develop personality measures that are situation-specific. To illustrate, rather than looking for a general trait of self-confidence, the marketer should measure the self-confidence of the consumer in evaluating different brands within a product category. Similarly, anxiety as measured by most personality tests is of little help in segmentation research, whereas anxiety as related to the physical or social risks involved in the purchase of a particular brand has significant implications for the marketing executive. Until sufficient research has been conducted to develop personality and other variables that are specific to market situations, there is little reason to believe in the effectiveness of such criteria for most segmentation problems.[19]

Life-Style Segmentation

Life-style segmentation is a relatively new technique that involves looking at the customer as a "whole" person rather than as a set of isolated parts. It attempts to classify people into segments on the basis of a broad set of criteria.[20]

Life-Style Dimensions. The most widely used life-style dimensions in market segmentation are an individual's activities, interests, opinions, and demographic characteristics. Individuals are analyzed in terms of (1) how they spend

---

[17]Franklin B. Evans, "Ford vs. Chevrolet: Park Forest Revisited," *Journal of Business* (October, 1968), pp. 445–455.

[18]As reported in Robert D. Buzzell, Robert E. M. Nourse, John B. Matthews, Jr., and Theodore Levitt, *Marketing: A Contemporary Analysis* (2d ed.; New York: McGraw-Hill Book Co., 1972), p. 142.

[19]Nariman K. Dhalla and Winston H. Mahatoo, "Expanding the Scope of Segmentation Research," *Journal of Marketing* (April, 1976), p. 37.

[20]This section is based primarily on Joseph T. Plummer, "The Concept and Application of Life-Style Segmentation," *Journal of Marketing* (January, 1974), pp. 35–37.

FIGURE 7-8   Life-Style Dimensions

Activities	Interests	Opinions	Demographics
Work	Family	Themselves	Age
Hobbies	Home	Social issues	Education
Social events	Job	Politics	Income
Vacation	Community	Business	Occupation
Entertainment	Recreation	Economics	Family size
Club membership	Fashion	Education	Dwelling
Community	Food	Products	Geography
Shopping	Media	Future	City size
Sports	Achievements	Culture	Stage in life cycle

Source: Joseph T. Plummer, "The Concept and Application of Life-Style Segmentation," [*Journal of Marketing*, (January, 1974), p. 34.]

their time, (2) what areas of interest they see as most important, (3) their opinions of themselves and of the environment around them, and (4) basic demographics such as income, social class, and education. Figure 7-8 presents a partial list of life-style dimensions.

The first step in life-style segmentation is to determine a basis for defining the market. In most instances, life-style research is used to examine the differences among heavy users, light users, and non-users of a particular product or service. Other useful criteria include brand usage rates and even product attitude data. Once the target segments have been determined, life-style research can be used to describe the target customers in depth. This description assists the firm in determining its communication strategy as well as in deciding how to position the product in order to maximize its sales potential. If, for example, research indicates that members of the target group feel a strong need to be with other people, the product advertisements might picture a variety of social settings showing how the product helps satisfy that need.

Illustration: Bank Credit Cards. In a 1974 life-style segmentation study, male users of bank credit cards were found to have a life-style differentiating them significantly from men who do not use bank cards. Bank card users tend to perceive themselves as socially active and urbane and as belonging to an upper socioeconomic class in terms of income, position, and education. You can picture the male bank credit card user arriving home from a busy day at the office, enjoying a cocktail and a pleasant meal, and then rushing off to some civic activity. This image derives from the fact that the credit card user tends to agree with the following statements much more than do non-users:

1. I would rather live in or near a big city than in or near a small town.
2. I often have a cocktail before dinner.
3. I enjoy going to concerts.
4. I like to think I am a bit of a swinger.
5. I expect to be a top executive within ten years.
6. I spend too much time on the telephone.
7. I buy at least two suits a year.
8. I usually dress for fashion, not for comfort.

The life-style of the female bank credit card user is consistent with that of the male. She tends to be an active individual of relatively high socioeconomic status, who belongs to many social organizations and who is concerned with her appearance. Interestingly, she apparently tends to fantasize more than women who do not use bank credit cards. This is evident in her agreement with such statements as:

1. I would like to spend a year in London or Paris.
2. I would like to own and fly my own airplane.
3. I would like to become an actress.

This type of input gives marketing and advertising executives a great deal of useful information for selecting promotional appeals and advertising media. Although this approach may be faulted because it is based primarily on perceived or anticipated behavior rather than on actual behavior, advertising messages frequently appeal to what people *want* to happen rather than what really happens or is likely to happen. Consequently, life-style segmentation analysis can be a useful approach in many situations.

Geographic Segmentation

Geographic considerations are useful in segmenting many markets. Since the role of geography varies somewhat between consumer and industrial markets, we will analyze the two separately.

Consumer Markets. People from different areas may demand different types of products to fulfill the same basic need. In some situations, such differences in preference are the result of basic climatic differences; in others, the result of differing traditions and cultures. Surprisingly, for example, the demand for coffee varies across the United States. Industry research indicates that while instant coffee accounts for almost 30 percent of the total coffee market in the United States, it represents 39 percent of the market in the East and only 19 percent of the market in the West. In addition, people in the West drink their coffee much stronger. Use is typically 50–60 cups per pound of ground coffee in the West and 60–70 cups per pound in the East. Overlooking such geographic idiosyncrasies can mean the difference between profit and loss.

Industrial Markets. Industrial markets in the United States are much more concentrated than consumer markets. Massachusetts, Connecticut, New York, New Jersey, Illinois, Ohio, Michigan, and Pennyslvania contain a disproportionately large percentage of the industrial market. Firms selling to industrial markets, therefore, are in a better position than consumer goods companies to concentrate their sales staffs in a few specific geographic areas for maximum impact on sales. The automobile industry, for example, is headquartered in Detroit, while the textile industry is centered in New York and North Carolina.

Segmentation by Consumption: Heavy vs. Light Users

There is a principle in marketing which states that 20 percent of a firm's customers account for 80 percent of its sales. Although this relationship does not always hold true, it seems inevitable that a small percentage of a firm's customers will purchase the majority of its merchandise. Many salespeople for industrial product companies concentrate their efforts only on one or two customers. In these situations, the salesperson almost becomes an external consultant to the customer firm, knowing the product and service needs of the firm, when orders will be placed, and who in the firm makes the purchase decision. Thus, the firm is able to specialize its offerings to the needs of the largest and most important customers.

One difficulty with such a market segmentation strategy is that current light users are left to fend for themselves. Although this strategy may appear wise in the short run, the seller may lose potential market opportunities as the light users expand or develop new applications for the merchandise. Even taking this problem into consideration, however, it is difficult to justify why the seller should not spend most of its time and effort on the best customers.

ALTERNATIVES TO MARKET SEGMENTATION

Although market segmentation is undoubtedly an important and, in many cases, the only marketing strategy available to the firm, there are some alternative marketing strategies that are also useful in specific situations.[21]

Undifferentiated Marketing

Undifferentiated marketing treats the market as an aggregate and focuses on what consumers have in common rather than on what makes them different. When pursuing a strategy of undifferentiated marketing, the firm ignores the possible existence of viable market segments. Undifferentiated marketing relies on large advertising expenditures to convince the market of the merits of the product in question. An excellent example of a consumer product sold via undifferentiated marketing is Prestone Antifreeze. Prestone's advertising and promotion concentrates on the universal need of automobile owners to prevent engines from freezing in the winter and boiling over in the summer. Prestone knows that nothing would be gained by trying to market the product to different income, geographic, or life-style segments of the market. In other words, a differentiated strategy would be inappropriate.

Concentrated Marketing

With a strategy of market segmentation or undifferentiated marketing, the firm strives for as large a piece of the total market as possible; with **concentrated marketing** on the other hand, the firm aims at only a portion of the market. In essence, it selects one segment of the market and concentrates its efforts on that particular group of customers. Often a firm can compete very effectively in one segment because of production, promotion, and distribution economies that result from such specialization. In addition, the firm normally develops a better understanding of the needs of its particular market segment than do firms competing in many market segments. There are numerous illustrations of firms that have adopted a strategy of concentrated marketing. For

---

[21]The following sections are based on Philip Kotler, *Marketing Management: Analysis, Planning, and Control* (3d ed.; Englewood Cliffs, N.J.: Prentice-Hall, Inc., 1976), pp. 151–155.

Colleges and universities with major athletic programs know that they must segment their market for athletics if they are to generate sufficient support for and interest in their teams. Different messages and appeals must be sent to each target segment. What are the various market segments and what messages are sent to each?

High School Athletes. Colleges start to recruit outstanding high school athletes in their junior year by sending them letters expressing an interest in their accomplishments and raising the possibility of scholarship offers. In their senior year, the most gifted athletes are asked to visit the campuses of interested colleges. Sometimes, coaches or recruiters visit the athletes at home. Parents are told not only of the quality of the athletic program, but also of the strengths of the school's academic programs.

Students. If the team is doing reasonably well, the student body will want to support the team by attending games. To encourage attendance, students are given a discount on tickets, and special events such as bonfire rallies are held before big games.

Faculty. Faculty support is essential since college athletes occasionally must miss class. Keeping faculty informed of this fact can make the athlete's life less difficult. Also, athletic programs, in the end, are controlled by faculty commit-

tees. To keep them interested in athletic programs, faculty members are given discounts on season tickets. Many schools sponsor weekly luncheons where team coaches meet with interested faculty to discuss the previous week's contest and any upcoming games.

Contributors. This segment is made up of people who contribute financially or in some other way to the college. Typically, these people are sent season ticket applications and invited to receptions before and after games. They are also given an opportunity to meet with team coaches several times during the year.

Alumni. Alumni publications usually feature special articles on athletic programs. Alumni are also sent season ticket applications.

General Public. Finally, the general public is invited to buy tickets to the various athletic contests. People in the community stay in touch with the college and its athletic programs by reading the sports section of the local newspaper and by watching television interviews with coaches and players. Holders of season tickets are usually sent a renewal application at the end of each season.

See if you can identify these segments at your school. Is the proper message getting through to each segment? Are **you** getting the message?

Marketing & You

years Volkswagen produced and marketed only lower-priced, economy cars. Rolex makes only expensive watches, aimed at wealthy people who are looking for something in a watch other than the time. Both are good examples of a concentrated strategy.[22]

SEGMENTATION VS. ALTERNATIVE STRATEGIES: FIVE DECISION CRITERIA

There are five factors that the firm should examine in deciding whether to adopt a market segmentation strategy or one of the alternatives. Are segment characteristics measurable? Is the segment accessible? Does the firm have the resources needed for segmentation? Are products or markets actually homogeneous? Are there competitive forces in the product's market?

Measurability of the Segments

Critical to any segmentation program is the firm's ability to isolate and measure the buyer characteristic(s) that will serve as the basis for segmenting the market. If such characteristics cannot be found and measured, the firm will have no choice but to employ a different segmentation variable or to adopt an undifferentiated marketing strategy. For example, if a manufacturer of men's suits cannot measure the importance of "status" in selecting a suit, then the firm cannot use that variable as a basis for segmenting the market.

Accessibility of the Segments

The degree to which the firm can reach its chosen market segments with a focused promotional effort is the second factor in the selection of an overall marketing strategy. Some television shows, for example, attract particular segments of the viewing public, while others seem to draw equally well from all viewing segments. Table 7-2 presents the characteristics of adult male television viewers for three programs: "Baretta," "Meet the Press," and "Pro Bowling Tour." This information, along with the characteristics of adult female television viewers, is collected weekly by the W. R. Simmons and Associates research firm for all nationally broadcast television programs. Data are made available on a fee basis to advertising agencies and to major advertisers. This type of data is vital to the firm trying to reach a particular market segment. If that segment is not accessible, the firm will probably choose to adopt a strategy of undifferentiated marketing rather than one of market segmentation.

Company Resources

We have already seen that to adopt a strategy of market segmentation, the firm must have the financial, production, and personnel resources necessary to

---

[22]The following sections on decision criteria are based on Ronald E. Frank, William F. Massy, and Yoram Wind, *Market Segmentation* (Englewood Cliffs, N.J.: Prentice-Hall, Inc., 1972), pp. 27–28; and Philip Kotler, *Marketing Management; Analysis, Planning, and Control* (3d ed.; Englewood Cliffs, N.J.: Prentice-Hall, Inc., 1976), p. 143.

TABLE 7-2 Characteristics of Adult Male Television Viewers

Demographics	"Baretta"	"Meet the Press"	"Pro Bowling Tour"
Percentage of total U.S. viewer audience	16.8	1.9	4.8
Marital status			
Married	70.6	82.7	76.2
Single	18.0	10.9	16.4
Widowed, separated, divorced	11.4	6.5	7.4
Total	100.0	100.1	100.0
Occupation			
Professional	9.2	12.8	9.4
Managerial	13.0	17.6	11.5
Clerical	7.9	9.8	7.7
Craftsperson	18.3	7.7	12.7
Other employed	28.4	10.1	19.4
Not employed	23.3	42.2	39.3
Total	100.1	100.0	100.0
Race			
White	84.0	98.9	95.6
Black	14.5	.8	4.1
Other	1.5	.3	.3
Total	100.0	100.0	100.0
Age			
18–24	20.4	1.2	14.7
25–34	22.9	16.9	11.6
35–54	34.7	25.2	27.7
55 and older	22.0	56.7	46.1
Total	100.0	100.0	100.1
Education			
Attended college	24.1	34.2	30.4
Graduated high school	41.6	21.5	40.1
Did not graduate high school	34.3	44.4	29.5
Total	100.0	100.1	100.0
Household Income			
≥$15,000	42.6	43.3	45.3
$14,999–$10,000	28.2	14.0	20.7
<$10,000	29.1	42.6	34.0
Total	99.9	99.9	100.0

Note: Many of the columns do not add to 100 because of rounding.

Source: 1976–77 Study of Selected Markets and the Media Reaching Them, W. R. Simmons & Associates Research.

appeal to the entire market. If the firm is weak in any one of these areas, it should consider instead a strategy of market concentration. Lack of resources is one reason American Motors has chosen to concentrate its efforts on the economy-car market.

Product and Market Homogeneity

The more homogeneous a class of *products*, the less likely consumers will be to perceive differences among competing products. The typical buyer, for example, is not able to distinguish between one orange and another, or between one square yard of sheet metal and another. As a result, suppliers of these products usually pursue an undifferentiated marketing strategy. Likewise, the more homogeneous the *market*, the more likely suppliers are to adopt a strategy of undifferentiated marketing.

Competitive Forces

Lastly, competition is one of the most important variables in selecting a market segmentation strategy. In the early stages of its life cycle, when a product faces little or no competition, the firm can afford to provide only one item for the entire market because the consumer has no alternative supplier. However, as competition develops and as the buyer is given several products from which to choose, the firm must begin to focus on the needs of specific market segments if it is to achieve its sales objectives. Hence, a segmentation or concentration strategy will likely emerge.

Underlying any segmentation decision or strategy is the careful selection or classification of markets to be served. Let's examine one very helpful technique for selecting markets.

MARKET SELECTION

As indicated previously, there is no one best way to classify markets. If, however, the firm decides to adopt either a market segmentation strategy or a market concentration strategy, it must then confront the problem of how to subdivide the aggregate market. The market-grid approach is one analytical tool for segmenting markets.

The Market Grid

Under the **market-grid concept**, the market is viewed as a matrix divided by relevant segmentation criteria.[23] Each cell within the matrix represents a smaller, more homogeneous market. This approach focuses on the needs of prospective customers, not on the product. The analyst may develop several different matrices before the market is fully defined. Normally, the analyst begins with general segmentation criteria and then proceeds to apply increasingly more specific criteria.

To illustrate the use of the market-grid technique, assume that you have been asked to analyze the housing market in the United States. What segmen-

---

[23]The market-grid concept was first introduced by E. Jerome McCarthy in *Basic Marketing* (5th ed.; Homewood, Ill.: Richard D. Irwin, 1975), p. 70.

FIGURE 7-9 First-Round Market Grid for Housing

GEOGRAPHIC FACTORS

	North	East	South	West
Apartments				
Duplexes				
Houses				

BENEFITS

tation criteria would you use? One reasonable way to begin would be to develop a matrix (see Figure 7-9) that incorporates both geographic considerations and the benefits that prospective consumers look for in their housing. For geography, we have divided the nation into four major regions: the North, South, East, and West. Further geographic segmenting might be necessary and could include, for example, the Northeast and Southwest. The important point is that houses in one area of the country are different from those in other areas because of the differing life-styles and cultural patterns of their owners. In the same way, the vertical portion of the matrix in Figure 7-9 represents the first-level benefit that people seek from a home — whether they want to live by themselves (houses), with another family (duplexes), or with a number of other families (apartments).

Assume further that we have decided to concentrate our efforts on single-family homes located in the South. We may now want to divide that market again to determine whether we should concentrate our efforts on a more homogeneous market. Figure 7-10 shows that we have selected social class and stage in the family life cycle as the second-round segmentation criteria. Although other variables may also be appropriate, a family's social class does dictate to some extent where in the community the family is likely to live as

FIGURE 7-10 Second-Round Market Grid for Housing

STAGE IN THE FAMILY LIFE CYCLE

	Single	Newly Married	Married with Children
Lower Class			
Middle Class			
Upper Class			

SOCIAL CLASS

well as what image it will want the house to convey. Stage in the family life cycle, on the other hand, provides insight into the number of houses the family may have previously owned, the family's current financial situation, as well as into how many bedrooms, bathrooms, and playrooms the family will need.

We may want to divide the market several more times. There is no set number of grids that can or should be developed. For some products, it would be appropriate to divide the market into even more homogeneous units. However, this is a decision that can only be made after careful study of the specific product under investigation.

Marketing Mix Decisions

After determining the structure of its market, the firm then develops or modifies the marketing effort for each of its target segments. Specifically, the marketing manager integrates the marketing mix variables of price, product, communication, and distribution into a sound marketing strategy for each segment. The purpose is to maximize the organization's chances of achieving its sales objectives. Some questions that will have to be answered for each market segment include:

Product
How many models should be manufactured?
How high should product quality be?
What type of warranty should be given?
How should the product be positioned with respect to the competition?
What image should the product have?
Should the firm manufacture the product itself or purchase it from another supplier?

Price
What will the product's price be?
Will seasonal discounts be offered?
Will trade discounts be offered?
Is the market sensitive to price changes?

Communication
What theme should be used?
What media should be used?
How should promotion be evaluated?
Is there a role for public relations?

Distribution
Where should the product be sold?
Should the firm handle its own intermediary functions?
Should intermediaries be employed? If so, what type?
What levels of inventory should be maintained?

The market segmentation strategy chosen is a key input to the marketing manager's most important decisions. Once the manager has a sound understanding of the markets to be approached, intelligent decisions about product, price, communications, and distribution can be made. The next several chapters will focus on these decisions.

summary points

1. The key reason for using market segmentation is because many markets are heterogeneous. Therefore, different segments have different needs for any given product. Different market segments also respond differently to various promotional strategies. In addition, market segmentation is consistent with the marketing concept.

2. At least four forces have led many firms in the United States to adopt market segmentation strategies: (1) new economies of scale, (2) greater affluence of the U.S. society, (3) increased competition, and (4) new areas of segmentation research.

3. For a firm to adopt a market segmentation strategy, it must be able to bear increased costs in the areas of product design and manufacture. It should also anticipate increased marketing inventory costs, promotion costs, and managerial costs.

4. Demographic variables are useful in many market segmentation studies; they include income, social class, ethnic background, age, and stage in the family life cycle.

5. When the firm segments its markets on the basis of the benefits that people perceive in the product, the strategy is called benefit segmentation.

6. Psychological and attitudinal variables have been only partially successful in segmenting markets. In the future, the use of more situation-specific personality variables may turn this situation around.

7. Life-style segmentation classifies people in terms of their spending patterns, interests, opinions of themselves and their environment, and basic demographics.

8. Geography can be an effective segmentation variable in both consumer and industrial markets. In the consumer sector, geographic segmentation is often based on climatic or cultural differences; in the industrial sector, on the extent of industrial concentration.

9. Many firms segment their markets on the basis of heavy users and light users, and then concentrate their promotional and sales efforts on their best customers.

10. There are two alternatives to a strategy of market segmentation: undifferentiated marketing and market concentration. Undifferentiated marketing tries to reach the entire market with one product; concentrated marketing involves selling a few market segments only.

11. In choosing a market strategy, the firm must determine the measurability of each segment, the accessibility of each segment, the availability of company resources, the extent of product and market homogeneity, and the level of competition.

12. The market-grid technique is useful in defining market segments.

questions for discussion

1. Is the market for laundry soap heterogeneous? How would you segment the market for laundry soap?

2. Give an example of a product that is not physically changed when it is sold to two or more market segments.

3. What forces have led to the increased use of market segmentation? Will these forces continue to be present in the 1980s?

4. Discuss the role of market segmentation in the planning process.

5. Why have demographics been so useful in market segmentation strategies? Will they play as important a role in the 1980s as they have in the 1960s and 1970s?

6. Construct a benefit segmentation strategy for a firm selling wristwatches.

7. How successful have psychological and attitudinal variables been in segmenting markets? What can be done, if anything, to make them more effective?
8. Do you agree with the following statement: "Life-style segmentation is the best segmentation strategy developed for consumer and industrial products because it looks at the individual as a whole person"? Explain your answer.
9. Is market segmentation a strategy that all firms should pursue? Explain.
10. Why are so few products marketed by means of undifferentiated marketing?
11. Explain why Volkswagen changed its marketing strategy from concentrated marketing to market segmentation.
12. Develop a market grid or set of market grids for women's coats.

Avery Griffith successfully sold life insurance as a broker for several medium-sized life insurance companies for seven years in Chicago. Griffith decided he should start an independent agency in which other sales representatives could assist him in the work. After investigating several locations for Griffith Insurance Agency (GIA), Griffith selected Lake Forest, Illinois. He contracted for space in Market Square, a fashionable shopping center located in the center of Lake Forest.

cases
part 2
case 4
griffith
insurance
agency

Staff and Services

Griffith was a broker for several companies, having available a wide variety of policies. In addition, his C.L.U. training prepared him for assisting with trust arrangements, and other problems involved in the insurance programs of high-income clients. As his vice president, Griffith employed Alan Williams, who had worked four years in the underwriting department of a major casualty insurance company. He graduated from a large state university in the South, and could best be described as a political "ultraliberal." Initially two sales representatives were employed. Edwin P. Corkin, a middle-aged salesperson for a local heating and air-conditioning firm, was slightly grayed and distinguished looking. He was active in civic organizations and respected by many people. The other representative, Jonathon T. McCormick, was the son of a socially prominent family in Lake Forest. McCormick was 22 and had just been graduated from Yale University with a major in history.

Griffith was considering using the slogan "the North Shore's most comprehensive insurance and financial planning service" to express the agency's desire to totally service the needs of its clients. Griffith and Williams had developed several innovations to accomplish their objectives. One of these was a computerized service that took basic information about clients and projected their total insurance needs at varying ages. Griffith also planned to sell mutual funds and expected to form a separate firm to handle common stocks. Griffith felt this would permit him to become a truly complete financial counseling service.

Griffith Insurance Agency case is taken from *Cases in Consumer Behavior*, 3d ed., by Roger D. Blackwell, James F. Engel, and David T. Kollat. Copyright © 1969 by Holt, Rinehart and Winston, Inc. Adapted by permission of Holt, Rinehart and Winston.

The Market

GIA was located in Lake Forest but served both the village of Lake Forest and the adjacent village of Lake Bluff. These were two of the high-income suburbs of Chicago that extended along Lake Michigan. The combined population of Lake Forest, Lake Bluff, Highland Park (just south of Lake Forest), and Libertyville (West of Lake Bluff) was just under 40,000.

Chicago's Community Renewal Program published a ranking of the most desirable communities on a socioeconomic basis using as criteria the percentage of professional workers, average years of schooling, and family income. In a recent year, Lake Bluff ranked third out of the 250 Chicago suburbs in both education and percentage of professional workers and ranked 20th in family income. On a weighted scale, this provided a ranking of fourth as a desirable "status" suburb in the Chicago area. Lake Forest had higher family income but a considerably lower rating on education and was 53rd in percentage of professional workers. This lower rating gave Lake Forest a status level of 32nd in the Chicago area.

Griffith thought that these data were somewhat misleading because he felt Lake Forest to be among the highest status level communities in the Chicago area, considerably higher than Lake Bluff. Griffith felt that the true situation was at deviance with the situation indicated by the data because Lake Forest was a much more heterogeneous community.

Griffith cited the real estate situation as further evidence of the social class situation in the two communities. Most houses in Lake Bluff were selling between $95,000 and $110,000, with few deviations. In Lake Forest, however, there was a great deal of deviation, and sale prices ranged from $25,000 to $400,000 and more. The building permits issued in Lake Forest indicated that the average cost of *new* homes was $99,000, with much less deviation than among the older homes of the community.

The Promotional Strategy

Griffith planned that the agency's promotion would connote that the agency was designed for the upper-middle, lower-upper, and upper-upper social classes. He hoped not only to reach this market directly, but also to serve other social classes in the area. Griffith believed that if the image were attractive to upper classes, the middle classes would also want to do business with the agency. If he designed it as a middle-class agency, however, he believed that the upper classes would not be attracted to the agency.

Griffith decided to establish a series of seminars on personal financial planning that would be of interest to high-income local residents. He doubted that attendance would be high, but hoped that the seminar offer would generate readership of his advertising, create awareness of the agency, inform the public of his intention to offer complete financial services, and help establish an image for the agency. The speakers for the seminar included a well-known tax consultant, a Northwestern University professor presenting his short-term forecast of economic conditions, a University of Chicago professor presenting an analysis of the relative performance of the major mutual funds, and Williams and Griffith describing recent innovations in insurance offerings.

A 12-week local advertising schedule was planned to inform the public of the seminar series and of the opening of GIA. Primary media were the *Lake Forester* and *Lake Bluff Review*, weekly suburban newspapers, and radio stations which served the North Shore area. A pre-seminar meeting was to be advertised by a direct mail promotion consisting of a carefully selected mailing of engraved invitations to the social elite of Lake Forest. The first seminar was an overview of the entire series and an explanation of the agency's intention to provide a personalized, comprehensive insurance service. This pre-seminar was the direct responsibility of McCormick, who selected the guests and planned the program.

Since Griffith wanted the advertisements to connote an upper social class image, a highly respected Chicago advertising art studio was employed to prepare high-quality cuts far above the quality of the typical newspaper ad. The tone of the ad was formal, the type was light, and there was a great deal of white space. The overall effect of the ad was a reserved, dignified image.

Griffith showed the advertising plans to an account executive for a Chicago advertising agency. The account executive disagreed with Griffith's plan. Instead, his analysis of the situation was that members of the upper classes preferred to purchase their life insurance from long-time associates and college friends and that Griffith was unlikely to get much of their business. Though Griffith realized that he would have difficulty getting the upper-class business, he thought he eventually would get it because of his superior and comprehensive service. He also stated that he would be satisfied to receive business from the middle groups in Lake Forest-Lake Bluff because these people represented a group far above average in their insurance needs. Also, Griffith pointed out that 30 percent of the population in these two suburbs moved each year, thereby generating large members of new potential customers in the area.

The account executive argued that the upper-class image created by Griffith would be interpreted as a snob appeal by the rest of the residents. As a result, they might not want to patronize Griffith for fear that they were not really wanted and that they would feel uncomfortable with Griffith personnel. According to the account executive, the campaign would not reach the upper-class groups and would alienate the middle groups; therefore, it should not be undertaken.

1. Should Griffith proceed with the seminars designed to interest high-income families?
2. Should the proposed advertising be run?
3. What policies should be adopted by Griffith with respect to the facilities in his office, the personnel recruited and trained, and the segmentation strategy of the agency?

---

case 5
northern
chemical
company

Marketing executives at Northern Chemical Company, headquartered in Minneapolis and a world leader in the manufacture and sale of chemicals, metals, plastics, pharmaceuticals, and consumer products, were wrestling with a new concept in building roofs on industrial and commercial buildings. Whatever marketing efforts they decided on would have to be consistent with the attitudes of a complex array of contractors, roofers, and architects.

In the past, Northern had manufactured only plastic insulation for roofing. This insulation was prefabricated into rectangular boardstock of two by four feet, and of variable thicknesses necessary to meet the customers' desired insulating requirements. The product had not been very profitable for Northern.

Northern Chemical Company case by C. Merle Crawford, with the research assistance of Kenneth A. Epstein, Division of Research, the University of Michigan. Used with permission of C. Merle Crawford.

The Buying Process

On new construction or total roof replacement, the owners of the building play no essential role. They hire architects and give them certain guiding parameters — site, height, size, purpose and operating conditions. The architect then develops the design and material specifications for the roof. Even subsequent management reviews rarely concern the roof itself unless there is a question of overall building shape or a necessity to reduce costs.

A third party, the general contractor, also has little knowledge regarding roofing and has little influence on design or materials. Such matters are turned over to the fourth party, the roofing subcontractor, whose workers actually build the roof. The subcontractor influences the architect directly and indirectly through feedback on the ease and success of the architect's plans, and is the only party to significantly influence the architect.

Experimentation and innovation on roofing are not really in the architect's best interest. Experimentation is usually expensive, since worker unfamiliarity slows installation. Experimentation also requires a trust in manufacturers' products which architects do not have. Unfavorable past experiences with new products have resulted in a deep-seated distrust of new products and the firms producing them. Architects question laboratory research results because some past tests did not correctly identify product deficiencies or simulate the realities of application.

Subcontractors are even more resistant to change than architects. Their conservatism is based primarily on roofing labor conditions. New products often require extensive applicator retraining, and since retraining reduces an applicator's productive time, it reduces a subcontractor's income. Furthermore, worker re-education is an arduous task; roofing workers are not usually receptive to change. In addition, subcontractors also equate new products with increased callbacks. Some products have been introduced prematurely in the past and unanticipated repairs and adjustments have been necessary. Finally, the manufacturer frequently lacks field experience in application, and consequently tends to underestimate application costs. If roofers rely on the manufacturer's projections, their profits may be reduced. Yet, roofers haven't had the experience to make their own estimates.

At the same time, few subcontractors have actually blocked introduction of new roofing products or designs, since they are rarely asked for advice during the specification writing stage. Most roofers bid for every job for which they can compete, and their strongest urge is to keep the work force busy even if it requires using new materials or design. Once the bid is won, only minor changes are permitted.

Northern's View of the Market

In addition to the normal problems of entering a new market, Northern was considered a newcomer to roofing, and moreover, a newcomer that did not understand the market. Architects and roofing contractors pointed to their plastic foam, a roofing product marketed many years before a need was established. Comments from architects and roofing contractors regarding Northern's sales force ranged from "unexceptional" to "technically incompetent in roofing."

On the positive side, nonresidential roofing was a large market, totalling perhaps $640 million in the U.S. alone. Northern also noted that firms competing for this market did not do so effectively. Manufacturers had a strong product orientation and failed to base their plans on market needs. Lack of marketing skill was demonstrated by their weak sales efforts and limited services. Finally, the roofing market was plagued with poor workmanship, poor quality of materials, and high liability. Fifteen percent of all roofs failed within five years.

Northern's new roofing concept was a patented system which modified the usual application of roofing materials. The system eliminated the major causes for premature built-up roof failures. It was expected to perform much better than the conventional roof system, and the patent allows Northern to control the installation of the system. Even though Northern did not make any roofing materials other than insulation, the system allowed it to assure a good job because the insulation took most of the abuse in a properly installed roof.

Marketing Research

Northern's marketing research yielded several conclusions about the typical roof installation procedures with which the new system would compete: (1) the workmanship of roofing crews was the worst of all the construction trades; (2) the materials used in roofing had no production specifications at all and varied from job to job; (3) no special instructions or supervision had been provided to the roofers for the proper application of the plastic foam insulation; (4) owners and general contractors were apathetic — they wanted the roof on first and fast so all the other trades could work — and thus jobs were rushed and quality fell accordingly; (5) competition among the suppliers and the applicators was so intense that products were introduced with very little research and development. Quality was poor because the low prices wouldn't permit otherwise.

1. Is this illustration of an industrial buying process more complex than most? Explain.
2. How can Northern help the decision makers realize that the firm has a quality product that they should seriously consider?
3. How would you attempt to introduce this product to the market?
4. Who makes the decision to include the Northern product?

---

case 6
cliff peck
chevrolet

In November, 1977, a new automobile dealership was opened in the growing northwest section of Austin, Texas. The two principals who established the dealership, Harold Pannel and Jack Izard, were extremely pleased about the prospects for their new dealership. They were confident that widespread consumer acceptance of the Chevrolet product line, coupled with the healthy and fast-growing Austin market, would produce a winning combination.

Cliff Peck Chevrolet Case © by John H. Murphy, associate professor of advertising, The University of Texas at Austin.

The Automobile Market

The shortages and high prices of gasoline have had a devastating impact on the automobile industry. Automobile sales nationwide fell more than 20 percent for the first half of 1979. The only bright spot was the extraordinary demand for small domestic cars. In 1978 compact and subcompacts comprised 47.7 percent of all sales; during the first half of 1979 almost 60 percent of the cars sold were compacts or subcompacts. However, automakers found that 85 percent of customers who had purchased a subcompact in response to the 1973 Arab oil embargo moved up to a larger car for their next purchase.

Chevrolet's product line now features a front-wheel-drive car called the Citation. It boasts the exterior dimensions of a subcompact, impressive operating economy, the interior room of a mid-sized car, and as much luggage capacity as many full-size sedans. The Citation is also 800 pounds lighter than the Nova it replaced in the Chevrolet line. Other Chevrolet offerings include the Caprice Classic, Impala, Monte Carlo, Malibu, Camaro, Monza, Chevette, Corvette, wagons, recreational vehicles, the Suburban, and pickups. Thus, Chevrolet offers a wide product assortment to prospective new car buyers.

There are two Chevrolet dealers in Austin that compete with Cliff Peck — Capitol Chevrolet and Henna Chevrolet. Henna leads in sales, with Capitol sales at an estimated 85 percent of Henna sales and Peck sales at 80 percent of Henna sales. Capitol has been in Austin for over 50 years, and tends to use more TV advertising than either Peck or Henna. Presently, Capitol calls itself "Your Chevrolet Capitol." Henna tends to advertise heavily in newspapers, and its slogan is "Austin's Favorite Dealer."

Research Project

In order to provide continuous research input for use in advertising evaluation and planning, Cliff Peck Chevrolet and McLane Advertising have commissioned two research studies. A local advertising and marketing research firm, Metropolitan Research Services (MRS), has been retained to conduct an initial benchmark study and a follow-up survey. After a series of meetings with the client and the agency, MRS developed a two-phase research plan.

Phase I of the study is to provide an initial measure of the awareness, knowledge, and attitudes of target prospects of Cliff Peck Chevrolet. Such measures, when repeated at regular intervals, can be used as a control device for the promotional activities of the dealership.

A random sampling of 300 male adult heads-of-household living within a 6-mile radius of the dealership will be contacted by telephone. This sample area includes approximately 30 percent of Austin residents and 35 percent of the families in Austin with a mean income in excess of $19,000. Therefore, the areas selected for inclusion in the sample include the best prospects for the dealership based on accessibility to the dealership and upon socioeconomic considerations. MRS designed questions to measure the respondents' unaided recall and aided recall of automobile dealerships generally and of Cliff Peck Chevrolet specifically. Questions covering identification of slogans, attitudes toward automobile dealerships, automobile purchase decisions, and several demographic variables are also included.

Phase II of the research program is to use the same questionnaire and sample as Phase I. During the time period between Phase I and Phase II, the advertising slogan and the theme used by Cliff Peck in its campaign is to be modified. Also, other changes will include models advertised at different times, the total budget allocated to the campaign, and the emphasis on specific variables such as location, service, and price which are promoted in Peck's advertising.

The research director at MRS thinks that Phase II will provide indications of past successes and future directions of Cliff Peck advertising. The information provided from the study will help determine whether current advertising expenditures are sufficient, given the firm's goals. It may also suggest content changes in current promotion.

MRS estimates that the first phase of the research will cost $11,500 and the second phase, $8,000. Before Izard gives the final go-ahead on the research he wants to ensure that what has been proposed by MRS will meet his firm's needs.

1. Are there any significant errors in the research designed by MRS that would limit the data's usefulness?
2. Is Phase II necessary? If so, how long of a time interval should exist between Phase I and Phase II?
3. Do you feel that Izard should utilize MRS's services for the proposed study?

case 7
north american
yachts

Don Norris recently assumed responsibility for directing the activities of a new division of Glastron Boats. The new division, North American Yachts (NAY), was formed to manufacture and market sailboats. Glastron's top management believed that expansion into the sailboat field was a logical move for Glastron, and would serve as a hedge for Glastron against the adverse effect of possible future fuel shortages on the demand for powerboats in its current line.

North American Yachts presently produces one model, the North America 23 (NA 23) which is a trailerable, family cruising sloop which sleeps four. Initially, NAY planned to develop a strong regional distribution and marketing program for the NA 23 in the southwestern region of the United States prior to implementing a national marketing effort. However, Norris's previous experience convinced him that NAY should undertake a national marketing program immediately.

Norris feels that the NA 23 competes directly with competitors' trailerable sailboats in the 21- to 23-foot range. Catalina Yachts, the first firm to mass-produce fiberglass sailboats, is presently the largest manufacturer in the market. Catalina's image is so favorable that it does no advertising. Most of NAY's competitors are located on the West Coast. Table 1 describes sailboat retail sales by size.

TABLE 1   Sailboat Retail Sales by Size, 1975

	Percentage of All Boats Sold	Percentage of Total Dollars Sold
Under 12 feet	47	10
12–20 feet	43	40
Over 20 feet	10	50

Source: *Boating Industry*, May 1976.

North American Yachts is adapted and reprinted with permission from *Advertising Management* by Charles H. Patti and John H. Murphy. Grid Publishing, Inc., Columbus, Ohio, 1978 pp. 195–207.

The Market

A number of considerations are crucial in understanding prospects for the NA 23, according to Norris. First, anyone who considers a boat is shooting for a dream. A person may really like a big boat, but would be willing to settle for less just to get out on the water.

Second, although the spring and summer are the big selling seasons, prospects are thinking about and deciding on sailboats all year. Further, the decision to purchase a boat, and its type, model, and accessories, is becoming more of a family decision. Also, as the family life cycle changes so does the type of boat desired. For example, young couples with no children have a different set of requirements and expectations than the middle-aged couple with older children. The concentration of sales by areas of the country is mainly a function of population and climate.

Third, in terms of special interest publications, three magazines are most popular among sailboat buffs — *Sail, Yachting*, and *Rudder*. Each publication enjoys national distribution.

Finally, the market for sailboats has undergone some important changes in recent years. Young couples with relatively high combined incomes are a new and increasingly attractive market. Further, the old "traditional" sailor, complete with blue blazer and yacht club membership, has been joined by some other important groups: racers, young couples, transitions, middle managements, and small boaters (see Table 2).

TABLE 2   Buying Groups in the Sailboat Market

Young Couples	Working couples, no children, who own a cat or dog and live in small houses or apartments; 25- to 30-foot boats wanted, ranging from Spartan to Summer Cottage; active in the outdoors and concerned with ecology; little sailing experience.
Transitions	Older couples who want to trade in powerboats for low-performance sailboats; influenced by media in concern over environment and energy.
Middle Managements	Husbands are white-collar workers, wives do not work; desire medium-range sailboats with lots of equipment; frequently are in market for used boats.
Small Boaters	Blue-collar heads of household who purchase boats on a whim or as a result of family pressure.
Traditionals	Big boat sales; customers may know a great deal about sailing or nothing at all; comfort, style, and appearance are central; peer pressure is important.
Racers	Most informed clients; racing is a serious business to them.

Establishing a Dealership Network

As would be expected, NAY has been concentrating on establishing a strong dealer network. Norris considers the quality of the local dealer as the single most important factor in determining the ultimate success of NAY (with the exception of the product itself). In attempting to obtain the best dealer in each market area, NAY must convince present dealers already handling a competitor's boat to drop it in favor of NAY. According to Norris, the following factors are of major concern to a dealer who is deciding which manufacturer's dealership organization to join:

1. The product and its consumer appeal
2. The profit potential of the product for the dealer
3. Stability of the manufacturer's reputation — will it be around for the long haul, and able to deliver boats?
4. Service and warranties — how well will the manufacturer back its product and dealers?

Management felt that NAY offered prospective dealers an extremely good opportunity on all of these points.

1. What market segments should NAY approach?
2. What media should NAY use to reach their market segments?
3. Design a marketing strategy that would be effective in promoting NAY sailboats?

3

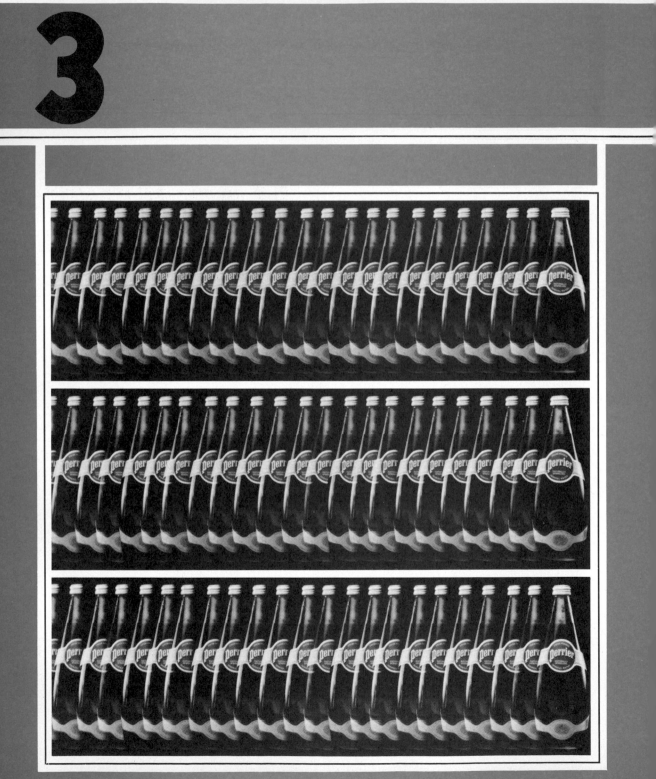

Product

You are now ready to begin investigating the components of a marketing program. Those components over which the firm has some degree of control are discussed in Parts 3, 4, 5, and 6.

Part 3 establishes the importance of a firm's product offering and its impact on the total marketing program. The need for a planned flow of new product ideas cannot be overemphasized.

Chapter

Topics discussed in Chapter 8:

1. A product as more than just a physical item.
2. Product classification as either industrial or consumer goods.
3. A five-stage technique for evaluating products.
4. The product life cycle concept and its application.
5. The functions of a product or brand manager.
6. The objective of product branding as well as the attributes of a good brand name or design.
7. The three primary functions of packaging and related environmental problems.

Some marketing executives have boasted that they have sold an inferior product at an exorbitant price. Although such actions may be the test of a good salesperson, they are not representative of a good product manager. One of management's most important responsibilities is to ensure that its products are as good as, if not better than, those of its competitors. We begin our study of product management by looking at what a product really is.

WHAT IS A PRODUCT?

In beginning our discussion of product management, it is essential that we clearly understand what a product is and is not. It is *not* merely a physical item; rather, a **product** represents a bundle of satisfactions or utilities to the purchaser. Since people have different tastes and preferences, and often different needs for the same item, products represent different levels of satisfaction to individual buyers.

The satisfaction that a product yields is a function of a number of variables including how the product is perceived, where it can be purchased, its reputation for reliability, the location of service installations, its warranty, and its physical design. As an example, for many years IBM has had a very large share of the computer market. Many small competitors, as well as large ones such as General Electric, have been forced out of the market. There is no question that IBM makes extremely fine mainframe computers, but so did many of its former competitors. What separates IBM from other firms in the computer industry is the wide variety of its auxiliary equipment and computer programs (software), its extensive service network and field sales organizations, and its *reputation* for producing reliable, high-quality products. Awareness of these various satisfactions and utilities, and not simply the physical features of the product itself, is integral to successful product management.

PRODUCT CLASSIFICATIONS

Products are broadly classified as either consumer goods or industrial goods. These categories differ not only in the physical products they include, but also in the techniques used to develop and market them effectively.

Consumer goods are produced for sale to individuals and families for personal consumption. In contrast, **industrial goods** and services are sold to commercial enterprises, government agencies, and nonprofit institutions for use in the production of their goods and services or for resale to other industrial customers. *Thus, the intended customer is the major distinction between consumer and industrial goods.*

FIGURE 8-1   Characteristics of Convenience, Shopping, and Specialty Goods

Characteristics	Convenience Goods	Shopping Goods	Specialty Goods
Examples	Milk, cigarettes	Furniture, vacuum cleaners	Expensive watches and jewelry
Price	Small profit margin, very competitive	Moderate profit margin	High profit margin
Turnover	High inventory turnover, over 25 times per year	Moderate turnover, 3-24 times per year	Low turnover, less than 3 times per year
Distribution	Many intermediaries, location critical	Several intermediaries	Few intermediaries, location not very important
Communication	Mass advertising, standardized theme	Personal selling, mass advertising, P.O.P. displays	Highly trained, personal selling, specialized for each area.
Replacement rate	Frequently purchased	Occasionally purchased	Seldom purchased
Adjustment	No adjustment for purchaser	Minor adjustment	Often custom designed
Searching time	Low, first available product is purchased	Significant searching time	High, customer seeks out particular brand

Consumer Goods

Consumer goods are classified into three categories: convenience goods, shopping goods, and specialty goods.[1] It is important that we understand the basic differences among these products, even though what is a convenience good to one person may be a shopping or even a specialty good to another, because each requires distinct promotional and distribution strategies. Figure 8-1 presents an overview of the characteristics of each of the three product types.

Convenience Goods. Convenience goods are products that the consumer purchases frequently, immediately, and with a minimum of effort. They are products for which the consumer feels that the cost of making price and quality comparisons outweighs the expected gain from such efforts. Examples of convenience goods include such items as milk, magazines, soaps, and canned peaches.

Normally, it is not possible to differentiate competing convenience goods from one another. Because of the basic similarity of convenience goods, such as milk products or cigarettes, the manufacturer and the distributor must be willing to invest considerable sums in advertising to remind the public of the existence and merits of their products. Also, the homogeneity of convenience goods, in conjunction with the heavy advertising expenditures, frequently results in highly competitive conditions leading to small per-unit profit margins. Many retailers claim they make little or no profit on convenience goods.

Finally, convenience goods are manufactured in such a way that they cannot be modified or adjusted to fit the particular needs of any one customer. If the buyer does not like the convenience item the way it is, another brand or item may be the only solution. There is neither the expertise nor the profit margin at the retail level to customize any product for the buyer.

To market convenience goods successfully, the retailer must realize the importance of locating close to the consumer. Location is one of the reasons that the Southland Corporation has been so successful over the last 50 years. Today, Southland has more than 5,000 Seven-Eleven "neighborhood stores." Its advertising emphasizes the convenience of the Seven-Eleven stores.

Shopping Goods. Shopping goods are items for which the potential customer normally examines such factors as quality, price, and style before making a purchase decision. The buyer seeking shopping goods usually feels that the expected gain from making price and quality decisions outweighs the cost of such comparisons. Examples of shopping goods include refrigerators, televisions, draperies, and automobiles.

It is critical that the manufacturer and the retailer of shopping goods provide the shopper with the information needed to make an intelligent decision. Easy-to-comprehend information on such factors as product warranty, price,

---

[1]For more information on consumer goods, see Louis P. Bucklin, "Retail Strategy and the Classification of Consumer Goods," *Journal of Marketing* (January, 1963), pp. 50–55; and Richard H. Holton, "The Distinctions Between Convenience Goods, Shopping Goods and Specialty Goods," *Journal of Marketing* (July, 1958), pp. 53–56.

and cost of service is essential in the marketing of shopping goods. If consumers are not provided with this data voluntarily by the manufacturer or retailer, many of them will turn to another brand.

A second characteristic of shopping goods is that their profit margins tend to be somewhat higher than those of convenience goods. Higher margins permit the retailer to employ salespeople who have some expertise with the product and who are trained to discuss the merits of the different shopping goods carried by the retailer. For example, if you were to enter an appliance store to buy a microwave oven, a competent salesperson would be able to explain the advantages of each line in the store. Frequently, the salesperson will recommend one brand to the individual who wants digital control and a heat probe, and another to the customer looking for the product offering the best value. Higher profit margins also enable the retailer to provide some "adjustments" in the product to fit the needs of the consumer. As an example, many refrigerators are not factory-equipped with ice makers but have been designed so that the retailer can easily install one should the customer so desire.

Although salespeople play a very important role in the marketing of shopping goods, promotion by point-of-purchase displays and mass advertising is also essential. Advertising frequently is used to tell the public of an upcoming "sale." Point-of-purchase displays are used to draw the customer's attention toward key product features and away from competing products.

Specialty Goods. Specialty goods are products for which people are willing to make a special purchasing effort. A product is a specialty good if the customer, prior to feeling a need for the product, knows what brand he or she would purchase. A specialty good entails a high degree of customer loyalty; the effort at shopping, therefore, does not involve comparing one brand against another but finding a store that carries the item in question. For example, if a consumer decides that only a Rolex watch will do, then this watch has become a specialty product for that consumer. Therefore, when it is time to purchase a watch, it is likely that this individual will visit only those jewelers that sell Rolex watches. The classic example of a specialty good is a Rolls Royce. A specialty good, however, does not necessarily have to be that expensive.

Specialty goods do have higher profit margins and higher prices relative to convenience or shopping goods. For the most part, manufacturers of specialty goods sell their products on the basis of product quality, reliability, and image rather than on the basis of price. Usually, the person who purchases an expensive specialty item is not as concerned about price as the average consumer.

The selection of the correct retailer in a community is a very important decision for the manufacturer of a specialty good. Normally, the manufacturer will sell to only a very limited number of retailers (often only one) in any particular market. If the decision is a poor one, the manufacturer is, in effect, not represented in the market. Manufacturers will be very concerned about a store's image and the expertise of its sales staff. In the case of shopping goods, and especially convenience goods, dealer selection is not as critical because several dealers represent the manufacturer in a given market.

Industrial Goods

As Figure 8-2 indicates, industrial goods and services can be subdivided into at least eight classifications ranging from heavy equipment to consumable supplies. Even though a few of these items — such as typewriters, portable power tools, and cleaning supplies — may be sold for personal consumption as well as for industrial use, the vast majority of these products are purchased for industrial use only. In addition, those items sold in both markets are sold through different channels of distribution and employ significantly different promotional strategies. Let us turn now to the strategic variables affecting the *sale* of industrial goods and then to the industrial *buying* process.

Strategic Variables in Selling Industrial Goods.[2] In designing a marketing strategy, the firm selling to industrial users must analyze the four variables that are a part of any marketing plan: price, product, distribution, and communication. The strategies designed for each variable will be different for industrial goods than for consumer goods. To illustrate, competitive bidding is widely used to establish prices for industrial products; it is rarely if ever practiced in the consumer sector. In addition, for those industrial items with a standard price there may be several discounts — based either on the quantity purchased or on how much time the purchaser takes to pay for the product — that are not usually available for consumer goods.

Product planning is frequently more difficult in the industrial sector because the manufacturer may operate at several different market levels. For example, pulp and paper companies often operate as suppliers of pulpwood, paper, and corrugated boxes. Each of these items is used to make the next item in the series and is also sold to competing firms. Similarly, General Electric manufactures engines for the locomotives it sells to the railroad industry, and

FIGURE 8-2 Types of Industrial Goods and Services

Classification	Example
Heavy equipment	Machine tools, trucks, tractors, blast furnaces
Light equipment	Typewriters, portable power tools, measuring instruments
Construction	Factories, office buildings, docks
Component parts	Motors, gears, pumps, semiconductors
Raw materials	Coal, iron, limestone
Processed materials	Steel plate, plastic sheeting, plywood, chemicals
Services	Repair and maintenance, design, consulting
Consumable supplies	Small tools, electricity, cleaning and maintenance materials

Source: Adapted from E. Raymond Corey, *Industrial Marketing: Cases and Concepts*, 2d ed., © 1976. Adapted by permission of Prentice-Hall, Inc., Englewood Cliffs, N.J.

---

[2]This section is drawn from E. Raymond Corey, *Industrial Marketing: Cases and Concepts*, 2d ed., pp. 1–5. © 1976. Adapted by permission of Prentice-Hall, Inc., Englewood Cliffs, N.J.

The purchase of an automobile is probably your largest financial commitment — second only to a house. Let's look at a few ideas that might help **you** to shop for a car.

Which Car Is Right? First you must ask yourself how you plan to use a car. Will it be used for cross-country trips, or just for getting around town? Will the car normally carry one or two passengers, or will it be used regularly for car pools? Is fuel efficiency more important than status? What you expect of a car largely determines what kind of car you should buy.

What Does the Warranty Cover? Although all new car warranties appear to be the same, they are not. For example, AMC's "Buyer Protection Plan" covers more problems than do the warranties of most other automakers. While all U.S. automakers offer an extended warranty on new cars, the terms and cost of the warranties often differ. Finally, the warranties on foreign cars are often for 24 months, but the buyer must agree to maintain a dealer-sponsored service program which can be quite expensive.

How Much Should You Pay? Before you begin negotiating price, determine how much the dealer paid for the car by checking magazines such as *Edmond's New Car Buyer's Guide*. Bear in mind that cars in short supply usually sell at list price, whereas cars not in demand can be purchased at significant savings. Consult the business section or the classified ad section of your local newspaper to find out which cars can be purchased at discount prices.

What Will Service Cost? After your warranty expires or with most used car purchases, you're on your own when it comes to maintenance costs. To estimate service costs, read the results of extended-use tests which are regularly published in magazines such as *Consumer Reports, Road & Track*, and *Car & Driver*.

Order or Purchase from Inventory? Although it is tempting to purchase a new car from the dealer's current inventory, it may be a mistake. If you buy a car from inventory that is equipped with unwanted extras, you may have to pay as much as $1,000 to $2,000 more than if you order the car with only the equipment you want.

Think Before You Act! Visit several dealers. Find out the advantages and disadvantages of competing models and dealers. Get several price quotations. If you live in a small city where each automaker has only one dealer, it may be worthwhile to visit dealers in other nearby cities. Be skeptical about claims of better service if you buy locally. The manufacturer is the one offering the warranty on the car and each of its dealers honors that warranty because they are well paid by the manufacturer to do so.

Marketing & You

also sells its diesel engines as components to competing locomotive manufacturers.

The consumer sector and the industrial sector also differ markedly in the areas of distribution and communications. Whereas most items in the consumer sector are sold in retail outlets, products in the industrial sector are usually sold by salespeople who call on customers at their places of business. In addition, the technical expertise of the salesperson plays a much greater role in the marketing of industrial products. To communicate with customers, manufacturers of industrial products rely primarily on trade journals, direct mail, and salespeople to convey their advertising messages. Only occasionally do they use mass media aimed directly at the final consumer to "pull" the product through the channel. DuPont has done this with its promotion of Orlon and Dacron by featuring high-fashion clothing made of these products. Since DuPont does not make the end product, its objective is to develop brand recognition on the part of the consumer and the retailer with the hope that this interest will stimulate the clothing manufacturer to utilize DuPont's products.

Industrial Buying Process. As discussed in Chapter 5, the process through which industrial goods are purchased is quite different from that used for consumer goods. First, all industrial goods have **derived demand**; that is, the demand for industrial goods is dependent on, or derived from, the ultimate demand for the consumer goods into which they are transformed. To illustrate, automobile manufacturers purchase sheet metal not because they want to own sheet metal but because they use it to build the cars demanded by the consumer. This implies that the sellers of industrial goods must carefully monitor final consumer demand for the products of the immediate purchaser in order to forecast their own sales effectively. This situation of derived demand also means that no matter how good the industrial firm's marketing plan may be, its sales may decline significantly at times because demand is down for the critical consumer product.

Second, industrial buyers are paid to make rational economic decisions; they usually are not paid to order the cheapest item. Most buyers consider quality as well as price. The item giving the best service over the longest period of time will have a significant advantage when the final decision is made.

Finally, the purchasing process for industrial goods is likely to involve a group of people, not just one individual. Therefore, it is important that the seller determine who will be involved in making the group decision so that these people can be approached individually in promoting the merits of the product.

PRODUCT EVALUATION PROCEDURE

The most important product strategy question in any manufacturing firm is: what products should be introduced, continued, or phased out? The firm must make important decisions with regard to individual *product items, product lines*, and its *product mix*.

A **product item** is the individual product or service. To illustrate, Gillette produces a single-edge razor, a double-edge razor, a twin-blade razor, and an adjustable twin-blade razor. Each of these distinct products is a separate item;

in contrast, a **product line** refers to a category or group of products. All the shavers Gillette sells represent one product line. The depth of a product line refers to the number of items the firm offers within that line. Many firms feel that it is important to have a great depth within each product line so that they can appeal to as many customers as possible.

The **product mix** consists of all the lines or categories of products that the firm sells. Accordingly, Gillette's product mix includes shavers, replacement blades, shaving creams, deodorants, and lighters. Normally, a firm will try to maintain a certain consistency among the products in its mix so that customers will associate new items with the firm's reputation in that area. In the case of Gillette, each line, with the exception of lighters, involves personal-care grooming products.

There is a step-by-step procedure that management can use to make product decisions. Although the procedure is not fail safe and therefore will not always lead to the "correct" decision, the firm that carefully follows these steps will increase its likelihood of taking proper action.

Figure 8-3 illustrates the five distinct phases required for optimal product evaluation. Each of these phases is analyzed in detail below.[3]

Definition Phase

First, management must clearly define the *product item or line* and the *market* under investigation. Specific parameters are essential at this stage or the analysis will be too general to be useful. Assume that Colgate-Palmolive sells five brands of soap, each of which has been on the market for a different length of time and faces different levels of competition. To complicate this matter further, some of these soaps may have potential in the consumer sector that differs greatly from their potential in the industrial sector. Similarly, a soap's sales potential may be good in the United States and only fair in Western Europe and South America. Therefore, the analyst must be careful to define clearly which product item or items and which markets are under investigation if the results are to be meaningful.

Data Collection Phase

During this phase the firm collects the data that will permit it to evaluate the potential of the product and market under investigation. The analysis begins by examining the *sales history* of the product both for that firm and for the industry as a whole. The product can then be identified as being in one of three categories — declining, stable, or growing. The following criteria are frequently used for categorizing:

- **Declining** — negative growth in sales during the previous 12 months.
- **Stable** — 0 percent to 10 percent increase in sales during the previous 12 months
- **Growing** — greater than 10 percent increase in sales during the previous 12 months.

---

[3]The following discussion is derived primarily from Yoram Wind and Henry J. Claycamp, "Planning Product Line Strategy: A Matrix Approach," *Journal of Marketing* (January, 1976), pp. 2–9, with permission of the American Marketing Association.

FIGURE 8-3 Product Evaluation Procedure

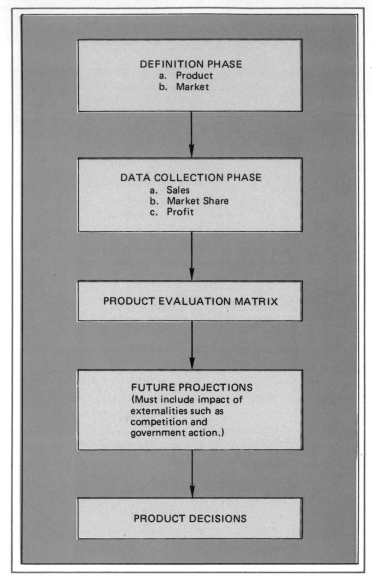

Once the sales histories for both the product and the industry have been determined, the firm must estimate its product's share of the total market. Secondary data sources such as the A. C. Nielsen Company or the Market Research Corporation of America can provide very accurate market share data. If data are not available the firm may have to rely on industry experts for informed estimates. Again, although individual circumstances may greatly modify the categories used to evaluate market share, the following categories are appropriate in many situations.

- **Marginal** — market share less than 10 percent.
- **Average** — market share between 10 percent and 24 percent.
- **Leading** — market share 25 percent or more.

The last data that must be collected concern the profitability of the product in relation to the firm's objectives. It is clearly management's responsibility to define the profit objectives of each product and market. Once accomplished, it is easy to determine whether the actual profits of a given product or market are below profit objectives, above profit objectives, or on target.

Product Evaluation Matrix

After the necessary data have been collected, the figures on industry sales, company sales, market share, and profit should be combined into a comprehensive product evaluation matrix, such as the one shown in Figure 8-4. To illustrate the application of the matrix, the figure presents hypothetical paths for two products. Product A has been in a growth industry for two of the last three years. In 1976 it was in a stable industry with declining sales; its market share was marginal, and its profits were below target. In 1977, however, the industry for Product A developed into a growth industry and the firm's sales of the product stabilized, although its share of the market remained marginal and profits were below target. By 1978 the market share for Product A had reached a situation of average growth, and for the first time in three years the firm achieved its target profit objectives for that product.

Product B's situation is much worse than Product A's. By 1978 Product B was in a declining industry. Its sales dropped from 1976 to 1977; and while it was able to sustain an average market share for 1976 and 1977, its market share became marginal in 1978. Can you spot the one positive note about Product B? It is that the firm has thus far been able to meet its profit objectives for this product.

FIGURE 8-4 The Product Evaluation Matrix: A Hypothetical Example Tracing Two Products Over Three Years

Industry Sales	Market Share	Decline — Below Target	Decline — Target	Decline — Above Target	Stable — Below Target	Stable — Target	Stable — Above Target	Growth — Below Target	Growth — Target	Growth — Above Target
Growth	Leading					A 1978				
Growth	Average				A 1977	•— — —•				
Growth	Marginal				•					
Stable	Leading									
Stable	Average	A 1976								
Stable	Marginal	•								
Decline	Leading		B 1977		B 1976					
Decline	Average				•					
Decline	Marginal	•— — —•	B 1978							

— — — — — projections

Source: Adapted from Yoram Wind and Henry J. Claycamp, "Planning Product Line Strategy: A Matrix Approach," *Journal of Marketing* (January, 1976), p. 5, with permission of the American Marketing Association.

Future Projections

The above analysis, which looks at four indices of product performance over time in one matrix, permits the analyst to answer the question "where are we?" with respect to the product in question. However, to use the product evaluation matrix to make future marketing decisions, the analyst must project what will happen in the future assuming no major changes occur in the product's marketing strategy or in competitive conditions. In the case of our hypothetical Products A and B, the projection lines in Figure 8-4 show that Product A will probably move into the above-target range for its profits, while Product B will likely no longer be able to sustain its profit objectives. After the initial future projection is made, the analyst may wish to modify the projections assuming adjustments are made in the product's price, distribution, or advertising strategies. Similarly, if it is reasonable to assume that a major competitor will modify its product strategy in some way, the future projection can take this element into consideration.

Product Decisions

At this stage, the marketing manager must determine what should be done with the product in the future. The decision alternatives are:

1. Do not significantly change either the product or its marketing strategy.
2. Do not significantly change the product, but do modify its marketing strategy. This modification may consist of changes in price, distribution, and/or communications strategies.
3. Change the product. Changes may involve substantial product modifications to fit the needs of a new group of customers or only minor product changes to make the product more acceptable to current customers. Regardless of the significance of the change, it will normally require some modifications in the product's marketing strategy.
4. Discontinue the product. Eliminating the product immediately may be required, or the product may be phased out in an orderly fashion so as to maximize whatever revenues and profits are left.

Once the marketing manager has completed the product evaluation process, final adjustments can be made in the product's pricing, distribution, and advertising strategies. At this point, too, marketing managers will look at the product from another perspective — that of the product life cycle.

THE PRODUCT LIFE CYCLE

The concept of a **product life cycle** implies that successful products move through rather predictable stages. They are introduced, their sales increase rather rapidly until a point at which they level off, and eventually they are replaced by newer products. The product life cycle concept is particularly valuable because it helps the marketing executive forecast the sales of any given product. The product's profits, as well as the marketing strategy, will vary significantly depending on where the product is in its cycle.[4] In looking at the product evaluation process, we found that it was necessary to classify a product's sales history into the decline, stable, or growth stage. We now adopt a slightly more sophisticated approach and analyze a product sales model with five stages.

Stages in the Product Life Cycle

The "life story" of many successful products shows that they move through five stages, illustrated in Figure 8-5. Their sales rise relatively slowly at first. In this **market development** stage, only a few people, those who enjoy being innovators, purchase the product. During the second stage, **rapid growth**, sales rise faster than at any other point in the product's life cycle; the product has "caught on," and many people want to be among the first to purchase it. In the **turbulence** stage, the rate of sales increase for the product declines as new competitors begin to take sales away from the original manufacturer. The fourth stage, **maturity**, may last for an extended period of time. At this point, an increase or decrease in the product's sales is tied primarily to the basic health of the economy. Finally, a product enters the **decline** stage when many of its customers begin to switch to other products that come closer to meeting their changing needs. Figure 8-6 summarizes the tactical adjustments that a firm must make over the life cycle of a product. The following

FIGURE 8-5 The Product Life Cycle

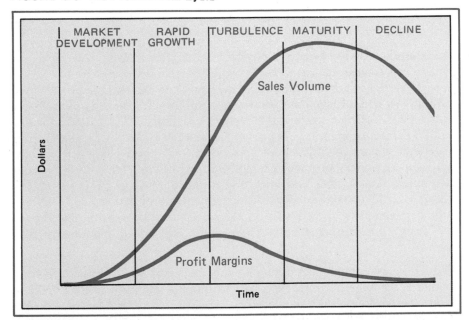

[4]Rolando Polli and Victor Cook, "Validity of the Product Life Cycle," *Journal of Business* (October, 1969), pp. 385–400.

discussion examines the overall strategy that should be followed for the product during each of these five stages.

Market Development. When a product is actually *new*, it has little, if any, direct competition. Therefore, the primary objective of the firm at this stage is to attract a sufficient number of purchasers to justify continued expenditures for product research and development and for the creation of a long-term distribution structure. Consequently, the firm concentrates its communication expenditures on persuading the public that it should purchase the *type* of product in question; it is not especially concerned whether customers actually buy its product. This strategy, called **primary demand stimulation**, is well illustrated in RCA's early advertisements for color television, which stressed the benefits of color television in general with only minor mention of the manufacturer. During market development, the firm must monitor its financial position closely. Although prices may be very high during this stage, marketing and production costs will also be elevated, so the product will probably lose money. Many good products have failed to reach the market because the manufacturer was not able to raise the required short-term capital to successfully launch and maintain the product.

Rapid Growth. During this second stage, many new firms enter the market. Often, however, demand is so strong that the industry cannot supply all of the products that are needed. As a result, prices remain high and, for those firms that have established good cost-control procedures, substantial profits are possible. During this stage, it is critical for the firm's long-term prosperity that it establish a strong dealer structure to help support the product when prices fall in the future.

Turbulence. Survival becomes the objective during this stage, and the keys to survival are a well-established dealer structure and good cost-control procedures. The citizen's band (CB) radio industry is an excellent example of an industry that has recently gone through the turbulence stage. For more than a decade, E. F. Johnson was by far the largest producer of CBs. In 1975 the firm had 25 percent of the total CB market and sales in excess of $100 million. In 1978 they announced the sale of their primary CB production facility. Other CB manufacturers that have recently dropped out of the business include Gemtronics, Xtal, UTAC, Fulcomm, and Regency. Many of the firms still producing CB radios have excellent distribution structures and are supported by large corporations such as Radio Shack and General Electric; or, like Browning, Tram, and Polamar, they are supplying a high-priced, high-margin market.[5]

Maturity. The central goals during the maturity stage are to defend the firm's market share against competition and to monitor the market continually to determine which product modifications would attract customers away from competitors. At this stage in the product life cycle, a 1 to 3 percent shift in market share is considered significant. Also, since only minor differences usually separate a product from its competitors by the time it reaches maturity, creative advertising becomes very important. How the product is perceived by

[5]Dick Cowan, "CB in Action," *Sarasota Herald Tribune*, December 25, 1977, p. 11.

FIGURE 8-6   Tactical Adjustments Over the Product Life Cycle

	Market Development	Rapid Growth	Turbulence	Maturity	Decline
Competition	No direct competition.	Competitors enter market.	Extreme competition; many firms leave industry.	Number of competitors stabilizes; few if any new competitors.	Decline in number of competitors as a result of reduced consumer interest.
Profits	No profits; high production and marketing costs.	Highest profit period; prices high while costs decline with economies of scale.	Profits decline with falling prices.	Per-unit profit low; total profit is function of cost control and large volume sales.	Profit low unless virtually all competitors leave industry.
Product Design	Limited number of models; frequent product modifications.	Expanded number of models; frequent product modification.	Large number of models; annual models begin to appear	Large number of models; design change only at times of annual model introduction.	Constant pruning of unprofitable models.
Pricing	Very high, no competition.	High; to attract new customers prices are reduced.	Competition forces prices down.	Prices stabilize at relatively low level.	Prices may rise; must maintain prices at level at which firm makes a profit.
Communications	Primary demand stimulation, publicity and personal selling important.	Selective demand stimulation; large amount of mass promotion.	Selective demand; large amount of mass promotion and dealer promotions.	Selective demand; large amount of mass promotion and dealer promotions.	Reduced communication expenditures; no sales or dealer promotions.
Distribution	Selective determination of new dealers; high margins to dealers to justify their carrying and servicing the products.	Expand number of dealers; dealer margins decline; vital to have well stocked inventory at dealer levels.	Extensive number of dealers; margins greatly reduced; product service important.	Extensive number of dealers; margins greatly reduced; product service critical.	Phase out unprofitable dealers.

Source: Adapted from Chester R. Wasson, *Dynamic Competitive Strategy and Product Life Cycles* (Austin, Texas: Austin Press, 1978), pp. 256–257.

the public is a critical concern during this stage. In the 1960s the Coca-Cola Company revamped its promotion strategy with advertising that stressed teenagers and young adults drinking and singing about Coke. Do you remember the "I Want to Teach the World to Sing" campaign? This promotion was a significant change from Coca-Cola's strategy that had focused on the theme of Coke as an effective thirst quencher.

Decline. Usually, the primary strategic objective in the period of decline is to get as much profit out of the product as possible while demand for the product still exists. As a result, during the decline stage the firm is reluctant to invest substantial resources in either production or marketing. It is also possible that enough competitors will leave the market that a firm can profitably serve for an indefinite period of time those customers who still want the product. In this situation, the reduced competition may allow prices to rise, and the manufacturer may feel comfortable investing in the product's future. One product beginning to move into this category is the reel-to-reel tape deck. As the less-complicated cassette machines become more refined, it is likely that people will gravitate toward them. However, it is also likely that a relatively small group of people who believe that cassettes do not have the proper sound reproduction capability will remain interested in reel-to-reel equipment. Those few electronic firms continuing to produce this equipment may be able to generate reasonable profits.

Now that you are familiar with the product life cycle concept, let's look at the ways marketers use the concept to manage both new and existing products.

Usefulness of the Product Life Cycle

The product life cycle concept has been criticized by many individuals who maintain that it is useless because products tend to have unique sales growth patterns.[6] Although we would not dispute the notion that the slope of a product's sales curve will vary with such factors as the "newness" of the product, how close it comes to meeting customers' needs, and how fast competition enters the market, we maintain that the product life cycle concept can be very useful in managing both new and established products.

New Products. The notion that successful products go through a life cycle forces management to try to forecast what the sales of the new product will be over time. Unfortunately, there is no magic method or checklist permitting management to forecast sales of a product correctly in all instances. Yet, it is also clear that the proper use of market research does help management make an educated guess — a ballpark figure — as to what the product's sales will be. This forecast in turn permits the development of a rational plan for modifying pricing, communications, and distribution strategies over time to achieve market acceptance. It also forces the firm to anticipate when competition will enter the market and to estimate the impact competitive entries will have on the

---

[6]See, for example, Nariman K. Dhalla and Sonja Yuspeh, "Forget the Product Life Cycle Concept," *Harvard Business Review* (January-February, 1976), pp. 102–112.

product. If, after the product is introduced, sales do not follow the forecast, the marketing plan can be modified or the forecast can be reevaluated.

Without the planning made possible by a sales forecast, developing and monitoring a marketing strategy would be impossible. Without a strategy, the marketing manager can do little more than react to sales with a series of short-range measures which are designed only to solve the immediate problem.

Existing Products. When a business is evaluating the possibility of entering the market for an existing product, the product's stage in its life cycle becomes very important. Firms are usually attracted to existing products because they feel they can make a large return on their investment. A common error that many executives make is to analyze a product rather early in its life cycle and then to expect the profit margins existing at that time to continue for the life of the product. We know, however, that as more firms enter the market, prices and profit margins decline. Therefore, what appears in the rapid growth stage to be a very profitable item may turn out to be only marginally profitable when it reaches the turbulence stage. Management can avoid this costly error by determining where the product currently is in its life cycle and then forecasting how much time will elapse before it moves on to the next stage.

A second use of the product life cycle for existing products is to force management to realize that a series of sequential actions are required to maintain the product's sales and profits. That is, advanced planning must be directed at stretching out the life of the product. Figure 8-7 illustrates an extended life cycle for a product. Notice that at point A, when original uses for the product had leveled off, the firm took action that had the effect of pushing product sales upward. The firm repeated its product-extension tactics at points B, C, and D, thereby dramatically increasing the product's sales and profits.

How can a firm extend a product's life cycle? There are several actions a firm can take. For instance, it can

1. Promote more frequent use of the product among current users.
2. Develop more varied uses for the product among current users.
3. Create new users for the product by enlarging the market.
4. Find new uses for the basic product.

As a classic example of the successful use of a product life-extension strategy, General Foods Corp. employed all of the above tactics to revitalize sales for its product, Jell-O. It stimulated the frequency of use (tactic 1) by increasing the number of flavors offered from six to more than a dozen. Greater variety of use (tactic 2) was promoted by demonstrating how well Jell-O worked in salads. The company established new users (tactic 3) for the product by illustrating its value in a fashion-oriented weight control program. Finally, General Foods introduced new uses for Jell-O (tactic 4) by developing a flavorless product that could be used as a substitute for gelatin to help women strengthen their fingernails.[7]

---

[7]Theodore Levitt, "Exploit the Product Life Cycle," *Harvard Business Review* (November-December, 1965), pp. 81–94.

FIGURE 8-7   Extensions of a Product's Life Cycle

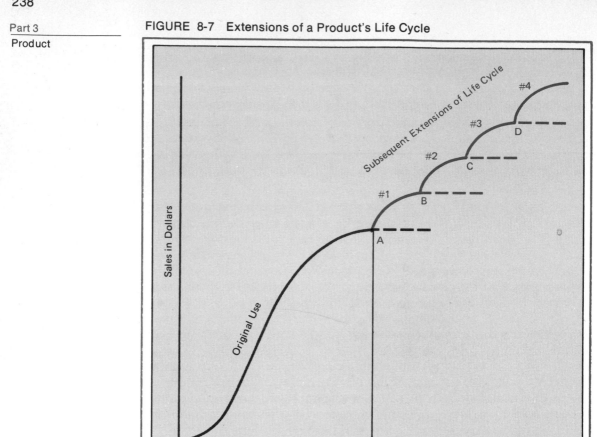

We will now shift attention from the product itself to how it can be managed within the organizational setting. While there are a variety of methods to accomplish this task, the use of product managers is worthy of special attention.

PRODUCT MANAGERS

The functions of product or brand managers can be traced to such single-product entrepreneurs as E. H. Stuart, who introduced Carnation Evaporated Milk. Stuart not only sold the milk door to door but also was in charge of production, advertising, inventory, and research. His fate clearly depended on the success of Carnation Evaporated Milk and he alone was responsible for decisions relating to the product. Today's brand managers have been called "bureaucratic entrepreneurs." Although they are judged by the success of their products, we will see that product managers seldom have the decision-making authority of the individual entrepreneur.[8]

The Purpose of the Product Manager

The product management system represents an attempt to create decentralized profit centers for each of a firm's products. With this system, one person is in charge of coordinating all of the firm's efforts for a particular product. The product manager, who is also called a *brand manager* or a *product planning manager* in some organizations, begins working with a new product by developing a marketing plan and a sales forecast. Once this plan has been approved by the overall product management hierarchy, the product manager must convince the firm's advertising, sales, and distribution officials of the merits of the product's marketing program. Once the product is in the market, the product manager closely monitors its sales pattern in order to evaluate and recommend adjustments in the product's sales and promotional programs. Finally, it is the product manager's responsibility to suggest modifications in the product as well as to recommend new products for the firm.

The Procter & Gamble Co. was a pioneer in using the product management system. P&G is divided into 50 brand groups, each of which has one product manager and several assistant product managers.[9] The product manager assigns each of the assistant product managers one or more areas of responsibility for that product. They work with corporate specialists on their product's advertising copy, media planning, sales promotion, package design, marketing research, and sales forecasting. To illustrate, if the members of the brand group for Tide detergent wanted to change the Tide package design, they would first work with the art and package design departments. Then the sales department would help evaluate how the new package would affect shelf space, stacking, special displays, and trade reaction. Marketing research would run tests to determine consumer reaction to the new package, while the manufacturing department would develop cost data for producing the new container.

The product management system seems to work best in large, multiproduct firms when the sales volumes of individual products are large enough to be significant and yet not so large as to be vitally important to the firm's survival.[10] When the firm *is* dependent primarily on a single product, it is most appropriate for the firm's top marketing officer to play the role of product manager. PepsiCo, Inc., for example, is essentially a one-product firm. Although it produces several secondary products, the sales of these products are related to the major one, Pepsi-Cola. As a result, it has not been difficult for the top marketing officer at PepsiCo to coordinate all of the firm's marketing efforts for that product.[11] However, in firms like P&G which have numerous impor-

---

[8]Stephens Dietz, "Get More Out of Your Branch Management," *Harvard Business Review* (July-August, 1973), pp. 127–129.

[9]"The Brand Manager: No Longer King," *Business Week* (June 9, 1973), pp. 59–60.

[10]*Ibid.*

[11]Richard M. Clewett and Stanley F. Stasch, "Shifting Role for the Product Manager," *Harvard Business Review* (January-February, 1975), pp. 65–73.

tant products, it is essential that each product has one person who monitors all aspects of its performance.

Authority vs. Responsibility of the Product Manager

The major difficulty with the product management system is that although product managers are given a great deal of responsibility, they have relatively little authority to see that the product is marketed according to the original plan. The organization chart in Figure 8-8 illustrates the problem. In this situation, which is typical of most product management structures, the individual product managers report to a group product manager, who in turn reports to the director of product management. No one in the product management hierarchy has any control over the functional areas of marketing. This situation creates frustration and conflict in the organization; the product manager must try to direct people who do not work in the product hierarchy to do what is best for the product. To accomplish this goal, product managers must often rely on the soundness of their arguments as well as on the levels of marketing expertise that they are perceived to have within the organization. Even these tactics may not bring the desired results.

Successful Use of Product Managers

With all the conflicts that the product management system involves, it is somewhat surprising that it is so successful. The real key to its success is that

FIGURE 8-8   A Typical Product Management Organization Structure

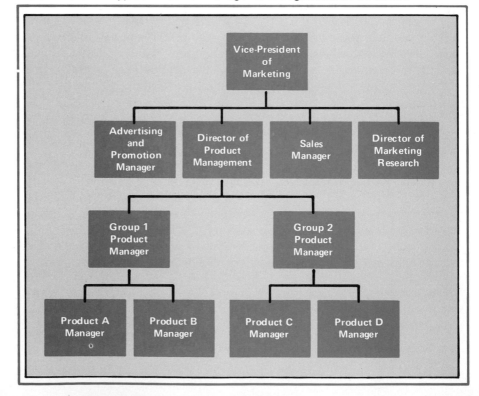

the business's top corporate officers are dedicated to the concept that one person is primarily responsible for each of the firm's products. If the officers are successful in communicating this idea to the rest of the organization, the system has a good chance of working. Without top management's vigorous support, however, the product manager will not have enough clout to gain the necessary cooperation from such areas as sales, advertising, and marketing research.

One new approach that some businesses have adopted to improve their product managers' chances of success involves giving the product managers more of a market orientation. Traditionally, product managers have been responsible for increasing the product's sales in all markets. This approach tends to break down when a product is sold in many different markets. As an example, the H. J. Heinz Co. modified its product management system when it realized that selling ketchup to retail grocers who make a profit on each bottle sold, and selling ketchup to restauranteurs, who give the product away, required such different strategies that one individual could not give the product the attention required to service both markets adequately. As a result, the firm now has two product managers for ketchup — one for grocery store sales and the other for restaurant sales.

The alternative to the use of product managers is to have one person in the organization responsible for all aspects of all products that the firm sells. This person normally would be the individual in charge of marketing. Although this approach works quite well for companies that have only a few products, it does not provide enough attention to individual products if the firm sells a number of items. Here, an individual must be given the responsibility of ensuring that sufficient attention is given to each product and that each is properly marketed.

BRANDING

The American Marketing Association defines a **brand** as "a name, term, sign, symbol, or design or a combination of these, which is intended to identify the goods or services of one seller or group of sellers and to differentiate them from those of competitors."[12] Stated simply, a brand is the means by which the firm identifies itself to customers. When a seller has been granted legal protection for a brand such that it may not be used by anyone else, it is called a **trademark**. In this section, we will analyze the marketing objectives for brands, examine the differences between manufacturer and distributor brands, and look at the characteristics of an effective brand name or design.

Objective of Branding

The purpose of branding is to help establish some limited form of "monopoly" power over the customer. The brand tells the customer that a particular firm or organization is responsible for the product. If this firm or organization has a reputation for producing high-quality merchandise, it is more likely that the consumer will be willing to pay a somewhat higher price for the product or

---

[12]Ralph S. Alexander, *A Glossary of Marketing Terms* (Chicago, Ill.: American Marketing Association, 1960), p. 9.

at least will select that product from among the array of potential competitors with little or no comparison shopping. Either alternative will result in larger revenues for the seller and what economists call "monopoly" profit.[13] Specifically, branding has three main objectives: seller identification, repeat sales, and new product sales.

Identification of Seller. The single most important aim of branding is to identify the seller. Interestingly enough, a look at the Russian television industry demonstrates just how important this objective is. In the Soviet Union, brands historically have been considered representative of the U.S. capitalistic system and therefore undesirable. A few years ago, however, several Russian factories began producing identical 17-inch television sets. Although there was apparently a great demand for televisions, consumers refused to purchase the sets and inventories piled up. After a great deal of research, the answer became quite clear: one factory consistently produced inferior sets. Since consumers could not tell whether the set they were purchasing was manufactured by the "lemon" factory or by a high-quality factory, they stopped buying televisions altogether.

Eventually the Russian television industry adopted a very practical approach to this problem and began placing "factory marks" on televisions to identify the manufacturer (see photo at left). Today in the Soviet Union, factory marks, or trademarks, are placed on many products to tell the buyer more about the origin of these products.[14]

Repeat Sales. Once an organization has effectively identified itself to a customer through its brand name, the satisfied customer will seek that company's products for repurchase. In addition, brands are instrumental in word-of-mouth and mass-media advertising. If, for example, the Campbell's Soup Company sold all its products under store labels, a satisfied customer would have to communicate pleasure not only with the product but also with the place of purchase in order for word-of-mouth promotion to be effective. In the same way, without its brand name, Campbell's could not take advantage of national or even local advertising. Because of the economies of scale in advertising, it is relatively expensive to redesign a campaign to fit each local market. However, many of you can no doubt identify the "Mm-mm-good" and "Mandhandlers" campaigns used by Campbell's.

New Product Sales. A firm with a well-established brand name, especially one denoting quality to the public, will have a much easier time introducing new products than will a relatively unknown company. When a firm such as Westinghouse, DuPont, or General Motors introduces a new product it will probably receive a positive response from many people who have had good experiences with its products in the past. For example, Gillette Co. banked heavily on the power of its reputation when it introduced the Cricket lighter. Because Gillette had no previous experience in the lighter business, some of

---

[13]The term *monopoly* in this context derives from the fact that the consumer does not necessarily purchase the product that generates the highest quality/price ratio.

[14]Theodore Levitt, "Branding on Trial," *Harvard Business Review* (March-April, 1966), p. 28.

the company's executives felt that the name *Gillette* would not help Cricket sales. The prevailing opinion, however, was that Gillette had a good name for producing high-quality products and that this reputation would prove beneficial to the Cricket lighter. Although it is always difficult to determine exactly why a new product succeeds or fails, the Cricket lighter has been very well received by the public.

Family Brands vs. Individual Brands

When most, if not all, of a firm's products bear the same brand name, they are said to be sold under a **family brand**. An illustration is Heinz 57 Variety brand name, which is carried on many Heinz products. We have just pointed out that a family brand makes it easier for a firm to introduce a new product to the market. It also tends to stimulate the sales of existing products in the firm's line. Why then do some firms choose to sell each of their products under a different brand name? There seem to be two answers: to protect existing products and to stimulate internal competition.

Protecting Existing Products. Shoppers sometimes perceive two or more of a firm's products as essentially the same even though they have different technical characteristics and differ considerably in price and quality. In such situations the firm usually makes an effort to differentiate its products from one another, especially when introducing a new, inexpensive product to the market. The concern here is to prevent the new product from jeopardizing sales of an existing, more expensive product. As an illustration, several well-known manufacturers of expensive watches decided that it was time to move into the lower-priced watch market. But what might happen at the jewelry counter if one of these firms puts its name on an inexpensive watch? It is not hard to imagine a situation in which a shopper, always on the lookout for a bargain and perceiving no difference between the two watches except price, decides to buy the inexpensive one. One way to prevent such "trading-down" is to market the new, inexpensive item under a separate brand name, i.e., as an individual brand.

Stimulate Internal Competition. A second reason why a firm might adopt an individual branding strategy is to stimulate competition within the organization. To illustrate, in the highly competitive laundry soap business, successful manufacturers typically offer a variety of products to the market; each product stands alone in the market and, in effect, competes against the products of other firms as well as against the other soaps produced by the same company and sold under a different name. This strategy tends to keep the marketing department on its toes. Procter & Gamble and Colgate-Palmolive both incorporate this strategy.

Battle of the Brands

For some time, manufacturers wielding national brands have waged war in the marketplace against retail distributors wielding private label brands. A manufacturer's branded product is sold under the same brand name across the United States. Examples of manufacturer's brands include Westinghouse appliances, Green Giant vegetables, and Sunkist oranges. In contrast, a private label product is sold under a brand name created specifically by the distributor. Examples include Craftsman tools at Sears, Ann Page products at A&P supermarkets, and Top Frost and Scotch Buy products at Safeway supermarkets. The so-called battle of the brands is usually fought over control of the distribution channel, since whoever controls distribution controls profits.

Who Controls the Channel? Manufacturers typically believe that they know more about marketing their products than anyone else does. Distributors or retailers often feel just as strongly about their ability to market these same products. Manufacturers hold that if they can control the marketing variables — price, product, distribution, and communication — they can create a strategy producing the best results for themselves as well as for the retailers. Retailers counter this rationale by arguing that because they deal directly with the final consumer, they know more about the consumer's needs than does the manufacturer. Also, many retailers feel that they are selling in a unique market which forces them to modify product strategy to compete effectively. An illustration would be the sale of men's shirts at $15.95 when they are promoted nationally at $19.00. Because of the local market conditions, a retailer may feel compelled to reduce the price of the shirts below the "suggested retail price," or be unable to sell enough shirts to make a profit.

Overriding the issue of who should make strategic decisions is the issue of customer loyalty: Is customer loyalty with the distributor or the manufacturer? As discussed earlier, one of the key reasons for using brands is to stimulate repeat sales. A manufacturer hopes to persuade customers, through effective communication and a reputation for quality, to search out its products. In contrast, many retailers would like customers to be loyal not to the manufacturer but to the store and to the products that can only be purchased there. Saks Fifth Avenue, a store that specializes in expensive clothing, has done an excellent job of marketing a line of private-label garments that can be purchased only at Saks.

Profit Implications. The profit position of retailers varies a great deal depending on whether they are selling private-label products or national brands. Cost savings that result from little or no promotion often permit the retailer to price a private-label product from 10 to 40 percent below its national-brand counterpart.[15] These price reductions often make it much easier for retailers to sell a sufficient quantity of merchandise to make a reasonable profit. In addition, as a study of grocery store prices and margins indicated, supermarkets not only price private-label products lower than national brands but also achieve greater profit margins with them. As detailed in Table 8-1, of the seven categories of grocery products examined, all private-label items sold for less than the national brands, and in six of the seven categories the profit margin for private-label products was higher than for the manufacturers' brands.

When the retailers can sell less expensive products and still bring in a greater profit, it is not difficult to see why so many of them are interested in carrying private-label merchandise.

---

[15]Barbara Davis Coe, "Private Versus National Preference Among Lower and Middle-Income Consumers," *Journal of Retailing* (Fall, 1971), p. 62.

TABLE 8-1 Profit Margins of Grocery Products

Product Category	Average Retail Price per Case*		Average Percentage Gross Margin*	
	Distributors' Brands	Advertised Manufacturers' Brands**	Distributors' Brands	Advertised Manufacturers' Brands**
Frozen orange juice concentrate	$ 8.74	$11.57	22.0%	23.0%
Frozen green beans	4.94	6.42	37.2	30.5
Canned green peas	4.76	5.54	25.8	21.2
Canned peaches	6.24	6.54	18.5	18.1
Catsup	4.46	5.51	17.3	16.5
Tuna fish	12.72	15.46	23.8	19.2
Evaporated milk	6.52	7.49	12.6	11.2

*The data shown are averages based on a survey of 7 to 12 food chains (the number of chains reporting varies from one product category to the next).
**The data reported here are for a typical advertised manufacturer's brand. All other data are averages of all distributors' and advertised manufacturers' brands in the product categories shown.
Source: Robert D. Buzzell, et al., Marketing: A Contemporary Analysis (New York: McGraw-Hill Book Co., 1972), p. 361.

What Makes a Brand Name Good?

In selecting the actual brand name, four rules of thumb should be considered:

1. The name should be short, easy to spell, and easy to understand. Examples: Jell-O, Tide, Wisk.
2. The brand name should be appropriate for the product. If possible, it should emphasize the product's major attribute. Examples: Swingline stapler, Right Guard deodorant, D-Zerta, Kool-Aid, Gaines Burgers.
3. A brand name should be distinctive. Examples: Xerox, Exxon, Zest.
4. A brand name should be easy to remember. Examples: Betty Crocker, Uncle Ben's, Soft and Pretty, Windex.

Although it may not be possible to incorporate all four considerations into the name of a particular product and still have it legally protectable, it is important to make sure that the brand name selected will stand the test of time. A few years ago, Esso Corporation decided to standardize its brand name across its various subsidiaries. To accomplish this task, Esso spent millions of dollars on research to determine potential names. The company's problem was particularly difficult because the new name had to be acceptable not only in the United States but also in the many foreign countries where Esso does business.

Once the firm decided on the new name, Exxon, it spent well over $100 million to inform its customers of the change.

After a firm selects its brand name, it must ensure, through trademark registration, that the name is legally protected in the United States, as well as abroad if the firm intends to sell its products internationally. For example, more than 500,000 brand names are registered with the United States Patent Office. More than 20,000 new names are added to the patent list each year.[16]

PACKAGING

Packaging is significantly more important today than it was 20 years ago. Presently, U.S. manufacturers spend more than $35 billion annually on packaging, exceeding the expenditures of U.S. industry on advertising and marketing research combined.[17] The primary force behind the "packaging revolution" has been the spread of self-service retailing. The use of automatic machinery for counting and measuring products seems to be the easiest way to achieve productivity gains in marketing. In addition, in a self-service world, the package must perform such functions as describing and selling the product — functions which were once handled by salespeople. We now look at the functions of packaging, the distributor's perspective on packaging, and the environmental problems created by packaging.

Functions of Packaging

Protection of the product is still one of the most important functions of packaging. In recent years, great strides have been made in the development of new materials providing added protection at reduced costs. Today, packaging also performs three marketing functions: product differentiation, product information, and symbolic image.

Product Differentiation. In many cases, the package is the primary vehicle used to differentiate a product from its competition. When a consumer walks through a supermarket that contains several thousand items, the package must catch the consumer's eye, hold his or her attention, and stimulate interaction between the consumer and the product. Consider the phenomenal success of L'eggs hosiery and the role packaging has played in it — truly a classic example of product differentiation through packaging.

Product Information. The package frequently provides a great deal of information for the user. Depending on the item, the package may include detailed instructions on how to use the product; information about the contents, value, and price of the product; as well as a warning about potential hazards involved in its use. The firm should make every effort to ensure that the average purchaser will have no difficulty understanding what is printed on the package. Del

[16]"The Name Is the Game," *Sales Management* (May 1, 1969), p. 55.

[17]William G. Nickels and Marvin A. Jolson, "Packaging — The Fifth "P" in the Marketing Mix," *Advanced Management Journal* (Winter, 1976), p. 13.

Monte, for example, led the way in providing nutrition-related information on its canned food products.

Symbolic Image. The package may also be used to provide a certain social-symbolic meaning. To illustrate, an expensive perfume may be packaged in a fine crystal container, not because the crystal will protect the perfume better than plain glass, but because the package relays the message that this product is of high-quality. In the same manner, a fine liqueur requires a bottle that is considerably different from one used for an 89¢ bottle of wine. The marketer must insist that the image conveyed by the product's package be consistent with the social-symbolic image conveyed by the product itself.

Thus far, we have talked about packaging only at the consumer level. What about packaging's role in the distribution process?[18]

Packaging and Distributors

Packaging also includes the manner in which the product is sent to intermediaries for distribution to the final consumer. The packaging executive must be intimately familiar with the distribution process in order to design containers that make the distributor's job easier. The average supermarket, for example, stocks more than 8,000 items. Container design for a product distributed primarily through supermarkets must take this fact into account. The carton must be strong yet easy to open, and it must be convenient to handle with the type of materials-handling equipment that most supermarkets have.

One successful program of packaging for the distributor involved GTE Sylvania, Inc., which was having a difficult time convincing supermarkets to provide additional shelf space for its light bulbs. Recognizing the concern of the retailer for efficient shelf restocking, the company designed a shipping carton that easily converted into a compartmentalized selling rack. As a result, the retailer was able to set up the Sylvania display in two minutes rather than the usual 30.

Packaging and Environmental Problems

Today, more than 70 percent of the combined sales of beer and soft drinks involve no-deposit, no-return bottles. As our society has become more concerned with environmental protection, we have become less tolerant of the broken bottles, crushed cartons, and bent cans littering our streets. At the same time, many cities are having a great deal of difficulty finding enough land to establish sanitary landfills to accommodate the growing amount of garbage produced by our society.

There appear to be two partial solutions to the U.S.'s package disposal problem. First, throw-away containers can be banned from the market, thereby forcing people to buy beer and soft drinks in returnable bottles. Oregon passed such a law in 1972, and it has been quite effective. A study by the Environ-

---

[18]Much of the following discussion has been adapted from Nickels and Jolson, *Ibid.*, pp. 13–21.

mental Protection Agency (EPA) indicated that roadside litter subsequently declined 81 percent in test areas in that state.[19]

Unfortunately, there are some very important problems with the Oregon solution. For example, it tends to put supermarkets in the recycling business. The significant costs of handling empty bottles are usually passed on to consumers in the form of higher prices. In addition, the EPA believes that if the deposit is raised high enough to ensure that most containers will be returned, "counterfeiters" will then manufacture bottles to collect the deposits.

A second partial solution to the package disposal problem is the development of more recycling plants. Such plants recycle returned packages into steel, aluminum, fertilizer, glass, plastics, or even a combustible material with half the heating strength of coal. Recycling not only conserves our limited resources and reduces the nation's energy expenditures, but it also lessens the need for sanitary landfills. The major difficulties with recycling are that buyers have a strong preference for products made entirely of "virgin" ingredients and have generally been unwilling to make the effort to return containers to the place of purchase or to a recycling plant.[20]

summary points

1. A product is not just a physical item; it also encompasses such non-physical features as reputation for reliability, warranty protection, ease of purchase and financing, and speed of delivery.

2. Consumer goods are sold to individuals and families for personal consumption. They are usually divided into three classifications: convenience goods, shopping goods, and specialty goods.

3. Industrial goods and services are sold to commercial enterprises and governments for resale to other enterprises or for use in the production of other goods and services. Eight classifications of industrial goods include heavy equipment, light equipment, construction, component parts, raw materials, processed materials, services, and consumable supplies.

4. A product item is the individual product; a product line refers to a category of products; and the product mix includes all the lines that the firm sells.

5. A five-phase procedure for evaluating the present and future potential of products includes: the definition phase, the data collection phase, the product evaluation matrix, future projections, and product decisions.

6. Many successful products move through five stages in their life cycle: market development, rapid growth, turbulence, maturity, and decline. Each stage generates different profit margins and requires unique marketing strategies.

7. The primary objective of the product management system is to create profit centers where one person is responsible for coordinating all of the firm's efforts for a particular product.

[19] "Oregon: A Test Case for Returnable Containers," *Business Week* (July 28, 1973), pp. 76–77.

[20] For more information on packaging and the environment, see: William N. Gunn, "Packagers and the Environmental Challenge," *Harvard Business Review* (July-August, 1972), pp. 103–112; and Tom Alexander, "The Packaging Problem Is a Can of Worms," *Fortune* (June, 1972), pp. 105–202 *passim*.

8. The most significant problem for product managers is that they are given a great deal of responsibility but relatively little authority.

9. The primary functions of branding are to identify the seller, to promote repeat sales, and to make it easier for the firm to introduce new products.

10. The "battle of the brands" refers to conflict between the manufacturer and the distributor over control of a brand's channel of distribution.

11. Four rules for establishing brand names suggest that they must be: short and easy to spell, appropriate for the product, distinctive, and easy to remember.

12. The major functions of packaging include protecting the product, differentiating the product, serving as a vehicle for information about the product, and enhancing the product's image.

13. Packaging must also take into account the needs of market intermediaries and protection of the environment.

1. Describe the various product attributes for an item such as Chanel No. 5 perfume.
2. How does a firm's marketing strategy change when it starts selling consumer goods and stops selling industrial goods?
3. Compare and contrast convenience goods, shopping goods, and specialty goods. Give examples of each.
4. Explain the product item, line, and mix distinction. Give an example to illustrate the distinction.
5. Why is it necessary to define the product item or line as well as the market under investigation when conducting a product evaluation?
6. What is the role of a product evaluation matrix in a product evaluation procedure?
7. Assume that you are a marketing manager for a firm that produces expensive slide rule calculators. The product has now reached the maturity stage. What marketing strategy should you recommend to your superiors?
8. Most experts agree that not all products pass through the same life cycle. Why then is it important to study the product life cycle?
9. Under which business environments does the product management system seem to work best? As discussed in the text, the authority of brand managers is rarely matched to their responsibility. How would you begin to solve this problem that seems to be inherent to the product manager approach?
10. Describe in your own words the primary objectives of branding. What problem does a manufacturer typically encounter when marketing products under a brand name?
11. What is meant by "battle of the brands"? Who do you think should win this battle?
12. Will packaging be more important to the marketing manager ten years from now than it is today?
13. How would you deal with the environmental problems caused by packaging?

Topics discussed in Chapter 9:

1. What is meant by a "new" product.
2. The reasons why firms introduce new products.
3. A comparison of internal product development and product development through acquisition.
4. The four types of new product management organizations.
5. A six-stage model for new product development.
6. The causes of new product failure.
7. The hidden costs of weak products as well as a system for eliminating unprofitable products.
8. The diffusion of innovations

The process by which new products are introduced to the marketplace is of critical importance to any firm that is operating in a highly competitive marketplace. While the firm's present profit position is largely a function of its ability to effectively market its existing products, the organization's future rests on its ability to successfully introduce new products. We begin our discussion of new product development by looking at what is really meant by a new product.

WHAT IS NEW ABOUT A "NEW" PRODUCT?

Relatively few of the many products introduced to the market each year are entirely new. To be considered as such, these products would have to perform a completely new function for the buyer. Therefore, let's define a **new product** as one which either performs a new function or provides a significant improvement over existing products. To illustrate, when the slide rule became widely available, it performed a new function, but the slide rule calculator represented only a product improvement to the customer. Yet both would have been considered new products when they were introduced. Other common examples of new or substantially improved products are the diesel train locomotive, jet planes, instant cameras, transistors, freeze-dried coffee, and cathode-ray computer display terminals (CRTs).

It is important for the firm marketing a new product to determine what the customer perceives as new about the product. This information is vital to the development of the product's marketing plan. Figure 9-1 lists seven new product attributes that make it easier for the firm to sell a new product and six attributes that make it more difficult. For example, the Polaroid Corp., in introducing its Pronto camera, stressed such features as the camera's low price,

FIGURE 9-1   Ways in Which a Product Is New

Attributes Making It Easier for the Seller	Attributes Making It More Difficult for the Seller
• Lower price. • Greater convenience in use. • More dependable performance. • Easier to purchase in terms of time, place, or credit. • Positive conspicuous consumption. • Positive new appearance. • New markets.	• More complex methods of use. • Unfamiliar patterns of use. • Unfamiliar benefits. • Unimportant benefits. • High risk of costly errors. • Negative new appearance.

Source: Adapted from Chester R. Wasson, "What Is 'New' About a New Product," *Journal of Marketing* (July, 1960), p. 54.

ease of use, and dependability in comparison to other instant cameras. Polaroid was fortunate with this product in that it did not have any negative new product attributes to overcome.

In contrast to Polaroid's success, Magnavox may encounter more difficulty in promoting its video-disc system. While the video-disc system is less expensive than its major competition, videotape systems, it does not allow recording of programs from television. This lack of flexibility may be perceived by consumers as a serious shortcoming. Magnavox must make a well-planned marketing effort to emphasize the advantages of the video-disc compared to videotape systems — advantages such as price, easy storage of programs, availability of specific educational and entertainment materials — if it wants to be successful in selling its product.

WHY FIRMS INTRODUCE NEW PRODUCTS

Businesses introduce new products for the purpose of increasing their profit positions. Profit goals may be missed without the help of new products. This tends to force even conservative managers to establish procedures for seeking out and evaluating new products. The following discussion centers on four specific stimuli that lead firms to introduce new products.

Sales Growth Objectives

Many corporations establish sales growth objectives of 10 to 30 percent per year. Although the marketing department can conceivably achieve these sales goals by selling more of what the firm currently produces, it is often easier to gain new sales by introducing new products. One study of marketing executives indicated that they attributed 85 percent of projected sales growth to new products or acquisitions. Sixty percent of this growth was attributed to internally developed products.[1]

Excess Production or Distribution Capacity

At times, firms introduce a new product simply because they have excess production or distribution capacity. Whether production facilities are used at 50 percent or 100 percent of capacity, the firm still incurs such fixed expenses as depreciation, insurance, and plant security. Therefore, a new product that might not otherwise be of interest to the firm may represent an opportunity to offset the fixed overhead expenses on the excess plant. Several years ago, the Gillette Co., makers of Gillette safety razors, considered selling blank cassettes through its normal distribution channels. The safety razor division sales manager felt that employees could devote up to 10 percent of their time without hurting the sales of Gillette's other products.[2]

Competition

A specific action or threat of such action by competition frequently motivates a business to introduce and market a new product. Chevrolet introduced its Camaro because of the success of the Ford Mustang; Ford introduced the Lincoln Versailles in response to the success of the Cadillac Seville. In jumping into the market, the "me too" company realizes that it made a mistake by not recognizing the potential of the product but does not wish to compound its error by staying out of the market any longer. In much the same way, a firm may choose to enter a market in order to prevent a competitor from exploiting the market first. In this case it is the threat of a competitive action, rather than a specific past action, that inspires the firm to act.

Completion of the Product Line

Another reason for introducing a new product is to complete the company's existing product line. In these situations, adding a new product often stimulates the sale of existing products. Beech Aircraft Corp.'s decision to add a trainer to its product line illustrates this strategy. Beech had specialized in expensive single- and twin-engine airplanes but had not offered its own trainer. Eventually, executives of the firm concluded that they were losing sales each year because people tended to buy a plane made by the manufacturer of the one in which they learned to fly. Therefore, to increase the sale of its more expensive planes, Beech introduced a trainer called the "Musketeer."

MAKE-OR-BUY CONSIDERATIONS

Once a firm decides to introduce a product to the market, it can either develop the product internally or buy out a firm that is currently producing the

---

[1]Philip R. McDonald and Joseph O. Eastlack, Jr., "Top Management Involvement with New Products," *Business Horizons* (December, 1971), p. 24.

[2]Steven H. Star, Nancy J. Davis, Christopher H. Lovelock, and Benson P. Shapiro, *Problems in Marketing* (5th ed.; New York: McGraw Hill Book Co., 1977), p. 15.

FIGURE 9-2 Internal Development Vs. Acquisition

Factor	Internal Development	Acquisition
Antitrust complications	None	Possible problem
Profitability	Larger profits	Quicker profits
Risk	More risk	Less risk
Management	No duplication	Possible duplication

product. As discussed in Chapter 3, the Federal Trade Commission has ruled consistently that any merger of two businesses resulting in significantly reduced competition is a violation of federal antitrust laws. In addition to this and other legal issues discussed in Chapter 3, there are three factors that must be considered in a make-or-buy decision: potential profitability, risk, and personnel requirements. These factors are outlined in Figure 9-2 and discussed below.

Potential Profitability

Compared to internal development, a merger or acquisition typically yields the business *quicker* profits because the product in question is already under production. As a result, the acquiring firm does not have to undertake such time-consuming activities as plant construction, test marketing, or sales force training. Instead, the new product can be sold immediately.

The profit potential, however, is greater if the new product is developed internally because the organization is able to keep the entrepreneurial rewards for itself. If one firm purchases another in order to acquire a successful product, it pays the market value for the business, which will have been enhanced owing to the success of the product in question. Therefore, the so-called entrepreneurial return from the new product remains with the original owners of the acquired business.

Risk

Typically, less risk is associated with a new product acquired through merger than with a product developed internally. As we will see later in this chapter, a firm may examine 50 or more new product ideas before developing one new product. In addition, as many as half of all new products never generate a satisfactory return. Such risk is greatly reduced when a product is acquired through merger because the acquiring firm has an opportunity to carefully examine how the product has been received by the market. If the product has done well, then it will probably continue to do well in the foreseeable future.

Personnel Requirements

One advantage of a merger is that it often yields the acquiring firm needed management and personnel skills. In fact, the objective of the merger may not be so much to gain a particular product as it is to obtain the services of important executives. Unfortunately, in some cases the added personnel may lead to unnecessary duplication; for example, where the firm had one director of marketing, it may now have two. Such a situation inevitably leads to the painful process of terminating a number of qualified people.

As a general rule relatively little duplication will result if the product is acquired through merger and is maintained as a separate division with its own manufacturing and marketing personnel. However, duplication of personnel is likely to occur if the acquired product is fully integrated with the rest of the firm's products. Obviously, there will be no duplication if the product is developed internally.

NEW PRODUCT MANAGEMENT

While many companies today are generally well organized and well managed, a considerable number are poorly prepared to evaluate and manage new product opportunities. This lack of preparation or expertise is a major problem for U.S. industry in a world where new products are rapidly replacing older ones. Though new product management can take one of many forms, we will focus on venture management, new product committees, new product departments, and new product managers.

Venture Management

The purpose of a **venture management team**, made up of people from the different functional areas of the enterprise, is to evaluate a new product idea and, if the product appears to have profit potential, to carry it through to commercialization. Venture teams differ significantly from regular business committees in that they are tightly structured groups of people who spend all their time on the new product. The goal is to free a group of highly talented, enthusiastic individuals from bureaucratic obstacles and day-to-day operating problems.

Truly enterprising venture teams are market oriented, not product or process oriented. Venture teams seek out opportunities with growth potential considerably greater than that of the economy as a whole. Therefore, the venture team must continually ask itself such questions as: What business is our firm in? Are there any unmet consumer needs that we could serve? This type of logic has stimulated General Mills to enter the game and toy business. It is apparent that General Mills has a talent for manufacturing ready-to-eat cereals, but the management of General Mills feels that the firm's chief asset is its ability to market products to preschool children and their mothers. Within this market segment, General Mills sees crafts, games, and toys as profitable growth opportunities.[3]

Characteristics of Venture Teams. Although the approach of each organization to venture management varies somewhat depending on its history and character, most successful venture teams have five characteristics in common.

---

[3]Mack Hanan, "Corporate Growth Through Venture Management," *Harvard Business Review* (January–February, 1969), p. 47.

Multidisciplinary. Venture team members typically are drawn from such predominantly technical areas as design engineering, application engineering, production, marketing research, and finance. The interaction of individuals with different specialties is essential for the successful operation of a venture team. In addition, although some members of the venture team stay with a specific product idea as long as it is under consideration, many other people are phased in and out of the project in response to changing product development requirements.

Organizationally Separate. In almost all cases, the successful venture team is separate from the permanent departmental, functional, or divisional structure of the organization. The generation of a continuing stream of new ideas about the product in question requires that the permanent members of the team not be involved at all in the day-to-day operations of the company. The organization chart shown in Figure 9-3 depicts the relationship of the venture team to the rest of the firm. Although the members of the team represent the four main functional areas of the organization, they report to the new ventures department as long as they are associated with the new product.

Supported by Top Management. It is essential that top management actively support the new venture concept. This is why in Figure 9-3 the new

FIGURE 9-3 Venture Team Organization

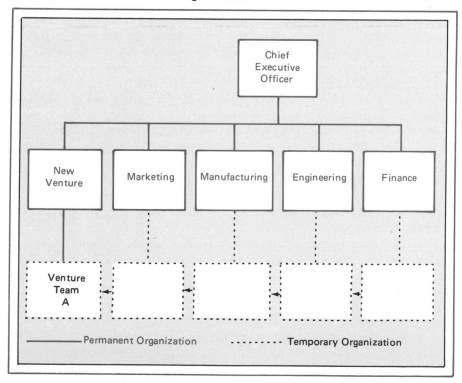

Source: Adapted from Richard M. Hill and James D. Hlavacek, "The Venture Team: A New Concept in Marketing Organization," *Journal of Marketing* (July, 1972), p. 47.

venture department reports directly to the chief administrative officer of the firm. Without the vigorous support of top management, venture teams tend to become entangled in the bureaucratic structure of the organization.

Entrepreneurial in Spirit. An entrepreneurial spirit is achieved by bringing together a small group of bright people, by freeing them from traditional job responsibilities, and by permitting them to pursue fresh ideas. In addition, most businesses have heightened the spirit of entrepreneurship by allowing venture team members to share in the profits of the product once it reaches the market. Ultimately, the degree of entrepreneurial spirit and the success of the team depend upon the manager of the venture group. The best new venture managers seem to have broad company experience. They have demonstrated initiative, imagination, and a strong drive to succeed. Their most important characteristic, however, may be their willingness to let other people take credit for the success of the team and for a successfully commercialized new product idea.

Flexible in Life Span. Virtually all successful venture teams operate free from the pressure of strict deadlines. Although they function within the general guidelines of a development plan with several phases or checkpoints, the completion schedules are loosely defined. Also, some new products may take much longer to develop than others. Unrealistic deadlines, in general, tend to stifle potentially profitable projects before they have had time to develop fully.

Analysis of Venture Teams. The primary advantage of a venture team is that it is a tightly knit group of individuals dedicated to introducing a new product into the market. Organizationally, the venture team is structured to permit a large firm to regain its original entrepreneurial spirit, at least to the extent of the product idea under investigation. The inherent flexibility of the venture team to respond to the changing needs of the marketplace is difficult to duplicate under any other management system.

Venture teams, however, have three significant disadvantages. First, they are expensive. As stated above, venture teams are made up of representatives from the various functional areas of the firm. Team members are selected because they are bright, articulate, and hard working; as a result, they also tend to be well paid. Venture teams are also expensive because they require staff assistance as well as supporting facilities if they are to be truly independent of the rest of the firm.

A second disadvantage of the venture approach is the difficulty of finding the right person to head the team. As one corporate executive has said, "Personnel with highly developed entrepreneurial skills are not that abundant in large corporations." In addition, many division managers are not willing to permit one or more of their brightest employees to leave their divisions to join the venture team. At times, this unwillingness has resulted in venture teams that are not as well staffed as they might otherwise be.

The last disadvantage of venture teams relates directly to their primary advantage — namely, their dedication to new product development. Some venture teams become emotionally involved with the success of the new product. When this occurs, the venture team may lose sight of its twin objectives — to evaluate a new product opportunity and then to market the product successfully. Many new product ideas must be dropped before they reach the market; if the venture team is unwilling to recognize a product's fatal flaws, it could cost the company a great deal of money. This potential problem can be overcome only by the careful selection of the venture team manager as well as by sufficient supervision by top management.[4]

Because of these disadvantages or because firms have not grown to the point where they have begun to lose their entrepreneurial flair, some firms have chosen other organizational structures to accommodate new product development.

Alternatives to Venture Teams

A firm deciding not to employ the venture team approach may elect to utilize new product managers. These individuals perform the same functions as do product managers, as discussed in Chapter 8, but work only with new products. Other alternatives to venture teams include new product committees and new product departments.

New Product Committees. Many firms use new product committees to evaluate new products. The new product committee usually is made up of the president of the firm along with managers from the major functional areas. Once this committee approves a new product idea, it is turned over to the marketing department for actual introduction to the marketplace. A new product committee has the advantage of bringing together people with different backgrounds to work on a common problem. In this sense, the committee is often successful in stimulating brainstorming sessions within the organization. In addition, it often serves as an effective system of organizational communication.

Unfortunately, new product committees sometimes fail to make the correct decisions because their participants work only part-time for the committee. As a result, committee members devote only limited time and energy to the new product because they are embroiled in their own day-to-day departmental problems. Other difficulties with new product committees are that they make decisions slowly and their decisions are frequently "committee compromises," which tend to satisfy no one completely.

If a firm decides to use new product committees, the following guides should be observed:

1. Management must establish in writing the committee's responsibilities and management's understanding of these responsibilities.
2. The committee must have formal agendas and minutes of the proceedings.
3. A strong leader must be appointed to chair the committee. If the leader selected is not the president of the company, it must be a senior department head.
4. Representatives of each department must be included on the committee. However, the committee must also be kept small enough to be manageable.[5]

New Product Departments. Many successful corporations, such as General Electric, have established new product departments. These departments fea-

---

[4]David S. Hopkins, *Options in New Product Organization*, (New York: The Conference Board, 1974), pp. 42–43.

[5]*Ibid.*, pp. 44–45.

ture a relatively small staff of analysts whose primary responsibility is to evaluate the market potential for new products. Once a product has been approved by the new product department and by top management, it is given to the marketing organization. Normally, the director of the new product department reports directly to the chief executive officer of the corporation.

The primary advantage of new product departments in comparison to new product committees is that members of the former spend all their time evaluating new products. Consequently, new product ideas are less likely to get lost in the bureaucracy. Unfortunately, new product departments typically do not have the authority to carry out their assigned responsibilities; thus they often must rely on their "influential authority" to obtain the necessary cooperation from the various functional areas of the firm. This situation frequently requires the president of the business to become involved in settling minor disagreements among departments. This exaggerated dependence on the chief executive can lead to mistrust among executives and a general stifling of initiative and innovation.[6]

Each firm must carefully weigh the advantages and disadvantages of each organizational structure for handling product development. Criteria for this decision include human and financial resources of the firm, time constraints, and compatibility with the existing organization.

DEVELOPING NEW PRODUCTS

Once the firm has chosen the appropriate managerial framework, it can begin the actual process of developing new products. A six-stage model describing the development of new products, as shown in Figure 9-4, can be used with any of the new product management systems discussed above.

Stated simply, the model shows that after the idea generation phase the firm concentrates its efforts on eliminating new product ideas from further consideration as quickly and as efficiently as possible in order to identify those products with the best chance of commercial success. It is with these products that the firm then goes to the marketplace. Accordingly, as Figure 9-4 indicates, after the completion of each stage beyond idea generation, a decision must be made whether the new product should be terminated, sent back for review and possible modification, or be sent forward to the next stage in the product development process. An important study by the consulting firm of Booz, Allen & Hamilton, Inc., found that approximately 58 ideas are needed to generate one new product. As shown by the curve in Figure 9-5, 46 of these new ideas fail and are eliminated during the product evaluation stage. Of the 12 remaining ideas, five are terminated during the economic analysis because of a lack of profit potential, four do not pass successfully through the product development stage, and two do not survive the market test. This leaves only one idea out of the original 58 that is destined to be commercialized.

---

[6]Chris Argyris, "Today's Problems with Tomorrow's Organizations," *Journal of Management Studies* (February, 1967), p. 31.

FIGURE 9-4 New Product Development Process

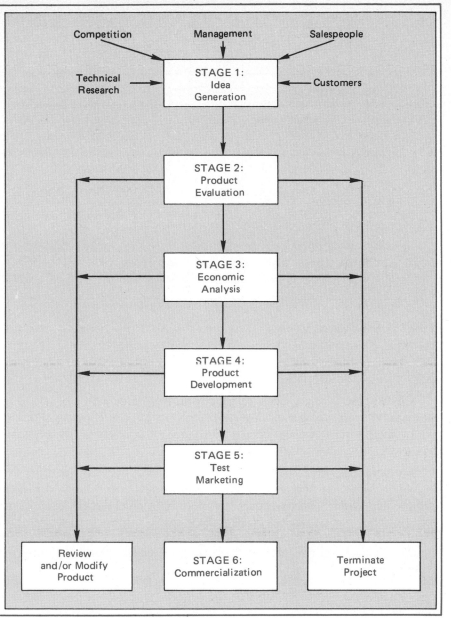

Stage 1: Idea Generation

New product ideas come from a variety of sources. Since these ideas represent the company's future, management must do everything economically feasible to encourage the flow of new product ideas. Although many firms do almost nothing to generate new ideas, others have implemented rather sophisticated programs.

FIGURE 9-5 Mortality of New Product Ideas

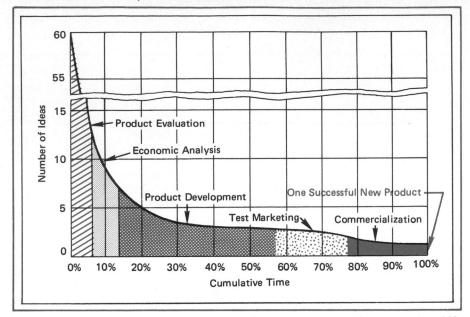

Source: Booz, Allen & Hamilton, Inc., 1968.

Sources of New Ideas. Where do firms get new product ideas? They get them from customers, salespeople, top management, their competitors, and their technical research staff.

Customers. The customer represents an important source of new product ideas for many companies. Consumer product firms and industrial product manufacturers alike receive literally thousands of unsolicited ideas for new products each year from current customers.

Salespeople. Salespeople are some of the most neglected and yet most promising sources of new product ideas. Salespeople spend the vast majority of their time talking with customers, and they learn what people do or do not like about the current product offering. As a result, it makes sense for a business to establish formal lines of communication between the sales force and the new product planning staff so that new product ideas can easily travel up the organization.

Top Management Personnel. Members of the firm's top management often have excellent ideas for new products. Frequently, these individuals have many years of experience in the industry, and have developed a sixth sense for determining what type of products the market is most likely to accept. Top management can also play an important role in defining those markets in which new product personnel should be concentrating their efforts.

Competition. Many new products are produced by modifying products that have already been developed and introduced by the competition. In reality, patents give relatively little protection to the inventor. Therefore, new product personnel should carefully analyze what new products the competition has introduced or might introduce. In the case of an industrial product, the future activity of the competition can be discerned by talking with customers; for consumer goods, watching what new products the competition is test marketing can be productive.

Technical Research Staff. Some large corporations spend significant sums of money on pure research. DuPont's Central Research Department specializes in the search for new knowledge without specific commercial objectives. While this type of research has led to such important products as nylon, most firms are not able to afford large departments dedicated to pure research. Thus most businesses concentrate their research efforts on using current technologies to create new products.

Brainstorming. If a firm is not satisfied with the number of new product ideas currently under consideration, it may wish to take some positive action to stimulate new ideas. One of the most useful techniques in this regard is **brainstorming**, wherein a small group of individuals with diverse backgrounds is brought together, presented with a problem, and asked to develop several solutions. This approach serves to generate a set of alternative solutions for the problem. In addition, the synergistic effect of one person's ideas on another's ideas often stimulate new problem-solving possibilities.

Brainstorming was first utilized in Alex F. Osborn's advertising agency, Batten, Barton, Durstine, and Osborn. Osborn suggests four rules that must be followed in brainstorming. First, session members should not be allowed to criticize the ideas of others; specific solutions to the proposed problem are evaluated later. Second, the wilder the idea, the better; no attempt should be made to constrain the imaginations of the participants. Third, the participants should be encouraged to think of as many ideas as possible; the more ideas, the better the chance that one will eventually be useful. Fourth, the participants should be encouraged to build on each other's ideas. Often, it is a combination of ideas, not just one idea alone, that leads to the development of a new product.[7]

Stage 2: Product Evaluation

The objective of the product evaluation stage is to eliminate new product ideas that are not compatible with the firm's long-term mission. The Booz, Allen & Hamilton study mentioned earlier in this chapter indicated that almost 80 percent of new product ideas are eliminated during this stage of the product development process. A helpful tool in screening out product ideas is the product evaluation matrix.[8] Use of the matrix involves determining which performance factors should be used in evaluating new products, deciding how the factors should be weighted, and ascertaining the new product's compatibility with each of the performance factors.

Performance Factors. The performance factors in the product evaluation matrix consist of those factors that the firm feels are important for the success-

---

[7]Alex F. Osborn, *Applied Imagination* (3d ed.; New York: Charles Scribner's Sons, 1963), pp. 155–156.

[8]Barry M. Richman, "A Rating Scale for Product Innovation," *Business Horizons* (Summer, 1962), pp. 36–44.

TABLE 9-1 Product Evaluation Matrix for a Hypothetical Product

Performance Factors	Relative Weights (A)	Product Rating* (B)											A × B (C)
		Very Poor 0	.1	.2	.3	.4	.5	.6	.7	.8	.9	Very Good 1.0	
Potential sales volume	0.25								x				0.175
Level of competition	0.15									x			0.120
Compatibility with marketing	0.20						x						0.100
Compatibility with production	0.10							x					0.060
Patent protection	0.05					x							0.020
Similarity to existing products	0.10						x						0.050
Environmental compatibility	0.10									x			0.080
Recycling potential	0.05										x		0.045
Total	1.00												0.650

*Rating scale: 0–0.4, poor; 0.41–0.75, fair; 0.76–1.00, good.

Source: Adapted with permission from material in Barry M. Richman, "A Rating Scale for Product Innovation," *Business Horizons* (Summer, 1962), pp. 37–44, copyright 1962 by the Foundation for the School of Business at Indiana University; and from Charles H. Kline, "The Strategy of Product Policy," *Harvard Business Review* (July–August, 1955), pp. 91–100.

ful introduction of a new product. These factors vary depending on the needs of each firm. Table 9-1 illustrates a hypothetical product evaluation matrix consisting of six traditional business factors and two social factors. The presence of the business factors requires little explanation; the social factors are included if for no other reason than because the federal government and many state governments are beginning to require firms to be responsible for their actions. The environmental compatibility factor considers whether the new product's manufacturing process will pollute the environment and whether the product itself will damage the environment once it is introduced. The recycling potential factor measures how easily the product can be reprocessed for further sale after it has been used.[9]

Factor Weights. The weights assigned to the performance factors indicate the importance of each product introduction factor. In the example in Table 9-1, the analyst believes that potential sales volume and compatibility with the firm's current marketing operations are the two most crucial performance factors. In addition, the analyst feels that the less competition the product faces, the better its chances of success. The two least important factors are patent protection and recycling potential. The weights for all factors sum to 1.0.

Product Ratings. The new product ratings indicate how the product scores on each factor. A score of 0.0 is very poor while a score of 1.0 is very good. The product in Table 9-1 receives its highest score (0.9) in terms of recycling potential and its lowest score (0.4) in terms of patent protection. It is important to point out that with a factor such as level of competition, a score of 0.8 indicates that the analyst feels the product will face relatively little competition.

Once the product rating is finished, the relative weights are multiplied by their corresponding ratings. The resulting numbers are then summed to obtain a total score for the product. In our example, the product has a combined score of 0.65. The next step is to compare this score to those of other products under consideration in order to determine which products warrant further analysis. In general, a score of 0.76 or above is considered to be quite good.

The product evaluation system is certainly not a perfect tool for screening new product ideas. If the analyst uses the wrong performance factors or the wrong weights, or scores the product incorrectly, the total score will be meaningless. The matrix, however, does have the advantage of forcing the analyst to rank each product with a common set of weighted factors. In addition, it is relatively easy to complete, and it permits new product ideas to be ranked against each other.

Stage 3: Economic Analysis

The purpose of the third stage in the product development process is to evaluate whether or not the proposed product will be profitable to the firm. This stage forces the analyst to make some "heroic" assumptions as to the product's expected revenues and costs. Although some people find this step uncomfortable, the alternative of not estimating a product's potential profit prior to the test market stage is unwise. The two best ways to perform this

---

[9]Dale L. Varble, "Social and Environmental Considerations in New Product Development," *Journal of Marketing* (October, 1972), pp. 11–15.

economic analysis are to develop a pro forma income statement or to conduct a market share study.

Pro Forma Income Statement. To develop a pro forma income statement, it is necessary to estimate the expected revenues and costs of the product in question. Under usual conditions, the firm's accounting department can generate quite accurate estimates of the projected manufacturing, marketing, and distribution costs associated with various production and sales levels. The more new technology that is required to produce the product, however, the more difficult the cost projections become.

Unfortunately, the revenue side of the pro forma statement is often very difficult to forecast accurately. Chapter 6 discussed four techniques for forecasting sales: jury of executive opinion, composite of sales force opinions, index of buying power, and time-series analysis. Although each of these techniques can be useful in certain circumstances, the task of forecasting new product sales is very risky. Assuming a relatively accurate sales forecast for the product is possible, the resulting pro forma income statement permits the analyst to determine whether the expected profit is sufficient for the product to proceed to the next stage of analysis.

Market Share Projections. When the analyst feels that it is not possible to make an accurate sales forecast, the market share approach to economic analysis can be useful. This approach can also be used to provide a "second opinion" if a pro forma statement is developed. Market share analysis involves tying a product's break-even point to the existing industry sales for the product. The **break-even point** is defined here as that quantity of unit sales at which the product's total revenue is equal to its total costs. In other words, it is the point at which the incoming revenue from the product pays all fixed and variable expenses but does not generate any profit for the firm. The higher the industry market share required for the product to break even, the smaller the chance of the new product succeeding.

To find a good illustration of market share analysis, we need only look at the Gillette Co. again. Several years ago, as mentioned previously, Gillette was considering the introduction of a line of blank recording cassettes. As a part of its analysis of the product's market potential, Gillette estimated the break-even point for blank cassettes at 6,700,000 units and industry sales at 38,000,000 units. Accordingly, Gillette would have to win 17.8 percent of the blank cassette market in order for its product to break even. The break-even point of 6,700,000 units does not mean a great deal in and of itself, but when expressed as a percentage of industry sales it does give some indication of whether the product is likely to be profitable. In this case, Gillette decided to abandon the idea of marketing blank cassettes.[10]

The primary difficulty with market share analysis is that it requires an existing product to serve as the basis for comparison. As a consequence, in the case of a truly new product, market share analysis is not of much use. A second problem is that market share analysis tends to be conservative — that is, it assumes that the new product will obtain a share only of the existing market. In other words, all sales are at the expense of the competition, and there is no

---

[10]Star, *et al., op. cit.*, pp. 6–21.

expansion of the market as a result of the new product. Typically, however, new products do tend to increase total industry sales significantly. In Texas, for example, when Southwest Airlines began operating a fleet of jet planes between Houston, Dallas, and San Antonio, the existing carriers initially felt that the total number of seats sold on these intrastate runs would not be sufficient for any of the carriers to make a profit. However, just the opposite occurred; Southwest generated enough new business that each of the existing carriers was able to operate profitably.

Stage 4: Product Development

Until the product development stage, the new product is little more than an idea. In Stage 4, the firm is forced to commit significant financial and personnel resources to the product. The outcome of this stage is the development of one or more prototypes of the products. Take a look at the prototypes of GM's X-car in the photos at right. The primary objective of the product development stage is to test the ability of the firm to manufacture the product at an acceptable cost level. If the product represents a technological breakthrough, this stage is also useful in determining whether the firm's scientists and technical staff will be able to develop the required technology.

Once the prototype is developed, the firm must begin tentative branding and packaging decisions. These decisions can be modified later depending on the results of test marketing. However, it should be remembered that a product is not just a physical object, rather it represents all those elements, including packaging and branding, that influence the customer's perception of its quality, value, and desirability.

Stage 5: Test Marketing

At this stage more than 96 percent of new product ideas have already been eliminated. Typically, one or two of the products reaching this stage will eventually be commercialized. You will recall from Chapter 6 that the objective of test marketing is to reduce decision risk, not to eliminate it. Based on the information obtained during this stage, the firm not only decides what product to market but also how it should be marketed.

A difficult question that many marketing executives must face at this stage in the new product development process is who should perform the test marketing. If a business is large enough to support its own marketing research staff, it may want to test market the product itself. Using in-house personnel for the test-marketing stage reduces the possibility of news about the product escaping prematurely to the firm's competitors. On the other hand, some large businesses utilize outside consulting firms in order to obtain more objective answers.

Stage 6: Commercialization

It used to be said that after a new product had gone through the first five steps of the development process, there was little the firm's marketing executives could do but pray. This is not the case. The firm begins the commercialization phase by completing, or revising, the new product's brand, packaging, and promotion strategies in light of the findings of the test market stage. The firm also needs to train its salespeople and dealers as to the merits of the product and its advantages relative to those of the competition.

Also, most new products are "rolled out" to the market, which means that they first may be introduced in one area of the country and then, if successful, sold in other areas. Typically, marketing analysts monitor the product's sales closely to determine what segments of the market are purchasing the product, how dealers are reacting to the product, and what the competition has done to counter it. This information is then used to modify the product or its marketing strategy as it is introduced into new markets. As a result, the commercialization phase may last two or more years and involve several product or strategy modifications.

WHY NEW PRODUCTS FAIL

The failure rate of new products in the United States is appalling. Although estimates vary, one study by the Conference Board indicated that the failure rate for new industrial products is 20 percent; for service industry offerings, 15–20 percent; and for consumer products, 40 percent.[11] These figures are particularly astonishing when one realizes that fully half of the products reaching the test market stage are not introduced to the market and that more than 96 percent of new product ideas are eliminated prior to test marketing. In short, U.S. industry spends a great deal of money on products that never return any profit to their firms. Let's examine why product failure risk has increased so much during the last several years and look at six of the most common reasons for product failure.

Management Risks in New Products[12]

Unquestionably, the risk associated with new products has increased considerably. Partially responsible is the dramatic rise in investment required for new products; in some industries it has tripled in less than ten years. Also, today's investments in new products are less able to be transferred from one activity to another than they were a few years ago. In the production area, most expenditures are concentrated in single-product equipment and in automated systems; in the marketing area, it takes larger and larger promotional expenditures to shape positive consumer attitudes toward a new product.

Another reason for increased new product risk is government regulation. In the automobile industry, for example, recent legislation requires substantial industry investments for improved safety and emission standards which, at least now, do not appear to coincide with the short-range desires of the public. Such regulations drain away money that might have been used for new products and also force the firm to market unwanted products at an inflated price. As a consequence, the firm must sell more units in order to break even and must wait longer before the product pays for itself.

---

[11]David S. Hopkins and Earl L. Bailey, "New Product Pressures," *The Conference Board Record* (June, 1971), p. 20.

[12]This section is based on material in Thomas A. Staudt, "Higher Management Risks in Product Strategy," *Journal of Marketing* (January, 1973), pp. 4–9.

Many college students have thought of new product or service ideas as a result of class discussion, introspection, visits with professors, or informal meetings with fellow students. One of the most successful of these ideas was Frederick Smith's Federal Express Corporation. While attending graduate school at Yale, Smith developed a plan for an airline specializing in the delivery of small packages to customers on a rush basis. Today, his firm has yearly revenues in excess of $120 million.

What made Smith's idea so good? Exactly the same thing that makes other good ideas good — Smith's proposed service was different and better than anything available on the market at the time.

Do you think that **you** might have a good idea for a new product or service? If you think you do, first ask yourself: "How is my product (service) idea different from current competitive products? Is it better than products already on the market?" It may be that your idea is not for a new product or service but rather for a new method of distribution — you've thought of a way to deliver a product to the market at lower cost.

If the new product meets the test of being different and better, ask yourself another question: "How will the competition react to the new product?" If the new product can be easily copied by competitors, then your chances of success are probably small. In contrast, if the product involves some unique service or product characteristic that cannot easily be copied, then your chances of success are much better. In the case of Federal Express Corporation, the giant airlines were too interested in moving people to bother with moving small packages. When they finally recognized their mistake, Federal Express had become a well-established business capable of defending itself against large competitors.

Another thing you might also consider is the cost of manufacturing and distributing your product. Will these costs necessitate such a high selling price that the people who may need and want your product simply cannot afford to purchase it? Is it technologically possible to even produce your product at all? Think also about the timing of your introduction. Some new product ideas have become obsolete while still on the drawing board.

Whatever you do, don't take your new product or service idea lightly! If it meets the above tests and is truly a better way of meeting the needs of consumers, then you, like Frederick Smith, may be able to turn your idea into a marketable and profitable product or service.

Marketing & You

Causes of Failure

Table 9-2 summarizes the results of a study on the causes of new product or service failure in the United States. The results do not vary significantly from one industry to another.

TABLE 9-2 Six Principal Causes of Failure of New Products or Services

Cause of Failure	Percentage of Companies Citing*
Inadequate market analysis	45
Product problems or defects	29
Lack of effective marketing effort	25
Higher costs than anticipated	19
Competitive strength or reaction	17
Poor timing of introduction	14

*Percentages total to more than 100 because some companies reported multiple causes of failure.

Source: David S. Hopkins and Earl L. Bailey, "New Product Pressures," *The Conference Board Record* (June, 1971), p. 20.

Inadequate Market Analysis. As shown in the table, the failure to research the market sufficiently is cited by almost half the companies as contributing to new product failure. This lack of research often is a result of unreasonable pressure applied by top management after a competitor has introduced what appears to be a successful new product. Comments such as "we can't let them steal our market" and "we're certainly not going to abandon this business to our competitors" often lead to hasty and unwise marketing decisions.

Other products fail because the firm does not recognize the importance of understanding the needs of the consumer. One metal-working machine company official stated that research on one promising new product was conducted "purely as an engineering exercise, without reference to opinions and evaluations from sales and marketing personnel. A net result was the design and manufacture of machines that exemplified engineering's concept of the ultimate in engineering achievement. Unfortunately, these were not the products that were most marketable."[13]

Product Deficiencies. Nearly 30 percent of the responding firms indicated that product deficiencies of one kind or another sabotaged the product's prospects of success. These deficiencies were often quite obvious and should have been recognized before the introduction of the product. Frequently, a product's problem is that, even though it performs adequately, it does not offer any significant advantage over competitive products already well established in the market. Before a new product is introduced, therefore, the firm should be able to answer the question: "What does the new product do differently and better

---

[13]J. Hugh Davidson, "Why Most New Consumer Brands Fail," *Harvard Business Review* (March–April, 1976), p. 120.

than existing products?" If the answer is "not much," then the odds are great that the product will not succeed.

Lack of Effective Marketing Effort. Many firms fail to give a new product the extra attention it needs after it has been introduced to the market. Many marketing executives show a tendency to "move on to something else" before the new product is really able to stand on its own. Unfortunately, this tendency can prove fatal because the marketing strategies of almost all new products require modifications once the firm has had an opportunity to evaluate customer reactions to the product.

Many businesses also make the mistake of attempting to sell a product in markets in which they have little, if any, experience. All too often, a hasty entry into a new market leads to product failure, not because the product is bad but because the firm does not understand the service, promotion, or distribution requirements of the market. A conservative, although often profitable, strategy for a firm in this situation is to sell or license the product to a company with a proven record of success in the market. The Singer Company, for example, a long-recognized leader in the sewing industry, tried marketing business machines. Because of unfamiliarity with the market, Singer was unsuccessful, and finally sold that division.

Higher Costs than Anticipated. When a new product costs more to produce than originally anticipated, it may have to carry a price that is too high for the market. In such cases, the firm must decide whether to sell the product at a loss or to discontinue it. In any case, the firm will not want to produce the product if revenues are not greater than or equal to the direct variable costs associated with the product.

Competitive Strength or Reaction. Most of the reasons why new products fail seem to be largely within a company's control. Other factors, such as the reaction of competitors, are outside the control of the firm introducing the product. Nevertheless, the firm should anticipate competitive reaction and incorporate these expectations into the product's marketing plan; otherwise sales projections are likely to be exaggerated. Although the impact of competition seems to occur more frequently in the consumer products industry, it also occurs with industrial products.

Poor Timing. Occasionally, a firm introduces a "good" product for which the market simply is not ready. However, more often the new product is introduced after the demand for the item has already been satisfied by another firm. This situation has become even more serious as more and more new products must be approved for sale by a federal regulatory agency. The proper certification often adds six months to a year to the planned introduction time.

The nation's largest and most famous new product disaster, the Edsel, failed at least partly because of the timing of its introduction. The Edsel, shown at right, was introduced at the beginning of a recession. Its competitors — Buick, Pontiac, and Oldsmobile — weathered the recession because they had an established clientele. Although the Ford Motor Company was aware of the difficulty of marketing an expensive new car during a recession, it proceeded with the Edsel's planned introduction since it had already spent a considerable amount of money on production and distribution.

PRODUCT ABANDONMENT

Very few businesses put much effort into deciding what products to phase out of existence. While it is relatively painless to introduce a new product, withdrawing a product from the market is a bit like abandoning an old friend.

According to one study, only 31 percent of the 500 largest companies in the United States have written procedures for guiding product elimination.[14] Two aspects of this problem are worthy of examination: first, the hidden cost of products that sell poorly and, second, a system for managing product abandonment decisions.

Hidden Costs of Poor-Selling Products

The costs of sustaining a weak product are not simply the losses that it incurs. No cost accounting system is finely tuned enough to allocate fully the following hidden costs:

1. Weak products demand a disproportionately large amount of management's time.
2. Weak products require frequent price and inventory adjustments.
3. Weak products involve short production runs and expensive setup costs.
4. Weak products require significant amounts of attention from advertising and sales personnel that might otherwise be spent on making successful products more successful.
5. The negative image of weak products may cast a shadow over the firm's other products.[15]

In addition to these hidden costs, perhaps the greatest cost of a weak product is its effect on future new product ideas — as the firm struggles to maintain a poor product, it is not able to give new products the attention that they deserve. Therefore, future profits are sacrificed in an attempt to keep old products alive.

Product Abandonment Procedures

Product abandonment decisions are too important and involve too many areas of the company for one person to handle alone. Therefore, in many situations, it is advisable to establish a corporate team of high-level executives, made up of representatives from the marketing, manufacturing, and finance departments, for the purpose of reviewing products that are candidates for elimination from the company's line. Typically, the marketing executive is responsible for discussing the firm's marketing strategy, customer relations, the product's future sales potential, and any prospective new products; the manufacturing executive describes any scheduling, production, or inventory problems related to the product; and the finance executive shows what the company's profit position would look like if the product were eliminated. In

---

[14]Richard T. Hise and Michael A. McGinnis, "Product Elimination: Practices, Policies, and Ethics," *Business Horizons* (June, 1975), pp. 27–28.

[15]Reprinted by permission of the *Harvard Business Review*. Excerpt from "Phasing Out Weak Products" by Philip Kotler (March–April, 1965), p. 109. Copyright © 1965 by the President and Fellows of Harvard College; all rights reserved.

addition, some firms also include on the team a representative from the personnel office; this individual discusses the redeployment of personnel resulting from a product elimination decision.

Early Warning Criteria. The product review committee, as described above, should establish a system for analyzing each of the firm's products periodically. Since many firms feature a relatively large number of products — in some cases, 1,000 or more — some sort of screening procedure is helpful for identifying products requiring detailed study. Therefore, the first decision of the review committee is to define appropriate product identification criteria. Although the list varies depending on the particular situation, the following criteria should be considered.[16]

Sales Trend. If sales of the product in question have been declining for a considerable period of time, it may indicate that the product is in the maturity or decline stage of the life cycle.

Price Trend. A downward trend in the price for a new product may be anticipated as a part of the product's introduction strategy. However, if the price of an established product is dropping, then the product may be in trouble.

Profit Trend. A declining profit, expressed as a percentage of either sales or invested capital, should raise questions about the product's continued existence.

Substitute Products. When a new product enters the market that is both a substitute for and a significant improvement over one of the firm's existing products, it should consider withdrawing the original product from its line.

Product Effectiveness. If a product loses its effectiveness, the firm should consider withdrawing it from the market. For example, a household bug spray that is no longer effective because insects have developed a resistance to it should be withdrawn.

Executive Time. The more time that executives must spend on an established product, the stronger the argument for abandoning it. As indicated earlier, sick products require constant attention; often this time can be better spent on other products.

Product Abandonment Checklist. Once the review committee has established the early warning criteria, it can combine them in a checklist similar to the one shown in Table 9-3. This checklist forces the review team to determine how the product scores on each criterion. For example, a neutral ranking in regard to "product sales trend" implies that product sales have been stable; a negative ranking on the "price trend" criterion suggests that the price of the product has been declining. Assigning scores of 3 for negative, 2 for neutral, and 1 for positive permits the review team to average the product's score for the seven criteria. For the product abandonment example in Table 9-3, the average score is 2.33 which would indicate that the product is in trouble. Normally, the firm would want to look closely at any product with a total score of 2

---

[16]*Ibid.*, pp. 106–118.

TABLE 9-3 Product Abandonment Checklist

Early Warning Criteria	Rating		
	Negative (3)	Neutral (2)	Positive (1)
Product sales trend	☐	☑	☐
Price trend	☑	☐	☐
Profit trend	☑	☐	☐
Substitute products	☐	☑	☐
Product effectiveness	☐	☐	☑
Executive time	☑	☐	☐
Average score = 2.33 (14 ÷ 6).			

or greater. If the time available to the review committee is limited relative to the number of products requiring investigation, it can rank the products according to their mean scores and investigate those products at the top of the list.

The product review committee can make the product abandonment checklist system as sophisticated as it wishes. Many early warning criteria are available in computer memory banks and can be utilized easily.[17] In addition, the firm may choose to weight some criteria more heavily than others, such as was done with the new product evaluation matrix discussed earlier. It is important to remember, however, that once the results of the product abandonment checklist are available, the review committee will have to spend a substantial amount of time analyzing the products determined to be in trouble. For example, one product with a poor score may be maintained because it completes a product line, whereas another with the same score may be eliminated because the company's long-term future prospects rest in other markets.

After the firm has decided to eliminate a product, it must still determine how quickly the abandonment should be accomplished. The alternatives range from dropping the product immediately to phasing it out over an extended period of time. This decision can be made only after looking carefully at such factors as current inventory levels, contractual and ethical obligations to dealers and final customers, and redeployment of personnel and capital associated with the product. Regardless of when the product is terminated the firm may decide to maintain a supply of parts for those products currently in the hands of consumers.

---

[17]For an excellent discussion of a more sophisticated, computerized approach to product abandonment, see Paul W. Hamelman and Edward M. Mazze, "Improving Product Abandonment Decisions," *Journal of Marketing* (April, 1972), pp. 20–26.

DIFFUSION OF INNOVATION

Up to this point, we have analyzed new products from the perspective of the seller. We have discussed why firms introduce new products, how they do so, and how they eliminate unsuccessful products. However, an examination of new products is not complete without a discussion of how new products are adopted by society. This process is known as the **diffusion of innovation**.

Everett Rogers had done much to stimulate diffusion research. His research has many implications for the marketing executive designing a new product strategy. The Rogers model of diffusion has three main components: the adoption process, adopter categories, and attributes of innovations.[18]

The Adoption Process

It is well recognized that an individual's decision to adopt an innovation is not an instantaneous act. Rather, it is a five-stage process that sometimes takes place over an extended period of time:

1. **Awareness Stage.** The individual learns of a new idea but lacks specific information about it.
2. **Interest Stage.** The individual develops an interest in the innovation and looks for additional information.
3. **Evaluation Stage.** The individual decides whether the product is worth trying.
4. **Trial Stage.** The individual buys the product or tests the innovation to see if it should be used regularly.
5. **Adoption Stage.** The individual adopts the innovation.

Not all people go through each of the stages in the adoption process. Many times people begin the product adoption process but stop when they find the product unsuitable. Others skip a stage in order to adopt the product more quickly. A consumer may skip the interest stage if the product does not require the individual to assume a high degree of risk.

The marketing executive should thoroughly understand how products are adopted because an innovation can become "stuck" at any point in the adoption process. Before Oldsmobile introduced the diesel V-8 engine, it provided the broadcast and print media with a series of stories on the development of the new engine. This step helped create awareness on the part of the consumers at very little cost to the company. Once the car was introduced, specific advertisements were aimed at creating interest in the concept of diesel automobile transportation as well as at providing prospective customers with enough information to evaluate the merits of the diesel engine.

Adopter Categories

People do not adopt innovations at the same rate. Some are quite venturesome and enjoy being the "first person on the block" to own the new

---

[18]The following sections are adapted from Everett M. Rogers, "New Product Adoption and Diffusion," *Journal of Consumer Research* (March, 1976), pp. 290–301; Everett M. Rogers and Floyd Shoemaker, *Communication of Innovations* (2d ed.; New York: The Free Press, 1971); and Everett M. Rogers, *Diffusion of Innovations* (New York: The Free Press, 1962).

FIGURE 9-6 Adopter Categorization on the Basis of Innovativeness

Source: Everett M. Rogers and F. Floyd Shoemaker, *Communication of Innovation*, 2d ed., p. 182. Copyright © 1971 by The Free Press, a division of Macmillan Publishing Co., Inc.

product, whereas others don't buy a new item until it has been purchased by nearly everyone. It is possible to group people into different classifications according to their degree of innovativeness. This section looks at those five adopter categories as well as at the special role of "early adopters" in the diffusion process.

Five Adopter Categories. Figure 9-6 depicts the five adopter categories. The curve shown in the figure represents a normal distribution of the buyers in a potential market. The **innovators**, about 2.5 percent of the population, are eager to adopt new products; venturesomeness is practically an obsession with them. In addition to enjoying risk, the innovator must be sufficiently wealthy to be able to purchase a product with the understanding that it may not be successful. The second group, **early adopters**, make up approximately 13.5 percent of the population. These people are well integrated into the social system and are often leaders in the community.

The third adopter category is the **early majority** (34 percent of the population). The people in this category can best be described as deliberate; while they frequently interact with community leaders, they rarely are leaders themselves. The **late majority**, who adopt a product after the early majority, view innovations from a cautious, skeptical perspective. These people usually act out of economic necessity or unrelenting peer pressure. The **laggards**, the fifth group and 16 percent of the population, are the last people to accept the innovation. They have the most local perspective in that they interact primarily with people within their community. The primary reference point for the laggard is the past. Figure 9-7 presents a detailed profile of each of the adopter categories.

Role of Early Adopters. The above classification of adopters emphasizes that the firm introducing a new product should focus its promotional and sales ef-

FIGURE 9-7 Profile of Product Adopters

Adopter Category	Percentage of Population	Salient Values	Personal Characteristics	Communication Behavior	Social Relationships
Innovators	2½%	"Venturesome." Willing to accept risks.	Youngest age; highest social status; largest and most specialized operations; wealthy.	Closest contact with scientific information sources; interaction with other innovators; relatively greatest use of impersonal sources.	Some opinion leadership; very cosmopolitan.
Early adopters	13½%	"Respected." Regarded by many others in the social system as role models.	High social status; large and specialized operations.	Greatest contact with local change agents.	Greatest opinion leadership of any category in most social systems; very locally oriented.
Early majority	34%	"Deliberate." Willing to consider innovations only after peers have adopted.	Above-average social status; average-sized operations.	Considerable contact with change agents and early adopters.	Some opinion leadership.
Late majority	34%	"Skeptical." Overwhelming pressure from peers needed before adoption occurs.	Below-average social status; small operation; little specialization; small income.	Secure ideas from peers who are mainly late majority or early majority; less use of mass media.	Little opinion leadership.
Laggards	16%	"Traditional." Oriented to the past.	Little specialization; lowest social status; smallest operation; lowest income; oldest.	Neighbors, friends, and relatives with similar values are main information sources.	Very little opinion leadership; semi-isolated.

Source: W. Thomas Anderson, Jr., adapted from Everett M. Rogers, *Diffusion of Innovations* (New York: The Free Press, 1962), pp. 169–189.

forts on the early adopters. Although innovators purchase the product first, they are generally not well-enough respected in the community to serve as opinion leaders. In contrast, many segments of society look to the early adopters for advice and information about an innovation. If early adopters cannot be convinced of the merits of the product, its chances of success are greatly diminished.

In terms of market strategy, early adopters respond more to different types of new product information than do early majority, late majority, or laggard adopters. Early adopters are more interested in technical details, scientific information, and statistical tests of performance of the innovation; followers look to the opinions of individuals who have already purchased the product.

Attributes of Innovations Bearing on Acceptance

The rate of adoption differs substantially among new products; some innovations are readily accepted whereas others are adopted only gradually. Several characteristics determine how quickly a new product is accepted by society. Rogers has defined these characteristics as relative advantage, compatibility, complexity, divisibility, and communicability.

Relative Advantage. In order to be adopted at all, an innovation must be perceived as representing an improvement over existing products. Thus, **relative advantage** is defined as the degree to which the new product is *perceived* as superior to existing products. The relative advantage may range from evident dollar savings to aesthetic appeal. The real challenge to the seller is to communicate the advantages of the new product in comparison to those products already available.

Compatibility. The degree to which an innovation is compatible with existing norms and products will increase its chances of rapid adoption. If the new product is a major change from older ones, educational and training programs and materials should be provided to the customer to facilitate the transition. Although the computer represented a drastic change from existing information and accounting systems, adoption of the computer was facilitated by educating customers about its use. In general, the more the innovation is in conflict with existing norms, the harder the firm must work to eliminate that conflict.

Complexity. Complex products tend to be adopted more slowly and with greater effort required of both the marketer and the buyer. Accordingly, product design and development, promotional materials, and sales presentations are tools that should help the customer understand how to use the product. Marketing department personnel must be aware at all times that prospective customers are not as informed about the product as they are.

Divisibility. The degree to which a new product can be used on a small scale for trial purposes tends to facilitate adoption. Promotions involving small samples of food products or drugs usually produce satisfactory trial results. Since risk is one of the major considerations in the adoption process, divisibility is a very important factor in the diffusion of the innovation. As a result, the seller should not discourage trial orders; if the product is good and if the customer is happy with the results of the trial purchase, then repurchase can usually be expected.[19]

Communicability. Communicability refers to the degree to which the attributes of an innovation are visible or can be communicated to others. The more easily people can see the importance of the innovation, the more quickly the innovation will be adopted. An illustration of the importance of communicability is provided by preemergent weed killers, which are sprayed on a field before weeds develop. Despite the advantages of this product, the rate of adoption was quite slow because other potential users were unable to see any dead weeds.

summary points

1. A new product performs a new function or provides a significant improvement over existing products.

2. Firms introduce new products primarily for four reasons: (1) to meet sales objectives, (2) to utilize excess production or distribution capacity, (3) to prevent other firms from gaining a competitive advantage, or (4) to complete a product line.

3. A product acquired externally generates smaller but quicker profits than one developed internally. Other factors affecting a make-or-buy decision include the possibility of antitrust complications, the risk associated with the product, as well as the personnel requirements involved.

4. Venture management teams are designed to recreate an entrepreneurial spirit within the organization by evaluating new product ideas and carrying the most profitable-appearing ones through to commercialization.

5. Venture teams draw their members from predominantly technical areas in the firm. They should report directly to a senior officer in the firm, and they should be separate from the firm's regular organizational structure. Typically, venture teams operate free of rigid deadlines.

6. Venture teams tend to be quite expensive, and it is often difficult to find the right person to lead the team. At times, team members may become emotionally involved with their products.

7. The alternatives to venture teams include new product managers, new product committees, and new product departments.

8. The firm should employ a systematic six-stage technique for developing new products. Idea generation, the first stage, yields many new product possibilities from many diverse sources.

9. The objective of the second stage, product evaluation, is to eliminate as many new ideas as possible that are not consistent with the objectives of the firm.

10. During the economic analysis stage of the new product development process, the firm develops either a pro forma income statement or a market share projection.

11. The end result of the fourth stage, product development, is the creation of prototypes evaluated during the test marketing (fifth) stage.

12. New products are often "rolled out" during the sixth stage of the new

---

[19]For research illustrating this point see Robert W. Shoemaker and F. Robert Shoat, "Behavioral Changes in the Trial of New Products," *Journal of Consumer Research* (September, 1975), pp. 104–109.

product development process — commercialization.

13. The risks associated with new products have increased significantly during the past several years.

14. Inadequate market analysis and product deficiencies are the main reasons for new product failures.

15. A product abandonment procedure allows the firm to extricate itself from unprofitable products in a systematic manner.

16. Diffusion of innovation refers to the process of new product adoption by society. The Rogers model of diffusion is composed of the adoption process itself, adopter categories, and attributes of innovations that bear on their acceptance in the marketplace.

questions for discussion

1. In your own words, what is meant by a "new" product?
2. What factors do you think encouraged General Motors to introduce its new X-cars in 1979? (An example of an X-car is the Chevrolet Citation. See the prototype X-car on page 265.)
3. What factors should a firm consider in deciding whether to produce a new product internally or to acquire one by merger?
4. What are the important characteristics of venture teams?
5. Compare and contrast the four new product management schemes. Which one would you suggest for a family-owned tool-and-die shop? For a large multinational corporation? Support your answers.
6. Describe the new product development process.
7. What is meant by brainstorming? What can be done to make a brainstorming session more productive?
8. What are the major drawbacks of a product evaluation matrix?
9. What is the best way to perform an economic analysis of a new product?
10. Do you think that the risk associated with new products will increase or decrease during the next decade? Why?
11. What can be done to reduce the cost of new product failure?
12. What costs does the firm experience when it refuses to drop a failing product from its product line?
13. Early warning criteria can help the firm determine when one of its products is beginning to decline in value. Evaluate the relative importance of these criteria.
14. What does the diffusion of innovation theory, as described by Everett Rogers, have to offer the marketing executive?

cases part 3

case 8 diaper sweet

Diaper Sweet is manufactured and marketed by the Consumer Products Group of the A. E. Staley Manufacturing Company. The firm's sales are in excess of $300,000,000 of which approximately 19 percent come from consumer products. In addition to Diaper Sweet, the Consumer Products Group is responsible for such products as Sta-Puff Fabric Softener, Sta-Flo Starches, Cream Corn Starch, Staley Corn Oil, and Cream Corn Starch Baby Powder.

While Diaper Sweet has contributed profits to Staley for a number of years, in only three of the last eight years has Diaper Sweet met the profit objectives that

Diaper Sweet case by William P. Dommermuth, Southern Illinois University at Carbondale. Copyrighted by original author and used with permission.

have been set for it. Recently, Diaper Sweet sales have been declining at about the same rate as has the generic product group that it belongs to.

Diaper Sweet is a powdered laundry product for use as a presoak and washing aid. Its primary use is for diapers and other baby items including bibs, blankets, sheets, pants, etc. The product can also serve as an aid in washing many non-baby items and is especially effective with nylon, lingerie, uniforms, dacron, orlon, and other synthetics, helping to remove the "yellowness" often developed by synthetics. It can be used in the kitchen for such jobs as removing odors from dish towels and cloths and deodorizing refrigerators and garbage cans.

Diaper Sweet has four primary ingredients: a germicide which kills bacteria, a bleach which whitens both synthetics and cottons, a cleaning agent which aids in the removal of soil deposits, and a water softening ingredient. A major feature of Diaper Sweet is the fact that it inhibits odor formation by controlling or destroying odor-forming bacteria during the *entire* use cycle of the fabric.

Distribution

The preponderance of sales for Diaper Sweet (over 85 percent) are made through grocery stores. Diaper Sweet is also available in other outlets such as discount houses, although distribution coverage in such outlets is not as strong as that in the grocery market. It is not available through drugstores.

While Diaper Sweet is marketed on a national basis, the distribution pattern, in terms of percentage of available outlets carrying the product, varies significantly in different parts of the country. The heaviest coverage is on the West Coast where virtually 100 percent of the outlets stock either one or both sizes. In contrast, 80 percent of the retail outlets in the West, 50 percent in the Midwest, and none on the East Coast carry Diaper Sweet. This is largely due to heavy competition from the one directly comparable product, which is strongest in the East and Midwest.

As noted before, virtually all of the sales are made through grocery supermarkets. The untapped potential in discount and drugstores remains something of an unknown. The nature of the available sales force is not highly compatible with selling in either of these types of outlets and, in the case of drugstores, the gross margin potential is also considered to be a serious handicap.

Advertising and Sales Promotion

The typical media schedule for the last several years has included *Mother's Manual* (three insertions), *Baby Care Manual* (four insertions), *Expecting* (four insertions), and *Parents* (three insertions). The common practice of Diaper Sweet has been to include a coupon in its advertising which allows the customer to purchase the product at 10¢ off the retail price.

An extensive sampling campaign is conducted providing sample packs of Diaper Sweet to new mothers before they leave the hospital. The cost is roughly 10¢ per sample distributed, and the total amount of money allocated for this purpose is somewhat higher than the amount spent on magazine advertising. Research has shown that this type of sampling increases Diaper Sweet's market share by approximately 2 percent.

The Nature of Potential Customers

First-time mothers are thought to be especially good prospects for Diaper Sweet because of their strong concern to take excellent care of their first baby and because they are likely to repurchase the product with the arrival of subsequent children. It is also felt that the strongest appeal is to families with incomes of approximately $15,000 or more who can better afford the cost of providing their children with such extra care.

One major problem faced by marketing management is the fact that this product is "outgrown" when the child no longer requires the use of diapers. An estimate of about a 2-year use period is considered standard, meaning that there is a heavy turnover of customers with a consequent need to continually persuade new prospects of the product's merits.

Assumptions regarding the nature of the consumer's attitudes toward diaper care products is based primarily on executive judgment and several small studies. The major points of this research are the following. First, caring for diapers is thought of as a chore that must be done. It is accomplished as easily and quickly as possible. Users do not agree on one best way to clean diapers. Second, one half of the subjects interviewed used additives such as Diaper Sweet while the remaining half did not.

Third, those who do use an additive in the diaper pail do so primarily to prevent the development of a strong odor. It is believed that germs are eliminated in the washing cycle, due to the hot water used, and in the dryer, because of the extremely hot air.

Fourth, a prewash or soak in the washing machine is very popular because the washing machine does the actual work. Fifth, only after a baby develops a diaper rash for the first time does the user take an active interest in the alternative techniques for laundering diapers.

Finally, women will utilize reduced price coupons only if they regularly use a product or have become sufficiently interested in trying a product.

1. How would you position Diaper Sweet in a product evaluation matrix? Assuming no changes are made in Diaper Sweet's strategy, where do you feel the product will be positioned in the future?
2. What stage of the product life cycle is Diaper Sweet in now?
3. Can Diaper Sweet's marketing strategy be modified so that the product is more attractive to markets beyond diapers? What changes in Diaper Sweet's strategy would you suggest?

---

case 9
durafashion
kitchen utensils

Durafashion Kitchen Utensils is one of the largest producers of kitchen utensils in the United States. From the founding of the firm until the middle 1960s, new products had come from a process that might be described as ad hoc. A person or persons had an idea for a product and suggested it. If the idea survived internal criticism and was aggressively backed by its proponents, it was eventually accepted by top management and added to the product line. Such ideas had come from customers and potential customers and within the firm from sales representatives, industrial engineers, the product repair department, and the purchasing department. The company had tried to instill in all employees a sense of duty to constantly monitor the product line with the objective of suggesting logical additions.

Durafashion Kitchen Utensils case by Thomas V. Greer, *Cases in Marketing* (New York: Macmillan Publishing Co., 1979), pp. 113–117. Used with permission.

A New Product Committee

In the middle 1960s a new products committee was established to consider new product development. At first the group met each time that enough suggestions had accumulated to warrant a meeting. Later it adopted a periodic meeting schedule of once every three months. The new products committee was composed of a person from production, one from the finance and accounting office, one from purchasing, one from sales, and the marketing research director.

If this committee was impressed favorably with the idea, it might ask the marketing research director to conduct a commercial feasibility study. It might also ask the engineers to study physical feasibility, or both studies might be requested. Based on the outcome of these studies, the committee either recommended to the company president, Roy Bannerman, that the product be added to the line or it recommended that the work on the idea be abandoned. Most people in the company seemed to be pleased that this approach to new product development was more systematic, objective, open-minded, and thorough than the old ad hoc approach had been. Using this new approach to the development of products, Durafashion Kitchen Utensils Company had doubled the depth of its product line, and annual sales had risen from $8,000,000 in the middle 1960s to a current figure of $13,000,000. Profits had risen by 59 percent in the same period of time.

About a year ago, Todd Lewis, the new director of marketing research, was appointed to the new products committee. In addition, he was appointed chairman of the committee by the president of the corporation, whereas previously the committee had chosen its own chairman. Lewis immediately entered into negotiations with a commercial designer and stylist and after a few weeks entered into a 12-month contract with him. These actions surprised most people in the company. Subsequently, it became common knowledge that Lewis had secured the permission of the president before talking with the outside designer and again before signing the contract. While the association with the outside designer had created some hostility for Lewis in the company, and even a little from the committee, it soon became apparent that the outsider had supplied some valuable ideas and had modified some Durafashion employees' ideas to the point that commercial prospects were excellent for two new products and two redesigned old products. The total cost to Durafashion for the outside designer's services was $30,000.

The Life Cycle Concept

Lewis had introduced additional uncertainty by asserting that products have a life cycle and that the manufacturer benefits to a different extent and incurs different costs in the various parts of the product's life cycle. The prevailing sentiment in the company and among its competitors had always been that once in the line products remained indefinitely or until they showed a sustained period of unprofitable sales. Many people thought that the systematic reevaluation of every item in the entire product line led to premature abandonment of products, premature redesign of products, and an emphasis on extremely minor modifications. They argued that in a resource-conscious society waste could be unpopular and even damaging to a corporate image. However, proponents of the idea argued vigorously that efficiency was served when an organization gave none of its products the benefit of the doubt. It had long been thought that American society was receptive and sympathetic to change, and that perhaps change itself represented a form of utility to the American consumer.

Within Durafashion, the production manager, Dale Redding, voiced some reservations about Lewis and his proposals. He noted the possibility of shorter production runs, new or more frequently modified tooling and dies, and the discomfort and fatigue of frequent change of duties on production workers. He also noted that published research has shown that one may find only one or two commercially feasible ideas out of every 500 ideas that were formally studied.

A New Product Department

Todd Lewis also proposed a new products department consisting of a permanent staff including at least the following: a chemist, a metallurgist, a home economist, a cost accountant, and a marketing researcher. The proposed unit would have extensive laboratories. Lewis's estimate of the capital investment required for such laboratories was $120,000. He said that there should be a standing liaison committee made up of people from all over the company who would serve fixed terms to ensure accurate and timely communications with the new products department. According to his recommendation, product suggestions could still come from anywhere but would flow to the new products department for physical research, cost research, and preliminary market feasibility studies. If they survived these types of investigation, the suggestions would go to the marketing research department for final commercial evaluation and perhaps a test market. If they survived again, they would proceed to the company president for his approval.

1. Should each of Durafashion's products be evaluated regularly?
2. How would you evaluate Durafashion's current process for evaluating new products?
3. Is the new product development process that Todd Lewis developed an improvement over Durafashion's current system? What changes if any in Todd Lewis's new approach would you recommend to the president of the company?

4

Communication

What image comes to mind when you hear the word "communication"? Perhaps two people talking to each other, maybe your favorite (or least favorite) television commercial, or maybe a brochure received in the mail?

Marketers must choose from among many ways of communicating to the buying public the benefits, or selling points, of their products. They must get and keep your attention long enough to inform you.

Part 4 looks at some of the ways marketers communicate with their markets. There are many questions to be answered before an effective communications package can be developed.

Topics discussed in Chapter 10:

1. The firm's external communication process.
2. The role of advertising in the firm.
3. Managing the advertising effort.
4. The effective use of sales promotion.

Advertising is a significant force in our economy and an integral part of our lives. On the average day each of us normally sees or hears hundreds of advertisements. To the marketer, advertising provides a way to communicate the selling message of a product, service, or institution to the public. Over the years, such technological developments as radio and television have enabled the marketer to reach the public more quickly, powerfully, and economically. This chapter begins by looking at a model of the firm's external communication process.

THE FIRM'S EXTERNAL COMMUNICATION PROCESS

Communication is very important in the marketing process. The interaction of consumer and salesperson and the exchange of information between the buyer and the seller are indispensable to the distribution of goods and services in the U.S. economy. Mass communication is a virtual necessity in today's business environment owing to the growth in the number and size of markets and to the many types of products offered for sale.

Different marketers emphasize different types of communications in their marketing strategies. Most rely on mass communication, but a few, such as the Avon Corporation, Amway Products, and the Latrobe Brewing Company, still favor face-to-face approaches to selling. Latrobe, brewers of Rolling Rock beer, benefits from consumers' perception of Rolling Rock as a hard-to-get beer, as is still the case with Coors beer in most eastern markets. An executive with Latrobe's advertising agency expressed the firm's communications philosophy as follows: "We let the beer sell itself. To me, the best advertising in the world is word-of-mouth advertising."[1] This approach differs considerably from that of Procter & Gamble, whose advertising budget reached $460 million in 1978.[2]

The model in Figure 10-1 shows the external communication process of the firm. The firm's marketing and communications strategy takes into account the major marketing variables — price, product, and distribution — and also the firm's corporate image or identity. The marketing variables are the essential inputs to the firm's overall campaign design. The **communication mix** is divided into the **promotional mix** and the **public relations mix**. The primary elements of the promotional mix are personal selling, sales promotion, and advertising. The firm's corporate image is communicated to the public through the public relations mix. The elements of the public relations mix are

[1] "We Don't Change Beer — Why Change Ads?" *Advertising Age* (May 16, 1977), p. 102.
[2] "100 Leading National Advertisers," *Advertising Age* (August 28, 1978), p. 1.

FIGURE 10-1   The External Communication Process of the Firm

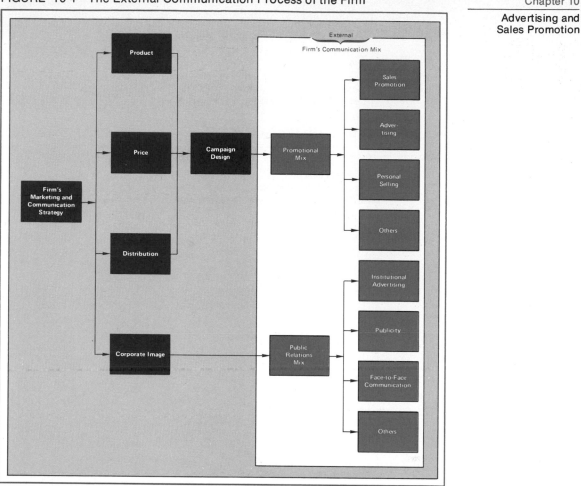

institutional advertising and publicity and face-to-face communications, such as audiovisual presentations or company tours. Chapter 11 focuses on the personal selling function while the remainder of this chapter focuses on the promotional mix, dealing first with advertising, and then sales promotion.

THE ROLE OF ADVERTISING

The American Marketing Association defines **advertising** as "any paid form of nonpersonal presentation and promotion of ideas, goods, and services by an identified sponsor."[3] Advertising is not the same as **publicity**, which is a form of communication sent by a firm to the media in the hope that it will be published or broadcast but for which media space or time has not been purchased. Advertising also is different from personal selling since there is no face-to-face communication between the advertiser and the audience. Finally,

---

[3]Ralph S. Alexander and the Committee on Definitions, *Marketing Definitions* (Chicago: American Marketing Association, 1963), p. 9.

advertising is to be distinguished from **sales promotion**, which refers specifically to displays, participation in trade shows or fairs, free samples, premiums, and contests.

Advertising Today

Figure 10-2 shows the annual increase in advertising expenditures in the United States from 1880 to 1978 as compared to annual growth in the Gross

FIGURE 10-2   Total U.S. Ad Expenditures and Percentage of GNP, 1959–1978

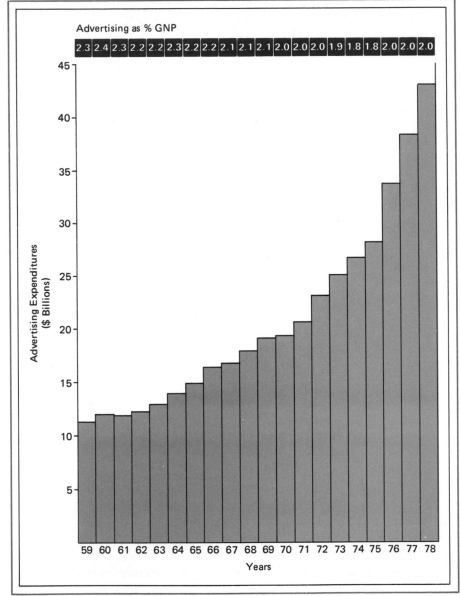

TABLE 10-1 25 Leading National Advertisers, 1978

Rank	Company	Ad Dollars (In Millions)	Rank	Company	Ad Dollars (In Millions)
1	Procter & Gamble	$554.0	13	AT&T	172.8
2	Sears, Roebuck & Co.	417.9	14	General Mills	$170.0
3	General Foods	340.0	15	Mobil Corp.	163.0
4	General Motors Corp.	266.3	16	PepsiCo Inc.	156.0
5	K mart	250.0	17	Beatrice Foods Co.	150.4
6	Philip Morris Inc.	236.8	18	Unilever	145.0
7	Warner-Lambert Co.	211.0	19	Norton Simon Inc.	144.6
8	Ford Motor Co.	210.0	20	Esmark Inc.	141.4
9	Bristol-Myers Co.	192.8	21	RCA Corp.	140.0
10	Chrysler Corp.	188.9	22	Coca-Cola Co.	138.8
11	American Home Products Corp.	183.0	23	McDonald's Corp.	136.8
12	R. J. Reynolds Industries	182.6	24	Johnson & Johnson	134.0
			25	U.S. Government	128.5

Source: Reprinted with permission from "Estimated Annual U.S. Ad Expenditures: 1959–1978," *Advertising Age* (September 10, 1979), p. 45. © 1979 by Crain Communications, Inc.

National Product (GNP). Total advertising expenditures have grown at an accelerated rate during the past 30 years, reaching $43 billion in 1978. When expressed as a percentage of GNP, however, advertising expenditures have remained fairly stable (around 2 percent). Table 10-1 shows the 1978 advertising expenditures of the 25 leading advertisers in the United States.

Objectives and Functions of Advertising

Advertising's basic objective is to inform the public about the firm and its products, and to persuade potential buyers that the firm's products are better than those of its competitors. Most companies expect advertising to increase both sales and profits. More generally, the purpose of advertising is to induce potential customers to respond favorably to the offerings of the firm or organization. This objective can be achieved by providing useful information, by changing consumer attitudes, or by showing how the firm's products or services can satisfy consumer needs.

While advertising, in its most traditional sense, is used as a tool for selling products, its scope is not restricted to its commercial function. More and more nonprofit organizations are using advertising to encourage people to save energy, to stop smoking, or to participate in charity programs. Advertising is used extensively to promote political candidates, as well as to inform the public about consumerism, nutritional practices, and various national goals and programs. Finally, advertising is used to generate public awareness of and goodwill toward institutions, associations, and interest groups. In the last few years, especially, corporations have advertised simply to inform the public about their

FIGURE 10-3 An Example of Corporate Advertising

The way to develop energy resources is to pool human resources.

As a company that produces many forms of energy, Conoco has many different human resources, too.

And because our people—44,000 in all—talk to each other and work with each other, they learn from each other.

For example, borrowing seismic techniques used to hunt for oil, our people have helped coal miners avoid the dangers of drilling into old, uncharted mines that are flooded with water.

And one bit of learning has come full circle: First, our engineers adapted oil production techniques to drill horizontally into coal seams before mining, to remove potentially hazardous methane gas. So more coal can be produced.

Now we've adapted this horizontal drilling system to get a petroleum deposits that were previously too difficult to tap. So more oil can be produced.

When resourceful people work together, the result is more energy for everybody.

(CONOCO)

Doing more with energy.

To learn more about what we're doing with energy, write Dept. H. Continental Oil Company, Stamford, Conn. 06904.

Courtesy: Conoco Inc.

business practices, goals, and concerns for the important social and economic issues of the day. Figure 10-3 shows an example of this type of advertising.

Advertising and the Marketing Mix

Advertising is a tool used to achieve specific marketing objectives; it is not an end in itself, but rather just one element of the marketing mix. There are no magic formulas for combining the various elements into an effective mix. Market situations change so fast and so often that the marketing manager must be flexible, emphasizing different aspects of the marketing mix as business conditions change. For this reason the firm can direct its efforts in one year, for example, to the development of new products and in the next to the establishment of a distribution network for existing product lines. The advertising function, therefore, is subordinate to the overall marketing plan of the firm and is influenced by whatever environmental forces may affect the plan.

Advertising and the Product. As stated in Chapter 8, a product is not merely a physical object designed to perform a specific function; rather it is made up of psychological and social as well as physical attributes. For example, people view a Ferrari not just as a means of transportation but also as a luxury item — the epitome of wealth, excitement, and high social status. The buyer of a Ferrari obtains not only a car, but also all the satisfaction of ownership and the image of wealth and power. Generally speaking, consumer satisfaction results from a product's functional design as well as from its package, brand name, color, quality, services, warranties, and image. Any of these attributes can be stressed in an advertising campaign.

Positioning. There are more than 500,000 registered trademarks in the United States. It is impossible, of course, for any one individual to remember all of these trademarks, or all of the products available on the market at any given time. It is important, therefore, for a product to acquire a position in the minds of consumers relative to other products with which they are already familiar. Otherwise, the product may be forgotten. Advertisers use the technique of **positioning** to build readily identifiable images for their product.

An example of positioning a product is the advertising campaign that transformed 7-Up from just another soft drink to the "Uncola," and gave it a distinct identity in relation to the more popular cola drinks. Implicit in the use of the positioning strategy is the recognition of the current market positions of competitive products and the establishment of a new position for the advertised product, rather than the displacement of competitors from entrenched positions of strength.[4]

Several other examples of successful advertising campaigns relying on the positioning concept can be found. The classic example is Avis's "We try harder" campaign. Avis had been losing money for more than 13 years, but when the company proudly positioned itself as no. 2 in the car rental business, revenues began to increase substantially.

B. F. Goodrich is another example of a company that has used the positioning concept successfully. Generally speaking, a company with a name similar to that of a much larger company, which also happens to be an industry leader, will have a hard time establishing a separate image for itself. Thus, advertisements paid for by the smaller company may ultimately benefit the larger company. Such was the case with Goodrich and its rival, Goodyear. In order to identify the company more clearly in the minds of consumers, Goodrich developed an advertising campaign around the fact that it is "the company without the blimp." By positioning itself in relation to Goodyear and its well-

---

[4]Jack Trout and Al Rice, *The Positioning Era* (New York: Ross Cappinelle Colwell, Inc.), p. 17.

known promotional trademark, Goodrich has been able to considerably increase consumer recognition of its products.

Not all product positioning campaigns have been successful, however. For example, Singer Business Machines, Mennen's Protein 29 line, and Diet Pepsi have all had positioning problems. Typically, such campaigns fail because management attempts to make a product all things to all people, to introduce a new product by relying on an already-established brand name, or to push an overly wide product line in the hope that each product will benefit from a single campaign. In some cases, management simply may not understand positioning as an advertising tool.

Positioning is not an easy proposition — choosing a niche in the marketplace and building consumer awareness must be done systematically. Research on consumer awareness of competing brands, long-range advertising planning, and careful consideration of the total marketing program must take place before the positioning campaign is launched. Finally, the creative effort must be integrated into the overall marketing program in order to achieve the desired level of market penetration and consumer awareness.

Advertising New Products. The introduction of new products to the marketplace has been a major factor behind the growth of the U.S. economy. Indeed, since the Industrial Revolution, U.S. businesses have been oriented toward the production and development of new products. Today, customers expect better and improved offerings, both at the consumer and the industrial level.

Advertising is the major tool for making consumers aware of new products. An example is the advertising campaign of Savin Business Machines, Inc., designed to introduce its newest copier in a market dominated by Xerox. Savin's aim was to establish itself as no. 3 in the office copier market, behind Xerox and IBM. The campaign strategy was to promote the Savin copier as better than the Xerox 4000 model. Positioning its product toward the smaller, convenience user, Savin appears to have made significant headway.

Advertising and Price. Advertising is an important tool to communicate to customers changes in the price of a product. Special price deals, price reductions for introductory purposes, or end-of-season price changes more effectively attract potential buyers when advertised. In many cases, price may be the most important information for purchasing decisions. This is especially true for products such as milk, eggs, meat, and generic brand products.

High prices may also be emphasized successfully by advertising. For some products, especially high prices are perceived by consumers as a sign of product quality. This is the case, for example, for Joy, the perfume by Jean Patou which is advertised as "the most expensive perfume in the world."

Advertising and Distribution. Advertising also provides support to other marketing functions, such as distribution. Advertising can help move products through the distribution channel by stimulating demand for the goods. Advertising reminds current users of the product, it attracts potential users, and it may even increase demand by suggesting new uses for the product. As an example, Arm & Hammer baking soda is advertised as being useful in eliminating food odors from the garbage disposal and the refrigerator. The message is that baking soda is not just for baking.

Four Types of Advertising

Advertising can be directed to members of the trade channel, industrial buyers, or to the general public. The objectives and format of trade or industrial advertising often differ radically from those of retail advertising or national advertising. Even though more money is spent annually on retail advertising, the fact that the total dollar volume of industrial sales is greater than the dollar volume of consumer sales gives some idea of the economic importance of trade and industrial advertising.

Trade Advertising. The purpose of trade advertising is to communicate with members of the distribution channel such as agents, wholesalers, or retailers. Most firms with nationally advertised products depend upon trade papers and magazines to reach their channel members. Examples of such publications include *Hardware Retailer* and *Supermarket News*. Trade papers can also be found at a more local level, for example, *Texas Food Merchant* and *Southern Hardware*. The advertisement in Figure 10-4 is typical of much trade advertising.

Advertising to trade channels is more informative and detailed than consumer advertising, relying more on rational appeals than emotional ones. Such advertising usually describes the products offered, makes suggestions as to their handling and presentation to the public, and points out the advantages to the distributor of carrying the products. Contests, sales training courses, store displays, and other promotional tools are also used to encourage dealers to carry a particular line of products. Trade advertising serves an important function, but because of its reduced visibility it is not often regarded as such by advertisers.

Industrial Advertising. A company selling materials, machinery, tools, parts, or equipment to another company uses industrial advertising in order to reach potential buyers. The market for industrial goods differs from the market for consumer goods in that industrial buyers are fewer in number and more readily identifiable than their consumer counterparts. Also industrial buyers are often more knowledgeable about the product category and are more interested in the informational content of advertisements. Industrial advertising is designed specifically to reach purchasing agents, production engineers, and in general, managers who control spending within the firm. An example of industrial advertising is shown in Figure 10-5.

Retail Advertising. The purpose of retail advertising, performed mostly by local merchants and service organizations, is to encourage people to buy consumer products either in person, by mail, or by phone. Some retailers advertise both nationally and locally; JCPenney and Sears, for example, advertise products and services on national television and in local newspapers. Many franchise operations, such as McDonald's, rely on national media for their advertis-

FIGURE 10-4 An Example of Trade Advertising

Courtesy: Swingster Premium Wearables

ing and restrict local promotions to coupons, price specials, and other special events.

National retail advertising differs greatly from local retail advertising. Whereas national advertising is primarily institutional and attempts to foster brand loyalty, local advertising is concerned specifically with making a sale. The local retailer is faced with continual changes in style, prices, and types of

FIGURE 10-5 An Example of Industrial Advertising

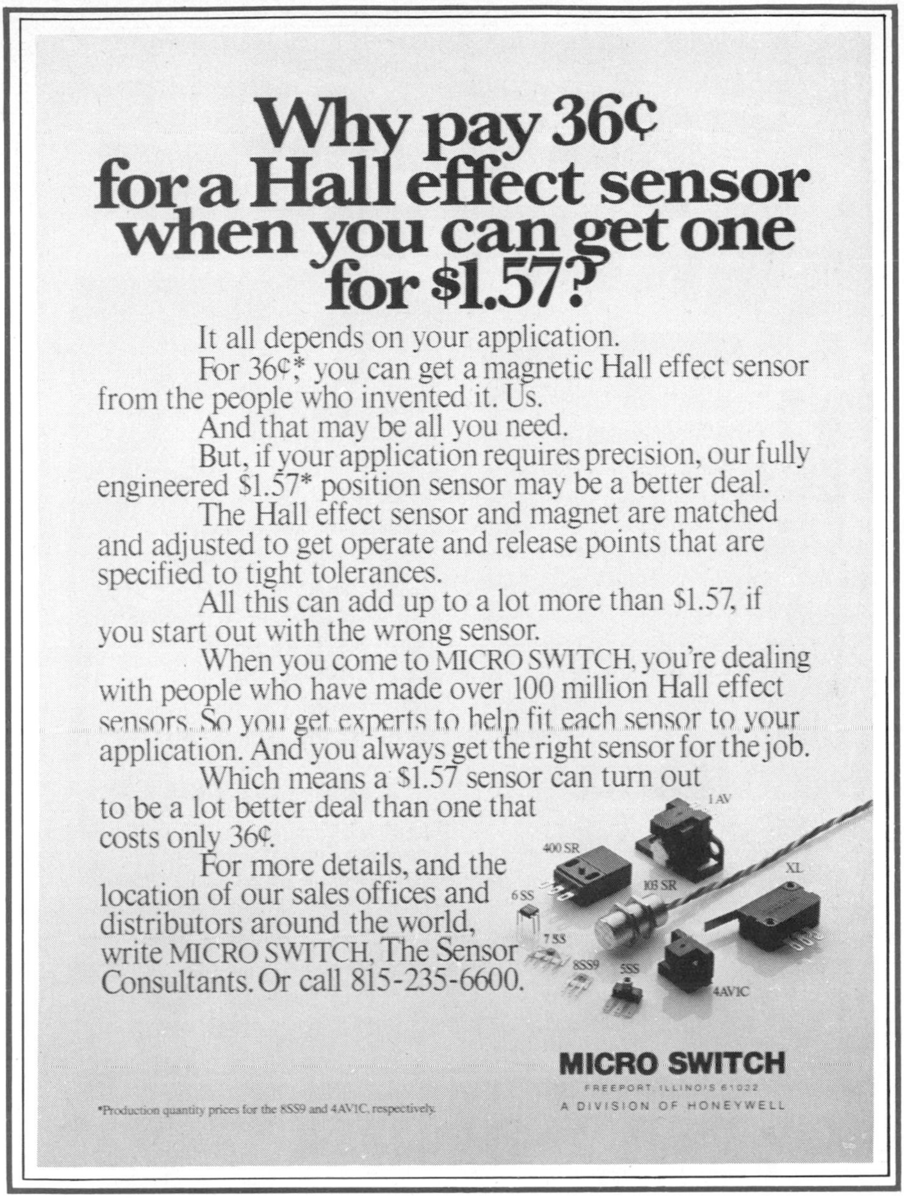

Why pay 36¢ for a Hall effect sensor when you can get one for $1.57?

It all depends on your application.

For 36¢* you can get a magnetic Hall effect sensor from the people who invented it. Us.

And that may be all you need.

But, if your application requires precision, our fully engineered $1.57* position sensor may be a better deal.

The Hall effect sensor and magnet are matched and adjusted to get operate and release points that are specified to tight tolerances.

All this can add up to a lot more than $1.57, if you start out with the wrong sensor.

When you come to MICRO SWITCH, you're dealing with people who have made over 100 million Hall effect sensors. So you get experts to help fit each sensor to your application. And you always get the right sensor for the job.

Which means a $1.57 sensor can turn out to be a lot better deal than one that costs only 36¢.

For more details, and the location of our sales offices and distributors around the world, write MICRO SWITCH, The Sensor Consultants. Or call 815-235-6600.

MICRO SWITCH
FREEPORT, ILLINOIS 61032
A DIVISION OF HONEYWELL

*Production quantity prices for the 8SS9 and 4AV1C, respectively.

Courtesy: Micro Switch, a Division of Honeywell

products handled and must communicate these changes to customers on a regular basis. Figure 10-6 shows an example of retail advertising.

One kind of retail advertising is **cooperative advertising**, in which the cost of advertising is shared by the retailer and the manufacturer on a percentage basis. A 50-50 arrangement is common. Cooperative advertising is widely practiced in the United States. The main benefits of cooperative advertising for manufacturers are that it encourages promotion of their products by retail out-

FIGURE 10-6   An Example of Retail Advertising

lets, it gives them a local tie-in, and it reduces their advertising costs. Cooperative advertising also benefits the local retailer by lowering advertising costs and by providing more "professional" and better quality advertisements. It also gives the small retailer a tie-in with a national campaign, which may enhance the prestige and image of the store.

Cooperative advertising, however, does have some disadvantages. The manufacturer incurs additional bookkeeping expenses and may have little control over the content of local ads. The retailer is often at a disadvantage because an ad provided by the manufacturer is usually national in orientation, not local, and because it emphasizes the manufacturer rather than the retailer. The retailer also must bear additional bookkeeping costs.

National Advertising to Consumers. The advertising of products or services directly from the manufacturer to the consumer or potential buyer is used to create awareness for the products or services, to reinforce or establish brand loyalty, and to inform consumers of new products, product changes, or new uses for existing products. National advertising to consumers is a very important competitive tool, especially in markets where thousands of products are offered to consumers simultaneously. This type of communication provides important information to potential buyers and allows them to easily discriminate among market offerings. For examples of national advertising aimed at consumers, tune into any of the network, prime-time television programs. Nearly every commercial will be sponsored by manufacturers of nationally distributed products — manufacturers such as Procter & Gamble, General Motors, Kellogg's, or General Foods.

National advertising directed to consumers and to the general public may have as an objective to create a corporate image or to change people's attitudes toward a firm or toward an institution. An example of this type of communication is the recent effort made by major U.S. oil companies to convince the public that their high profits are necessary to provide the capital for the development of new types of energy.

The objective of most national advertising is not to make a sale, but rather to emphasize those qualities of a particular product, service, or organization which are instrumental in developing awareness and favorable attitudes on the part of the general public. This is known as the promotion of **selective demand**. In the case of products purchased on impulse, such as chewing gum or soft drinks, national advertising, along with distribution, may be the only two factors responsible for a sale.

National advertising is sometimes used to increase *primary demand* for a product. Here advertising emphasizes a total product category rather than a particular brand or company. Recall, for example, the advertising for orange juice from Florida, California prunes, and the "Drink Milk" campaign sponsored by the National Dairy Association.

MANAGING THE ADVERTISING EFFORT

An advertisement, as it is seen by the public, is the result of the combined efforts of many people from many different functional areas of the organization. The marketing research experts develop a profile of target customers and market needs; product managers, sales personnel, and financial managers allocate the advertising budget, establish the product line, and choose the channels of distribution; artists and copywriters design the advertising message; media planners, agency executives, and media salespeople make the media and scheduling decisions; and so on.

Managing the firm's internal focus is one problem faced by those who organize and execute the advertising effort. Environmental influences may also significantly affect advertising decisions. Legal and social constraints, for example, pose a continuous challenge to the creative advertising effort. This section looks at the steps involved in managing the advertising effort — specifically, setting advertising objectives, establishing the advertising budget, developing the creative appeal, selecting the appropriate media, and evaluating the advertising effort.

Setting Advertising Objectives

A crucial step in any management effort is the establishment of operational objectives. In order to determine criteria for decision making and measurement standards for evaluating the advertising effort, management must first establish advertising objectives.

There is always a temptation to express advertising objectives and to measure advertising effectiveness in terms of product sales. Reaching the sales goal, however, is not necessarily an indication of advertising performance since many other factors influence product sales, including product availability, price, and the existence of substitute or complementary products. Consequently, it is advisable to think in terms of product recognition, advertising recall, brand awareness, and change in consumer attitudes as advertising objectives. The relationship between advertising and these variables is much more direct and measurable than the relationship between advertising and actual sales. Although other factors may also affect recall and awareness — such as in-store shelf exposure, word-of-mouth communication, and reference group influences — advertising is the major force in establishing brand identity.

DAGMAR — An Approach to Advertising Planning. One of the most widely used methods for advertising planning is known as **DAGMAR** — defining advertising goals for measured advertising results.[5] The DAGMAR approach defines an advertising goal not as a sales quota but as a specific effect to be produced in a defined target audience over a given period of time. In terms of the effect produced, an advertisement can either make the consumer aware of the existence of a product, provide the consumer with information about it, convince the consumer of the product's advantages over competitive offerings, or actually encourage the consumer to purchase the product. This "hierarchy-of-effects" model is based on the assumption that the consumer passes through the stages of *awareness, understanding, preference, conviction*, and finally *action* in making any given product purchase decision. The practical

---

[5]See Russell H. Colley, *Defining Advertising Goals for Measured Advertising Results* (New York: Association of National Advertisers, 1961).

value of DAGMAR is that it expresses advertising objectives as explicit, psychologically defined effects and measures advertising performance in terms of these effects.

The implementation of DAGMAR involves several steps. First, the advertiser investigates the market in terms of available merchandise, buyer motives, and advertising messages. Then the market position of the product in question is assessed on a hierarchy-of-effects scale. How aware are prospective buyers of the product to be advertised? How much knowledge do they have of the product? What are their attitudes toward the product? Do they need to be made aware of the product or do they simply need to be encouraged to buy it? Finally, the firm develops specific operational objectives to reach the communication, or hierarchy-of-effects, goals set for the product.

The DAGMAR approach is a useful planning tool because it directs the creative effort, facilitates the elaboration of measurable goals, and allows the integration of behavioral science theory into advertising management. Several other planning models have since been introduced in an effort to provide rational approaches to advertising planning. A fairly straightforward approach, DAGMAR still remains in use. Whatever method is employed, however, setting objectives should always be the first step in the planning process.

The Role of Research in Setting Objectives. The purpose of advertising is to induce a behavioral or attitudinal change. The success of an advertising campaign depends on the number of people both exposed to and affected by the advertising message. As a result, it is necessary to tailor the advertising message to the needs, interests, and level of product awareness of the target audience or market in order to produce the intended effect. In this regard, it has been said that, "The real measurement of advertising effectiveness comes before the fact rather than after."[6] This statement suggests that the success of an advertising effort depends primarily upon the quality of preliminary research and the accuracy of the target audience profile, i.e., the identification of target markets, rather than upon the advertisements themselves. An audience profile usually involves an analysis of the audience's demographic characteristics, size, needs and wants, attitudes, habits, and preferences. It is on the basis of these descriptive traits, identified through research, that the advertising effort is built. In addition to collecting audience profile data, primary research is also particularly useful in indicating whether consumers are likely to try a new brand.

Secondary research can provide much useful demographic information. Panel research data, gathered by such research firms as Simmons Market Research Bureau and the A. C. Nielsen Company, furnish the advertiser with information on the media habits of different consumer groups. It is possible with such data, for example, to determine whether heavy users of shampoo read *Seventeen* or *Family Circle* magazines, or watch M*A*S*H or *Archie Bunker's Place* on television.

Finally, research is of use in pretesting the effectiveness of a sample message or creative appeal. In-depth interviews, consumer juries, word-association

[6]Howard L. Gordon, "Yes, Virginia, Research Helps Make Better Advertisements," *Journal of Marketing* (January, 1967), p. 64.

tests, and other measures of audience response tell the advertiser whether the message is achieving the desired objective.

A savings and loan institution in central Texas provides an example of how research can contribute to the establishment of advertising objectives. Although the S&L in question was not facing a crisis, management was concerned about its competitive position and declining market share. Accordingly, primary research was undertaken to profile S&L users in the community and, in particular, users of this facility; to determine why area residents save and what their attitude is toward savings and loan associations; and to measure public recall and awareness of local S&L advertising. Secondary research was useful in identifying general economic trends in the community. On the basis of this research, top management was able to specify a target audience for its advertising effort, the attributes of the organization to be stressed in the advertisements, and a measurable advertising objective expressed in terms of a desired level of advertising recall and awareness.

Establishing the Advertising Budget

Deciding how much money to spend on advertising is not easy. The type of product involved, the competitive structure of the industry, legal constraints, environmental conditions, and many other factors influence the productivity of advertising expenditures. Profiling the current state of these variables is hard enough, but it is also necessary to forecast the future business environment since advertising expenditures must be budgeted like any other expense. Several methods, ranging from quite simple to relatively sophisticated ones, are available for setting advertising budgets.

The "All-You-Can-Afford" Method. Since small firms have limited financial resources and working capital, they often must resort to the "all-you-can-afford" approach to advertising budgeting. Under this approach, the firm first makes its unavoidable expenditures and satisfies its immediate financial obligations, and then allocates all the cash it can reasonably afford to advertising. The advantage of this approach is that it avoids unnecessary spending and waste. On the other hand, the firm sacrifices the incremental sales revenues that might have been generated by additional advertising expenditures. Although most commonly used by small firms, this method is also occasionally practiced by large companies. In this case, whatever cash is left after budgeting for expenditures and profit is allocated to advertising.

The all-you-can-afford method of budgeting is based on the erroneous assumption that the advertising function is independent of the firm's other marketing functions. It may be the only alternative available to some advertisers, but it is far from being an ideal solution to the problem of setting advertising budgets.

The Percentage-of-Sales Method. One of the most common ways to establish an advertising budget is to calculate the budget as a percentage of either past sales or projected sales. For example, a firm may set the advertising budget for a product equal to 5 percent of the previous year's sales for the product. Thus, if total product sales last year were $80 million, the firm will spend

$4 million ($80 million × 0.05) in advertising the product during the coming year.

The percentage-of-sales method has several advantages. First, if the advertising formula has been successful in the past, it may be successful in the future — past decisions may have yielded the most efficient allocation of advertising money. Second, the percentage-of-sales method permits a clear understanding of how the budget is allocated to the different elements of the marketing program. Third, it is affordable; thus the firm need not worry about overspending. Fourth, provided that the method is used by all the firm's major competitors, it allows for a certain stability in the level of advertising within the industry. Also, assuming that the market has reached its potential, it tends to minimize the occurrence of advertising wars among competitors.

The major disadvantage of the percentage-of-sales method is that the level of sales determines the level of advertising — the actual functional relationship would seem to be the reverse — with a year's lag time. Therefore, if the firm has not been spending enough money on advertising to gain a competitive advantage for its products, the continued implementation of the percentage-of-sales method will only perpetuate the mistake. Also, if a firm has been systematically overspending, it will continue to waste resources. If the percentage-of-sales method is used, it is preferable that a percentage of projected sales be allocated rather than a percentage of last year's sales. At least this way, the expenditure is tied to current activity and conditions rather than to those of past years.

The Competitive-Parity Method. The competitive-parity method is often used in industries dominated by a small group of large firms. Under this approach, each firm adjusts its advertising budget so that it is comparable to that of the leading firm in the industry. The assumption behind the competitive-parity method is that the industry leader, with its more accurate and timely market information, is likely to have allocated its advertising budget in an optimum manner. In addition, firms typically are reluctant to depart from the industry norm out of the fear that if they did, a competitive price or advertising war would ensue. A more conservative approach, that of maintaining the status quo, is thus preferred.

Many of the disadvantages of the percentage-of-sales method also apply to the competitive-parity method. For example, if the industry as a whole has been advertising below the optimal level, a large potential market may remain untapped. The firm, therefore, may be bearing a large opportunity cost for not taking advantage of underdeveloped markets. Likewise, if the industry has reached the maturity stage of its sales life cycle, all the firms in the industry may be overspending.

Another problem with the competitive-parity method is that it assumes that the product offerings and corporate images of all firms in the industry are identical. The ''all-other-things-equal'' assumption rarely holds true in market situations. Even though Goodyear and Goodrich may be selling comparable tires at comparable prices, the names of the firms, their images, and even whether or not they have a blimp may be instrumental in determining where the consumer buys tires. Similarly, this method does not consider the influence of creative appeal and the choice of media on advertising budget efficiency. The creativeness of the message and the use of local rather than national media can totally change the way potential buyers perceive the advertisement and hence the product.

The competitive-parity method does have some advantages, however. It is likely to prevent competitors from making inroads into the firm's market share — that is, if the firm keeps pace with the level of expenditures of its competitors, a drastic change in its market position is unlikely. This method is easy to implement because it does not require complicated sales forecasts or appraisals of future market conditions. Finally, it is attractive to those firms that want to budget their marketing expenditures in advance, without contending with uncertainties or contingency planning.

The Objective-and-Task Method. The last approach to setting the advertising budget, the objective-and-task method, is designed to provide the firm with a series of decision rules relating to its advertising activities. It establishes the advertising budget on the basis of specific tasks needed to accomplish an agreed upon objective. For example, if a firm wishes to increase consumer awareness of its product by 10 percent, it develops an advertising budget based on all the tasks involved in achieving this objective.

The objective-and-task approach is conceptually superior to the others because it assumes that the level of brand recognition and brand sales varies with the level of advertising. In the case of new products, it enables the firm to establish a complete promotional plan in the absence of data about future sales or competitive action.

The problem with the objective-and-task method is that the relationships between advertising and consumer attitudes, perceptions, and purchase behavior are not at all clear. A certain amount of personal judgment is necessary in order to determine how much and what kind of promotional effort is required to reach each target objective.

In view of the variety of budget allocation methods available and the controversy as to which method is best, the notion of "insurance" may serve as an appropriate rationale for setting advertising budgets.[7] Advertisers should begin by deciding whether they even need to advertise in the first place. The value of advertising in a given situation depends on whether and to what extent the sales or consumer recognition of a product would suffer if advertising support were withdrawn. If they would not suffer, then advertising is of only marginal importance to the firm. But if product sales or consumer recognition would be negatively affected, which is usually the case, then advertising is needed to reduce the probability, or risk, of a competitor making an inroad into the firm's market share. The advertising manager must then quantify such risk in terms of dollars and allocate financial resources to the advertising budget up to the point where the total dollar value of the perceived risk equals the advertising budget. In effect, advertising acts as insurance by reducing market risk and protecting the firm against a sudden decline in market share.

More information and research is needed about the effects of advertising so that the budgeting process can become more efficient and objective. Until

---

[7]David Corkindale, "A Practical Way to Set Advertising Budgets," *Marketing* (August, 1978), pp. 28–30.

more analytic methods are available, firms will resort to simplified and subjective budget allocation methods, thereby potentially hurting the overall efficiency of their marketing plans.

Developing the Creative Appeal

Once the firm has formulated advertising objectives and identified target markets, it must then translate the objectives into a campaign theme and specific advertising appeals. Developing the campaign strategy involves consideration of the product, the overall tone of the campaign, the possible use of a spokesperson, the intended effect, and perhaps the firm's competitive environment. Copy and graphic appeals are then combined, rough ads developed, and finished advertisements produced. Many firms also pretest their campaign themes and copy appeals.

Let's take a closer look at what is considered in creating the advertising for a product.

Creative Strategy. The development of the creative strategy for a product begins with clearly defined objectives. These objectives may focus on the functional characteristics of the product, the perceived psychological rewards for the buyer, the product's social value, or its personality. Whatever creative theme is chosen, it will be reflected in the individual advertisements comprising the product's ad campaign.

The individual advertisements in the campaign may contain written copy, photographs or other visual devices, dialogue, live action or animation, or a combination depending on the media and the creative appeal selected for each ad. For example, written copy may be chosen for print ads which are to focus on new uses for an old product or on reasons why the product is superior to existing market offerings. Such copy may or may not be used with visual devices depending on the purpose of the ad. On the other hand, a graphic image may be the central part of the ad, and the copy is secondary or eliminated altogether. Figure 10-7 illustrates how dramatic photography is used to promote McDonald's hamburgers, while the copy (the written message) is secondary.

An advertisement may also appeal to the audience's emotions; it may use humor to catch the audience's attention, or it may employ research evidence or demonstrations as proof of product performance. Finding the best focus for the ad's message is crucial to the success of the advertising effort. To that end, we'll now discuss some specific copy considerations, the choice of a spokesperson for the product, and whether or not to use humor in the advertisement.

Copy Considerations. Several copy appeals have been used by advertisers to increase recall, to improve recognition, and to spur brand adoption. One such appeal is the interrogative headline. A famous example is "Wouldn't you really rather have a Buick?" For many years advertisers have believed that interrogative headlines are more effective than declarative headlines. Research, however, has not been able to find any evidence to support that belief.[8]

---

[8]James H. Myers and Arue F. Haug, "Declarative vs. Interrogative Advertisement Headlines," *Journal of Advertising Research* (September, 1967), pp. 41–44.

FIGURE 10-7 McDonald's Uses a Strong Graphic Image to Enhance Its
Creative Strategy

U.S.D.A. Inspected 100% Beef.   Weight before cooking 4 oz. (113.4 gm.)

100%

Pure beef. Pure pleasure. That's what you get in every Quarter Pounder with cheese sandwich.

A lean and unmistakably good taste of 100% pure, domestic beef including cuts of chuck, round and sirloin.

No fillers. No additives.

Simply pure lean beef, leaner than the ground beef most people buy.

And for cheese lovers, there's not one, but two melted slices of our rich and golden cheese. All tucked into a freshly toasted, sesame seed bun.

It's your Quarter Pounder with cheese. And we make it 100% for you.

Nobody can do it like McDonald's can™   McDonald's

© 1979 McDonald's Corporation

Courtesy: McDonald's Corporation

A second frequently encountered appeal relies on social pressures or peer group influence to promote product purchase. An example of this appeal is the "ring-around-the-collar" advertisement that was used so successfully to promote Wisk laundry detergent. The homemaker in the ad is made to feel embarrassed by her husband's dirty shirts and resolves to use Wisk in order to avoid further humiliation. Is such a strategy more effective for some products than for others? Research has not yielded a definite answer yet, but this technique does appear to be useful in accelerating the adoption of certain new products.

A third copy technique discussed frequently in the literature is the use of sexual appeals. This practice is distasteful to some, and special interest groups have tried to stop advertisers from relying on blatant sexual appeals. In at least one study, it was found that sexual appeals do not affect a person's recall of an advertisement.[9] In fact, the researcher found that the subjects were less likely to recall brand names in ads employing this appeal than in ads with an alternative appeal.

Choosing a Spokesperson for the Product. If a spokesperson is to be used in developing the advertising appeal, that person should be selected on the basis of his or her credibility, attractiveness, familiarity, and power as a spokesperson. For example the use of experts, trustworthy witnesses, celebrities, or just "common folks" can determine how the product is perceived by the public. If potential buyers identify themselves with the source, they will be more likely to pay attention to the advertisement.

Many advertisers believe that notable and well-respected people are more credible sources than unknown people. Accordingly, the use of movie actors, retired politicians, and sports heroes has become increasingly popular in advertising. Such celebrities are used to sell just about every type of product or service. Perhaps you've seen the ad shown in Figure 10-8.

Other advertisers use unknown people in their appeals in the belief that the average consumer identifies more closely with someone of similar social class than with a famous personality. Testimonials such as taste tests, the "Crest test," or even the "candid camera" approach, where the spokesperson is not aware that the conversation is being filmed, are all ways of using ordinary people to increase advertising credibility.

There are no set procedures for determining the most credible advertising sources. Creativity, experience, and research tests all play a role in the selection of the most appropriate source.

Humor in Advertising. During the past decade, some advertisers have come to believe that humor increases advertising credibility. Alka Seltzer, Benson & Hedges, and Volkswagen are three examples of companies with highly successful, humorous advertising campaigns. Many other companies have not been so lucky in relying on humorous advertisements to increase brand awareness.

Sternthal and Craig, who have researched humor in advertising, present some conclusions and guidelines regarding the use of humor in advertising:

1. Humorous messages attract attention.
2. Humorous messages may detrimentally affect comprehension.
3. Humor may distract the audience, yielding a reduction in counter-argumentation and an increase in persuasion.
4. Humorous appeals appear to be persuasive, but the persuasive effect is at best no greater than that of serious appeals.

---

[9]Major Steadman, "How Sexy Illustrations Affect Brand Recall," *Journal of Advertising Research* (February, 1969), pp. 19–22.

FIGURE 10-8   Minolta Uses a Sports Celebrity as a Spokesperson for Its Products

Bruce Jenner, world record holder, Olympic decathlon.

Courtesy: Minolta Corporation

5. Humor tends to enhance source credibility.
6. Audience characteristics may confound the effect of humor.
7. A humorous context may increase liking for the source and create a positive mood. This may increase the persuasive effect of the message.

8. To the extent that a humorous context functions as a positive reinforcer, a persuasive communication placed in such a context may be more effective.[10]

While more research needs to be conducted on the actual effects of humor in advertising, the findings of Sternthal and Craig are important and useful to marketing executives.

Copy Testing. Copy testing is a diagnostic procedure enabling the firm to avoid repeating past mistakes. Although it does not measure the effectiveness of each and every advertisement perfectly, it can indicate how well an ad performs in a test situation relative to other ads. While copy research needs to be improved because it does not answer all of advertising's crucial questions, it can help the firm avoid major creative errors.

Today, advertisers rely on many types of copy testing to pretest advertisements and campaigns — for example, recall and consumer attitude tests. On the other hand, recognition tests and comprehension tests are still used but are no longer considered very valuable. In general, behavioral, attitudinal, and opinion measures appear to be the best predictors of future sales behavior and the most reliable indicators of advertising copy effectiveness.

Selecting Media

Once the creative appeal has been developed, the advertising manager chooses an appropriate mix of communications media to reach the target audience and allocates the advertising budget among the media chosen. Frequently used media include television, radio, newspaper, magazine, and billboard. The choice of media depends not only on the objectives of the campaign but also on the characteristics of each medium, the target markets, and the message. For example, the **reach** (the total audience a medium actually covers) varies by medium; the readers of *Sports Illustrated* may not be the people who listen to FM radio or watch daytime television. Also, if the advertising message is concise or involves a product demonstration, the medium should be visual. If the message is complicated, the medium should be newspaper, magazine, or other vehicles suited to the communication of a relatively large amount of information.

A second media consideration is the establishment of a media schedule. The medium's **frequency** (the number of times an individual or household is exposed to a medium) has an important effect on whether the advertisement or the product advertised will be remembered by the consumer. Several linear programming models have been developed in order to determine the most effective media schedule given a set of budgetary constraints for the firm. ADMOD and MEDIAC, for example, are programs designed to maximize the reach and frequency of the message within a specified budgetary constraint and set of media alternatives.[11]

---

[10]Brian Sternthal and C. Samuel Craig, "Humor in Advertising," *Journal of Marketing* (October, 1973), p. 17.

[11]David A. Aaker and John G. Myers, *Advertising Management* (Englewood Cliffs, N.J.: Prentice-Hall, Inc., 1975), p. 471.

Evaluating the Advertising Effort

One of the most important tasks of the advertising manager is to evaluate the performance of the advertising effort in terms of the previously agreed upon objective. Whether the objective was to increase sales, to increase brand recall and recognition, or to change consumer attitudes, it must be quantifiable and measurable.

Measuring Sales Results. Sometimes, the advertising effort is designed solely to produce short-run sales. An example of such an effort is the type of ad frequently seen in the newspaper or heard on the radio announcing a special one-day sale. *It is important to note that advertising alone cannot be considered responsible for changes in product sales.* This is particularly true if the period of time involved is long enough for other variables to affect sales — variables such as the product's demand elasticity, changes in competitive offerings, changing economic conditions, and the carryover effects of past advertising. For this reason, sales response is an acceptable measure of advertising effectiveness only for short-term campaigns when the relevant environmental variables are not expected to change significantly.

Measuring Advertising's Communication Performance. The hierarchy-of-effects model (DAGMAR), discussed earlier in the chapter, has been widely adopted by advertisers because it enables them to evaluate advertising effectiveness in terms of a psychologically defined purchase process. The model is particularly useful when the advertising objective is to improve product image or to increase brand loyalty.

The model, however, has one major shortcoming — that is, it assumes that awareness, understanding, preference, conviction, and action occur in a neat and predictable sequence. We know, for example, that some of the steps are omitted in the purchase of a convenience or impulse item; the consumer may buy an item immediately after becoming aware of it, without either obtaining more information about it or weighing its advantages relative to those of competitive offerings. It is necessary, therefore, to recognize that not all purchases involve each of the steps. Nevertheless, the hierarchy-of-effects model does provide a yardstick for measuring the communications effectiveness of advertising.

Several independent research institutions investigate various aspects of advertising effectiveness. Readership and audience data for many types of media are monitored and provided by the Audit Bureau of Circulations, the A. C. Nielsen Company, the American Research Bureau, W. R. Simmons & Associates, and others. Likewise, a number of institutions furnished advertisers with measures of advertising recognition and recall; Starch Inra Hooper and Gallup and Robinson provide such information on key magazines and advertisements.

In addition, individual firms can develop their own techniques for assessing advertising effectiveness. These techniques may involve generating research data on the firm's customers and identifying any special market conditions.

Have *you* ever become involved in college or university fund-raising efforts? Undergraduate student leaders of the College of Business Administration (CBA) of The University of Texas at Austin did when they decided to establish a $40,000 scholarship fund in the name of Foster Parker, president of Brown & Root Construction Company and a graduate of the college, who had died two years earlier.

The Product. The students realized that their fund-raising efforts would be more successful if they gave donors something in return for their gifts. A bronze western-style belt buckle emblazoned with the insignia of the university and the CBA seemed to be the perfect solution. The buckles were individually numbered and were to be given in return for a donation of $20 or more. The cost of producing each buckle was $6.50.

Target Audience. Current students and faculty members as well as interested friends and alumni of the university comprised the target market for the buckle. Faculty members were contacted by a representative of the CBA student council; students were given an opportunity to purchase the buckles before and after class at a number of tables set up for that purpose. Former students and friends of the university were reached through traditional advertising and sales promotion techniques.

Positioning. The product was positioned as a first-class, limited-edition belt buckle representing the university and the many contributions that Foster Parker had made to the school over the years.

Copy. Advertising copy stressed that revenues from the sale of the belt buckle would be used to fund a permanently endowed scholarship in the name of Foster Parker. Brief statements by the dean of the college and the CBA student president in the ads stressed the importance of providing financial aid to needy students.

Media Selection. Posters were displayed at strategic locations around the campus to tell students about the belt buckle. Advertisements were placed in three airline magazines at no cost to the college. The university alumni magazine which had a circulation of 100,000, provided a half-page ad at no cost.

Sales Promotion. Alumni were sent a one-piece mailer emphasizing the contributions of Foster Parker and the need to provide a permanent "living" memorial to him. It was sent out two months after all the initial advertisements had been placed to take advantage of the product awareness created by the ads.

The campaign easily exceeded its goal and the students gained some very valuable experience from marketing an idea.

Marketing & You

SALES PROMOTION

Sales promotions are yet another way of communicating with customers and potential customers. Examples of sales promotion devices include point-of-purchase displays, free samples, coupons, premiums and gifts, two-for-the-price-of-one offers, direct mailings, and trading stamps. The major objectives of sales promotion are:

1. To motivate people to try a product that they had not purchased before, or had only purchased on occasion.
2. To induce people who are currently using the product to buy and use more of it.
3. To keep existing customers and reinforce and maintain their purchase patterns for the product.
4. To suggest new uses of a product, e.g., baking soda to disinfect the bathroom and deodorize the refrigerator, so that existing customers will use more of it for different purposes.
5. To strengthen the image or the competitive position of a product. This can be done by repeating the advertising message over a long period of time.[12]

Sales promotions are a very important element in the promotional mix. They enhance product recall and recognition, and increase the trial rate for new products.

It is almost impossible to determine annual dollar expenditures on sales promotions in the United States; there are simply too many activities that could be classified as sales promotions but that are not separately measured or accounted for by firms. The A. C. Nielsen Company has estimated that the number of coupon promotions, for example, grew from 20.3 billion in 1972 to more than 60 billion in 1977, or 200 for every person in the United States.[13] Some of the most common sales promotions are discussed below.

Point-of-Purchase Displays

One very important promotional tool is the point-of-purchase (POP) display. The purpose of a POP display is to direct the attention of the shopper to the product. Almost any product can be promoted successfully by means of such displays. For example, when Hanes decided to introduce its new lower-priced line of pantyhose, L'eggs, it used special display racks in supermarkets to call attention to the new product. The attractively designed display racks (see photo at left) contributed considerably to the product's fantastic success.

Samples

The use of samples to induce potential customers to try new products is widespread, especially among manufacturers of food, household products, and pharmaceuticals. Recently, Beecham Products used this promotional tool to introduce its new toothpaste, Aqua-Fresh. Beecham mailed a small sample of

---

[12]John Young, Scott Paper Company, as quoted in Eugene S. Mahani, "Premium 'Tie-Brakers' Stand Out in Marketplace Glut," *Advertising Age* (May 3, 1976), p. 39.

[13]Louis J. Haugh, "New Marketing Woe: It's Coupon Clutter," *Advertising Age* (December 26, 1977), p. 1.

the toothpaste to households in selected markets at the start of the national advertising campaign for the product. The free samples allowed people to try the product for a few days to see whether or not they liked it.

To be an effective promotional device, samples should be given to as many people as possible. Not surprisingly, therefore, free samples can be an expensive form of promotion. Also, samples are effective only if the product distributed is actually superior to competitive products already on the market and if the consumer is able to perceive the superiority without much difficulty.

Free samples can be a very useful way of changing product image. In general, due to either past advertising or common usage, some products have a masculine image or a feminine image. As an example, hair-coloring products are perceived by most people as feminine products. In a study by Hamm and Perry, when male consumers were given free samples of a product with a feminine image and provided with promotional material explaining how the product could be used by men, the image of the product changed. The male subjects, because they had a chance to try the product for themselves, no longer related the use of the product to a particular sex. The researchers concluded that free sample distribution can help change consumer attitudes toward a product and increase the likelihood of purchase.[14]

Coupons

A coupon is a certificate entitling the holder to special savings on a product or to a cash refund if a given product or group of products is purchased. Coupons are designed either to attract new users or to encourage past users to make repeat purchases. Coupons can also be an especially effective brand-switching incentive. Typically, coupons are distributed by mail, printed in newspapers or magazines, or inserted in merchandise packages.

The widespread use of coupons by advertisers has caused problems concerning their redemption. Coupons, in effect, are cash substitutes; accordingly, they invite fraud and misrepresentation, which can considerably reduce their effectiveness as a promotion tool.[15]

Premiums and Gifts

Premiums and gifts are another popular form of sales promotion. Manufacturers of cereals, candies, and other food products frequently use this technique to build brand loyalty and to encourage repeat sales. Sometimes, a premium will be tied to a recent national or regional event. Accordingly, in 1976 several corporations offered bicentennial gifts to their customers in exchange for proofs of purchase.

Sale premiums can take the form of either trade premiums and bonuses, or consumer premiums. Trade premiums are given to dealers, retailers, and distributors to encourage them to sell more of the product in question. Consumer premiums are given to shoppers in order to encourage them to buy the product.

[14]B. Curtin Hamm and Michael Perry, "The Effect of a Free Sample on Image and Attitude," *Journal of Advertising Research* (August, 1969), pp. 35–37.

[15]For more information on coupon fraud, see "Feds Smash Profitable Coupon Fraud Operation," *Advertising Age* (June 9, 1975), p. 21; and "Bait and the Sting: Coupon Fraud Indictments Termed Only Tip of Iceberg," *Advertising Age* (December 18, 1978), p. 1.

The use of sales premiums in promotional campaigns appears to have increased considerably in recent years.[16] Another trend is the increased use of free mail-in premiums for multiple proofs of purchase. Many firms allow customers to obtain free mugs, T-shirts, or more expensive gifts in exchange for boxtops, labels, or other proofs of purchase. Sales premiums are sometimes distributed within the product package itself, such as a free towel in each box of Breeze, a powdered detergent.[17] These premiums, known as **container premiums**, are often substitutes for cents-off promotions, which businesses have grown increasingly reluctant to offer.

Contests and Sweepstakes

Contests also serve as promotional tools. One of the most successful consumer contests is Pillsbury's "America's Bake-Off," held annually for the past 30 years. In 1976 the total budget for the contest was around $2 million, and Pillsbury awarded a total of $81,000 in premiums.[18] In a sweepstakes, on the other hand, prizes are awarded on the basis of chance alone. Sweepstakes are often employed as a tool to sell magazine subscriptions. The Publishers' Clearinghouse annual sweepstakes is a good example of this type of promotion. The success of a sweepstakes depends on the product promoted, the quantity and value of the prizes awarded, and the amount of advertising support behind it. State lottery laws regulate the administration of sweepstakes.

Trade Show Exhibits

Trade show exhibits, one of the earliest and most popular forms of sales promotions, are used by manufacturers to arouse retailers' or dealers' interest in their products. Trade shows are growing increasingly more important in the U.S.; in 1976, for example, at the 31st National Hardware Show, more than 175,000 items were displayed.[19]

Trade shows usually involve only a particular industry or industry segment. Companies typically participate in trade shows to introduce new products, to train sales personnel, to promote their corporate image, to gauge the market for a prototype product, to take product orders, and to conduct market research.[20] Trade show exhibits can be a highly effective way of communicating to a target audience at relatively low cost.

Trading Stamps

As a retail-sponsored sales promotion, trading stamps are a kind of bonus given to shoppers for buying merchandise at certain stores. Usually, one stamp

---

[16]See "Future Spring from Coupons to Premiums," *Advertising Age* (May 2, 1977), p. 1.

[17]Mahani, *loc. cit.*

[18]William A. Robinson, "Top Promos of '76 Show Topic, Pertinence and Thoroughness," *Advertising Age* (April 11, 1977), p. 71.

[19]Robert Chew, " 'Serious' Handyman Is Prime Hardware Target," *Advertising Age* (August 23, 1976), p. 8.

[20]Suzette Cavanaugh, "Setting Objectives and Evaluating the Effectiveness of Trade Show Exhibits," *Journal of Marketing* (October, 1976), pp. 100–103.

is given for every ten cents worth of products purchased. Stamps can be redeemed for either cash or merchandise at redemption centers or through catalogues. Sperry & Hutchinson, maker of S&H Green Stamps, is one of the largest national stamp companies. While stamps were very popular in the 1960s, their popularity waned considerably in the 1970s.

Product Demonstrations

Demonstrations are used to promote a wide variety of products, including automobiles, carpet sweepers, sewing machines, and microwave ovens. Product demonstrations usually take place at the point of purchase. They can be a very effective form of sales promotion if the demonstrator is successful in involving the prospect in the demonstration. This is why automobile dealers attempt to get prospects to actually drive the car they are considering buying. There is some truth in the phrase, "try it, you'll like it."

1. A firm's communications mix is divided into the promotion mix and the public relations mix.

2. Advertising is defined by the American Marketing Association as "any paid form of nonpersonal presentation and promotion of ideas, goods, and services by an identified sponsor."

3. The purpose of advertising is to induce potential customers to respond favorably to the goods, services, or ideas offered by the organization.

4. Positioning is used to build an identifiable image for the firm's product by choosing a niche for the product in the marketplace.

5. Advertising can be directed to members of the distribution channel, industrial buyers, or to the general public.

6. An advertising effort begins with the establishment of objectives. These objectives provide the basis for management decision making, budgeting, and evaluating the effectiveness of the advertising effort.

7. Advertising objectives can be expressed in terms of sales, product recognition, recall, brand awareness, or change in buyer attitude.

8. According to the hierarchy-of-effects model in the DAGMAR approach, a purchase decision involves

the steps of awareness, understanding, preference, conviction, and action.

9. Of the methods available for establishing an advertising budget, the objective-and-task approach is the most conceptually sound because it assumes that brand recognition and product sales vary with the level of advertising. This approach involves numbering all the tasks needed to accomplish a specified objective and assigning a dollar amount to the tasks.

10. Developing the creative appeal for an advertisement involves setting copy objectives, choosing a spokesperson, and deciding on techniques that will best communicate the ad's message.

11. Media are selected for a particular advertising campaign and schedules are planned on the basis of reach, frequency, and budgetary constraints.

12. Evaluating the advertising effort's effectiveness can be accomplished by measuring sales results or communication performance.

13. Sales promotion techniques include point-of-purchase displays, free samples, coupons, premiums, contests and sweepstakes, trade show exhibits, trading stamps, and product demonstrations.

summary points

1. Explain the difference between the firm's promotional mix and its public relations mix.
2. Describe the objectives and functions of advertising.
3. Why is it important for managers to be concerned about how their firm's products are positioned in the market?
4. Compare and contrast trade, industrial, and retail advertising.
5. Do you think that the DAGMAR approach is an effective tool in planning the advertising effort? Explain.
6. Evaluate the advantages and disadvantages of the various methods of establishing the advertising budget.
7. Assume that you have been hired as a marketing consultant to your college or university. Develop a creative appeal that could be used to attract new undergraduate students.
8. How should an advertising effort be evaluated?
9. Is sales promotion an important tool for most businesses?
10. What types of sales promotion tools would you use for the following products: canned soup, industrial lubricants, lawn care services, and home furnishings?

11 Managing Personal Selling

"Nothing happens until a sale is made." This phrase is one that many marketing people and especially salespeople are fond of quoting. Although it is not completely true, since many other areas of the firm contribute a great deal to the firm's success, it is fair to say that if the product or service is not sold, all the other efforts of the firm have been in vain. This chapter is very important not only because selling is critical to the firm's success, but also because there are more high-paying professional positions in selling than in any other area of marketing. In addition, many young men and women who eventually move into marketing management positions begin their careers in sales.

THE SALES STEREOTYPE

The image of selling held by most college students is one lacking in status, security, and creativity — certainly a position in which a college education would be wasted. To dispel this image, we will contrast the commonly held stereotype of the used car salesperson with the actual procedures and responsibilities of the professional sales representative.

The Stereotype: The Used Car Salesperson

It is easy to conjure up an image of the stereotypical used car salesperson who is promoting a product that looks good on the outside, "a cream puff," but which has probably been involved in a head-on collision on a figure-eight racetrack. The question is always in the back of our minds, "How much sawdust has been put in the transmission to keep it from making noise?" We may also feel that the used car salesperson uses deceptive sales tactics to make us buy the car, without caring whether or not it fits our needs: "After all, 'research' has shown that cars with 450-cubic-inch engines run more efficiently than a straight six." Finally, we may expect that to close the sale the used car salesperson will use high-pressure lines like: "Since this car is such a good value, there are several other people who are interested in buying it. You had better act now or it won't be here when you get back."

The Professional Salesperson

While undoubtedly there are salespeople who fit the used car stereotype, there are a great many more highly *professional* sales representatives who act in a very responsible manner. For example, an IBM computer sales representative begins each sale by attempting to determine what the real needs of the customer are, and then works to design a package of computer hardware and software that will solve the customer's problems in the most efficient manner possible. Here, there is never any question about the quality of the equipment, about the company's willingness to stand behind it, or about the high professional standards of the sales representatives.

The point is that there are a great many honest, hard-working used car salespeople, as well as computer salespeople, who want to see that customers get products that they really need and can afford. Yet, we have tended to stereotype the role of the salesperson in a way that is not fair to the selling profession and in most cases is not even accurate.

OPPORTUNITIES IN SELLING

There are many exciting opportunities for people in selling. Let's look at the career opportunities in selling, the freedom that sales representatives enjoy, and the financial rewards of selling.

Career Opportunities

A large number of companies provide a set of varied career tracks for people who enter selling careers. As Figure 11-1 indicates, once individuals have obtained initial sales training and have had some experience as sales

FIGURE 11-1 Career Paths for Salespeople

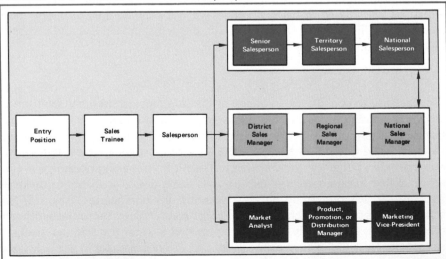

reps, they may pursue a career in sales, sales management, or marketing management.

Sales Avenue. In most firms there will be a larger number of openings in sales positions than in either of the two management career paths. One electronics firm differentiates between three positions on their sales career path: senior salesperson, territory salesperson, and national salesperson. In this firm, as the salespeople progress, they are permitted to call on larger and larger accounts and are given more authority to negotiate contracts in the firm's name. Promotions within the sales career path are accompanied by a higher base salary along with other nonfinancial incentives.

Sales Management Avenue. The opportunities are numerous and varied for salespeople aspiring to move up this career avenue. Advancement comes in the form of supervisory responsibility over other sales representatives. The position may be designated, depending on the firm, as district manager, branch manager, division manager, or field sales supervisor. To achieve success in such an assignment, aspirants must be able to communicate sales knowledge and skills to others in order to achieve results through their efforts. Depending on the organizational structure of the firm, such professionals may, in addition to their ''people'' responsibilities, be responsible for market analysis, sales forecasting, and, in some cases, the management of local inventories. A definite promotional ladder leads from the first-echelon post in field sales management to the position of national or general sales manager.

Marketing Management Avenue. Field sales experience is viewed by many companies as essential for advancement to marketing management positions. Such firms believe that for personnel in product, promotion, or distribution management to understand how their positions interact with the marketplace they should spend some time as a sales rep. If a marketing management career path is followed, the initial assignment is likely to be that of market analyst. In this capacity, the individual will be asked to examine a problem that deals with one of the key functions of marketing, such as product promotion or distribution. Upon completion of that assignment, the analyst will be asked to make recommendations to management on how the problem should be resolved.

New marketing management employees may be rotated through several market analyst positions to give them a feeling for the different types of marketing problems that exist in the organization. When this process is completed, they are assigned to one of the specific functional areas of marketing management. As individuals successfully complete a management assignment in a functional area, they may be moved to other areas for training or they may be given additional management responsibility as group managers in charge of several areas of marketing.

In Figure 11-1, it is also important to note the arrows drawn between the sales, sales management, and marketing management career paths. These arrows indicate that there is movement between career paths, not only within career paths, for individuals who begin their careers in selling. For example, an individual beginning on the sales career path as a salesperson and then advancing to senior salesperson, could then move to either a sales management or a marketing management position. There are also situations, although less frequent, where it is advantageous for the individual to leave a management position and return to a high-level sales position.

Freedom from Direct Control

Individuals who do not like to be closely supervised but who still want the protection of working for an organization find that selling provides an excellent opportunity for them. Many salespeople operate virtually as independent business people. They plan their own schedules, create their own sales strategies, and often go several weeks without face-to-face contact with their supervisors. Sales reps who are successfully obtaining orders for the company in a legal and ethical fashion, are frequently free to function in whatever way they choose. For example, they may decide to work 13 hours on Thursday and take Friday off completely. For those individuals who want to be their own boss, selling comes closest to providing them with the independence that they seek than most other positions with an organization.

Financial Rewards

In addition to the significant nonmaterial rewards associated with selling, salespeople have an opportunity to earn an excellent living. Table 11-1 presents the total compensation figures for sales trainees, salespersons, senior salespersons, and sales supervisors for 1974 to 1979. It is interesting to note that not only are these people well paid, they also have experienced significant increases in compensation. While the sales trainee's compensation has risen

TABLE 11-1 Average Total Compensation for People in Sales Positions

	1974	1975	1976	1977	1978	1979	Percentage Change 1974–1979
Sales trainee	$ 9,895	$11,975	$12,588	$13,750	$15,217	$14,763	49.2%
Salesperson	15,126	17,114	17,592	19,410	20,252	22,359	47.8
Senior salesperson	19,566	21,766	22,768	24,003	26,530	26,256	34.2
Sales supervisor	22,100	25,720	26,143	28,919	31,575	32,919	48.9

Source: American Management Association, Executive Compensation Service, *Sales & Marketing Management* (February 25, 1980), p. 60.

from $9,895 in 1974 to $14,763 in 1979, the average senior salesperson's compensation has increased from $19,566 to $26,256. In a highly competitive economy such as ours it is reasonable to assume that salespeople will continue to be well compensated for their efforts. We now turn our attention to properly managing the sales organization.

THE SALES ORGANIZATION

During the last 20 years, sales departments have undergone dramatic changes in terms of their responsibilities to their organization. Sales managers must now realize that they no longer *are* the marketing department, but rather they work *for* the marketing department. We need to examine two facets of the sales department operation: the role of the marketing-oriented sales manager and managing the sales department by objectives.

The Marketing-Oriented Sales Manager

As a firm adopts the marketing concept, it is usually forced to make major organizational changes. In a firm still embracing the production orientation, the sales department is typically run by a vice-president of sales who reports directly to an executive vice-president or to the president of the business. The chief sales executive has regular and direct contact with the top management of the business. In the marketing-oriented firm, sales operations are functionally a part of the marketing department. The sales manager reports to the vice-president of marketing, who in turn reports to top management.

Under the marketing concept, are the chief sales executive and the sales department any less important? The answer is yes. The sales department is still primarily responsible for generating orders on a day-to-day basis and for hiring, motivating, training, and managing the sales force, the largest group of people within the marketing department. However, sales executives are no longer responsible for setting all policies on how the product should be distributed to the final customer. When the chief sales executive reported directly to the top management of the firm, all other marketing decisions were forced to fit the requirements of the sales department. Now the sales department must be considered as merely one of the important elements in the marketing process.

Profit Responsibility. In the past, before the widespread adoption of the marketing concept, the sales manager was primarily responsible for selling as many units of the firm's products as possible. The emphasis was clearly on volume. Under the marketing concept, the firm and the sales manager redirect their efforts toward making profitable sales. As discussed in Chapter 1, this concern with profit may mean in some cases eliminating customers whose orders are too small to justify a sales effort or even products that cannot sustain a sufficient profit margin. To achieve profitable sales, sales managers are expected to coordinate their efforts with their firm's advertising, sales promotion, product planning, marketing research, and physical distribution.

The Sales Manager and Marketing Management. All too often, sales executives do not appear to be planning oriented. Apparently, the interest of sales managers in achieving sales volume makes it difficult for them to make long-range decisions. Sales managers may simply be too busy to take time away from "bringing in the business" to plan for the future. Regardless, many times the sales manager's only contribution to the planning effort is to make sales projections on a few major accounts. This limited use of sales management personnel is not in the best interest of the organization. Instead, sales managers should be asked to perform a number of functions that are critical to the firm. These functions include:

1. Providing a channel for the transmission of information from field sales personnel back to marketing management — information on changing market conditions, the success of new products, and competitors' actions.

2. Meeting with other members of management about the various strategic alternatives available to the business.
3. Working with other members of management to estimate volume and market projections that are realistic for each alternative strategy as well as which alternatives are the most attractive.

If the sales manager functions in the above manner, the company can be assured that the best available information and strategic alternatives are presented to marketing management before a decision is made. In addition, the sales organization will act as an integral part of the marketing department and not as an independent sales force, which unfortunately is the case in far too many organizations.[1]

Managing the Sales Staff

Sales staffs are very difficult to manage effectively. In addition to all the normal problems of line managers, sales managers must attempt to motivate salespeople with whom they have only limited contact. A salesperson may be on the road for several days or even weeks and have no face-to-face contact at all with sales management. Thus, the sales manager must take special care to ensure that the objectives of each salesperson are consistent with the overall marketing objectives of the firm. Finally, the sales manager must be able to evaluate individual salespeople though they may be operating in vastly different competitive environments.

Management by Objectives. One method which many sales managers have found to be effective for managing sales forces is management by objectives (MBO). In **management by objectives** sales managers and salespeople jointly identify performance goals and strategies for reaching these goals. These agreed-upon objectives are then utilized to evaluate the performance of each salesperson. The MBO process is diagramed in Figure 11-2.

Setting Objectives. The first step for the sales manager in setting objectives is to identify areas of responsibility that are considered important to the firm's marketing objectives. Once this identification has been completed, specific objectives must be established for each responsibility area. For example, a key responsibility area might be sales volume; the specific objective might be to increase sales volume by 20 percent. Other illustrations of responsibility areas and specific objectives are presented in Figure 11-3. If the sales staff participates in setting objectives, many motivation and performance evaluation problems can be eliminated. At the least, each salesperson will understand the criteria against which sales performance is being measured.

Planning Strategies. In creating a strategy or set of strategies to permit the salesperson to accomplish objectives, the sales manager and the salesperson make a good team. The sales manager will normally have a broader range of experience and may be able to advise the salesperson about strategies that have worked for other members of the sales force. In contrast, salespeople have a great deal of familiarity with their sales territories — familiarity that

---

[1]B. Charles Ames, "Build Marketing Strength into Industrial Selling," *Harvard Business Review* (January–February, 1972), p. 59.

FIGURE 11-2 The Process of Managing by Objectives

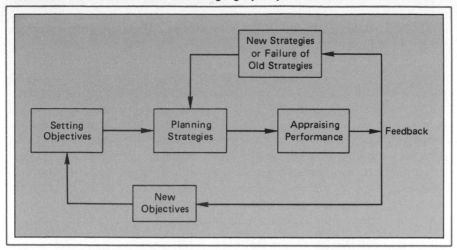

Source: Ramon J. Aldag and Donald W. Jackson, Jr., "Managing the Sales Force by Objectives," *MSU Business Topics* (Spring, 1974), p. 54. Reprinted by permission of the publisher, Division of Research, Graduate School of Business Administration, Michigan State University.

should permit them to tailor the sales manager's experience to their individual sales situations.

Performance Appraisal. Performance evaluation should be an ongoing process; the sales manager and the salesperson should periodically review progress toward agreed-upon goals. The salesperson may fail to reach objectives

FIGURE 11-3 Possible Objectives in an MBO Program

Responsibility Areas	Possible Objectives
Sales volume	Increase sales volume by 20 percent.
Gross margin of goods sold	Keep average gross margin of goods sold at 10 percent.
Number of calls per day	Increase the number of calls per day to four.
Order/call ratio	Increase order/call ratio to 30 percent.
Average order size	Increase average order size to $100 by eliminating a certain type of account.
Expenses and expense ratios	Reduce cost per call to $30, reduce cost per order to $60, reduce the ratio of selling expense to net sales to 20 percent.
New accounts	Generate ten new accounts per year.

Source: Adapted from Donald W. Jackson, Jr. and Ramon J. Aldag, "Managing the Sales Force by Objectives," *MSU Business Topics* (Spring, 1974), p. 55. Adapted by permission of the publisher, Division of Research, Graduate School of Business Administration, Michigan State University.

for any one of at least four reasons. First, the objectives may simply be unrealistic. Objectives should be high enough that they afford a challenge yet not so high that they are unachievable. Second, the objectives may be sound but the strategy for achieving them may be poorly formulated, in which case the strategy must be reconsidered. Third, uncontrollable environmental variables may make it impossible for the salesperson to reach an objective. For example, an economic recession usually hits the capital equipment and durable goods industries the hardest; an industrial goods sales rep, therefore, may find it all but impossible to meet a sales quota when the economy slows. Here, in response to an environmental change, the sales manager and salesperson will have to reformulate the objectives and possibly even the sales strategy. Finally, a salesperson may not reach the sales goal simply because he or she is not effective. In this case, the sales manager will have to make some tough decisions. Is the individual's problem due to a lack of product knowledge? Would additional training help? Should the salesperson be replaced?

Integrating MBO with Other Policies. If MBO is to be successful, it must be integrated with other corporate policies. Most critically, it must not conflict with the sales compensation plan. If salespeople are to be encouraged to sell more of a product, they must be provided with some sort of motivating compensation plan, such as a commission arrangement. Nothing confuses salespeople more and destroys a compensation plan quicker than offering inadequate monetary compensation for each unit of product sold, while at the same time directing salespersons through an MBO plan to sell aggressively. Sales contests and sales training sessions must also be closely integrated with MBO.

Clearly stated objectives can also be helpful to a sales manager at hiring time, for they alert prospective employees to management's expectations of salespeople. Let's look now at the recruiting and selection process.

RECRUITING AND SELECTING SALESPEOPLE

Businesses invest substantial resources in recruiting and selecting salespeople. There are two critical reasons why they do so. The most obvious reason is that the company must have good people who can properly represent the firm to its customers. As indicated earlier, if the sales effort is ineffective, the rest of the firm's activities are wasted.

The second reason is due to the often excessive turnover rates in sales departments. One study found that nearly 50 percent of all insurance agents leave their employer within the first year and that 80 percent leave within three years.[2] Because of the cost involved in hiring and training a salesperson, a firm will not begin to turn a profit on a salesperson until that person has been employed for at least a year. Therefore, when a firm experiences a high level of sales personnel turnover, most of its profits are coming from a relatively small group of salespeople — the rest are actually a drain on the organization. One way to overcome this problem is to have an efficient recruiting and selec-

---

[2]David Mayer and Herbert M. Greenberg, "What Makes a Good Salesman," in Harper W. Boyd and Robert T. Davis, *Readings in Sales Management* (Homewood, Ill.: Richard D. Irwin, 1970), p. 281.

tion program. We begin our discussion of the topic by looking at the legal constraints on hiring salespeople.

The Legal Aspects of Recruiting Sales Personnel

Major changes in personnel practices have occurred since the Civil Rights Act of 1964. Two federal government agencies, the Equal Employment Opportunity Commission (EEOC) and the Office of Federal Contract Compliance (OFCC), have issued guidelines designed to ensure that employers do not violate any of the civil rights laws. These guidelines establish important limitations on the use of standardized tests for hiring, promotion, or retention decisions. The guidelines cover personality tests, qualifying personal history forms, scored interviews, and interviewer rating schemes. Both the EEOC and OFCC stipulate that these tests may be administered only if it can be shown empirically that the trait or item being tested correlates significantly with critical factors in the work environment. The tests must also be administered in a manner that does not discriminate on the basis of race, color, religion, sex, age, or national origin.[3]

Although most discrimination lawsuits are based on race or national origin, the law also prevents firms from discriminating on the basis of age or sex. A firm *does* have the right to inquire as to an applicant's date of birth for the purpose of maintaining personnel files, computing insurance benefits, or formulating retirement plans. Age, however, must not be a factor in the hiring decision, and the applicant should be so informed. Regarding sex discrimination, which has presented problems for some employers, the law is very clear on the point that a job must be open to both men and women with very few exceptions (notably, an actress, a model for menswear, or a restroom attendant). As a result of federal legislation, many women have begun careers in sales.

Sales Job Description

Before a firm begins an active search for new salespeople, it must formulate an accurate **job description** — a description of the objectives of the sales position and how the salesperson is expected to accomplish these objectives. To write such a description, several questions must be answered: What is the title of the job? To whom will the salesperson report? How much supervision will be provided? How much planning is involved in the selling process? Does the salesperson have to manage a staff? How much technical expertise will the salesperson need? Will the salesperson actually have to install the equipment that is sold? How much imagination is required in the sales position? What compensation plan is to be used?

Although there is no sure way to develop a totally accurate job description, the following nine-step procedure has proven effective for many companies:

1. Prepare a questionnaire for sales personnel, asking them to list the main objectives of their job together with the major functions and subfunctions performed in doing the job effectively.

---

[3]Richard R. Still, Edward W. Cundiff, and Norman A. P. Govoni, *Sales Management: Decisions, Policies, and Cases* (3d ed.; Englewood Cliffs, N.J.: Prentice-Hall, 1976), pp. 231–232.

2. Prior to receipt of the completed questionnaires, have all executives interested in sales activities write down their conceptions of the salesperson's job objectives and the functions they feel should and should not be performed in achieving them.

3. Survey customers to find out what they believe should and should not be the functions of a company salesperson.

4. Tabulate the information received.

5. Reconcile differences revealed by the three viewpoints, write a concise statement of job objectives and prepare a detailed list of activities that sales personnel are to perform.

6. Classify the activities into major functional groups, such as sales, service, territory management, sales promotion, executive, and goodwill duties.

7. Determine what a salesperson needs to know, the qualifications necessary to perform designated activities, and the reasons that necessitate performance of each activity. Assemble this information into a written job description.

8. Submit the written job description to salespersons for discussion and recommendations and make alterations as required.

9. Periodically revise the job description, following the preceding eight steps, when changes in products, competition, the economic climate, or customers' demands require a review of job objectives and the activities involved in reaching them.[4]

Qualifications Needed for the Sales Position

Once the firm has developed a job description, it can then determine the type of person needed to fill the job. Karl von Clausewitz, the great Prussian militarist and father of modern military strategy, classified his recruits as either active or lazy, intelligent or dumb. He is quoted as saying,

> If . . . they are active and intelligent, I make line officers of them; lazy and intelligent men make excellent staff officers, and lazy and dumb men make perfect privates. But if they are dumb and active — I have them shot.[5]

Although the Clausewitz scheme for placing people in military positions is quite simple, most sales executives find that they live in a world much more complex than that of Clausewitz and that they do not have Clausewitz's authority. Two general characteristics have been identified as being needed for most sales positions; other factors vary with the job.

General Characteristics. The two basic qualities that every salesperson must have are empathy and ego drive. **Empathy** is the ability to understand the customer's problems, that is, to see problems as the customer sees them. Empathy enables the salesperson to anticipate the customer's reaction to a sales presentation and thereby to adjust the presentation accordingly.

The second factor, **ego drive**, makes the salesperson feel a personal stake in the success of each sales attempt. Ego-driven salespeople feel that their customers are there to assist them in fulfilling their desires for recognition, success, and personal achievement. In effect, each sale becomes a kind of conquest. The self-image of a salesperson tends to improve dramatically when a sale is made and to diminish when a sale is lost. Salespeople must have strong

---

[4]*Ibid.*, p. 233. Reprinted by permission of Prentice-Hall, Inc., Englewood Cliffs, N.J.

[5]Henry Lavin, "Not Wanted: 'Aggressive Salesmen'," *Management Review* (May, 1972), p. 7.

egos, because the nature of selling is such that even the most successful sales-people fail on many sales attempts.

Dyadic Relationship. In addition to the important role played by empathy and ego drive, a substantial amount of research has shown that a dyadic relationship exists between the salesperson and the prospective customer. That is, the personal reaction of the prospective customer to the salesperson is a key determinant of sales.[6] As Table 11-2 shows, customers who agree to make a purchase usually know more about the salesperson and the company involved and feel more positively toward them than do those who do not make the purchase. What this means for sales managers is that they should employ people who can get along well with their customers. That fact is especially significant when competing firms are offering basically the same products.

The same line of research also has shown that the likelihood of a sale increases with the perceived similarity between the salesperson and the customer. This relationship holds true for physical characteristics (e.g., age, height), objective variables (e.g., politics, smoking). It is also interesting to note that the *perceived* similarity for such factors as religion and politics is much more important than the actual similarity in belief or outlook between salesperson and sales prospect.[7]

It is quite true that many short people can sell equally well to both tall and short people, just as it is true that smokers, by controlling their habits, are able

TABLE 11-2   Comparison of Sold and Unsold Prospects' Recall and Attitudes Towards Salesperson Who Called on Them

Interaction Indicator	Percentage Sold	Percentage Unsold
Consider salesman a friend.	31	6
Consider salesman an expert.	67	55
Salesman liked me as a person.	78	60
Salesman enjoys his job.	95	75
Salesman enjoyed talking to me.	98	71
Prospect knew salesman's name.	76	32
Would introduce salesman to my business friends.	92	78
Would introduce salesman to my social friends.	89	79
Salesman represents the best company.	20	10
Denied agent's call.	0	20
Company A, not represented by salesman, is best.	18	17
Total dyads	(45)	(104)

Source: This table, drawn from "Selling as a Dyadic Relationship — A New Approach," by Franklin B. Evans, published in *American Behavioral Scientist* (May, 1963), pp. 76–79, is reprinted by permission of the publisher, Sage Publications, Inc.

---

[6]Edward A. Riordan, Richard L. Oliver, and James H. Donnelly, Jr., "The Unsold Prospect: Dyadic and Attitudinal Determinants," *Journal of Marketing Research* (November, 1977), pp. 530–537.

[7]Franklin B. Evans, "Selling as a Dyadic Relationship — A New Approach," *American Behavioral Scientist* (May, 1963), p. 78.

to sell to nonsmokers. Nevertheless, the real implication of the research on dyadic selling relationships is that the sales manager should attempt to hire people with backgrounds similar to those of prospective customers. Therefore, a salesperson who is to represent a company to technically oriented customers should have a sound technical background in order to communicate effectively. This logic has led many textbook publishers to hire ex-teachers to sell their books. These individuals know how teachers think and they understand the process by which textbooks are selected.

Sources of Salespersons[8]

The type of individual recruited for sales positions is a function not only of the job description and qualifications needed to fill the job but also of the amount of sales training a firm is able to provide. If the firm needs technically trained people but is unable to provide the training itself, it will have to hire individuals who already possess the required expertise. In contrast, if the firm is able to offer its own training program, it is in a better position to hire the best people available, not just those who are already technically prepared. The five primary sources of sales representatives are recent graduates, current salespeople, other employees within the firm, sales representatives from other firms, and employment agencies.

Recent Graduates. Graduates from high schools, trade schools, junior colleges, and universities have a variety of sales careers open to them. For example, high school graduates can be trained to be very effective retail salespeople. In contrast, graduates of four-year colleges and advanced degree programs frequently see sales as a path to management positions.

The Firm's Current Sales Force. The firm's current sales force can be an important source for leads on new salespeople. Since these salespeople have an understanding of what it takes to successfully sell the firm's products, they are in an excellent position to identify individuals who might be successful as sales reps for their company.

Sales representatives also tend to know most of the people who sell in their territories by meeting them in clubs, at customers' offices, at airports, and in hotels and restaurants. Since salespeople have one very important thing in common — their careers — they tend to talk freely with one another. Leads to available sales personnel may come from these talks.

Finally, salespeople come in contact with many people on a daily basis, some of whom may want to enter selling as a career. A good example again is the textbook sales rep, who, as often as not, was recruited from a position in a college bookstore or from a teaching position by a company salesperson.

Other Employees of the Firm. Another potential source of new salespeople are employees who have other jobs in the firm but would like to try a career in selling. Production people or engineers, for example, have excellent knowl-

---

[8]This section is adapted from W. J. E. Crissy, William H. Cunningham, and Isabella C. M. Cunningham, *Selling: The Personal Force in Marketing* (New York: John Wiley & Sons, Inc., 1977), pp. 411–413. Reprinted by permission of John Wiley & Sons, Inc.

edge of a firm and its products; thus if the firm is selling highly technical products, these people may be prime candidates for selling positions.

Competitors' Employees. Typically, management is reluctant to hire salespeople away from competitors. This practice, referred to as "pirating," is not looked upon favorably. One reason why a firm might want to pirate another company's sales force is quite obvious: these salespeople, if trusted employees of the competitor, may have valuable information about the company, its products, and its customers. It is clear, however, that a firm is acting unethically if it attempts to spy on competitors by hiring their salespeople.

The major advantage of hiring someone away from a competitor is that that individual has experience in the industry and understands the market and the needs of the various customer groups. It is also good for the firm, from time to time, to hire an experienced sales rep from the outside just to get a different perspective on how to attack old problems. This action helps to reduce "inbreeding" and to make other employees of the firm more creative. Finally, salespeople newly hired from a competitor may bring their old loyal customers with them.

Employment Agencies. Employment agencies refer potential salespeople to sales managers in return for a fee. Most sales managers feel that employment agencies are not particularly useful in recruiting new salespeople and that qualified salespeople do not have to use employment agencies in order to find a job. One problem with employment agencies is that their personnel often do not fully understand the needs of the sales manager; as a result, they recruit unqualified people. This problem can be remedied, and the employment agency can serve a useful referral function, if the sales manager takes the time to carefully describe the type of person being sought.

The Selection System

Once sales candidates have been recruited, the firm must evaluate them. This evaluation begins with an initial screening of candidates in which the firm attempts to learn as much as possible about each candidate without investing much time and effort. For those individuals who pass the initial screening, the firm will seek personal and job references and arrange for additional rounds of interviews and tests.

Screening. Screening of candidates, whether at a university campus or at the home office, typically will be conducted by a member of the firm's personnel office. The interviewer at this time will have two objectives. The first objective is to inform the applicant as to the type of sales position available in the firm, the nature of the products that are to be sold, compensation policies, and general career opportunities in the organization. Not surprisingly, the second objective is to determine whether the interviewee is qualified for the available sales position. Although it is difficult to make this decision after only a 30-minute interview, recruiting personnel are trained to look for certain characteristics that mark the successful salesperson.

Application Form and Letters of Recommendation. The application form is used to obtain descriptive information about the individual — name, date of birth, level of education, work experience, social security number, and marital status. Some organizations have found that lengthy forms, sometimes as long as five printed pages, can provide useful information. Longer forms might include questions about hobbies, travel, personal financial history, and job aspirations.

Letters of recommendation may be useful, but there are difficulties associated with them. Many salespeople in the process of changing jobs request that the interviewing firm not contact their current employer. Although such a request is understandable because the applicants do not want to jeopardize their current job, it makes it more difficult for the hiring firm to accurately appraise them. A second difficulty is that very seldom will someone write a critical letter of recommendation. Some people are afraid of being sued for libel if they indicate their true feelings about the individual, whereas others just want to be nice to a departing associate. The sales manager may alleviate this problem somewhat by telephoning the person who wrote the letter of recommendation for more information about the applicant.

In-Depth Interviews. Up to this point in the selection process, the applicant will have dealt primarily, if not exclusively, with personnel employees. An applicant who has passed the initial screening conducted by the personnel office will be invited back to the firm for several in-depth interviews. During these sessions, the applicant will meet with several representatives of management — typically, the sales manager, assistant managers, and possibly the director of marketing. These contacts are important because frequently more than one person in the organization is involved in the hiring decision. It may be that the sales manager is looking for a first-rate career salesperson, whereas the marketing manager wants someone who will stay in sales for only a few years and then move into product management or advertising. In addition, various members of the management team will have different perspectives on company needs; this diversity will help the applicant understand the organizational dynamics of the firm.

No matter how hard management tries to give the prospective employee a good understanding of the sales position, it cannot do it as well as an experienced sales representative. Many organizations, therefore, will ask a prospective employee to spend two days visiting the firm, the first day meeting with management and the second day traveling with a salesperson. Even if the individual does not accept the position, the day spent with the salesperson will usually be rewarding.

Psychological Testing. Over the years, a great deal of effort has been directed toward the development of psychological tests that will predict whether an individual has the ability to become an effective salesperson. Although some consulting firms in the field of psychological testing have trumpeted the merits of their tests, most psychologists and sales managers now do not place much faith in the predictive ability of these tests.[9]

---

[9]For a good summary of psychological testing in selling, see E. A. Johns, "The Use of Tests in the Selection of Salesmen," *British Journal of Marketing* (Autumn, 1968), pp. 185–199.

The Hiring Decision

The decision whether to hire a particular individual for a sales position should be made by a line manager — preferably, the person for whom the new employee will be working. If individuals are hired by others and simply assigned to the sales managers by personnel people, the sales managers are not likely to feel the same level of interest in or loyalty to the new employees that they would if they had hired the individuals themselves. In addition, if the new employee does not work out, it is too easy for the line manager to blame the failure on the personnel department rather than to work with the employee more closely to identify and resolve problem areas.

Another important reason why sales managers, not staff assistants, should make the hiring decision is that sales managers know a great deal more about sales and the type of people with whom they can work. Sales managers should interview several prospects that have made it through the initial screening; then hire the individuals that appear to have the best chance of succeeding in the organization.

ALLOCATION OF SALESPEOPLE

One of the sales manager's primary responsibilities is to assign each salesperson to prospective accounts. The objective, of course, is to maximize the profitability of the representative and the firm by ensuring that the salesperson's time is allocated properly to each account. This section begins by looking at three key factors that must be evaluated when making territory allocation decisions — workload, territory potential, and territory size.

Workload

All current and prospective accounts should be classified according to their potential sales volume. Such classification permits the sales manager to allocate selling time in relation to the potential sales volume of each account. Exceptions to this system of allocation will, of course, result from long-standing personal relationships or exclusive sales account relationships. In the latter case the salesperson involved may have to devote even more time to an account in order to ensure that the customer receives all the products needed to operate profitably. The sales manager cannot permit representatives to take their best accounts for granted.

Territory Potential

Each sales territory must have sufficient sales potential to enable the salesperson to earn a living wage. If sufficient sales volume does not exist, the firm has one of two alternatives. First, the salesperson can be withdrawn from the territory and not reassigned to it until sufficient potential develops. The firm may continue to have some presence in the market by selling via direct mail or the telephone or by employing a manufacturer's agent as its representative.

As graduation approaches, you have at least tentatively decided on a career path. You are now ready to begin interviewing with prospective companies. Let's look at the recruiting process from *your* perspective.

The Resume. The first step in the recruiting process is to develop a neat, organized, professional-looking resume. Include basic biographical data, your telephone number, and your address. Design your resume to emphasize your achievements in school. Highlight the positive! If your grades were good, display this information prominently. If you were especially active in campus organizations, draw attention to that fact on the resume. List any jobs you've held — tell who, what, where, and how long — and any awards that you have received while in college.

The Initial Interview. The first interview usually takes place in your college's placement office and lasts no more than 30 minutes. The purpose of this interview is simply to provide time for you and the recruiter to get acquainted. It is also a screening device by which the more qualified candidates are separated from the less qualified. So, come well-dressed, do some research on the company, find out what kind of people the company is seeking, and appear interested in what the recruiter has to say. Your enthusiasm for the firm and its industry is often what the recruiter remembers most about you.

The Second Interview. If all went well during the first interview, you may be asked to visit (expenses paid) the company headquarters or one of its district offices. The people you talk with during the office visit will try to do two things: (1) sell you on what the company has to offer and (2) decide whether you are the kind of person they're seeking. Although you should never be overconfident, the fact that you were invited for a second interview means that you have a good chance of being offered a job. Businesses just will not spend money and time on you unless they think you have what it takes to work for them.

What If You Are Not Successful? First, remember that almost everyone gets a job eventually. Even colleges with very successful placement programs rarely place more than 65 percent of a graduating class; the other 35 percent get jobs through friends, family connections, professional placement firms, or by visiting the offices of prospective employers. If you're having trouble finding a job, speak candidly with your placement director. You may learn something about yourself — your interview style, manner of dress, attitude, or preparation — that may be having a negative effect on recruiters. By being aware of the problem, you can then begin to solve it. Good luck!

Marketing & You

The second alternative is to subsidize the salesperson's income by using the profits from other territories to cover the low-potential territory. The subsidizing may be either an increase in salary, or an adjustment in the formula used for calculating commissions. Such action is taken when the territory is thought to have substantial long-term potential.[10] The use of straight salary and commissions in compensation plans is discussed later in the chapter.

Determinants of Sales Territory Size

The work pattern of salespeople varies depending on the firm's specific situation and its competitive environment. If certain factors are not considered carefully, the firm is likely to misallocate its sales resources. Consider the following factors as determinants of sales territory size.[11]

Nature of the Product. In the case of a consumer good with a rapid turnover, the salesperson will have to call on each account frequently. In contrast, industrial products, which usually last a long time, do not require the salesperson to call on accounts as often. Therefore, the person selling industrial durable goods will be able to carry more accounts than the person selling high-turnover consumer goods.

Channels of Distribution. A salesperson dealing only with wholesalers will not have as many accounts within a given area as the salesperson dealing primarily with retail customers. Neither, however, will that salesperson have as many accounts as the person selling door to door.

Stage of Market Development. When dealing in new markets, sales territories tend to be larger than in older, better-established markets. Because of the uncertainties associated with new markets, the territory must be larger to provide the sales representative with sufficient potential sales volume.

Intensity of Market Coverage. If the firm's products must be distributed intensively, then the size of its sales territories will be relatively small. In contrast, for firms selling to a few accounts on a selective or exclusive basis, the sales territories are likely to be very large.

Competition. How strong is the competition, and how aggressive is top management in attempting to take sales away from competitors? The size of each salesperson's territory varies inversely with the strength of the competition and the aggressiveness of top management.

The Quality of the Sales Force. If the firm has an experienced, highly productive sales force, it will be able to work with fewer representatives and larger sales territories. In contrast, if the firm is new or if it has not been able to maintain a competitive sales force, it must resort to more salespeople.

---

[10]John D. Louth, "Establishing Sales Territories," in Victor P. Buell, *Handbook of Modern Marketing* (New York: McGraw-Hill, 1970), pp. 68–69.

[11]William J. Stanton and Richard H. Buskirk, *Management of the Sales Force* (Homewood, Ill.: Richard D. Irwin, 1978), pp. 489–490.

Establishing Sales Territories

The first step in establishing sales territories is to select the basic geographical control unit. The firm then applies simple economic analysis to determine how it should allocate its sales force.

Select the Basic Geographical Control Unit. The most commonly used control units are states, counties, cities, metropolitan areas, and zip codes. Sales territories are established by combining a group of control units. The sales manager will want to ensure that the control unit itself is as small as possible. When control units are too large, areas with high sales potential may be hidden. Also, if the control units are selected properly, they will remain stable over a number of years. This stability makes it possible to reconstruct sales territories by simply recombining control units rather than by starting over and identifying control units again.[12]

Determine the Work Load for Each Control Unit. After choosing control units, it is relatively easy to determine how much time the firm should invest in each control unit. To demonstrate, Table 11-3 has been constructed to represent a control unit of an electrical supply house in Wisconsin. Here, the sales manager has calculated the yearly and monthly number of hours that must be spent for each type of account. This control unit has two class-one accounts, each of which should be called on 15 times per year at an average length of eight hours per call. As a result, the business will invest 240 hours per year, or 20 hours per month, on these two class-one accounts. In a similar manner, the sales manager has calculated the required amount of sales time for each of the four remaining classes of accounts and then has totaled the required hours for each account. The sales manager finds that an average of 91.9 hours per month will be spent servicing the control units.

The firm must also calculate the travel time between the sales rep's office and each account in the control unit. The sales manager can simply estimate the travel time for each account and then sum these amounts to obtain a total for the control unit.

TABLE 11-3 Hypothetical Workload for Control Unit #45

Account Class	Number of Accounts	Number of Calls Per Year Per Account	Average Time Per Call (Hours)	Total Yearly Hours	Total Monthly Hours
1	2	15	8	240	20.0
2	4	12	6	288	24.0
3	7	10	5	350	29.2
4	10	6	3	180	15.0
5	11	2	2	44	3.7
				1,102	91.9

---

[12]Still, *et al., op. cit.*, pp. 358–359.

Assign Salespeople to Control Units. The last step in establishing sales territories is to assign each salesperson to one or more control units. To do so, the firm must estimate how much selling time each representative has in a month. The average month has 21 working days. From this figure the sales manager must subtract the amount of selling time lost for such activities as sales meetings, sales training sessions with suppliers, interviews with prospective salespeople, and other administrative duties. Subtracting three days per month for these nonselling activities leaves the salesperson with a total of 18 days, or 144 hours, for on-the-road selling.

Referring to the example in Table 11-3, a salesperson having 144 available hours and already assigned Control Unit #45, which required only 91.9 hours per month, could be assigned additional control units until the 144-hour limit is reached.

SALES COMPENSATION

Sales compensation plans are often very difficult to administer. Salespeople like to be rewarded immediately for their performance. As a result, many compensation plans are designed to make the individual feel like an independent entrepreneur. Also, salespeople tend to be highly paid. The average income for a senior commission sales rep in the United States was just under $30,000 in 1979.[13] What this means for the firm is that if it makes a mistake in designing its sales compensation system, it can end up wasting a great deal of money. This section begins by looking at the objectives of a sales compensation plan and then analyzes three types of compensation plans.

Objectives of Sales Compensation Plans

The objectives of all compensation plans are the same — namely, to reward salespeople for superior performance, to control and direct the sales effort, and to attract and develop effective salespeople. Fortunately, these objectives do not directly conflict with one another.

Correlate Results with Rewards. Ideally, payments to representatives should reflect the amount and quality of their work. Two examples illustrate the problems involved in matching compensation to performance. First, two salespeople may work equally as hard but one receives an order immediately, whereas the other may have to wait months for a sale from a similar account. Second, one salesperson may sell $200,000 worth of merchandise and the other $400,000 worth. The first salesperson may be much more valuable to the firm because the sales potential of his or her territory may be only 25 percent as great as the potential of the second salesperson's territory. These types of problems are not easy to deal with because many compensation plans are tied closely to immediate results.

---

[13]This figure is derived from adjusting data presented in *Sales & Marketing Management* (February 26, 1979), p. 60.

Control and Direct the Sales Force. Besides selling, most salespeople provide many other services to their customers and to other employees of their firm. To the customer, they provide free consulting services about products, financing, installation, inventory maintenance, and product servicing. In many cases, the salesperson may provide valuable engineering services to the customer before and after the sale. The sales rep is often expected to provide marketing intelligence data, to train new salespeople, to coordinate sales programs, and to evaluate the sales potential of new products. To the extent that these additional services are important, they should be considered when designing the sales compensation plan. Otherwise, salespeople may not be sufficiently motivated to perform them.

Attract Good Salespeople. A good compensation plan should attract qualified applicants for sales positions and should encourage effective salespeople to remain with the firm. Both the amount of money paid and type of plan used are important. Some firms, particularly in the retail industry, pay their new employees less than competitive rates. The management of these firms justify their comparatively low wage rates by arguing that the industry is "more exciting" and offers more opportunity for personal advancement than others. Frequently, these arguments do not hold much water and result in the firm losing many good prospective employees. Even when its recruiting process works well, a firm occasionally will hire the wrong person. The compensation system is one way to identify these individuals: poor salespeople will not make their quotas, nor will they earn large commissions or bonuses.

Types of Sales Compensation Plans

There are three basic types of sales compensation plans: straight salary, commission, and a combined salary-commission plan. As Figure 11-4 indicates, the use of commissions and other incentives has become increasingly common.

FIGURE 11-4. How Companies Are Changing Sales Compensation Plans

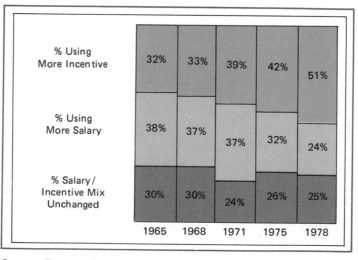

Source: Research Institute of America, "Sales Compensation '78," *Sales & Marketing Management* (April 9, 1979), p. 19.

Straight Salary. Under a straight salary plan, salespeople receive the same amount of compensation regardless of how much they sell. The primary advantage of a straight salary plan is that it enables the firm to control the sales force's efforts. A sales manager who believes that salespeople should be calling on new accounts, selling new products, or servicing old ones, can simply direct them to do so, even if it means sacrificing short-term sales. A second advantage of a straight salary plan is that it is easy to administer; the sales manager need not be concerned with complex incentive formulas based on either sales or profits.

Salary-based plans are often criticized because they do not provide sufficient incentive. Although this is a valid criticism, the incentive problem can be partially overcome by frequent salary adjustments.

Straight Commission. Under a straight commission system, the salespeople are compensated only when they make a sale; thus, such a system involves very little risk to the firm. Salespeople are motivated because the more they sell, the more money they make.

However, there are several difficulties associated with the commission plan. Commision representatives are basically independent business people; they follow company directives only when they feel it is in their best interests to do so. Specifically, they will push a new product aggressively only if they expect it to have a beneficial effect on their incomes. In the same way, commission salespeople frequently do not provide the expected level of ongoing service for products already sold because their compensation is tied to sales, not to service or to any other type of consideration.

Another important disadvantage of a straight commission plan is the risk to the salesperson — that is, when sales drop for any reason, the salesperson faces an immediate decrease in income. This uncertainty can be partially offset with a **draw**, i.e., giving the salesperson a specified level of income each month. At the end of certain periods, typically six months or one year, the commission salesperson and the company settle their accounts. If commission earnings have been more than the salesperson's draw, the firm pays the extra amount. However, if the commissions are less than the draw, the salesperson must either work for several months without a draw or give some of the draw back to the company.

Combination Salary and Incentive Plans. A combined salary incentive system attempts to take advantage of the good points of both plans. The salesperson is paid a salary that is not a function of the number of units sold. Therefore, the salesperson does not have to worry about extreme variability in income, and the firm has a right to ask the salesperson to perform nonselling duties since not all compensation is tied directly to sales. The salesperson, however, also receives incentive pay — in some situations, a commission fee for every unit sold, and in other cases, primarily when the salesperson must be responsible for a large variety of nonselling activities, a bonus once or twice a year.

One difficulty with the combination plan is determining the base salary and the commission percentage. In other words, how much of the salesperson's income should come from salary and how much should come from commissions. Generally speaking, the more selling expected of the individual, the greater the amount of incentive pay that should be built into the system. Although combination plans are quite complex, they often are the best compensation system available to management.

DEVELOPING SALES REPRESENTATIVES

The common but erroneous belief that "sales representatives are born, not made" has done more to hinder the acceptance of sales training programs than any other factor. In this section, we consider who should be trained, the factors influencing the content of sales training, and the importance of reinforcement to successful sales training programs.

Who Should Be Trained?

Should the firm concentrate its sales training programs on newly hired people or on its experienced salespeople? In dealing with seasoned representatives, should the firm direct its efforts to its less productive salespeople or to those who exceed their quotas month after month? These are important questions for the sales manager. Possible answers are suggested below.

There is no question that all sales recruits, no matter what their selling experience, must go through some training if for no other reason than because they need to learn about company policies and products. Those with little or no selling experience may also be required to attend seminars and role-playing sessions on selling.

The salesperson with many years of selling experience with the firm should also participate in sales training sessions from time to time. Typically, these training sessions are designed to acquaint the sales force with the firm's new products. However, many firms also use these meetings to introduce promising new sales techniques.

Research has shown that it is far more effective to focus on making a good representative better than to try to change the marginal salesperson into an above-average performer. The person who takes the time to learn more about selling not only will be among the company's best sales representatives but also will get a great deal more out of formal training sessions.

Factors Influencing Sales Training Content

Although the content of sales training programs varies depending upon the particular needs of the firm, at least three factors govern the selection of training program material.[14]

Experience Level of Trainees. Not surprisingly, new employees with no selling experience will need the most training. In this regard, the firm should acquaint new salespeople with company history, the firm's organizational structure, sales policies, products, markets, competition, selling techniques, and ter-

---

[14]Kenneth R. Davis and Frederick E. Webster, Jr., *Sales Force Management* (New York: Ronald Press, 1968), pp. 478–481.

ritory management. The length of the training program depends on the nature of the firm's business. For example, a person selling encyclopedias door to door may need no more than a week of training, whereas a sales engineer may be required to spend as much as two years learning about the product before making a first sales call.

A new employee with some previous sales experience, on the other hand, will usually require less formal training than the inexperienced recruit. Many firms customize programs to fit experienced sales recruits since no two of them have the same background. Sending these people through a standardized sales training program would probably be a waste of time.

New Products and New Markets. A firm that regularly introduces new products will need to hold frequent product training sessions. These sessions may be a part of another sales meeting or they may involve sending the salesperson to the production facility for training.

In the same manner, a firm that decides to modify its marketing plan may be required to offer sales retraining programs. Consider the case of a firm that decides to mass market an industrial-strength detergent that previously had been sold only to corporations and businesses. If the firm plans to use the same sales force, it will probably have to invest a substantial amount of time and effort in a retraining program because the new consumer market involves an entirely new distribution channel. Where salespeople had previously called on purchasing agents, they now will have to sell to supermarkets and convenience stores.

Changes in Company Policies. Changes in corporate personnel policies is the third factor influencing the content of the sales training programs. For example, if the firm were to change the sales compensation plan, management, no doubt, would hold a conference in order to explain the changes to those affected.

Follow-up: The Best Training

All too often, upon completion of the sales training program, salespeople are simply sent back to the field and told to apply what they have learned in the classroom. If training is to make individuals more effective salespeople, there must be some way for sales managers to reinforce the classroom lessons. Four ways of providing follow-up are listed below:

1. Newsletters reviewing the material presented in the sales training session.
2. Video cassette tapes sent out to district sales offices.
3. "Self-administered" exercises enabling the salesperson to work on sales problems.
4. Visits by sales managers, including observation of the salesperson during several sales calls.[15]

The sales manager should realize that the participants of a sales training program will return to the field with varying degrees of understanding of the classroom lessons. Some may leave the program with a firm grasp of a few

[15]Donald S. Hammalian, "Follow-up: The Best Training Investment of All," a special report in *Sales & Marketing Management* (December 12, 1977), p. 65.

specific lessons, whereas others may leave with a good feel for all the material only to revert to their old habits after a few weeks. Therefore, the sales manager must be willing to work with each trainee individually.

In addition to individual attention, the sales manager should try to use positive reinforcement. Salespeople need to feel that the sales manager is more interested in their future successes than in their past failures.

MOTIVATING SALES PERSONNEL

Motivation is one of the most important factors behind personal success. Generally speaking, sales managers spend more time attempting to motivate their salespeople than do other function managers with respect to their employees. This section examines why salespeople require extra encouragement, the theory of job enrichment, and the use of contests to motivate sales pesonnel.

Why Sales Personnel Require Additional Encouragement

Why salespeople need additional encouragement rests with the nature of the sales job. Selling is typically characterized by alternating states of exhilaration and depression. In the course of a day, a salesperson may receive one large order and lose two others. It is very difficult for most people to "lose" so openly as does a salesperson having to report back to the office without a single order. Furthermore, many representatives spend long hours away from their families, which often leads them to believe that they are not being fair to their spouses and to their children.

Extra encouragement is also needed because many sales reps tend to become apathetic. They call on the same customers year after year. Since they often develop close personal relationships with their customers, they come to believe that creative selling is no longer necessary. As a result, the sales call slowly degenerates into a social meeting that concludes with the question, "How many units do you need today?" Unfortunately, the customer may get to the point where the answer is "none." Later that day, when a competing salesperson arrives on the scene and takes the time to learn about the customer's product or service needs, the customer finds that a purchase really is necessary.

Finally, salespeople are isolated from their colleagues most of the time. As a result, it is difficult for them to develop any real team spirit. However, if the sales manager can generate some enthusiasm for meeting group performance standards, the sales performance of each member of the team should improve.[16]

Job Enrichment

Although there are several approaches to motivating employees, many experts now believe that people are most likely to be motivated when they feel

---

[16]Still, *et al., op. cit.,* pp. 305–306.

FIGURE 11-5 Factors Affecting Job Attitudes

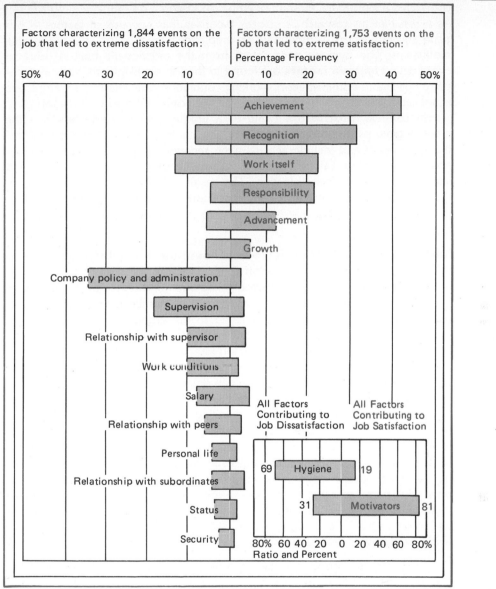

Source: Reprinted by permission of the *Harvard Business Review*. Exhibit from Frederick Herzberg, "One More Time: How Do You Motivate Employees?" (January–February, 1968). Copyright © 1968 by the President and Fellows of Harvard College; all rights reserved.

that they have some control over their jobs and when they receive public recognition for a job well done. To understand how salespeople might best be motivated, let's look at Frederick Herzberg's notion of hygiene vs. motivators.[17]

[17]Frederick Herzberg, "One More Time: How Do You Motivate Employees?" *Harvard Business Review* (January–February, 1968), pp. 56–58.

Hygiene vs. Motivators. Frederick Herzberg, a well-known psychologist, has conducted a substantial amount of empirical research on employee motivation. As a result of his research, Herzberg theorizes that two sets of factors — hygiene and motivators — determine an employee's level of job satisfaction and motivation. The hygiene needs stem from the individual's built-in drive to avoid pain. **Hygiene factors** are found in the job environment, such as company policy and administration, working conditions, and salary. If an employee is not satisfied with job hygiene, he or she will not be satisfied with the job.

In contrast, **motivators** relate to a unique human characteristic — the need to grow psychologically. In the industrial setting, motivators are a part of the job content and include achievement, recognition, the work itself, and responsibility. Figure 11-5 illustrates a composite of factors involved with job satisfaction and job dissatisfaction. The results of Herzberg's study of more than 1,600 people indicated clearly that motivators are the primary cause of job satisfaction and that hygiene factors are the primary cause of job dissatisfaction.

Enrichment Possibilities for Sales Positions. To provide incentive to sales personnel through reliance on motivators, the sales manager first must carefully evaluate each sales position to determine whether or not it can be "enriched." Job enrichment programs involve an identification of the responsibilities that reasonably can be delegated to the employee, in this case, the salesperson. The basic principle is that each job should require a level of skill commensurate with the skill of the person hired for it.

Generally speaking, the more highly trained and professional the sales force, the more responsibility the firm can delegate to its salespeople. Areas of responsibility that might be added as the salesperson gains more experience include recommending sales quotas, directing team selling efforts made on the salesperson's account, determining route patterns, and deciding which accounts deserve extra attention. Again, it is important to point out that if the hygiene factors are not handled satisfactorily, salespeople will become unhappy and probably leave. However, to truly motivate salespeople, the firm must give them an opportunity to assume responsibility and then recognize them publicly for their success.

Sales Contests

Sales contests are used quite often to stimulate sales or to achieve some specific sales objective. In a study of 1,400 subscribers of *Sales & Marketing Management*, it was found that 62.7 percent of the subjects used merchandise or travel incentives to motivate their sales personnel. It is interesting to note that reliance on such incentives varies significantly by industry. Manufacturers of consumer goods are more likely to use incentive programs than industrial or commodity firms. In the study, 96 percent of food products manufacturers used merchandise or travel incentives, whereas only 29 percent of primary metal manufacturers used such incentives.[18]

---

[18]Sally Scanlon, "Moving It," *Sales & Marketing Management* (April 11, 1977), p. 35.

TABLE 11-4 Objectives of Sales Contests

Objective	Rank Order	Number of Mentions
Find new customers.	1	273
Obtain greater volume per call.	2	208
Get better territory coverage.	3	189
Promote special items.	4	175
Overcome seasonal sales slump.	5	165
Get better balance of sales.	6	124
Get renewal of business from former customers.	7	115
Introduce a new product or line.	8	114
Stop or slow a sales decline.	9	108
Develop new sales skills.	10	95
Ease an unfavorable inventory position.	11	91
Lower selling costs.	12	67
Sell higher quality products.	13	62
Improve sales service to customers.	14	61
Build better product displays.	15	50
Get better sales reports.	16	37
Reduce selling time.	17	24
Eliminate returns and mistakes.	18	13
All other.	—	26

Source: Richard R. Still, Edward W. Cundiff, and Norman A. P. Govoni, *Sales Management: Decisions, Policies, and Cases* (3d ed.; Englewood Cliffs, N.J.: Prentice-Hall, Inc., 1976), p. 321. Reprinted by permission of Prentice-Hall, Inc.

Theoretically, sales contests are used because they provide recognition, one of Herzberg's key motivators. In practice, sales contests have been shown to increase sales dramatically. A study conducted at the University of Indiana resulted in the development of the list of sales contest objectives shown in Table 11-4. The first and third most frequently mentioned use of contests — "find new customers" and "get better territory coverage" — are designed to encourage sales personnel to generate more sales in markets with untapped potential. The second most frequently mentioned use — "obtaining greater volume per call" — is designed to increase sales to current customers.

As an illustration of the cost effectiveness of contests, *Sales & Marketing Management* magazine estimated that in 1977 sales executives in the United States spent $3 billion on incentive programs that generated $40 billion in extra sales.[19] In a more specific, yet typical, example, several years ago Singer found itself in a sales slump. Although its commercial clients do not normally purchase business machines in the summer, Singer launched a sales contest entitled "Singer Summer." The program involved the firm's salespeople and their families, all of whom were sent a well-coordinated barrage of promotional material including wall posters, scorecards, and children's T-shirts. Although the grand prize was a week in Spain, "Singer Summer" also involved weekly

[19]Scanlon, *op. cit.*, p. 33.

bonus checks as well as interim merchandise prizes. At the end of the contest, Singer sales were up $3.8 million at a total cost of only $300,000.[20]

summary points

1. The image of a salesperson as a "huckster" who tries to get the buyers to purchase unneeded products at inflated prices is a common stereotype. Most salespeople are professional, hard-working individuals who are trying to sell products which meet customers' real needs.

2. People who enter the selling profession have an opportunity to pursue sales, sales management, and marketing management careers. In addition, selling also provides freedom from direct control and excellent financial rewards.

3. Under the marketing concept, the sales manager reports to the vice-president of marketing rather than directly to top management. The sales manager's concern is less with sales volume than with profitable sales and strategic planning.

4. Management by objectives involves the joint identification of performance goals and work strategies by sales managers and members of the sales force.

5. Federal legislation makes it unlawful to discriminate in the recruiting and hiring of sales personnel.

6. A sales job description must be developed and the qualifications needed for sales positions must be identified. Two essential characteristics of the successful salesperson are empathy and ego drive.

7. The major sources of new sales personnel are recent graduates of institutions, current salespeople, nonselling employees of the firm, salespeople from other firms, and employment agencies.

8. Some of the steps in selecting applicants for the firm's sales force are initial screening, review of completed application forms and letters of recom-

mendation, in-depth interviews, and psychological testing.

9. Both the allocation of the sales force to accounts and the work pattern of individual salespeople depend on territorial potential, the nature of the product, the channel of distribution, the stage of market development, the desired intensity of market coverage, the strength of the competition, and the quality of the firm's sales force.

10. The basic steps in establishing sales territories are: (1) select the appropriate geographical control unit, (2) determine the workload for each control unit, and (3) assign salespeople to control units.

11. The objectives of a sales compensation plan are to reward salespeople for superior performance, to control and direct the sales effort, and to attract and develop effective salespeople.

12. The three types of sales compensation plans are straight salary, straight commission, and a combined salary-incentive plan.

13. Sales recruits as well as experienced salespeople can benefit from well-designed training programs. It is usually more productive to focus on making the good salesperson better than on changing the marginal salesperson into an above-average performer. A key ingredient of any successful sales training program is follow-up by the sales manager.

14. Salespeople usually require more encouragement than other members of the firm. Job enrichment, as a technique for motivating sales personnel, involves the delegation of as much responsibility as possible to the salesperson. Sales contests are another very effective way of motivating the sales force.

---

[20]John H. Stevenson, "It's a Good Time for Innovation," *Sales & Marketing Management* (April 8, 1974), pp. 22–23.

1. What is your image of a sales representative? On what is this image based?
2. Which aspects of selling are most attractive to you? Which are the least attractive?
3. Is the sales manager less important in a firm that has adopted the marketing concept than in one that still holds to the production orientation? Explain.
4. Explain the process of management by objectives. Is this a good tool for sales managers to use? Why or why not?
5. What qualifications are needed in a sales representative?
6. Is there any one source of new sales representatives that works best for most firms? Explain your answer.
7. Describe the selection system you would employ to hire sales representatives. Would psychological testing play an important role?
8. Analyze the approach presented in this chapter for allocating salespeople. What changes, if any, would you suggest?
9. If you were a sales representative, would you prefer to be paid on the basis of a straight salary, straight commission, or a combination system? Explain your rationale.
10. How important are sales training programs?
11. What is meant by job enrichment? How can the jobs of sales representatives be enriched?
12. What role do sales contests play in motivating sales representatives?

Big Surf is a 20-acre recreation facility located in Phoenix, Arizona, that has over 600 feet of sandy beach and palm trees surrounding a pump-filled, 500,000-gallon reservoir. Perfect 5-foot-high waves are produced every 50 seconds, providing a 360-foot-long ride to the beach. The huge reservoir is 20 feet wide, 160 feet long, and 47 feet high and holds the water and the hydraulic head that creates the waves. In addition to the surfing and swimming facility, Big Surf has a 300-foot water slide, a food and drink concession, an equipment rental service (for surfboards, rubber rafts, etc.), locker facilities, pinball arcade, and a surf shop which sells swimwear, sunglasses and suntan oil.

The Market

Between 1960 and 1974 the population of the Phoenix area increased 45 percent. Phoenix's median age is 24.6 years, with more than one third of the household heads under 35 years. Because of its warm, dry climate, Phoenix is a popular leisure and recreation area. Much of the area's leisure activities revolve around water. Phoenix has nearly 25,000 private swimming pools and 4,500 public and commercial pools (apartments, motels, etc.). In a 90-day period, 51 percent of the area's population go boating or swimming at least once.

Since 1971, the under-21 group has continued to represent the bulk of the Big Surf customers and is still considered the primary market. The next most important target market for Big Surf are the young marrieds with one or two small children.

Inland Oceans, Inc. — Big Surf is reprinted with permission from *Advertising Management* by Charles H. Patti and John H. Murphy (Grid Publishing, Inc., Columbus, Ohio, 1978), pp. 159–167.

These two groups constitute 52.8 percent of the Phoenix metro area population. Another target market for Big Surf are organizations. Big Surf offers an attractive recreation facility for any group with 25–10,000 members. Educational, religious, political, social, community service, and commercial organizations are among those that have rented the entire Big Surf facility for private affairs.

Big Surf Promotion

Since the opening of Big Surf a number of promotional tools and techniques have been used to create awareness and stimulate attendance. In 1969 and 1970, the firm relied primarily on publicity and advertising. News releases, press kits, open houses, and promotional literature were all used to inform potential customers that Big Surf was a new and unique facility that offered an exciting recreation activity. Big Surf also used advertising extensively to encourage attendance by offering a variety of special promotions.

Most of this early advertising and publicity emphasized the surfing activity, and there was a concentrated effort to attract a portion of the 26,000 student population of nearby Arizona State University. While it is difficult to assess the effectiveness of the early promotion, management felt that these efforts contributed heavily to making Big Surf known as one of Arizona's recreation attractions.

In January, 1972, Big Surf's management decided that most of the "awareness" communications task had been accomplished through its promotional efforts and as a result advertising expenditures were reduced substantially. In 1972, total spending for advertising and publicity was $63,000 — less than a third of 1970 and 1971 expenditures.

Also, attendance data indicated that Big Surf was not attracting the college market. Despite numerous promotions aimed at the college market, high school teenagers and young families were identified as the primary source of customers. Consequently, advertising directed to the college market was minimized, and more high school and "family-oriented" promotional themes were initiated.

Finally, customer research and attendance data indicated a growing interest in the Big Surf facility but a declining interest in surfing. This increased interest in the overall water facility was substantiated by rental equipment receipts which showed a 40 percent increase in rubber raft rentals and a 25 percent decrease in surfboard rentals. A 1974 survey of Big Surf customers showed that swimming was the most preferred activity for 81.5 percent of all visitors, rafting was second (57.4 percent) and surfing was third (14.6 percent).

TABLE 1   Big Surf Advertising Media Expenditures

Medium	1973	1974
Television	$33,317	$ 0
Radio	13,154	19,096
Newspapers	15,557	8,904
Total	$62,028	$28,000

Increased use of Big Surf by families encouraged Inland Oceans to pursue this market more aggressively, and during 1973 and 1974 more advertising was directed to family promotions. It was also during 1973–1974 that group sales began to represent a significant portion of Big Surf's total attendance. Groups were reached primarily by direct mail and inquiries about rental of the facility were then completed by telephone or personal call by a Big Surf representative to the interested group.

As Table 1 indicates, Big Surf has used most of the major advertising media during the past two years. In the past, the selection of media has been determined by the limitations of the size of the budget and management's "feelings" about the relative effectiveness of an individual medium.

1. Which target market should Big Surf attempt to attract?
2. What should be Big Surf's advertising objectives?
3. Using the target market and advertising objectives which you have established, develop a media plan that will best contribute to the success of Big Surf.

---

case 11
clemson meat
company

The Clemson Meat Company is a family-owned meat processing and packing company which sold high-quality perishable meat products directly to retail grocers and supermarkets. The company had been started in the 1930s, and the main processing plant was located in a large western city. The company's sales volume, about $85 million a year, had been increasing about 10 to 12 percent a year, and management expected this growth rate to continue.

However, like most meat packers, Clemson operated on a narrow net profit margin. In the previous year Clemson had incurred a small loss. The company had no control over the price of live hogs, its main raw material. Consequently, Mr. Peter Jauch, the vice-president of sales, was looking for a way to cut sales operating expenses in the hope of contributing to profit.

The Meat Market

The Clemson products were divided into six categories. Each salesperson sold the full line. The six product groups and their share of the company's sales were as follows: fresh pork, 60 percent; weiners, 12 percent; bacon, 12 percent; ham, 6 percent; sausage, 6 percent; and lunch meats, 4 percent.

Since meat products are perishable, orders had to be filled very quickly. Clemson's small size made it flexible enough to receive orders one day and ship them the next. Clemson sold in 14 western states. The company sold to some 3,500 accounts, but Mr. Jauch estimated that the potential in these states was about three times that number. Clemson sold primarily to retailers. Each salesperson handled 6 or 7 large accounts. In the Colorado market, for example, two retail supermarket chains — King Soopers and Safeway — accounted for about 85 percent of Clemson's sales. In general, the retail accounts had been decreasing in number but increasing in average size. Consequently, Mr. Jauch believed that the company could continue its growth without adding more salespeople, at least for the next couple of years.

Clemson Meat Company case by William J. Stanton and Richard H. Buskirk, *Management of the Sales Force*, (5th ed.; Homewood, Ill.: Richard D. Irwin, Inc., 1978), pp. 290–293. © 1978 by Richard D. Irwin, Inc.

Clemson's major competitive advantages were its flexibility and its modern production facilities. For example, the company operated a hot dog machine which manufactured 30,000 weiners per hour. The company's major limitation, as Mr. Jauch saw it, was that Clemson was too small to advertise as heavily as its major competitors.

The Sales Compensation Plan

Clemson's 22 sales representatives had a thorough knowledge of meats and the meat industry. They usually were hired from competitive firms. They were paid with a combination salary and bonus plan. Salaries ranged from $700 to $1,000 a month. The bonus, a percentage of salary, was based on how much a sales representative exceeded his or her quota. Tonnage quotas in each of five categories of processed meats were assigned to each sales representative. These quotas were based on past sales, as adjusted for current economic conditions and market outlook. The quotas and bonuses were computed quarterly.

The bonus was a certain amount paid for each ton of meat sold in excess of quota. To encourage a balanced selling job of all products, management set limits for the bonuses in each category of processed meats. For example, the total bonus paid for selling hot dogs could not exceed 12 percent of salary. These limits in the other product categories were as follows: hams, 6 percent; sausage, 12 percent; lunch meat, 12 percent; and bacon, 10 percent. Thus, a sales rep's total bonus for all products was limited to 52 percent of his or her salary. Most other firms in the industry paid their sales forces a straight salary.

The salespeople were also provided with unlimited expense accounts but were required to submit itemized statements. Clemson allowed its sales force to grant an allowance or discount of four cents per pound as a concession to customers in special situations.

Is a New Compensation Plan Needed?

Recently, it has been brought to Mr. Jauch's attention that the sales of three sales reps were fluctuating about 500,000 pounds from one three-month period to the next. This represented 10 to 12 percent of the average four to five million pounds of meat sold by each salesperson during a quarterly period. Apparently, in order to exceed their volume quotas, these individuals were convincing some of their customers that they needed more meat than was actually the case. The retail buyers consequently would be overstocked one period and would underbuy the next period in order to balance things out. Fluctuations of this sort caused production inefficiencies, thus increasing costs.

Upon further investigation of past records, Mr. Jauch discovered that on virtually all of their orders, these same three sales representatives were shaving 4 cents a pound from the list price which is allowed only as a special price concession. Thus, Clemson was not realizing its planned profit margins in these territories. Moreover, sales on low-margin products far exceeded sales of high-margin items. As a final point, Mr. Jauch felt that the travel and business expenses of these sales reps were much too high.

Each of the three sales representatives involved had been with Clemson for over ten years and was well established in his or her territory. Each handled a number of large accounts. These salespersons were very good — they knew meat and could sell it. They liked to write up big orders. They consistently won or came close to winning the annual sales contest for the greatest volume sold. They also had the highest earnings last year.

1. Are the three sales representatives marketing oriented?
2. Should major changes be made in Clemson's compensation plan for its system? If so, what would you recommend?

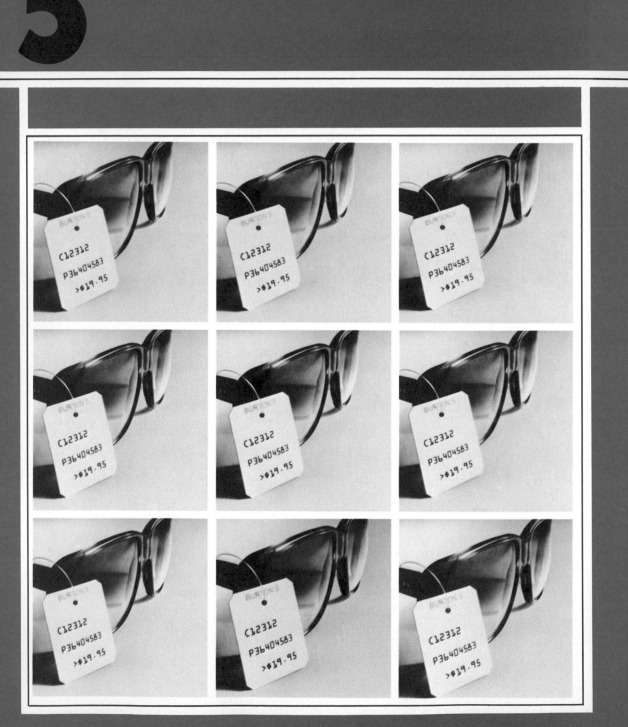

5

Pricing

Sixty dollars or $75, $49.95 or $50.00? Have you ever wondered just who determines the price you pay for products? In many, though certainly not all cases, you do! Probably no other variable receives as much attention (and criticism) from customers as does pricing.

Part 5 tackles the problem of pricing both new and existing products. The pricing decision is constantly, or at least periodically, under review, since a change in almost any aspect of the marketing program bears directly upon the price to be charged for the product.

12 Pricing Policies

What price to charge for a product is among the firm's most critical decisions. This decision has an effect on how the product is perceived by the public, on who buys it, and on how profitable the firm will be. Although marketers have given a great deal of attention to pricing, there are still many pricing issues that have not been resolved.

THE MEANING OF PRICE

The **price** of a product or service is what the seller feels it is worth, in terms of money, to the buyer. Normally, prices in the United States are fixed by the seller, although in some instances they are negotiated by the buyer and seller. This section of the chapter looks at both fixed and negotiated prices as well as at the factors that most firms consider when setting prices for their merchandise.

Fixed vs. Negotiated Prices

For most consumer products, the seller sets the price and the customer either buys the product at that price or not at all. As an example, if you go to a stationery store to buy a ballpoint pen, you do not negotiate the price with the sales clerk. If the price is higher than you anticipated, you might choose not to buy the product, but generally you do not try to bargain for a lower price for the product.

In a number of situations, however, in both the industrial and consumer sectors of the economy, prices are not fixed, but subject to negotiation. All new cars, for example, display the manufacturer's suggested retail price. Depending on the make and model of the car, the time of year, and the competition in the immediate geographic market, the customer may be able to obtain a substantial reduction from the suggested retail, or sticker, price. To some extent, the size of the reduction depends on how much the customer knows about the automobile business — costs, markups, trade-ins, what is meant by "dealer preparation" — and the negotiating skills of the customer. In large cities, where several dealers represent the same manufacturer, it is much easier for the customer to negotiate price than in small single-dealer towns and cities.

Important Factors in the Determination of Price

How is price determined? What factors does the seller consider in making a pricing decision? As shown in Figure 12-1, the cost of the product, the goals of the company or store, competitive pressures, the characteristics of the typical customer, and the general economic environment all affect the pricing decision in one way or another. How and to what extent they affect price, of course, depends on the product itself.

Cost of the Product. Under normal conditions, the seller does not sell a product below its cost. **Loss leaders**, which are products that the seller promotes in order to get people into the store, are the exception. For example, a supermarket may advertise a special on whole milk in the hope that the low price of milk draws people into the store to buy not only milk but other grocery items as well.

FIGURE 12-1   Critical Factors in the Determination of Price

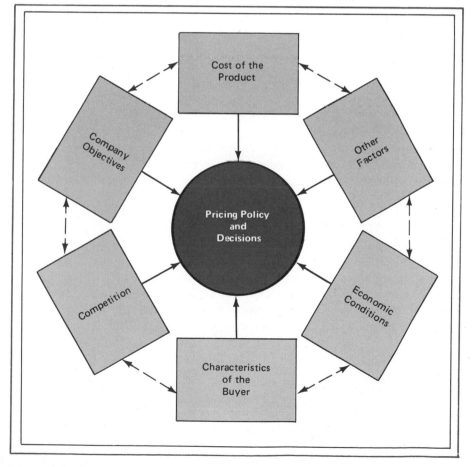

Company Objectives. The objectives of the firm play an important role in determining its pricing strategy. One of General Motors' objectives for the Chevette is to capture a large share of the price-conscious market for subcompact cars. Accordingly, GM attempts to price the car as low as possible. The Cadillac Seville, on the other hand, is designed to appeal to a much smaller, less price-conscious segment of the new car market. Consequently, it is not necessary for GM to make such a concerted effort to control the Seville's sticker price.

Competition. The more intense the competition, the more care the firm should exercise in making pricing decisions. In addition, the greater the similarity between a firm's products and those of its competitors, the more it must depend on price to sell its merchandise. One reason why a Mercedes-Benz has been so expensive is that U.S. automobile companies have only recently introduced cars designed to compete with it. For years Mercedes-Benz stood alone in its product class, and therefore commanded a higher price.

Characteristics of the Buyer. Before setting a product's price, sellers must know their customers — their needs, income, and shopping patterns. If prospective customers are affluent, then they may not be particularly concerned about price. In fact, they may actually seek out products with high price tags. In contrast, members of a primarily middle-class target market may be more interested in obtaining lower priced, good value products.

Economic Conditions. The sale of many products is a function of the nation's economic health. In a healthy and expanding economy, people buy more products and can afford to pay higher prices for them. In a recessionary economy, on the other hand, people have less disposable income. As a result, many firms attempt to stimulate overall product demand by lowering their prices, much as the federal government stimulates the economy by lowering taxes or increasing spending.

A great many other factors, such as the time of year and the seller's inventory level, affect the pricing decision. The specific combination of factors that most affect the pricing decision depends on the unique business situation of the firm.

PRICING'S ROLE IN SOCIETY

The price mechanism is one of the most important forces in the U.S. economic system. It performs three vital functions: comparison, stimulation, and rationing. This section examines each of these functions and shows how they influence our lives.

Comparison

The price of a product allows the buyer to estimate its value, or worth, relative to other similar products. Frequently, consumers and even industrial purchasing agents are not sure of the value of a particular product. If interested in a high quality product, they may assume that "you get what you pay for" and thus buy the most expensive product on the market.

The theory that shoppers typically equate price with quality has been tested numerous times. In two such studies, the researchers found that the subjects tended to be less satisfied with lower priced products than with higher priced products.[1] This trend was found to be true for a wide variety of merchandise — cooking sherry, razor blades, table salt, aspirin, floor wax, and liquid shampoo.

Stimulation

The price mechanism performs a stimulation function — that is, the higher the price of the product, the greater the total revenues, and therefore the more the firm is willing to produce. The sugar market in 1974 exemplified this principle. During that year the price of sugar increased even faster than the price of oil. A combination of rising demand and reduced supply (as a consequence of bad weather) caused the price of raw sugar to rise from 10.75 cents per pound in January to 54.5 cents per pound in November. This dramatic price increase had two effects. First, the high price *stimulated* an increase in the amount of land allocated to the production of sugar. Second, consumers reduced their consumption of sugar by more than 8 percent. Per capita consumption of sugar in the United States dropped from 103.5 pounds per year to 95 pounds per year. The combination of these two factors forced the price of sugar back down to 11.5 cents per pound by May of 1977.[2] This example shows not only that high price stimulates production but also that the market is very dynamic, capable of adjusting quite rapidly to the price or quantity of goods available.

Rationing

In the U.S. economic system, the price mechanism determines who purchases what. As a product becomes more expensive, fewer people are able to buy it. Although the credit system at times distorts the rationing function of price, it is still apparent that goods are rationed through pricing decisions. For example, the higher your income, the more likely you will be able to purchase an expensive home. While you may earn a great deal of money and still not purchase an expensive home, very few people on limited salaries are able to purchase for cash or even finance expensive houses.

THE IMPORTANCE OF PRICE IN THE FIRM'S MARKETING STRATEGY

We have seen that price is a critical economic and marketing concept. However, we must also ask ourselves, "How important is price to the firm's marketing success?" A widely publicized study in 1964 asked business execu-

---

[1]See Harold V. Leavitt, "A Note on Some Experimental Findings About the Meaning of Price," *Journal of Business* (July, 1954), pp. 205–210; and D. S. Tull, R. A. Boring, and M. H. Gonsior, "A Note on the Relationship of Price and Imputed Quality," *Journal of Business* (April, 1964), pp. 186–191.

[2]"Sticky Slump," *Time* (May 23, 1977), p. 71.

tives to list the five policy areas most important to their firm's marketing success. Only 50 percent of the respondents listed pricing among the top five; product research and development, market research, management of sales personnel, advertising and sales promotion, and customer service all ranked ahead of pricing. The researcher's explanation was as follows:

> To compete successfully in a setting characterized by oligopolistic firms offering rival products to a customer-oriented market, the firm must be customer-oriented. In appealing to the customer, management finds success in utilizing the non-price facets of competitive activity, adjusting its strategy to the needs and desires of the buyer.[3]

It appears, however, that major changes have occurred in the economy since this research was conducted. A study undertaken in 1975, which sought to replicate the 1964 research, reached a dramatically different conclusion.[4] Table 12-1 compares the 1964 and 1975 studies and shows that *marketing executives now rank price as the most important factor* in their company's success. It is not that the firms are no longer customer-oriented. Rather, it appears that many buyers today are not as willing to pay a high price for style and distinctiveness; instead, they want to receive a good value for their dollar expenditure.

This finding was partially documented by the answers to a second question in the 1975 study, which asked the executives to identify the *environmental*

TABLE 12-1   Comparison of 1964 and 1975 Rank Orders of the Importance of Various Marketing Activities

Marketing Activity	1975 Rank Order of Importance	1964 Rank Order of Importance
Pricing	1	6
Customer services	2	5
Sales personnel management	3	3
Product research and development	4	1
Marketing cost budgeting and control	5	9
Physical distribution	6	11*
Market research	7	2
Marketing organization structure	8	7
Advertising and sales promotion planning	9	4
Distribution channel control	10	8
Extending customer credit	11	11*
Public relations	12	12

*Tied for 10 and 11.

Source: Robert A. Robicheaux, "How Important Is Pricing in a Competitive Strategy?: Circa 1975," *Proceedings of the Southern Marketing Association* (1975), p. 57.

---

[3]Jon G. Udell, "How Important Is Pricing in Competitive Strategy?" *Journal of Marketing* (January, 1964), p. 48.

[4]Robert A. Robicheaux, "How Important Is Pricing in Competitive Strategy?: Circa 1975," *Proceedings of the Southern Marketing Association* (1975), pp. 55–57.

TABLE 12-2   Importance of Various Issues to Corporate Performance

Issues	Frequency of Mention in Top Five (Sample = 74)
Inflation	72
The energy crisis	66
Recession	64
Environmental pollution problems	48
Materials shortages	34
Unemployment	23
Middle East tensions	13
Moral decay in the U.S.	9

Source: Robert A. Robicheaux, "How Important Is Pricing in Competitive Strategy?: Circa 1975," *Proceedings of the Southern Marketing Association* (1975), p. 56.

variables with the most impact on their business. Table 12-2 shows that of the 74 executives interviewed, 72 said that inflation, a price factor, was among the five most important variables. The next two variables, the energy crisis and the recession, also are essentially pricing concerns. Apparently, executives now believe that consumers are much more price conscious than they were a decade or two ago. As a result, firms have grown increasingly concerned about the role of price in their overall marketing strategy. Let us now look at how a firm begins to price its merchandise.

A MODEL FOR PRICING DECISIONS

The pricing decision involves a series of separate events, actions, and decisions. As Figure 12-2 indicates, the firm first establishes its *corporate mission*, which in turn dictates its *marketing objectives*. As discussed in Chapter 1, the firm's *mission* is stated in broad enough terms so that it can easily adjust to the changing needs of its customers. In contrast, the firm's marketing objectives are specific at any moment in time; they should be stated in terms of particular markets and particular products, specifying market share as well as sales and profit goals.

Once the marketing objectives are formulated, marketing management develops marketing programs for each product. This step involves relating product decisions to distribution, communication, and pricing. As the program evolves, the firm must decide on its **pricing objectives**, which represent the firm's overall pricing goals or targets. The next steps involve outlining **pricing policies**, followed by determining how the firm should establish its price, i.e., what its **pricing tactics** will be. In Figure 12-2, pricing policies are located between objectives and tactics because policies provide the framework through which the firm translates its pricing objectives into the actual market pricing tactics. We will examine objectives and policies in greater detail in later sections of this chapter. Chapter 13 deals with pricing tactics. In the final step, the firm implements its pricing decisions.

FIGURE 12-2 A Model for Pricing Decisions

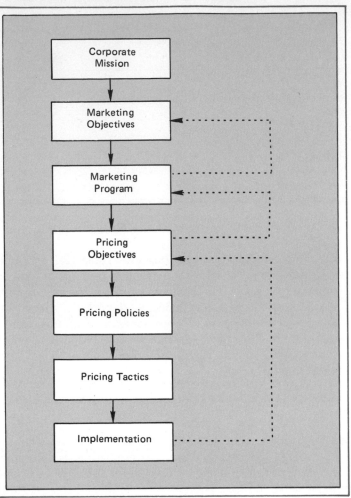

Figure 12-2 also has several feedback loops. After a price is implemented and the market has had a chance to react, management must decide whether the designated price is such that the firm is meeting its pricing objectives. If not, the firm may wish to recycle through the pricing policies and tactical decisions to establish a new price. The original marketing objectives may no longer be feasible, thereby necessitating a change in the objectives and the market programs.

PRICING OBJECTIVES

Many social critics believe that business corporations in the United States price their products so as to maximize profits, not an altogether despicable goal in a capitalistic society. Although some business people choose profit maximization as their primary business objective, the evidence is quite clear that most firms are more interested in a *satisfactory* return rather than in a *maximum* return. A **satisfactory return** is defined as one large enough to continually attract individuals to invest their savings in the firm by purchasing its stocks or bonds. A satisfactory return will also have to be competitive with those achieved by the more profitable, well-established firms in the country. This willingness on the part of most executives to accept a satisfactory return rather than a maximum return is the result of the fact that most business people are socially responsible citizens who feel that profit maximization is not their business's only concern. In addition, most executives do not know how to maximize their profits even if this was their primary concern.

The most comprehensive study to date on the pricing objectives of large firms was undertaken by Lanzillotti.[5] He found that firms tend to have one predominant pricing objective, although most have collateral pricing objectives as well. The most common primary pricing objectives were target return on investment, cost-plus pricing, target market share, and meeting or matching competition. Figure 12-3 presents the pricing objectives of the 20 major U.S. firms studied by Lanzillotti.

Target Return on Investment

Target return on investment (ROI) was the most common pricing objective mentioned by the firms investigated. Fifty percent of the firms cited this as their principal pricing goal, while three other firms cited it as one of their collateral pricing goals. The average target return was 14 percent after taxes, with figures ranging from 8 percent to 20 percent.

Firms naming target return on investment as their pricing goal tended to operate in markets in which they are the dominant competitive force. Examples include General Electric, General Motors, Alcoa, and U.S. Steel. It is also interesting to note that new products were singled out for target ROI pricing. Why? Because new products have no close rivals in the marketplace, and thus by definition, they cannot be priced in relation to competitive offerings. Also, the firm would not want to invest in the development and introduction of a new product unless it were expected to achieve a reasonable return, which is specified as the target ROI.

Cost-Plus Pricing

Cost-plus pricing is the practice of determining a product's selling price by adding a certain predetermined percentage to its cost. U.S. Steel, Alcoa, and DuPont used cost-plus pricing as one of their pricing goals. In Lanzillotti's study, these firms indicated that since they had been able to achieve an adequate return during difficult economic times, they would not charge as much as as the market would bear during good times. Many firms using target ROI pricing for new products employ the cost-plus method for existing products.

Target Market Share

Achieving a maximum or minimum share of the market was listed by the 20 firms surveyed almost as frequently as target return on investment as the

[5]Robert F. Lanzillotti, "Pricing Objectives in Large Companies," *American Economic Review* (December, 1958), pp. 921–940.

FIGURE 12-3 Pricing Objectives of Large Firms

Company	Principal Pricing Objectives	Collateral Pricing Objectives
Alcoa	20% ROI; higher on new products.	"Promotive" policy on new products; cost-plus.
American Can	Maintenance of market share.	Meeting competition; cost-plus.
A&P	Increasing market share.	General promotion.
DuPont	Target ROI — no specific figure provided; cost-plus.	Charging what traffic will bear; Maximum return for new products.
Esso	"Fair-return" target — no specific figure given.	Maintaining market share; price stabilization.
General Electric	20% ROI after taxes.	Maintaining market share.
General Foods	33⅓% gross margin.	Full line of food products; maintaining market share.
General Motors	20% on investment (after taxes).	Maintaining market share.
Goodyear	"Meeting competitors."	Maintaining position; price stabilization.
Gulf	Follow price of most important marketer in each area.	Maintain market share; price stabilization.
International Harvester	10% ROI after taxes.	Market share: less than dominant in any market.
Johns-Manville	ROI greater than last 15 years' average.	Market share not greater than 20%; cost-plus.
Kennecott	Stabilization of prices.	
Kroger	Maintaining market share.	Target return of 20% on investment before taxes.
National Steel	Matching the market.	Increase market share.
Sears Roebuck	Increasing market share.	Realization of traditional return on investment 10–15% after taxes.
Standard Oil (Ind.)	Maintain market share.	Stabilization of prices.
Swift	Maintenance of market share.	
Union Carbide	Cost-plus.	Promotive policy on new products.
U.S. Steel	8% ROI after taxes.	Target market share of 30%; cost-plus.

Source: Robert Lanzillotti, "Pricing Objectives in Large Companies," *American Economic Review* (December, 1958), pp. 924–927.

most important pricing goal. In most cases market share was stated as a maximum. In other words, these firms price their products so as to limit their share of the market, thereby avoiding antitrust problems. This concern would not be as prevalent, of course, among smaller firms or among firms enjoying a patent or innovative monopoly. For example, DuPont, which holds patents for cellophane and nylon, made no mention of shooting for a specific maximum share in these markets.

Meeting or Matching Competition

In most cases, firms attempting simply to meet the prices of their competitors do not really have a pricing policy of their own. In effect, they let other firms make the pricing decisions for their industry. This generalization does not hold up in all cases, however. For example, in the Lanzillotti study, DuPont seemed to have a policy of adopting the market price only for those products for which it did not have a leadership position. Other firms appeared to have a policy of preventing competition. One illustration was A&P's policy of localized price reductions to make life difficult for other supermarket chains when they open new stores near an existing A&P store.

Small vs. Large Firms

Lanzillotti conducted his study on large firms partially because he was interested in looking at firms that were masters of their fate to a significant degree and hence in a position to adjust their prices to fit company goals. But what are the pricing objectives of small or medium-sized firms? The answer seems to be twofold. First, some small or medium-sized firms provide something *special* to the market, and therefore have some control over their destiny. These firms probably have a mix of pricing objectives very similar to those of large firms. Second, small or medium-sized firms competing directly with large firms and without special merchandise usually price their goods at the market price, which normally is established by the most powerful firm in the industry.

PRICING POLICIES

As indicated previously, pricing policies provide the framework and consistency needed by the firm to make reasonable, practicable, and effective pricing decisions. Although policies in any area of management are difficult to develop, firms with a well-established set of pricing policies usually make consistently better pricing decisions than firms without such policies.

The correctness of any pricing policy depends on such variables as managerial philosophy, competitive conditions, and the firm's marketing and pricing objectives. Recognizing that there is no set of magically correct pricing policies, we will look at six fundamental areas of pricing policy: new product pricing, price discounts, price lining, transfer pricing, pricing in times of uncertainty, and geographic price considerations.

New Product Pricing

There are two diametrically opposed strategies for new product pricing: skimming and penetration. Each has its own advantages and disadvantages.

Price Skimming. Price skimming is the practice of introducing a new product at an artificially high price. By artificially high, we mean a price level that the

A house may be the largest single purchase of **your** life. Whether you buy a new house or an old house, one of the most important questions you must answer is, "How much should I pay for any given house?"

For new houses, the builder will usually set the price according to a cost-plus formula. There will not be much room to negotiate unless the house has been on the market for some time or the builder has gotten into financial difficulties.

The situation is more complex for old houses. Many times, the asking prices on old houses are unreasonably high, either because sellers believe that there is no house quite like theirs or because they have heard rumors that sellers of similar houses are making a killing. Unfortunately, most real estate agents do not discourage this practice because they need the listings. Realizing, then, the problems involved in pricing an older house, how do you go about formulating an offer?

Comparable Houses. Find several houses that are similar to the one you're considering. For how much are they selling? Determine the approximate price per square foot for each of the comparable homes, and use it as a yardstick in determining whether the house is underpriced or overpriced relative to the market. Be sure to account for any "extras," such as a swimming pool, privacy fence, sprinkling system, or quality construction, in the market comparison.

The Price of a New Home. If you're buying an older house, you may want to ask a builder how much it would cost to build the same house today. A new house normally sells for a 10–20 percent premium over a five- to seven-year-old house because it has all new appliances, new carpeting, and looks fresher inside and out. Remember, however, that new houses do not usually come with a nice lawn and landscaping, which can add considerably to the cost of a house.

Location. Consider the location of the house. A house in one area may sell for considerably more than the same house in a less prestigious area. Also, are houses in the neighborhood expected to increase or decrease in value relative to the community as a whole? If you don't know the community, talk to people who live and work in the area or to your real estate broker.

The Offer. Do not be afraid to make an offer significantly below the asking price of the house. Never pay more than you think it is worth. If the house has been on the market for a long time or if the seller has already moved, he or she may be willing to accept a lower price. Finally, never act precipitously. Look at the house several times and don't make an offer until you have thoroughly studied the market.

Marketing & You

FIGURE 12-4 Skimming Pricing

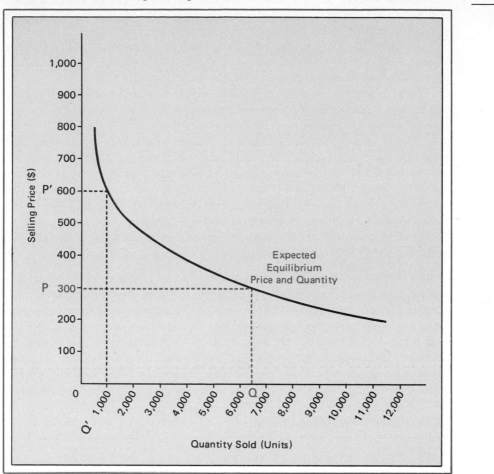

market will not be able to sustain in the long run. The management of a firm using price skimming realizes that as competition develops it will be forced to reduce the price of the new product. A skimming strategy works best when there are many buyers willing to pay a premium to be among the first owners of the product.

Figure 12-4 shows how price skimming works. Assume in this case that the market price for our new product is expected to stabilize at $300. But before the competition introduces a similar product, our firm, by adopting a skimming strategy, is able to sell a number of units at a considerably higher price, for example 1,000 units at a price of $600 each. A skimming approach, in effect, enables the firm to segment its market according to how much people are willing to pay for the product. The firm initially sells its merchandise to that segment of the market willing to pay extra for the product and to own it early in its life cycle. As competition develops and the market becomes saturated, the firm reduces the price in order to appeal to a broader market. In Figure 12-4, the firm could introduce the product at $600 and then let the price slide down the curve until it reached the expected equilibrium level of $300.

Another benefit of price skimming to the firm is that it helps minimize some of the risk inherent in new product introduction. Since most firms are not in a position to pump money into a new product on a long-term basis, a skimming policy enables them to recover their initial product investment quickly, thereby freeing funds for reinvestment in other projects. In general, the shorter the payback period for a new product, the less risk is involved.

Not surprisingly, the greatest problem with price skimming is that it attracts competition. The firm with a successful price-skimming strategy and the resulting above-average return can expect the competition to introduce similar products. The Reynolds Pen Company is the classic example of a firm that used price skimming successfully. Reynolds introduced the ballpoint pen in 1945 with an initial investment of only $26,000. The pen cost 50 cents to produce but was originally priced at $12.50. In less than a year, new competitors had driven the market price for ballpoint pens down to less than $1.00, but not before Reynolds had ceased operation with total after-tax profits of more than $1.5 million. More recently, electronic calculators and digital watches have been successfully introduced through the use of price-skimming strategy.

Penetration Pricing. Penetration pricing is the practice of introducing a product at a low price. Under this strategy, the firm expects to sell a large number of units to a price-sensitive market. Everyday staple goods are normally introduced using penetration pricing. For instance, when a new laundry soap is put on the market, very few people are willing to pay a premium to be among its first users. Realizing this fact, the manufacturer introduces the product at a price that the market will be able to support in the long run. Figure

FIGURE 12-5 Penetration Pricing

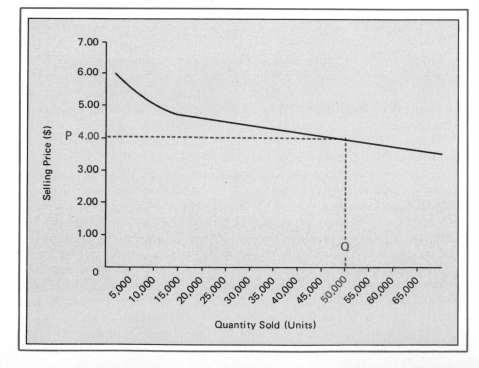

12-5 illustrates how penetration pricing works. Although the figure shows that the firm could initially charge a little more than the expected market price of $4.00, there is little incentive to do so. By reducing the price from $6.00 to $4.00, the firm is able to increase expected sales from 1,000 units to 50,000 units.

An advantage of penetration pricing is that it tends to discourage competitors from entering the market since there is little opportunity for them to make an unusually high return on investment. As a result, many potential competitors elect not to enter the market and to pursue more attractive investment opportunities instead. Another advantage of penetration pricing is that it enables the firm to reduce its costs substantially because of a higher volume of production. For many products, economies of scale can result in cost savings of 50 to 75 percent or more to the manufacturer. Consequently, the firm may want to hold down the price of the product in order to stimulate demand, to increase total sales, and thus to achieve production economies of scale.

The only major problem with penetration pricing is that it prevents the firm from capturing those additional profits resulting from the fact that, at least initially, many people might be willing to pay a substantially higher price for the product. If this segment of the market does not appear to be large, however, the firm should employ the penetration strategy. Conversely, if many people are willing to pay a premium, the firm should consider adopting the skimming strategy.

Price Discounts

Most products have an established **list price**, which is the publicly announced price for which the firm expects to sell the product. It is called a list price because many manufacturers and distributors publish a list of prices for their products in a folder or book which is then made available to their customers. However, depending on the firm's competitive position, the time of year, the quantity purchased, and the terms of trade in the industry, the buyer may be able to obtain a discount, or reduction, from the list price. Most of the types of discounts discussed below are applicable for resellers as well as for final customers.

Quantity Discounts. Many firms offer discounts if the customer purchases a large order. Depending on the firm, the order size may be calculated in terms of dollar volume or in number of units purchased. The purpose of a quantity discount is to induce customers to purchase more units than they would otherwise. By increasing sales, a quantity discount helps the firm capture some significant economies of its own. Typically, it costs the seller less per unit to sell a large order than a small one. For example, a large order does not entail much more paperwork than a small order; nor does it require that much more of a salesperson's time. In addition, the seller can pass inventory cost savings on to the buyer. That is, a certain amount of merchandise must be maintained by the seller in order to meet demand. A large individual order, rather than many small orders occurring over time, means in effect that the buyer is carrying inventory for the seller. This feature can result in dramatic cost savings for the seller.

There are two types of quantity discounts — cumulative and noncumulative. With a **cumulative quantity discount**, the buyer need not purchase

merchandise all at once but instead may order goods over a period of time —
two weeks, a month, six months, or a year. The greater the cumulative amount
purchased, the greater the discount. Although the seller does not reap the
economies of scale and inventory possible when a customer buys all items at
once, cumulative discounts do serve to tie the customer to the seller. For example, some hardware stores use a slight variation of this plan when selling
paint. The first three gallons are sold at the manufacturer's list price; purchases
over and above three gallons are sold at a 10 percent discount. Although the
quantity discount period is stated as three months, store managers frequently
extend the period to please loyal customers.

Under the **noncumulative quantity discount** policy, whether or not the
customer receives a discount depends entirely upon the size of the individual
purchase. Each sale is independent, and the size of the discount, if any, is
computed on the number of items purchased at a particular time. This approach reduces selling and inventory expense but does not build customer
loyalty to the same extent as the cumulative discount approach.

Seasonal Discounts. Many firms offer their customers seasonal discounts;
that is, if the customer purchases an item during a specified time of the year, a
discount from the regular list price will be given. To the firm with sales volume
varying greatly over the year, a policy of seasonal discounts offers several advantages. Most importantly, it smoothes out the sales pattern and pushes inventory from the seller to the buyer. An excellent example is Christmas cards.
The buyer, whether a reseller or the final consumer, can expect to pay full list
price for Christmas cards during November and the first 24 days of December.
Thereafter, retailers may offer discounts of up to 75 percent on any Christmas
cards left in stock. A retailer who keeps these cards until next season will have
to inventory, insure, and finance them. Since this alternative is costly, the retailer usually discounts them. In the same manner, stores that purchase their
cards earlier than usual can obtain a significant discount from the manufacturer.

Promotional Discounts. Many firms and stores put products on sale in
order to encourage customers to purchase items they would probably not otherwise buy. A sale of this type may also result because the product has not sold
as well as management had anticipated. Thus a **markdown**, a reduction from
the original selling price, is necessary to induce people to buy the product.
Such promotional discounts are common in the clothing industry. A classic
example is the Nehru jacket, introduced in 1965. Although fashion designers
thought that Nehru jackets would be in great demand, they were wrong —
consumers never showed any real interest in them. As a result, a great many
department stores had to offer discounts of up to 90 percent.

A final type of promotional discount is known in the trade as a **loss
leader**. As mentioned earlier, a loss-leader product is sold below cost in order
to stimulate its sales as well as sales of other products. Grocery stores frequently advertise products at or below cost. For example, with a coupon from
the grocery, a shopper may be able to buy a package of hamburger buns for
only five cents. In this case, the store's management is betting that the cus-

tomer will come into the store because of the advertised special and then buy enough other items to offset the cost of the loss leader and the promotional campaign.

The Federal Trade Commission and the attorney general offices of many states have shown growing concern over promotional discounts. Deceptive practices, such as marking up a product one day and then putting it "on sale" the next, are illegal. In addition, a firm advertising a sale must stock enough of the sale items to meet reasonable demand. Finally, a store cannot participate in bait-and-switch advertising, a practice occurring when a store puts a product on sale with the intent of switching customers over to another, more expensive product once they have entered the store. These and other deceptive trade practices were discussed in more detail in Chapter 3.

Cash Discounts. It is a common practice in many industries to offer members of the distribution channel cash discounts if they pay for the purchase in full within a specified period of time. An invoice reading "net 30 days" means that the seller is not willing to give a discount for early payment and that the entire amount due must be paid within 30 days. In contrast, many invoices read "1/10, net 30," which means that the seller is offering the buyer a 1 percent discount if the bill is paid in full within ten days; if the buyer chooses not to exercise this option, the invoice is due in full within 30 days.

From a marketing perspective, the firm may wish to offer cash discounts for at least two reasons. First, it may want to encourage the prompt payment of bills. Second, trade practices in the industry may be such that the firm cannot afford *not* to offer cash discounts. Although "1/10, net 30" may not seem like a large discount, the buyer must pay the full amount of the bill within another 20 days regardless. Since there are 18.25 20-day periods per year and assuming that the terms of trade are "1/10, net 30," the buyer, in effect, can earn 18.25 percent interest by paying promptly — a significant return, even in today's economy.

Price Lining

In a pricing decision, it is important to bear in mind that the product is likely part of a larger merchandise line. Because of this fact, and because some products are traditionally priced within clearly defined ranges, the firm may not be totally free in choosing prices for its products. The practice of pricing merchandise within traditional or market-determined price ranges is known as **price lining**. A good example is men's clothing. A retailer of men's clothing normally carries three lines, or grades, of clothing. A college-oriented store might have $90, $125, and $180 suits; $5.50, $7.50, and $10.50 ties; and $9.50, $12.50 and $18.50 shirts.

Price lining allows the *customer* to narrow the decision-making process. That is, the customer first decides how much money to spend for a suit. The wise customer then looks only at those suits falling within that specified price range. Price lining allows the *retailer* to carry less overall inventory; rather than stocking suits at all prices, the retailer need only stock three lines, or grades, of suits. Finally, to the *manufacturer*, price lining means that its products must be priced within traditionally accepted price ranges.

To price a product within the proper range, the manufacturer begins with the retail price and moves backward.[6] If the objective is to compete in the $125 price line for suits, the manufacturer works backward from $125 to determine how much to charge wholesalers so that they can in turn sell the product profitably to retailers, who then add their own customary markups. As an illustration, if the manufacturer wants its suits to sell for $125 at the retail store, it would realize that the retailer cannot afford to pay more than $75 to the wholesaler. In the same way, if the wholesaler is to sell the suit for $75, it must not pay more than $50 to the manufacturer. If everything works according to plan, each link in the distribution chain makes a profit, and the customer pays $125 for the suit. But if the manufacturer is unable to make a profit at the price arrived at through this procedure, the manufacturer will have to adjust costs downward, try a higher price zone, or price between two price zones.

Transfer Pricing

Many corporations sell products from one of their divisions to another. A corporation transferring products in this fashion must concern itself with how much to charge the buying division. A good example of **transfer pricing**, as it is called, can be found in the many divisions of AT&T. Western Electric, the manufacturing arm of the Bell telephone system, builds telephones and sells them to South Central Bell and the many other local telephone affiliates in the Bell system. Both Western Electric and South Central Bell are part of AT&T and are expected to contribute to overall corporate profitability. Thus, Western Electric cannot simply give telephones and related equipment to Bell system affiliates. The most commonly used methods for setting transfer prices are the market price system and the cost-based system.[7]

Market Price. Typically, if a market price exists for the transferred product, it is used as the firm's internal transfer price. This system has the benefit of letting a division's profits represent real economic contributions, which makes it possible to compare the division with an independent company of the same type. In addition, division management is under the same competitive cost-control pressure as an independent company. Finally, management need not spend a great deal of time negotiating a transfer price since the price charged is based on the market price.

Cost-Based Price. If a market price does not exist or cannot be estimated, then the transfer price of the product is usually based on its cost. Under this approach, known as cost-based transfer pricing, management decides how cost is to be calculated and the level of profit margin that will be allowed. Inefficiencies in the selling division, however, should not be passed on to the buying division in the form of high prices. Therefore, the transfer price is calculated using standard costs per item, which are provided by the firm's cost accountants. If the seller's actual cost exceeds the standard cost, then the seller is required to sustain the loss, unless external factors, such as unanticipated cost increases for labor or raw material, have significantly affected unit costs.

---

[6]Mark Alpert, *Pricing Decisions* (Glenview, Ill.: Scott, Foresman & Co., 1971), p. 111.

[7]Robert N. Anthony and John Dearden, *Management Control Systems* (Homewood, Ill.: Richard D. Irwin, 1976), pp. 280–283.

If the selling division markets the product to external firms, then the profit margin for internal sales should be the same as that for external sales. When the seller does not sell outside the firm, however, the markup should be based on typical markups in the industry or on the profitability of similar products made by other divisions.

Transfer pricing is a difficult but critically important strategic pricing problem for many firms. To evaluate the performance of divisional management when most of the division's sales are internal requires that the transfer price be as realistic as possible. Only when the transfer price is realistic can the firm determine just how effective its managers are and whether the division should continue to manufacture and sell the product.

Pricing in Times of Uncertainty

Rampant inflation, shortages of raw materials and supplies, and high interest rates have made today's pricing decisions much more complex and riskier than those of even a few years ago. Many firms have been forced to accept lower profits or gamble on raising prices in order to maintain historical profit levels. In the case of price-sensitive products, for example, the alternative of raising list prices has often backfired; many of the firm's customers simply switch to competing products. We now look at some ways that firms can indirectly raise prices or at least maintain past profits without directly raising prices.

Reduction in Discounting. In many industries over the years, salespeople have discounted the price of their merchandise to loyal customers in order to close the sale. This practice has made list prices for many products almost meaningless. One way to discourage indiscriminate discounting and thus maintain profits, is to prevent salespeople from reducing prices without the approval of their sales managers. A less drastic approach — and one less onerous to the sales force — is to modify the compensation system such that the salespeople are paid not according to sales volume but according to profits generated. Table 12-3 shows the differences in a salesperson's commission when it is

TABLE 12-3   Comparison of Commissions Based on Sales and Profits

Item	Commission Based on Sales		Commission Based on Profits	
	List Price	Discounted Price	List Price	Discounted Price
Price	$100.00	$80.00	$100.00	$80.00
Cost	60.00	60.00	60.00	60.00
Profit before commission	40.00	20.00	40.00	20.00
Commission	10.00*	8.00*	10.00**	5.00**
Profit	30.00	12.00	30.00	15.00

*Salesperson receives 10 percent of sales price.
**Salesperson receives 25 percent of profit before commission.

based on profit rather than on sales. In this example, the salesperson receives the same commission under either system if a price discount is not offered. However, under the sales-based commission system, when the salesperson reduces the price from $100 to $80, the company's profit declines from $30 to $12, while the salesperson's commission falls only $2, from $10 to $8. In contrast, under the profit-based compensation system, a sales price discount means more profit for the firm ($15) and a smaller commission for the salesperson ($5). As a result, the salesperson is likely to think twice before offering sales discounts.

Pricing at Time of Shipment. A rather drastic but often necessary way to control prices is to quote an estimated price at the time of the sale and then to set the final price at the time of shipment. The usual procedure is to notify the customer of the final transaction price just prior to shipment. Moreover, some firms operate under extremely favorable competitive conditions and have taken the added step of applying post-sale price increases after shipment without prior notification. This practice can be detrimental to the firm's long-term relationship with its customers. When competitive conditions change, these firms often find that many of their "old faithful" customers are only too happy to change over to suppliers with a more reliable pricing policy.

Escalator Clauses. Escalator clauses are becoming more and more a part of industrial sales contracts. These clauses allow the seller to raise the price of merchandise under contract to a buyer if costs increase prior to delivery. Normally, an escalator agreement includes a description of the cost element subject to escalation (e.g., labor or raw materials), a stipulation of the indices by which the changes are to be measured (e.g., the consumer price index), the frequency of adjustment, and the limits of the increase or decrease.

Several years ago, Westinghouse signed a number of long-term contracts to deliver nuclear fuel, at a specified price, to power plants then under construction. The company made the mistake of assuming that, in the years ahead, it would be able to provide nuclear fuel at then-current market prices. When the price of nuclear fuel increased dramatically, Westinghouse lost a great deal of money because its earlier nuclear fuel contracts did not contain escalator clauses.

Escalator clauses have two major problems, however. Many customers will not agree to escalator clauses because of the uncertainty surrounding the eventual sales price. Escalator clauses also cause problems for the seller when the value of the measuring index falls while other product costs increase, leading to a situation where the firm is forced to sell the product for less than the initial estimated price even though its real cost has increased.

Indirect Price Increases. A firm can raise prices indirectly by reducing the terms of its sales discounts. As an example, instead of offering a 2 percent discount for payment within ten days, the terms could be changed to 1 percent or the discount could be eliminated entirely and payment due in full upon receipt of the statement. As stated previously, however, competitive industry practices may prevent a firm from tightening its terms of trade.

Another indirect way for the firm to increase the price of its merchandise is to reduce product warranties. A few years ago, U.S. automobile manufacturers reduced their warranties from 24 months to 12 months. In effect, this action meant an increase in the price of automobiles.

The problem with indirect price increases is that predicting the reaction of the market is not always possible. Although there is no evidence that the automobile industry's warranty changes caused any great economic hardship for the affected dealerships, changes in terms of trade have been known to do so. One St. Louis manufacturer, in order to increase its profits, eliminated quantity discounts to distributors only to learn that the distributors relied almost totally on trade discounts to move the firm's products.

Unbundling of Services. Sometimes, a firm selling a package of items — the actual product, peripheral equipment, replacement parts, and special services — at a discount for one price decides to price each item separately. The result of this unbundling of goods and services is a higher total cost to the consumer and thus greater revenues for the firm. When unbundling services, however, the firm should analyze carefully the market segments for each of the products or services. For instance, a small institutional service firm in Tennessee found when it unbundled its product mix and priced each item separately, it was not equally competitive in each product market. The resulting revenue increase for some of the items was more than offset by the sales decline for some of the others.[8]

In summary, the firm's pricing policies must allow for adjustments as market conditions change. Some products will be able to support outright price increases and to restore healthy profit margins. With other products, however, the firm may have to find creative and more subtle ways to maintain profit margins.

Geographic Price Considerations

Another pricing issue is the assignment of transportation costs. One way for the firm to deal with this issue is to determine how much it would charge for the merchandise if picked up at the factory, and then to make a policy decision concerning the assignment of freight and delivery costs. The firm, however, must consider both the marketing and legal implications of this decision. Alternative pricing approaches include FOB pricing, uniform-delivered pricing, zone-delivered pricing, and freight-absorption pricing.

FOB Pricing. FOB, meaning *free on board*, is a common term in transportation. Under **FOB pricing**, the seller loads the merchandise aboard a transportation vehicle (hence, free on board), at which time the buyer takes title to the merchandise. The buyer is then responsible for any transportation charges beyond that point.

The usual procedure is to state **FOB factory**, meaning that the buyer pays all transportation charges after the merchandise leaves the place of manufacture. The seller's net price is therefore the same for all customers, whereas the total cost to the buyer is a function of the selling price plus appropriate freight charges.

---

[8]Joseph P. Guiltinan, "Risk-Aversive Pricing Policies: Problems and Alternatives," *Journal of Marketing* (January, 1976), pp. 10–15.

FOB pricing does present some marketing problems, however, in that customers farther from the factory pay more for the product. The result is that the firm is less competitive when customers are located near another supplier and when freight costs constitute a significant percentage of the buyer's total cost. The manufacturer can counter this problem by changing the terms of trade to **FOB-delivered**. Here, the manufacturer pays the entire cost of delivery to the buyer. You will recall from our discussion of the Robinson-Patman Act in Chapter 3, that it is illegal to discriminate in the services or prices offered to customers. Consequently, a seller offering FOB-delivered prices to one customer may have to offer them to all customers.

Uniform-Delivered Pricing. Under uniform-delivered pricing, the seller charges all customers the same delivery price regardless of their location or the transportation charge involved. In effect, those buyers located close to the seller subsidize the freight charges of those located far away. The Supreme Court has held uniform-delivered pricing to be legal when the manufacturer charges all customers the same price.[9]

Uniform-delivered pricing is used primarily when the transportation charges are a relatively small part of the total cost of the product. In addition, such resellers as furniture stores use uniform-delivered pricing when they believe that "free" delivery strengthens their market position. In addition to improving a firm's competitive position, this pricing strategy has two other advantages. First, it makes pricing decisions much easier — all customers pay the same price. Second, it makes it easier to conduct national price promotion campaigns.

Zone-Delivered Pricing. A zone-delivered pricing system is simply a modification of uniform-delivered pricing. Under the zone system, the seller divides customers into geographic zones and then charges the customers within each zone the same price. The result is that each customer in the zone pays an average transportation cost for the product. It also means, in effect, that buyers nearest the seller in the zone subsidize buyers located farther away.

The zone system is used to determine the cost of long distance telephone services. Manufacturers of food and hardware items use zone-delivered pricing to minimize price competition and also to simplify the calculation of transportation charges for their many wholesale and retail customers.

The only legal problem with zone-delivered pricing is similar to that found with FOB-delivered pricing, that is, all competing buyers must be in the same zone so that there is no question of price discrimination on the part of the seller. This problem is especially difficult in the densely populated areas of the Northeast.

Freight-Absorption Pricing. Freight-absorption pricing is used to offset some of the problems that arise with FOB-factory pricing. As stated earlier, the buyer located far from the factory is at a competitive disadvantage under FOB-factory pricing. To remedy this situation, the manufacturer may be willing to absorb some of the freight costs. Normally, a manufacturer using a freight-ab-

---

[9]*Federal Trade Commission v. A. E. Staley Manufacturing Company*, 324 (U.S. 745, 1945).

sorption system quotes a distant customer the factory price plus the freight cost charged by the competing manufacturer located nearest to the customer.

Freight-absorption allows the firm to expand its market far beyond its normal economic boundaries. It makes particularly good sense for a firm with high fixed costs and low variable costs, since freight absorption helps cover fixed costs by generating extra customers.

The legal parameters of freight-absorption pricing are quite clear — it is legal if it is done by a firm independently and not in collusion with competitors. In addition, the current interpretation of the Robinson-Patman Act by the courts is that firms can use freight-absorption pricing to *meet* competitors' prices but not to *undercut* them. If practiced correctly, freight-absorption pricing can actually reduce spatial monopolies and thereby increase competition.

summary points

1. Five factors that the firm should consider when making a pricing decision are the cost of the product involved, company objectives, the competition, characteristics of the buyer, and the overall economic situation.

2. The price mechanism plays three critical roles in the U.S. economic system: it measures the relative value of goods, it stimulates production, and it rations scarce products.

3. Because of changing economic conditions, pricing decisions are more important today than they were a decade ago.

4. In the model for pricing decisions, pricing objectives represent the firm's pricing goals. Pricing policies, in turn, provide the framework through which the firm translates its pricing objectives into the actual market pricing tactics.

5. Target return-on-investment pricing has been the most common pricing objective among large firms. Other common pricing objectives include cost-plus pricing, target market share, and meeting or matching competition.

6. In pricing new products, the firm can charge either a high price (skimming) or a low price (penetration).

7. Many customers do not pay list price for merchandise. Quantity, seasonal, promotional, and cash discounts all are important pricing considerations for a firm.

8. Sometimes firms are forced to price their products within relatively narrow price lines. This practice is known as price lining.

9. Transfer prices between one division of a company and another can be either market prices or cost-based prices.

10. There are at least five strategies for maintaining margins during periods of uncertainty: reduction in discounting, pricing at time of shipment, escalator clauses, indirect price increases, and unbundling of services.

11. Freight costs, with their various legal and marketing implications, are an important element in the firm's pricing policy. Alternative pricing approaches include FOB pricing, uniform-delivered pricing, zone-delivered pricing, and freight-absorption pricing.

questions for discussion

1. Other than automobiles, what retail products in the United States are subject to price negotiation? How might the economy of the United States differ if the prices of most products were negotiated between the buyer and seller rather than set by the seller?

2. In selling a new fighter plane to the U.S. Air Force, what factors might a firm such as McDonnell Douglas consider when establishing its price?

3. What are the three vital functions performed by the price mechanism in the U.S. economic system? Are these functions as important in the industrial sector as they are in the consumer sector?

4. Do you expect that pricing decisions will be more important to businesses in the mid-1980s than they are today? Explain.

5. Explain the relationship between pricing objectives, pricing policies, and pricing tactics.

6. Why is target return on investment the most commonly used pricing objective? Are there any forces operating in the U.S. economy that may make ROI any less important in the future as a pricing objective?

7. What is the difference between price skimming and penetration pricing?

8. What is the rationale, from the seller's perspective, of using each of the following types of price discounts: quantity discounts, seasonal discounts, promotional discounts and cash discounts?

9. Define price lining. Under what operating circumstances is price lining an important consideration for the seller?

10. Which method for setting transfer prices is best for the seller? Explain.

11. In times of high inflation, how can a firm maintain its profit position without appearing to raise the prices of its products?

12. What is the difference between FOB-delivered and FOB-factory pricing? Why would a firm utilize an FOB-delivered pricing policy?

13. Why is freight-absorption pricing used? What are the strategic implications of using freight-absorption pricing?

13 Pricing Tactics

There is no single best way to set prices; each pricing technique has its advantages and disadvantages in a particular decision situation. This chapter analyzes the various approaches to establishing price; it also discusses the advantages and disadvantages of each approach and the conditions favoring the use of a particular pricing technique. The last section of the chapter examines a five-step procedure used to insure that all important pricing factors are considered when the firm establishes prices for its products. We begin by looking at cost-oriented pricing.

COST-ORIENTED PRICING

Many firms establish the price of a product on the basis of its cost. This approach, known as **cost-oriented pricing**, is the most frequently used pricing strategy in U.S. business today. Although cost-oriented pricing does not involve a consideration of demand, most pricing executives attempt to estimate the likely impact of a cost-derived price on the demand for the product.[1] U.S. firms commonly use one of three types of cost-oriented pricing: markup pricing, variable-cost pricing, and break-even pricing.

Markup Pricing

Markup pricing is the practice of setting a price by adding a fixed percentage to the cost of the product. Markup pricing is widely used by wholesalers, retailers, and other firms that sell many different types of products. It would be difficult and time consuming for these firms to determine the "correct" price for each of their products. Consequently, they use standard markups for broad product categories. For example, a department store might set its markup on men's clothing at an average of 40 percent over cost, the markup on women's clothing closer to 60 percent, and the markup on fine jewelry as high as 125 percent. Markups differ because of competition in the product class, product turnover, and the risks associated with selling each product.

How Markup Prices Are Calculated. As indicated above, **markup** is the difference between the cost of a product and its selling price. Stated another way, it is the amount of money added to the cost of a product to determine its

---

[1]Mark I. Alpert, "Pricing in an Era of Rapid Change," in Gerald Zaltman, *Annual Review of Marketing* (Chicago: American Marketing Association, 1978).

TABLE 13-1 A Markup Chain for a Hypothetical Product

Price Components	Manufacturer $	%	Wholesaler $	%	Retailer $	%
Cost	$40.00 =	75%	$53.33 =	70%	$ 76.19 =	60%
Markup	13.33 =	25	22.86 =	30	50.79 =	40
Selling Price	53.33 =	100%	76.19 =	100	126.98 =	100

*To calculate the manufacturer's selling price algebraically, assume that .75x = $40, where x = the selling price for the manufacturer; $40 = the cost of the product; 75% = the percentage of the final selling price that equals the manufacturer's cost.

selling price. Typically, markup is stated as a percentage of selling price, although it may also be stated as a percentage of cost. To illustrate, assume that a retailer pays $10 for a shirt. If $5 is added to the cost, the markup is either the percentage of selling price, 33⅓ percent ($5 ÷ $15), or the percentage of cost, 50 percent ($5 ÷ $10).

In either of the above cases, the cost figure used in calculating the markup is the *direct cost* of acquiring the product. In our shirt example, however, the retailer's cost accountant might show that in addition to the amount that the retailer must pay the manufacturer for the shirt, which is the direct cost, there is also $2 of overhead cost that must be allocated to each shirt. Overhead costs include rent for the building, electrical and insurance costs, and salaries for sales and administrative personnel. The markup must be sufficient to cover these additional costs and also to contribute to the firm's profits. In our example, the $5 markup allows the retailer to pay the overhead costs associated with selling the shirt and to realize a profit of $3.

Table 13-1 illustrates a markup chain for a product when markup is defined as a percentage of selling price. The total cost of manufacturing each unit of the product is $40. Assuming a 25 percent markup to achieve profit objectives, the manufacturer would have to charge $53.33, which in turn becomes the cost of the product to the wholesaler. At the end of this chain, the retail price has risen to $126.98 as a result of the 25 percent markup at the manufacturing level, the 30 percent markup at the wholesale level, and the 40 percent markup at the retail level.

Problems with Markup Pricing. The mechanical application of markup pricing involves three important problems. First, markup pricing does not take into consideration the demand for the product; that is, if a firm applies the same markup to all its products, it may underprice some and overprice others. As an example, the manager of a women's junior apparel clothing store knows that, as a result of current styles, blue jeans command a greater markup over cost than dressier slacks. A store with a single markup for women's slacks misses the opportunity to make additional profits from the high demand item, while also possibly losing sales of the dressier slacks, which might benefit from a lower markup.

A second problem is that real overhead may vary substantially from one product to the next. To illustrate, men's suits usually command a higher

TABLE 13-2   Sales and Stock Turnover Rates for Two Stores

Factors	Store A	Store B
Sales	$5,500,000	$3,000,000
Markup*	10%	20%
Markup in dollars	$ 550,000	$ 600,000
Turnover rate	50 times/year	8 times/year
Average inventory	$ 110,000	$ 375,000
Inventory cost (30%)	$ 33,000	$ 112,500
Profit**	$ 517,000	$ 487,500

*Defined as a percentage of sales.
**Defined as markup in dollars less inventory costs.

markup than men's dress shirts, since it takes more of the salesperson's time to sell a suit than to sell a shirt. In addition, once the suit is sold, the store must pay for the cost of alterations, which it would not have to do with a shirt. Allocation of overhead is always a difficult task.

The third problem with the mechanical application of markups is that a high markup may actually reduce profits by slowing the firm's stock turnover. **Stock turnover** is defined as the number of times the average inventory for the firm is sold in one year. To illustrate, assume that a firm sells $1,000,000 worth of merchandise annually. If the value of the inventory on hand at any one time averages $50,000, then the firm "turns," or sells, its inventory 20 times per year ($1,000,000 ÷ $50,000).

Table 13-2 shows the relationship between sales, stock turnover, and profits. Store A has annual sales of $5,500,000; the markup as a percentage of sales is 10 percent, yielding a total dollar markup of $550,000. Store A's turnover rate is 50, which means that the firm's average inventory is worth $110,000. Assume further that the cost of carrying the inventory is 30 percent of the inventory's worth ($33,000), which covers insurance, the cost of borrowing money, and maintenance of the inventory. Gross profit, then, is the difference between the total dollar markup ($550,000) and inventory cost ($33,000), or $517,000. For Store B, however, the higher markup (20 percent) has reduced sales to $3,000,000 and the stock turnover rate to 8 times per year. Although the total dollar markup is higher than Store A's, the firm's overall profit has declined because of the extra cost of carrying inventory. Though this trade-off does not hold in all situations, the firm should monitor the effect of markup adjustments on the turnover rate so as to achieve the best possible profit position.

Many firms avoid these problems by applying different markup percentages, not only by product category but also by item within a particular category. The firm then regulates the markup on the basis of price sensitivity, competition, the real cost of selling the item, and anticipated turnover rates. A study by the National Retail Hardware Association found that less than 100 items carried by the average hardware store are sold primarily on the basis of price. These are products such as hand tools and window fans that help establish the store's pricing image. The association recommended that its members classify the approximately 5,000 items sold in the typical hardware store into six categories on the basis of price sensitivity. Price-sensitive items might receive a markup of 10 percent or less; items not particularly price sensitive might be marked up as much as 75 percent or more. This practice was a definite departure from the historical pricing policies of hardware stores in which all products were marked up 50 percent.[2]

Variable-Cost Pricing

Marketing executives often find that a product's likely market price is not high enough to cover the total cost of manufacturing or acquiring it. Should such a product be produced or not? In the long run, a product must generate revenue in an amount at least equal to total production or acquisition costs. In the short run, however, variable-cost pricing teaches us that the firm can profitably produce some items that are priced below their total cost.

Before examining variable-cost pricing, it is first necessary to define two terms: variable costs and fixed costs. **Variable costs**, as the name implies, vary with the level of production or sales. If a firm stops manufacturing a product, the variable costs associated with that product end immediately. That is, the manufacturer can lay off the employees who produce the item and stop purchasing the raw materials from which it is made.

In contrast, **fixed costs** do not vary with the level of production or sales. The salaries of top executives, depreciation on equipment, and insurance continue whether the firm manufactures the product or not. Fixed costs are assigned to the product by the firm's cost accountant. Although the accountant will try to assign these costs in a way that logically reflects how they are associated with the item, in many cases the assignments are somewhat arbitrary.

The Key Principle in Variable-Cost Pricing. In the short run, a firm should produce and market a product when the revenue generated by the product is greater than its total variable costs. Revenue in excess of variable costs is known as the **contribution margin**, and it is used to absorb part of the firm's total fixed costs. To illustrate, Table 13-3 presents revenue and cost data for a watch company. The question is whether the company should con-

TABLE 13-3 Variable-Cost Pricing by a Hypothetical Watch Company

Factors	Electronic Watch	24-Jewel Wind-Up Watch	Automatic Self-Winding Watch
Revenue	$650,000	$300,000	$400,000
Variable costs	−200,000	−200,000	−410,000
Gross margin*	$450,000	$100,000	($ 10,000)
Fixed costs	−100,000	−130,000	−50,000
Profit	$350,000	($ 30,000)	($ 60,000)

*Defined as revenue less variable costs, and in this case it is the contribution margin.

---

[2]"Handbook Teaches Dealers How to Sell," *Printer's Ink* (March 27, 1959), pp. 65–69.

tinue to produce all three watches. The answer is no — the firm should stop production of the automatic self-winding watch immediately. Not only is the firm losing money on the product ($60,000), but the variable costs for this model are greater than its revenue. Although by discontinuing the automatic self-winding watch the other two products are forced to absorb its fixed costs ($50,000), the firm still saves $10,000 ($60,000 − $50,000). The result is that total profit increases from $260,000 to $270,000.

The firm should continue to sell the 24-jewel watch even though it appears to be losing money; the revenue from the product is greater than its direct variable costs. In this case, the contribution to gross margin is positive ($100,000). If the firm produced only the electronic watch, however, it would have to absorb the fixed costs not only of the automatic self-winding watch ($50,000), but also of the 24-jewel watch ($130,000). As a result, the fixed costs of the electronic watch would jump from their current $100,000 to $280,000, thereby reducing the firm's total profits to $170,000. For the time being, the firm must absorb all of the fixed costs even if the product is no longer produced. Therefore, in the short run, as long as the product's revenue is greater than its variable cost, production should continue.

Constraints and Risks. We must emphasize that in the long run the firm must cover all of its costs if it is to survive. Therefore, although the firm could continue in the short run to sell the 24-jewel, wind-up watches below total cost, it would not want to do so indefinitely. It is also important to note that even though the automatic self-winding watch should be discontinued, the manufacturer may choose not to do so. For example, the product may be new on the market, and the firm may have anticipated the losses and be willing to continue production because of the item's potential profits. Or the watch may occupy an important position in the firm's product line. Thus, if discontinuing production of the automatic watch meant that its dealers would be less willing to carry its electronic watches, the firm might well decide not to take the watch out of production.

The major risk associated with variable-cost pricing is that such a strategy occasionally triggers a price war, resulting in profit losses for all the firms in the industry. An excellent example of such a price war occurred when TWA introduced two round trip flights a day from Chicago to Los Angeles, offering significantly lower fares for passengers in the coach class. The airline assigned old, fully depreciated, narrow-bodied 707 jets with 184 seats instead of the usual 145 seats for these flights. The idea was to generate enough revenue to cover the variable costs of each flight (fuel, food, personnel expenses). By reducing the ticket price and the quality of service at the same time, TWA hoped to attract price-conscious customers while leaving the regular business and tourist market to the other airlines. TWA's competitors, however, fearing a mass exodus of passengers to TWA, petitioned the Civil Aeronautics Board for permission to match TWA's fare on their regularly scheduled flights. The result was that on the Chicago-Los Angeles route, all four carriers lost money.[3]

[3]Brenton Wellings, Jr., "Why Price-Cutting Backfires in the Airline Industry," *Business Week* (October 10, 1977), pp. 116–118.

Break-Even Analysis

Break-even analysis enables the market executive to estimate the impact of various prices on the firm's profit position. At the break-even point, total revenues equal total costs; thus the **break-even point** for any product is defined as the number of units sold at which product revenues just match total product costs. At sales in excess of the break-even point, the firm begins to earn a profit. The break-even point is calculated using the following formula:

$$\frac{\text{total fixed costs}}{\text{unit selling price} - \text{unit variable cost}} = \text{break-even point in units.}$$

Consider the case of a product with an $80 selling price, variable costs of $30 per unit, and associated fixed costs of $10,000. The break-even point for this product is 200 units, calculated as follows:

$$\frac{\$10,000}{\$80 - \$30} = 200 \text{ units}$$

Viewing this relationship another way, if the firm sold 200 units at a margin of $50 per unit (selling price − variable costs per unit), it would generate $10,000 in revenues, just enough to cover the product's fixed costs.

The break-even relationships are shown diagrammatically in Figure 13-1. The fixed-cost line is horizontal, indicating that fixed costs do not change with the level of production. Variable costs are added to the fixed costs and increase as the level of production increases. The total cost line is the sum of total variable costs and total fixed costs. Finally, the total-revenue curve is the price per unit multiplied by number of units sold. The higher the price, the steeper the angle of the revenue curve. The total revenue curve intersects the total cost line at the break-even point — in this case, at 200 units and at total revenue of $16,000 ($80 × 200 units).

FIGURE 13-1   **Break-Even Analysis**

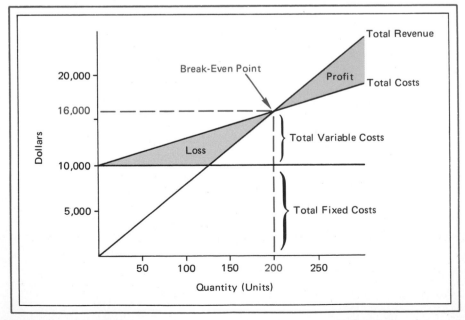

Flexible Break-Even Analysis. Break-even analysis tells the firm how many units of a product it must sell in order for total product revenues to equal total product costs, but not whether it can actually sell that number of units at the specified price. Break-even analysis gives no indication of the *correct* unit price in terms of demand and other competitive factors, only the break-even sales volume for a particular price. This limitation can be overcome, at least partially, through **flexible break-even analysis**. Under this approach, the analyst draws a series of total revenue curves, each based on a different price for the product in question. On the basis of experience or market research studies, the analyst then estimates the expected sales volume for the product at each price. Finally, these estimate points are connected to form a demand curve showing how total revenue varies with price.[4]

Figure 13-2 uses the data in Figure 13-1 to demonstrate flexible break-even analysis. As shown in Figure 13-2, a price of $130 per unit yields the greatest profit because the distance between the demand curve *DD'* and the total-cost line is greatest at that price. Assuming the demand estimates are correct, the advantage of this approach is that it shows the cost-revenue rela-

FIGURE 13-2 Flexible Break-Even Analysis

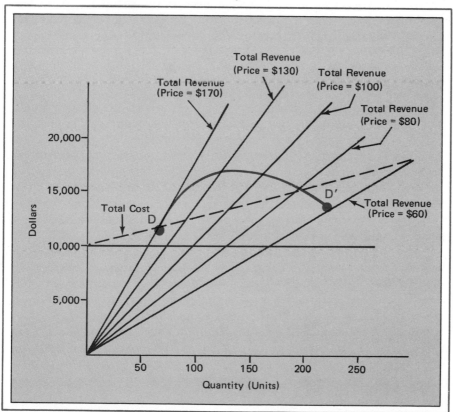

[4]For more information on flexible break-even analysis, *see* Edward R. Hawkins, "Price Policies and Theory," *Journal of Marketing* (January, 1954), pp. 233–240; and Mark I. Alpert, *Pricing Decisions* (Glenview, Ill.: Scott, Foresman & Co., 1971), pp. 39–42.

tionship for each of a series of price alternatives, thereby enabling the firm to select the price yielding the greatest profit.

Evaluation of Break-Even Analysis. Break-even analysis is an excellent management tool for analyzing the relationship between costs and revenue. It is particularly helpful when examining new product opportunities. For example, it can be used to determine the break-even sales volume at a specified price and, in light of this break-even volume, whether the firm can expect to sell enough additional units of the new product to generate a reasonable profit. Also, break-even analysis enables the firm to see quickly the impact of various price levels on the firm's break-even position.

Even with the advantages of flexible break-even analysis, however, there still remains the problem of static variable and fixed costs. Break-even analysis assumes that the variable costs associated with each additional unit are the same and that total fixed costs remain constant, regardless of the level of production. Although these assumptions are true for some products, they are not true for all products. In fact, costs can fluctuate a great deal with changes in the level of production. Break-even analysis also assumes that the selling price does not change with the number of units sold. Again, for many businesses and in many market situations, this assumption is not reasonable. As an illustration, many sellers offer a quantity discount to customers purchasing a large order, which would not be consistent with the assumption of a linear revenue curve in break-even analysis.

Target Return on Investment

When considering the introduction of a new product, marketing executives often must determine whether they will be able to price the product high enough to achieve a specified or target return on investment. If the product, for one reason or another, cannot be priced sufficiently high, management may decide against introducing it.

As we saw in Chapter 12, Alcoa, DuPont, General Motors, and many other firms rely heavily on this technique, known as target-return-on-investment pricing. It is also used by most publicly regulated utilities, which must justify their rates on the basis of the amount of invested capital.

Target-return pricing can be implemented in conjunction with break-even analysis. The first step is to estimate the amount of capital required for the manufacture of the product in question and then to specify a required rate of return. The dollar return figure is calculated and then added to the fixed cost figure in the numerator of the break-even formula. To illustrate, again assume that the selling price of the product is $80, unit variable costs are $30, and total fixed costs are $10,000. Further assume that the required investment is $20,000 and that the firm desires a 25 percent return on investment, that is, a $5,000 return ($20,000 × 25%) before taxes. The target-return break-even point is calculated as follows:

$$\frac{\text{fixed costs} + \text{required return}}{\text{price} - \text{variable costs per unit}} = \text{target return break-even point}$$

$$\frac{\$10,000 + \$5,000}{\$80 - \$30} = 300 \text{ units.}$$

FIGURE 13-3   Target Return Break-Even Analysis

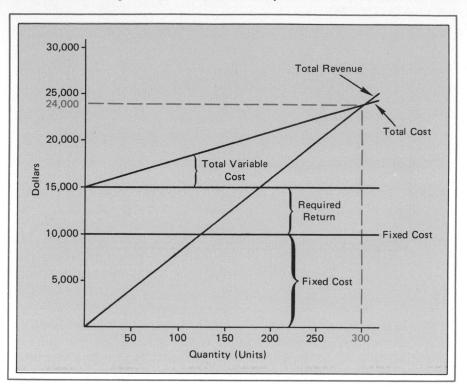

Note that 300 units is not the break-even point; rather it is the number of units that the firm must sell in order to achieve 25 percent investment return. Any sales over and above 300 units would contribute to profits in excess of the 25 percent return on investment. If total sales were less than 300 units, the firm would be falling short of its target return objective.

The next step in the analysis is to decide whether the target figure of 300 units is reasonable given a selling price of $80 and current demand conditions. It may be necessary for the firm to lower the selling price, thereby increasing the number of units that must be sold before the firm reaches its return objective of $5,000. Figure 13-3 diagrams target-return break-even analysis.

DEMAND-ORIENTED PRICING

We have just looked at how costs are used to establish prices. Although the simplicity of cost-oriented pricing is its primary advantage, the demand for the product may also be an important consideration when setting price. Demand factors are particularly relevant when the firm is selling a product in several distinct market segments, each with a different level of demand for the product. To understand the nature of demand, we now look at movement along the demand curve, shifts in the demand curve, and elasticity of demand. We conclude with an analysis of two demand-oriented pricing techniques: differential pricing and psychological pricing.

FIGURE 13-4 A Typical Demand Curve

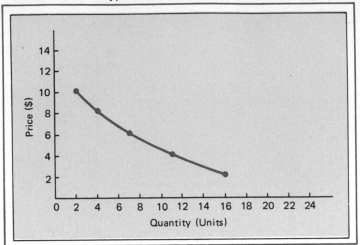

Movement Along the Demand Curve

For most products, demand is a function of price — demand increases as price decreases, and vice versa. Since the typical demand curve is downward sloping, the tendency of demand to vary inversely with price is referred to as *movement along the demand curve*. Figure 13-4 depicts this relationship. As price is reduced from $10 to $2 per unit, sales increase from two units to 16 units. The demand curve slopes downward because, as price decreases, new buyers begin to purchase the product and previous buyers begin to purchase more of it.

The price of energy provides an excellent example of downward-sloping demand. A few years ago, when natural gas cost only 20¢ per thousand cubic feet, many people installed gas heating systems in their homes and proceeded to set their thermostats at 78° or higher, showing little concern for either the supply of energy or its cost. In recent years, however, as the price of natural gas rose to more than $3 per thousand cubic feet in many areas of the country, consumers began to look seriously at alternative sources of heat — electrical heat pumps, solar energy, and wood burning stoves, to name a few. In addition, many people with gas heat began to turn their thermostats down to levels previously considered uncomfortably cold.

Shifts in Demand

A shift in the entire demand curve is to be distinguished from movement along the demand curve. Such shifts are not caused by price, but by one of the more fundamental forces of demand, such as a change in consumer tastes or preferences. Figure 13-5 illustrates both a positive and a negative shift in demand. When the shift is positive, the firm can expect to sell a greater quantity of its products at each price level. Thus, in the diagram the demand curve shifts to the right. Assuming the positive shift shown in Figure 13-5, the firm could

FIGURE 13-5 Shifts in Demand

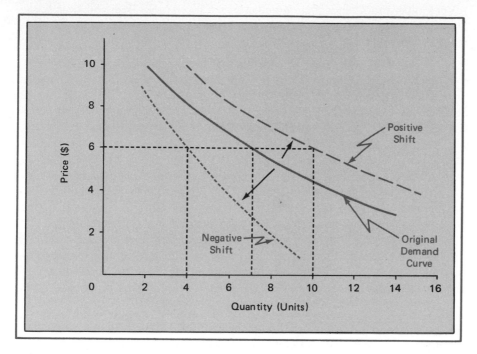

expect to sell ten units at a price of $6 each, whereas with the original demand
curve it could expect to sell only seven units at that price. A negative shift has
the opposite effect — at a selling price of $6, demand drops to four units. In
other words, the demand curve moves to the left. The major forces underlying
shifts in demand are consumer tastes and preferences, the size of the market,
the level of consumer income, and the range of goods available.

Consumer Tastes and Preferences. Of the four forces underlying shifts in
demand, the most important is consumer tastes and preferences. When consumers become more favorably disposed to a product, the demand curve for
the product shifts in a positive direction (to the right). Conversely, if consumers
view the product less favorably, the demand curve shifts in a negative direction
(to the left). When the Arab oil embargo created an energy shortage in 1974,
the demand for small, fuel-efficient cars increased dramatically. In short, the
demand curve for this product shifted positively and the automobile companies
were able to sell more small cars at each price level. By 1975, however, the
embargo had been lifted and energy problems were less pressing; consequently, U.S. consumers reverted to their large cars, rapidly losing interest in
the smaller models. As a result, the demand curve for small cars shifted negatively and sales at each price point on the curve dropped.

Size of the Market. The number of consumers in the market has a significant
impact on demand. The greater the increase in the size of the market, the more
the demand curve shifts to the right; conversely, the greater the decrease in the
number of consumers, the more it shifts to the left. As an illustration, the decline in the birthrate in the U.S. has caused a negative shift in the demand for

baby care products. This decline has led manufacturers of baby care products to seek other markets for their merchandise. For example, Johnson & Johnson now promotes its baby shampoo as a product not only for babies but also for women who want to have baby-fresh hair.

Level of Consumer Income. As the real income of consumers increases, they are likely to buy more products. Therefore, for most products an increase in real income causes a positive shift in demand, whereas a decrease in real income has the opposite effect. One exception, so frequently cited by economists, is the Irish potato market. Theoretically, during a depression the people of Ireland buy more potatoes than they did before the drop in their real income. Why? Because they are forced to switch from expensive foods, such as meat, to less expensive potatoes. A second illustration is the automobile market. During the severe recessions of 1965, 1974, and 1979–80 many U.S. car buyers switched from General Motors, Ford, and Chrysler products to the smaller, less expensive automobiles manufactured by American Motors. In 1965, while the big three producers suffered significant sales decreases, AMC's market share swelled to a record 6.6 percent. Similarly, during the first six months of 1974 and the last six months of 1979, AMC sales increased 15 percent, whereas industry sales declined 20 percent. These examples, however, represent the exception to the rule, not the rule itself.

Range of Goods Available. The introduction of a new product or service to the market usually causes a negative shift in the demand curves of competitive products or services. To illustrate, assume a small town is adequately served by three dry cleaning stores. What happens when a fourth is opened? All else being equal, total demand for each of the existing stores will decline. In the same manner, if one of the three existing stores goes out of business, the demand curve for each of the remaining stores will shift to the right — that is, total demand for each store will increase.

Elasticity of Demand

When the price of a product or service is changed, what effect will the resulting change in demand have on total revenue? Will total revenue increase, decrease, or stay the same? This question can be answered only if we know the slope, or **elasticity**, of the product's demand curve. If a reduction in the price of a product results in the sale of enough additional units to increase total revenue for that product, then the product is said to have an **elastic** demand curve. Figure 13-6(A) shows an elastic demand curve — when the selling price of the product is lowered from $10 to $5, total revenue increases from $50 ($10 × 5 units) to $125 ($5 × 25 units). The firm increased total revenue by decreasing unit price because the percentage decrease in price was less than the percentage increase in quantity demanded. The market for this product appears to be very *price sensitive* — in other words, demand is highly elastic. Conversely, assuming the same elasticity of demand, if the firm increased the price of the product from $5 to $10, total revenue would decline.

The demand curve for a product is said to be characterized by **unitary elasticity** when a change in price has no effect on total revenue. Looking at the unitary elastic demand curve in Figure 13-6(B), we see that total product revenue at a selling price of $10 per unit is equal to total revenue at $5 per

FIGURE 13-6 Types of Elasticity of Demand

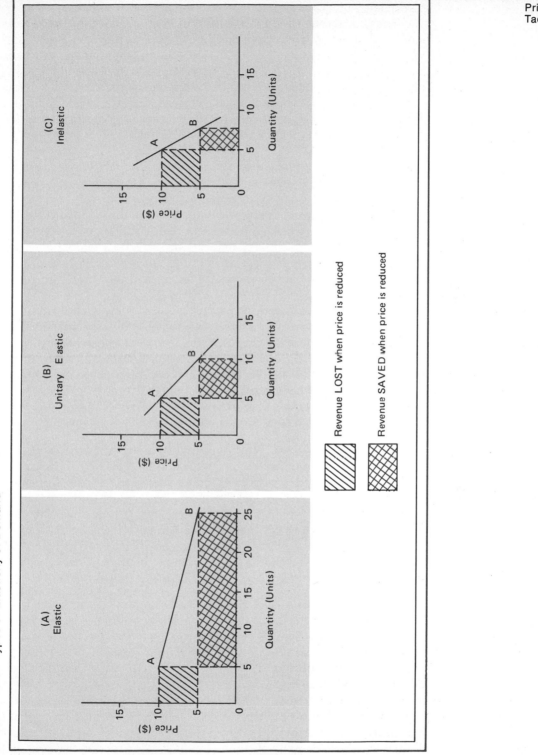

unit. In other words, the percentage decline in price was offset exactly by the percentage increase in the number of units sold.

Finally, demand is said to be **inelastic** when a reduction in price results in a decrease in revenue. An inelastic demand curve is shown in Figure 13-6(C). When the price is reduced from $10 to $5, the number of units sold increases from five to only seven. Therefore, the percentage reduction in price was not offset by a corresponding increase in the quantity demanded. Similarly, under conditions of inelastic demand, a price increase generates greater total revenue because the reduction in the number of units sold is more than offset by the higher price received for each unit sold.[5]

What Makes Demand Elastic or Inelastic? Two factors affect a product's sensitivity to price. The more important of the two is the availability of product substitutes. The more competition a product faces — that is, the greater the availability of product substitutes — the more elastic the demand curve for that product. When all products in a class are basically alike, people tend to purchase the least expensive one. Laundry soap provides a familiar example. Although most consumers do feel some loyalty for a particular brand, they will probably switch to a competing brand if the price of their brand increases substantially.

The second factor underlying product elasticity is the relative importance of the product in the consumer's budget. Expensive items, especially those requiring a high percentage of an individual's budget, tend to be very price sensitive (elastic demand); items requiring only a small percentage of the budget are less sensitive to price (inelastic demand). It follows, then, that "big-ticket" items such as automobiles have elastic demand curves, whereas chewing gum and other inexpensive products have inelastic demand curves. As a result, we see a great deal of price promotion for automobiles but little for chewing gum.

Evaluation of Elasticity. Typically, elasticity of demand for a product varies throughout the range of feasible prices for that product.[6] When describing the elasticity of demand for a particular product, therefore, the pricing analyst must specify the relevant price range. For example, a recent study of the public's response to increases in the price of electricity indicated that for relatively small increases (10 to 50 percent), people were willing to make an effort to reduce consumption. However, a major price increase (51 to 100 percent) did not result in a significant additional reduction in the amount of energy consumed. Why? Consumers apparently had made all the sacrifices they were willing to make at the 50 percent price increase level. They were willing to cut back on

---

[5]The formula for measuring elasticity of demand (E_D) is the following:

$$E_D = \frac{\% \text{ change in quantity demanded}}{\% \text{ change in price}}$$

When E_D is greater than 1, demand is elastic; when it is equal to 1, demand is unitary; and when it is less than 1, demand is inelastic. See Paul A. Samuelson, *Economics* (11th ed.; New York: McGraw-Hill, 1979) for additional explanation of the mathematics of elasticity.

[6]Kent B. Monroe, "Measuring Price Thresholds by Psychophysics and Latitudes of Acceptance," *Journal of Marketing Research* (November, 1971), pp. 460–464.

the use of air conditioners but not to turn off their televisions or to disconnect their refrigerators. In short, the demand for electricity was relatively elastic for price increases of up to 50 percent but relatively inelastic for increases of greater than 50 percent.[7]

It is also important to recognize that elasticity is difficult to measure, not because the mathematics of elasticity are obscure but because of the difficulty of estimating the shape of the demand curve for most products. Many techniques have been developed to measure demand curves, including statistical analyses of the relationship between sales and price over time, in addition to market surveys, the subjective judgment of executives, and laboratory experiments. Although each of these approaches may prove useful in particular situations, none of them provides an error-free solution.[8]

Even with the problems of estimation, elasticity is still one of the most important and useful concepts that economics has given the marketing executive. When attempting to price a product characterized by inelastic demand, the executive knows that it is probably impossible to maximize total product revenue simply by increasing its price. Instead, the executive typically will choose to compete on the basis of nonprice factors, such as the technical expertise of the firm's salespeople (for industrial goods) or the quality of its distribution outlets (for consumer goods). In contrast, if demand for the product is elastic, every effort should be made to ensure that the final price is competitive. The marketing executive need not know the exact numerical elasticity of demand in order to incorporate the concept of elasticity into the planning process.

With the concept of elasticity in mind, let us turn now to two types of demand-oriented pricing: differential pricing and psychological pricing.

Differential Pricing

A common type of demand-oriented pricing is **differential pricing**, defined as the sale of a product at price differentials that do not correspond directly to differences in cost.[9] Differential pricing is practiced when the market is composed of several distinct segments, each of which has a different elasticity of demand for the product in question. The firm attempts to sell the product at a high price in market segments characterized by inelastic demand and at a low price in the segments characterized by elastic demand.

---

[7]William H. Cunningham and Sally Lopreato, *Energy Use and Conservation Incentives: A Study of the Southwestern United States* (New York: Praeger Publishers, 1977).

[8]For an excellent discussion of methods of estimating demand, see Mark I. Alpert, *Pricing Decisions* (Glenview, Ill.: Scott, Foresman & Co., 1971), pp. 75–108; Lee Adler and James D. Hlavecek, "The Relationship Between Price and Repair Service for Consumer Durables," *Journal of Marketing* (April, 1976), pp. 80–82; Ira J. Doloch, "How Subscription Prices Affect Magazine Sales," *Journal of Advertising Research* (April, 1977), pp. 31–36; and Brian T. Ratchford and Gary T. Ford, "A Study of Price and Market Shares in the Computer Mainframe Industry," *Journal of Business* (April, 1976), pp. 194–218.

[9]Frederic M. Scherer, *Industrial Pricing: Theory and Evidence* (Chicago: Rand McNally College Publishing Co., 1970), p. 125.

Types of Differential Pricing. Differential pricing is normally based on one of the following factors: time, product, location, or customer.[10] In terms of time, the demand for a product frequently varies over the business cycle — by the season, by the day, or even by the time of day. Christmas cards sold at a premium in November and December are marked down heavily during January. Similarly, resort hotels in Florida charge higher rates in the winter than they do in the summer. Bars and restaurants offer "happy hours" during the afternoon, selling drinks at about half their usual price in order to attract customers during what might otherwise be a slow period.

Differential pricing is product-based when a manufacturer sells two slightly different products at substantially different prices. Typically, the price difference is not justifiable on the basis of cost. As an illustration, consider the case of a contractor who builds a house in a middle-class section of town, charging $35 per square foot. The contractor then adds a few minor trim items to the design and builds the same basic house in an upper-class area, selling it at $40 per square foot even though the extra cost per square foot is only $2. In this situation, the higher price of the second house reflects the demand for the location rather than the actual cost of the house. In short, the contractor is using differential pricing to increase revenue.

Location-based differential pricing is also practiced widely. Theater tickets are an excellent illustration: a seat close to the stage is usually priced higher than a seat at the back of the theater, even though the installation and maintenance costs of each are the same.

The final type of differential pricing is based on the customer. Some people are simply better than others at negotiating price. This ability is extremely important in many areas of the world, where prices are negotiated for almost all items. In the United States, we see such bargaining in only a few consumer goods markets, such as housing and automobiles. To use automobiles as an example, there is no question that the buyer who understands the negotiation process and who has taken the time to find out the cost of the car to the dealer as well as the asking price of other dealers frequently strikes a better bargain than the uninformed buyer.[11]

Requirements for Effective Differential Pricing. The implementation of a strategy of differential pricing depends on the existence of two or more market segments with distinct elasticities of demand. Further, buyers in the lower-priced segment must not be able to resell their purchases to buyers in the higher-priced segment. Even if these conditions are met, the firm still may not find it profitable to adopt a differential pricing strategy. Such a strategy implies that the firm's objective is to charge as high a price as possible to each of its market segments. Although this objective may lead to high profits in the short run, it may also alienate many customers, as the Honda Motor Company found out when it introduced the Accord to the U.S. market. The car was so popular with customers in the United States that Honda could not satisfy de-

---

[10]Philip Kotler, *Marketing Management: Analysis, Planning and Control* (Englewood Cliffs, N.J.: Prentice-Hall, 1976), pp. 257–258.

[11]See such publications as *Edmond's New Car Buyers Guide* for the dealer's cost of the car. Advertisements in newspapers will also give a good indication of competitive conditions within a local automobile market.

mand. As a result, some dealers began to sell the car at a premium over list price. Honda worked to discourage this practice because of the resulting bad publicity.

Psychological Pricing

The term **psychological pricing** suggests that some noneconomic or psychological factors enter into the determination of prices. Not all people perceive and react to price in the same way. What is a bargain to one person may be the ticket to a better, more prestigious life for another. Similarly, people's tastes and preferences differ. Two common types of psychological pricing are prestige pricing and odd/even pricing.

Prestige Pricing. As we have seen, the typical demand curve is downward sloping, i.e., a price reduction is accompanied by an increase in demand. In contrast, the demand curve associated with prestige pricing is backward bending. As the example in Figure 13-7 illustrates, up to a selling price of $10, price increases are associated with more purchases; above $10, however, product demand slackens and the curve bends backward, indicating fewer sales.

FIGURE 13-7 The Backward-Bending Demand Curve Associated with Prestige Pricing

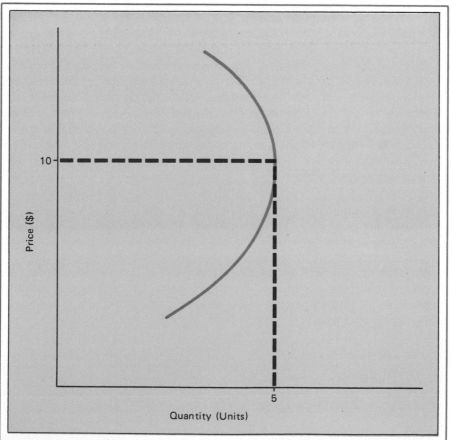

For prestige pricing to be effective, several, if not all, of the following characteristics should be present. First, large quality differences should exist between available products. Second, the typical consumer should not be able to judge these quality differences. Third, a high level of risk should be associated with making the wrong decision and obtaining a poor quality product. Fourth, the product in question should be visible to people who have an influence on the buyer — that is, people will see the buyer's new product and judge the individual by it, or at least have an opinion about the purchase. All of these factors encourage the consumer to view price as an indicator of quality.[12]

Assume, for example, that you have been invited to your boss's house for dinner. You would like to bring along a bottle of good wine, but you don't know much about wines. You know, however, that you don't want to walk in the front door carrying a bottle of a totally inappropriate wine. Since you are not a wine connoisseur, you will tend to associate quality with price; therefore, within a certain price range, the higher the price, the more likely you will be to purchase the wine.

A second illustration of prestige pricing is provided by the Curtis Mathes Television Corporation, which advertises its television as the most expensive in the U.S. and "darn well worth it." Curtis Mathes believes that a segment of the overall television market wants the best and is willing to pay a higher price to get it.

Both the wine example and the Curtis Mathes example involve products for which there are significant quality differences — not all burgundies are the same and not all television sets are the same. Moreover, these quality differences are not always apparent to the typical consumer. Without the price tag or the label, how does one tell the difference between Chateau Rothschild and table wine? Who examines a television's solid-state circuitry before deciding whether to buy it? The wrong decision involves immediate or substantial risk for the buyer — a social blunder or a flickering, blurry picture. Finally, both purchases are somewhat visible to the buyer's friends, colleagues, or superiors. To a great extent, people are judged by the appropriateness, intelligence, and tastefulness of their purchases.

Odd/Even Pricing. Odd/even pricing has developed from the belief that consumers are more likely to buy a product at an odd price, such as $1.95, than at an even price, such as $2.00. Although there is some question whether consumers really do react positively to such small differences in price, there is no question that retailers price their products in this manner. In a study conducted in 1,865 supermarkets in 70 cities, 64 percent of the prices investigated ended in a "9" and 19 percent ended in a "5". Only 1 percent of the supermarket prices ended in a "0."[13]

---

[12]Mark I. Alpert, "Pricing in an Era of Rapid Change," in Gerald Zaltman, *Annual Review of Marketing* (Chicago: American Marketing Association, 1978), pp. 127–128.

[13]Dik Warren Twedt, "Does the '9 Fixation' in Retail Pricing Really Promote Sales?" *Journal of Marketing* (October, 1965), pp. 54–55.

FIGURE 13-8 Demand Curve Under Odd/Even Pricing

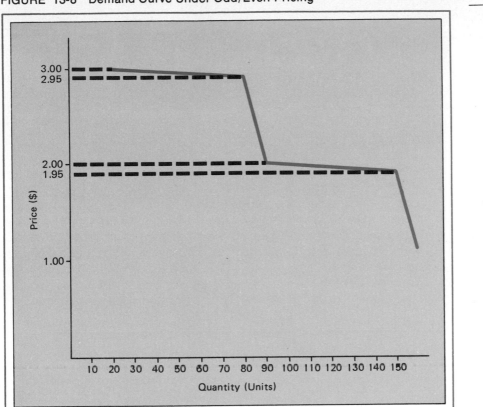

Figure 13-8 shows the demand curve for a hypothetical product with an odd/even pricing dimension. If the firm were to charge the odd price of $1.95, it could expect to sell 150 units. If, however, the firm raised its prices to the even amount of $2.00, it would sell only 90 units. The demand curve is very elastic between these two price points. In addition, in this example, raising the price from the $2.00 to $2.95 would result in lost sales of only 10 units. The demand curve is very inelastic between the even and the much higher odd price; consumers are almost as willing to pay $2.95 as $2.00 for the product.

According to one popular theory, stores initiated odd prices in order to force cashiers to record the sale, thereby eliminating shrinkage at the cash register.[14] Presumably, if customers used exact change to pay for a product priced at $2.00, for example, some cashiers might simply stick the money in their pockets. However, if required to make change, they would be forced to record the sales in order to open the cash register. Very possibly, odd pricing has become standard practice in many industries as a result of small companies following the lead of large companies who, for one reason or another, adopted an odd-even pricing strategy.

---

[14]*The Price Is Right* (St. Louis: The Garvey Corporation, 1964), p. 6.

Assume that **you** have been chosen to head a campus committee which is sponsoring a rock concert. You have already chosen the musical group. Now, how much are you going to charge for a ticket? In deciding on a ticket price, consider each of the following steps.

Set Your Profit Objectives. Is the rock concert expected to generate a profit, break even, or operate as an event subsidized by the college? Let's assume in this case that you would like to earn a modest profit or at least break even.

Estimate Demand. Next, you'll want to estimate demand at each price level you are considering. Ask yourself the following questions: How good are the musicians? How popular or well known are they? Or, as an economist might put it, how price sensitive is the demand for this band? Will a high price discourage people from buying tickets — people who might purchase tickets at a slightly lower price? Remember that there is a point at which the market will decide to just stay home. What else is happening around town or on campus on the night of the concert? How much do people normally pay for entertainment? Would they pay more to come to your concert? Finally, how have audiences responded to these musicians in the past? For how much did tickets sell at their previous engagements?

Decide on Concessions. Do you plan to make any money by selling soft drinks, food, or beer? If so, it may be possible to reduce the ticket price because of the anticipated revenues from concessions.

Figure Costs. How much do you have to pay the musical group? Using the techniques that you have learned in this and other classes, you will want to estimate the break-even point in terms of tickets sold for each alternative price level. Remember that fixed costs will include not only the band's cost, but also the cost of the concert hall, ads, clean-up, security, as well as some administrative expenses.

Estimate Profits. Once you have estimated ticket demand for each alternative price and you have figured your fixed and variable costs, you can now estimate your profit (loss) at each price. Then, compare these various profit levels with your original profit objectives.

Set the Ticket Price. Choose the price where the estimated profit level most closely matches your profit objectives. In this case, since we are assuming that you would like to earn a modest profit for your efforts, choose a price just above the price at your estimated break-even point.

Marketing & You

COMPETITIVE BIDDING

Many sales are finalized when sealed bids are opened and the contract is awarded to the lowest bidder. Prior to the opening of the bids, suppliers meet with the customers in order to determine their needs and to convince them that they should be placed on their "qualified bidder" list. The qualified bidders list is the all-important list of suppliers that a customer believes can provide the specified product or service. Competitive bidding is used by many private companies as well as by state and federal agencies purchasing standard items. In these situations, price is often the only variable by which the buyer can differentiate among suppliers. In this section we examine how most suppliers draw up competitive bids as well as the various factors influencing the formulation of a bid.

Decision Rule — Expected Profit

Although a number of highly sophisticated bidding models have been developed, most can be reduced to the basic premise that the supplier is attempting to maximize **expected profit**, that is, the amount of profit that the supplier would receive on the average from a particular bid. To implement this decision rule, the supplier must estimate the profit associated with each of a number of potential bids, as well as estimate the probability of winning the contract with each of the bids.[15]

Table 13-4 illustrates how a supplier can use the expected profit rule to formulate a bid. If the firm were to bid $30,000 and win the contract, it would receive a profit of $500. Notice that as the bid increases, profit also increases. Raising the bid does not result in additional costs, only increased profits. The third column in Table 13-4 lists the subjective probability of the supplier winning the contract at each of the bid prices. These probabilities are determined on the basis of what the supplier knows about the purchaser and general competitive practices in the industry.

The expected profit for a particular bid is calculated by multiplying the probability of winning the contract by the profit associated with that bid. As stated above, a successful bid of $30,000 results in profit of $500, but because the probability of winning the bid is only 0.80, the *expected* profit is $400. Usually, the supplier selects the bid with the highest expected profit. In the example presented in Table 13-4, the supplier would very likely bid $45,000 for the contract since this bid yields the highest expected profit, $5,425. Bids higher than $45,000 entail much lower probabilities and, therefore, lower expected profits.

---

[15]For information on more sophisticated approaches to competitive bidding, see James E. Reinmuth and Jim D. Barnes, "A Strategic Competitive Bidding Approach to Pricing Decisions for Petroleum Industry Drilling Contractors," *Journal of Marketing Research* (August, 1975), pp. 362–365; Michael H. Rothkopf, "A Model of Rational Competitive Bidding," *Management Science* (March, 1969), pp. 362–373; and Lawrence Friedman, "A Competitive Bidding Strategy," *Operations Research* (February, 1956), pp. 104–112.

Pre-Bid Decisions

The expected-profit decision rule works best when the supplier bids on a number of projects simultaneously. The supplier does not expect to win all of these contracts; in fact, most suppliers bid on more projects than they could reasonably undertake because of the low probability of winning all of them. In addition, three factors may force the supplier to put in a bid that does not yield the highest expected profit: available plant capacity, bidder objectives, and follow-up opportunities.[16]

TABLE 13-4 Competitive Bidding and Expected Profits

Bid	Profit	Probability of Winning the Contract	Expected Profit
$30,000	$ 500	.80	$ 400
35,000	5,500	.70	3,850
40,000	10,500	.50	5,250
45,000	15,500	.35	5,425
50,000	20,500	.25	5,125
55,000	25,500	.15	3,825
60,000	30,500	.10	3,050

Available Plant Capacity. A supplier with unused plant capacity may decide against putting in a bid with the highest expected profit in favor of the bid with a much greater probability of winning. In Table 13-4, for example, the bid of $45,000 yields the highest expected profit, but the firm has only a 35 percent chance of receiving the contract. Wanting to utilize excess plant capacity, the supplier might choose a lower bid, say, $35,000, since the probability of winning the contract with this bid is 0.70, twice as high as the probability of winning with the $45,000 bid.

Bidder Objectives. Company objectives may range from profit maximization to survival. The expected profit decision rule leads to profit maximization. However, if the objective is simply to survive, the firm may price very close to its variable cost in order to contribute to overhead and to keep the labor force intact. In the situation presented in Table 13-4, a bidder fighting for survival might bid $30,000 or even lower in order to win the contract and to survive until more profitable business conditions develop.

Follow-up Bid Opportunities. The supplier may also put in a bid that does not represent the highest expected profit because of the prospect of lucrative future contracts. In many situations, the recipient of an important contract will have significantly improved chances of winning larger and more profitable contracts with the customer in the future. Consequently the firm may bid low in order to maximize long-term profits. Similarly, new suppliers, seeking an opportunity to demonstrate their abilities, may decide to bid low in order to win contracts and hence get their feet wet in the industry.

[16]The following sections are adapted from Stephen Paranka, "Competitive Bidding Strategy," *Business Horizons* (June, 1971), pp. 39–43.

COMPETITION-ORIENTED PRICING

In many situations, the pricing techniques discussed above are neither feasible nor practical. Sometimes, competitive forces are so strong that marketing executives are not able to set their own prices. In such situations, the firm must meet the market price if it is to sell enough merchandise to survive. Two opposing economic conditions lead to competition-oriented pricing: pure competition and oligopoly.

Pure Competition

For pure competition to exist in a market, several conditions must be present. First, there must be many manufacturers selling homogeneous products to many buyers. Second, there must be no government intervention. Third, each buyer and seller must have perfect information. Fourth, all products must be sold at the prevailing market price. Finally, both human and capital resources must be free to move to the location yielding the highest return on investment.

Although no major markets in the United States meet all the criteria for pure competition, a number are sufficiently competitive that their prices are established by the marketplace and not by the unilateral action of any particular buyer or seller. Two examples are the U.S. agricultural and bond markets. In these markets, prices normally cannot be influenced by any one buyer or one seller. However, the federal government regulates these markets quite closely. For example, when President Carter stopped much of the nation's exports of agricultural products to the Soviet Union in 1980, he also closed the agricultural commodity market for several days.

Oligopoly

Most of the nation's largest and best-known industries are oligopolies, and include the steel, aluminum, and automobile industries. The distinguishing element of an oligopolistic market is the existence of a few large sellers and many buyers. Each seller knows the strategy of competitors and responds as much to competitive pressures as to the needs of the marketplace. The result is usually inflexible prices.

Kinked Demand Curve. Typically, the characteristic price rigidity of oligopolistic competition is explained by the theory that the firm reacts one way when a competitor reduces prices and another when a competitor raises prices. That is, oligopolistic firms tend to follow a price reduction so as not to lose sales to the firm that initiated the reduction. On the other hand, they tend not to match a price increase because, by maintaining their current price, they may be able to pick up customers lost by the firm initiating the price increase. As a result, oligopolistic firms learn to administer their prices in a rigid manner; each firm knows that it is more profitable to agree tacitly on a common industry price than to modify price repeatedly.

This inflexibility of price leads to what economists call a **kinked demand curve**, illustrated in Figure 13-9. Point A in the figure is the long-term equilibrium price. The demand curve is kinked at point A because, for price increases above the equilibrium price, demand tends to be very elastic (D_1A). That is,

FIGURE 13-9 Oligopoly: Kinked Demand Curve

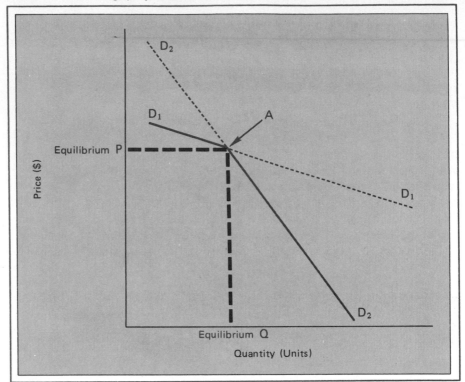

price increases result in declining product revenues, assuming of course that the firm's competitors hold the line on prices. In contrast, for prices lower than the equilibrium price, demand tends to be inelastic (AD_2); price reductions do not increase revenues because competitors also lower their prices. Thus, price in an oligopolistic industry tends to remain — in a sense, inflexibly — at the equilibrium price.

Price Leadership. A second explanation for competition-oriented pricing in an oligopolistic industry is that, over time, one firm emerges as dominant in the industry. The selling prices set by this firm become the prices for the entire industry. Both price fixing and price leadership caused few legal problems before the passage of the antitrust laws discussed earlier in Chapter 3. Since these laws now forbid firms from conspiring to set industry prices, today price influence in an oligopolistic industry is typically exercised as price leadership. Most price leaders periodically announce price changes in trade journals or in the *Wall Street Journal*, and the rest of the firms in the industry match the new price. Of the last eight price increases in steel, seven have been initiated by the industry leader, U.S. Steel Corporation. The courts have consistently held that as long as the members of the oligopoly do not conspire in any way to set prices, price leadership is not illegal.[17]

[17]For an interesting case analysis of price conspiracy, see Richard A. Smith, "The Incredible Electrical Conspiracy, Part I," *Fortune* (April, 1961), pp. 132–191 passim; and Richard A. Smith, "The Incredible Electrical Conspiracy, Part II," *Fortune* (May, 1961), pp. 161–225 passim.

A MULTISTAGE APPROACH TO PRICING

This chapter has presented a set of independent pricing techniques commonly used by business firms in the United States. It is important to be aware of the various approaches because there is clearly no one best way to set prices; each technique has certain advantages and is applicable under certain market conditions. Unfortunately, all too often, business managers rely on one pricing technique without considering alternative methods or the impact of the price adopted for one product on the rest of the organization's products, on its resellers, or even on the government. This concluding section of the chapter presents a multistage approach to pricing. This approach is designed to help the pricing analyst narrow the range of price alternatives by ensuring that all relevant factors in the pricing decision are taken into consideration.[18] We begin by reviewing the pricing decision model presented at the beginning of Chapter 12.

Pricing Decision Model: A Review

The price of a product should be the result of a logical decision process. This procedure begins with an examination of the firm's mission along with its marketing objectives and programs. This information provides the basis for determining the pricing objectives, which result in the establishment of pricing policies and tactics. While Chapter 12 dealt primarily with pricing objectives and policies, this chapter has focused on the last element in the pricing process — pricing tactics. Unfortunately, all too often, pricing analysts forget that prices must be consistent with the firm's objectives and policies as well as with the overall marketing strategy for the product.

To illustrate, AT&T recognizes that much of its long-distance transmission capacity is underutilized during nonbusiness hours. Consequently, it encourages consumers to make more long-distance telephone calls after 5:00 p.m. and on weekends and holidays. To provide such encouragement, AT&T has devised a promotional program emphasizing the pleasure of talking with distant friends and loved ones. Integral to this program is a set of price discounts for long-distance calls made during nonpeak hours. The company's objective is to increase the use of its equipment during nonpeak hours; its marketing mission is to encourage individual consumers to make more long-distance calls during these times. It supports these objectives with a well-integrated set of price discounts, and informs customers of these discounts through an extensive promotional campaign. Take a look at a typical ad in this campaign shown in Figure 13-10.

Sequential Steps in Establishing Price

With a clear understanding of the firm's mission, objectives, policies, and strategy, the marketing executive is ready to establish the product's price. Ideally, setting the price for a new product or changing the price of an existing product should involve each of the following steps:

---

[18]Adapted, by permission of the publisher, from *Pricing Strategies*, by Alfred R. Oxenfeldt, © 1975 by AMACOM, a division of American Management Associations. All rights reserved.

FIGURE 13-10 An Ad Promoting Long-Distance Calls During Nonpeak Hours

Courtesy: AT&T Long Lines.

1. Determine the cost of the product.
2. Estimate the demand for the product at various prices.
3. Estimate the reaction of competitors to alternative prices.
4. Evaluate the impact of each price on complementary products.
5. Determine how resellers will react to each proposed price.
6. Assess the impact of each price on the rest of the product's marketing strategy.
7. Determine whether any of the prices will be likely to result in legal action from the government.
8. Choose the final price.

Figure 13-11 shows that each step in the pricing decision reduces the range of alternative prices for the product. That is, as the firm moves from cost and demand factors to government considerations, the range of prices is narrowed to the point where the analyst selects the best alternative from among the small set of realistic price alternatives still available.

Cost Considerations. Production costs tend to impose a price floor on the eventual selling price of a product. Unless the firm is able to cover its full costs in the long run and its variable costs in the short run, it will have to discontinue production. When considering a new product, the firm's accountants may estimate all relevant costs — direct variable, overhead, selling and administrative costs — and then apply a higher-than-normal markup to reflect the extra risk associated with a new product. The firm also can use break-even analysis, flexible break-even analysis, or variable-cost pricing in setting this initial price floor.

Demand Considerations. The second step involves an examination of the product's target market and its intended image. These demand considerations enable the firm to determine both a ceiling price and the potential, if any, for differential pricing with respect to the product's various market segments. For example, if a firm were marketing a prestige product to high-income customers, the pricing analyst would expect the product to have an inelastic demand curve and, therefore, to merit a relatively high price. Demand considerations might also favor the marketing of a lower-quality version of the product to a larger, more price-sensitive group of consumers. The outcome of such differentiation might be greater total revenue for the firm.

Reaction of Competition. How will the price of the product affect competitors? In the case of a new product, the adoption of a price-skimming strategy usually encourages other firms to begin producing a similar product. Competitors are attracted by the higher-than-average returns associated with such a strategy. The adoption of a penetration strategy, on the other hand, usually means that the profit on each unit sold will be lower but that competitors will be less likely to enter the market.

In the case of existing products, the question concerns the effect of a price change on other firms in the industry. If our firm initiates a price change, what will our competitors do: raise prices, lower prices, or hold the line on prices? In a highly oligopolistic industry, we can expect that most firms will follow a price reduction by an industry leader but not necessarily a price increase. If others in the industry do not follow suit, the firm initiating the price hike usually finds that its customers have begun to switch to other suppliers. How competitors react to a price change really depends on how the product is perceived by its customers. Generally speaking, in oligopolistic industries as well as in less concentrated industries, the less a product is differentiated from its competitors, the more likely competitors will be to follow a price change.

Impact on Complementary Products. The pricing analyst next decides whether the agreed-upon price for the product is likely to hurt the sales of other products marketed by the firm. For example, IBM sells complete computer systems, not only mainframe computers but also high-speed printers, computer programs, and other software. Raising the price of printers might hurt sales of this item but also, and more to the point, it might hurt the sales of mainframe equipment and computer programs. Generally speaking, when a firm sells products closely related to one another, the pricing decision for one product must take into consideration the probable impact on the others.

Reseller Considerations. Demand considerations view price from the perspective of the final consumer. Many items, however, must first go through a reseller (either wholesaler or retailer) before they are made available to the final consumer. Therefore, in calculating the suggested retail price, the manufacturer must also take into consideration the fact that the reseller needs to make a profit too. If the markup is not sufficient, the reseller may charge more than the suggested retail price for the item, or else refuse to carry it.

Price bargaining between manufacturer and reseller begins with the normal trade margins for the product under consideration. If a manufacturer wants the reseller to provide extra benefits, such as no-cost service or installation, the manufacturer may have to offer the reseller a higher-than-average margin. If the price determined on the basis of demand, cost, and competitive factors does not give the reseller a satisfactory profit, the manufacturer may have to adjust the dollar figure further. Chapter 14 will discuss in greater detail how members of the distribution channel interact with one another.

Impact on Marketing Strategy. The price established for a product must be consistent with the product's overall marketing and promotional strategy. For example, a high quality product can more easily carry a higher price. The same holds true for a prestige product targeted to a fairly small, affluent segment of the population.

Manufacturers can usually sell products at slightly higher prices to retailers if the manufacturers promote the products themselves. If retailers are expected to advertise the products, the manufacturers will probably have to charge less or expect retailers to add higher markups. This is why cigarettes, for example, involve such small markups at the retail level and furniture much higher markups.

Government Considerations. Many local, state, and federal laws affect pricing decisions. As stated earlier, the law is clear on the point that business firms may not set prices in a collusive manner. In addition, firms are not normally permitted to charge different prices to different distributors for the same product. At times, the government itself has established prices for particular products. You might want to review the legal environment for pricing discussed in Chapter 3.

Establishing the Price. At this point the firm has narrowed the range of possible prices to the point where it can now select how much to charge for its product. It should be apparent that this system is built upon a series of assumptions as to how a product price will affect such factors as resellers' profits and complementary products. In the same way the system has assumed certain demand and cost considerations. If these assumptions are incorrect, then the firm will not arrive at the best price. However, if they are well thought out, the firm has an excellent opportunity to select an acceptable price for its merchandise if it follows the logical flow of events that are prescribed in the multistage approach to pricing.

FIGURE 13-11 A Multistage Approach to Pricing

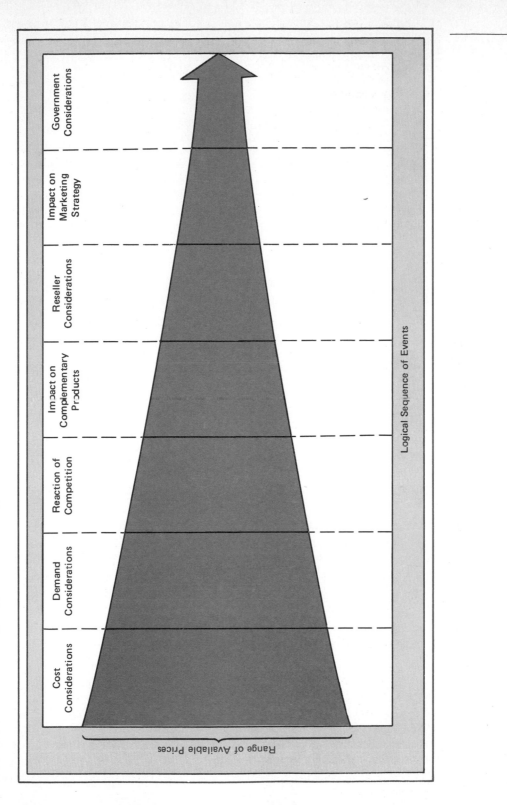

Government Considerations

Impact on Marketing Strategy

Reseller Considerations

Impact on Complementary Products

Reaction of Competition

Demand Considerations

Cost Considerations

Logical Sequence of Events

Range of Available Prices

summary points

1. Cost-oriented pricing is the simplest and most commonly used pricing technique.

2. Markup pricing involves the addition of a fixed percentage to the cost of the merchandise.

3. Variable-cost pricing enables the firm to price below its full costs but still to contribute to fixed overhead.

4. Break-even analysis permits the pricing analyst to estimate the impact of various prices on the firm's profit position.

5. The break-even point for a product is the number of units the firm must sell in order for product revenues to equal total product costs.

6. Flexible break-even analysis combines traditional break-even analysis with an estimate of demand for the product.

7. New product pricing decisions frequently employ the target-return-on-investment technique.

8. Movement along the demand curve is the result of a price change; a shift in the demand curve is the result of more fundamental market forces.

9. Elasticity measures the sensitivity of total product demand to a change in price. Demand may be elastic, unitary, or inelastic.

10. Differential pricing refers to the practice of selling a product at different prices to different customers when such price differences do not reflect actual cost differences.

11. With some prestige products, the higher the price, the more consumers are willing to buy the product. Also consumers may be more likely to buy a product with an odd-numbered price than with an even-numbered price.

12. The key decision rule in competitive bidding is to maximize expected profit, not actual profit.

13. In pure competition or under oligopolistic conditions, the firm sets its prices on the basis of competitive market forces.

14. The multistage approach to pricing provides the pricing analyst with a systematic scheme for cutting down the overall range of pricing alternatives.

questions for discussion

1. Why is markup pricing used so frequently? What are the disadvantages of markup pricing and how can they be overcome?

2. Assume the production cost of a product is $65 and the manufacturer wants a 40 percent markup. How much should the manufacturer charge for the product?

3. What is the objective of variable-cost pricing? What risks are associated with variable-cost pricing?

4. Compute the break-even point for a product with a selling price of $75 and unit variable costs of $40. Assume that fixed costs are $10,000.

5. How can the marketing executive use flexible break-even analysis to price a product?

6. How can the marketing executive use break-even analysis in deciding whether to develop a new product or not?

7. Distinguish between a shift in demand and movement along the demand curve.

8. Define elastic, unitary elastic, and inelastic demand. What factors affect a product's sensitivity to price?

9. How is the concept of price elasticity useful to the marketing executive?

10. How can differential pricing increase the profitability of the firm? What dangers, if any, are associated with differential pricing?
11. What is prestige pricing? Odd/even pricing?
12. How is expected profit calculated in a contract bidding situation? Under what circumstances might a firm choose not to submit the bid yielding the highest expected profit?
13. What is meant by a kinked demand curve? Is competition-oriented pricing for an oligopoly still governed by a kinked demand curve in times of rapid price inflation?
14. Explain the use of the multistage approach to pricing. Do you see any weaknesses in this approach?

cases
part 5

case 12
united
techtronics

United Techtronics (UT) was founded in Boston in 1959 by Dr. Roy Cowing. Prior to that time, Dr. Cowing had been an associate professor of electrical engineering at MIT. Dr. Cowing founded UT to manufacture and market products making use of some of the electronic inventions he had developed while at MIT. Sales were made mostly to the space program and the military. Sales grew from $100,000 in 1960 to $27 million in 1976.

The Video Screen Project

The objective of the video screen project was to develop a system whereby a television picture could be displayed on a screen as big as 8 to 10 feet diagonally. In late 1976, one of UT's engineers made the necessary breakthrough. The rest of 1976 and the first few months of 1977 were spent producing working prototypes. Up until June, 1977, UT had invested $600,000 in the project.

Extra large-screen television systems were not new. There were a number of companies who sold such systems both to the consumer and commercial (taverns, restaurants, and so on) markets. Most current systems made use of a special magnifying lens that projected a regular small television picture onto a special screen. The result of this process is that the final picture lacked much of the brightness of the original small screen. As a result, the picture had to be viewed in a darkened room. There were some other video systems that did not use the magnifying process. These systems used special tubes, but also suffered from a lack of brightness. UT had developed a system that was bright enough to be viewed in regular daylight on a screen up to 10 feet diagonally. Dr. Cowing felt that it would take at least two to three years for any competitor to duplicate the system.

Competition

A number of large and small companies were active in this area. Admiral, General Electric, RCA, Zenith, and Sony were all thought to be working on developing large-screen systems directed at the consumer market. Sony was rumored to be ready to introduce a 60-inch diagonal screen system that would retail for

United Techtronics case by Kenneth L. Bernhardt and Thomas C. Kinnear, *Cases in Marketing Management* (Dallas, Texas: Business Publications, Inc., 1978), pp. 405–407. © 1978 by Business Publications, Inc.

about $2,500. A number of small companies were already producing systems. Advent Corporation, a small New England company, claimed to have sold 4,000 84-inch diagonal units in two years at a $4,000 price. Muntz Manufacturing claimed one-year sales of 5,000 50-inch diagonal units at prices from $1,500 to $2,500. Dr. Cowing was adamant that none of these systems gave as bright a picture as UT's. He estimated that about 10,000 large-screen systems were sold in 1976.

Cost Structure

Dr. Cowing expected about 50 percent of the suggested retail selling price to go for wholesaler and retailer margins. He expected that UT's direct manufacturing costs would vary depending on the volume produced (see Figure 1). He expected direct labor costs to fall at higher production volumes due to the increased automation of the process and improved worker skills. Material costs were expected to fall due to automation. The equipment costs necessary to automate the product process were $70,000 to produce in the 0–5,000 unit range, an additional $50,000 to produce in the 5,001–10,000 unit range, and an additional $40,000 to produce in the 10,001–20,000 unit range. The useful life of this equipment was put at five years. Dr. Cowing was sure that production costs were substantially below those of current competitors including Sony.

FIGURE 1 Estimated Production Costs of UT's Video Screen System

	Volume		
	0–5,000	5,001–10,000	10,001–20,000
Raw materials	$ 480	$460	$410
Direct labor	540	320	115
Total direct costs	$1,020	$780	$525

Dr. Cowing wanted to establish a position in the consumer market for his product. He felt that the long-run potential was greater there than in the commercial market. With this end in mind he hired a small economics research consulting firm to undertake a consumer study to determine the likely reaction to alternative retail prices for the system. These consultants undertook extensive interviews with potential television purchasers, plus examined the sales and pricing histories of competitive products. They concluded that: "UT's video screen system would be highly price sensitive or elastic across a range of prices from $500 to $5,000 both in a primary and secondary demand sense." For every 10 percent decline in price they could expect to sell between 30–40 percent more video screen systems.

1. Does UT have a clear cut pricing policy? If so, what is it? If not, what should it be?
2. Should UT adopt a penetration or a skimming pricing policy? Explain your answer.
3. Develop a marketing strategy for UT's video screen system.

Port-Marine is a sailboat manufacturing company which was formed three years ago in Portland, Maine. Revenue from sales in the first full year of operation totaled $225,000. Sales increased to an estimated $1,240,000 in the present year. The initial product line consists of three different types of fiberglass sailboats. The P/M-17 is a small day cruiser with berths for two adults and two children, and sail area of 130 square feet; it weighs one-half ton and has an overall length of a little over 17 feet.

The P/M-34 is a relatively large motor sailer that sleeps seven people in three separate compartments. The main saloon contains an adjustable dining table, a complete galley, and a navigator's compartment. The aft cabin, which is entered by a separate companion way, contains a double berth, wardrobe, wash basin, and lockers. The toilet and shower are situated between the fore cabin and the main saloon. The boat has a sail area of 530 square feet, weighs about five tons, and has an overall length of 33 feet, 8 inches.

The P/M-36 was designed for a different purpose. While the P/M-17 and P/M-34 are oriented toward a family approach to sailing, the P/M-36 is first and foremost a sailing craft. It does have two berths, a small galley, and toilet facilities, but the emphasis is on sailing and racing rather than comfort. The boat has a sail area of 420 square feet, weighs a little less than four tons, and has an overall length of 35 feet, 10 inches.

Two Channels of Distribution

The president of the company began to market the sailboats by visiting East Coast dealers in order to evaluate their showrooms, service and marina facilities, and marketing capabilities. His next step was to persuade some of the most likely candidates to visit the factory and to evaluate the sailboats firsthand, and secondly, he offered to sell them a P/M-17 on consignment. That is, the dealers could return these boats to Port-Marine if they were unable to sell them to customers. Virtually all of the subsequent sailboats sold to the dealers were sold only after the dealers had firm orders from their customers. Thus, the dealers did not have to provide any capital to finance these sales.

In order to improve the relatively weak position of the company in this channel of distribution, the president decided to try to develop another channel. His idea was to advertise and sell directly to the final customers, and thus eliminate the dealers in these transactions. His intention was to improve the company's bargaining position with its dealers. He selected a number of the leading newspapers in the major cities in the East and placed large, four-column ads in these papers, describing the sailboats and instructing interested buyers to contact the company directly. Although this was a new approach in the sailboat industry, approximately 25 percent of the orders received in this current year was received directly from the final customer. The negative aspects of this approach are the very large advertising expenditures and the fact that the company is not staffed to operate in this way. In addition, a number of the dealers have voiced strong objections to the direct marketing approach since their customers could purchase the boats cheaper from the manufacturer than from the dealer.

Port-Marine case by James H. Sood, *Situations in Marketing* (Dallas, Texas: Business Publications, Inc., 1976), pp. 76–81. © 1976 by Business Publications, Inc.

TABLE 1 Marketing Results and Plans

	First			Present Year			Proposed Plan		
	No.	Average Price	Revenue	No.	Average Price	Revenue	No.	Average Price*	Revenue
P/M-17	20	$ 2,500	$ 50,000	120	$ 3,000	$ 360,000	240	$ 3,300	$ 792,000
P/M-29	—	—	—	—	—	—	40	20,000	800,000
P/M-34	4	35,000	140,000	20	40,000	800,000	30	44,000	1,320,000
P/M-36	2	17,500	35,000	4	20,000	80,000	4	22,000	88,000
	Total Revenue		$225,000			$1,240,000			$3,000,000

*Estimated prices to cover anticipated increases in costs.

The P/M-29

Port-Marine is also about to announce the introduction of the P/M-29, which has an interior similar to that of the P/M-34. The new boat is a motor sailer that sleeps six people in three separate compartments, is 28 feet, 9 inches long, weighs four tons and has a joined cabin space and a separate aft cabin, small galley, toilet and shower facilities, and 12 horsepower diesel engine. Because of a new construction technique the company is able to offer the boat at $20,000. The company is now concerned that the sales of this product might have an adverse effect on the sales of the P/M-34.

TABLE 2 Variable and Fixed Cost Analysis

Variable Cost Analysis

The variable production costs for labor, materials, and parts and equipment have been averaging 65 percent of the manufacturer's selling price for all boat types.

Fixed Cost Analysis

	Present Year	Estimated Next Year
Total production costs	$ 70,000	$125,000
Total production design costs	130,000	190,000
Total administration costs	50,000	75,000
Marketing costs		
Salaries	35,000	65,000
Advertising	130,000	175,000
Boat shows	45,000	60,000
Sales promotion	31,000	30,000
Travel expenses	23,000	30,000
Total marketing costs	$264,000	$360,000
Total fixed costs	$514,000	$750,000

Pricing Sailboats

There are three current ideas concerning the pricing of motor sailers. The predominant theory is that, most generally, price is a function of the overall length of the boat; however, a number of sailing people believe that the overall weight of the craft is a more accurate basis. The third group consists of those people who argue that neither of these ideas holds water, and that the price is a function of the special features and equipment. Tables 1 and 2 present data concerning the revenues and costs of the Port-Marine sailboats.

1. Assuming that the fixed costs are allocated to each boat in the same proportion as the respective revenue produced by each boat type, calculate the break-even point for each type of boat for the present year and for the coming year.
2. Assuming that the fixed costs are allocated to each boat by the estimated number of each type of boat to be produced, calculate the break-even point for each type of boat for the present year and for the coming year.
3. Evaluate the approximate impact of each of the two different channels of distribution on the pricing of the sailboats.
4. Evaluate the three methods for pricing large sailboats; by overall length, by weight, or by special features and equipment.

6

Distribution

Products may travel a long distance and through many hands in getting from the manufacturer to your door. Or they may be manufactured in your hometown and be sold directly to local residents.

Within the past week you have probably purchased items in a suburban shopping center, in a downtown shopping area, perhaps from an exclusive boutique or a giant discount store. These options for consumers do not occur by accident but rather are part of the carefully planned distribution strategies of the nation's manufacturers.

In Part 6 we discuss the remaining controllable variable in the marketing mix — distribution. Producers must make decisions about the intensity of market coverage, the types of intermediaries to be used, and how to ship products to waiting customers at a reasonable cost.

14

Channels of Distribution

1. The structure of the channel of distribution and the role that society plays in its development.
2. The distribution channel as an integral part of the firm's marketing strategy.
3. Planning and organizing a channel of distribution.
4. Guidelines for selecting distributors.
5. Sources and solutions of conflict among independent members of the channel.
6. Evaluation and control of distributors by suppliers.

The efficiency of its channel of distribution is often what separates a successful firm from an unsuccessful firm. Some companies apparently feel that if they simply manufacture a product demanded by society, it will somehow magically spread throughout the marketplace and into the hands of the consumer. Most businesses soon come to realize that they must spend as much time working with their distribution structure as they do with any other element of the firm's strategy. Channel planning is complicated by the fact that the distribution structure is often made up of several independent firms that do not necessarily follow the manufacturer's lead with respect to every pricing, promotion, or distribution decision.

CHANNELS OF DISTRIBUTION — A DEFINITION

A **channel of distribution** may be defined as "an organized network of agencies and institutions which, in combination, performs all of the activities required to link producers with users, and users with producers in order to accomplish the marketing task."[1] The channel permits the seller to locate and supply the users of its merchandise, and allows the buyer to find and obtain the products it desires.

While channels of distribution are often thought of as static networks, in reality they are dynamic, i.e., new channels are continually being established and existing ones modified. As an illustration, a manufacturer of proprietary drugs may restrict the distribution of a new suntan lotion to drugstores until it has developed the production capacity to produce enough of the product for larger markets. The manufacturer can later modify the distribution channel to include wholesalers selling to variety stores and supermarkets as well as to drugstores.

---

[1]Reavis Cox and Thomas F. Schutte, "A Look at Channel Management," *Proceedings of the American Marketing Association* (Chicago: American Marketing Association, Fall, 1969), p. 100.

It is important to point out that a new channel of distribution is normally created because both buyers and sellers need it in order to do their jobs effectively. For example, SmithKline Corporation, maker of Contac cold medicine and Sea and Ski suntan products, depends on 400 drug wholesalers and more than 35,000 drugstores to distribute its products. By contrast, Drug House, Inc., one of the nation's largest drug wholesalers, expects its supplier, Smith-Kline, to perform a number of services that assist it in selling merchandise to the retailer, such as packaging products in easy-to-handle shipping cases. Without this type of cooperation, consumer prices would be much higher.[2]

Structure of Distribution Channels

Figure 14-1 depicts the typical channels of distribution for consumer and industrial products. These examples are not meant to be all-inclusive; rather a virtually unlimited variety of distribution networks exists in the U.S.

In the consumer sector the most frequently used channels consist of a wholesaler and a retailer, or just a retailer. If there is an intermediary, such as a wholesaler, involved, this is an **indirect channel**. If no intermediary is used, then it is a **direct channel**. Some manufacturers have been successful in selling directly to final consumers. For example, both Avon and Fuller Brush have well-established sales forces that call on customers in their homes; the Singer Corporation has a large number of wholly owned retail establishments distributing its merchandise. However, these firms are the exceptions to the rule; most manufacturers do not sell directly to the consumer either because they are not large enough or because they feel that independent wholesalers and retailers can distribute their merchandise more efficiently. Finally, some consumer goods manufacturers utilize agents to sell their merchandise to wholesalers. Agents, which are discussed in detail in Chapter 15, do not take title to the goods they sell.

The industrial sector tends to have shorter channels of distribution than the consumer sector — that is, fewer independently owned firms, middlemen, between the manufacturer and the end user. At least three reasons account for the shorter channels characteristic of industrial distribution networks. First, the sale of manufactured goods frequently involves very high-priced merchandise. Normally, the higher the price, the greater the profit, and therefore the easier it is for the manufacturer to staff its own sales force. Second, some manufactured goods are so technical that most wholesalers do not have the required specialized training to sell the products effectively. Third, many manufactured goods require frequent service. Therefore, the manufacturer needs to be in direct contact with the buyer. Products such as computers, dynamometers (engine testing devices), and electrical power plant equipment are sold directly to the user.

A More Complex Illustration. Although Figure 14-1 depicts the channels of distribution for many consumer and industrial products, the channels for particular products can be more complex. As an illustration, the channel of distribu-

---

[2]*Ibid.*

FIGURE 14-1 Channels of Distribution for Consumer and Industrial Goods

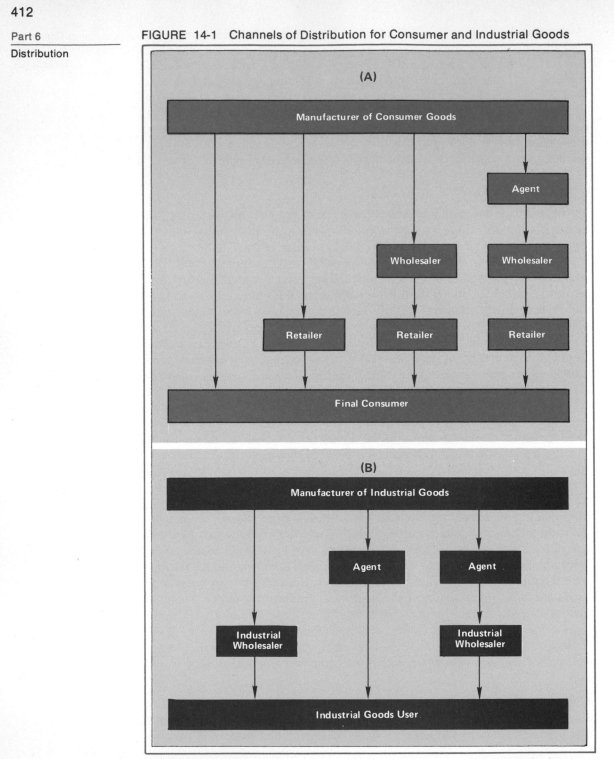

tion for magazines and paperback books may look like the network shown in Figure 14-2. Magazine publishers may find it profitable to approach consumers on a direct mail basis or to work with subscription agents. Paperback publishers

FIGURE 14-2 Channels of Distribution for Publishers of Magazines and Paperback Books

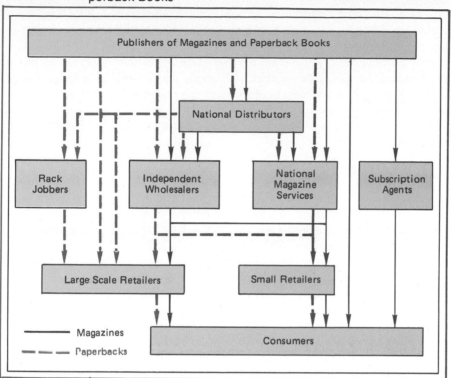

Source: Edwin H. Lewis, "Descriptions and Comparison of Channels of Distribution," in *Handbook of Modern Marketing*, edited by Victor P. Buell (New York: McGraw-Hill Book Company, 1970), Section 4, p. 6.

may use the services of a rack jobber (a specialized wholesaler who sells directly to large supermarkets) or they could distribute directly to large retailers.

While the channel network in Figure 14-2 appears quite complex, it is in fact much more efficient than the normative channels shown in Figure 14-1. Multiple channels reflect the publisher's wish to reach various market segments in the most efficient and profitable manner. In a highly competitive economy, firms constantly must seek better and often more complex ways to get their merchandise to the user.

Flows in the Channel of Distribution. So far, we have illustrated only the flow of the product in the channel. That is, as the product moves down the channel, ownership passes from the manufacturer through the intermediaries to the end user. However, more than just the product flows through the channel. In addition to money to pay for the merchandise, promotional materials and people move through the system. The manufacturer may send salespeople to call on wholesalers and retailers while simultaneously advertising directly to the final user. Also, sales figures and other market research data flow from the user back to the manufacturer. This data flow helps the manufacturer determine whether its products are selling, to whom they are selling, and possibly, why they are selling. Other types of information continually flowing between channel members concern the quantity of inventory at each point in the channel, future production runs, service requirements, and delivery schedules.

Also, *risk* has a tendency to move back and forth between channel members. To reduce its risk, the manufacturer wants the wholesalers and retailers to inventory as much merchandise as possible. Similarly, the intermediate members of the channel want the manufacturer to hold large inventories so as to reduce the risk of being stuck with goods the consumer no longer wants. The product may move very well through the channel, but if the other flows are not planned properly the channel will fail to perform as a whole. Figure 14-3 illustrates the typical flows that take place in the channel of distribution for raincoats.

Society and Distribution Networks

Several factors other than the specific needs of the buyer and seller shape the channel of distribution. These other factors stem primarily from a given society's state of economic development as well as from its political, social, and cultural objectives. A nation with a highly developed economy will necessarily have well-established travel arteries and warehousing facilities, permitting materials to flow efficiently between producers and users. In addition, it will have a highly developed banking and credit system to facilitate the exchange of title to products. In less developed economies, on the other hand, distribution channels are shorter, less formal, and are usually made up of people personally acquainted with one another. The informality of these channels along with the lack of large capital investments in the distribution structure makes it difficult for less economically developed nations to export goods and ensures that imported merchandise will be very expensive.

National objectives — whether political, social, or cultural — may not have an obvious impact on distribution, yet they are still important. A classic illustration can be found in the distribution network for Alaskan crude oil. From a distribution efficiency perspective, this oil should be shipped to Japan. However, the U.S. decided for strategic and economic reasons to reduce its volume of imported oil. Therefore, the Alaskan oil is shipped to Texas, refined, and then sent to the rest of the nation via pipelines. While this procedure reduces the U.S.'s reliance on imported oil, it is not as efficient as exporting Alaskan oil and importing oil from the Organization of Petroleum-Exporting Countries (OPEC) for use in the East and Midwest.

IMPORTANCE OF THE CHANNEL OF DISTRIBUTION

The channel of distribution is vital to the firm for two reasons: first, it is an integral part of the firm's overall marketing strategy, and second, it involves commitments on the part of each channel member.

Marketing Strategy

A business marketing strategy consists of a set of decisions in the areas of pricing, product selection, communications, market segmentation, and distribu-

FIGURE 14-3 Typical Flows in the Channel of Distribution for Raincoats

Source: Adapted from Philip Kotler, *Marketing Management: Analysis, Planning, and Control* (Englewood Cliffs, N.J.: Prentice-Hall, Inc., 1976), p. 278.

tion. For the strategy to be effective each decision must be coordinated with the others. The distribution program is designed to deliver the right product at the right time to the right customer at the lowest possible price.[3] If these objectives are not met, sales will be lost. If a consumer goes to a supermarket to purchase hamburger and the supermarket is sold out, the customer may go to another store. The first store loses the sale and, more important, runs the risk of losing future business from that customer.

It is also important that the firm's promotion program be coordinated with its distribution program. Nothing is more irritating to the marketing manager than to find that a promotional strategy for a particular product has stimulated demand that the firm is unable to meet because of early stockouts and poor inventory planning. On the other hand, physically moving the product to the market without adequate promotional support will result in excess inventories, which could force the firm to reduce the price of its product.

In some cases, distribution considerations may actually dictate what type of product the firm sells and how it prices and promotes the product. Companies such as Procter & Gamble and General Foods make excellent products that are well advertised and competitively priced. However, one of the most important factors that separates these companies from their smaller competitors is the size and effectiveness of their distribution networks. Therefore, when a new product is being considered by Procter & Gamble or General Foods, they make sure that it is compatible with their current distribution system.

Channel Member Commitments

Channel decisions often involve long-term commitments limiting the flexibility of channel members. Thus, if the firm makes a major error in its channel decisions, it may lose substantial profits before the mistake can be rectified. The following case illustrates this point:

> A leading manufacturer of toiletry products distributes exclusively through drug wholesalers and drug chains. As a result of heavy spending on promotion, advertising, and personal selling, it has built up a strong consumer demand for one of its lines and, hence, inventory commitments by dealers. Nearly two thirds of total industry sales in this line, however, are sold through nondrug trades, and this proportion is increasing. Members of these trades want the firm's products but the firm has resisted modifying its distribution strategy.[4]

Why has this toiletry company refused to modify its distribution structure? Although the answer is very complex, it revolves around two fundamental issues. First, it is often difficult to justify selling one product through a special channel of distribution while the rest of the firm's products are sold through a different channel. A salesperson can call on an account and sell several products in about the same time it would take to sell one product. Second, travel time, meal expenses, and billing expenses are nearly the same whether the salesperson is selling one or several products. Therefore, the cost per unit is much less when the firm is selling several products.

---

[3]John Magee, "The Logistics of Distribution," in Donald J. Bowersox *et al.*, *Readings in Physical Distribution Management* (New York: MacMillan, 1969), pp. 179–184.
[4]Cox and Schutte, *op. cit.*, pp. 99–100.

Businesses are also reluctant to modify their channels of distribution because consumers associate the firm's products with one channel. No one can be sure how the consumer will react when the product is taken out of one channel and placed in another. Several years ago Bulova decided to sell its watches in selected drugstores, rather than just in jewelry stores, in order to reach a larger market. Would customers change their perception of Bulova watches? Would they conclude that Bulova watches had deteriorated in quality? Deciding that it could not take this risk, Bulova introduced a new watch, the Caravelle, for drugstore distribution.

The channel of distribution performs many vital tasks for the manufacturer. Five of the most important functions of the channel of distribution are summarized in Figure 14-4. Each is discussed in more detail in Chapter 16. In principle, these functions could be performed entirely by the manufacturer as well as by a group of independent middlemen. Therefore, in thinking about how to plan and organize a channel of distribution, the first question that must be answered is why do so many manufacturers use independent intermediaries to sell their merchandise? Other questions concern channel leadership and intensity of distribution.

Use of Independent Intermediaries

There are several reasons why manufacturers generally prefer to use independent intermediaries rather than to own the channel themselves. First, most firms do not have the capital required to own the entire channel of distribution. As an illustration, General Motors has more than 18,000 independent dealers that sell and service its automobiles. If the average dealership were worth $3

FIGURE 14-4   Functions of the Channel of Distribution

Contacting	One of the most important functions of the distribution channel is contacting purchasers or potential purchasers of the product.
Sorting	By buying a large number of products in large quantities, and then dividing and rearranging them into suitable combinations for the buyer, intermediaries greatly facilitate the distribution process.
Stimulating Demand	Intermediaries help the manufacturer sell merchandise through personal selling and advertising.
Maintaining Inventory	Since marketing intermediaries, such as wholesalers and retailers, maintain inventories of the merchandise they sell, products are at all times closer to the point of purchase than they would otherwise be.
Transmitting Marketing Information	The channel of distribution serves as an excellent conduit for information flowing between the market and the manufacturer.

million, which is a conservative figure, General Motors would have to raise $54 billion to purchase all its dealers — a great deal of money even for the world's largest manufacturing corporation.

Second, most manufacturers believe that independent channel members can perform distribution functions more efficiently than they can. Very simply, most manufacturers feel that they cannot match the experience, specialization, contacts, and scale of operations of independent intermediaries. Therefore, they have come to the conclusion that it is easier for them to make money producing products and letting someone else distribute them.

Who Should Lead the Channel of Distribution?

At one point, it was felt that the question of channel leadership was unimportant — there was no need for a channel leader because the firms were independent and acted in their own best interests. However, in today's complex marketplace, the channel leadership question is important if for no other reason than coordination among channel members can reduce overall distribution costs. Let's now look at two key sources of power in the channel as well as at alternative channel leaders.

Sources of Power. The primary bases for power in the distribution channel are economic and position power.[5] Economic power manifests itself in the concentration of capital resources. The owner of capital is able to employ the best, most experienced, and most expensive management team, to hire market research personnel, and to improve communications among channel members and with the consumer. Position power stems from the location of the firm in the channel. The key consideration in terms of position power is access to markets. Small retailers and wholesalers can bring only a few customers into the channel. As a result, their position power is very weak relative to large firms.

Alternative Leaders. Since small retailers have little position or economic power, they are not candidates for channel leadership. In contrast, large manufacturers are potential leaders, although even small manufacturers can serve as channel leaders. While the limited economic power of a small firm reduces its chances for control, such a firm can assume substantial position power if it has a product in strong demand. A manufacturer — whether large or small — exercises control by offering or withholding its product from particular intermediaries. In addition, the manufacturer is the only organization in the channel in the position to develop a complete marketing program, covering such matters as product introduction, advertising and public relations strategy, and the selection of wholesalers and retailers. The manufacturer's position strength begins to slip when the product matures and competitors begin to develop many similar, if not superior, products. At this point, intermediaries are in a position to pick and choose among the manufacturers and the product lines they will handle.

A basic limitation to the channel power of even the largest manufacturers is simply that, in most circumstances, they cannot establish their own retail out-

---

[5]This section is adapted from Robert W. Little, "The Marketing Channel: Who Should Lead This Extra-Corporate Organization?" *Journal of Marketing* (January, 1970), pp. 31–38.

lets. Therefore, they must cooperate with channel intermediaries if their products are to reach the marketplace.

The large multilevel merchandisers are also candidates for channel leadership. These firms are retail-wholesale integrated organizations representing a corporate chain or some type of voluntary relationship among retailers or wholesalers. In addition to economic power, multilevel merchandisers have a great deal of position power because they control access to large markets. In fact, they can reduce the risk of new product failure by ensuring the manufacturer access to these large markets. The position power of these merchandisers is especially strong when numerous product sources are available. Almost every day we come in contact with one of these multilevel merchandisers: examples include Sears, Montgomery Ward, the May Company, Dayton-Hudson's, Federated Department Stores, and any of the numerous supermarket chains.

Differential Advantage. Unfortunately, there is no obvious or definitive answer to the question of who should lead the channel of distribution. What is important is that one organization within the channel assumes the leadership role so that products can be most efficiently brought to the marketplace. In any given channel, the entity with the greatest differential advantage will become the leader. The differential advantage of the manufacturers resides in the fact that they produce the products demanded by society; the advantage of the multilevel merchandisers is the fact that they deliver the manufacturers' products to the market. Differential advantages are usually temporary and can only be maintained through continued innovation.

Degree of Distribution

The degree of intensity of distribution refers to the relative availability of a product to the consumer. Three levels of distribution intensity are generally recognized: intensive, exclusive, and selective. **Intensive distribution** is defined as that level of distribution whereby a product is made available to the public through as many retail outlets as possible. This strategy tends to maximize the product's sales if for no other reason than the customer will be widely exposed to it. Intensive distribution, however, does mean that the manufacturer will have to employ a large sales force in order to stay in contact with the large number of intermediaries necessary to supply the market. Examples of products distributed intensively are cigarettes, candy, milk, and beer.

Exclusive distribution, the opposite of intensive distribution, is that type of distribution whereby a product is made available through one or only a few outlets in any one trading area. This strategy generally involves low distribution costs to the manufacturer since only a few salespeople are required to facilitate movement of the product to the market. It also tends to create a harmonious relationship between the middleman and the manufacturer, each of whom feels a part of the other's organization. That cooperation is essential if the product is to succeed. Illustrations of products sold via exclusive distribution are expensive watches, fine china, and sterling silver.

Of course, intensive and exclusive distribution represent the extremes on a continuum of distribution intensity — from a great many product outlets to a very few. Accordingly, **selective distribution**, located at the middle of the continuum, is that level of distribution whereby a product is sold by a number of retailers but not by all the retailers in a community that could carry it. Examples of items that are marketed selectively are television sets, dishwashers, and carpeting.

Consumer Expectations. The most important determinant of a product's intensity of distribution is where consumers expect it to be sold.[6] For example, if consumers expect to find the product only at exclusive shops in large cities, then the manufacturer would not want to have it carried by drugstores. In contrast, a product such as homogenized milk, with relatively little brand loyalty, should be sold through as many retail outlets as possible.

In Chapter 8, we classified consumer goods into three categories — convenience goods, shopping goods, and specialty goods — depending on how much effort was involved in making the purchase. Convenience goods are purchased frequently, immediately, and with a minimum of effort; shopping goods are those products for which the consumer is willing to spend a significant amount of time examining such factors as price, style, and quality before making a decision. In contrast, a specialty good is a product characterized by strong brand loyalty and for which the consumer is willing to make a special purchasing effort.

The terms convenience, specialty, and shopping may also be applied to store patronage. **Convenience stores** are those stores for which the consumer, before a need for some product arises, possesses a preference map that indicates a willingness to buy from the most accessible store. **Shopping stores** are those stores for which the consumer has not developed a complete preference map relative to the product he or she wishes to buy, thereby necessitating a search to construct such a map before purchase. Finally, those stores for which the consumer, before a need for some product arises, possesses a preference map that indicates a willingness to buy the item from a particular establishment even though it may not be the most accessible one are called **specialty stores.**[7]

By integrating the product and store definitions, we can create a classification system for predicting, based on consumer buying behavior, the type of distribution strategy that a firm will employ for any given product. Take a look at Figure 14-5. If the consumer either feels that the product is a specialty good or prefers to buy it from specialty stores, then in all probability the product will be distributed selectively or exclusively. Also, products enjoying a high degree of brand loyalty are not likely to lose sales if they are not available through a large number of retail outlets. However, products for which consumers have little brand loyalty and that are not likely to be purchased on a store loyalty basis, will probably require intensive distribution. The manufacturer simply cannot count on consumers going out of their way to purchase the product.

Marketing Mix. The second important variable affecting the intensity of distribution includes the other elements of the marketing mix — product, price,

---

[6]This section is adapted from Burton Marcus *et al., Modern Marketing* (New York: Random House, 1975), pp. 548–551.

[7]Louis P. Bucklin, ''Retail Strategy and the Classification of Consumer Goods,'' *Journal of Marketing* (October, 1962), p. 53.

FIGURE 14-5 Cross Classification of Types of Products and Stores

Stores / Products	Convenience Stores	Shopping Stores	Specialty Stores
Convenience Goods	**Intensive Distribution** Consumer purchases most readily available product from nearest store.	**Selective Distribution** Consumer indifferent to brand but shops several stores to obtain the best deal.	**Selective Distribution** Consumer prefers specific store but does not care which brand is purchased.
Shopping Goods	**Intensive Distribution** Consumer purchases from assortment at closest store.	**Selective Distribution** Consumer looks at both brand and store.	**Selective Distribution** Consumer prefers specific store and examines the several brands that the store carries.
Specialty Goods	**Selective Distribution** Consumer purchases favorite brand from closest store.	**Selective or Exclusive Distribution** Consumer has strong preference for product but looks among several stores to obtain the best deal.	**Exclusive Distribution** Consumer has a strong preference for both store and product.

Source: Adapted from Louis P. Bucklin, "Retail Strategy and the Classification of Consumer Goods," *Journal of Marketing* (October, 1962), pp. 53–54.

and communications.[8] How often is the product purchased? How is it used? What are its service requirements? Will a fashion change affect sales? All these questions have an impact on distribution intensity. As an illustration, a product such as a television, for which the dealer is normally required to maintain a service department, is generally sold via selective distribution. Intensive distribution would not be appropriate because the number of retailers capable of servicing the product is limiited; exclusive distribution would not be suitable because of insufficient brand loyalty. Expensive watches, also requiring a service department on the part of the retailer, are usually distributed exclusively through well-established stores. A community of 500,000 rarely has more than three authorized Rolex watch retailers, while it may have as many as 50 Timex dealers.

The price the manufacturer charges middlemen often determines what type of distribution outlets will carry the product. The higher the retailer's profit margin, the more ancillary product services the retailer can be expected to perform. Retailers with exclusive distribution rights for a given product usually expect to have a high markup or profit margin on each unit sold in order to offset the costs of high-priced salespeople and the service facilities. However, products distributed intensively have a much smaller markup because customers usually do not need the assistance of salespeople to make the purchase. Items sold in a self-service (convenience) store provide a classic example.

As we have indicated, promotion and channel decisions also affect each other. In the case of intensive distribution, the retailer is expected to do little more than provide display or shelf space for the product. Any mass-media advertising, therefore, is usually paid for by the manufacturer. Here, the manufacturer is said to "pull" the product through the channel of distribution by creating a general need or demand for the product. As an illustration, many retailers prefer not to sell cigarettes since they are not very profitable. However, the convenience store retailer not carrying cigarettes knows that consumers may go elsewhere to purchase not only the cigarettes but also other, more profitable items. In contrast, the margins for products distributed exclusively are high enough for the retailer to provide sales support or a "push" strategy, as well as some local advertising.

Because of the important role played by channel members, we must now look at the process of selecting them.

SELECTING CHANNEL MEMBERS

The selection of members of the channel of distribution is a critical decision for the firm. It is important to realize that a manufacturer need not use the same channel of distribution to reach all the users of its product. Some key factors that should be considered when determining which intermediaries to

---

[8]This material is adapted from Bruce Mallen, "Selecting Channels of Distribution for Consumer Products," in Victor P. Buell, *Handbook of Modern Marketing* (New York: McGraw-Hill Book Company, 1970), pp. 4–24, 4–26. See also Leo V. Aspinwall, "The Marketing Characteristics of Goods" and "Parallel Systems of Promotion and Distribution" in *Marketing Classics*, edited by Ben M. Enis and Keith Cox (3d ed.; Boston: Allyn and Bacon, Inc., 1977), pp. 295–314.

include in the channel of distribution include financial and personnel resources, competition, and availability of distributors.[9]

Financial and Personnel Resources

The firm's own financial resources may limit the range of available distribution network options. A manufacturer with limited capital usually will have to employ an intermediary to sell the product to the consumer regardless of whether it is the most profitable way to distribute the product. As an illustration, the Smithville Company, a medium-size manufacturer of dinnerware and coffee mugs, adopted a channel strategy of utilizing manufacturers' representatives to call on its small suburban retailers and using its own salespersons to call on the larger urban accounts. Although the firm wanted to use an in-house sales force for all of its accounts, it could not do so economically for those accounts with only limited sales potential. In addition, the greater the resources of the manufacturer, the more likely it will be able to exercise control over channel intermediaries through the use of special promotion campaigns, displays, and mass advertising. Similarly, if the manufacturer does not have the marketing expertise to distribute a new product, a middleman will probably be utilized.

Competition

How do competing firms distribute their products? Do they utilize intensive, selective, or exclusive distribution? Do they employ outside intermediaries or do they perform the distribution function solely with company personnel? These are important questions not because the competition is always right, but because the firm may have to change its distribution policies in response to some change in the distribution practices of its competitors. A few years ago General Electric decided that it would no longer attempt to control the retail prices of its small electric appliances and that, instead, it would sell them through mass-merchandise outlets. This change in distribution strategy forced other appliance manufacturers to reexamine their distribution policies in order to remain competitive with GE.

Availability of Distributors

Many manufacturers face the problem of convincing distributors to carry their products. If distributors do not believe in the product, they will not be willing to invest the time and money necessary to sell it. Distributors may also carry a competitive product with a strong sales record. Many distributors do not like to jeopardize relationships with their important suppliers by starting to sell competing products.

Assuming the manufacturer does have a high quality product, how can it persuade the best distributors to carry the merchandise? One method is to offer incentives, such as a training program for the distributor's sales force, including

---

[9]The following sections on selecting channel members drawn from material in Roger M. Pegram, "Selecting and Evaluating Distributors," *Studies in Business Policy*, No. 116 (New York: The Conference Board, 1965).

transportation and living expenses. Another way is to provide free consulting advice in the areas of purchasing, inventory control, order processing and handling, and financial management. For example, the Norton Company, which manufactures industrial abrasives, has designed a cost accounting and profitability measuring system now used by virtually all of its distributors.

Manufacturers can also encourage distributors to carry their products by offering advertising and sales promotion assistance, often in the form of free promotional literature or point-of-purchase displays. They can also provide outright advertising grants or cooperative advertising programs to assist a distributor's own advertising program. A manufacturer that is unsuccessful in attracting a distributor can either sell the product directly or utilize a distributor with less immediate potential.

Selection Criteria

Manufacturers often find it difficult to formulate a set of specific procedures to guide the selection of channel intermediaries. An executive of a nonferrous metal company offers the following reason:

> Among general-line metal distributors, there are no two alike. This is because they have different managements, operate in different localities, and have different capitalizations, different patterns of business, and different numbers and grades of personnel. There are even differences between distributors of similar size and with similar markets because the different kind of effort they expend will produce dissimilar patterns of business. Because of these wide differences, we cannot reduce selection to a uniform, detailed procedure of a routine nature.[10]

Although personal judgment is helpful, it is also necessary to evaluate each prospective distributor in relation to a uniform set of criteria. Without these criteria it is difficult, if not impossible, to evaluate one potential distributor against another. Figure 14-6 presents a list of 21 questions which should be asked when selecting a distributor. Five potential problem areas are worthy of special attention here.

Credit and Finance. Virtually all manufacturing firms look closely at the financial positions of prospective distributors. Financially shaky distributors will not be able to commit the resources required to maintain necessary inventory levels or sales programs. Even worse, a distributor could go out of business, thereby forcing the manufacturer to look for a new intermediary. Manufacturers are also concerned about whether distributors, or resellers, are in a position to extend credit to their accounts. The ability to offer credit is particularly important in the construction industry where such credit is a common trade practice. A Dun & Bradstreet credit rating is the usual source for determining a prospective distributor's financial position.

Distributor Sales Strength. Does the prospective distributor have a strong enough sales force to ensure that the product lives up to its market potential? The firm selecting a distributor must be concerned with both the size and the expertise of the distributor's sales staff. How many full-time salespeople does the distributor employ? Does the distributor have sufficient inside or telephone

---

[10]*Ibid.*, p. 21.

FIGURE 14-6   Checklist for Selecting a Distributor

1. What is the caliber of the head of the distributor's organization? Does the firm have the respect and confidence of the community?
2. Does the distributor carry any conflicting lines or products?
3. Does it have a well-trained, smoothly running organization?
4. Is it adequately financed?
5. Is it making money?
6. Does the distributor have plant equipment and facilities for handling the line?
7. Does it have an adequate and well-informed sales team?
8. Does it have other products that fit in and harmonize with our line?
9. Does the distributor have a sales training program? Does it allow suppliers to participate in its training programs?
10. What is the average educational background of its personnel?
11. Are its personnel marketing-minded? Do they have the interest and ability to promote our product?
12. Is the distributor willing to appoint one executive to concentrate on our line and be responsible for it? Who would that person be and what are the qualifications of that individual?
13. Does the distributor cover its territory thoroughly?
14. Does it penetrate through to customers, executives, engineers, and operating people, or does it cover only the purchasing agents?
15. Will the distributor accept a quota and make a reasonable effort to meet it?
16. Will it accept and use our promotional materials in accordance with our marketing program?
17. Does the distributor have the courage to maintain reasonable margins when times are tough?
18. Does it have a good setup for giving continuing service to customers in order to maintain customer goodwill for our product?
19. Will the distributor welcome our executives for conferences and sales meetings?
20. Will the distributor give us the names and home addresses of its inside and outside salespeople so we can quickly send information to them?
21. If our line is small, is the distributor willing to feature it and push it?

Source: Adapted from Ferdinand F. Mauser, *Modern Marketing Management: An Integrated Approach* (New York: McGraw-Hill Book Co., 1961), p. 338.

staff to back up the outside sales force? Although measuring the quality of the distributor's salespeople is not easy, it is possible to evaluate their formal technical training. Since it is the distributor's salespeople who actually sell the product to the end user or to another reseller, the manufacturer wants them to be skilled professionals, not just order-takers.

Inventory and Warehouse Practices. The manufacturer also wants to be sure that the distributor is willing to carry enough inventory to meet customer demand. Before signing a distributor agreement, many manufacturers require prospective dealers to indicate how large a product inventory they would be willing to carry. A second concern is whether warehousing and other distribution facilities are adequate to handle the merchandise, especially when the product involved requires special handling. The Coors Beer Company insists that its distributors use refrigerated trucks to keep their beer as fresh as possible. These trucks sell for as much as $36,000 each.

Management. Does the prospective distributor enjoy a good reputation in the community? Many problems can develop when a firm uses unethical distributors, as shown in the following case involving two farm equipment distributors. One of the dealers, thinking that the other was selling products in its territory, hired a private detective to break into the competitor's place of business and to destroy any records found on the premises. After four such break-ins in one month, the burglar was caught, resulting in the cancellation of the distributorship for the first dealer as well as in lost sales for the farm equipment manufacturer.

The second management consideration, as most manufacturers realize, is that in the long run sales are directly related to the management ability of the distributor. Although managerial skill is difficult to judge, it is possible to look at a distributor's ability to plan distribution strategies, to control inventory levels, to set objectives, and to train employees.

Because there are differences in managerial skills, there are bound to be areas of both conflict and cooperation among members of the channel of distribution. Let's turn attention to the problem areas, and some of the techniques available for resolving conflicts.

CONFLICT AND COOPERATION

Some business executives feel that any form of conflict among channel members is dysfunctional. According to this line of reasoning, a channel characterized by cooperation is more efficient than one characterized by discord. In contrast, other people — including the noted economist John Kenneth Galbraith — feel that a lack of conflict breeds complacency, making it more difficult for the system to accept innovation.[11] Regardless of which belief is held, the fact remains that a considerable amount of conflict normally does exist within a distribution channel. Figure 14-7 presents several typical examples of channel conflict.

Three types of channel conflict are generally recognized:

1. **Horizontal Conflict.** Horizontal conflict is between two marketing institutions at the same level in the channel. An example is competition between two supermarkets.
2. **Intertype Conflict.** This type of channel conflict results from the use of different types of distribution outlets in the same market area, such as a specialty store, a department store, and a mail order outlet.
3. **Vertical Conflict.** Vertical conflict is among members of the same channel of

---

[11]See Larry J. Rosenberg and Louis W. Stern, "Toward the Analysis of Conflict in Distribution Channels: A Descriptive Model," *Journal of Marketing* (October, 1970), pp. 40–46; and Michael M. Pearson, "The Conflict Performance Assumption," *Journal of Purchasing* (February, 1973), pp. 57–69.

FIGURE 14-7 Illustrations of Channel Conflict

> A manufacturer promises an exclusive territory to a retailer in return for the retailer's "majority effort" to generate business in the area. Sales increase nicely, but the manufacturer believes it is due more to population growth in the area than to the effort of the store owner, who is spending too much time on the golf course.

> A fast-food franchisor promises "expert promotional assistance" to retailers as partial justification for the franchising fee. One of the retailers believes that the help is anything but expert and that the benefits do not correspond with what was promised.

> A franchisor insists that franchisees should maintain a minimum stock of certain items that are regularly promoted throughout the area. Arguments arise as to whether the franchisor's recommendations constitute a threat. For their part, the franchisees are particularly concerned about protecting their trade name.

> Many major oil companies market a line of "private label" TBA items — tires, batteries, and accessories — in addition to their petroleum products. By various means, they attempt to urge their service station operators to promote the private label. The selling of competing national brands is discouraged, although it cannot be prevented. However, the station operator may see competing brands as easier to sell and perhaps more profitable. Because of heavier advertising, national brands are better known and more attractive to the consumer.

Source: The first three examples are taken from Robert E. Weigand and Hilda C. Wasson, "Arbitration in the Marketing Channel," *Business Horizons* (October, 1974), pp. 39–40. The fourth example is from William P. Dommermuth, "Profiting from Distribution Conflicts," *Business Horizons* (December, 1976), p. 6.

distribution. Disagreement between a manufacturer and a wholesaler over inventory policies is an example of vertical conflict.[12]

The following discussion will center on vertical conflict. We begin by analyzing three common areas of vertical conflicts and look at sources of conflict, sources of cooperation, and methods of resolving channel conflicts.

Sources of Conflict

Figure 14-8 lists the kinds of conflict that frequently occur between manufacturers and retailers. Three of the most important sources of conflict in the channel of distribution include goals, roles, and the acts of exchange.

Goals. In a distribution channel some general goals may be accepted by all members, such as delivering the product at a competitive price to the consumer. However, each firm in the channel has its own specific goals, which are a function of the problems and opportunities that it faces. Unfortunately, the

---

[12]Joseph C. Palmountain, Jr., *The Politics of Distribution* (Cambridge, Mass.: Harvard University Press, 1955), pp. 24–57.

FIGURE 14-8 Areas of Conflict Between Retailer and Manufacturer

Issue	Manufacturer Perspective	Retailer Perspective
Price	Retailer demands low price.	Manufacturer demands high price.
Inventory	Retailer will not carry adequate inventory.	Manufacturer wants the retailer to carry excess inventory.
Payment terms	Retailer is often delinquent in payments.	Manufacturer expects immediate payment.
Advertising	Retailer does not promote product.	Manufacturer's cooperative advertising budget is inadequate.
Product line	Retailer carries only established products.	Manufacturer wants the retailer to carry slow-moving, unprofitable products.
Competition	Retailer insists that the manufacturer not sell to competing retailers.	Manufacturer sells to more than one retailer in a competitive area.
Market research	Retailer does not provide timely market information to the manufacturer.	Manufacturer does not do adequate market research.

goals of individual channel members often are incompatible. The manufacturer may wish to expand the sales of a new product while the retailer refuses to invest the required capital needed to sell additional products.

Roles. Each firm in the distribution system has several roles to play, depending upon its position. These roles involve such decision areas as (1) the range of products provided to the market, (2) target markets served, and (3) services rendered to other channel members. Conflict develops whenever channel members cannot agree on the assignment of roles ("who does what"), or when a particular channel member does not perform as expected. An example of the first source of conflict can be found in the case of a manufacturer who expects its retailers not to sell competitive products while the retailers feel that such sales are essential to their business.

The Act of Exchange. At times, suppliers and manufacturers look upon resellers as customers who must be persuaded, manipulated, or even fooled. According to the marketing concept, it makes no difference whether the reseller is perceived as a customer or a channel member. Regardless, resellers must be assisted and served at a reasonable profit. Unfortunately, much conflict exists within the channel because the suppliers want to get as high a price as possible for their product while the reseller (buyer) attempts to bargain for

Your college or university is a kind of distribution channel — **you** are the consumer and the professor is the producer or service vendor trying to provide you with a certain set of knowledge. Most of the time, the relationship works and is mutually beneficial. When it doesn't work, the reason may be due to conflicting goals, roles, or expectations with respect to performance evaluation.

Goals. Unfortunately, the goals of the professor may not be the goals of the student. The professor's goal may be to present information to the student in an understandable, interesting, and challenging manner. In contrast, the student's goal may be to get through the course with a minimum expenditure of energy. Or the professor may want to devote time and energy to research, not to teaching, but the student wants to learn as much as possible about the subject.

Roles. Just as conflicts arise when manufacturers and wholesalers disagree on their roles, conflicts can also arise when students and professors disagree on their roles. The professor may see his or her role as one of stimulating thoughtful discussion, providing a good set of lecture notes, or helping students with research projects. The professor may view the student as a colleague in the quest for knowledge or simply as a notetaker or dunce. The student may want the professor to play the role of classroom entertainer, unapproachable guardian of wisdom, or concerned mentor. In turn, the student may see his or her own role as one of dutifully recording all utterances of the oracle, of conducting as much independent inquiry as possible, or of just doing enough work to "get by."

The Exchange Act. The evaluation of the student by the teacher represents a type of exchange or transaction. The method of evaluation may in itself cause conflict. The professor might select multiple choice examinations and a term paper for evaluative purposes, while the student might feel that an essay exam would be better. In addition, conflict can arise if the student believes that the professor has not evaluated work fairly.

Most students and professors realize that they have more to gain through cooperation than through conflict. When voluntary cooperation does break down, most colleges and universities have some formal arbitration system for resolving disputes. A third party arbitrator such as a dean or a department chairperson is often appointed. The U.S. Supreme Court has ruled that if a college or university provides due process for the appeal of student grievances and if there is no illegal discrimination, then the courts will not interfere in the arbitrator's decision.

Are you doing all you can to facilitate the exchange?

Marketing & You

the lowest possible price. The conflict in the exchange process is normally resolved through the negotiation process.

Solutions to Channel Conflict

One common solution to a problem, or conflict, within the channel is for the parties involved simply to discontinue their working relationship. As indicated above, this resolution often leads to reduced profits for both parties as well as to dissatisfied customers, who must now search out new ways to obtain the merchandise they want. When long-term service commitments are involved, the situation becomes even more complex.

An alternative to severing a business relationship is to resolve the conflict through litigation. Here, a fair and impartial court attempts to determine whether one of the parties has been harmed and, if so, what the remedy should be. Although litigation leads to a final public decision, it is expensive and time consuming. In addition, the firms involved in the dispute often find it difficult to work together again after a tough court battle. The alternative to litigation is arbitration.

What Is Arbitration? Arbitration is a process of negotiation and conflict resolution whereby a third party is brought into the dispute to act as an impartial judge. This judge or arbitrator determines not only whether certain items of evidence should be admitted into the proceedings but also who is the party at fault and what should be done to resolve the dispute. At the arbitration hearing, both parties agree that they will abide by the arbitrator's decision.

An Illustration of Arbitration. Carling Brewing Company has a very unusual and forward-thinking arbitration agreement with its distributors. When a dispute between Carling and a distributor develops, the distributor submits the facts in the case to the president of Carling. If the president fails to resolve the conflict to the distributor's satisfaction within ten days, the distributor's case is submitted to a three-person arbitration panel. What is unique about the Carling system is that while arbitration is optional to the distributor, it is not to Carling. If the distributor selects arbitration rather than, for example, litigation, Carling has no alternative; it must submit to such arbitration. The rules to be used in the arbitration proceedings are those of the American Arbitration Association. Carling and the distributor each select one arbitrator; the third member of the arbitration panel is selected jointly. Although it is preferable to resolve channel conflicts informally and without a special hearing, arbitration is a reasonable alternative to litigation for many channel problems.[13]

Voluntary Cooperation

Although we have discussed channel conflict at length, there is a great deal of voluntary cooperation within the channel. Most channel members realize that they have more to gain by cooperating with one another than by fighting. In truth, all members have a common goal, namely, to sell a product; only in

---

[13]Robert E. Weigand and Hilda C. Wasson, "Arbitration in the Marketing Channel," *Business Horizons* (October, 1974), pp. 39–40.

the division of the profit do they have a potential conflict. Thus most channel participants eventually come to the conclusion that they would be better off increasing the size of the profit pie than bickering over the size of each member's piece.

Suppliers can assist distributors in many ways and, thereby, promote voluntary cooperation within the channel. Many suppliers provide missionary salespeople (salespeople who are involved more in building goodwill for the firm rather than in directly generating sales) to assist the distributor in selling the product. These missionary salespeople spend most of their time training the distributor's salespeople on how to sell the product more effectively. Missionary salespeople will also occasionally make a joint sales call with a distributor's sales staff to assist the distributor in landing especially large or important accounts.

A second form of cooperation emanating from the supplier is promotional assistance. Suppliers often provide free sales promotion literature to the reseller in the hope of increasing product sales. Many suppliers also feature a cooperative advertising program (see Chapter 10) whereby they agree to fund a certain percentage of the reseller's advertising efforts. Finally, many suppliers sponsor sales contests, awarding prizes ranging from token gifts to major, all-expense-paid trips to those members of the reseller's sales force who have sold the greatest amount of the supplier's product.

The supplier can also assist channel members by providing consulting services at little or no cost. Typically, the larger the supplier, the more services it can provide. Specific consulting services include estimating sales quotas by territory and type of customer, studying market potential, and offering inventory planning and control. Other areas where the large supplier might offer assistance are accounting, finance, office procedures, and site selection.

It is important to understand that this cooperation is not a one-way street; all members of the channel must see themselves as working with one another for a common goal — meeting the needs of the buyer profitably. Some specific ways that channel members can cooperate with one another are listed in Figure 14-9.

EVALUATION AND CONTROL OF DISTRIBUTORS

What factors should suppliers consider when evaluating the performance of the independent resellers in their distribution channel? What can the supplier do to control the channel of distribution? Suppliers must answer these questions if they are to have an effective distribution system.

Evaluation of Independent Distributors

By far, the single most important variable in the evaluation of distributors is sales performance. If the distributor is able to meet sales objectives consistently, the supplier will want to continue their relationship. In evaluating sales performance, the supplier may wish to analyze sales to the distributor or the sales of the distributor's product to its customers. These two sales figures are rarely identical and may be quite different.

FIGURE 14-9   Methods of Cooperation

 1. Cooperative advertising allowances.
 2. Payments for interior displays including shelf-extenders, dump displays, "A" locations, aisle displays, etc.
 3. Allowances for a variety of warehousing functions.
 4. Payments for window display space, plus installation costs.
 5. Detail people who check inventory, put up stock, set up complete promotions, etc.
 6. Demonstrators.
 7. Free goods.

 8. In-store and window display material.
 9. Mail-in premium offers to consumer.
10. Preticketing.
11. Automatic reorder systems.
12. Delivery costs to individual stores of large retailers.
13. Liberal return privileges.
14. Contributions to favorite charities of store personnel.

15. Contributions to special store anniversaries.
16. Training retail salespeople.
17. Payments for store fixtures.
18. Payments for new store costs, for more improvements, including painting.
19. Payments of part of salary of retail salespeople.
20. Time spent on actual selling floor by manufacturer, salespeople.
21. Inventory price adjustments.
22. Store name mention in manufacturer's advertising.

Source: Edward B. Weiss, "How Much of a Retailer Is the Manufacturer?" reprinted with permission from the July 21, 1958, issue of *Advertising Age*, p. 68. Copyright 1958 by Crain Communications, Inc.

Suppliers analyze sales figures by comparing (1) the distributor's historical sales volume with current sales volume, (2) the performance of different resellers, and (3) the actual sales figures with previously established sales quotas.[14]

Historical Sales Trends. The analysis of historical sales trends includes looking at the distributor's current sales in contrast with sales in the prior time period as well as comparing current sales with sales of one year earlier. In making such comparisons, the distributor is often asked to break down sales by product or product class, by type of customer, and by customer industries. Figure 14-10 shows the procedures used by Kimberly-Clark to analyze each of its resellers on both a monthly and quarterly basis.

Comparison of Resellers' Sales. Many suppliers attempt to evaluate the performance of a reseller by comparing the sales performance of each reseller with the sales of all other resellers. One technique is to compute the average sales volume for all the firm's distributors and then to compare each distributor's performance with the average distributor. This comparison can be done

[14]Pegram, *op. cit.*, pp. 109–114.

FIGURE 14-10   Reports of Distributor Sales Issued by the Kimberly-Clark
Corporation

> The following periodic sales tabulations are provided as a statistical basis for Kimberly-Clark Corporation's evaluations of distributors performed by their salesmen and regional field sales managers:
>
> **1.** Monthly to each Kimberly-Clark territory salesman and his regional field sales manager, a report of all Kimberly-Clark sales to merchants for his sales territory broken down by merchant branch house, by delivery destination, by product grade; and showing for each breakdown the pounds shipped for the current month, the pounds shipped for the previous year-to-date vs. current year-to-date and the net dollars invoiced for the previous year-to-date vs. current year-to-date.
>
> **2.** Quarterly to each Kimberly-Clark merchant, his Kimberly-Clark territory salesman, and the regional field sales manager, a report of all Kimberly-Clark sales to that merchant branch house, broken down by product grade, and showing for each breakdown, the pounds sold to (that merchant) for the previous year-to-date vs. current year-to-date, and the net dollars invoice for the previous year-to-date vs. current year-to-date.

Source: Roger M. Pegram, "Selecting and Evaluating Distributors," *Studies in Business Policy*, No. 116 (New York: The Conference Board, 1965), p. 109.

using a variety of sales data, including total sales, sales by type of product, and rate of sales growth. A second approach requires that the supplier evaluate each distributor's sales performance with the average performance of the supplier's best distributors — usually those in the top 10 percent. Most firms using these techniques break down the data into sales regions; they also distribute the results to their own sales staff at the end of the analysis. Doing so helps the supplier's salespeople identify the distributors in their areas most in need of assistance.

Sales Quotas. Suppliers should be sure that their sales expectations for distributors are reasonable. Quotas can be expressed as total units sold, total dollar revenues, or market share. Depending on the sophistication of the supplier, quotas can be set for a line of merchandise or even for individual products. The supplier then evaluates the distributor by comparing actual performance to the sales quota. It is also useful to look at how successful the other distributors have been in meeting their quotas when evaluating any particular distributor.

Other Evaluation Factors. As indicated previously, if a distributor is generally living up to expectations, the supplier is not likely to spend much time evaluating the distributor's sales performance. However, this may be a mistake; close evaluation of some other important factors or variables could enable the supplier to help the distributor increase sales or avoid potential problems.

These other evaluative factors are the same factors a supplier looks at when selecting a new distributor. As an example, a distributor lacking a well-trained sales force will soon begin to experience difficulty selling the product. In the same way, a distributor in a weak financial position may not be able to borrow enough money to maintain inventory at required levels. Other factors include the quality and type of competitive products the distributor carries, the distributor's overall management ability, and inventory and warehouse procedures.

Control of the Distribution Channel

Ideally, no entity in the channel should have to worry about "controlling" the other channel members: all members somehow, magically, agree on the mission of the channel, and the various distribution activities are allocated among channel members without conflict or disagreement. The opposite of this situation is coercion; i.e., the major power sources within the channel require the other members to cooperate with their policies or run the risk of losing future business. Some large national retailers have been accused of wielding this type of power over small distributors that sell virtually all their merchandise to the national retailer. Several other ways of controlling the channel are discussed below.

Territorial Restrictions. The supplier adopting a selective or exclusive distribution structure can more easily control the distributor's activities. If the supplier sells through every possible outlet, the distributor will not feel like a partner in the distribution system. In contrast, the more exclusive the distribution structure, the more the reseller will value the relationship with the supplier. As a result, the reseller will be more willing to cooperate with any reasonable requests made by the supplier.

Promotion. Suppliers can control the activities of their resellers through the type and amount of promotional assistance they provide. If suppliers want a reseller to advertise the product, they can offer the reseller a cooperative advertising allowance. The reseller enjoys using advertising that is paid for in part or in total by someone else. A second type of promotional control is the literature and promotional layout material provided by suppliers to resellers. This material is designed by professional advertising people to present a supplier's product in the best possible light. By providing attractive display and other promotional materials, the supplier is able to control how the product is presented to the final consumer.

Pricing. Some suppliers feel they must control the price of their product at each level in the distribution channel. At one time, the fair trade price mechanism accomplished this objective. Although fair trade pricing has had a long history, it was never really successful in controlling prices, and Congress repealed the fair trade legislation in 1977.[15] Under the fair trade legislation, suppliers could control prices by simply refusing to do business with distributors who did not adopt their pricing scheme. Although this is still done by some firms, it is no longer legal. The courts have consistently ruled that once title passes from the supplier to the reseller, the supplier has no right to tell the distributor how to price the products.

The only legal way for suppliers to control prices is to persuade the other channel members that it is in their best interest to adopt the suggested price

---

[15]For more information on fair trade laws, see James C. Johnson and Louis E. Boone, "Farewell to Fair Trade," *Business Topics* (Spring, 1976), pp. 22–26.

schedule. The suppliers can reinforce their suggestions by advertising the product at a specified price and by attaching a price ticket to the product. However, suppliers cannot force resellers to accept a given pricing strategy.

Services and Delivery of Merchandise. Some suppliers try to control their distributors by providing additional services to firms willing to accept their control. Such services may involve assistance in promotional planning, credit practices, inventory control procedures, or even more rapid delivery from the supplier. While they may be effective tools to "whip" the distributors into line, they are also probably illegal. The Robinson-Patman Act, discussed in detail in Chapter 3, makes it illegal to charge different prices to different buyers for products or services of similar grade or quality. According to judicial interpretation of this law, suppliers providing inventory control assistance to one retailer must provide a similar service to their other customers.

While suppliers can try to control the activities of their distributors, they cannot do so through coercive methods. In the short run, the supplier may be able to bully small resellers; in the long run, this strategy will lead to lawsuits and treble-damage penalties.

summary points

1. Channels of distribution permit sellers to locate and supply the users of their merchandise, and allow buyers to find and obtain the products they desire.

2. Channels of distribution in the industrial sector tend to be shorter than those in the consumer sector.

3. In addition to product and title flows, four other flows occur in the channel of distribution — payment, promotion, information, and risk.

4. A nation's level of economic development will affect commercial distribution networks.

5. The firm's distribution strategy is an integral part of its overall marketing strategy.

6. Channel-of-distribution decisions often involve long-term commitments that do not permit much flexibility.

7. Independent intermediaries tend to be used because manufacturers lack the capital and expertise to perform distribution functions themselves.

8. Who leads the distribution channel is a function of the economic and position power of each channel member.

9. The most important determinant of the intensity of a product's distribution is consumer expectation. A second determinant is the overall marketing strategy used to sell the product.

10. In selecting members of a channel of distribution, the firm must analyze its own financial and human resources, the way in which competitors distribute their products, and the availability of distributors.

11. Important selection criteria include the credit and financial situation of potential distributors, their sales strength, their inventory and warehouse practices, and their management abilities.

12. Three of the most important sources of conflict within the channel of distribution involve goals, roles, and the price of the product.

13. Arbitration offers several important advantages in resolving disputes among channel members.

14. When evaluating a distributor, it is important to look at historical sales trends, comparisons of various distributor sales patterns, and the distributor's success in meeting sales quotas.

15. Manufacturers can control the policies of their distributors through territorial restrictions, the amounts and types of promotional assistance, and suggested list prices.

1. What is a channel of distribution? Describe it in your own words.
2. The industrial sector of the economy tends to have shorter distribution channels than the consumer sector. Why?
3. Analyze the various flows within the channel of distribution. Are these flows significantly different for consumer goods than for industrial goods?
4. Why is the firm's channel of distribution strategy so vital to its marketing efforts? Is the distribution strategy any more important than other aspects of the firm's marketing strategy?
5. Why do so many manufacturers use independent intermediaries to distribute their products? Is there any reason to believe that manufacturers will use fewer independent intermediaries in the future?
6. Who do you feel should lead the channel of distribution? In the future, will it be more or less important for the channel to have a leader?
7. What is meant by intensity of distribution? How important is this concept to the marketing executive?
8. What factors should be considered when selecting channel members? Is the relative importance of these factors likely to change in the future?
9. What are the major sources of conflict in the distribution channel?
10. In the future, do you think that arbitration will play a more important role in resolving disputes within the channel of distribution?
11. What factors should the supplier consider when evaluating independent distributors? Under what conditions would a distributor who is meeting a sales quota be terminated by the supplier?
12. What tools does a supplier have available to control independent members of the channel? Which of these tools are the most effective? Explain.

15 Retailing

We often think of retail stores as "mom-and-pop" operations; in reality, however, some chains such as Sears and Montgomery Ward generate sales in excess of several billion dollars each year. These are professionally managed firms that utilize very sophisticated marketing strategies. In an effort to compete with national chains, many smaller retail and wholesale businesses also employ college-trained marketing specialists and have become sophisticated in inventory control, advertising, marketing strategies, and buying.

One of the most exciting aspects of retailing is that it provides such a wide variety of opportunities. Students with an entrepreneurial interest should take note of the fact that 85 percent of retail establishments in the United States are operated by an individual or firm with but a single store. In contrast, for students who look forward to careers with large corporations, Table 15-1 shows that in 1978 the 20 largest retailers in the United States employed almost two million people and had sales in excess of $120 billion. We begin our discussion of retailing by examining the different types of retail institutions.

CLASSIFICATION OF RETAILERS

Four major types of retail institutions worthy of mention include specialty stores, supermarkets and convenience stores, general merchandise outlets, and nonstore retailing. Each of these four types has developed a unique marketing strategy.

Specialty Stores

Specialty stores concentrate their efforts on meeting a particular market need. Often, they sell only one type of product, such as clothing, jewelry, or furniture. Specialty stores are usually small owner-managed businesses. However, there are many examples of medium-sized, limited-line chains, such as Hughes, Hatcher, and Suffrin in Detroit, a chain of more than 40 men's stores. Successful specialty stores compete effectively against giant department and discount stores because they have a better feel for the needs of their particular market segments and because they can adjust more quickly to

TABLE 15-1 Twenty Largest Retailing Companies (Ranked by Sales), 1978

Rank	Company	Sales ($000)	Net Income ($000)	Net Income as Percent of Sales	Number of Employees
1	Sears, Roebuck (Chicago)	$ 17,946,336	$ 921,523	5.1%	430,000
2	Safeway Stores (Oakland)	12,550,569	146,118	1.2	144,243
3	K Mart (Troy, Michigan)	11,812,810	343,706	2.9	213,347
4	JCPenney (New York)	10,845,000	276,000	2.5	211,000
5	Kroger (Cincinnati)	7,828,071	84,596	1.1	63,539
6	Great Atlantic & Pacific Tea (Montvale, N.J.)	7,288,577	4,791	0.1	81,000
7	F. W. Woolworth (New York)	6,102,800	130,300	2.1	142,579
8	Federated Department Stores (Cincinnati)	5,404,621	197,896	3.7	115,000
9	Montgomery Ward (Chicago)	5,013,514	119,367	2.4	107,700
10	Lucky Stores (Dublin, California)	4,658,409	80,400	1.7	55,000
11	Winn-Dixie Stores (Jacksonville)	4,444,255	84,014	1.9	55,500
12	American Stores (Wilmington)	3,737,634	26,596	0.7	43,790
13	Jewel Companies (Chicago)	3,516,352	41,142	1.2	33,400
14	City Products (Des Plaines, Illinois)	3,312,600	64,000	1.9	53,300
15	Southland (Dallas)	3,076,532	57,097	1.9	37,000
16	Dayton-Hudson (Minneapolis)	2,981,234	264,905	8.9	35,000
17	Food Fair (Philadelphia)	2,785,899	(52,518)		30,000
18	May Department Stores (St. Louis)	2,622,918	90,004	3.4	62,000
19	Albertson's (Boise)	2,268,970	36,421	1.6	24,440
20	Rapid-American (New York)	2,169,732	44,433	2.0	50,000
	Total	$120,366,833	$2,960,791		1,987,838

Source: *Fortune* (July 16, 1979), pp. 164–165.

changing market conditions. Specialty stores are not as burdened with bureaucratic procedures as larger stores and, as a result, are able to spot and react more quickly to new opportunities.

Supermarkets and Convenience Stores

Supermarket owners recognize that consumers tend to shop at the nearest supermarket. As a result, they attempt to locate their new stores in the middle of a residential area not otherwise conveniently served. Finding an ideal location becomes more difficult each year, however, as large supermarket chains such as Kroger and Safeway look for new places to establish stores.

In addition to store location, it is important for a supermarket's customers to perceive its prices as competitive and its meat and produce departments as offering superior quality. Inflation has made shoppers much more sensitive to price changes. A can of peas with a succession of price stickers on it, each price higher than the last, makes the supermarket look bad in the eyes of the consumer. Meat and produce are the two departments where a supermarket can differentiate itself from its competitors in terms of quality. If the store consistently offers fresh produce and well-cut meat, it may be able to take business away from other supermarkets. In contrast, frozen foods offer few opportunities for differentiation — the only thing a store can do with frozen corn is to offer a lower price.

Traditionally, supermarkets find it difficult to make enough money to generate the capital needed to build new stores. Today, supermarkets make slightly less than 1 percent after-tax profit on each dollar's worth of merchandise sold because the gross margin (sale price to cost of goods sold) on most *food items* is only 18 to 22 percent. To solve this problem, supermarkets have been stocking more and more *nonfood convenience items*. This practice of selling nonrelated lines of merchandise is called **scrambled merchandising**. Many of these products, most of which are also sold in drugstores, carry a gross margin as high as 40 to 50 percent. As long as the margin on food items remains so low, supermarkets will continue to expand into nonfood items.

Although the vast majority of grocery products are sold through supermarkets, an increasingly important factor in food retailing today is the convenience store, which often functions as a "mini-supermarket." Convenience stores carry many of the food and nonfood items the supermarkets carry, but they do not have the variety of brands or package sizes. Convenience store shoppers recognize that they are paying more per unit of merchandise purchased. They are willing to do this because the average size of their purchase is very small (less than $2.00), and because they value the convenience of being able to make their purchases very quickly.

One of the most successful convenience store chains is Southland Corporation's 7-Eleven chain. Southland owns more than 5,500 stores, generating over $3 billion in sales annually. According to the firm's president, one of 7-Eleven's major advantages is that it operates in so many markets; thus, if a product or an idea proves successful in one market, it can be transferred quickly to all of the 7-Eleven stores. The Slurpee, a semi-frozen drink that was sold originally in only one store, today is sold throughout the 7-Eleven chain.[1]

---

[1] Allen Liles, *Oh Thank Heaven!* (Dallas: The Southland Corporation, 1977), p. 252.

General Merchandise Stores

General merchandise stores, as the name suggests, carry a wide variety of products. The two traditional general merchandise outlets are department stores and discount stores. Recently, we have also seen the development of "hypermarkets."

Department Stores. Before World War II, large department stores such as Hudson's in Detroit and Macy's in New York were the dominant retail outlets. They provided complete lines of merchandise ranging from kitchen appliances to expensive china. Practically any nonfood item could be purchased at a full-line department store.

Gradually, these department stores began to lose their customer base as the urban middle class discovered the comforts and convenience of suburban life. Since department stores were slow to react to this population shift, many sales were lost to the new, more conveniently located discount department stores as well as to the two large mail-order firms, Sears and Montgomery Ward. Executives of most downtown department stores eventually realized that they had to locate their stores in outlying suburban neighborhoods or else risk a continuing erosion of their markets. Accordingly, by 1974, branch outlets generated 72 percent of the sales of those department stores having annual sales of more than $1 million.[2] Today, the figure has undoubtedly reached 80 percent.

In a related and equally important trend, several department stores have moved out of their traditional geographic and customer markets. New York's Bloomingdale's has opened full-line department stores in Washington, D. C., and in Florida; Atlanta's Rich's is moving both south and west; and I. Magnin of Los Angeles is going national.[3] Although different reasons underlie each of these moves, the basic rationale is the same; i.e., department stores, if they are to survive and prosper, must follow the migration pattern of the public. For some stores, these moves have created logistics problems; nontheless, geographic diversification is the only option if these department stores are to maintain their historical growth rates.

Discount Stores. Over the years the term discount store has been used to refer to several different types of retail outlets. When they first appeared in the early 1950s, discount stores sold name-brand items at low prices. They specialized in selling such items as watches, jewelry, electrical appliances, silverplated tea sets, and luggage. Typically these stores offered neither delivery nor credit services to the buyer. Two operations that are still quite similar to the original discount store concept are Service Merchandise and Best Products.

In the early 1960s a dramatic change took place in the discount world. Outlets such as Kresge's K-Mart and Jupiter, Korvette, Arlans, Stop and Shop, Shopper's Fair, and Gibson's began to sell little-known brands of products at low prices. In the process, they quickly attracted a large number of price-conscious shoppers. For example, K-Mart's sales went from virtually nothing in

---

[2]Delbert J. Duncan and Stanley C. Hollander, *Modern Retailing Management: Basic Concepts and Practices* (9th ed.; Homewood, Ill.: Richard D. Irwin, Inc., 1977), p. 22.

[3]"Federated: The Most Happy Retailer Grows Faster and Better," *Business Week* (October 18, 1976), pp. 74–80.

1962 to $1.3 billion in 1967. During that five-year period, Kresge opened 215 K-Mart and Jupiter stores.[4]

The magazine *The Discount Merchandiser* estimates that more than 6,700 discount stores currently operate in the United States selling more than $33 billion worth of merchandise.[5] The most common characteristics of these stores are as follows:

1. Merchandise assortments are limited to the most popular items, colors, and sizes.
2. Low price is the stores' major attraction.
3. Self-service operations predominate. Cashiers are located at checkout terminals, not in each product department.
4. The stores keep long hours and are usually open on Sundays.
5. The stores are usually large, ranging in size from 50,000 square feet to more than 200,000 square feet.
6. The physical plant is inexpensive and the interior fixtures spartan.
7. Ample free parking is generally available.

Although discount stores have continued to be popular, their sales growth rates have not kept pace with inflation, primarily because of some misinformed managerial decisions with regard to store location and also because of a general absence of internal control procedures. These stores also have faced stiff competition from specialty chain stores such as Tandy's Radio Shack, which concentrates on a single category of low-priced merchandise, as well as from some large supermarkets that may allocate up to 40 percent of their shelf space to low-priced nonfood items.[6]

Hypermarkets. The hypermarket is a type of discount general merchandise store that was developed in Germany. Often very large stores, many in excess of 250,000 square feet, hypermarkets sell grocery products as well as almost any other product sold by department stores. Like regular discount stores, they specialize in low-price, high-turnover merchandise. Much of the merchandise is nonbranded. Hypermarkets achieve substantial cost savings by simplifying their unpacking and display procedures; products are sold from large racks, usually in their original shipping cartons.

The most significant entry of a hypermarket into the United States has been Fed-Mart, a San Diego-based discount chain recently purchased by a German firm. Forty Fed-Mart discount stores eventually will be converted to hypermarkets. While it is still too early to tell whether they will be successful in the United States, hypermarkets do represent a dramatic, imported retail innovation.

Nonstore Retailing

The three major types of nonstore retailing are vending machines, door-to-door sales, and catalogue sales. Each of these is an important source of merchandise for many consumers.

---

[4]William R. Davidson, Alton F. Doody, and James R. Lowry, "Leased Departments as a Major Force in the Growth of Discount Store Retailing," *Journal of Marketing* (January, 1970), p. 46.

[5]"The True Look of the Discount Industry," *The Discount Merchandiser* (May, 1976), p. 30.

[6]Duncan and Hollander, *op. cit.*, p. 23.

Vending Machines. The sale of merchandise from vending machines represents approximately 1 percent of the nation's retail sales. Although sales from vending machines have grown consistently during the last decade, the relative market share of vending machines has not changed significantly.

Most items sold through vending machines are used quickly and in close proximity to the machine itself. Therefore, it is important that the machines be located near the potential consumer. Even though vending machines can be quite profitable, they also have several significant disadvantages. For example, the finality of the purchase makes it difficult, if not impossible, for the consumer to return an item. In addition, of course, the machine cannot answer questions about the product — maybe someday even this will change! Finally, the vending machine provides only historical sales data to the seller. Only when one of the products in the machine stops selling does the owner of the machine realize that a problem exists. Well-trained salespeople, on the other hand, can spot the beginnings of a sales decline before demand has ceased entirely.

The distribution of products through vending machines requires less labor and fewer advertising expenses. But most, if not all, of these advantages are offset by the high equipment depreciation expenses as well as by location expenses. In terms of location expenses, vending machine operators typically pay 9 percent commission on a short-term lease for a location with heat, light, and power.[7]

Door-to-Door Sales. Traditionally, the door-to-door salesperson has been an independent entrepreneur selling products by calling directly on customers in their homes or places of business.[8] Although door-to-door selling is still common, it has been partially replaced by salesperson-sponsored "parties," such as those organized by Tupperware in which a host or hostess supplies food and refreshments in return for a gift from the sponsoring company. The value of the gift depends upon the amount of the company's products sold at the party.

Although many different products are sold door-to-door, successful ones have the following four characteristics:

1. Dependable quality.
2. Unconditional guarantee.
3. Subject to effective demonstration.
4. Potential for repeat sale.

The first two product characteristics reassure the customer as to the quality, dependability, and reliability of the product. Such reassurance is essential because most people tend to be skeptical, perhaps justifiably so, about the quality of merchandise sold door-to-door. The third characteristic is important because one of the advantages of door-to-door selling is that the salesperson is there to show precisely how the product can be used. This is why Avon and Viviane Woodward train their salespeople to be fashion consultants, not just order-

[7]For more information on vending machines, see Malcolm L. Morris, "Growth Parameters for Automatic Vending," *Journal of Retailing* (Fall, 1968), pp. 31–45; and Douglas J. Dalrymple, "Will Automatic Vending Topple Retail Precedents," *Journal of Retailing* (Spring, 1963), pp. 27–31.

[8]This section adapted from Michael Granfield and Alfred Nicols, "Economic and Marketing Aspects of the Direct Selling Industry," *Journal of Retailing* (Spring, 1975), pp. 33–50.

TABLE 15-2 Commission Schedules for Three Direct Selling Firms

	Viviane Woodward	Amway	Bestline
Door-to-door salesperson			
Inactive salesperson	30%	30%	30%
Active salesperson	40%	40%	40%
Area superior	10% + 1% overwrite	15% + 1% overwrite	12% + 2% overwrite
District superior	10% + 1% overwrite	——	8% + 2% overwrite
Regional supervisor	1.5%	1.5%	1.5%

Source: Michael Granfield and Alfred Nicols, "Economic and Marketing Aspects of the Direct Selling Industry," *Journal of Retailing* (Spring, 1975), p. 44.

takers. In general, if the product cannot benefit from a demonstration, it should not be sold door-to-door. Finally, in order to take advantage of the personal contact established between the customer and the salesperson, the product should be amenable to repeat sales. Fuller Brush has been successful at developing repeat sales by encouraging its representatives to call on their customers regularly.

One of the most important success factors for a door-to-door sales firm is recruiting enough qualified salespeople. Success at selling door-to-door requires working long hours. The commission schedule reflects this fact by paying supervisors not only on the basis of how much their subordinates sell but also on the basis of how much any person they personally have recruited into the firm sells. This type of schedule is called an *overwrite*. The commission schedules for three firms in the direct selling industry are presented in Table 15-2.

Catalogue and Telephone Sales. Many businesses solicit sales through catalogues or by telephone. Take a look at any Sunday newspaper and notice that many advertisements feature mail-order coupons which indicate that telephone sales will be accepted. Sears, the largest retailer in the U.S., began as a mail-order house and still does approximately 21 percent of its business through its catalogue. Today, Sears' catalogue department receives 40 percent of its sales through the mail, 50 percent via telephone, and the rest through over-the-counter catalogue sales.[9] Many other large department stores receive more than 10 percent of their total sales via telephone or mail order.

Shopping by mail or telephone permits the customer to avoid the problems associated with bad weather, traffic, inadequate parking, and overcrowding at the shopping center. Mail or telephone shopping is particularly helpful to working people who may not have the time to visit several stores. For their part, most retailers encourage mail or telephone orders. Such orders, they feel, represent business that they would not get if they limited themselves to in-person sales only. The few retailers who have tried to discourage this type of

[9]Duncan and Hollander, *op. cit.*, p. 477.

shopping have done so on the assumption that they could generate more sales if their potential customers came into the store and browsed.

Several studies have attempted to identify the type of individual who typically purchases by mail or telephone. In general, the in-home shopper is looking for convenience. Demographically, the mail or telephone shopper tends to have a better-than-average education, the head of the household has a relatively high status job, and total family income is greater than the family income of the out-of-home shopper.[10] Although it is always difficult to forecast the future of any marketing institution, it seems reasonable to assume that as shopping centers become more congested and as more women enter the job market, mail-order and telephone sales will become increasingly important.

Turning now from nonstore retailing, we look at a long-time fixture on the retailing scene, the chain store.

GROWTH AND IMPACT OF CHAIN STORES

The first real chain store in the U.S. was the Great American Tea Company, founded in 1859. The business, which later changed its name to the Great Atlantic and Pacific Tea Company (A&P), sold primarily tea, spices, and coffee. Other early chains were Woolworth's (1879), Kroger (1882), S. S. Kresge (1897), and JCPenney (1902). The impact of chain stores on retailing has increased significantly since their introduction. As a group, they now account for more than 30 percent of all retail sales in the United States.[11] This figure is particularly impressive when one remembers that 95 percent of the retail stores in the United States are owned by one person or one firm.

Chain stores may be specialty outlets (Radio Shack), grocery stores (Kroger or Winn-Dixie), or general merchandise outlets (Montgomery Ward). They may even be one of the three types of nonstore retailing establishments — both Sears and Montgomery Ward, as stated earlier, still make a large percentage of their sales via catalogue or telephone. However, to be classified as a chain store, the retailer must own two or more retail outlets and sell the same type of products to similar markets.

Major department stores, such as Bloomingdale's and I. Magnin, are chain stores in the sense that they operate a number of stores within their markets. However, even though they are both owned by Federated, they are not thought of as members of a chain, because they formulate their own marketing strategies and purchase their own merchandise to fit the needs of their particular markets. In contrast, the operating philosophy of Sears, the U.S.'s largest chain, is to utilize the same basic marketing approach to reach "middle-class hometown Americans" regardless of whether they live in the North or the

---

[10]See Isabella C. M. Cunningham and William H. Cunningham, "The Urban In-Home Shopper: Socioeconomic and Attitudinal Characteristics," *Journal of Retailing* (Fall, 1973), pp. 42–50; Peter L. Gillett, "A Profile of Urban In-Home Shoppers," *Journal of Marketing* (July, 1970), pp. 40–50.

[11]William H. Bolen, *Contemporary Retailing* (Englewood Cliffs, N.J.: Prentice-Hall, Inc., 1978), p. 11.

Are **you** considering a career in retailing? One way you can get retail experience is to work for a large retail chain or department store. After learning about the business, you may decide to open your own store. The following are factors that you should consider in the purchase of an existing retail establishment.

Why Is the Store Being Sold? Find out precisely why the owner wants to sell. Talk to the owner's banker, the store's employees and suppliers, the manager of the mall or shopping center, as well as any customers whom you can locate through the store's credit files.

The Competition. Who are the store's competitors? Is the competitive situation likely to change in the future? Check the strengths and weaknesses of each competitor.

Location. Is the store located in a favorable area? If not, it may be easier starting a new store in a better location rather than trying to overcome a bad location through advertising and merchandising.

Goodwill and Inventory. Two primary assets of any retail establishment are its reputation or goodwill and its inventory — when you buy a store, you buy these assets! Assess the store's reputation by comparing it to the reputations of its competitors. Check the inventory to be sure that it is all there and that it is made up of salable merchandise, not just obsolete goods.

Suppliers. Does the store currently buy from good suppliers? Will the terms of trade be the same, better, or worse for you than they are for the current owner? If you're interested in finding new suppliers, will you be able to buy merchandise from them at a reasonable price?

Physical Structure. If you are buying the building as well as the retail business, have a competent architectural engineer evaluate the building. If repairs are necessary, obtain an estimate of their cost. If someone other than the retailer owns the building, be sure you understand all terms of the lease.

Financial Analysis. Examine the store's books carefully and develop *your own* pro forma profit-and-loss statements and balance sheets. These will give you an indication of the cash requirements, profitability, and general financial condition. Evaluate the retail store like any other investment prospect: What is the expected return? How much risk is involved?

Where to Get Help. The management and marketing faculties of your college or university should be able to help you, or they can at least tell you whom to contact. Your bank and the Small Business Administration (SBA) can also be of great assistance. The SBA can also help in the actual financing of your store.

Marketing & You

FIGURE 15-1 Sears' Business Philosophy for the 1980s

> Sears is a family store for middle-class hometown Americans.
>
> We are the premier distributor of durable goods for these families, their homes, and their automobiles.
>
> We are the premier distributor of nondurable goods that have their acceptance base in function rather than fashion.
>
> We are valued by middle-class America for our integrity, our reputation for fair-dealing and our guarantee.
>
> We are not a fashion store. We are not a store for the whimsical, nor the affluent. We are not a discounter, nor an avant-garde department store.
>
> We are not a store that anticipates. We reflect the world of Middle America, and all of its desires and concerns and problems and faults.

Source: Jerry Knight, "Sears' Business Plan Leaked," Washington Post Service, *Austin American Statesman*, December 10, 1978, p. C10.

South, in big cities or in small towns, downtown or in the suburbs. Figure 15-1 presents the six tenets of the Sears approach to the market for the 1980s.

Tight Controls

One of the most important aspects of successful chain store management is maintaining tight controls at each retail outlet. Radio Shack has been as successful as any new chain store in recent years. In 13 years Radio Shack has gone from 9 stores and $14 million in sales to 5,600 retail outlets and sales in excess of $700 million. To control its growing, nationwide retail network, the Tandy Corporation, owner of the Radio Shack chain, requires weekly sales reports and monthly profit-and-loss statements. In addition, store inventories are taken every three months, at which time the firm's computer automatically reorders enough inventory to give each store a four-month supply. Every other week, each store manager receives a computer-printed form listing the firm's "top 100" and "top 400" selling items. The purpose of this procedure is to provide a quick guide for local managers to make sure that their stores do not run out of merchandise.[12]

The Story of W. T. Grant

W. T. Grant appeared to be a healthy retail chain in 1972 — the firm operated 1,200 stores and generated $38 million in profits on sales of $1.6 billion. Four years later, it was forced to go out of business. In the process, its bankers lost $234 million, its suppliers lost $110 million and 80,000 people lost their jobs. What went wrong?

Although there is no easy answer to this question, it is clear from an examination of Grant's record that the firm violated virtually every rule of successful chain store management. First, each store operated almost as if it were independent of the chain. Second, the chain moved too rapidly into building new

---

[12]Irwin Ross, "Charles Tandy Never Stops Selling," *Fortune* (December, 1976), pp. 178–185.

FIGURE 15-2 Comparison of K-Mart and W. T. Grant

K-MART	W. T. GRANT
No credit.	Easy credit — each store acted as a credit office.
No trading up — dedicated to discounting.	Traded up unsuccessfully to furniture and large appliances.
Leases stores — more money available for merchandise.	Owned stores.
National promotion.	Primarily local store promotion — led to competition between Grant stores.
Tight management control.	Poor controls — easy for store managers to manipulate inventories.
All central purchasing.	Up to 80% of merchandise ordered independently by store manager.
Stores operated identically.	Store managers were almost independent.
Strong top management.	Weak top management — corporate office did not understand what was happening. Too much expansion. Weak outside directors.

Source: "Those 1,250 Ks Stand for Kresge's K-Mart and the Key to Success," *The Wall Street Journal*, March 8, 1977, p. 1; "Investigating the Collapse of W. T. Grant," *Business Week* (July 19, 1976), pp. 60–62; and Rush Loving, Jr., "W. T. Grant's Last Days — As Seen from Store 1192," *Fortune* (April, 1976), pp. 109–114.

stores; from 1969 to 1973 it opened 369 stores, the effect of which was to place a heavy strain on its personnel and financial resources. Third, it jumped into the credit business without an investigation of the implications of credit sales; during its last year of operation, Grant had $500 million worth of credit card receivables of which half were uncollectible. One of the outside auditors said, "Grant was flying blind with no controls and was wide open to abuse."[13]

In contrast, most successful chain store operations are well controlled almost to the point where individual stores have no personality of their own. What a good chain store loses from its inability to adjust rapidly to each of its markets, it more than makes up for in economies of scale in purchasing and in proven, centralized management techniques. Figure 15-2 contrasts one of the most successful chain stores, K-Mart, with W. T. Grant.

FRANCHISING

A **franchise** is a contractual relationship under which the franchisor permits the franchisee to sell its products under a strict set of rules, to display the

[13]"Investigating the Collapse of W. T. Grant," *Business Week* (July 19, 1976), pp. 60–62.

FIGURE 15-3 Franchising's Share of the Retail Market (In Billions)

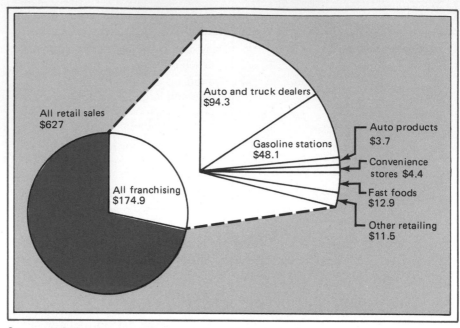

Source: U.S. Department of Commerce, *Franchising in the Economy, 1974–76* (Washington, D.C.: U.S. Government Printing Office, 1976), p. 6, in Delbert J. Duncan and Stanley Hollander, *Modern Retailing Management: Concepts and Practices* (9th ed.; Homewood, Ill.: Richard D. Irwin, Inc., 1977), p. 28.

franchisor's sign, and to call upon the marketing and operating assistance of the franchisor, if required. In return, the franchisee pays the franchisor a fee or royalty payment in order to be a member of the franchise system and to derive the benefits therefrom. Most experts agree that the central ingredient to a successful franchising system is a group of highly motivated franchisees who are willing to work long, hard hours. A few years ago, Arthur Treacher Service System, a home service company, turned down more than a million dollars worth of franchise offers because they came from absentee owners.[14]

Franchising is not a new phenomenon in the United States. The first franchise system in this country was the Singer Sewing Machine Company. In 1898, General Motors began to market its automobiles through independent franchised dealers. By 1915, franchising had become the primary means for selling and servicing automobiles as well as for distributing petroleum products. As depicted in Figure 15-3, the U.S. Department of Commerce estimates that in 1976 franchise retail establishments accounted for more than $175 billion worth of retail sales — well over 20 percent of the national total. The vast majority of these sales still comes from automobile and petroleum-related products and services.

---

[14]Alfred R. Oxenfeldt and Donald N. Thompson, "Franchising in Perspective," *Journal of Retailing* (Winter, 1968–1969), pp. 3–13.

There are several distinct advantages and disadvantages to franchising. Often what seems to be an advantage to one of the parties in the contract is a disadvantage to the other. Figure 15-4 outlines this situation. We look at franchising first from the franchisor's perspective, then from the franchisee's viewpoint.

Franchisor's Perspective. The major advantage of franchising from the perspective of the franchisor is that it allows the franchisor to expand distribution of its product without making a major capital expenditure. The franchisee is usually expected not only to pay the franchisor a fee for the right to open up a retail franchise, but also to raise all the money required to build and equip the facility. These requirements eliminate or greatly reduce the capital outlays required of the franchisor. In the franchisee, the franchisor has as a representative, a hard working, locally oriented individual. Since this person is responsible for hiring all the local staff, most of the personnel problems of a wholly owned chain simply do not exist for the franchisor.

Another significant advantage for the franchisor is that several sources of revenue can be built into the franchise contract. These sources of revenue include an initial fee to obtain the franchise, a percentage of gross operating revenues, and profits from selling the necessary supplies to the franchisee. As an example, several large successfully franchised hamburger restaurants charge more than $500,000 for the outlet, take up to 5 percent of the gross sales, and

FIGURE 15-4 Advantages and Disadvantages of the Franchise System

Franchisor's Perspective	Franchisee's Perspective
Advantages	**Advantages**
1. Little capital required.	1. Initial training by franchisor.
2. Rapid expansion.	2. Reputation of franchisor.
3. Local orientation.	3. Continual advice from franchisor.
4. Lack of human resource commitment.	4. Less risk.
5. Several sources of revenue.	
6. Highly motivated franchisees.	**Disadvantages**
	1. Large amount of capital required.
Disadvantages	2. Too much money paid to franchisor.
1. Lack of control over franchisee.	3. Franchisee finds it difficult to adapt to local market conditions.
2. Must share profits with franchisee.	4. Too much control by franchisor.
	5. Contract written to benefit franchisor.

supply the outlets with products ranging from hamburger to napkins and computer forms.[15]

The most important disadvantage to the franchisor is that some control of franchise operations is lost. If the franchisee does not keep the facility properly maintained, it reflects badly on the franchisor. Also, if the franchisee chooses to operate the business in an unusual manner, such as adjusting operating hours, there may be little the franchisor can do about it. In extreme cases, the franchisor can withdraw the franchisee's license, but this drastic measure frequently results in lost sales for the franchisor and possibly even a court battle (see the Marinello case in Chapter 3). Another disadvantage is that the franchisor gives up potential profits by franchising rather than operating as a chain. This disadvantage does not apply to every business, however, since some hard-working franchisees make more money for their franchisors than the franchisors could themselves.[16]

Franchisee's Perspective. The most important advantage of franchising to the franchisee is the assistance provided by the franchisor in establishing the business. Such assistance can include site location recommendations, help in obtaining local bank financing, and instruction in the day-to-day operation of the facility. Once the franchisee is in business, the franchisor may sponsor training programs for the franchise owner's staff at the franchisor's headquarters and provide on-site consulting services to the franchise owner. The franchisee also benefits a great deal from the franchisor's reputation. When people travel, they may not know anything about the reputation of the Holiday Inn in Cincinnati, but they are familiar with Holiday Inn's national reputation. As a result, they are more likely to reserve a room at the Holiday Inn in Cincinnati than at an independently operated motel in that city.

One of the most significant disadvantages to the franchisee is that he or she normally is expected to raise most of the capital required to begin operations. A hamburger fast-food restaurant may cost the franchisee $50,000 or more for the right to sell the hamburgers, plus as much as $150,000 to construct and equip the building. A second problem, particularly for successful franchisees, is that a considerable portion of the operation's gross receipts is channeled back to the franchisor. Successful franchisees may also feel that they receive relatively little help from the franchisor and that they probably could do almost as well if they were not associated with the franchisor.

A third problem arises when the franchisee believes that the franchisor does not understand unique local conditions. This problem is especially acute if the franchisee is not permitted by the franchise agreement to adjust the marketing strategy to meet the needs of the local market. Finally, the franchisee may feel that the franchise agreement has been written primarily for the benefit of the franchisor. Unfortunately, this feeling is not an unfounded fear. Many contracts have been written that clearly define the obligations of the franchisee but are ambiguous about the corresponding obligations of the franchisor.

---

[15]For more information, see Milton Woll, "Sources of Revenue to the Franchisor and Their Strategic Implications," *Journal of Retailing* (Winter, 1968–1969), pp. 14–20.

[16]John P. Shelton, "Allocative Efficiency vs. X Efficiency: A Comment," *American Economic Review* (December, 1967), pp. 252–258.

Problems with the Franchise System

Unquestionably, franchising does provide several important benefits to the economy. It does train individuals to operate successful businesses that provide an income to the franchisee, to employees, and to suppliers. In addition, franchising does promote consistent quality and service, since franchisors do set quality standards. However, franchising does have two problems.

Opportunity for Small Business People. There is no question that franchises provide an opportunity for people to establish profitable businesses. One must remember, however, that many franchises are expensive and require a significant capital expenditure on the part of the franchisee. As a consequence, many small business people are not able to participate in franchises. Although a Chevrolet dealership, by government definition, is clearly a small business, the fact that the buyer must come up with well over $1 million to purchase the dealership suggests that the individual is not the poorest person in town.

Trend Toward Wholly Owned Franchise Systems. The past few years have seen the emergence of a trend toward company-owned chains and away from franchised stores. In 1960, only 1.2 percent of the fast-food franchises were company owned; in 1971, 11.3 percent were company owned; and today, the figure is much closer to 20 percent. The primary reason for this trend is that some franchisor executives believe that company-owned outlets are more profitable than franchised outlets. John Y. Brown, past president of Kentucky Fried Chicken, has stated: "We'll make more profit from 300 company-owned stores than we will from 2,000 franchised outlets.[17]

While this trend is certainly not a major threat to society, it may imply that the franchise system, as we have known it, is being redefined. Rather than as an opportunity for local people to be assisted by a large corporate advisor, a franchise may come to be viewed as nothing more than a marketing research outpost. If the local franchisees work out, they will be bought out; if they do not, they will merely become franchise casualties. If franchising is moving in this direction, the prospective franchisee must become aware that his or her role in the franchise system is going to be significantly different than it was just a few years ago.

STORE IMAGE

A store image is much more than a composite of its physical plant, products, or services. While a store image is partially a function of these factors, it also has an emotional or psychological aspect. Some individuals are attracted to a store because it has a warm, trustworthy atmosphere; others may view the same store as cold and unpleasant. The point is that it is impossible to objectively define or precisely predetermine a store image. Rather it is customer perception that determines the image.

---

[17]Shelby D. Hunt, "The Trend Toward Company-Operated Units in Franchise Chains," *Journal of Retailing* (Summer, 1973), p. 6.

The Importance of Store Image

A store's image may be its most important asset. A positive image will yield the following benefits to the retailer:

1. Since the store is generally perceived in a favorable light, a positive interpretation will be placed on almost anything the store does.
2. Customers will make a significant effort to purchase merchandise from the store.
3. Customers will tend to forgive the store for errors, such as being out of stock in a product category.
4. When people have little to do, they will go "shopping" or "browsing" at the store.[18]

To appreciate the importance of image, we need only look at the JCPenney organization. Traditionally, JCPenney has been identified as the retailer to small-town America; the store was seen as selling soft goods in a bargain-basement atmosphere to price-conscious customers. It specialized in such unglamorous lines as underwear, children's clothing, linens, and work clothes. Penney's is now attempting to transform its image to that of a moderately priced department store emphasizing higher-priced fashion clothing and housewares. The thinking behind this image change is that the firm will be able to make more money if it can persuade its current customers to buy higher-margin fashion goods.

For JCPenney this is a high-stakes gamble. If the image change should misfire and confuse the public, the firm could lose much of its current customer base without attracting the sought-after new customers. This is essentially what happened to Sears in 1974–75 when it attempted, unsuccessfully, to upgrade its image and margins. Sears abandoned the strategy in early 1975 after profits fell almost 25 percent. For JCPenney's strategy to succeed, its sales margin must be high enough to support the extra amount of advertising required to change its image and then to continue to promote its more expensive lines of merchandise. In the first year of the image transformation, Penney's spent an additional $50 million on advertising and store displays that emphasized Penney's new line of merchandise (see Figure 15-5). Finally, some of Penney's store managers may not be able to make the transformation to a higher-fashion outlet. As a result, substantial sums of money may need to be spent on retraining executives and hiring new store managers.[19]

Image-Building Procedures

There are no sure ways to create a positive store image; each situation must be analyzed as unique. However, a procedure that has worked well for many retailers is to identify store image characteristics that are perceived as important by the store's potential customers.[20] Although these factors vary

---

[18]Alfred R. Oxenfeldt, "Developing a Favorable Price-Quality Image," *Journal of Retailing* (Winter, 1974–1975), p. 9.
[19]"JCPenney's Fashion Gamble," *Business Week* (January 16, 1978), pp. 66–74.
[20]The following procedures are based on Oxenfeldt, *op. cit.*, pp. 12–13.

FIGURE 15-5   JCPenney's Advertisement Emphasizing Fashion.

Very terry.

The thick, textured plush of terry.
Beautiful. And bountiful. With roomy
dolman sleeves that give you a definite
fashion swagger. Poly/cotton in rich
colors for misses' sizes. $12

This JCPenney
is

°1980 JCPenney Co., Inc.

Courtesy: JCPenney Co., Inc.

widely from store to store, Figure 15-6 presents nine common factors in store
image. The second step is to determine how the store ranks in terms of these
factors, as well as how competing stores match up to them. This ranking and
comparison is important if for no other reason than it provides a data base
against which the final plan to change or build the store's image will later be
judged for its effectiveness.

The next step is to decide what image the store should have. At this point,
the retailer should recognize that the store cannot be *all things to all people*. A

FIGURE 15-6   Nine Store Image Attributes

Merchandise	The five attributes considered here are quality, selection or assortment, styling or fashion, guarantees, and pricing. Merchandise itself is taken to mean the goods and services offered by a retail outlet.
Service	The attribute areas are service-general, salesclerk service, presence of self-service, ease of merchandise return, delivery service, and credit policies of the store.
Clientele	Social class appeal, self-image congruency, and store personnel are included as attributes of this factor.
Physical Facilities	This attribute category covers the facilities available in a store to include such things as elevators, lighting, air conditioning, and washrooms. It may also be used by a customer to include store layout, aisle placement and width, carpeting, and architecture.
Convenience	Three factors have been identified that fit into this classification, namely, convenience-general, locational convenience, and parking.
Promotion	Within this summary grouping one finds sales promotions, advertising, displays, trading stamps, and symbols and colors.
Store Atmosphere	This attribute category consists of what the author would dub atmosphere-congeniality. This refers to a customer's feeling of warmth, acceptance, or ease.
Institutional Factors	Within this grouping is the conservative-modern projection of the store, and also the attributes of reputation and reliability enter the picture.
Post-Transaction Satisfaction	This classification of attributes would include such areas as merchandise in use, returns, and adjustments. In essence, was the consumer satisfied with the purchase and with the store?

Source: Jay D. Lindquist, "Meaning of Image," *Journal of Retailing* (Winter, 1974–1975), pp. 31–32.

positive image in one market segment may actually be an unfavorable image in another.

The retailer is now ready to formulate a plan for modifying its image. In this respect, the retailer should realize that a new or better image is much easier to create if real changes in decor or operating practices accompany the image change. As an example, the management of the largest supermarket chain in Texas, The H. E. Butt Grocery Company (HEB), thinks of its stores as "friendly." Rather than just running an advertising campaign showing smiling store clerks, HEB held a series of meetings with its personnel to emphasize the importance of treating customers in a friendly manner. Once this step was accomplished, HEB was able to utilize mass advertising to point out that its stores were indeed friendly places to shop.

After identifying the image elements perceived favorably by the public, ranking the store in terms of these factors, choosing an overall image, and then designing a plan to advance this image, the last step for the retailer is to monitor the results of the image transformation effort. Such performance monitoring enables the retailer to determine whether the project has been cost effective and, if not, what new steps should be taken to further modify the store's image.

Store Management and Consumer Congruence

Do retail executives understand the image that consumers have of their stores? If not, it may explain why so many retailers fail to understand why consumers do not patronize their stores as heavily as they expect. A major study on this topic was conducted with four department stores included in the research. The findings were quite conclusive: store executives tended consistently to overrate their stores. Department store managers seemed to have a better understanding of how consumers perceived their merchandise offerings than they did of the less tangible attributes of service, sales personnel, and store congeniality. These findings suggest that managers of mass merchandising outlets are product-oriented, and that intangible factors in the marketing program are not considered to be significant.[21] If this is true, then a great many customers are lost each year because the store just "does not feel right." Retail managers are not able to prevent or stop this customer loss because they do not realize that they have an image problem.

RETAILING MIX

Although marketing is vital to the success of any business, it is especially crucial to success in retailing. The retailer must begin by selecting the right type of merchandise for its market. In Chapter 5 we discussed the role of the retail buyer in merchandise selection in some detail. In addition, the retailer who does not price merchandise wisely, use the correct amount and types of advertising, and provide the right mix of customer service will be out of business very soon. Each of these variables is examined in other chapters in this text, but it is necessary here to look at them briefly from the retailer's perspective.

Pricing at the Retail Level

The price the retailer pays for a product is the single most important factor determining how much the consumer pays for the product. For a retailer with a

---

[21]Dev S. Pathak, William J. E. Crissy, and Robert W. Sweitzer, "Customer Image Versus the Retailer's Anticipated Image," *Journal of Retailing* (Winter, 1974–1975), pp. 21–28.

large number of items, such as a supermarket or a clothing store, it is impossible to set prices by estimating the demand for each and every product. Instead, the retailer determines the selling price of each product by simply adding a fixed percentage to its cost, an amount sufficient to result in an overall store-wide margin. Figure 15-7 shows the anatomy of a retail selling price. From the retailer's perspective, the expense portion of the margin in Figure 15-7 is the cost of operating the store and includes items such as electricity, insurance, and employees' salaries. The cost of goods sold is the actual dollar amount the store paid for the merchandise it has sold.

The question of product demand often enters the store manager's mind for the first time when merchandise begins to accumulate on the store shelves. This problem may have resulted from purchasing too much of a product or from purchasing the wrong product. When the retailer marks down or reduces the price of the product, the expectation is that the lower price will stimulate enough sales to reduce inventory levels at the store.

As stated in Chapters 12 and 13, the primary exceptions to the rule that demand is not central to setting retail prices are price lining and psychological

FIGURE 15-7 Anatomy of a Selling Price

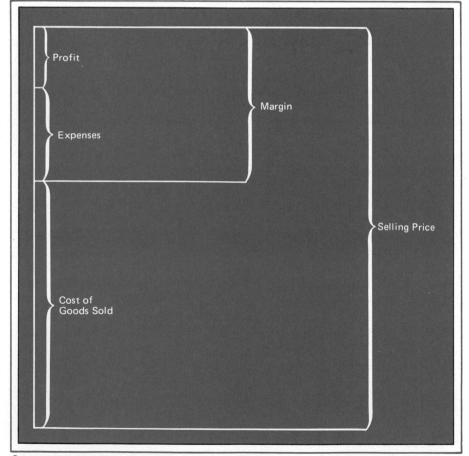

Source: Adapted from Ronald R. Gist, *Basic Retailing: Text and Cases* (New York: John Wiley & Sons, Inc., 1971), p. 325.

pricing. Price lining refers to the practice of pricing items within certain demand price ranges. An example would be shirts priced in the $10–12 range and the $18–22 range. Psychological pricing is based on the assumption that the consumer is willing to buy more of some products as the price increases. Examples include expensive wines or fine watches. The point here is that the buyer cannot evaluate these products objectively and, therefore, uses price as the means for comparing the value and quality of alternative products.

Finally, price is often the key variable in determining a store's image. For example, a discount store, with its "priced-to-go" image, charges less for its products and offers few customer services. Such stores incur fewer expenses and hence require a lower margin on each item sold. At the opposite end of the spectrum are stores such as Saks Fifth Avenue or Nieman Marcus, both of which specialize in selling high-quality, high-margin products to customers demanding a great deal of individual attention.

Promotion at the Retail Level

The retailer is faced with making many tough promotion decisions. In terms of mass advertising — such as television, radio, and newspaper — the store manager must carefully define the store's target market, select appropriate media, and formulate a broadcast or print schedule. For example, a national advertiser such as Sears might face the decision of buying commercial time on *The Lawrence Welk Show* or on *The Tonight Show*. The decision is important because the viewing audiences of these programs may be entirely different.

In-store displays are often very effective in selling products. To promote products successfully in this manner, the retail manager must not only keep display windows attractive but also make the interior decor interesting to the prospective customer. Take a look at the innovative and eye-catching display at right from Z.C.M.I.'s department store in Salt Lake City. Product demonstrations may also be used. For example, supermarkets periodically sponsor in-store cooking demonstrations of food products.

Some retailers have an advantage in that they are able to participate in manufacturers' cooperative advertising programs, as discussed in Chapter 10. Most store managers spend a significant amount of time ensuring that they use their cooperative advertising allowances effectively.

Finally, it should be remembered that advertisements reflect store image. Therefore, retailers wanting their stores to be thought of as high-fashion establishments should develop copy and choose media accordingly. In contrast, if the store is a discount house specializing in low-price items and providing few services, its advertisements should reflect this retailing orientation.

Service at the Retail Level

Not surprisingly, the amount of service that a store provides its customers is largely a function of what kind of store it is. To illustrate, a convenience store provides practically no service to its customers. If a customer cannot find a product, the cashier, rather than a salesperson, may simply point to its location in the store. Convenience outlets and their personnel offer few other services, except for the fact that the stores are usually open late at night and on Sundays.

In contrast, a specialty store, such as a small hardware store, survives by its ability to advise the customer on how to use the products it sells. This service function costs money. As a result, the margin on hardware products purchased at a specialty store often is slightly higher than the margin on the same product at a store such as Sears, which does not give the shopper quite as much individual attention.

A store can offer many other services in an attempt to attract customers. Depending on the product, these services might include maintenance and repair facilities, product guarantees in addition to those offered by the manufacturer, and a policy of accepting product returns. Each of these services costs the retailer. Consequently, the retailer must either accept a lower profit margin or pass the cost on to the customer. However, many people apparently are willing to pay a little more for a product if they are confident that the seller will stand behind it.

RETAIL MARKET AREA

We now analyze a retailer's geographic market first from the perspective of trading area and then from the perspective of site location. The discussion of **trading area** is concerned with determining the geographic area from which the retail outlet draws its customer base. The site location section addresses the question of where the retailer should locate the business once the trading area has been defined.

Trading Area

Knowledge of the trading area is critical to the development of a successful retail marketing strategy. The trading area must be defined to ensure that all the retailer's prospective customers are being reached through promotional efforts. For example, a retailer located in a major shopping center may need to advertise in several different urban newspapers to notify potential customers of a sale. The trading area concept is also important for retailers who must install and service their products. Many appliance retailers refuse to service equipment beyond a certain distance from the home store. There are several techniques available for determining the trading area of existing businesses or for predicting the trading area of proposed retail outlets.

Existing Businesses. It is relatively simple and inexpensive to calculate the trading area for an existing retailer. The usual procedure is to ask people in the store where they live. Another easy approach involves recording the license numbers of automobiles in the store parking lot and then determining the addresses of the owners by examining license bureau records. Either of these techniques permits the retailer to determine where customers live and to plot these locations on a map. Studies of this type have led to four important trading area generalizations:[22]

---

[22]David L. Huff, "Defining and Estimating a Trading Area," *Journal of Marketing* (July, 1964), p. 34.

1. The proportion of people utilizing a shopping area varies with their distance from the center. The longer it takes to drive to a shopping area, the less likely people will be to make the trip.
2. The proportion of customers patronizing a shopping area varies with the breadth and depth of the merchandise carried. The more goods carried, the farther people will travel to visit the shopping area.
3. The distance that people are willing to travel varies with the type of product sought. Consumers will travel only short distances for convenience goods but they may go great distances for specialty goods.
4. The attraction of any one shopping area is affected by its proximity to other shopping areas. Consumers will rarely drive by one small shopping center just to visit another small shopping center.

Forecasting Trading Areas. It is important to estimate trading areas before a store or shopping center is built. An investigation of this type can help avoid the selection of an unfavorable retail site location. Since a retailer's site selection is essentially a segmentation decision, every effort should be made to ensure a match between the store's offering and its prospective clientele. A widely used model for forecasting trading areas was developed by David Huff. The Huff Model calculates the probability that an individual will patronize a shopping center. That probability is a function of the size of the shopping area, the travel time required for the individual to reach the shopping area, and a parameter that reflects the difference in travel times that individuals are willing to expend for various products.[23]

Site Location

Not surprisingly, there is no magic system for ensuring that the retailer selects the best site for a store. Also, the best site in terms of generating traffic may be so expensive that the store could not operate profitably. The four variables underlying a site decision — the shopping behavior of customers, traffic flow, accessibility, and the location of competing stores — are discussed below.

Shopping Behavior of Consumers. Undoubtedly, shopping behavior is the most important of the four variables. As discussed in the previous chapter, a store selling convenience goods must be located close to the customer if it is to do any business at all. In the same way, a store selling furniture (a shopping good) or a store featuring expensive china (a specialty good) does not have to be located very near the consumer. In fact, it may be more advantageous for outlets selling shopping goods to be located near enough to one another that consumers can easily make product comparisons in one shopping trip. Many cities, for example, have an automobile row, such as Livoroni Avenue in Detroit, which has more than 50 automobile dealers along a ten-mile section of the street.

---

[23]See David L. Huff, "A Probabilistic Analysis of Consumer Spatial Behavior," in *Emerging Concepts in Marketing*, edited by William S. Decker (Chicago: American Marketing Association, 1963), p. 446; and David L. Huff, "Defining and Estimating a Trading Area," *Journal of Marketing* (July, 1964), p. 34.

Traffic Flow. How many prospective customers pass by the store as a normal part of their everyday activities? If the store is to be located in a mall, how many people visit the mall? And when they enter the mall, will their shopping patterns be such that they walk by the store? Simple traffic flow questions such as these are not hard to answer. In terms of how many people drive by a specific store or shopping center, most cities keep good records that are open to the public. The potential traffic at a mall can be estimated on the basis of traffic patterns in other, similarly designed malls.

Accessibility. In addition to traffic flow, each prospective store site should be evaluated as to how easy it is for the store's customers and its employees to get to it. Location experts suggest that after a map of the area has been thoroughly studied, the surrounding area itself should be viewed from the air in order to spot places of potential traffic congestion. The following specific points should be analyzed:[24]

1. Distance in miles and travel time from the prospective store to the customers' and employees' homes.
2. Availability of public transportation.
3. Amount of traffic congestion and variability of traffic congestion as a function of time of day and day in the week.
4. Parking convenience.
5. Width of street and width of walking areas near stores (prospective customers do not like to be jostled when approaching the store).
6. Location of the store in the block, if situated along a city street, or within a mall, if in a shopping center.

Location of Other Stores. The location of other stores is also an important consideration in site selection. In most new shopping centers, so-called anchor

FIGURE 15-8   Aerial Photograph of Florence Mall, Florence, Kentucky

Courtesy: Florence Mall, Florence, Kentucky

[24]Delbert J. Duncan and Stanley C. Hollander, *Modern Retailing Management: Basic Concepts and Applications* (Homewood, Ill.: Richard D. Irwin, Inc., 1977), p. 101.

stores are located at the ends of the mall. These anchor stores are very large, often more than 100,000 square feet in size. Smaller specialty stores prosper from the traffic of inside mall shoppers who move from one large store to another. Figure 15-8 illustrates a large shopping mall in Florence, Kentucky, with four anchor stores — Sears, JCPenney, Pogue's and Shillito's.

RETAIL LIFE CYCLE

The concept of a product life cycle, analyzed in some detail in Chapter 8, has been accepted by most marketing practitioners. There has also been suggestion of a life cycle of retail institutions. Let's look at the four stages of that cycle and the implications of an institutional life cycle for retailing.[25]

Stages in the Life Cycle

The life cycle of retail institutions involves four distinct stages: early growth, accelerated development, maturity, and decline. The development and strategy of the retail institution will vary dramatically as it moves through the life cycle.

Early Growth Stage. The first and most exciting stage in the retail life cycle is the early growth period. When a new approach to retailing represents a major departure from other retailing practices, it usually enjoys a significant differential advantage in the marketplace. The advantage may arise from a new cost control procedure resulting in reduced selling prices, or from a unique feature such as better product assortment, more convenient shopping, better location, or a more effective use of advertising.

Figure 15-9 illustrates the relationship between profitability and the institutional life cycle. During the early growth period, the retail institution's differential advantage usually generates rapid sales increases. Profits, however, may lag as the new institution works out the problems associated with the innovation and achieves the economies of scale necessary for profitable operations.

An excellent example is the supermarket. Its differential advantage lies in its operating economies; by eliminating credit and delivery, and by utilizing self-service, supermarkets are able to operate with margins of 12 percent rather than the 20 percent or more required for traditional neighborhood groceries.

Accelerated Development Stage. During the accelerated development phase, the business and the volume of sales activity expand rapidly. The result of this growth is usually a dramatic increase in the market share of the innovative retail institution. At the same time, other firms begin to adopt the innovation or to create retaliatory programs. Accordingly, after discount stores had been in operation for several years, J. L. Hudson's, a large department store in Detroit, adopted a pricing philosophy that it would not be undersold by any

---

[25]The following sections are adapted by permission of the *Harvard Business Review* from ''The Retail Life Cycle'' by William R. Davidson, Albert D. Bates, and Stephen J. Bass (November–December, 1976), pp. 89–96. Copyright © 1976 by the President and Fellows of Harvard College; all rights reserved.

FIGURE 15-9 The Institutional Life Cycle in Retailing

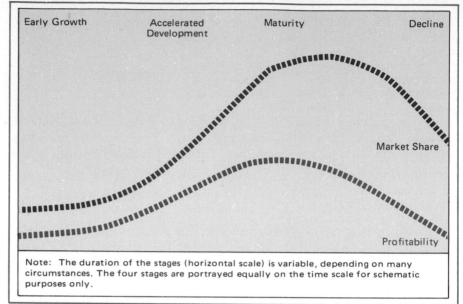

Note: The duration of the stages (horizontal scale) is variable, depending on many circumstances. The four stages are portrayed equally on the time scale for schematic purposes only.

Source: Reprinted by permission of the *Harvard Business Review* from "The Retail Life Cycle" by William R. Davidson, Albert D. Bates, and Stephen J. Bass (November–December, 1976), p. 91. Copyright © 1976 by the President and Fellows of Harvard College; all rights reserved.

store in town. Hudson was then price competitive with any discount store located in its market area.

Profits at the beginning of the accelerated development stage are quite strong. Sales increases result in substantial economies of scale, which together produce healthy profits. By the end of the period, however, profits attributable to the innovation may decline markedly as a result of the increased costs stemming from the need for large staffs, added services, and the more detailed internal control procedures required to operate a multiple-unit retail institution.

Maturity Stage. The market share of the innovative firm begins to level off during the maturity phase. There are at least three reasons for this leveling off. First, entrepreneurial managers who were so successful earlier in creating and building the new retail institution may not have the talents to control a large, complex organization. Second, the retail institution may have expanded beyond the optimal size, which tends to breed excessive, unprofitable competition within the industry. Third, management is likely to face competition from new retail institutions. The result is reduced sales along with declining profits at the end of the maturity phase.

Decline Stage. The last stage in the institutional life cycle is decline. This phase may be postponed through skillful, creative management and the adoption of new strategies to fend off retail competition. Usually, however, these measures provide only short-term solutions. Eventually, as the decline gains momentum, market share drops, profits become marginal at best, and investors take their capital elsewhere.

Implications of the Institutional Life Cycle

The major implication of the institutional life cycle is that retail management must remain flexible in dealing with changing markets and institutions. A retail organization cannot permit itself to become "locked in" to one management philosophy. Figure 15-10 presents some of the management activities appropriate to each stage in the retail life cycle. The market characteristics present in each stage of the cycle are also summarized in Figure 15-10. The ability of a retailer to adapt is especially critical when one realizes that the life cycle for retail institutions has become progressively shorter; firms simply no longer have the extended development phases during which to generate surplus profits for the leaner years ahead. To illustrate, whereas downtown department stores took as long as 80 years to reach maturity, home improvement centers introduced 100 years later did so in only 15 years.

A second implication is that retail managers must attempt to extend the profitable portions of the maturity stage by appealing to new segments of the market. For example, consider Macy's department store in New York. Macy's began as a large store selling a variety of basic merchandise such as clothing and housewares. As the suburban population shift became apparent, the firm moved to the suburbs in order to better serve its migrating market. At the same time, the store modified its image to that of a fashion department store and changed its product mix accordingly. This adaptation to the needs of New York's suburban fashion-conscious consumers resulted in a substantial increase in profits for an institution clearly in its maturity stage.

SHOPPING CENTERS

The shopping center, truly a U.S. institution, first appeared in the mid-1950s. Since that time it has gone through several phases. Let's review the evolution of shopping centers and the various types of shopping centers, and speculate on their future.

Evolution of Shopping Centers

The introduction of shopping centers in the U.S. was primarily a result of basic shifts in migration patterns. The flow of people to the cities in the early 1900s was followed by the appearance of a new retail institution, the large downtown department store, which grew in importance as the urban market grew. However, in the early 1950s, the middle class began to move to the suburbs, thereby creating the need for a new marketing institution. Families that had moved out of the cities to avoid the congestion, pollution, and lack of parking would certainly not be willing to go back downtown to do their regular shopping and face all these troubles again. In addition, there was a growing interest in one-stop shopping and in extended shopping hours.[26]

---

[26]The following two sections on the advantages and disadvantages of shopping centers are based on William H. Bolen, *Contemporary Retailing* (Englewood Cliffs, N.J.: Prentice-Hall, Inc., 1978), pp. 87–90.

FIGURE 15-10   Market Characteristics and Management Activities in the Retail Life Cycle

Area or subject of concern	Stage of Life Cycle Development	Innovation	Accelerated Development	Maturity	Decline
Market Characteristics	Number of competitors	Very few	Moderate	Many direct competitors; moderate indirect competition	Moderate direct competition; many indirect competitors
	Rate of sales growth	Very rapid	Rapid	Moderate to slow	Slow or negative
	Level of profitability	Low to moderate	High	Moderate	Very low
	Duration of innovations	3 to 5 years	5 to 6 years	Indefinite	Indefinite
	Investment/growth/ risk decisions	Investment minimization: high risks accepted	High levels of investment to sustain growth	Tightly controlled growth in untapped markets	Minimal capital expenditure and only when essential
	Central management concerns	Concept refinement through adjustment and experimentation	Establishing a preemptive market position	Excess capacity and "overstoring"; prolonging maturity and revising the retail concept	Engaging in "run out" strategies
Appropriate Retailer Actions	Use of management control techniques	Minimal	Moderate	Extensive	Moderate
	Most successful management style	Entrepreneurial	Centralized	"Professional"	Caretaker

Advantages of Shopping Centers. Today's shopping centers are considered traffic (pedestrian) generators. As mentioned earlier, most large centers have two or more anchor stores such as Sears, JCPenney, or a large local department store. These stores are strategically located such that shoppers must pass many small stores in order to go from one anchor store to the next. Accordingly, these smaller stores, perhaps without much drawing power of their own, benefit from the increased foot traffic.

Shopping centers also are modern in appearance and structure. The atmosphere of most centers built today is completely controlled, not only within each store but also in enclosed walkways connecting the stores. Also, the centers are well-planned, using natural light, green plants, and bright colors, often in dramatic contrast to the old appearance of many stores located in central business districts.

Finally, there is a general belief among retail experts that well-planned shopping centers are truly synergistic marketing institutions. This synergism is said to result from the fact that there is so much merchandise on display that many more people are attracted to the shopping center than would otherwise visit any one store individually. The stores within a planned shopping center participate in cooperative programs designed to attract people to the center. These activities, which are spelled out clearly in the store lease, require each store to participate in sales, special promotions, and community events. By working together to promote these activities, the store managers can generate a great deal more excitement and interest among consumers than if they operated alone.

Disadvantages of Shopping Centers. The major difficulty with shopping centers is that retail space is expensive. To receive all of the benefits of a well-programmed shopping center, the store owner may have to pay more than $40 per leased square foot. This figure is as much as 30 percent more than rental costs in a comparable freestanding store. Many retailers also believe that stores located in a mall will lose some of their identity, especially if the shopping center requires that the store signs fit into the center's general motif.

Another serious disadvantage is that retailers in a poorly managed center may face problems beyond their control. Normally, this situation occurs when the center does not have the proper mix of stores. If there are too many shoe stores, for example, each shoe store will have a difficult time surviving. Other management problems may include inadequate maintenance or an insufficient number of mall events. Figure 15-11 suggests 35 questions that should be answered before a prospective store owner decides to move into a shopping center.

Types of Shopping Centers

There are three basic types of shopping centers: neighborhood, community, and regional. Figure 15-12 compares each of the centers on the basis of five major criteria.

Neighborhood Shopping Centers. The neighborhood shopping center is the smallest of the three types. The major tenant usually is a supermarket and/or a large drugstore. Visually, the center is often a strip of stores with its

FIGURE 15-11 Checkpoints for Evaluating Shopping Center Locations

1. Who is the shopping center developer?
2. How long has he been developing real estate?
3. What are his financial resources?
4. With whom has he arranged for the financing of the center?
5. How's his reputation for integrity?
6. Who performed the economic analysis? Does the report cover both favorable and unfavorable factors?
7. What experience has the economic consultant had?
8. Has an architectural firm been retained to plan the center?
9. Has the architect designed other centers? Have they been successful from a retailing standpoint?
10. Who will build the center? The developer? An experienced contractor? An inexperienced contractor?
11. Has the developer had experience with other centers?
12. What is, or will be, the quality of management for the center?
13. Will the management have merchandising and promotion experience? (Some developers are large retailers rather than real estate operators.)
14. What percent of the leases have been signed? Are they on a contingent basis?
15. Has every facet of the lease been carefully studied?
16. Is the ratio of parking area to selling area 3-to-1 or more?
17. Has sufficient space (400 square feet) been assigned to each car?
18. Is the parking space designed so that the shopper does not walk more than 300 to 350 feet from the farthest spot to the store?
19. What is the angle of parking space? (Ninety degrees provides the best capacity and circulation.)
20. What is the planned or actual car turnover? (3.3 cars per parking space per day is the average.)
21. Is the number of total spaces adequate for the planned business volume? (Too many spaces make the center look dead; too few openly invite competition around the center.)
22. Does the parking scheme distribute the cars so as to favor no one area?
23. Is there an adequate number of ingress/egress roads in proper relationship with the arrangement of parking spaces?
24. For the larger centers, a ring road is preferable. Is this the case?
25. Is the site large enough for the type of center?
26. Is the size sufficiently dominant to forestall the construction of similar shopping centers nearby?
27. Is the center of regular shape? If not, does the location of the buildings minimize the disadvantage of the site's shape?
28. Is the site sufficiently deep? (A depth of at least 400 feet is preferred; if less, the center may look like a strip development.)
29. Is the site level? Is it on well-drained land?
30. Does the center face north and/or east?
31. Can the center be seen from a distance?
32. Are any structures, such as a service station, located in the parking area? (If so, do they impede the site's visibility?)
33. Is the site a complete unit? (A road should not pass through the site.)
34. Are the buildings set far enough back on the site that the entire area may be seen?
35. Are all the stores readily accessible to each other, with none having an advantage?

Source: John Mertes, "Site Opportunities for the Small Retailer," *Journal of Retailing* (Fall, 1963), p. 44.

FIGURE 15-12 Indicators of Types and Sizes of Shopping Centers

	Neighborhood Shopping Centers	Community Shopping Centers	Regional Shopping Centers
Average gross floor area	40,000 sq. ft.	150,000 sq. ft.	650,000 sq. ft.
Range in gross floor area	30,000–75,000 sq. ft.	100,000–300,000 sq. ft.	400,000 to over 1,000,000 sq. ft.
Coverage of minimum site area	4 acres	10 acres	40 acres
Minimum support	1,000 families (7,000–20,000 people)	5,000 families (20,000–100,000 people)	70,000 to 300,000 families (250,000 or more people)
Leading tenant	Supermarket or drugstore	Supermarket, drugstore, or variety or junior department store	One or more department stores

Source: Walter D. Stoll, "Characteristics of Shopping Centers," *Traffic Quarterly* (April, 1967), p. 161.

own parking facilities. Most neighborhood centers do not sponsor regular shopping center events, but rely heavily on the convenience of the center to compete against the larger malls.

Community Shopping Centers. A community center is designed to serve approximately five times the number of people that a neighborhood center serves. In addition to a supermarket and/or a drugstore, the community center is likely to have a medium-sized department store as well as from five to 15 smaller specialty shops. The attraction of the community center is its greater depth of merchandise and its convenient location. It is likely to have several major center events each year in order to generate publicity and to attract customers.

Regional Shopping Centers. Regional centers are designed to attract large numbers of people who can be expected to drive significant distances to reach them. As a result, these centers often have two or three major anchor stores in addition to more than 100 specialty stores. This type of center sponsors events on almost a weekly basis in order to draw customers. Because of their size and the significant automobile traffic they generate, it is important that regional shopping centers have access to major cross-community streets, if not expressways. For many communities, regional centers have almost become new central business districts.[27]

The Future of Shopping Centers

At least two things can be said with some degree of certainty about the future of shopping centers. First, there will be fewer new ones, and they will be

[27]See Joseph B. Mason and Morris L. Mayer, *Modern Retailing: Theory and Practice* (Dallas, Tex.: Business Publications, Inc., 1978), pp. 483–484.

smaller than the giant regional centers of today. There is likely to be less demand for shopping center sites than there was a few years ago, because many of the best locations in growth communities have already been taken. Also, the high cost of borrowing money, along with the expected modest growth in disposable family income, will tend to make the construction of giant new centers a very risky venture.

Second, it is likely that more downtown shopping centers will be constructed or revitalized. This expected trend is partially the result of the fact that many department store managers have come to the conclusion that their stores located in suburban centers benefit from the reputation of the downtown store. Also, many people seem to miss the activity and services of the central city and would be willing to move back downtown if given the opportunity to shop in a safe, modern environment.[28] Finally, the increasing cost of energy will force large numbers of people to move into town, closer to their place of employment.

In the future, downtown centers will be environmentally controlled, when feasible, integrating shopping, eating, working, and living complexes. Stores will be connected to one another in some way, with minimal exposure of customers to the weather or to traffic congestion. The Broadway Plaza in Los Angeles (shown at left) is an excellent prototype of these centers. Broadway Plaza is a two-level shopping mall containing 30 specialty shops, and a Broadway-Hale anchor department store. It is adjoined by a 32-story office building, a Hyatt Regency Hotel, and a number of restaurants.

summary points

1. There are four types of retail institutions: specialty stores, supermarkets and convenience stores, general merchandise stores, and nonstore retailing.

2. Specialty stores specialize in meeting a specific market need. Convenience stores operate as "mini-supermarkets."

3. The three types of general merchandise stores are: department stores, discount stores, and hypermarkets.

4. Each of the three forms of nonstore retailing — vending machines, door-to-door sales, and catalogue sales — has its own set of market advantages.

5. For chain stores to be successful, their managements must exercise tight controls over their operations.

6. For franchisors, the most significant advantage of the franchise system is that it enables them to expand their operations rapidly with only limited capital.

7. For franchisees, the most significant advantage of the franchise system is that they are able to obtain a great deal of planning and operating assistance from the franchisor.

8. A positive store image will help a retail outlet in numerous ways, but many store executives fail to even realize that their stores have images.

9. The retailer must customize its marketing mix to fit the particular market segment being served.

10. The retail trade area must be determined from which the retail outlet draws its customer base.

11. Site location decisions are a function of the shopping behavior of consumers, traffic flow, accessibility of the location, and the location of other stores.

[28]"Suburban Malls Go Downtown," *Business Week* (November 10, 1973), pp. 90–94.

12. The existence of the retail life cycle forces firms to be flexible in dealing with changing needs in the marketplace.

13. A shopping center is advantageous to the retailer because it draws large numbers of people. However, there are two problems associated with shopping centers: they are expensive to build and lease, and they offer the individual retailer little control over the immediate selling environment.

questions for discussion

1. Distinguish among the various marketing strategies employed by the different types of retail establishments.
2. Which type or types of retail establishments do you think will experience the greatest sales gains in the 1980s? Explain your answer.
3. What is the chief ingredient in the success of chain stores? Is this ingredient important for all chain stores?
4. Why are the advantages of franchising to the franchisor often disadvantages to the franchisee? Analyze the advantages and disadvantages of franchising from the perspective of society.
5. What is meant by store image? How can a store successfully transform its image?
6. What elements are included in the retailing mix? How does the retailing mix vary from the marketing mix that has been discussed in this text?
7. How should a retailer establish both its trading area and its site location? Is either one of these problems more important than the other?
8. Discuss the implications of the retail life cycle.
9. What are the advantages and disadvantages of shopping centers from the perspective of the retailer?
10. Which type of shopping center do you feel will experience the most growth in the 1980s — neighborhood, community, or regional? Explain your answer.

16

Wholesaling

Wholesalers have been the targets of social critics throughout recorded history. Wholesalers are the institutions who stand between the manufacturer and the retailer and who supposedly dig their hands into the payment stream without contributing much to society in return. Despite such harsh and constant criticism, the number of wholesalers has continued to expand. We begin our study of these ''villains'' by defining the wholesaling function, a vital step if we are to understand the role of wholesaling in the economy.

THE NATURE AND SCOPE OF WHOLESALING

There is no universally accepted definition of a wholesaler. Some people feel that any firm providing a significant discount from a product's list price is a wholesaler. For example, someone suggesting that ''I can get that for you at wholesale,'' probably means he or she can buy a product for you at a price significantly less than the list price. However, that definition may not be entirely accurate. For our purposes, a **wholesaler** is defined as a firm that assists the producer in selling products to other wholesalers, retailers, or businesses that, in turn, sell the product to ultimate consumers or use it to produce something else. Wholesalers sell large quantities of merchandise but do not deal directly with ultimate consumers. This definition is consistent with our usage of the term in Chapter 5.

While the success of manufacturers depends on their ability to make products for selected markets, the success of wholesalers depends on their ability to serve selected markets. The most significant resource for wholesalers is their intimate knowledge of the product and the service requirements of their customers. Historically, a wholesaler's service function and contribution to economic efficiency rested on an ability to deliver rapidly a broad assortment of products to customers.[1] Although product delivery is still critical to the wholesaler's success, many wholesalers have expanded their service base to include bookkeeping, computer operations, inventory control services, and even pri-

---

[1]Richard S. Lopata, ''Faster Pace in Wholesaling,'' *Harvard Business Review* (July-August, 1969), p. 135.

TABLE 16-1   Statistical Data on Wholesale Trade in the U.S.

	Number of Establishments (Thousands)	Sales (Billions of Dollars)	Inventories (Millions of Dollars)	Number of Employees (Thousands)
Manufacturer Operations				
Sales branches				
(with inventory)	26.8	$ 221.5	$14,574.3	606.3
Sales offices				
(without inventory)	13.6	230.4	——	200.2
Merchant Wholesaler	307.2	676.1	67,035.6	3,368.2
Merchandise Agents and Brokers				
Brokers	4.8	30.6	62.8	36.7
Commission agents*	6.2	20.9	174.0	41.4
Manufacturer agents	19.9	48.4	310.1	96.1
Selling agents*	1.2	7.1	45.0	10.9
Auction companies	1.7	10.8	31.9	32.4
All others	1.4	12.6	54.9	5.9
Total U.S.	382.8	$1,258.4	$82,288.6	4,398.1

*Estimated by authors based on U.S. Bureau of the Census data published in 1976 in the *Census of Wholesale Trade, 1972*.

Source: U.S. Bureau of the Census, *Census of Wholesale Trade, 1977* (Washington, D.C.: U.S. Government Printing Office, 1980).

vate-label merchandise. We will examine several of the wholesaler's most important functions later in this chapter.

As to the importance of wholesaling, it is quite easy to see how vital wholesaling is to the U.S. economy. Take a look at Table 16-1. In 1977 wholesale sales topped $1.2 trillion ($1,200,000,000,000) while retail sales barely exceeded $1 trillion. Even though wholesale prices are substantially lower than retail prices, total wholesale sales exceed total retail sales because wholesale products are often sold several times before they reach the retailer.

The data in Table 16-1 also points out the importance of wholesalers in the economy. There are about 382,800 wholesale establishments in the United States that in aggregate maintain more than $82 billion worth of inventory and employ almost 4,400,000 people. Total employment in the industry grew at an annual rate of 3 percent during the period 1975–1979. Later in this chapter we will discuss the different types of wholesalers, but from Table 16-1 you can already see that full-service merchant wholesalers are the dominant factor in the wholesale industry.

FUNCTIONS OF WHOLESALERS

"We eliminate the middleman and pass the savings on to you." How often we hear these words on local television advertisements! Advertisers using this pitch are saying they can save money for us because they deal directly with the manufacturer. We have already seen that wholesaling represents a significant amount of the business activity of the U.S. economy. But does the wholesaler play a useful role in distributing products to the final consumer? Would we really save money if wholesalers were eliminated? To answer these questions, we will look at the eight critical functions performed by wholesalers.

Contacting

The single most important function of the distribution channel is to contact current customers and potential customers. The Gillette Company sells its products through 500,000 retail outlets via 3,000 wholesalers. There simply is no way that Gillette could economically contact each of its retail outlets if it did not use wholesalers. To illustrate this point, Figure 16-1(A) shows that in a system of three manufacturers, three customers, and no wholesalers, a minimum of nine contacts, or exchanges, are necessary for each manufacturer to reach each customer. In contrast, in Figure 16-1(B) if one wholesaler enters the system, the number of transactions drops to six. This simple demonstration

FIGURE 16-1   Transactions in the Distribution Structure

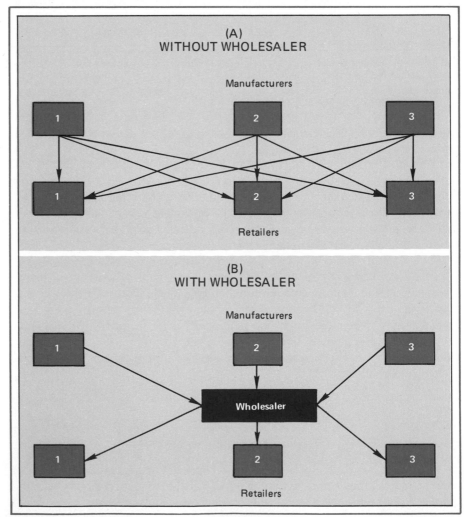

makes the unrealistic assumption that the cost of any two transactions (manufacturer-wholesalers, wholesaler-retailer, or manufacturer-retailer) is the same; nonetheless, it is still true that if the number of transactions can be reduced, the distribution channel will operate more efficiently.

Sorting

Wholesalers within the distribution channel perform two vital sorting tasks. First, the intermediaries buy in large units and divide, or sort, the purchases for resale to other organizations. The result is lower transportation costs. For example, an electronic supply wholesaler can purchase electric motors from Westinghouse by the boxcar load. As a result, per unit transportation costs are much lower than if each motor were shipped individually from Westinghouse by parcel post.

Second, sorting occurs when the intermediary buys many different goods from several manufacturers and rearranges them into more suitable combinations for resale. For example, a plumber needing materials for the construction of a new house would find it more convenient to go to one plumbing wholesaler for plastic and copper pipe, fixtures, and tools than to purchase each product from a different supplier. If the plumber did use four different outlets, the real cost of purchasing the merchandise would be substantially greater because of the additional shopping time involved.

Demand Stimulation

The intermediaries in the channel also help the manufacturer sell merchandise. This function, known as demand stimulation, varies from one type of product to another. In some cases, it involves personal selling on the part of the wholesaler. Wholesalers for Gillette, for example, employ more than 20,000 salespeople to call on retail accounts to make sure that they are well-stocked with Gillette products. Well-constructed advertising and sales promotion campaigns are also used. Wholesale advertising usually takes the form of advertisements in local trade journals and sales promotion displays utilized by retailers. Occasionally, wholesalers also provide cooperative advertising grants to retailers for specific products.

Inventory Maintenance

Another function of the wholesaler is to store merchandise before delivery to the final user. When a wholesaler is included in the channel, inventory levels throughout the system are usually lower than when a wholesaler is not included. To demonstrate, Table 16-2 shows a hypothetical situation in which three retailers each expect to sell 100 units of a product. In addition to the 100 units of base stock, each retailer also carries ten units of safety stock to cover unanticipated demand. Total inventory in the system, therefore, is 330 units. However, a wholesaler, when included in the system, can deliver the base stock to each retailer and then maintain the ten units of safety stock for whichever retailer requires them. Thus total inventory is reduced to 310 units.

The point of the example is that it is possible to predict unanticipated demand in an entire industry or geographic market area by studying sales trends,

TABLE 16-2 Effect on Inventory Levels of Utilizing a Wholesaler

Without a Wholesaler	Retailer A	Retailer B	Retailer C		Total
Base stock	100	100	100		300
Safety stock	10	10	10		30
Total inventory in system					330

With One Wholesaler	Retailer A	Retailer B	Retailer C	Wholesaler	Total
Base stock	100	100	100	0	300
Safety stock	0	0	0	10	10
Total inventory in system					310

but it is not possible to predict which particular retailer will experience the unexpected increase in demand. Without the wholesaling function, therefore, each retailer is forced to carry safety stock. The presence of a wholesaler in the system eliminates this need because the wholesaler can make deliveries on short notice. In a real situation, each retailer would probably carry some safety stock, but certainly less than if there were no wholesaler in the channel.

Information Transmittal

The wholesaler is one of the primary communication links between the marketplace and the manufacturer. A manufacturer can easily become isolated from customers when several levels of intermediaries are introduced into the distribution channel. If the manufacturer is to make products that continue to satisfy the needs and wants of customers, it must have timely and reliable information about product sales and about future customer wants and needs. One function of the wholesaler is to transmit this information back to the manufacturer.

Transportation

The wholesaler is often responsible for delivering the product to the buyer. In many cases the wholesaler also installs the product, if required, or places the product on the shelf. Many of the products delivered to the supermarket by a wholesaler are actually placed on the shelf by the wholesaler and not by store personnel. Still, the most important transportation function for the wholesaler is to provide rapid delivery of merchandise to the buyer.

Financing

Wholesalers often finance the products they sell to their customers. Typically, credit is extended for the normal billing cycle, usually 30 days, with a discount given if the bill is paid early within some specified time period.

In addition, some wholesalers occasionally agree to finance inventory in order to help a new buyer get established. A small new retailer may be given up to 90 or even 120 days to pay for the merchandise if the wholesaler believes that the new store is a reasonable credit risk and that it has the potential to become a very good customer. Needless to say, the wholesaler who helps the new retailer in this manner creates a great deal of goodwill.

Managerial Assistance

The last important function of the wholesaler is to provide managerial assistance to customers — for example, taking inventory for the buyer, designing an advertising campaign, or developing a computerized inventory control and purchasing system. Although relatively few wholesalers have the technical staff to offer this last type of assistance, it is reasonable to expect that more and more full-service wholesalers will begin to provide highly technical assistance to their customers in the future.

TYPES OF WHOLESALERS

The 382,800 wholesalers in the United States are broadly classified into three groups by the federal government: manufacturer-owned operations, merchant wholesalers, and merchandise agents and brokers. As Table 16-3 indicates, operating expenses, or the cost of doing business as a percentage of sales, vary a great deal among the different types of wholesalers. The reason is because some wholesalers perform many more services for their customers than do others. This section begins by examining wholesaling operations owned by manufacturers.

TABLE 16-3 Operating Expenses as a Percentage of Sales
for U.S. Wholesalers

Type of Wholesaler	Percentage
Manufacturer-Owned Operations	
Sales offices (without inventory)	3.1%
Sales branches (with inventory)	8.9
Merchant Wholesalers	12.7
Merchandise Agents and Brokers	
Manufacturer agents	6.6
Commission agents	4.8
Selling agents*	3.2
Brokers	3.2
Auction companies	3.0
Other	2.3
Total U.S. wholesalers*	10.5%

*Estimated by authors based on U.S. Bureau of the Census data published in 1976 in the *Census of Wholesale Trade, 1972.*

Source: U.S. Bureau of the Census, *Census of Wholesale Trade, 1977* (Washington, D.C.: U.S. Government Printing Office, 1980).

Manufacturer-Owned Wholesalers

In the previous section we saw that wholesalers perform several important functions in order to assist manufacturers in delivering their products to the ultimate consumers. Each of these functions can be performed by manufacturers themselves or by independent businesses. Keep in mind, however, that the functions must be performed; they cannot be eliminated. In reality, manufacturers must be able to generate substantial sales for their products in a given market before they can economically consider establishing their own wholesaling facilities. When they do establish such facilities, they may be either a sales office or a sales branch.

Sales Offices. A manufacturer-owned sales office may employ only one or two salespeople and a secretary. Sales offices do not maintain inventory. When a sale is made, the merchandise is delivered directly from the manufacturer to the buyer. In some cases a salesperson from the sales office will assemble the product on the premises of the buyer and then service the product for a specified period of time.

Why would a firm want to use a sales office rather than an independent wholesaler? Operation of a sales office may be more economical than dealing with a private wholesaler. This is not often the case, however, because the wholesaler is able to spread costs over a large number of products supplied by a variety of manufacturers, whereas the sales office is supported entirely by the sales of one organization. A second reason for establishing a sales office is that a manufacturer may not be able to locate a good wholesaler to carry its products. Many wholesalers, for example, refuse to sell directly competing products. The final and most important reason is that a sales office gives the manufacturer complete control over how its products are sold. That is, by maintaining a sales force, arranging for financing, and providing technical assistance to the buyer, the manufacturer keeps in touch with the changing needs of the market and thus is able to sell more merchandise.

Sales Branches. The major differences between a sales branch and a sales office is that the former maintains inventory and the latter does not. Therefore, the salesperson at a sales branch is able to deliver products more quickly to the customer. As Table 16-3 shows, the operating expenses for a sales branch are much greater than for a sales office primarily because of inventory carrying costs.

A sales branch is also often much larger than the sales office and, as a result, is able to provide more services to its customers. It is not unusual for sales branches to provide quite sophisticated managerial assistance to their clients as well as to participate in credit evaluations and to collect money on overdue accounts. General Electric Supply Corporation, a subsidiary of GE, maintains sales branches in most major cities in the United States. These offices are major distribution outlets that differ from other electrical supply wholesalers only in that they carry primarily General Electric products.[2]

---

[2]Richard H. Buskirk, *Principles of Marketing* (4th ed.; Hinsdale, Ill.: The Dryden Press, 1975), p. 364.

Merchant Wholesalers

For our purposes, we will divide the government classification of merchant wholesalers into full-service and limited-service wholesalers. More than 80 percent of the wholesalers in the United States are full-service merchants.

Full-Service Merchant Wholesalers. Depending on the industry or the geographic location of the industry, full-service merchant wholesalers are called distributors, jobbers, merchants, or dealers. These wholesalers take title and possession of the products they sell. They also provide a full range of services to their customers. The four most important types of full-service wholesalers are listed and described below.[3]

Wholesale Merchants. Wholesale merchants do most of their buying and selling within domestic markets. In addition to the usual marketing services, they also install and service the equipment they sell. Some wholesale merchants carry a broad line of merchandise, whereas others specialize in one line of merchandise, such as materials handling equipment.

An excellent example of a full-service wholesale merchant is Wetterau, Inc., a wholesale grocer located in Hazelwood, Missouri.[4] The key to this firm's annual sales of $830 million is that it provides a complete line of services to its customers in addition to offering a wide variety of merchandise. These services include lease programs, store design and actuarial services, financing packages, and training for all store personnel from executives to cashiers and bookkeepers. Wetterau even has a construction subsidiary that builds supermarkets.

Rack Jobbers. Rack jobbers are relatively new to the wholesale business. They specialize in fast-moving, nonfood merchandise, such as toys, health and beauty aids, and magazines. The primary customers of rack jobbers are supermarkets. Rack jobbers relieve supermarket managers of the responsibility of merchandising their products by supplying the rack or shelves on which the merchandise is displayed and by keeping the displays well stocked. Look again at the L'Eggs Boutique on page 310. The L'Eggs Boutique is one of the most successful racks supplied and maintained by rack jobbers. The supermarket's only responsibility is to provide space for the merchandise and to collect the money for the items that are sold. It then remits a previously agreed-upon percentage of the revenue to the rack jobber. The economic rationale for rack jobbers is that they permit supermarkets to carry a wider variety of merchandise than they could handle if required to rely on their own marketing expertise.

Terminal Grain Operators. Acting as wholesalers, terminal grain operators receive grain from local county elevators rather than directly from farmers. They in turn sell the farm products to milling companies, distillers, brewers, and exporters. They also have facilities for screening, cooling, and drying grain, and most also have facilities for reclaiming grain that has accumulated foreign matter in transit.

---

[3]The following sections are adapted from Richard M. Hill, "Marketing Through the Wholesaler/Distributor," in Victor P. Buell, *Handbook of Modern Marketing* (New York: McGraw-Hill Book Co., 1970), Section 4, pp. 74–80.

[4]See "Wettereau: A Maverick Grocery Wholesaler," *Business Week* (February 14, 1977), pp. 121–122.

TABLE 16-4 Functions of Limited Service Wholesalers

Functions	Cash-and-Carry Wholesalers	Drop Shippers	Truck Wholesalers	Mail-Order Wholesalers
Takes title	X	X	X	X
Contacting	X	X	X	X
Sorting	X	limited	X	X
Demand stimulation	limited	X	X	limited
Inventory maintenance	X		X	X
Information transmittal		X	limited	
Transportation			X	X
Finance		X		
Managerial assistance		limited		

Export-Import Merchants. Export-import merchants specialize in selling imported goods in domestic markets or in selling domestically produced merchandise in foreign markets. Although this category of full-service merchant wholesalers represents only about 10 percent of the sales of full-service wholesalers, the typical export-import firm is quite large. Export-import merchants must maintain offices in a number of countries if they are to bring products and markets together successfully. In addition to the basic services that all other full-service merchant wholesalers offer their customers, both export and import firms provide various shipping, customs, and insurance services.

Limited-Service Merchant Wholesalers. Limited-service merchant wholesalers take title to the merchandise they sell but do not offer a complete line of services to their customers. Cash-and-carry wholesalers, drop shippers, truck wholesalers, and mail-order wholesalers are the most common types of limited-service wholesalers.[5] Table 16-4 identifies the functions that each of the limited-service wholesalers performs.

Cash-and-Carry Wholesalers. Cash-and-carry wholesalers provide neither credit nor merchandise delivery services. Instead, their customers must go to the warehouse, pay for the merchandise, and carry it away themselves. These wholesalers are used primarily by small retailers. Chain stores patronize them only for fill-in orders or for merchandise not immediately available through conventional wholesalers. Cash-and-carry wholesalers specialize in a limited line of fast-moving products that are always in demand.

Drop Shippers. Drop shippers do not perform any inventory function. Although they legally take title to the merchandise, they never have physical custody of it. Rather, the merchandise is ordered by the customer through the drop shipper who transmits the order to the producer. The drop shipper is responsible to the buyer for any delays in delivery and to the producer for remitting payments from the buyer. The products sold by drop shippers are large bulky items, such as building materials, for which there is a substantial economic advantage in avoiding the extra handling cost of transporting the merchandise to the wholesaler prior to its delivery to the customer.

[5]The following discussion is adapted from material in Hill, *loc. cit.*

Truck Wholesalers. Truck wholesalers provide many of the services of full-service wholesalers. Typically, they have a warehouse of fast-moving, nationally advertised products with which they daily stock their trucks. These wholesalers are usually aggressive salespeople skilled in selling, delivery, and collection. Dealing primarily with small retailers, they sell such products as fruits, cheeses, potato chips, bakery products, and tools for service stations. Their operating expenses are among the highest in the wholesale industry. Finally, they do not provide credit to their customers.

Mail-Order Wholesalers. Mail-order wholesalers operate in many different industries. As their name suggests, they provide no direct personal selling; rather, the customer purchases all merchandise from a catalogue by either mail or telephone. Mail-order wholesalers have lost many of their larger accounts as a result of intense competition from wholesalers who use salespeople to call on their clients.

Merchandise Agents and Brokers

Merchandise agents are unlike full-service and limited-service wholesalers in that they do not take title to their merchandise. They are compensated by either a commission or a brokerage fee. The functions of the various merchandise agents are given in Table 16-5.

Manufacturers' Agents. The most common type of merchandise agent is the manufacturers' agent. Since manufacturers' agents take the place of the manufacturer's sales force, they have no authority over price and distribution decisions. Manufacturers' agents normally represent several lines from noncompeting firms. For example, an agent might sell a line of radio and television antennas, hook-up wire, testing equipment, and miscellaneous electronic parts, each supplied by a different but noncompeting manufacturer. The economic rationale for manufacturers' agents is that because they represent several manufacturers and spread their fixed cost over several products, they can survive and prosper in a market not large enough to warrant a company salesperson.

TABLE 16-5   Functions of Merchandise Agents

Functions	Manufacturer's Agents	Selling Agents	Brokers	Commission Agents	Auction Companies
Takes title					
Contacting	X	X	X	X	X
Sorting	limited	X			
Demand stimulation	X	X	X		
Inventory maintenance	limited	limited		X	limited
Information transmittal	X	X	X	X	
Transportation					
Finance		X			
Managerial assistance	limited	X			

Selling Agents. Selling agents are similar to manufacturer's agents except that they have more authority. Whereas manufacturer's agents are primarily salespeople, selling agents handle all of the manufacturer's output and act as the firm's marketing department. They frequently have considerable authority over prices, terms of sale, and conditions of sale; moreover, they have no territorial restrictions. A problem with selling agents who control prices is that they have a tendency to reduce the price to make the sale easier. Although this can be disastrous for producers, it has a relatively small impact on selling agents, whose revenue is a function of total sales, not profit. Selling agents are common in a variety of industries, including textiles, industrial machinery, metals, chemicals, and canned foods.

Brokers. Brokers assist in the process of bringing together buyers and sellers but do not have a long-term relationship with either party. Brokers receive a fee for their services when the sale is completed. The fee is a percentage of the selling price. For most products, the fee is quite low (less than 5 percent) because the broker is expected to sell a large volume of merchandise.

Brokers are used a great deal in the food industry. Most vegetable processing plants hire a broker to supply them with market information. The broker is then responsible for selling the plant's output to other wholesalers and to supermarket chains at a minimum price that has been established by the vegetable processing plant. Once all the output has been sold, the relationship between the broker and plant is over until the next year or whenever they choose to work together again. Other familiar examples of brokers are stockbrokers and real estate brokers.

Commission Agents. Commission agents are most often found in agricultural markets. If farmers are unable or unwilling to sell their produce or livestock through a local dealer, they will ship it to a large central market where a commission agent will be responsible for maintaining and selling the goods. Although commission agents do not take title to the goods, they are usually permitted to sell them at the highest obtainable price. There is rarely any problem over prices because they are set by supply and demand at the time the goods are sold, and daily prices are well publicized in business and farm publications. Commission agents are paid a percentage of the selling price.

Auction Companies. Of all the wholesalers we have discussed, auction companies provide the fewest services to buyers and sellers. Typically, products are brought by the seller or the seller's agent to the auction company, where buyers are then invited to bid on them. The selling price is determined by supply and demand at the time of the auction. For its services, the seller pays the auction company a percentage of the selling price of each good. Auction companies are used to sell tobacco and other agricultural products, as well as used cars and trucks.

Wholesalers Servicing Industrial Users

Many of the wholesalers discussed above operate with equal effectiveness in both the industrial and consumer sectors of the economy. As an illustration, a manufacturer-owned sales office could be directed to sell industrial lubricants to manufacturing facilities or consumer detergents directly to supermarkets. A

Many college graduates with an entrepreneurial flair or an interest in selling go into real estate. A few are very successful, while most find selling real estate to be frustrating and unprofitable. Why is a career in real estate attractive to so many people? What does it take to be successful? Could *you* be successful as a real estate broker?

One of the obvious attractions of a real estate career is that it takes very little capital to get started. About all you need is a car and a brokerage license. Most properties in a city are listed through some type of a multiple listing service so that any broker can sell them.

A second advantage is that potential earnings are quite high. Real estate brokers are always paid on a commission basis. Hence, for the broker able to sell three times as much real estate as the average broker, the commission will be three times as high. There is really no ceiling on potential earnings. Also, many operating expenses, such as your car and office expenses, can be deducted from your income when calculating your personal income taxes.

Finally, a career in real estate can be entered on a part-time basis. In the morning you can work on your novel or catch a stringer of bass, and in the afternoon you can help your clients find just the right house or office space.

Typically, the success of a salesperson depends on selling ability and the characteristics of the product. Since all real estate brokers basically sell the same properties, they are not able to differentiate their product or to market a unique product. You can buy that nice bungalow on Alta Vista through Ms. Goodman, Mr. Fletcher, or Ms. Peacock.

The successful broker, therefore, builds up contacts from one sale to the next. If the broker has done a good job of matching the needs of the client to a particular piece of real estate, the client will be more likely to recommend that particular broker to friends or relatives wishing to buy or sell property. In this sense, real estate brokers are the ultimate marketing people; their success depends not only on how well they can sell, but also on how frequently past customers recommend them to new customers.

Thus, many brokers find that they do much better if they establish a good relationship with influential people in the community, especially with people who regularly come in contact with others just moving into the community. If you can meet the needs of your clients, you just may find that you not only have satisfied customers, but new friends as well.

Marketing & You

manufacturers' agent could work in a similar fashion. There are, however, two types of wholesalers that sell only to industrial accounts — industrial distributors and mill supply houses.

Industrial Distributors. Industrial distributors perform all the functions of full-service merchant wholesalers. However, they do not normally carry competing manufacturers' products. In addition, they attempt to stock a complete line of products for selected industries. In this way, they are able to meet practically all the supply needs of an industrial customer.

Industrial distributors are very useful for manufacturers not large enough to maintain their own sales offices. By using industrial distributors, manufacturers can avail themselves of excellent sales personnel and local industry contacts. Industrial distributors always take title to and possession of the goods they carry.

Mill Supply Houses. Mill supply houses carry a very large number of products for specific industries and act as full-service merchant wholesalers in that they perform a wide variety of functions for their customers. These functions include bringing a vast assortment of competing and noncompeting products together in one place. In this sense, mill supply houses are often referred to as industrial hardware stores. They also provide advice on how to sell products and finance merchandise sold to their customers. Mill supply houses are used a great deal in the drilling industry.

GEOGRAPHIC LOCATION OF WHOLESALERS

Wholesalers tend to be concentrated in large metropolitan areas. In fact, in the last census of wholesaling in the U.S., completed in 1972, nearly half of all wholesale transactions were made in the 15 largest urban areas, as illustrated in Table 16-6. The one exception to this pattern of concentration involves farm products, which are sold and inventoried at locations close to the farmer.

There are several reasons why wholesalers are located so close to one another. The first is simply that they need to be near the markets for their products. Many wholesaling operations survive on the basis of their ability to serve their customers quickly and reliably. Large metropolitan areas are where most of the U.S.'s industrial production takes place; therefore, the wholesaler serving industrial markets must be located near these same metro areas. In the same manner, consumer goods wholesalers must operate in large cities so as to be near the large consumer markets.

A second reason for the geographic concentration of wholesalers is that some industries tend to be highly concentrated in one or two locations. A classic example is the textile and clothing industry, highly concentrated in North Carolina and New York. Wholesalers who want to serve this industry must locate close to these areas or they will not be able to compete. The third and final reason for geographic concentration is that most corporations tend to locate their headquarters in a major city even though their production facilities may be scattered across the United States or around the world. If a corporate client does a significant amount of centralized purchasing, the wholesaler must be able to respond quickly to the requests of the firm's headquarters.

TABLE 16-6 Fifteen Largest Concentrations of Wholesale Transactions

Rank	Standard Metropolitan Statistical Area	1974 Population
1	New York, NY–NJ	9,526,700
2	Chicago, IL	7,006,400
3	Los Angeles–Long Beach, CA	7,004,400
4	Philadelphia, PA–NJ	4,822,400
5	Detroit, MI	4,389,900
6	Boston–Lowell–Brockton–Lawrence– Haverhill, MA–NH	3,905,600
7	San Francisco–Oakland, CA	3,158,900
8	Washington, DC–MD–VA	3,035,700
9	Nassau–Suffolk, NY	2,675,300
10	Dallas–Ft. Worth, TX	2,585,300
11	Houston, TX	2,392,100
12	St. Louis, MO–IL	2,386,300
13	Pittsburgh, PA	2,306,300
14	Baltimore, MD	2,152,400
15	Minneapolis–St. Paul, MN–WI	2,033,400

Source: Rankings of U.S. Standard Metropolitan Areas, U.S. Bureau of the Census, 1977.

VERTICAL MARKETING SYSTEMS

The relationships between wholesalers and manufacturers and between wholesalers and retailers often become strained. Chapter 14 discussed in some detail the reasons for these conflicts. Generally speaking, they arise because traditional distribution systems link together a set of independent organizations, each of which is concerned primarily with its own profitability. Although conflicts are usually resolved through the voluntary cooperation of channel members, an alternative approach to conflict reductions does exist, namely, the development of vertical marketing systems.

Types of Vertical Marketing Systems

Vertical marketing systems may be corporate, contractual, or administered. Each has grown in economic importance during the last ten years.[6]

Corporate Systems. For some time, corporations have been utilizing mergers and internal expansion to gain control of their distribution systems. Sherwin-Williams, a paint manufacturer, operates more than 2,000 retail paint stores; Hart Schaffner & Marx, a well-established manufacturer of men's clothing, has purchased more than 100 clothing outlets; and Sears has an ownership position in the various production facilities supplying approximately 30

[6]See Bert C. McCammon, Jr., "The Emergence and Growth of Contractually Integrated Channels in the American Economy," in Peter D. Bennett, Marketing and Economic Development (Chicago: American Marketing Association, 1965), pp. 496–515.

percent of its merchandise. Corporate vertical marketing systems are often a complete substitute for independent intermediaries, thereby allowing the firm to dictate the product's entire marketing strategy.

Administered Systems. Under an administered system, coordination is achieved through the leadership of a member firm, not through the ownership of the entire channel, as it is with corporate systems. Suppliers carrying highly demanded brands, for example, usually experience little difficulty in obtaining strong trade support for their marketing programs. Thus they tend to assume leadership roles in their distribution systems. In addition, many small manufacturers have been able to elicit the cooperation of wholesalers and retailers by using liberal distribution policies, which include such enticements as large trade discounts, financial assistance, and unusually large cooperative advertising allowances. These types of efforts, by encouraging resellers to accept the manufacturer's marketing programs, reduce conflict within the distribution system.[7]

Contractual Systems. The most rapidly growing vertical marketing arrangement is the contractual system. Under a distribution system of this type, independent organizations enter into a formal contract so as to coordinate their efforts to ensure maximum market impact for their products. Whereas leadership serves as the primary source of power in the administered channel, the nation's courts can be used by the members of a contractual system to require each member to live up to its responsibilities. The nationwide network of McDonald's restaurants is an excellent example of a contractual retail marketing system.

Benefits of Vertical Marketing Systems

The primary objective of vertical marketing systems is efficiency — that is, providing a better product to the final user at a price lower than that possible under a traditional distribution approach. There are several significant benefits, or efficiencies, of vertical marketing systems.[8]

Less Duplication. Since in a traditional marketing system each firm in the channel creates its own marketing strategy, there is often a great deal of functional overlap and duplication. In a vertical marketing system, however, as Figure 16-2 illustrates, if a manufacturer has done a good job in developing both a product and a price strategy, the wholesaler need not waste time working in these areas. In the same manner, if a wholesaler has created an effective retail distribution system to reach particular types of individuals, there is no need for the manufacturer to do the same thing. Duplication of effort is further minimized under a vertical system when promotional responsibilities are divided between the manufacturer, who designs the national promotion, and the wholesaler, who develops point-of-purchase displays for the retailer.

High Degree of Standardization. Standardization of activities in a distribution system or channel is normally required if large-scale physical distribution

---

[7]Donald J. Bowersox and E. Jerome McCarthy, "Strategic Development of Planned Vertical Marketing Systems," *Vertical Marketing Systems*, edited by Louis P. Bucklin (Glenview, Ill.: Scott, Foresman and Company, 1970), p. 59.

[8]The following sections are adapted from Michael Etgar, "Effects of Administrative Control on Efficiency of Vertical Marketing Systems," *Journal of Marketing Research* (February, 1976), pp. 14–15.

FIGURE 16-2 Division of Channel Strategy Responsibility in a Vertical
Marketing System

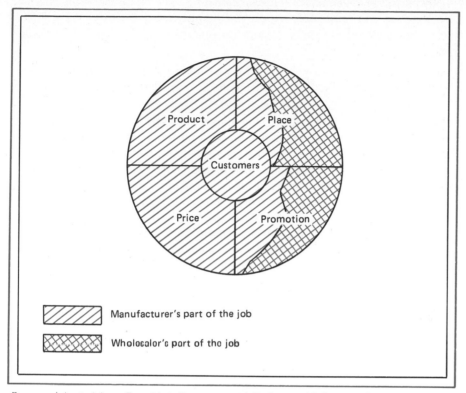

Source: Adapted from Donald J. Bowersox and E. Jerome McCarthy, "Strategic Development of Planned Vertical Marketing Systems," *Vertical Marketing Systems*, edited by
Louis P. Bucklin (Glenview, Ill.: Scott, Foresman and Company, 1970), p. 60.

technologies are utilized to reduce the costs of moving products from the producer to the consumer. In a traditional system, wholesalers may not be willing
to make the necessary investment in physical plant to distribute products effectively out of concern that if they lock themselves into special handling equipment, they will be too vulnerable to the demands of the manufacturer. However, in a vertical marketing system, each member of the channel makes a
long-term commitment to the other firms in the channel. As a result, wholesalers are more willing to invest in large-scale, product-specific equipment so as
to increase system efficiency.

Better Intrasystem Communication. The stable relationships among the
members of a vertical marketing system make possible the development of a
common language and a standard reporting format that facilitates intrasystem
communication. More accurate and faster communication means that the distribution system can adjust quickly to the changing needs of the end user. This
flexibility helps make vertical marketing systems significantly more efficient and
productive than traditional systems.

It is reasonable to expect that in the future wholesalers will become more
involved in vertical marketing systems. In some cases, they will act as system
leaders; in others, they will simply play a role in developing system strategy.

WHOLESALING IN THE 1980s

Increased involvement in vertical marketing systems by wholesalers is but one trend we can reasonably expect to continue into the 1980s. We will also likely see increased customer orientation and expanded usage of computer systems by wholesalers.

Increased Customer Orientation

In the past, merchant wholesalers have been concerned primarily with buying merchandise, physically storing it, and then selling it later at a profit. In the 1980s merchant wholesalers will have to be more attuned to meeting all the needs of their customers. For example, a petroleum distributor will want to be able to serve all the product needs of the service station and garage. In many fields, the wholesale firm will provide not only merchandise to the retailer but also credit checks, inventory management, computer services, and marketing support.

In materials handling, there will be more emphasis on meeting customer delivery schedules. Large regional warehouses will probably be established to serve a number of branch supply houses. The inventory make-up at each branch location will vary depending on the product requirements of the customers located closest to the outlet. Communication between regional warehouses and branch warehouses will have to be rapid and responsive to ensure that merchandise is moved quickly to where it is in greatest demand.

Expanded Computer System Usage

In an attempt to increase productivity, wholesalers will rely more and more on computers. Computers will be used not only to monitor inventory levels, but also to determine the most profitable product lines and to chart the buying history of each of the wholesaler's major clients.

Just a few years ago, only the largest wholesalers could afford a computer system for their operations. They not only had to purchase expensive hardware but also had to hire computer software specialists to design programs to fit their requirements. Today, most of the computer manufacturers have created canned computer programs that, with only minor modifications, can meet the needs of even the smallest wholesalers. The development of minicomputers, as well as the current large supply of inexpensive used computers, also makes it possible for small wholesalers to have their own computer systems.

summary points

1. A wholesaler is defined as a firm that assists the producer in selling products to other wholesalers, retailers, or businesses that, in turn, sell the product to the public or use it to manufacture another product.

2. The eight essential functions of wholesalers are contacting product customers, sorting goods into more suitable combinations for resale, stimulating product demand, maintaining inventory, transmitting information about the market to the manufacturer, transporting the product to the buyer, financ-

ing the product purchases of the customer, and providing managerial assistance.

3. The advantage to manufacturers of owning their own wholesaling networks, whether made up of sales offices or sales branches, is that they enable manufacturers to retain control over product distribution decisions. The result of such networks can be lower per unit distribution costs.

4. Most U.S. wholesalers are full-service merchants. They take title to and possession of their products and provide a complete line of services.

5. The most important types of full-service merchant wholesalers are wholesale merchants, rack jobbers, terminal grain operators, and export-import merchants.

6. Limited-service merchant wholesalers take title to their merchandise but offer only a few customer services. They are classified as either cash-and-carry wholesalers, drop shippers, truck wholesalers, or mail-order wholesalers.

7. Merchandise agents, compensated by either a commission or a brokerage fee, do not take title to their products. They can be manufacturers' agents, selling agents, brokers, commission agents, or auction companies.

8. Industrial distributors and mill supply houses sell only to industrial accounts.

9. Wholesalers tend to locate in large metropolitan areas in order to be near the markets for their goods and services and to be able to respond quickly to the centralized purchasing decisions of their clients.

10. Vertical marketing systems offer a way of reducing conflict among channel members. The three types of vertical marketing systems are corporate, administered, and contractual.

11. Vertical marketing systems reduce functional overlap and duplication in the channel, enable channel members to standardize operations, and allow for faster and more accurate intrasystem communication.

12. In the 1980s wholesalers will increasingly assume a customer and service orientation and will integrate computer systems into their operations.

---

questions
for
discussion

1. What is a wholesaler?
2. What role does the wholesaler play in the economy? Would we be better off without wholesalers? Explain.
3. What is the most important function of a wholesaler? Do you expect this function to change in the late 1980s?
4. Why is there less inventory in a distribution channel that includes a wholesaler?
5. What is the difference between a sales office and a sales branch? What criteria should a firm consider in deciding whether to open a sales office or a sales branch?
6. What is the difference between a full-service and a limited-service merchant wholesaler?
7. What is the role of merchandise agents in the economy?
8. What are the three types of vertical marketing systems? Define each.
9. Do you think that vertical marketing systems will be more important or less important ten years from now than they are today? Explain.
10. What changes do you feel will take place in wholesaling in the mid- and late-1980s?

1. The traffic, transportation, and physical distribution concepts.
2. The interrelationships between marketing and physical distribution.
3. The managing of the physical distribution function.
4. The legal forms of transportation as well as the five types of carriers.
5. Inventory management procedures.
6. Public versus private warehouse decisions.
7. Important changes facing the physical distribution function.

17

Physical Distribution

Physical distribution is the vital link connecting a firm with its customers. The primary objective of physical distribution is to create **time** and **place utility** — that is, to deliver a product at the right time to the right place. Although physical distribution activities have traditionally been thought of solely as cost centers, physical distribution can be one of the firm's most important revenue generators. If physical distribution is properly integrated with the rest of the firm's marketing effort it can be a very powerful tool in positively differentiating the firm from its competitors.

THE PHYSICAL DISTRIBUTION CONCEPT

Modern physical distribution is built upon concepts that were developed many years ago. We begin this chapter by looking at alternative distribution concepts as well as the role that total cost analysis plays in distribution.

Alternative Distribution Concepts

The movement of merchandise from the producer to the user is an old problem. Three approaches for handling this problem have evolved. While many modern firms have adopted the physical distribution concept, others still operate under the traffic or transportation concept.

Traffic Concept. The traffic concept, the narrowest of the three approaches, says that the primary role of the distribution function is to obtain the most favorable rates and routes for the movement of merchandise. Performance is measured in terms of cost per ton mile or some other similar standard. Freight bill audits and reports by the traffic department usually concern any cost savings achieved in the movement of merchandise.

Transportation Concept. The transportation concept, less restrictive than the traffic concept, focuses on minimizing total transportation and warehousing expenditures. Firms with a transportation concept typically operate with timely and accurate data on shipping and warehousing costs and take an aggressive approach to rate negotiation.

Physical Distribution Concept. The most sophisticated of the three approaches is the physical distribution concept. Businesses with a physical distribution orientation attempt to balance a concern for cutting transportation and warehousing costs with customer servicing, manufacturing, and marketing considerations. Physical distribution executives deal with the distribution problem from a corporate rather than a functional point of view. They realize that often it is necessary to operate some elements of the distribution system below peak efficiency in order for the complete system to function efficiently.[1] Just how does this concept of cost trade-off work?

The Total Cost Approach

Total cost analysis is an integral part of the physical distribution concept. According to the total cost approach, any decision concerning a particular element of the physical distribution system must be made in terms of its impact on the other elements in the system as well as on the system as a whole.

Trade-offs. Cost trade-offs result from the fact that the various cost elements of a distribution system often respond differently to a change in some independent variable. To illustrate, examine the costs shown in Figure 17-1 for the three distribution activities as they are influenced by the number of warehouses in the distribution system. Note that as the number of warehouses increases, transportation costs decline, primarily because bulk shipments can be made to the warehouses at low-volume rates. Also, the distance from a warehouse to any given customer is shortened, thereby reducing the high cost of shipping small-volume packages from the warehouse to the buyer. Therefore, the total cost of warehouse inbound and outbound activities declines as more warehouses are added to the system.

On the other hand, inventory and order processing costs show the opposite pattern. Inventory costs increase with the number of warehouses because more stock is needed to maintain the same level of stock availability. Order processing costs also increase but only if the additional warehouses act as order-processing points. To determine the optimal number of warehouses, the distribution manager must balance or trade off the conflicting costs. The goal is to minimize system cost, not the cost of any single element or function. Figure 17-2 presents examples of trade-off analysis in both the consumer and industrial sectors.

Elements in Total Cost Analysis. The real cost of distribution includes many elements not normally considered when studying distribution expenditures. Virtually any major distribution decision affects every other cost center in the organization. The following eight cost elements and their interrelationships are the most critical in evaluating distribution expenditures.[2]

---

[1]Robert P. Neuschel, "Physical Distribution — Forgotten Frontier," *Harvard Business Review* (March–April, 1967), p. 133.

[2]Raymond Lekashman and John F. Stolle, "The Total Cost Approach to Distribution," in J. Howard Westing and Gerald Albaum, *Modern Marketing Thought* (2d ed.; New York: The Macmillan Co., 1969), pp. 412–414.

FIGURE 17-1   Cost Trade-Offs in Selecting the Number of Warehouses

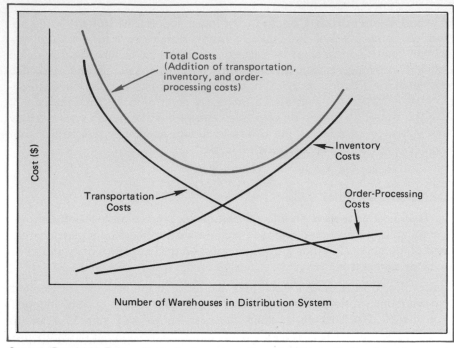

Source: Ronald H. Ballou, *Basic Business Logistics*, © 1978, p. 31. Reprinted by permission of Prentice-Hall, Inc., Englewood Cliffs, New Jersey.

1. **Warehousing.** In order to provide service to the distribution channel, the manufacturer must maintain some warehousing facilities. The alternatives range from one in-plant facility to a large network of local warehouses. Although customer service usually improves as the number of warehouses increases, the average size of the warehouse decreases. Smaller warehouses can lead to reduced efficiency and increased total costs, which ultimately could have a negative effect on the quality of customer service.

2. **Inventory Carrying.** Maintaining inventories at storage points close to the end user usually improves customer service, but it also increases total inventory and the cost of carrying the inventory. Therefore, inventory carrying costs are related both to warehousing expenditures and to the level of service desired.

3. **Inventory Obsolescence.** As the amount of inventory is increased in order to offer better customer service, inventory turnover is reduced. Large inventories, however, automatically expose the firm to greater risk of inventory obsolescence, especially in industries involving frequent model or style changes or perishable products.

4. **Cost Concessions.** Decisions by independent members of the distribution channel may affect the manufacturer's total distribution costs. For example, if a retailer constructs a large warehouse, it can accept larger, more economical shipments from suppliers, which results in lower costs to both the retailer and the supplier as well as lower prices to the final user.

5. **Transportation.** Many alternate transportation modes are available to suppliers and manufacturers, each involving a cost-benefit trade-off. Air is the fastest transportation mode but it is also more expensive than either rail or truck. An advantage of the slower rail and truck modes is that they serve as means of

FIGURE 17-2 Examples of Cost Trade-Offs

The Noxell Corporation, producer of Noxzema Skin Cream, Cover Girl makeup, and related products, was faced with a number of problems symptomatic of a logistics system in need of improvement. Some of these symptoms were excessive time to fill and deliver customer orders, inconvenience of orders not completely filled, too many order-filling errors, and high losses due to theft and damage. After careful replanning and coordination, which took into account trade-offs among transportation, inventory holding, and order-processing costs, several warehouses were closed, and an improved communications system was installed. Although higher freight expenses were incurred in addition to the investment in data-transmission equipment, these were offset by substantial reductions in inventory costs. At the same time, their national average delivery time was reduced. A net annual savings of $78,000 was realized.*

International Minerals and Chemical Corporation experienced rapid growth during the 1960s which put strains on its distribution system. The firm was concerned about rising storage and transportation costs and the slow or inefficient communication among the various distribution points in the system. Initially, the company had 44 public warehouses in its physical distribution system. However, a thorough analysis of logistics-cost trade-offs showed that the system could be trimmed to 13 warehouses without affecting customer service. Balancing transportation, inventory holding, and order-processing costs resulted in a 35 percent reduction in annual operating costs.**

*Jack Farrell, *Physical Distribution Case Studies* (Boston & Cahners Books International, 1973), pp. 1–8.
**Kenneth Hessler, "Assignment, Design, and Phase-In of a New Distribution System," *Transportation and Distribution Management* (January, 1965), pp. 35–43.

Source: Adapted from Ronald H. Ballou, *Basic Business Logistics*, © 1978, p. 3. Reprinted by permission of Prentice-Hall, Inc., Englewood Cliffs, New Jersey.

in-transit warehousing for manufacturers. A final point here is that the number and location of warehouses influence the cost of transportation — whether by rail, air, sea, or truck.

6. **Communications and Data Processing.** These important costs increase with the complexity of the distribution system and the level of service desired. A system with many warehouses usually entails increased costs for order processing, inventory control, payables, and receivables.

7. **Production or Supply Alternatives.** The cost of manufacturing varies widely depending upon the production process used and the volume of production. Ultimately, production decisions are affected by transportation and warehousing costs as well as by manufacturing costs.

8. **Customer Service.** Stockouts, lengthy delivery times, and excess variability in delivery schedules all result in lost sales. Any change in the distribution structure will have an effect on these and other elements of customer service. Although the extent of any lost sales is difficult to determine, lost sales must be considered when alternative distribution systems are being evaluated.

We must now turn attention to the relationships between marketing and physical distribution.

PHYSICAL DISTRIBUTION AND MARKETING

Marketing and physical distribution are closely related if for no other reason than that merchandise sold by the marketing department is delivered to the customer through the physical distribution system. Despite this rather obvious link, the two activities are frequently perceived as entirely different, perhaps because marketing is concerned directly with the customer and the generation of revenue, whereas physical distribution is concerned with cost control and cost minimization.

Much of the natural conflict between physical distribution and marketing can be reduced if one realizes that physical distribution is one of the most important sales tools of the firm. In many instances, in fact, about the only way a manufacturer can differentiate a product from competitive products is through refinements in the physical distribution system. The importance of the

TABLE 17-1   Mean Importance Ratings to Purchasing Agents for
Supplier Characteristics

Supplier Characteristic	Mean
Product quality	.176
Distribution	.171
Price	.161
Supplier management	.152
Distance to supplier	.114
Required order size	.108
Minority/small business	.078
Reciprocity	.046

Source: William D. Perreault, Jr., and Frederick A. Russ, "Physical Distribution Service in Industrial Purchase Decisions," *Journal of Marketing* (April, 1976), p. 5.

distribution function to marketing was shown in a study of 400 purchasing agents. As Table 17-1 illustrates, researchers found that the distribution service provided by the suppliers is only slightly less important to the purchasing agent than product quality and more important than price and the quality of supplier management. What distribution factors can help suppliers sell products? Let's look at four factors.[3]

Length of Order Cycle

A reduction in product delivery time, i.e., the total amount of time required for a supplier to fill an order, enables the buyer to reduce inventory size and thus inventory carrying costs. Reduced order cycles also release funds pre-

---

[3]The following four sections are adapted from P. Ronald Stephenson and Ronald P. Willett, "Selling with Physical Distribution Service," *Business Horizons* (December, 1968), pp. 79, 81, 83–84. Copyright 1968 by the Foundation for the School of Business at Indiana University. Reprinted by permission.

viously tied up in inventories and make them available for investment in other assets. The supplier who can significantly shorten the order cycle will have a substantial economic advantage when negotiating sales contracts.

Order Cycle Consistency

Isolated service and delivery failures occur in any business. When such failures are rare, they have little or no effect on the buyer-seller relationship. However, to the extent that competitive products are close substitutes for one another, the buyer is likely to expect superior, consistent service. Supplier consistency enables the buyer to make the repurchase process more routine, which lowers the costs of making and monitoring the reorder decision. In addition, a consistent reorder cycle allows the firm to carry both smaller safety stocks and smaller inventories.

Order Placement

A buyer can place an order either by mail or by some means of electronic transmission, such as telephone, telex, or telegraph. Mail order is inexpensive but tends to lengthen the order cycle and to make it less consistent; electronic transmission, expensive but fast, tends to reduce the order cycle and to increase its consistency. A seller investing in an electronic communication system must be able to convince the buyer of the cost and scheduling efficiencies involved, thereby gaining a competitive advantage in the marketplace.

Order Formulation

Most orders are formulated by the buyer. In such cases, there is little cost to the seller. On the other hand, if the seller provides a programmed reordering system or some other mechanism for formulating an order, there is a tendency for the customer to become dependent on the supplier. Although the programmed reordering system may be expensive for the seller, it does effectively take the buyer making routine repurchase decisions out of the market. In so doing, such a system reduces the seller's risk of losing the account and also may even decrease sales promotion costs.

PHYSICAL DISTRIBUTION MANAGEMENT

Responsibility for managing the physical flow of merchandise is frequently dispersed throughout the organization. Each department, while moving the product through its part of the overall production and distribution system, attempts to increase the efficiency of its operations. The problem with this approach, however, is that it makes it difficult for the firm to develop a truly firm-wide integrated distribution system. It also creates conflict within the organization.

As an example, because producers are traditionally oriented to economies of scale, the physical distribution function most often utilizes low cost, slow product delivery systems. However, this conflicts directly with the marketing department's desire for superior service, rapid product delivery, and a wide product assortment. We now analyze, first, an integrated physical distribution system, and second, the line and staff relationships within the system.[4]

Catalysts to Effective Physical Distribution Management

Each firm must evaluate the advantages and disadvantages of establishing a separate physical distribution department. Three factors frequently act as catalysts to move the firm to consider an integrated physical distribution system: the cost of physical distribution, the importance of customer service, and the attitude of top management.

Cost of Physical Distribution. For a firm to establish a physical distribution department, it must have significant physical distribution costs. A firm spending 35 percent of its sales dollar on distribution may be able to achieve dramatic cost savings with an integrated physical distribution department. In contrast, an organization spending only 3–5 percent is not a likely candidate for an integrated distribution system.

Importance of Customer Service. The more important customer service is to the firm, the more likely the firm is to develop an integrated physical distribution department. The problem, however, is that the marketing department alone is usually responsible for customer service. The chief marketing officer who feels that a physical distribution department will hinder the firm's ability to serve its customers will resist the creation of the department. This problem usually can be overcome by explaining to the people involved how a coordinated, centralized physical distribution effort will enable the firm to provide the same or better customer service than before, and at a lower price.

Top Management Support. Once the new physical distribution department is established and operating, it must have the active support of top management if it is to succeed. The new department will have to borrow resources from existing departments as it takes over some of the functions that they had performed in the past. Without top management support, the existing departments may resist many of the actions of the new physical distribution department. The best way to ensure top management support is to structure the new department on an equal footing with the finance, manufacturing, marketing, and other major functional departments. Without the confidence of top management and the necessary authority, the new department will not be able to achieve its objectives.

Line and Staff Responsibilities

In a traditional organization, line personnel are responsible for day-to-day management of the firm's operations. In a physical distribution department, line responsibilities include warehousing, order processing, inventory control, and transportation. In contrast, staff personnel are concerned with the develop-

---

[4]The following sections have been drawn primarily from Donald J. Bowersox, "Emerging Patterns of Physical Distribution Organization," *Transportation and Distribution Management* (May, 1968), pp. 53–56; and Harry J. Bruce and John G. Kneiling, "A Logical Look at Logistics," *Distribution Age* (November, 1966), pp. 41–44.

ment of new systems to meet future needs; consequently, their responsibilities include distribution cost analysis, planning and forecasting, and customer service.

Initially, a physical distribution department is staff oriented because integrating physical distribution activities is a relatively new concept requiring a great deal of study by the firm before it is implemented. Accordingly, during its early stages, the new physical distribution department is managed by a staff group, who evaluate approaches for integrating the distribution system, while the actual line activities are still performed by the functional departments.[5]

In some instances, appointing the physical distribution staff may be sufficient to provide the necessary integration. These individuals, acting as internal consultants, try to convince the managers of the various functional areas of the merits of a coordinated distribution system. Unfortunately, this type of staff system usually fails because the individuals themselves do not have the authority to integrate the physical distribution system. To solve this problem, it is necessary for the firm's top management to evaluate the staff's distribution plan and then to create a physical distribution line organization. Having done so, management must then ensure that close coordination is maintained be-

FIGURE 17-3 Management of the Physical Distribution Operations

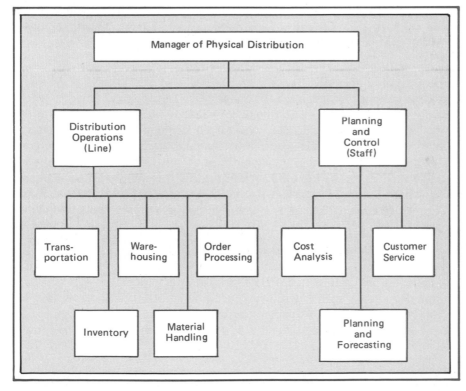

Source: Adapted from Wendell M. Stewart, "Physical Distribution," in Victor P. Buell, *Handbook of Modern Marketing* (New York: McGraw-Hill Book Company, 1970), Section 4, p. 67.

[5]For an excellent discussion of logistical organization, see Donald J. Bowersox, *Logistical Management* (New York: Macmillan Publishing Co., Inc., 1974), pp. 426–435.

tween the distribution line and staff organizations. Coordination can best be accomplished by appointing a manager of physical distribution, to whom both the chief line and chief staff manager will report. Figure 17-3 illustrated how a modern physical distribution department might look.

TRANSPORTATION

For most firms transportation is the single largest physical distribution expenditure. In 1980 more than $100 billion were spent on the movement of intercity freight in the United States. This figure represents a real growth rate, excluding inflation, of more than 60 percent during the last decade.[6] Our examination of transportation begins by looking at the legal forms of carriers, followed by the five major types of carriers.

Legal Forms of Transportation

Transportation carriers in the U.S. are classified as to their operating rights. Firms involved in interstate commerce are subject to the authority of the Interstate Commerce Commission (ICC), a federal regulatory body. Firms with strictly local operations are regulated by state transportation agencies. Common, contract, exempt, and private carriers, each with a different operating privilege, are discussed below.

Common Carriers. Most legal carriers are referred to as common carriers. A common carrier provides transportation services to any firm in its operating authority without discrimination. It receives a certificate of public convenience and necessity from the state or federal government. This certificate requires the carrier to publish its freight rates, which must be identical for similar types of merchandise. The common carrier may be authorized to transport any commodity, or its authority may be limited to the transportation of a single commodity, such as household goods, steel, computers, or petroleum products. The operating authority specifies the geographical area in which the carrier is entitled to operate as well as the nature of its service, whether scheduled or nonscheduled.

Contract Carriers. A contract carrier provides transportation services on a selective basis. It receives an operating permit to transport commodities based on a contract between itself and a shipper; the operating permit is for a specific commodity over a specified route. The fee for the service is negotiated between the carrier and the shipper. The contract carrier can haul commodities for more than one firm, and it can charge different rates to each of its customers.

Exempt Carriers. These carriers are exempt from direct regulation with respect to operating rights and prices. The exempt carrier status developed be-

---

[6]Ronald H. Ballou, *Basic Business Logistics* (Englewood Cliffs, N.J.: Prentice-Hall, Inc., 1978), p. 112.

cause of the powerful farm lobby which wanted agricultural products transported at rates cheaper than those provided by common carriers. Today, organizations lobbying for a variety of special interest groups have convinced Congress that their products should be shipped by exempt carriers. In addition, exempt status is granted to local transportation firms operating within specified trading zones around municipalities. These firms have been awarded exempt carrier status partly because the short-haul market in normal trading zones is so complex that it cannot be regulated effectively.

Private Carriers. When a firm provides its own transportation services, it is operating as a private carrier. To qualify as a private carrier, a firm must own (or control through lease arrangement) both the transportation equipment involved and the merchandise being shipped. Also, the transportation of the merchandise in question must be incidental to the primary purpose of the business. Although private carriers are generally exempt from transportation regulatory agencies, they are subject to state laws concerning safety equipment, weight restrictions, and licensing. An example would include trucks that are owned by General Motors to transport cars manufactured in Detroit to retailers in Lansing, Michigan.[7]

Selection of a Carrier

The major differences between the four types of carriers concern the number of operating restrictions and the degree of financial commitment required of the shipper. The number of restrictions determines the flexibility of the carrier. A private carrier, for example, may haul any of the shipper's product over any route but it does not transport the products of other firms.

Although private carriers often generate large cost savings for the shipper, they can prove to be quite expensive if not utilized fully. Establishing a private carrier as an in-house transportation service involves the investment of a substantial sum of money in equipment and personnel. On the other hand, common carriers do not require much of a financial commitment by the shipper. A contract carrier, as defined by the specific contract, requires a greater financial commitment than a common carrier but less than a private carrier. A reasoned decision as to what type of legal carrier to employ can be made only after the needs of the shipper as well as its financial and personnel resources have been determined.

Types of Carriers

Railroads, inland waterways, air, trucks, and pipelines are the five major ways of transporting intercity freight. Figure 17-4 illustrates that railroads have declined steadily in importance since 1930, whereas air, pipelines, and trucks have all increased their share of the market. The use of inland waterways has remained relatively constant at 18 percent.

---

[7]Donald J. Bowersox, *Logistical Management* (New York: Macmillan Publishing Co., 1974), pp. 151–152.

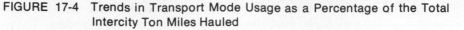

FIGURE 17-4   Trends in Transport Mode Usage as a Percentage of the Total Intercity Ton Miles Hauled

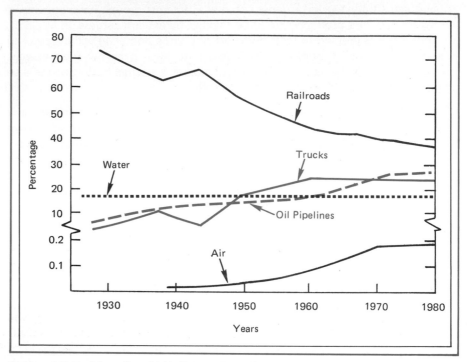

Source: Adapted from Ronald H. Ballou, *Basic Business Logistics*, © 1978, p. 118. Reprinted by permission of Prentice-Hall, Inc., Englewood Cliffs, New Jersey.

Railroads. Railroads are used primarily for transporting over long distances commodities that do not need to arrive quickly at their destinations.[8] Over the years the role of railroads has changed: 20 years ago the railroads carried a wide variety of products; today they haul primarily heavy manufactured goods and raw materials. As Table 17-2 indicates, railroads enjoy a substantial price advantage over trucks and airlines; the price per ton mile is less than half of that for trucks and less than 5 percent of the price of air transportation. The table also shows that, price-wise, barges and oil pipelines can offer significant competition to railroads.

Although U.S. railroads have experienced many problems lately, they have made significant efforts to regain their lost markets. Innovative marketing is evidenced by the new special cars purchased by many railroads, including "piggy-back" systems designed to transport complete truck trailers and also "stack-pack" and "Vert-a-Pac" automobile-carrying freight cars. The railroads have also created special "run-through" freight trains designed to move freight over long distances rapidly by eliminating time-consuming terminal delays. A good illustration is Santa Fe's Super C, an all-piggyback train operating on a 40-hour schedule between Chicago and Los Angeles. Assuming the railroads

---

[8]This section is drawn from "Common Carrier Capabilities I: Rail and Water Carriers," *Transportation and Distribution Management* (March, 1972), pp. 21–24.

TABLE 17-2 Freight Transportation Costs

Mode	Price (cents/ton mile)
Air	45.80
Truck	4.60
Rail	2.07
Pipe	0.31
Water	0.25

Source: U.S. Bureau of the Census, *Statistical Abstract of the United States, 1976* (Washington, D.C.: U.S. Government Printing Office, 1976), pp. 582–583.

raise enough capital for the required investment in new tracks and equipment, they should be able to stay competitive in the long-haul, heavy materials market.

Water. Shipment via inland waterway is one of the oldest methods of moving large quantities of merchandise. Although it is the least expensive mode in terms of cost per ton mile, transportation by water does suffer from several problems that limit its usefulness to all but a few commodities. First, cost-efficient utilization of waterways requires that both buyer and seller be located on a waterway; if the merchandise has to be transported any significant distance by rail or truck, the economies of ships and barges are greatly reduced. Second, inland waterways are affected by weather. For instance, the Great Lakes are shut down for all barges and transportation ships for four to five months each year. Finally, water transportation is very slow even when compared with trains; although freight trains normally average no more than 25 miles per hour, barge traffic moves at a much slower rate of six to nine miles per hour.

Shipping companies have recently begun to design ships to solve particular transportation problems. Examples include container ships and ships transporting truck trailers. Although it seems unlikely that the waterways will grow in importance in the transportation of general merchandise, they will remain competitive in the shipping of bulk commodities such as coal, bauxite, chemicals, and cement.

Air. Historically, air transportation has specialized in the movement of high value, light, perishable commodities such as flowers. Air freight continues to be much more expensive than other forms of transportation, but with the advent of jet aircraft, especially jumbo jets with their great lifting capacity, the airlines have become much more aggressive in seeking out new markets. One innovative freight service is United Airlines' Soft Touch container. This sealed box holds up to 10,000 pounds in a volume of 457 cubic feet. It includes a tie-down system to ensure a secure ride for its cargo. Soft Touch is now used by computer companies and other electronic firms as an alternative to truck transportation. Another new service offered by many airlines is a high-speed package service utilizing the airlines' baggage handling system. American Airlines' version is called Priority Parcel Service. A package, placed on the next American flight to the desired destination, can usually be picked up 30 minutes after the plane has landed.[9]

As a means for hauling freight, air transportation has many inherent advantages. For example, the cost of operation is partially subsidized in that airways and airports traditionally have been maintained with public funds. Although the airlines have been slow to develop the freight market, it seems clear that the jumbo jets, as well as the large specialized freight planes currently under development, will make air freight transportation even more economical than it is today.

Highways. Freight truck lines, which compete more directly with railroads than with airlines, tend to haul freight on relatively short, intercity runs. The average length for a haul via common carrier truck is 306 miles and only 166 miles for a privately owned carrier. The major advantages of truck shipment are door-to-door delivery (which unlike rail freight eliminates much of the expense of loading and unloading), the frequency and flexibility of service, and speed and convenience.

A major disadvantage of highway transportation, however, is that it is significantly more expensive than rail — 4.60 cents per ton mile for truck vs. 2.07 cents for rail. In addition, many types of cargo simply cannot be handled by trucks. In most states truck vans can be no longer than 40 feet and no wider than eight feet. Although specially designed equipment can carry larger loads, it is not very economical to do so over long hauls.[10]

Pipelines. In the past, pipelines have been used for transporting liquids such as crude oil. Although the product moves at a relatively slow speed (three to five m.p.h.), it moves continuously. In addition, whereas the fixed cost of building a pipeline is extremely high, operating costs are quite low if it is utilized at capacity. Also, transportation through pipelines is very dependable; it is almost completely automatic and, as a result, will not normally be affected by labor problems. Finally, weather disruptions of pipeline transportation are almost nonexistent.

A great deal of attention currently is being given to the movement of solids through pipelines, such as coal suspended in water. This mixture, known as slurry, is transportable at very low cost. One of the real problems with slurry, however, is the availability of sufficient quantities of water, especially in the western states. If this problem is overcome, pipelines could become a major carrier of some solid products.

INVENTORY MANAGEMENT

Besides transportation, physical distribution managers must also manage their firm's inventories. The primary rationale for maintaining inventories is that it is not physically or economically possible to handle each sale on a custom order basis. As a result, to satisfy customers' needs as well as to balance pro-

[9]"Common Carrier Capabilities II: Airlines and Trucklines," *Transportation and Distribution Management* (April, 1972), pp. 17–19.

[10]Ballou, *op. cit.*, pp. 140–141.

The largest common carrier and, in fact, the most expensive project ever undertaken by private industry is the Alaskan pipeline. The pipeline extends from ice-bound Prudhoe Bay 900 miles south to Valdez on the Gulf of Alaska. The project involved over 70,000 people and crossed 30,000 acres of land. In 1968, the cost of the pipeline was estimated at $900 million, but by the time the project was finished in 1977, more than $7.7 billion had been spent.

Why was the original cost estimate so low compared to the actual cost? The main reason was because project planners did not fully comprehend the strength of the environmental movement in the United States, and especially the impact of the National Environmental Policy Act of 1969. The intent of this act is to provide safeguards over any project crossing federal land by requiring an environmental impact statement as well as evidence that alternatives to the project in question had been carefully considered. The final environmental impact statement for the Alaskan pipeline totaled nine volumes. It dealt with every aspect of the pipeline, from potential threats to the permafrost (the permanently frozen layer below the earth's surface) to the impact of construction activities on the land, on the wildlife in the area, and on the people of Alaska.

When the pipeline was finally finished, more than half of it was built above ground to protect the fragile permafrost and tundra environment. As a measure of protection against earthquakes, the pipeline was built in a zigzag, trapezoidal pattern to give the system as much flexibility as possible.

The Alaskan pipeline was begun by Atlantic Richfield and Exxon after they discovered oil in the North Slope of Alaska. Eventually, five other oil companies joined in the venture. The pipeline is a common carrier licensed by the state of Alaska to transport crude oil.

On June 20, 1977, oil began to flow from Prudhoe Bay, and on August 1, 1977, the first oil-laden tanker, carrying 824,000 barrels of oil, headed for the state of Washington. The Alaskan pipeline was complete!

What does this adventure in physical distribution have to do with *you*? Look at the gasoline gauge in your car. The gasoline in your car right now might well be a product of Alaskan crude oil.

Source: James P. Roscow. *The Alaskan Pipeline: All You Ever Wanted to Know* (Englewood Cliffs, N.J.: Prentice-Hall, Inc., 1977).

Marketing & You

501

duction schedules, most firms find it necessary to maintain significant inventories both at the point of manufacture and in the distribution channel. Several questions arise: (1) how much inventory should be ordered? (2) when should inventory be reordered? and (3) how much safety stock should the firm maintain?

How Much Should Be Ordered?

The amount of inventory that should be ordered at any moment in time, the **economic order quantity** (EOQ), is primarily a function of the cost of maintaining the inventory once it is received and the cost of ordering the inventory. One of the key elements of inventory carrying cost is the amount the firm must pay to finance the required investment in inventory. This amount is primarily a function of the short-term interest rate on inventory-secured borrowing. A second element of carrying cost is the inventory service charges, which include any taxes that a state may levy on a firm's inventory as well as the cost of protecting the inventory (insurance) against loss from fire or theft. A third element is the expense involved in operating a warehouse, which varies somewhat depending on whether the firm owns the warehouse or simply rents space in one. The last element is the risk associated with carrying inventory. Many unfortunate things can happen to an inventory: it can be stolen; it can be damaged by flood, fire, or other accident; and it can also become obsolete. Inventory obsolescence, for which there is no insurance available, is particularly a problem in high fashion and fad industries where products may be in today and out tomorrow.[11]

When inventory is obtained from an outside vendor, the cost of ordering includes expenditures for postage, telephones, clerical assistance, purchasing agents' time, and receiving and handling. If a product is ordered internally, the ordering cost is augmented by production set-up costs. Depending on the nature of the product, the ordering cost may range from less than one dollar to many thousands of dollars.[12]

The more units of inventory the firm orders at any given time, the higher the cost of carrying the inventory but the lower the total ordering cost. This trade-off occurs because the more units of inventory ordered, the greater the average amount of inventory on hand, and accordingly, the fewer the number of orders that need to be placed during the year.

The following formula tells the firm how much inventory it should order (EOQ) to achieve the optimal balance between ordering cost and carrying cost.[13]

$$EOQ = \sqrt{\frac{2SO}{iP}}$$

---

[11]For more detailed information on the cost of maintaining inventory, see Bernard J. La-Londe and Douglas M. Lambert, "Inventory Carrying Costs: Significance, Components, Means, and Functions," *International Journal of Physical Distribution*, Vol. 6, No. 1 (1976), pp. 51–63.

[12]James Don Edwards and Roger A. Roemmich, "Scientific Inventory Management," *Business Topics* (Autumn, 1975), pp. 41–45.

[13]For a mathematical proof of the equation, see James L. Heskett, Nicholas A. Glaskowsky, Jr., and Robert M. Ivie, *Business Logistics: Physical Distribution and Materials Management* (New York: The Ronald Press Co., 1973), pp. 308–309.

where:

S = annual quantity sold in units.
O = cost of placing an order,
i = carrying cost per unit expressed as a percentage of selling price, and
P = dollar value at cost of one unit of inventory.

To illustrate how the EOQ formula is used, let us assume that a firm's expected annual sales are 4,800,000 units, the cost of placing an order is $2,500, the cost of carrying one unit in inventory is 24 percent and the dollar value of one unit is $10. The EOQ formulation is calculated as follows:

$$EOQ = \sqrt{\frac{2\,(4,800,000)\,(2,500)}{(.24)\,(10)}} = 100,000 \text{ units.}$$

The formulation can be understood more easily if you look at Table 17-3, which shows the ordering and carrying costs for ten alternative quantities. The

TABLE 17-3   Calculation of Order Costs, Carrying Costs, and Total Costs

Quantity Purchased Q (units)	Order Costs (S/Q) · O (dollars)	Carrying Costs (½) (Q · i · P) (dollars)	Total Costs
50,000	$240,000	$ 60,000	$300,000
60,000	200,000	72,000	272,000
70,000	171,400	84,000	255,400
80,000	150,000	96,000	246,000
90,000	133,300	108,000	241,300
100,000	120,000	120,000	240,000
110,000	109,100	132,000	241,100
120,000	100,000	144,000	244,000
130,000	92,300	156,000	248,300
140,000	85,700	168,000	253,700

S = annual quantity sold in units = 4,800,000.
O = cost of placing an order = $2,500.
i = carrying cost per unit expressed as a percentage of selling price = .24.
P = dollar value at cost of one unit of inventory = $10.
Q = quantity purchased in units.

Note: The carrying cost is calculated by multiplying ½ times (Q · i · P) because at the beginning of the period the firm has 100% of its inventory requirements on hand and at the end of the period it is out of inventory.

table shows that as the order size becomes larger, the ordering cost decreases and the carrying cost increases. Note that the total cost decreases until 100,000 units are purchased, after which it increases. Figure 17-5 presents the same data in graph form.

FIGURE 17-5 Trade-Offs Between Carrying Costs and Ordering Costs

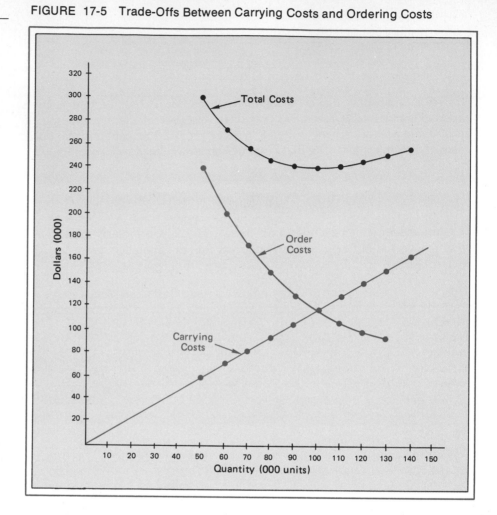

When Should an Order Be Placed?

The calculation of EOQ tells us how much to order but it does not tell us when to order. However, by knowing the EOQ, it is easy to calculate how many times annually the firm will have to place an order. In our example, with annual expected sales of 4,800,000 units and an EOQ of 100,000 units, the firm will have to order inventory 48 times during the year (4,800,000 ÷ 100,000). In order to determine exactly when an order should be placed, however, it is also necessary to know the pattern of demand for the inventory and the amount of time it takes for the inventory to arrive once the order has been sent.

Although the pattern of sales varies with the industry, many firms experience reasonably steady demand for their merchandise over much of the year. In the case of steady demand, an inventory pattern takes on a sawtooth appearance when graphed. We know that the firm will have to order inventory 48 times during the year, and therefore, that it should receive inventory every

FIGURE 17-6 Reorder Cycle

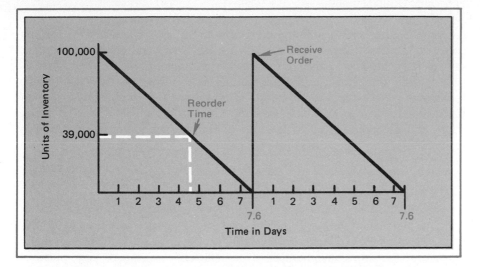

7.6 days (365 days per year ÷ 48 order periods). In other words, if the firm could somehow get delivery the instant it ran out of merchandise, it would reorder every 7.6 days. Since delivery is rarely instantaneous, the firm must estimate how long it takes the supplier to fill the order. In our example, assume a delivery time of three days. As Figure 17-6 shows, if the merchandise is ordered during the afternoon of the fourth day, it will arrive on the afternoon of the seventh day. In some situations, the delivery time is longer than the reorder cycle, in which case the firm must place a new order before it receives the previous order.

How Much Safety Stock Should Be Maintained?

Up to this point, we have dealt only with the inventory the firm expects to sell. This inventory is called **base stock**. The firm may also want to carry inventory in excess of what it reasonably expects to sell. This excess inventory is referred to as **safety stock**.

The amount of safety stock the firm should carry is determined by what happens in the event of a stockout. Does the firm offer a product so unique that sales are not lost but merely postponed? If so, the business need not be very concerned about running out of inventory because it will probably make the sale during the next reorder period. In contrast, if the firm is operating in a highly competitive market, a stockout could result in a sale being lost forever. In addition, the customer forced by a stockout to shop elsewhere may be very pleased with the new supplier and never return.

Two additional questions must be asked when evaluating the need for safety stock: How long does it take the firm to obtain a reorder? What is management's attitude toward stockouts? If a reorder can be delivered in a short time, there may be little reason for the business to carry a large safety stock. Regarding the second question, some managers feel that their firm must be able to satisfy 99 or even 100 percent of all its orders. If top management feels

this way, the firm will probably carry more safety stock than can be justified on economic grounds alone.

The problems of inventory management are perhaps most obvious in large grocery stores, where an offering of 10,000 to 16,000 separate items is quite common. To avoid some of the problems associated with inventory control, several large grocery chains have installed computerized check-out systems similar to the one shown in the photograph at left. Not only do such systems facilitate the check-out activity, but more importantly, they maintain a perpetual inventory record, alert management when stocks are low, and in many cases actually place the order when a predetermined inventory level is reached.

WAREHOUSING

The physical location and maintenance of inventory is not usually thought of as one of the critical factors in physical distribution. However, this is a major mistake. If the firm's merchandise is not efficiently managed, large sums of money will be wasted. Warehousing decisions are also important because they often involve long-term contractual arrangements. Here we look at the functions performed by warehouses, the relative advantages of public and private warehouses, and the use of automated warehouses in the physical distribution system.

Warehousing Functions

The primary function of warehouses is to provide safe, economical maintenance of inventories. Without efficiently operated warehouses, the firm would not be able to provide the level of service demanded by its customers. In addition, eight processing functions performed by warehouses have been defined:[14]

1. **Receives goods.** The warehouse receives merchandise delivered from outside transportation or an attached factory, and accepts responsibility for it.
2. **Identifies goods.** The appropriate stock-keeping units must be recorded, and a record made of the number of each item received. It may be necessary to mark the item by a physical code or tag. The item may be identified by an item code, a code on the carrier or container, or by physical properties.
3. **Sorts goods.** The merchandise must be sorted and assigned to the appropriate storage areas.
4. **Dispatches goods to storage.** The merchandise must be put away where it can be found later when needed.
5. **Holds goods.** The merchandise is kept in storage under proper protection until needed.
6. **Recalls, selects, or picks goods.** Items ordered by customers, for example, must be selected from storage efficiently and grouped in a manner useful for the next step.

---

[14]John F. Magee, *Physical Distribution Systems* (New York: McGraw-Hill Book Co., 1967), p. 73.

7. **Marshals the shipment.** The several items making up a single shipment have to be brought together and checked for completeness or for explainable omissions; the order records must be prepared or modified as necessary.
8. **Dispatches the shipment.** The consolidated order must be packaged suitably and directed to the right transport vehicle. Necessary shipping and accounting documents must be prepared.

Large firms typically invest substantial sums of money and management expertise to ensure that these processing functions are performed satisfactorily. Today, such concern means the large-scale use of computers to monitor the location of inventories as well as the use of automated inventory-processing machines.

Private vs. Public Warehouses

The firm has three basic warehousing alternatives: it can purchase its own warehouse, it can lease a warehouse, or it can utilize a public warehouse.

Private Warehouses. If a firm needs to store a large amount of inventory in one particular place, it should consider purchasing or leasing a warehouse. A major advantage of owning or leasing a warehouse is that it can be designed or selected on the basis of the specific needs of the firm. This advantage is particularly important to an organization with products requiring special care, such as exact temperature or pressure conditions.. Also, a private operation gives the firm greater control over the movement of its merchandise. With a public warehouse, the firm is just one of several customers, but if it controls its own warehouse, it can ensure better service schedules.

Private warehouses are also less expensive to operate than public warehouses, but only if the fixed cost of the warehouse can be spread over a large number of units. A private warehouse operating at less than 60 percent capacity is probably a major financial liability to the business. A final advantage of private warehouses is that extra space can be used to house other segments of the firm's operations; warehouses frequently provide office space for sales and service personnel.

Public Warehouses. If the business does not want to own its own warehouse or to control it through a long-term lease, it can rent space in a public warehouse. The services offered by public warehouses compare favorably in most respects with those of a private warehouse. In addition to the services listed in Table 17-4, some public warehouses also perform periodic inventory counts, initiate inventory restocking, process customer invoices, and provide general computer services.[15]

Whereas private warehouses are custom designed to meet the needs of a specific business, public warehouses serve a wide variety of customers. Nonetheless, a public warehouse can usually be grouped into one of five special-purpose categories:[16]

---

[15]John J. Coyle and Edward J. Bardi, *The Management of Business Logistics* (St. Paul, Minn.: West Publishing Company, 1976), p. 116.
[16]Ballou, *op. cit.*, p. 207.

TABLE 17-4   Public Warehousing Services Offered by 120 Large Public Warehouses

Service	Percentage of Firms Surveyed Offering Service
Inventory records	100%
Warehouse receipts	100
Storage	100
Break bulk handling	100
Marking and tagging	100
Over, short, damage reports	93
Prepaying freight	88
Local pickup and delivery	72
Accredited customer lists	72
Repairing	68
Packaging	52
Field warehousing	32
Bulk handling	28
Loans on goods in storage	23

Source: *Public Warehouse Study* (Washington, D.C.: McKinsey and Company, Inc., 1970).

1. **Commodity warehouses.** These warehouses handle only a single type of commodity, such as lumber, cotton, tobacco, or grain.
2. **Bulk-storage warehouses.** Some warehouses store and handle products in bulk form only, such as liquid chemicals, oils, or syrups. In some cases, product-mixing services may also be provided.
3. **Cold-storage warehouses.** These warehouses are controlled, low-temperature facilities that are used to maintain fruits, vegetables, frozen foods, and other perishable products.
4. **Household-goods warehouses.** Specialists in the storage and handling of furniture and other household articles, these warehouses are used by furniture manufacturers and household-moving companies.
5. **General-merchandise warehouses.** The true generalists in the public warehouse industry, these warehouses store any type of product not requiring special handling or processing.

The most significant advantage of public warehouses is that they do not require the firm to commit a large sum of money. The cost factor is very important to a firm with a cash problem since a large warehouse can easily cost between two and four million dollars. As a second advantage, public warehouses provide a great deal more flexibility than private warehouses. For example, they permit a firm to launch a new product on short notice and to withdraw it quickly from the market if it is not successful. No time is lost waiting for a warehouse to be constructed to store the new product. In the same manner, if the product fails, the firm can pull it off the market without being concerned about what will happen to its own warehouse expense. Recognizing this advantage, some firms augment their own private warehouse facilities by periodically renting public warehouse space. Also, if the business needs extra space because of a special promotion plan or for seasonal adjustment, such space can easily and economically be rented in a public warehouse.

The third advantage of public warehouses is that time-wasting management problems can be avoided because managerial responsibility is in the hands of someone outside the firm. As an example of how public warehouses can minimize headaches, the courts have ruled that, while a private warehouse can be picketed by a union, a public warehouse cannot be picketed when the employees of one of its customers are out on strike. Finally, renting public warehouse space may reduce the firm's tax payments. Many states have laws that define a firm as "doing business" within the state if that enterprise owns a building of any kind in that state. As a result, the firm may have to pay some form of corporate tax simply because it owns a warehouse within the state.[17]

Automated Warehousing

Any process that is repetitive, such as warehousing, is subject to automation. Today, there are many examples of large, fully automated warehouses. Most of the original designs were developed by the logistic command centers of the United States armed services. These military warehouses utilize punched tape or data cards and a computerized conveyor system which may be several miles in length. When an order is placed, a shipping container travels automatically to a dispenser, which on electronic command unloads the required item into the container. If more than one item is needed, the container travels to several bins to receive each item. Once all the merchandise has been assembled and packaged, the container is routed to a central shipping location.

In a fully automated warehouse, human labor may be used only to assign stock storage locations, to pack assembled materials, and to operate the warehouse's computer center. In addition to reducing the labor force necessary to operate a warehouse, automated inventory centers generally provide more rapid service to the customer. They also remove the manager from routine, day-to-day decisions, thereby providing much needed time to deal with long-range problems and planning.

Unfortunately, automated warehouses have encountered many problems. In some cases, firms operating such warehouses decided to modify their distribution structure and to switch to decentralized warehousing, with the result that there no longer was enough activity to justify the large fixed investment in equipment and computers. In addition, computers are always subject to malfunction; when this occurs, the entire warehouse must be shut down until the problem is solved. However, because of the large potential saving that accrues to the owner of an automated warehouse, it is only reasonable to expect that such warehouses will become increasingly popular in the next decade.[18]

THE FUTURE OF PHYSICAL DISTRIBUTION

Physical distribution has undergone some dramatic changes during the last decade. As indicated at the beginning of the chapter, only a few years ago the

---

[17]Coyle and Bardi, *op. cit.*, pp. 114–115.

[18]Heskett, *et al., op. cit.*, pp. 635–636.

firm spent most of its distribution efforts in traffic management, that is, comparing alternative transportation modes and selecting the carrier capable of providing the best service at the least cost. Today, the physical distribution executive deals with the entire distribution system and its interaction with the rest of the enterprise.

Energy Situation

The high cost of energy has begun to cause many changes in our way of life; it also has had significant impact on physical distribution. The most obvious impact of the energy shortage is that it is causing company managers to reevaluate their transportation networks. Many organizations have been forced to shift from high-speed delivery systems to slower, lower-cost alternatives. Another response has been the development of more efficient distribution and transportation systems. The energy efficiency of airplanes, trucks, and trains has improved markedly in the past ten years. New commercial aircraft, for example, have jet engines and wing modifications which make them 40 percent more energy efficient.

A less obvious impact on physical distribution has been the pruning of some product lines in order to lower production and distribution costs through energy conservation. A major television manufacturer recently announced in a full-page newspaper advertisement that in the future it would produce only one model of color television. The advertisement explained that such a policy would cut production and distribution costs, and thus save money for the consumer.

High Interest Rates

High interest rates also have a significant impact on how products are distributed. In the EOQ example presented earlier, we used 24 percent of the selling price of the item as the carrying cost per unit of inventory, which yielded an economic order quantity of 100,000 units and an order cycle of 7.6 days. If a more realistic 30 percent figure were chosen, the firm's EOQ would drop to 89,443 units and its order cycle to 6.75 days. The decline in both figures reflects the fact that higher carrying costs force the firm to inventory less merchandise and to order more often.

An additional ramification of higher interest rates is that firms are less willing to build private warehouses because they will have to pay higher fixed interest charges on borrowed capital. Long-term lease arrangements will also be less attractive because of increased annual lease payments. Therefore, firms will be more likely to utilize public warehouses even though they are less efficient and the per unit variable costs involved are somewhat higher. Unfortunately, like just about everything else, the price charged to the consumer will have to be increased to cover these additional costs.

Consolidated Shipments

One outcome of increased costs is expected to be greater consolidation of distribution services. Even competing companies will find it more efficient to share distribution facilities in order to reduce their individual distribution costs. The result will be less system duplication and greater utilization of existing capacity. Such cooperative activity is exemplified by Noxell Corporation in Cockeysville, Maryland, and McCormick and Co. in nearby Hunt Valley. The firms are located five minutes from each other and have many of the same customers. When the firms began co-loading operations, they were able to consolidate 40 percent of their shipments, which led to a significant savings on freight. In addition, they began shipping enough material together that they were able to establish faster, more dependable shipping schedules.[19]

In addition to direct cooperation enjoyed by Noxell and McCormick, increased utilization of freight forwarders and public warehouses can be expected in the near future. Freight forwarders specialize in the transportation of small shipments. They derive their income from the differences between the freight rates for small packages and the rates for carload and truckload shipments. Unfortunately, the effectiveness of freight forwarders has been greatly reduced since the Interstate Commerce Commission (ICC) began exercising tight control over their activities. If Congress decides to relax ICC control over freight forwarders, substantial new economies would be created for many businesses.

Computer Simulations

Generally speaking, management science has not lived up to its great promise in terms of applications involving distribution planning. The basic problem with management science is that, often, computational efficiency can be achieved only through the imposition of unrealistic assumptions, which tend to severely limit the model's usefulness. However, it is only reasonable to assume that management science will develop new techniques in the future that will permit the realistic evaluation of alternative distribution systems and the selection of the single most efficient system.

In the future, computer simulations should be able to deal effectively with such distribution planning questions as: How many distribution centers should be established? Where should they be located? How big should they be? Which distribution center should service each customer? How should the output from the manufacturing facilities be allocated to the various distribution centers? Given an acceptable customer service level, how do various distribution systems vary in cost?

The computer distribution simulation designed by Hunt-Wesson Foods provides a good illustration of the use of modern management science techniques.[20] The company produces tomato products, cooking oils, puddings, and many other products at its 14 locations; it distributes these products through 12 distribution centers. Because of a need for more distribution capacity, the com-

---

[19]Walter F. Friedman, "Physical Distribution: The Concept of Shared Services," *Harvard Business Review* (March–April, 1975), p. 25.

[20]Arthur M. Geoffrion, "Better Distribution Planning with Computer Models," *Harvard Business Review* (July–August, 1976), pp. 92–99. See also Donald J. Bowersox, "Planning Physical Distribution Operations with Dynamic Simulation," *Journal of Marketing* (January, 1972), pp. 17–25.

pany developed a computer model, with the result that three of the firm's distribution centers were modified immediately and many of the firm's customers were reassigned to new distribution centers. Hunt is saving well over $1,000,000 annually with no decline in the quality of customer service. Although computer models will never be any better than the data involved, it is likely that they will play an increasingly important role in the distribution process of the future.

summary points

1. The physical distribution concept is the most sophisticated of the three approaches to the problem of moving merchandise from the producer to the user. The traffic concept and the transportation concept are the other two approaches.

2. Total cost analysis is critical to the physical distribution concept. It requires that all decisions concerning one element in the physical distribution system be made in terms of their effects on the total system.

3. A firm's physical distribution capabilities can serve as an important sales tool for its marketing department.

4. Businesses which require excellent customer service and which spend a significant portion of their sales dollars on distribution should seriously consider establishing a physical distribution department.

5. Common carriers must provide transportation services to any firm without discrimination. Contract carriers receive an operating permit for movement of commodities for a specific set of shippers. Exempt carriers are not subject to state or federal legislation concerning operating rights or tariff charges.

6. Railroads and water carriers are used primarily for hauling heavy commodities over long distances. Airlines specialize in transporting high value, lightweight, perishable items. Trucklines haul freight on relatively short runs and offer door-to-door delivery.

Pipelines are used to move liquids continuously over long distances.

7. The economic order quantity (EOQ) minimizes the total of two costs: the cost of maintaining inventory and the cost of ordering inventory.

8. To determine when an order should be placed, the firm must know the product's EOQ, the pattern of demand for the product, and the inventory delivery time.

9. The more unique the product, the smaller the required amount of safety stock.

10. If a firm consistently has a large amount of inventory that must be stored in a particular location, it should consider establishing a private warehouse.

11. Large public warehouses provide flexibility to the user and offer many private warehouse services.

12. Automated warehousing reduces labor costs, provides more rapid service to the customer, and permits the manager to concentrate on long-range problems and planning.

13. The high cost of energy will force firms to shift to relatively slow, low-cost transportation alternatives. High interest rates will reduce the size of inventories and promote the use of public warehouses.

14. As distribution expenses increase, there will be more consolidation of shipments and greater use of computer simulations to select and test the best physical distribution system.

1. Evaluate the differences between the traffic, transportation, and physical distribution concepts.
2. What is meant by cost trade-offs in physical distribution?
3. How does physical distribution assist the firm's marketing efforts?
4. How do the cost of physical distribution, the importance of customer service, and top management support encourage the firm to adopt an integrated physical distribution system?
5. What are the four legal forms of transportation? What criteria should be used in selecting a form of transportation?
6. What are the differential advantages of each of the major transportation modes — railroads, water, air, trucks, and pipelines?
7. What is the rationale of the economic order quantity?
8. How does a purchasing agent know when to place an order?
9. How much safety stock should be maintained by the firm?
10. What are the advantages and disadvantages of selecting a private warehouse? A public warehouse?
11. How will physical distribution change in the future?

The beer industry has gone through several dramatic changes since prohibition was repealed. In 1930 there were almost 900 breweries operating in the U.S.; today, there are less than 80 breweries. Small breweries have been forced out of the market as large national breweries have expanded into their markets. Because of economies of scale, Schlitz, for example, can produce 9,110 barrels of beer per employee each year at an average cost of $1.08 per barrel. In contrast, Falstaff, the seventh largest brewer, produces only 2,277 barrels of beer per employee each year at a cost of $4.39 per barrel. Budweiser, Miller, Schlitz, Coors, and Pabst together account for more than 50 percent of the beer sold in the United States.

A second and more dramatic change in the industry occurred when the Miller Brewing Company was purchased by Phillip Morris in 1975. Phillip Morris had a great deal of experience in the marketing of tobacco products to consumers. The company used its know-how and financial resources to move Miller from the fifth largest selling beer to number two in less than five years. Phillip Morris recognized that the beer market is not made up of one large market, but consists of distinct market segments. As a result, Miller introduced several new beers, including Miller Lite, Clipper Dark Lite, and Lowenbrau. These products have been successful because they meet real needs in the marketplace and they have been heavily promoted. The other major breweries have been forced to reevaluate their entire marketing strategy to make sure that they will be able to remain competitive in the future.

Adolph Coors Company case is based on material in Charles G. Burck, "While the Big Brewers Quaff, the Little Ones Thirst," *Fortune* (November, 1972), pp. 104–106; Elliot Wendt, "Regional Brewers: How They Meet the Ad Challenge," *Beverage World* (March, 1978), p. 18; and William J. Schnick, Jr., "Homemade Imports," *Forbes* (October 15, 1977), p. 33.

Adolph Coors Company

Coors was established in 1873 by Adolph Coors in Golden, Colorado. Coors has always had a philosophy that the company should produce and market only the highest quality beer possible. To accomplish this objective, Coors uses only ingredients grown on Coors-supervised farms; no artificial ingredients are used in the brewing of Coors. In addition, Coors has the longest and the most expensive brewing cycle in the industry.

As a part of the emphasis on quality, Coors has never been willing to pasteurize its beer. Pasteurization, which requires that the beer be heated to an extremely high temperature, kills the bacteria in the beer and thereby slows down deterioration of the product. Coors feels that pasteurization in itself damages the flavor of the beer and therefore should be avoided. Coors has developed a process which requires its beer to pass through a long line of special energizer filters that eliminate most of the bacteria in the beer. While this process is more expensive than pasteurization, Coors feels that it results in a much better beer for the consumer.

The Coors philosophy of producing the best possible product has been very successful for the firm. While Coors is the fifth largest selling beer in the U.S., it spends 20 percent less per case on advertising than does Anheuser-Busch, Miller, or Schlitz. In addition, while comparative data is impossible to collect, industry insiders believe that even with its limited volume, Coors has consistently been the most profitable brewery in the nation.

Coors Distribution Program

Beer is sent from the brewery to local distributors. These distributors then sell the beer both to retail accounts and subwholesalers, who also sell to retail accounts. Normally subwholesalers sell to those accounts that the distributor feels are too small to warrant its servicing. While Coors uses the same channel of distribution as all other beer distributors, it expects a great deal more from its distributors than does any other major brewer.

As a part of Coors' quality control program it ships all of its beer in refrigerated railroad cars or trucks to its distributors. When the beer arrives it must be stored in a refrigerated warehouse at no more than 40°F. The Coors distributor delivers the beer to its retail accounts in refrigerated trucks, whereupon the distributor must convince the retail account that Coors beer will last longer and taste better if it is kept refrigerated. The distributor is then required to visit all of its retail accounts regularly to rotate the beer. This means that the beer that was sold earlier to the retail account is moved to the front of the retailer's display case and any new beer that is sold to the retail account is placed at the back of the case to ensure that the older beer is sold first. Finally, all Coors beer is dated so that the local distributor knows when it was brewed. Any beer that is 60 days or older that is discovered at the retail level is bought back by the Coors distributor and destroyed. This requirement ensures that all Coors beer at the retail level is fresh.

No other brewery requires that its wholesalers spend as much time and money to maintain the product once it arrives at the local level as does Coors. For example, Anheuser-Busch is the only other national brewer that requires that its product be refrigerated when it arrives at the wholesale level. Budweiser, however, is not refrigerated when it is shipped to the wholesaler, and the wholesaler is not required to deliver Budweiser to its retail accounts in refrigerated trucks.

The Problem

Coors is very much concerned about the impact that Miller has had on the beer industry. Executives are beginning to wonder if producing the best beer and distributing it through a highly controlled distribution structure is adequate. Coors' market share in several key states such as California has dropped from over 50 percent to approximately 35 percent. Some people feel that Coors has tried too hard to tell people what type of beer they should drink rather than responding to the real needs of the market. Finally, Coors is seriously considering expanding into other markets and even opening up an East Coast brewery. While Coors has never had any problem attracting potential distributors, it does require that the distributors spend more money to distribute their beer than do the other national breweries. If Coors' market share drops much more it will be more difficult for these dealers to make a reasonable return on their investments.

1. Does Coors appear to be market oriented?
2. Do you feel that Coors has adopted the best policy for distribution of its beer?
3. What potential conflict does Coors face in its channel of distribution?

Henderson's Men's Shop was a men's clothing store located in the downtown area of Austin, Texas, a city of about 285,000 people. The store featured high-quality men's clothing and accessories at moderate prices considering the quality products it carried. Henderson's had been at the same location for 32 years and enjoyed an excellent reputation for its clothing and personal, dependable, courteous service. Of the retailers in the city's downtown area, none had a more loyal clientele than Henderson's. The vast majority of Henderson's regular customers were from the upper-middle class.

Austin's downtown area had been allowed to deteriorate over the past several years. While it was not in as much disrepair as many cities, virtually nothing had been done to improve the situation. The results of the city's slip were businesses leaving for more attractive places and a noticeable decline in the number of people shopping downtown. In addition, two new shopping centers had been established in the past three years, one on the city's northern outskirts and one in the eastern suburbs.

Austin's Two New Shopping Centers

During the unsettling times for the downtown area, especially those of the past three years, Henderson's sales had increased, although at a significantly slower rate than was normal for the retail store. Mr. Henderson attributed the increase to the store's capturing some of the customers of clothing stores that had left the city. He felt that, were it not for other retailers' customers coming to his store, he would have experienced a decrease in sales in each of the past three years. His records showed that a few of his loyal customers had gone periods much longer than usual between purchases which led Mr. Henderson to suspect that they possibly were buying some of their clothes and accessories at other stores.

Henderson's Men's Shop case is reprinted with permission from Norman A. P. Govoni, Jean-Pierre Jeannet, and Terry F. Allen, *Marketing Problems: Cases for Analysis* (Columbus, Ohio: Grid, Inc., 1977), pp. 83–86.

When Austin's two new shopping centers were in the development stage, Mr. Henderson had been approached and he considered adding a branch store in the center or near the northern fringe of the city. This seemed to him to be more logical than the eastern center due to the lower socioeconomic characteristics of the eastern center's primary trading area and the general decor and tenant makeup of the shopping center. In the course of making his decision on whether or not to join the northern shopping center, Mr. Henderson considered several factors. On the positive side, he saw the following: It would be a new store in an expanding shopping area; prospects were good that the store would be profitable; many downtown shoppers were making their purchases at the shopping centers; there would be several complementary specialty shops that would undoubtedly benefit him; the two outstanding major chains, one a department store and the other a supermarket, would attract large numbers of customers and thus the center had a very high traffic potential; the desirable surroundings and decor of the overall shopping environment, and the characteristics of the shopping center's customers were consistent with his market.

On the negative side, were the following: high rental and common area costs for the shopping center location; a percentage of sales had to be paid out as part of the lease; much longer store hours; he would be tied to a ten-year lease at the shopping center; concern over the effect the new location would have on his downtown store; there was already a very reputable men's clothing store included in the center; and the two locations might be too much for one man to handle.

Mr. Henderson decided not to add a branch store in the new shopping center. When he informed the developer of his decision, Mr. Henderson was asked if he would consider moving his downtown store to the shopping center, thereby eliminating the need to run two stores. Mr. Henderson immediately declined the opportunity, stating that he strongly believed in downtown and that he would always keep his downtown store.

During the past year, Mr. Henderson had increased his advertising expenditure by over 50 percent and added television to the newspapers and radio stations he customarily used to spread his message. He also instituted a special "bargain days" promotion to go along with his two annual clearance sales. In addition, he took up sponsorship of Little League and Stan Musial League baseball teams. In light of the recent sales performance, Mr. Henderson was not satisfied with his extra promotional effort. He was contemplating cutting back to previous levels, unless he could be assured of more positive results.

Alternative Decisions

Mr. Henderson listed the following alternatives that he felt should be considered:

1. Keep the present store and step up his promotional effort.
2. Keep the present store and locate another store in the northern shopping center he rejected earlier, even though the sites now available were less-than-desirable in terms of both size and specific location within the shopping center.
3. Keep the present store and start a lower-quality, lower-priced branch operation at the eastern shopping center, which catered to a lower socioeconomic market, and where several sites were available that were ideal in terms of size and location in the center.
4. Close the downtown store and locate a similar store in the northern shopping center or a low-quality, low-priced store in the eastern shopping center.

5. Either keep or close the downtown center and move to the northern or other suburban area, not in a shopping center, and set up a shop consistent with the area's socioeconomic characteristics.
6. Sell the business outright and retire, which he could do comfortably, but not very happily.

1. Evaluate fully the advantages and disadvantages of each alternative listed by Mr. Henderson.
2. Can you think of any other alternatives?
3. What information should Mr. Henderson have before making a decision? How would he obtain it?
4. What should Mr. Henderson do? Why?

case 16
laredo boot
company

The Laredo Boot Company is a medium-sized manufacturer of cowboy boots. Company sales in 1979 were almost $30 million, most of which were concentrated in the fast-moving line of fashion boots. These boots have an average retail price of $85, with some of the fancier snakeskin types running up to $200. At present, more than 95 percent of Laredo's boots are sold in Texas, New Mexico, and Arizona. The only boots that are sold out of this tri-state area are sold to mail-order customers, who pay Laredo's standard suggested retail price for the boots.

The Marketing Mix

Laredo sells virtually all of its boots through three wholesale merchants located in each of the states in which Laredo does business. Laredo has always felt that it had a responsibility to advertise its products regularly in its market area. The firm budgets 2 percent of its estimated sales dollars to regional magazines such as *Texas Monthly* and *Arizona Highways*, newspapers, and selected spot television advertisements. Laredo has not used radio advertising since 1970.

Laredo has a cooperative advertising program with its distributors and their retail customers. Laredo has agreed to pay for half of any advertisements run by distributors or retailers if they use copy provided by Laredo. In each case, the reseller is permitted to display its name and store location in the ad. During the last two years, Laredo has spent approximately 3 percent of its sales dollars on cooperative advertising.

Laredo discourages its dealers from discounting its products. The firm's management feels that this type of activity would eventually lead the distributors to try to force Laredo to discount the product's price to them. Laredo believes that its products are competitively priced at the suggested retail price level and that there is no reason to cut into traditional profit margins. Laredo was sued several years ago by a retailer which had been cut off from receiving boots from the Texas distributor. The dealer claimed that the distributor and the Laredo Boot Company had conspired to stop providing Laredo boots because of the dealer's discounting practices. While many experts in the industry felt that conspiracy might have taken place, the dealer was not able to prove the allegation to the court's satisfaction.

A New Distribution Strategy

Maria Garcia, the niece of the president and principal owner of Laredo Boot Company, was named executive vice-president for marketing in September, 1980. Garcia feels that while Laredo has been very successful, the firm has not experienced any real growth during the last ten years. She would like to experiment with two new distribution strategies as well as with one new market.

First, Garcia believes that the Arizona distributor, which accounts for 25 percent of the firm's sales, has never really given Laredo boots the amount of attention and time that they deserve. This distributor (Arizona Boot and Saddle Company) sold boots, shoes, and a line of western work boots. Laredo boots represent 23 percent of its business. As a result of her unhappiness with the Arizona distributor, Garcia is carefully considering the alternative of selling directly to the retail accounts in Arizona. She realizes that it will be difficult to reach the 175 retail accounts located in Arizona, but she also believes that while some retailers may switch to another brand of boots most are loyal to Laredo and not to the distributor.

A second strategy that Garcia is considering involves opening retail outlets in some of the larger shopping centers in Houston and Dallas. These stores would be supplied directly from Laredo. This way, the firm has an opportunity not only to make profits on the products as they are produced, but also as they are sold at the retail level.

The new market that Garcia is considering is New York City. Many "in" people in New York are buying Texas-style clothing, and cowboy boots are very popular. Manufacturers such as Tony Lama have done quite well in this market. Garcia believes that while this fashion trend has been building for several years, it can be expected to continue for some time. While Garcia does not know the best way to reach the market, her intention is to use a manufacturer's representative to call on retail accounts. Realizing that this would be giving away some control over the product line, Garcia still plans to insist that retail accounts not discount the product. In addition, if the market in New York proves profitable, Garcia plans to make cooperative advertising available to the retail accounts there.

1. Do you feel that Laredo should sell directly to its retail customers in Arizona? What are the potential risks and rewards to Laredo if its products are sold directly?
2. Should Laredo establish its own stores in Houston and Dallas? How would the Texas distributors and the Houston and Dallas retailers be expected to react?
3. How should Laredo try to reach the potential market in New York City?

---

case 17
radiofleet, inc.

Radiofleet, Inc., operated a chain of electronic component stores with combined sales in excess of 40 million dollars. The central organization at Radiofleet decided on most important policy areas, such as buying and pricing. Advertising only recently had been decentralized to the store level. Day-to-day operations were left to the individual store managers. They controlled their own inventory levels, decided on store layouts, selected items for display, arranged for work schedules, and handled advertising and promotion.

Radiofleet's product line included virtually all types of electrical components currently available as well as a new line of home computers that sold for just under $700 and cost Radiofleet $350. Its two major warehouses stocked over 100 name brands. The stores carried most of the major brands of electrical products for homes, boats, mobile homes, and cars.

Radiofleet, Inc., case is reprinted with permission from Norman A. P. Govoni, Jean-Pierre Jeannet, and Terry F. Allen, *Marketing Problems: Cases for Analysis* (Columbus, Ohio: Grid, Inc., 1977), pp. 105–107.

Until about two years ago, Radiofleet, Inc., centrally arranged for all advertising and promotion of its stores. This included timing as well. As the chain grew, it became clear that each store would be better off if allowed to design its own promotional campaigns. Each store was allocated a monthly advertising allowance following a formula that incorporated past sales and market potential. Pricing policy was handled centrally and emphasized low margins with high turnover. Overstocked items, demonstration models, and used equipment were priced by each store following company guidelines. The company's retail price policy was aimed at "never being undersold by any competitor."

One of the more critical areas for Radiofleet was central buying. Due to its size, Radiofleet commanded large discounts from the five component distributors that were its major suppliers. Up to now Radiofleet had never dealt directly with manufacturers.

The stores' new minicomputer presented major problems for Radiofleet. During the product's first three months, Radiofleet reordered only once. In contrast, during the next six months, Radiofleet had been forced to reorder five times. Fortunately, relatively few sales had been lost since the minicomputer manufacturer had been able to deliver its merchandise in ten days. Radiofleet knew that demand had been quite consistent during the entire nine-month period it had carried the product. Demand was expected to be 300 units for the first year and 330 units for the second year. The cost of placing an order had been estimated to be $150.

In addition to the specific problems with the small computers, the company had been increasingly faced with supply problems. Often, individual stores ran out of stock on promoted merchandise at times when the two central warehouses were unable to come up with the supply. Occasionally, a store manager could obtain components from another nearby Radiofleet store, but this was costly because special trucking was necessary. Supply problems arose also when Radiofleet's regular distributor was unable to deliver the components. The greater the demands, the more frequently this happened. In such cases, Radiofleet had the option of waiting until the components arrived or of going outside its regular distributor network and buying the components without its customary discount. Both of these options led to increased costs. If the components could not be supplied in time, a potential sale might be lost.

Radiofleet was well aware of the costs of its inadequate logistics system. Partially, this was attributed to a lack of information flow between the central buying unit and the 40 stores. The lost sales due to stockouts were estimated to amount to 10 percent of sales. Since Radiofleet earned a contribution margin of 20 percent and a net margin of 3 percent of its sales, this loss in sales had a considerable impact on the company's earnings.

The Radiofleet management was considering only one possible course of action at the present time to improve its logistics system. The option was to expand its two warehouses at a net cost of $50,000 each. Increased interest costs and taxes would result in an annual expense of $30,000. Furthermore, the work force would have to be expanded, adding another $50,000 in annual costs. The expanded warehouses would then permit a larger inventory. Management estimated it would be possible to raise inventory from the current level of $5,000,000 to $6,000,000. However, carrying costs, running at about 20 percent of inventory, might also increase by as much as 2 percent.

1. Would the proposed warehouse expansion be profitable for Radiofleet?
2. What warehouse alternatives should Radiofleet consider?
3. Does the company need to make a change in its procedure for ordering its new line of home computers?

7

Marketing Specialties

Two areas of marketing that require rather specialized knowledge are the marketing of services and marketing in an international setting.

Although the marketing of services is similar to the marketing of products, differences do exist. Likewise, operating in an international market presents problems and challenges not encountered when serving a domestic market. Part 7 highlights these differences.

18

Marketing of Services

Marketing is defined in terms of both products and services. Marketing executives and theoreticians generally have focused their attention on products under the assumption that services are marketed in much the same way. While this may be true for many services, it certainly is not true for all services. In any case, this assumption has limited the amount of research undertaken on the subject of how services can be marketed most effectively. We begin by defining what is meant by a service.

WHAT IS A SERVICE?

It is not easy to define services precisely in a few words, or even in a few sentences. For many years, the American Marketing Association (AMA) defined **services** as "activities, benefits or satisfactions which are offered for sale, or are provided in connection with the sale of goods."[1] In order to clarify this somewhat unclear definition, the AMA cited amusements and transportation as examples of a service.

A better understanding of services can be gained if a product is seen as a noun and a service as a verb — that is, a product is a tangible object or device, whereas a service is a deed, a performance. In purchasing a product the buyer obtains an asset; in purchasing a service the buyer sustains an expense.

A second way to differentiate a product from a service has to do with utility. Does the utility of the purchase to the buyer derive from the physical nature of an object or from an action or performance? Using this approach, it is possible in some cases to distinguish unequivocally between a product and a service. For example, the satisfaction received in the purchase of a painting or other work of art stems from the tangible object itself. In contrast, the benefit provided by a certified public accounting firm is based exclusively on the rather intangible result of an act that it performs or service that it renders. In the first case no act is performed; in the second, no product is involved. Apart from such extreme examples, however, the distinction between the two is still not

---

[1] Committee on Definitions, *American Marketing Association, Marketing Definitions* (Chicago: American Marketing Association, 1960), p. 21.

always clear, since most products require some supporting services, and vice versa.[2]

A Molecular Model

A molecular model enables us to see that a firm's offerings, whether products or services, can be partly tangible and partly intangible.[3] Consider the purchase of an airline ticket and the purchase of a new automobile. As shown in Figure 18-1, the nucleus of the first type of purchase is an intangible transportation service; the nucleus of the second, a tangible product. Also, the two types of purchases differ dramatically in terms of whether they are dominated by intangible or tangible elements. Clearly, the airline's offering is intangible-dominant and does not involve transfer of ownership, as compared to the purchase of an automobile. The model can be completed by adding the re-

FIGURE 18-1   Molecular Models for Airlines and Automobiles

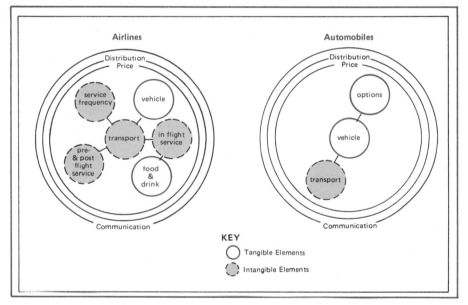

Source: G. Lynn Shoestack, "Breaking Free from Product Marketing," *Journal of Marketing* (April, 1977), p. 77.

maining marketing elements — price, distribution, and communications decisions — around the nucleus. The important point here is that the key marketing decisions depend on the makeup of the nucleus, specifically, whether it is dominated by intangible or tangible elements.

The molecular model makes it possible to position market offerings along a continuum as a function of their tangible and intangible elements. As shown in

---

[2]John M. Rathmell, "What Is Meant by Services?" *Journal of Marketing* (October, 1966), p. 33.

[3]This section is adapted from G. Lynn Shoestack, "Breaking Free from Product Marketing," *Journal of Marketing* (April, 1977), pp. 73–75.

FIGURE 18-2 Continuum of Market Offerings

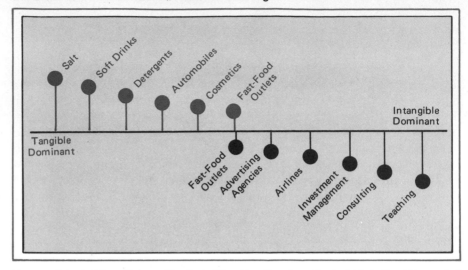

Source: Adapted from G. Lynn Shostack, "Breaking Free from Product Marketing," *Journal of Marketing* (April, 1977), p. 76.

Figure 18-2, consulting services and teaching are at one end of the continuum while salt and soft drinks are at the other. This framework can graphically put marketing opportunities into proper perspective. The more a market offering is characterized by intangible elements, the more difficult it is to apply the usual marketing tools developed and tested for products. These highly intangible offerings require different marketing techniques if they are to be sold successfully.

Characteristics of a Service

In addition to intangibility, services have three additional characteristics that differentiate them from products. These other characteristics require the marketing executive to develop special marketing programs for services.

Buyers Are Dependent on Sellers. When a seller transfers title to a product, the buyer normally has complete control over the product. In contrast, as stated above, the purchase of a service does not involve transfer of ownership. Consumption of the service is not possible without the participation of the seller, whether the seller is a public utility, a lawyer, or a football team. Therefore, the seller of the service is an integral part of the buyer's satisfaction, much more so than the seller of a product. The seller, therefore, must give special attention to the needs of the buyer.

A Service Cannot Be Inventoried. Whether the service seller is a university, a hospital, or a port authority, it must be able to create, or render, the service before a transaction can take place. A service cannot be stockpiled; as a result, the seller does not have the flexibility that inventory provides firms that manufacture or sell tangible products. The seller of a service must be concerned with peak load and excess capacity because wide fluctuations in demand cannot be smoothed over with inventory. A good example is the CPA firm which must work its employees as much as 15 hours a day in the weeks before the April 15 income tax submission deadline.

Performance Standards Are Difficult to Maintain. Finally, except for a few machine-intensive service industries, such as automated telephone systems, it is very difficult to maintain uniform performance standards for services. The quality of service varies not only among firms in the same industry (compare the output of several advertising firms), but also from one service transaction of the firm to the next. The basic reason for such variation in quality is that service industries are human-intensive. As a result, the managers of service firms typically must supervise their employees quite closely in order to ensure that they consistently meet customer service standards.[4]

THE SERVICE SECTOR

How big is the service sector in the U.S. economy? How fast is it growing? What has caused the service sector to grow so large in the United States? You may be very surprised by the answers to these questions.

The Importance of the Service Sector

The economy of the United States, slowly but steadily, has grown less manufacturing-based and more service-based. This gradual transformation is shown in Figure 18-3, which traces the growth of the durable goods, nondurable goods, and service sectors of the economy from 1960 to 1979. The im-

FIGURE 18-3 Growth in Three Sectors of the U.S. Economy, 1960–1979

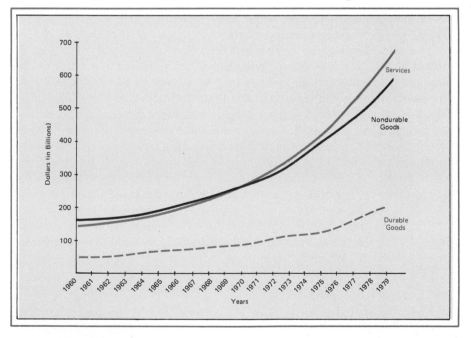

Source: U.S. Department of Commerce, *Business Statistics* (1979).

---

[4]John M. Rathmell, *Marketing in the Service Sector* (Cambridge, Mass.: Winthrop Publishers, 1974), pp. 6–7.

portance of the service sector in the economy can also be seen from the following statistics:

1. From 1947 to 1977, the slowest-growing industry in the service sector, retail trade, grew faster than the fastest-growing industry in the production sector, construction.
2. In 1976, more than two thirds of the entire U.S. work force were employed in service-related jobs.
3. In 1976, services (including government services) accounted for 65 percent of the gross national product.
4. More than 70 percent of all college graduates employed in the private sector currently work for service industries.
5. According to the forecast for the first five years of the 1980s, more than two thirds of all newly created jobs for college graduates will be in service industries.[5]

Reasons for Growth in the Service Sector

The most important long-range reason why the service sector has grown so rapidly in the United States, and in other Western nations as well, has been the creation of a large middle class with a substantial amount of cash available for discretionary spending. A service is just what the name implies — a job or action purchased by one person from another that the buyer cannot or does not want to perform. For many years most services were limited to the professions — lawyers, doctors, and dentists — and to domestic help. As our economy became more affluent, new services developed, including insurance companies, employment agencies, beauticians, travel agencies, catering services, housecleaning services, and many others.[6]

The second reason for growth in the service industry is the fact that the number of dwelling units in the United States has increased at a much greater rate than the population; the millions of babies born after World War II have now become active participants in the housing market. Smaller households mean fewer people to help with household tasks, more disposable income, and thus greater reliance on services procured in the marketplace. The third reason is the substantial increase in the number of working women who have neither the time nor the inclination to do many of the things around the house that their unemployed mothers did. As a result, many of them use service organizations to clean their houses, to do their hair, and to take care of their preschool children.

The final reason for the increase in the total amount of money spent on services is that the price of services has grown nearly 40 percent faster than the price of products. Why? Because wage increases are more easily offset by productivity increases in the manufacturing sector than in the service sector.[7]

---

[5]James Fitzsimmons and Robert Sullivan, *Service Operations Management* (New York: McGraw-Hill Book Co., 1981), pp. 5–11.

[6]Eugene B. Mapel, "The Marketing of Services," in Victor P. Buell, *Handbook of Modern Marketing* (New York: McGraw-Hill Book Company, 1970), Section 1, p. 41.

[7]Fabian Linden, "Service Please!" *Across the Board* (August, 1978), p. 42.

What Services Does the Family Purchase?

The average family spends more money on shelter than on any other service category. As Figure 18-4 indicates, almost 34 percent of the family service dollar goes to shelter, while at the other extreme less than 3 percent is spent on foreign travel. Of particular interest is the fact that income elasticities,

FIGURE 18-4   The Family Service Dollar, 1976

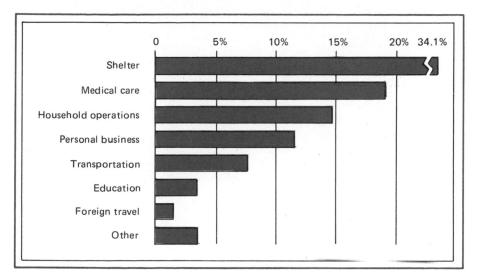

Source: U.S. Department of Commerce and The Conference Board in Fabian Linden, "Service Please!" *Across the Board* (August, 1978), p. 43.

which represent the percentage increase in consumer spending for each one percent increase in disposable income, vary significantly for each type of service. For example, as shown in Table 18-1, expenditures for services in general increase 1.16 percent for each one percent increase in disposable income. In contrast, expenditures for owner-occupied housing increase 1.62 percent for each one percent increase in disposable income, while expenditures on local public transportation actually decline when disposable income increases. Let's look at each major sector in the service economy as well as the future for each.[8]

Shelter. Since the early 1960s, total outlays for shelter have increased at a rate of nearly 5 percent compounded annually. The currently high interest rates for mortgage money can be expected to slow this growth rate somewhat — many families today are simply being priced out of the housing market. However, between now and late 1985, total population will increase by 7.5 percent and the number of families by 18 percent. Barring a major long-term economic downturn, it is only reasonable to assume that the pressure of many new families clamoring for affordable housing will again cause total outlays in this area to accelerate.

---

[8]Data in the following Sections are from *ibid.*, pp. 43–45.

TABLE 18-1   Service Income Elasticity Ratios, 1967–1976

	Income Elasticity Ratio
Services	1.16
Housing	
Owner-occupied	1.62
Renter-occupied	1.33
Household operations	1.08
Electricity	1.73
Telephone	2.23
Local transportation	−0.76
Intercity transportation	0.74
Medical care services	1.74
Personal care services	−1.23
Higher education	0.82
Foreign travel	0.63

Note: Income elasticity ratios denote real percentage increase in consumer spending for each 1 percent rise in real disposable income.

Source: Fabian Linden, "Service Please!" *Across the Board* (August,
1978), p. 43.

Medical Care. Rising costs as well as a more highly educated and older population have caused the medical care component of the service sector to increase considerably. However, even more important in this regard has been
the growth in the number of insurance plans for medical and hospital care.
Many of these programs are paid for in full or in part by the employer, or at
least are deducted from employees' wages. As dental care programs become
more widely available and as the general concern for health increases, it is
likely that the medical care component of the service economy will continue to
grow in the 1980s.

Household Operations. Although total outlays on home utilities have increased a great deal since 1970, the high cost of utilities in the 1980s will keep
real usage rates from growing significantly. Many families who once air-condi-
tioned their homes 24 hours a day in the summer have stopped doing so.
Many more families have lowered their thermostat settings as much as 10 degrees in the winter. These steps may not result in lower utility bills, but they do
reduce the total amount of energy consumed. One exception has been telephone service. After adjusting for inflation, expenditures on telephone service
have still risen at an annual rate of 7.2 percent, which has been much higher
than the corresponding growth in real income. Although it is difficult to account
for the increase in telephone usage, it may be attributable to the growing
number of teenagers and their use of extension lines and to increased reliance
on long distance as a means for family members to keep in touch with one another.

Personal Services. Personal service expenditures include brokerage fees,
legal fees, trips to the hair salon, to name a few. Expenditures in this service
category will increase only modestly in the 1980s, and they will be tied directly

to the health of the economy. When stock market prices fall, for example, stockbrokers find themselves with fewer customers — unless the market collapses and there is a selling panic. In the same way, when disposable money is scarce, most families postpone the legal expense involved in writing a will, and visits to the hair salon become less frequent.

Transportation. The transportation sector of the service economy includes both local transportation and intercity transportation. Expenditures on local public transportation have been declining at the alarming rate of 2.5 percent annually. The largest single reason for this decline has been shift of population from the city to the suburbs. In addition, pay raises and soaring energy costs have been passed along to the consumer in the form of fare increases, which has further served to deter public transportation ridership. Someday, if cities are able to move large numbers of people in and out of their central business districts, as many optimistic demographers predict will happen in the 1980s, the decline in local public transportation expenditures may be reversed.

In contrast, spending for intercity public transportation, primarily air travel, rose sharply in the 1960s and early 1970s. After a slump in the mid-1970s, spending increased again after the Civil Aeronautics Board authorized some degree of price competition among domestic airlines. The demand for domestic air travel proved to be surprisingly elastic as the public responded enthusiastically to the new lower fares.

Education. The education sector rises and falls with the demographic tidal wave. During the 1960s, as the post-World War II baby-boom generation entered college, the amount of real income spent on education increased significantly. However, more recently, owing to rising tuition costs and the fact that many college graduates cannot find jobs, there has been an absolute dollar decline in this sector. During the first half of the 1980s, the number of people of college age is expected to decline by 5 percent; as a result, there is every reason to believe that higher education will continue to suffer further declines in total dollar expenditures.

Foreign Travel. Foreign travel experienced substantial gains in the 1960s. Such gains generally were the result of economic prosperity in the United States and rising incomes bolstered by two-income families. Today, however, record levels of inflation worldwide and the weakening of the dollar relative to other world currencies make the foreign travel sector a target for real decline. The one bright spot on the horizon is the recent decrease in international airfares. However, even with the reduced costs of overseas flights, it seems likely that total expenditures of U.S. citizens abroad will continue to decline in importance.

STRATEGIC MANAGEMENT AND MARKETING OF SERVICES

In pure service industries, such as banking, public transportation, and management consulting, the transfer of a physical product to the buyer is incidental to the service provided. An example of such a "product" is a quarterly report sent by a savings and loan association to each of its depositors. Unfortunately, many managers in service industries view strategy from a product perspective despite the fact that such an approach may not be relevant to the delivery of services. This section outlines how the marketing of services differs from the marketing of products in terms of four areas of strategic management: (1) gaining a competitive edge, (2) cutting costs, (3) setting prices, and (4) introducing a new offering to the market.

Gaining a Competitive Edge

Every business attempts in some way to protect itself from the effects of competition. In product-oriented firms, capital is the most commonly used tool: the larger the firm, the greater the economies of scale, the lower the unit production costs, and the greater the profit margin. While many service industries do not have this luxury, many others do, especially those in equipment-based service businesses. An example is a commercial air carrier flying wide-bodied jet airplanes — a Boeing 747, Lockheed L-1011, or McDonald-Douglas DC-10. These airplanes cost the airlines considerably more than smaller jet aircraft but carry twice as many passengers and require only a few additional crew members. Another example is a multi-unit theatre — four screens but only one ticket taker, one cashier, and one soft drink and candy counter.

A second approach to gaining a competitive edge in product-based firms is through product differentiation, or brand identification, which can be critical to the long-term maintenance of markets. In the product sector, two good examples are Coca-Cola and Xerox, both of which have nearly become generic product names. Gaining an edge through service differentiation is more difficult but it can be accomplished. Many well-known consulting firms have been able to develop strong reputations in specific service areas, such as Burke in marketing research, Dun's Marketing Services in direct mail, and A. C. Nielsen Co. in data base management.

Cutting Costs

The usual way to reduce costs and to improve profit margins in the product sector is to substitute capital for labor. Capital is then used to purchase machines capable of performing certain tasks cheaper and more consistently than human labor. Many service industries have adopted this approach as well. For example, rather than maintaining paper files, many universities now keep student records on computer tape, which permits such tasks as degree checks and certifications to be done much faster than before.

In addition to relying more on capital, some service industries have begun to replace expensive labor with inexpensive labor for jobs that cannot be automated. Many tasks performed at law firms are routine and require little professional training; as a result, part-time law students and full-time paralegal assistants now prepare legal briefs and conduct routine research, freeing staff attorneys to occupy themselves with more important matters.

Setting Prices

Product-oriented companies have well-established cost formulas telling them exactly how much a product costs at various production levels. They then usually set their price as a function of cost and competitive factors. In service-based industries, price is often determined on the basis of value. Customers usually have a general idea of how much they should pay for a given service but are not sure because of the difficulty of comparison shopping. As a result, prices are often calculated by the seller in terms of how much the market will bear.

Interestingly enough, professional people can create a poor image for themselves if they price their services too low. Not often does one hear a person boast that he or she has the cheapest lawyer in town. In the same spirit, any experienced consultant knows that it may not be easy to sell a client on the merits of an expensive report, but that it certainly is much harder to build a convincing case for a *bargain* report. Purchasers of sophisticated consulting services are especially susceptible to the price-quality illusion because of the difficulty of ascertaining the real value of the service beforehand.

Introducing a New Offering to the Market

Most production firms employ research and development teams to design and test new products and to improve older ones. The development process is much more complex in service industries because the concern is with concepts rather than with products. As a result, test marketing is much more expensive and much less reliable. Consider the introduction of electronic funds transfer. Although the technology is available to create a cashless society, electronic funds transfer has not enjoyed wide acceptance. Consumers have not accepted the service out of concern for computer errors, invasion of privacy, and the maintenance of permanent personal data records.

Because of the difficulty of test marketing new services, which can sometimes be overcome if enough money is invested in research, there has been little real innovation but a great deal of imitation. When a firm offers a new service to the market that proves to be quite popular, other firms in the industry start offering a similar service. The classic example is the schedule of lower air fares initially tested by one airline on a few routes. When competing carriers saw the demand for these lower fares, they quickly reduced the prices of their flights as well.

THE MARKETING MIX FOR SERVICES

The marketing mix consists of the marketing research, product, communications, pricing, and distribution decisions made by the firm in order to deliver its service to the customer profitably. Many, if not most, of the product concepts discussed in this text also apply to services. The objective of this section, then, is not to develop totally new ways to market services but rather to look at the marketing mix from a service perspective.

Marketing Research

The objective of marketing research, as practiced in service industries and in product manufacturing firms, is the same — to reduce decision risk. According to the marketing concept, a service firm should carefully investigate the needs of the marketplace before it introduces a new service, since different market segments usually want slightly different services. As an illustration, well-

Many people enter the service industry as a franchisee of a national firm. Here are some hints on how to evaluate a franchise just in case such an opportunity comes *your* way.

Reputation of the Franchisor. When dealing with national firms such as McDonald's, Holiday Inn, or Chevrolet, you need not worry too much about their reputations. They are respected organizations. Of course, you should have an attorney read the franchise contract specifying your rights and obligations. Should a part of the contract be unacceptable to you, it is very unlikely that an established national franchisor would modify it just to please you. On the other hand, if you've never heard of the franchisor, first check on the reputation and track record of the firm. Your banker should be able to help you. In such cases, the franchisor may be a bit more flexible in the contract in order to line up needed franchisees.

Product Evaluation. What exactly will you be selling? Does the product or service seem to be a fad, or does it fill some long-term societal need? Even hamburgers, which seem to have tremendous staying power, do not *guarantee* a successful and lasting franchise.

Financial Analysis. How much does the franchise cost? What is your likely financial return? Are there additional operating and service fees payable to the franchisor? Are there immediate out-of-pocket costs? What is your break-even point?

Consulting Other Franchisees. Unless you're the franchisor's first franchise operator, you should be able to find other people who have already opened an outlet. Ideally, these other franchisees should range from unsuccessful to very successful. In general, find out how many hours you, as the franchise operator, will be required to work, whether the franchisor is willing to help the franchisee solve operating problems, and what types of management problems you should anticipate. If at all possible, you or your accountant should evaluate the financial statements of other franchisees.

Benefits of the Franchisor. Does the franchisor provide adequate training for new franchisees? Will the franchisor help you protect and maintain your market? Under what terms can your franchise agreement be terminated? Are there contractual provisions for resolving disputes between you and the franchisor? Or do you have to do everything the franchisor tells you to do or risk losing your franchise?

Act Slowly. There is usually no great hurry to sign a franchise agreement. A franchisor who is interested in you should be willing to give you and your lawyer, banker, and accountant time to evaluate the franchise agreement carefully.

Marketing & You

to-do families will probably want a summer camp for their children to be staffed by college students, to offer a complete package of programs, including horseback riding and art and music classes, and to have medical care facilities available at all times. The reason for sending the kids to camp may be more than just to give them a chance to "commune with nature." It may also be to give the parents an opportunity to take a cruise to the Greek Isles without being bothered by the trials and tribulations of parenthood. In contrast, a less well-to-do family may be willing to sacrifice such expensive extras as horseback riding or art and music classes to be able to send their child to summer camp. In addition to evaluating market segments and their purchase motives — both the *apparent motive* and the *underlying motive* — marketing research is useful in determining how often the service is purchased, who makes the purchase decision, and who actually procures the service.

Motivational research is often more useful than market surveys in the evaluation of a new service offering. A service represents an "idea," which frequently is easier to evaluate using storytelling techniques and focus groups (see Chapter 6). In addition, test marketing a service is usually much more complex than test marketing a product. First, there is no physical product to show the customer, only an idea, and second, the adoption period is much longer because the advantages of the new service may not be readily apparent. A good illustration is dental insurance, which would never have been introduced if the decision had been made on the basis of test marketing alone. In fact, overcoming the initial skepticism of the labor unions and many private individuals toward the idea took several years and a great deal of promotional literature from insurance companies.

Service Planning

As stated earlier in this chapter, one of the characteristic attributes of a service is that it requires the active participation of the seller. Similarly, it is important to remember that a service is not just the act, or performance, but rather all the features involved in convincing a buyer to purchase it. Such features include the location of the service, any warranties offered in connection with the service, and the reputation of the seller. One reason why many law firms spend a disproportionately large amount of money decorating their offices is because their clients want to believe that they are dealing with a prosperous, stable organization. This aspect of the service may be just as important in generating buyer confidence as the legal services themselves.

Services, like products, pass through a life cycle — they are born, prosper, and reach extended periods of modest profitability, after which most of them fail. Services still in the growth phase of the life cycle curve include telecommunications, health care, and leasing. Examples of services clearly past their growth peaks are motion pictures, watch repairing, and rail passenger service.[9] This pattern does not suggest that a firm should not enter a service industry in the mature or decline phase of the life cycle, but rather that more capital will be required to remain competitive during these phases and that the return on investment may not be as large as it might have been earlier in the life cycle.

---

[9]Rathmell, *op. cit.*, p. 59.

A second implication of the service life cycle is that many currently profitable services may someday be unprofitable. Weak services, like weak products, can be spotted early if the firm monitors sales, price, profit trends, as well as the impact of substitute products or services. Finally, the service life cycle tells us that the firm must remain flexible, modifying its market strategy as the product passes through the life cycle.

Service executives must also concern themselves with the depth and the breadth of the service line offered. Commercial banks are good examples of businesses that have attempted to increase the breadth of their services by becoming virtual financial department stores. In contrast, physicians have become increasingly specialized, thereby deepening but narrowing their service lines. The advertising business in recent years has been the center of an ongoing controversy over the issue of breadth versus depth. Many people in advertising favor full-service agencies capable of conducting market research and providing a complete market strategy package, whereas others argue that advertising agencies should concern themselves only with advertising problems. Interestingly enough, there seems to be a trend today toward the increasing specialization of advertising agencies. Examples of specialized agencies include the so-called creative houses, jingle-makers, media-buying agencies, and public relations specialists.[10]

Distribution

Many so-called experts dismiss the importance of the distribution channel in the marketing of services. Although it is true that some services, such as those provided by doctors and lawyers, are marketed through very short, direct channels, many others are not. In reality, about the only generalization that can be made about service channels is that the time and place utility of the channel is extremely important because services cannot be inventoried and demand varies considerably over time. To illustrate, consider the time and place utility of a telephone booth, emergency medical care, and an automobile repair garage.

Where the service is performed is an important consideration for the marketing manager. Geographically, the trend in service delivery today seems to be away from concentration and toward dispersion. A wealthier society, more education, increased emphasis on individuality, convenience, and self-actualization all favor the growing dispersion of service delivery points. Examples of such dispersion include neighborhood outpatient health clinics, community colleges, and the growing willingness of ballet companies, symphony orchestras, and other fine arts groups to market themselves to the public. Of course, there are several exceptions to the trend toward dispersion — most notably large banks, some of which are building new facilities in downtown urban areas, and physicians, many of whom are leaving suburban offices and moving to centralized office buildings located adjacent to hospitals. In the case of banks, branch banking notwithstanding, the preference for downtown seems to be a matter of historical precedent; with regard to doctors, increasing specialization in the

---

[10]*Ibid.*, p. 60.

FIGURE 18-5 Typical Terms Used for Pricing in the Service Sector

Nature of Services	Typical Price Terminology
Communications	Rate
Consulting and business facilitating	Fee, commission, retainer
Educational	Tuition
Financial	Interest
Health	Fee, charge
Household operations	Rate, charge
Housing	Rent
Insurance	Premium*
Legal	Fee, retainer
Personal	Charge
Recreational	Admission
Transportation	Tariff

*In the case of life insurance, premiums must be adjusted for dividends and cash surrender value (savings) to arrive at the true price.

Source: John M. Rathmell, *Marketing in the Service Sector* (Cambridge, Mass.: Winthrop Publishers, Inc., 1974), p. 72.

medical profession makes it advantageous for doctors to be near one another for referrals.[11]

The use of intermediaries is the final service distribution issue that should be addressed. Franchising has proven to be an effective way to deliver such services as automobile brake repair (Brake Check) and muffler replacement (Midas and Meineke) to the public. Where it is appropriate, franchising offers the advantages of specialized training and follow-up quality control checks. Nonfranchised intermediaries are also used in the service sector to make it easier for the buyer and seller to transact business. For example, travel agents book airline and hotel reservations; independent insurance agents develop insurance programs which may draw upon the policies of several insurance companies. In each of these cases, the customer contacts the intermediary, who in turn draws upon the resources of another organization(s) to develop the best possible package of services for the customer.

Pricing

Interestingly enough, the word "price" is not often used in the service sector. As Figure 18-5 indicates, consumers usually do not think of the price of a semester credit hour or of the price of an apartment. Figure 18-5 also suggests the great variety of environments in which service pricing decisions are made. In reality, what the multiplicity of environments means is that it is nearly impossible to make any useful generalizations about the pricing of services.

The government has regulated the prices of some services for many years. In most of these cases, the regulated firm occupies a monopoly position in its

---

[11]*Ibid.*, pp. 104–106.

market area and could charge an unreasonable price for its services, thereby reaping an excessive profit. Electrical and telephone utilities are examples of industries that the government regulates to prevent such abuses. Often, it is difficult for the regulatory authority to determine a fair price for these services because the firms involved have little incentive to keep costs under control.

A second type of regulated service involves such businesses as airlines and railroads. For many years, economists believed that the demand for transportation services was inelastic — that is, price cuts would not result in significantly greater ticket sales. Thus, if firms in these industries were allowed to price competitively, they would tend to set prices too low, eventually resulting in bankruptcy. In contrast to public utilities, transportation prices were regulated to prevent them from falling too low, not from rising too high. At least for the airlines, the economists were wrong with respect to the inelasticity assumption — price cuts in the late 1970s led to significantly larger profits!

The pricing of professional services has long been considered a topic that simply isn't discussed. For example, doctors and lawyers for many years were forbidden by the American Medical Association and the American Bar Association, respectively, from advertising their prices or their services. Both were expected to charge at least the minimum fee set for them by their professional associations. In a far-reaching case, the Federal Trade Commission found the American Bar Association (ABA) guilty of price conspiracy because of its attempt to punish lawyers for advertising their fees. Further, the Supreme Court has held that it is illegal for the ABA to restrain its members from advertising their fee schedules. It is only reasonable to assume that the American Medical Association will soon be forced to withdraw its sanctions against advertising.

How do firms or individuals set the price for their services? The answer, unfortunately, is what you might expect — the procedure depends on the nature of the service. As we stated earlier, price is often determined by how much the seller feels the buyer values the service. The result is often a situation where one individual can charge a much higher price than could another individual for the identical service because of the different reputations of the two sellers. For example, a lawyer that has an outstanding reputation can charge an inflated price for routine work, such as making out a will, simply because of the market value that society places on that good reputation. Cost-oriented pricing, however, is also a common pricing technique. It is used for such diverse services as automobile repairs, consulting, and education. With the exception of a few capital-intensive firms, the major cost of a service is labor. As the cost of labor increases, the price of services must also increase.

Capital-intensive services, such as public utilities, use rate-of-return pricing strategies. They attempt to convince their regulating agencies that they need to make a certain target rate of return on invested capital in order to generate a reasonable profit for their stockholders. Rate-making agencies and service firms often find it easy to agree on a percentage rate-of-return figure — what they disagree about is the amount of capital invested. The utilities argue that asset replacement cost represents the true level of investment; utility commissions, on the other hand, contend that assets should be valued at the actual amount paid for them — what accountants call the historical price. Needless to say, the historical price is usually much lower than the replacement cost.

Variable-cost pricing is another technique used by many service professionals. Medical doctors frequently charge low-income patients a lower rate. Doctors would argue that in doing so they are charging a fair price to those who can afford to pay and donating their services to those who cannot. In essence, it is understood that the demand for health care is inelastic — people simply must have medical attention when they need it regardless of the price. Lawyers and even consultants also sometimes use variable-cost pricing.[12]

Communications

Such communication functions as advertising and personal selling are much more difficult to perform for a service than for a product. With a service there is no physical item that the buyer can see or touch. Therefore, most services are promoted and sold on the basis of performing a useful *function* for the buyer, in contrast to many products, which are sold on the basis of their *physical* appeal. Insurance companies sell life insurance policies by pointing out that such policies protect the family — and thus perform a useful function — in the event the breadwinner dies. In the same way, the telephone company promotes extension phones on the basis of their convenience.

Service businesses typically equate advertising with marketing. Banks and other financial institutions have been notorious for making this mistake. Unfortunately, equating the two leads the organization to forget that the overall market for its services is made up of many distinct segments, and that service planning, distribution, and pricing decisions are key elements in the development of a successful service organization.

The promotion of nonprofit institutions, such as the United Fund and the American Heart Fund, is often quite low-key. The objective simply is to inform the public of the existence of the organization or its service mix. This approach may be a mistake. Although nonprofit organizations do not compete directly with one another in the marketplace, they do compete in the sense that each of us has only so much time or money to contribute to worthy causes. Thus, giving to one cause may mean not giving to another.

Nonprofit institutions communicate with many different audiences; each audience, or target market, may require a different type of promotion. For example, think of the many audiences of a university — alumni, current students, future students, legislators, regents, donors, faculty, and staff. Each group is different and must be dealt with differently.

As stated earlier, for many years lawyers and other professionals did not advertise their services. To do so was considered unethical and, even worse, in poor taste. These professions relied on word of mouth and various forms of public relations to tell the public about their services. Today, this situation has begun to change. Lawyers, for example, are beginning to communicate with the public via newspaper and occasionally via television. Although the number of lawyers using mass communication techniques is still small, it is reasonable to assume that the legal and other professions will rely increasingly on such techniques in the future.

---

[12]Rathmell, *op. cit.*, p. 78.

Finally, although advertising has been the focus of much of this discussion, personal selling is a most important promotional vehicle for some services. Many people develop a personal relationship with their life insurance agent, doctor, or dentist largely because they do not know much about either insurance or medicine, preferring instead to rely on the expertise of a trusted professional.

INCREASING THE PRODUCTIVITY IN THE SERVICE SECTOR

As mentioned earlier, the service sector has been the fastest growing component of the U.S. economy over the last ten years. The obstacle that could stop, or at least slow, the growth of the service sector in the 1980s is the continued increase in the cost of labor. Already, people are simply being priced out of the market for many services. The solution to this problem is obvious but difficult to implement — that is, increase the productivity of the service sector labor force.

The traditional way to increase productivity in a business is to provide more capital and more training per employee. To a limited extent, both approaches have been used in the service sector.[13] For example, fast-food franchises, such as McDonalds and Kentucky Fried Chicken, which sell a mix of products (food) and services (quick meals), have spent a great deal of money on the equipment needed to prepare food quickly and inexpensively. These firms also offer extensive training programs at their home offices for franchise owners and at individual store sites for franchise employees.

Although traditional methods of improving productivity should be employed in service organizations, it is also possible to use various marketing techniques to change consumer behavior, thereby increasing productivity indirectly. Three such techniques — modifying the timing of demand, involving the customer, and changing buyer expectations — are discussed below.[14]

Modifying the Timing of Demand

As indicated at the beginning of the chapter, service organizations frequently face capacity problems because they cannot inventory their services. If the organization employs enough people and invests enough capital to handle peak demand, then it may not be able to turn a profit because of the need to support excess labor and capital during off-peak periods. The logical alternative to increased spending as a solution to peak-capacity problems is to change buyer consumption patterns, specifically, to modify the timing of demand.

In the public service sector, an excellent illustration is the joint effort by downtown business firms in Manhattan and the Port Authorities of New York and New Jersey to stagger working hours by 30 minutes. This program has resulted in a 25 percent reduction in subway usage during the peak 5:00–5:15

---

[13]See Theodore Levitt, "Production Line Approach to Service," *Harvard Business Review* (September–October, 1972), pp. 41–52.

[14]The following sections are based on Christopher H. Lovelock and Robert F. Young, "Marketing Potential for Improving Productivity in Service Industries," in Pierre Eiglier *et al., Marketing Consumer Services: New Insights* (Cambridge, Mass.: Marketing Science Institute, 1977), pp. 111–118.

p.m. period and a 57 percent increase in usage during the more lightly traveled 4:30–4:45 p.m. period.

A similar impact can be gained via the pricing mechanism. For example, Steak and Brew restaurants found that they had empty tables on Mondays and Tuesdays, which led to reduced profits. Accordingly, they began to offer special product and price promotions on these nights.

Involving the Customer

For some service businesses, it is possible to increase productivity by having the consumer play a more active role in the performance of the service. The idea is that if some of the required labor is transferred to the buyer, then the service firm can become more productive. While this task is not always easy to accomplish, it has the potential for significant gains in productivity for the service firm.

Several years ago AT&T realized that it had to switch from primarily operator-assisted long-distance calls to direct dialing. Such a move had the potential of reducing AT&T's cost, increasing the reliability of its service, and making the firm less vulnerable to labor disputes. However, it also meant that long distance customers would have to be responsible for placing their own calls rather than asking the operator to do it for them. AT&T was under the mistaken impression that the public would quickly learn to stop calling the operator for assistance. Instead, after one year, nearly half of all long-distance calls were still being made through an operator. AT&T solved this problem by introducing special price discounts for direct dialing, which it announced through a nine million dollar advertising campaign stressing the financial advantages of direct dialing — "You save and we save, too." Currently, more than 75 percent of AT&T's long-distance calls are dialed directly by consumers. AT&T estimates that the direct dialing marketing campaign has resulted in annual productivity savings of $37 million.

Changing Buyer Expectations

In addition to modifying the timing of demand and involving the customer more in the actual delivery of the service, it may be possible, through the effective use of marketing communications, to convince the buyer to expect less service from the organization. The result is often a substantial increase in productivity. It was not very long ago that even in inexpensive restaurants busboys or waitresses were responsible for clearing off the table after the meal was eaten. Today, fast-food restaurants such as Burger King have been able to convince their patrons to clear off the tables before they leave the restaurant.

In some cases the service seller has been able to reduce the service the buyer expects and at the same time provide additional benefits to the buyer. A good illustration is express checkouts at some hotels and car rental services. While the express checkout service means that no clerk will help the customer with the paperwork, it also means that the buyer does not have to stand in line and waste valuable time. It is very important to point out that when the firm attempts to modify consumer service expectations, it should first determine, through marketing research, what aspects of the service are essential to the consumer. If the seller eliminates a portion of the service that buyers value a great deal it will be difficult to keep from losing a substantial amount of business to competitors.

summary points

1. A product is a physical object or device, whereas a service is a deed, performance, or benefit provided. A service can also be distinguished from a product on the basis of whether the utility or benefit involved in the purchase stems from a tangible object or from an intangible action of performance.

2. Three other distinguishing characteristics of a service are that buyers are dependent on sellers, a service cannot be inventoried, and service performance standards are difficult to maintain.

3. The economy of the United States has grown increasingly service-based, as shown by the fact that in 1976 more than two thirds of the entire U.S. work force were employed in service jobs.

4. The major sections of the service economy are shelter, medical care, household operations, personal services, transportation, education, and foreign travel.

5. Many managers in service industries make the mistake of viewing strategy from a product perspective.

6. A service firm can gain a competitive edge through economies of scale or through service differentiation.

7. A service firm can cut costs by substituting capital equipment for labor, and inexpensive labor for expensive labor.

8. In a product-oriented company, prices are typically set as a function of cost and competitive factors; in a service-oriented company, prices are set on the basis of value.

9. The introduction of a new service to the market is much more complex and risky than the introduction of a new product.

10. Motivation research techniques — storytelling and focus groups — are often more useful than market surveys in evaluating a new service offering.

11. Services, like products, pass through a life cycle — introduction, accelerated growth, maturity, and decline.

12. In terms of distribution, the trend today is toward greater geographic dispersion of service delivery points.

13. Cost-oriented pricing is commonly practiced in service industries, although the pricing of services, by and large, is less systematic and less objective than the pricing of products.

14. Most services are promoted and sold on the basis of their functional value rather than their physical appeal.

15. Productivity in the service sector, in some cases, can be increased through the traditional approach of providing more capital and more training per employee. It can also be increased by changing consumer behavior, specifically, by modifying the timing of demand, involving the customer in the performance of the service, and lowering buyer expectations.

questions for discussion

1. What is the difference between a product and a service?
2. How important is the service sector to the economy? Will the service sector be more or less important by the end of the 1980s than it is today?
3. Which services do you think will grow the fastest in the 1980s? Explain your answer.

4. Design a marketing strategy for a travel agency. How would this strategy differ from a marketing strategy for a national car rental agency, such as Hertz or Avis?

5. What are the most useful marketing research techniques for a service organization?

6. What are the implications of the service life cycle? Where is banking today in the service life cycle?

7. How important is the distribution channel to a service organization? What is meant by the statement that the trend in service delivery today is away from concentration and toward dispersion?

8. How are prices established in the service sector?

9. What particulars of the service sector have the greatest influence on how service companies communicate with their customers?

10. What techniques are available to make the service sector more productive? Which of these techniques has the best chance of improving the productivity of the service sector?

Topics discussed in Chapter 19:

1. Strategic planning for and the problems involved in international marketing.
2. The international environment affecting business operations abroad.
3. The advantages and disadvantages of standardizing market strategies.
4. The ways of entering foreign markets, such as indirect and direct exporting, establishing local subsidiaries, licensing, and joint ventures.
5. The role and importance of the multinational corporation in today's world.

Only a few years ago, there was little or no mention of international marketing in most marketing textbooks. The rationale was that the international community was not a very important segment to U.S. firms. Today most economists and business executives realize that the efficient movement of merchandise between countries means that additional profits can be generated for the firms' stockholders and that a higher standard of living can be delivered to more people at a lower cost.

It is important for firms which are housed primarily in the United States to be competitive in world markets. Figure 19-1 shows U.S. imports and exports from 1960 through 1979. Prior to 1971, the United States had a small positive surplus in international trade. However, only three times during the 1970s did the United States export more than it imported. This trade deficit has weakened the dollar abroad which serves to increase the price of merchandise that the U.S. imports, thereby increasing its rate of inflation. This situation could even lead to economic disorder on a worldwide scale if trading nations lost so much confidence in the dollar that they refused to accept it in international transactions. One of the best ways to overcome this negative trade balance is for the U.S. economy to be more productive in marketing goods to other nations. Strategic planning by businesses which are operating in international markets is the first step.

STRATEGIC PLANNING FOR INTERNATIONAL MARKETING

Strategic planning has become an accepted fact of life for most large and medium-sized firms in the United States. Although some do it much better than others, most firms recognize that they must at least attempt to plan for the future of their organizations. Unfortunately, in international marketing most businesses have had relatively little success with their planning efforts. The first section of this chapter discusses some of the inherent problems of international marketing planning as well as a useful international planning model.

FIGURE 19-1 U.S. Balance of Trade, 1960–1979

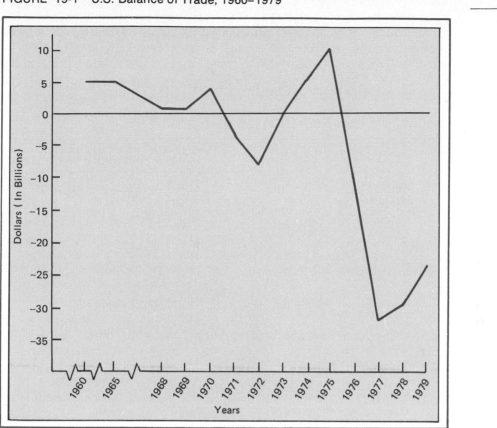

Source: U.S. Bureau of the Census, *Statistical Abstracts of the U.S. 1979* (Washington, D.C.:
U.S. Government Printing Office, 1979), p. 874.

Problems of International Planning

Many planning programs fail simply because top management does not fully support them. Planning is an expensive process, requiring large amounts of time from highly paid executives. In addition, the results of effective planning often take years to become apparent. One large European firm recently disbanded its planning department and terminated its vice-president. The firm's chief executive officer said, "Planning has not been discontinued; it had never gotten underway." When this type of impatience exists, international market planning is almost doomed to failure.

One of the most important benefits of international planning is its synergistic effect on the various independent operations of the company located in different countries. Unfortunately, this benefit can cause problems for international market planning. Most division managers are committed to achieving the profit objectives of their own units. If they spend a significant amount of time adapting their market plans to a wider international framework, they may be forced to compromise short-term profit objectives. Most international managers are simply not willing to jeopardize the profits of their division so that another division of the firm, located 5,000 miles away, can reach its objectives.[1]

Although the problems of planning for the future — namely, the expense involved and the need to consider the interests of the enterprise as a whole — are critical, they can be alleviated to some degree if the business has a strong home office. Central management, for example, can require international branches to plan for the future and can evaluate them at least partially on the

FIGURE 19-2   Domestic vs. International Planning

Domestic Planning	International Planning
1. Single language and nationality.	1. Multilingual/multinational/multicultural factors.
2. Relatively homogeneous market.	2. Fragmented and diverse markets.
3. Data available, usually accurate and easily collected.	3. Data collection a formidable task, requiring significantly higher budgets and personnel allocation.
4. Political factors relatively unimportant.	4. Political factors frequently vital.
5. Relative freedom from government interference.	5. Involvement in national economic plans; government influences business decisions.
6. Individual corporation has little effect on environment.	6. "Gravitational" distortion by large companies.
7. Chauvinism helps.	7. Chauvinism hinders.
8. Relatively stable business environment.	8. Multiple environments, many of which are highly unstable (but may be highly profitable).
9. Uniform financial climate.	9. Variety of financial climates ranging from over-conservative to wildly inflationary.
10. Single currency.	10. Currencies differing in stability and real value.
11. Business "rules of the game" mature and understood.	11. Rules diverse, changeable, and unclear.
12. Management generally accustomed to sharing responsibilities and using financial controls.	12. Management frequently autonomous and unfamiliar with budgets and controls.

Source: William W. Cain, "International Planning: Mission Impossible?" *Columbia Journal of World Business* (July-August, 1970), p. 58.

---

[1]William W. Cain, "International Planning: Mission Impossible?" *Columbia Journal of World Business* (July-August, 1970), p. 55.

basis of whether they have shown a willingness to cooperate with the firm's overall plan. However, a set of factors truly beyond the control of home office management complicates the planning process. These factors include language differences, market differences, the availability of market data, the relative stability of host governments, and financial climates. A list of these complicating factors, along with their differing effects on domestic and international operations, is shown in Figure 19-2. Despite these complications, market planning is absolutely essential.

A Model of International Market Planning

In many ways, the strategic planning process for international marketing is quite similar to that for domestic marketing. What differs are the questions that must be asked at each stage in the planning process. Figure 19-3 shows a planning model that includes each of the important elements in the international market planning process.

Stage 1: Establishing Objectives. Establish the objectives for each international unit. These objectives may be set forth in terms of either dollar sales or unit sales. In either case, top management of the division in question must have an opportunity to participate in establishing objectives. Local conditions — the peculiarities of the local market, the political and regulatory climate of the host government, and the cultural factors affecting relations with the work force — are far too important to divisional performance to have an individual located thousands of miles away decide what the division is to accomplish.

Stage 2: Environmental Analysis. The planner must carefully analyze the environment in which the division operates. Political, economic, social, and governmental differences among the various nations force the multinational enterprise to adapt its overall strategy to each of its particular markets or areas of operation.

Stage 3: Strategic Planning. The firm decides which market segments it will attempt to reach. It is during this stage that the enterprise designs its price, product, communication, and distribution strategies — i.e., its marketing mix.

Stage 4: Structure. The firm next decides how to carry out its marketing plan. For example, it must decide whether to hire an agency located in the host country to develop its advertising campaign. Also, it must decide who should be responsible for distributing the product to the retailer — should the firm perform the function itself or should it hire a local wholesaler? Other structural alternatives that must be considered include the use of joint ventures and licensing agreements.

Stage 5: Operational Planning. The firm places the product on the market. This stage implements the plans and strategies formulated in Stage 3.

Stage 6: Controlling the Marketing Program. The firm monitors its sales pattern to determine whether it is meeting its objectives. At this point, if the

FIGURE 19-3 The Multinational Market Planning Process

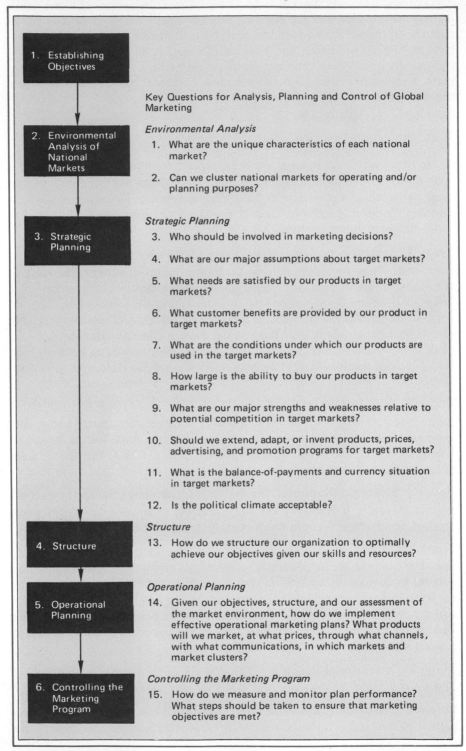

1. Establishing Objectives

2. Environmental Analysis of National Markets

3. Strategic Planning

4. Structure

5. Operational Planning

6. Controlling the Marketing Program

Key Questions for Analysis, Planning and Control of Global Marketing

Environmental Analysis

1. What are the unique characteristics of each national market?

2. Can we cluster national markets for operating and/or planning purposes?

Strategic Planning

3. Who should be involved in marketing decisions?

4. What are our major assumptions about target markets?

5. What needs are satisfied by our products in target markets?

6. What customer benefits are provided by our product in target markets?

7. What are the conditions under which our products are used in the target markets?

8. How large is the ability to buy our products in target markets?

9. What are our major strengths and weaknesses relative to potential competition in target markets?

10. Should we extend, adapt, or invent products, prices, advertising, and promotion programs for target markets?

11. What is the balance-of-payments and currency situation in target markets?

12. Is the political climate acceptable?

Structure

13. How do we structure our organization to optimally achieve our objectives given our skills and resources?

Operational Planning

14. Given our objectives, structure, and our assessment of the market environment, how do we implement effective operational marketing plans? What products will we market, at what prices, through what channels, with what communications, in which markets and market clusters?

Controlling the Marketing Program

15. How do we measure and monitor plan performance? What steps should be taken to ensure that marketing objectives are met?

Source: Adapted from Warren J. Keegan, "A Conceptual Framework for Multinational Marketing," *Columbia Journal of World Business* (November-December, 1972), p. 75.

firm is not able to meet its objectives, it can either modify its objectives if it decides they were not realistic or it can adjust its strategy in an effort to meet the established objectives.

THE INTERNATIONAL ENVIRONMENT

You'll recall from Chapter 2 how the domestic environment affects the firm — the constraints it imposes upon business operations as well as the opportunities it provides for new product ideas and new markets. Once again, it is necessary to examine environmental factors as we look at how a firm evaluates foreign markets. Here, we consider general factors such as political instability, host government factors, cultural influences, and economic factors, and how these factors affect international marketing.

Political Instability

In the United States and Canada we tend to take for granted the stability of our political systems. Unfortunately, as we look around the world, political stability seems to be the exception rather than the rule. In 1979 such instability and its sudden, potentially catastrophic effects were exhibited in Iran, where many U.S. firms did a great deal of business. When the Shah was overthrown by Ayatollah Khomeini and his followers, foreign business people were forced to leave the country with but a few days notice. Oil companies with large sums of money invested in Iranian distribution facilities will probably lose their entire investment. These same firms, even though they had been assured that they would continue to receive Iranian oil, were forced to redesign their entire distribution strategies when Iran stopped the flow of its oil to world markets. The ultimate consequence of political instability to firms with international operations is expropriation without reimbursement.

Expropriation. Expropriation means that the host country simply takes over the physical assets of the foreign company without providing any payment or compensation in return.[2] One of the stumbling blocks to full trade relations with China was the nationalization of U.S. assets in China after the Communists took power. The tentative settlement of this issue calls for China to refund 41 cents on the dollar to U.S. firms whose property has been nationalized.

Expropriation without reimbursement is relatively rare. Most foreign countries realize that multinational firms are needed to stimulate economic growth. These firms channel capital into the host country, pay taxes, employ a significant percentage of the work force, and, perhaps most important, attract other multinationals into making similar investments in the host country. Consequently, the takeover of even one foreign business can cause other firms to reconsider their investment plans, thereby effectively stopping the flow of international capital into the host country and slowing the rate of its economic growth. In addition, some multinational companies can perform certain production and distribution functions more efficiently than the host countries. For

---

[2]This section is taken primarily from Philip R. Cateora and John M. Hess, *International Marketing* (4th ed.; Homewood, Ill.: Richard D. Irwin, 1979), pp. 158–159, 164–165.

example, when Saudi Arabia nationalized Aramco, which had been producing oil in that country for many years, it paid the company a fair price for the expropriated assets. Today, Aramco still provides assistance to Saudi Arabia and markets most of the nation's exported oil.

Other Forms of Political Risk. Although expropriation is the most dramatic form of political risk, it is not the most common. Any of the following types of political risk is more likely to affect firms operating in foreign markets.

Exchange Controls. When a nation faces a shortage of foreign exchange, it often places controls on the movement of funds out of the country. These controls may be applied selectively to politically vulnerable foreign-owned companies or to all firms operating within the nation.

Import Restrictions. Many developing nations place high import duties on imported raw materials and manufactured products in order to protect small, domestically operated firms. For example, the duty on automobile parts imported to Brazil is more than 300 percent. Thus, when General Motors began to install air conditioners in their cars manufactured in Brazil, they had little choice but to buy the units from a local firm rather than to import them from the United States.

Tax Controls. When a host government uses its taxing authority to control investment and the profits of foreign companies, it is applying a political force. Oil companies often must face dramatic changes in the rates at which their foreign investments are taxed. In the early 1970s, Venezuela increased the tax on the profits of all foreign-owned oil companies to 65 percent of net income.

Price Controls. Products that are critical to the national interest, such as drugs, gasoline, or tires, are often subject to price controls. Such controls are typically imposed during periods of extreme inflation. When revenues are controlled and costs are permitted to increase, many local firms as well as the subsidiaries of international firms are forced to declare bankruptcy.

Labor Problems. The stronger the political power of organized labor in the host country, the more problems for the multinational. In extreme cases, organized labor can use its political power and its influence with government to have layoffs forbidden and to force the passage of legislation, in the case of a democracy, entitling laborers to a certain percentage of corporate profits. The more usual tactic is prolonged strikes. A few years ago, The Ford Motor Company decided to establish a new automobile parts plant in Brazil rather than in England, because its existing English plants averaged more than 30 days each year of labor-related work stoppages, whereas its existing Brazilian plant averaged less than five days.

Host Government Factors

Many multinational firms get involved with the political leadership of the host country in the hope that such involvement will reduce political and economic risk. Although a working relationship with the host government has several potential benefits, it also entails a considerable degree of risk.

Involvement in the Host Government. When local managers begin to play a behind-the-scenes role in the political processes of the host country, they are in an excellent position to ensure that profit restrictions are not placed on their firms. Some of the specific potential benefits are low income taxes, few currency restrictions, and the removal of restrictions on products imported into the host country. Typically, these advantages can be achieved only through bribery.

This approach to risk reduction has two basic problems. First, most business executives find bribery unethical. Although a bribe can be rationalized as a consulting fee that everyone pays, it is still a bribe. Second, in most countries, involvement with the host government means that the firm has taken sides in the political process. Unlike in the United States, opposing political parties in other countries, particularly in many developing nations, often disagree violently as to how the country should be run. If there is a change in government, either by revolution or by the democratic process, the multinational that supported the loser may face major problems. In the long run, apolitical businesses tend to get along much better with host governments.

The Sears Saga — Make a Contribution. The real key to success for the firm operating abroad is to make a significant contribution to the welfare of the host nation. If government leaders and the public think they are better off having the multinational firm in their country, then the firm is less likely to have onerous restrictions placed upon its operations.

Sears provides a good example of how farsighted business practices can benefit both the host country and the firm. When Sears began operations in Peru, it imported 80 percent of its merchandise sold there; today, it imports less than 10 percent, buying instead from 900 local Peruvian suppliers. Approximately 400 firms have been founded as a result of the willingness of Sears to buy from local manufacturers. Also, the Sears pension plan makes each of its Peruvian employees a stockholder of the firm.[3] Sears has used this same strategy successfully in Brazil, Mexico, and Spain. This and other examples of synergistic business practices indicate that foreign investment does not have to conflict with the social and economic development of the host country.

Cultural Factors

Chapter 4 discussed the meaning and importance of culture to marketing. Culture was defined as a set of values, ideas, attitudes, and other symbols and objects created by people which shape human behavior. Because cultural attitudes vary dramatically between countries, it is important for the marketing executive to look closely at a nation's cultural heritage before it introduces a product to that country. Figure 19-4 illustrates some of the problems that a Western executive typically experiences when doing business in India. The

---

[3]Jon Basil Utley, "Doing Business with Latin Nationalists," *Harvard Business Review* (January-February, 1973), p. 80.

FIGURE 19-4   Marketing in India

The first day of the new moon in India is considered a very bad day for conducting business. Many otherwise Westernized well-educated Indians simply will not become involved in nor associated with business affairs at this time, as they feel it is bad luck.

It would be considered very poor planning to advertise a product in a birthday or wedding setting with the models wearing black dresses or suits. It is simply not considered auspicious to display black at such pleasant occasions.

As to seasons of the year, the Hindu New Year, Divali, is considered an excellent time to do business and the Hindu makes it a specific point to transact a piece of business on that particular day for good luck, to open the way for good tie-in promotions and a receptiveness to forceful promotions at that time.

While English is widely used throughout India, for vernacular authenticity it is best to tailor the approach. For example, an advertiser could generally use Tamil dialect in South India, Hindu in North India, and Gujarati around Bombay.

The cow is a sacred animal to the Hindu in India. It would be extremely unwise for a food-product manufacturer to extol the joys of a beef sandwich. Similarly, Muslim beliefs preclude promotion in settings where ham or bacon are shown.

It would be a mistake to show a Hindu god in any kind of deodorant promotion. This would be the equivalent of running an ad in Western media for boot polish with the trade name of Jesus.

Source: *Printer's Ink* (February 21, 1964), p. 47.

marketing executive must be aware of the impact of culture on three elements of marketing strategy: product positioning, distribution policy, and communication policy.[4]

Product Positioning. How should a manufacturer position a product? Many international firms have found that a product must be positioned differently from one country to the next. As an illustration, when Renault introduced the Renault 5, its newest entry in the European small car market, it positioned the car in France as an amusing, fun car suitable for both urban and highway driving. Advertisements took the form of a cartoon strip showing a bouncy, chatty car with eyes and a mouth. In Germany, on the other hand, where purchasing a car is a serious matter, the advertisements stressed the Renault 5's modern engineering and interior comfort. In Finland, the emphasis was on solid construction and reliability, and in Italy, on the automobile's road performance.

Distribution Strategy. Culture also affects the choice of distribution strategy. In the United States, Avon and Tupperware have been successful in using

---

[4]The following sections are based on Susan Douglas and Bernard Dubois, "Looking at the Cultural Environment for International Marketing Opportunities," *Columbia Journal of World Business* (Winter, 1977), pp. 106–108.

homemakers as a kind of in-home sales force. In the case of Tupperware, female customers are encouraged through the use of discounts and other financial incentives to organize sales parties during which considerable social pressure is exerted on the guests to purchase Tupperware merchandise. This approach does not work in Europe because women there regard selling in the home as an intrusion of privacy. In addition, European women do not believe in profiting at the expense of their neighbors.

Communication Strategy. As indicated during the discussion of product positioning, the advertising theme for a product may vary from one nation to another. Renault was able to do this effectively with its Renault 5. Other phases of advertising also may have to be modified as a result of culture. For example, words and symbols may connote different things in different cultures. In a new car promotion, Chrysler-France translated the phrase "the original" that had been used in England to "the example" for its advertising campaign in Germany. The problem was that "die original" in German has a connotation of strange or odd, which was not what the firm was trying to communicate to the German public.

The choice of advertising media is also subject to culture. The British airline, BEA, found that its promotional theme emphasizing the reliability of British pilots was very successful when displayed in print media in all Western European countries with the exception of Italy. Research showed that it was less successful in Italy because of the importance of oral communication to Italians.

Economic Factors

Not surprisingly, multinational firms also face very different economic environments from one country to the next. The most significant differences occur between a socialist economy and a capitalist economy. Factors worthy of consideration include the state of economic development of a nation and its level of inflation.

Level of Economic Development. The level of economic development of a nation affects how products are sold logistically and to whom they are sold. In highly developed Western economies, it is easy to take modern commercial conveniences for granted — such as highways, railroads, air transportation systems, and warehouse facilities. In less-developed economies, it normally takes more time and money to move products from one location to another. In many cases, multinational firms have found it easier to establish their own air and truck fleets than to depend on the publicly available distribution systems of host countries.

In addition, multinational firms find that their customers vary significantly from more- to less-developed countries. In Brazil, the Ford LTD has been marketed successfully to wealthy people. It is not unusual at all to see a man or woman being driven around Sao Paulo in an LTD by a chauffeur. In the same way, Sears has found that people who shop in its Latin American stores tend to come from much higher social classes than do the majority of Sears shoppers in U.S. stores.

Inflation. The problem of rising prices is no longer confined to just a few unfortunate Central American countries. Table 19-1 illustrates the severity of the recent inflation experienced by the United States and many other nations. Regarding product management during periods of high inflation, U.S. executives may be able to learn a great deal from their colleagues in countries where inflation has been a way of life for many years.

TABLE 19-1   Inflation Rates in Selected Countries

	Percentage Change 1970–1977	Percentage Change 1976–1977
Austria	108.0	12.4
Belgium	75.0	7.4
Brazil	257.0	40.6
Chile	166,066.0	91.9
Egypt	66.0	12.9
France	83.0	8.9
West Germany	46.0	3.5
Hungary	25.0	8.5
Italy	137.0	18.5
Japan	104.0	8.5
Portugal	202.0	23.8
Thailand	73.0	8.1
USSR	0.0	0.0
United States	56.0	6.1
Zambia	99.0	19.8

Source: Data from *United Nations Statistical Yearbook, 1978* (New York: United Nations, 1979), pp. 690–696.

Although there is no one best way for a multinational firm to deal with inflation, it should strive to remain flexible in its pricing strategy. If prices rise rapidly in one nation, the multinational firm can profit by selling merchandise there that was manufactured in a nation with a lower rate of inflation. A multinational can also hedge against high inflation by investing in materials and equipment that are expected to increase in value. It may also be advisable under conditions of inflation for the firm to borrow money for capital investment because it will be able to pay off the loans with inflated and therefore less valuable currency. This hedge is especially effective when the rate of inflation is greater than the prevailing interest rate.

STANDARDIZATION OF INTERNATIONAL MARKETING STRATEGIES

When a firm enters a new national market, it usually must determine whether it should modify its marketing strategy to fit local market conditions. The following questions need to be answered. Does the product itself need to

What could be more glamorous than a career in international business? The opportunities for travel and for learning about new cultures are unsurpassed. Hong Kong, London, Singapore, Tokyo, Zurich, Berlin, Paris, Cairo, Mexico City, Riyadh, Montreal, Caracas — the list of international business capitals goes on and on. Do they sound like places where *you* would like to work?

Employment overseas has its financial advantages as well. For example, in developing nations one finds that the cost of living and effective tax rates are often significantly lower than they are in the United States, Canada, or Western Europe. But before you pack your bags, consider the following problems with employment in the international sector.

The Problems. Unfortunately, there are not very many positions available for citizens of the United States in overseas divisions of international companies. More than 20 years ago, it became apparent to most U.S. multinational firms that if they were to operate profitably abroad, they would have to develop strong, stable working relationships with host countries. One way to develop such relationships was to hire local citizens to fill key managerial positions. Today, in most large U.S. companies, only the president and/or the treasurer of the foreign division is a U.S. national — the remaining management personnel are local citizens.

However, most international firms regularly bring in specialists from the United States to provide consulting services to the international division. These specialists operate in the areas of marketing research, product planning, and inventory control.

Another more serious problem with overseas jobs has been the steady increase in political violence directed toward U.S. citizens working abroad. Such countries as Iran and Argentina come immediately to mind. Also, some developing nations are still experiencing double- and even triple-digit inflation. Such instability makes working and living in these areas difficult at best.

A Solution. If you're really interested in international business, don't despair. Many firms employ people at their U.S. headquarters to monitor world markets and overseas business operations. These positions can give you an opportunity to travel overseas while maintaining your home and family base in the United States. Occasionally, you may also be sent abroad as a consultant in your area of specialization to assist or train local citizens of the host country who have been hired to work in U.S. firms overseas.

The reward for excelling in these U.S.-based positions may just turn out to be a promotion to a high-level position overseas. Bon voyage!

Marketing & You

be changed? Are existing sales promotion and advertising campaigns applicable to the new market? Should the type of distribution network used in the firm's other foreign markets be replicated in the new market? There is no easy answer to any of these questions. However, the standardization of market strategy across national markets is one potentially effective approach.

An assessment of the pros and cons of standardization depends upon a prior assessment of the role of international sales in the firm's overall corporate strategy. If international sales represent a real opportunity for the firm to expand into new, permanent markets abroad, then the firm should consider customizing its product line and its marketing strategy to fit the needs of its local markets. In contrast, if international sales are merely an outlet for excess production capacity, then the firm should focus on finding international markets that are receptive to products that have already been developed for the domestic market.[5]

Advantages of Standardization

The advantages of a standardized marketing strategy lie mainly in the areas of cost efficiency, advertising efficiency, and idea utilization.

Production Cost Efficiencies. Although it may be possible for the firm to achieve higher total sales if its products are tailored to each individual national market, the firm can also increase its profit margin by taking advantage of cost economies. That is, by offering the same basic product in all of its national markets and thereby increasing the size of its production runs, the firm can begin to experience the benefits of production cost efficiencies. Moreover, research and development costs can be spread over a greater number of units. The benefit of cost reductions, of course, is that they make the firm's products, whether sold domestically or internationally, more profitable.

Advertising Efficiencies. If the firm utilizes the same advertising theme for all of its national markets, total advertising costs can be reduced significantly. Standardized advertising also provides a consistent image of the firm's products across its various markets. Consumers, today, are increasingly mobile, and encountering a common advertising theme from one country to the next tends to reassure them as to the sincerity of the advertiser and the quality and reliability of the product.

In Europe, magazines, newspapers, and radio and television broadcasts flow readily and with few restrictions across international frontiers. According to Young and Rubicam, an international advertising agency:

1. 40 percent of Dutch television viewers watch German broadcasts.
2. The magazine *Paris Match* has a circulation of 85,000 in Belgium, 26,000 in Switzerland, and a substantial readership in Germany and Italy.
3. More then 4 million French households listen to Radio Luxemburg, which also reaches 620,000 Belgian, 30,000 Swiss, and 100,000 Dutch families.[6]

---

[5]James Killough, "Improved Payoffs from Transnational Advertising," *Harvard Business Review* (July-August, 1978), p. 104.

[6]As reported in Robert D. Buzzell, "Can You Standardize Multinational Marketing," *Harvard Business Review* (November-December, 1968), pp. 104–106.

Given these statistics, it is apparent that standardized advertising can result in both cost efficiencies and customer relations benefits.

Utilizing Good Ideas. Marketing ideas that worked in one country may work in another. Certain advertising themes developed for one national market have been shown to have universal appeal. Advertisements for Levi's jeans have a casual, almost rodeo flavor wherever Levi Strauss products are sold; the Coca-Cola Company stresses the freshness and sparkle of youth in its advertising around the world.

Similarly, when a new product is developed in one country, it can be tested and then eventually produced and sold in other countries. An excellent example is the Chevrolet Chevette. This car was first produced in Brazil in 1972. The car was so successful that it is now produced in five countries, under the names Gemini, Kadett, and Chevette. General Motors is going one step further with its new J-Car, scheduled for production in the early 1980s. Parts for this car, a four-cylinder hatch-back sedan with front-wheel drive, will be produced in many different parts of the world. Eventually, the car will be sold in the United States, Europe, Canada, Africa, and Asia.[7]

Disadvantages of Standardization

The most significant disadvantage of standardization is simply that cultural, political, and economic differences among countries may make it all but impossible to use a single standardized marketing strategy. Unfortunately, many businesses assume that the underlying environmental variables, discussed earlier in this chapter, do not affect their marketing strategies either because these variables are the same everywhere or because they are not important.

Advertising is often the key component of the marketing strategy that the firm would like to standardize. Advertising can be broken down into two components: the buying proposal and the creative presentation. The buying proposal consists of the sales points that are the most persuasive and relevant to prospective customers. It is what the advertiser says. In contrast, the creative presentation is how the buying proposal is communicated to the public. Figure 19-5 illustrates the differences between the buying proposal and creative presentation for five products.

In many cases, it is possible to standardize the buying proposal. Appeals such as the cosmetic benefits of toothpaste, the conservative management of bank trust departments, and the heavy-duty cleaning power of detergents are practically universal. However, the actual creative presentation used to present the buying proposal may have to be modified to fit local conditions. A few years ago, a major soft-drink manufacturer lost a great deal of money in the Near East on a product advertised as "glacier fresh" and as providing an "avalanche of taste." Although the buying proposal, namely, the fact that the soft drink was a thirst quencher, is universal, the creative presentation made little sense to target consumers since few of them, living as they did in an arid climate, were able to make a positive connection between a soft drink and

---

[7]Bob Tamarkin, "GM Gets Ready for the World Car," *Forbes* (April 2, 1979), p. 44.

FIGURE 19-5   Buying Proposals vs. Creative Presentations

Product Category	Buying Proposal	Creative Presentation
Leisure-time vehicles	Off-the-road technology	Jeep's "We wrote the book on 4-wheel drive"
Toothpaste	Cosmetic benefits	Colgate's "Ring of Confidence"
Bank trust department	Conservative management	Chase Manhattan's "nest egg"
Laundry detergents	Heavy-duty cleaning	Procter & Gamble's "Tide gets out the dirt kids get into"
Airline travel	In-flight service quality	British Caledonian's "The airline other airlines hate"

Source: Reprinted by permission of the *Harvard Business Review*. Exhibit from "Improved Payoffs from Transnational Advertising" by James Killough (July-August, 1978). Copyright © 1978 by the President and Fellows of Harvard College; all rights reserved.

mountain snowdrifts.[8] Thus, standardized advertisements may be of limited utility across national and cultural boundaries.

Implications of Standardization

At a minimum, the firm should standardize its procedures for identifying target markets, establishing price policies, evaluating distribution mechanisms, and determining which advertisements are the most effective. If all divisions of the mutinational firm follow the same procedures in market evaluations, the home office will be assured that the marketing plan is at least systematic. An additional benefit of a standardized plan is that sales results from one country to the next are more amenable to comparison. Five factors influencing the extent to which the marketing plan should be standardized are discussed below.[9]

Type of Product. Certain products have truly universal sales appeals. Items such as razor blades, electric irons, automobile tires, and ballpoint pens are sold primarily on the basis of their physical characteristics. It is possible for the firm to standardize most, if not all, of its marketing strategy for such products.

Homogeneity of the Markets. The more alike people are in terms of their income, education, occupation, and similar characteristics, the greater the probability that they will purchase similar products. For this reason, it is relatively easy to standardize marketing strategies for most of the Western Euro-

---

[8]Killough, *op. cit.*, pp. 105–106.

[9]The following sections are based on Gordon E. Miracle, "International Advertising Principles and Strategies," *Business Topics* (Autumn, 1968), pp. 35–36.

pean nations. However, if a product is to be sold in Europe and in the Far East, the organization may have to formulate separate market strategies.

Interaction of International Consumers. The more consumers from various countries interact with the international marketplace, the more suitable is the environment for adopting a standardized marketing strategy. Such interaction could include reading newspapers or magazines from other nations, watching television or listening to radio broadcasts from other countries, or traveling from one nation to another. Thus, as Europe becomes more "internationalized," firms will begin to use European marketing strategies rather than simply Italian strategies or German strategies.

Availability of Marketing Services. Regarding the country or market in question, how available are advertising agencies, marketing research data, and commercial television and radio time? A market strategy developed for the United States may not be applicable in other countries because U.S. advertising relies heavily upon television. In some countries, the government owns the television stations and does not permit advertising. In others, advertising may be available, but large segments of the population are too poor to own television sets. The greater the differences between nations in terms of the availability of marketing services, the more likely the firm is to adopt a separate strategy for each national market.

Government Restrictions. All nations have laws regulating their markets. These laws influence how products are promoted, priced, and distributed. Australia, for example, has a law requiring that 85 percent of the component parts of all automobiles sold in that country be manufactured in Australia. In the case of General Motors' new J-car, the government has agreed to waive that provision because GM intends to build a large engine plant in Australia that will manufacture J-car engines for export all over the world.[10]

ENTERING FOREIGN MARKETS

Though many businesses lead profitable lives without ever selling internationally, an increasing number of firms are beginning to develop new markets abroad. Figure 19-6 gives six alternative approaches to selling products in foreign markets. Generally speaking, alternatives involving direct investment and an extensive financial commitment are associated with greater potential profits but also greater risk. Firms selecting these potentially more profitable alternatives usually must maintain a large staff of international experts. Each of the six alternatives is discussed below.[11]

Indirect Exporting

A firm selling its merchandise abroad but making no special effort on its own behalf is called an **indirect exporter**. Indirect exporting may entail foreign sales through domestic operations or export management companies.

---

[10]Tamarkin, *loc. cit.*
[11]The following sections are adapted from *International Marketing*, Second Edition, by Vern Terpstra. © 1978 by The Dryden Press, a division of Holt, Rinehart and Winston, Publishers. Adapted by permission of Holt, Rinehart and Winston.

Foreign Sales Via Domestic Organizations. Many businesses sell products in domestic markets that eventually are shipped abroad. In some cases, the domestic firm does not even know that its products have left the country. An example of this type of indirect exporting is a small domestic manufacturer that sells to the local buying office of a foreign department store.

A more organized approach to indirect exporting is to use an international trading company. In Japan, Mitsui and Mitsubishi distribute more than 50 percent of all products imported to that country. Trading companies provide all marketing services to the exporting firm. In most cases, trading companies prefer to take title to the merchandise once it leaves the manufacturer. Only occasionally will they agree to sell a product on a commission basis where they merely act as an agent for the exporter.

FIGURE 19-6 Alternative Methods for Selling Products in Foreign Markets

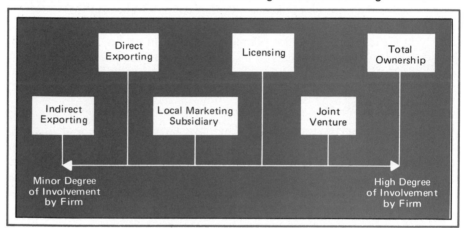

The services provided by trading companies, their vast market coverage, and their credit reliability make them attractive to domestic firms interested in selling abroad. The major drawback of international trading companies, from the point of view of the domestic manufacturer, is that it is not able to exercise control over whether the companies carry competing products or whether they even push the manufacturer's products at all.

Export Management Companies. An export management company (EMC) is an independent firm that provides most of the services of an in-house export department. Thus, EMCs are used primarily by firms that cannot afford their own export departments. The major advantage of an EMC is that it enables its users to obtain the services of an export department without having to bear alone the fixed costs involved in operating such a department. EMCs also provide instant information and management expertise to user firms and are paid only when they actually make a sale. As a result, there is relatively little risk to the individual user firm.

Unfortunately, some EMCs have taken on too many merchandise lines from unrelated businesses and thus have not been able to give each client firm the attention that it probably had anticipated. For its part, the EMC runs the risk of being too successful — that is, the client firm could capitalize on the markets developed by the EMC and move its own sales force into these markets. Accordingly, EMCs have been careful not to tie themselves too closely to any single manufacturer.

Direct Exporting

Under direct exporting, the manufacturer rather than the indirect exporter performs all the necessary export functions, including contacting local distributors, conducting the required marketing research, preparing export documentation, and setting prices. Direct exporting typically results in increased sales for the exporter. Whether it yields additional profits depends on whether the incremental revenues are greater than the extra costs associated with running an in-house export operation.

The choice between exporting indirectly or directly is analogous to the choice between selling the product through a manufacturer's agent or selling it through the firm's own sales force. In selling direct, the firm not only earns a higher return on its investment, but it also exercises greater control over how its merchandise is sold and which products are emphasized in the selling effort. Selling direct also puts the firm in a better position to gain information about the needs of its international markets. However, it does have the disadvantage of greater cost: the manufacturer must pay all the overhead expenditures involved in international marketing rather than sharing them with other exporters, as would be the case under an EMC arrangement. Most small and medium-sized businesses begin exporting directly only if they have already been successful marketing their products indirectly.

Local Marketing Subsidiary

Establishing a local marketing subsidiary abroad represents a third approach to developing international markets. This approach entails a greater financial commitment on the part of the exporter, and thus, greater potential profit and risk. Typically, when a firm begins to export directly, it uses local distributors to sell its merchandise in the new international markets. The firm simply does not have the expertise or knowledge of local conditions to sell its products in the intended markets, nor is it able or willing to establish a complete local distribution network and to assume all the costs involved. Very few international firms, in fact, can afford to accept the financial risks associated with establishing a local distribution system. The exception is high technology firms whose products and services are such that there simply is no way for a local firm to handle distribution and servicing. An example is IBM's computer division. When IBM enters a market, it establishes a complete distribution structure for its products. IBM moves very quickly to train local people in the selling of the products; these people are responsible to IBM, as are other IBM employees no matter where they are located.

Licensing

Licensing is a method for developing local production and marketing capabilities without investing capital in the local market. A licensing agreement is a contractual arrangement whereby the licensor (international company) gives the licensee (local company) either (1) patent rights, (2) trademark rights, (3) a copyright, or (4) expertise in how to produce and sell the product in question.

In turn, the licensee pays the licensor a fee. Receipts from foreign licensing agreements to U.S. firms should exceed $3 billion per year during the first half of the 1980s.[12]

Evaluation of Licensing. Licensing has many advantages for internationally oriented businesses. Since no capital is required, the license option is available to many small businesses that otherwise would not be able to enter foreign markets. Also, even multinational organizations with abundant capital may not have the expertise to manufacture and market products locally in other countries. In these cases, licensing agreements enable the firm to avoid many of the difficulties involved in establishing company-owned production and marketing facilities. Finally, many foreign governments favor licensing agreements over direct investment because licensing brings technology into the country without also bringing large direct foreign investments. As a result, it is frequently easier to obtain government approval for a license than for a direct investment.

Unfortunately, licensing agreements have several significant disadvantages. The most important is that the licensor loses some control over how its products are manufactured and sold. If the licensee turns out to be a disreputable firm, the reputation of the licensor could be damaged. Also, the more expertise that the licensor provides the local company, the greater the probability that the licensor may actually be training its future competition. When the agreement comes up for renewal, the licensee may decide that further assistance from the licensor is unnecessary. At this point, some licensees may even begin to expand their sales efforts into international markets.

Joint Ventures

If a business decides to go one step beyond licensing in terms of its commitment to an international market, it can purchase a percentage of a foreign business. This option is called a joint venture. Typically, the international firm supplies some capital and the required technology, while the local partner provides additional capital and the expertise needed to sell the product in the host country. The advantages and disadvantages of joint ventures should be analyzed from the perspective of a lesser commitment, such as licensing agreements, as well as from the perspective of a greater commitment, that of 100 percent ownership.

To Join or Not to Join. Compared to a licensing arrangement, a joint venture has four important advantages. The most significant is that the return on a joint venture, which involves an equity investment, is usually greater than the royalty payments under a licensing agreement. Other advantages include greater control over how the product is produced and marketed, more accurate feedback about how the market is receiving the product, and a greater opportunity for executives of the international company to gain operating experience in foreign markets. The major disadvantage of a joint venture, when compared to a licensing agreement, is that the firm must invest more capital and management time. Thus, if the product is not successful, the firm is likely to sustain greater financial losses than if it had instead entered a license agreement.

---

[12]*Survey of Current Business* (August, 1977).

In comparison to 100 percent ownership, joint ventures require less capital and, as a result, are more attractive to small and medium-sized firms. In addition, a firm can diversify its risk by entering joint ventures in several countries rather than by owning all of one company in one market. Also, the likelihood of government red tape, and even expropriation, is reduced when the international firm has a local partner. As an illustration, India has been slowly forcing multinational firms to surrender 51 percent of the ownership of their local subsidiaries to Indian control. After a great deal of consideration, IBM closed its entire Indian operation as a result of this request. IBM reasoned that it could not operate in an environment in which it did not exercise control over its operations. Most other firms have not taken such a strong position on this issue and thus have continued to operate in India.

Another disadvantage of joint ventures is that they often give rise to disputes among partners, especially when executives of the multinational enterprise feel that their firm is contributing more than its fair share of technology and management expertise. Other potential points of conflict concern the price of the products sold to the local firms (transfer pricing), the percentage of the profits reinvested in the local market, and the selection of new products for introduction to the local market.

Local Partners' Contribution. Joint ventures are particularly attractive to businesses during the early stages of a product's international life cycle. During these stages, it may be apparent to the multinational firm that foreign markets do exist for its products. The firm, however, may be reluctant to move forward because it does not have accurate information about each local market or much experience in producing and selling internationally. It is in this situation that a joint venture becomes an especially attractive market development approach.

The idea that knowledge of local market conditions is the most important contribution of the local partner to the joint arrangement was substantiated by a study of 63 managers of multinational firms. The study (see Table 19-2) was designed to determine the importance of eight factors in the selection of a local partner. Local environment was found to be the most important factor; management expertise, the second most important. Most multinational firms are content to provide the product and related technology and to let the local partner gather market data, develop market strategies, and deal with the local government bureaucracy.[13]

Total Ownership

Total ownership is the ultimate degree of commitment to a foreign market — the firm owns 100 percent of the foreign enterprise and has complete control over its operation. Conflict among partners cannot arise because there are no partners. Furthermore, 100 percent of the profits go to the international firm. The most important advantage of total ownership, however, may be that the international firm is able to weave its various foreign divisions into an inter-

---

[13]For further information on joint ventures, see Lawrence G. Franko, "Joint Venture Divorce in the Multinational Company," *Columbia Journal of World Business* (May–June, 1971), pp. 13–22; Richard W. Wright and Colin S. Russell, "Joint Ventures in Developing Countries: Realities and Responses," *Columbia Journal of World Business* (Summer, 1975), pp. 74–80.

TABLE 19-2 Importance of Local Partner Contribution to a
Joint Venture Agreement

Local Partner's Contributions	Average Importance Score*
General knowledge about the local environment	4.8
General managers	3.6
Marketing personnel	3.4
Better access for joint ventures' production than possible with 100% subsidiaries	3.3
Better access for goods shipped into joint ventures' markets	2.6
Capital	2.6
Access to local raw materials	2.5
Production, technical, and R&D skills	2.5

*The scale ranges from 0 = "no importance" to 6 = "very important."
Source: Lawrence G. Franko, "Joint Venture Divorce in the Multinational
Company," *Columbia Journal of World Business* (May-June,
1971), p. 19.

national production and marketing system that is capable of generating greater
incremental profits. This synergistic effect often is not possible with joint ventures because the local partner may have goals that are not consistent with the
overall objectives of the international firm.

The difficulties associated with 100 percent ownership are quite apparent.
The international firm must dedicate a great deal of capital and management
resources to operate the foreign subsidiary profitably. Although the capital is
not a problem for many large companies, international management expertise
may not be available in-house. Another problem is that many countries simply
forbid 100 percent ownership under the assumption that such ownership is an
attempt to take advantage of the local market without giving anything in return
to the host country. Even in countries that permit 100 percent ownership, the
international firm can expect to encounter more problems with the local
bureauracy than if it had organized its overseas enterprise as a joint venture.

THE ROLE OF MULTINATIONAL CORPORATIONS

The operating philosophy of a multinational corporation (MNC) is to sell its
products wherever in the world there appears to be a market for them. A true
MNC may have its headquarters in New York, have a French citizen as president, manufacture its products in Africa, market them in Canada, Western
Europe, and Latin America, and have its stock traded in five exchanges around
the world. Table 19-3 lists profits that 15 firms, which are usually thought of as
U.S. businesses, generate from outside the United States.

TABLE 19-3 Profits Generated Outside the U.S. by 15 Major
Businesses, 1976

Company	Percentage of Earnings from Foreign Operations
Black & Decker	40%
Coca-Cola	55
Ferro Corporation	65
H. J. Heinz	34
International Multifoods	45
International Systems and Controls	112*
ITT	39
Johnson & Johnson	48
Mattell	45
Merck	44
Revlon	23
Sirco International	63
3M Corporation	30
J. W. Thompson	59
F. W. Woolworth	59

*Reflects domestic loss.

Source: Reprinted from p. 260 of the August 19, 1977, issue of *Business International*, and p. 311 of the September 30, 1977, issue of *Business International*, with the permission of the publisher, Business International Corporation (New York).

The growth of MNCs was stimulated by several events after World War II. By the 1930s the world had learned that when one country imposed high tariffs in order to protect its home industries, other countries were quick to do the same. The general result of these national tariff barriers was a decline in would trade. After World War II, however, a series of steps were taken to relax trade barriers and to stimulate world trade. These steps included establishment of the International Bank for Reconstruction and Development (the World Bank) and the International Monetary Fund, the objective of which is "to facilitate the expansion and balanced growth of international trade" by stabilizing currencies and by helping countries solve balance of payment problems. Also the General Agreement on Tariffs and Trade (GATT) encouraged the development of multinationals by mandating a general reduction of trade barriers.[14] The next section examines several criticisms of the role of multinational firms in world markets as well as what role they play in improving society.

Criticisms of MNCs

Criticism of MNCs seems to focus on several major issues, including their normality and political power, their effect on the balance of payments, their exploitation of cheap labor, and their infringement on national sovereignty.

---

[14]Donald M. Kendall, "The Need for Multinationals," *Columbia Journal of World Business* (Fall, 1973), pp. 104–105.

Morality and Political Power. In a well-publicized case, Lockheed admitted spending more than $12 million to influence government policy in Japan. Although the exact reason for these payments is still unclear, several U.S. senators suggested that the objective was to promote a policy of rearmament in Japan. These payments may not have been bribery in the strictest sense, but they clearly represented an attempt on the part of Lockheed to influence the foreign policy of a sovereign nation.

Was Lockheed's action acceptable? What type of behavior should be expected from an MNC? In attempting to answer these questions, it is important to distinguish between small-scale "grease" payments and large-scale bribes. Although few societies condone grease payments to minor officials, such payments have become a way of life around the world. They can be useful in expediting licenses or in moving shipments more quickly through customs officers. Often, they are even viewed as a tax to compensate poorly paid public officials.[15]

We may not approve of grease payments, but they certainly are a standard business practice in many countries. The tougher question concerns the legitimacy of large-scale bribes. Many MNC executives, like many other people, feel that morality is a culturally bound, not an absolute, phenomenon. In other words, what is considered unethical in one country may be considered ethical in another. Proponents of this view argue that the U.S. has no right to project its own moral standards on the rest of the world, and that condemning bribery as an international business practice amounts to setting up a uniform moral code based on U.S. beliefs and customs. Moreover, if is argued, "If our firm doesn't provide the bribe, our competitors will."

The above argument is difficult for many people to accept. It implies, for example, that an MNC can operate one way in foreign countries and another in the United States. A reasonable middle ground on the issue of international business ethics has been stated by William I. Spencer, the chief administrative officer of Citicorp and Citibank. When asked whether U.S. business executives should be expected to have higher ethical standards than other business people in dealing with officials of foreign countries, Spencer stated:

> Of course we should expect, and demand, higher standards, but we've got to be careful how we draw the line. Consider the case of a corporation operating in a country where it's the accepted custom for people like import agents to take 1% off the top. Now, this can be bribery — but it can also be a sales commission. It's properly regarded as a sales commission, I think, if it's the accepted custom in the country and if the figure goes into the books. Now, the fact that some countries have such a custom doesn't mean we shouldn't deal with them. We may not like that kind of situation, but in our enthusiasm for our own moral codes I don't think we should try to write ethical standards for the rest of the world. We can, however, insist on proper accounting procedures consistent with our standards of business conduct.[16]

---

[15]Stephen J. Kobrin, "Morality, Political Power, and Illegal Payments by Multinational Corporations," *Columbia Journal of World Business* (Winter, 1976), pp. 105–106.

[16]William I. Spencer, "Who Controls MNCs?" *Harvard Business Review* (November-December, 1975), p. 97.

FIGURE 19-7 Citicorp's International Code of Conduct

> **1**
> We must never lose sight of the fact that we are guests in foreign coun-
> tries. We must conduct ourselves accordingly. We recognize the right of
> governments to pass local legislation and our obligation to conform.
>
> **2**
> Under these circumstances, we also recognize that we can survive only if
> we are successful in demonstrating to the local authorities that our pres-
> ence is beneficial.
>
> **3**
> We believe that every country must find its own way politically and eco-
> nomically. Sometimes we feel that local policies are wise; sometimes we
> do not. However, irrespective of our own views, we try to function as best
> we can under prevailing conditions.
>
> **4**
> We have always felt free to discuss with local governments matters directly
> affecting our interests, but we recognize that they have final regulatory au-
> thority.

Source: Reprinted by permission of the *Harvard Business Review*. Exhibit from "Who Controls MNCs?" interview with William I. Spencer (November–December, 1975), p. 99.
Copyright © 1975 by the President and Fellows of Harvard College; all rights reserved.

What Spencer seems to be saying is that an MNC must be flexible in its
dealings with foreign countries, but that it also should not get involved in any
financial arrangement that is not entered into its accounting records. As soon as
an attempt is made to cover up an action, the executive involved probably has
gone too far. This appears to be a more reasonable approach than simply
permitting officials of the firm to do whatever they think appropriate to increase
return on investment or than, at the other extreme, forbidding them from participating in any practice not commonly accepted in the United States. Citicorp's international code of conduct is presented in Figure 19-7.

Balance of Payments.[17] Many people believe that MNCs are responsible for
the recently severe balance of payments problems of the United States, as was
depicted in Figure 19-1, page 543. The evidence, however, does not substan-
tiate this claim. For example, U.S. multinationals have been generating more
than $3 billion per year in dollar inflows to the United States since 1955 on the
basis of only a $2 billion average annual capital outflow. Retained earnings of
foreign subsidiaries of U.S. corporations have grown at an annual rate of $1
billion. Notwithstanding the fact that the value of U.S. corporate assets abroad
has more than doubled in the last decade, direct foreign investment has not
substantially weakened the economic position of the United States. The cause
of the U.S. balance of payments problems is considerably more complex than
an explanation based on MNC-induced cash inflows and outflows.

---

[17]The following three criticisms are based on material in Emile Bench, "The Attack on the
Multinationals," *Columbia Journal of World Business* (November–December, 1972), pp. 15–22.

Exploitation of Cheap Labor. MNCs have also been accused of moving operations to less developed nations in order to exploit cheap labor. Again, the evidence seems to indicate otherwise. MNCs, in whatever country they operate, tend to be among the firms paying the highest wages. Not only do they pay higher wages but they also provide many fringe benefits to their employees that most local firms do not. Firms such as IBM and General Electric have led movements in South Africa intended to bring the races together in that nation. These companies not only pay their employees well but also refuse to discriminate on the basis of race or creed.

Infringement of National Sovereignty. MNCs have been accused of taking over nation states or, at the least, not permitting them to function as independent nations. To the extent that MNCs have tied national economies together, there may be a small bit of truth in this accusation. However, the real definition of national sovereignty rests with issues with which MNCs have nothing to do. Nations are able to levy taxes, maintain armies, license business activities, and nationalize property. Clearly, MNCs have none of these powers. MNCs recognize that national sovereignty is a fact that they must reckon with and adjust to if they are to accomplish their profit objectives.

A Convincing Argument for MNCs

The noted economist, John Kenneth Galbraith, has often been thought of as a critic of corporate society. However, in an important article published a few years ago, Galbraith pointed out that MNCs have been both economically and socially beneficial.[18] The beneficial effects of multinationals, as seen by Galbraith, are summarized below.

Lessening of Tariffs. The emergence of multinational firms has been accompanied by a general reduction of tariffs and other trade barriers. The best illustration is the European Economic Community, which came into existence because MNCs, and other influences, had begun to make the old national trading boundaries obsolete. Today, most products move freely among European nations, with the result that European products have become less costly because they are more efficiently produced and marketed. Continued high tariffs, on the other hand, would have made it all but impossible for MNCs to integrate their far-flung operations and grow to the size and importance that they have. The result would have been less efficient allocation of goods and services.

Pacifying Influence. During the last century, the steel, coal, and shipbuilding industries, among others, were the national allies of governments requiring large amounts of armament. Quite simply, these industries had an interest in creating international tension. Just the opposite is true of today's MNC: it operates in many different countries, and a war or even just the breaking of diplomatic relations between two nations could cost the MNC a considerable sum of money in lost trade. Therefore, MNCs have worked behind the scenes to help reduce international tension.

Local Management Power. In large corporations, power does not reside with the owners (i.e., stockholders) but rather with management. For MNCs to

---

[18]John Kenneth Galbraith, "The Defense of the Multinational Company," *Harvard Business Review* (March-April, 1978), pp. 83–93.

operate efficiently, power must be delegated to management, especially local managers who are experienced in the idiosyncrasies of local market conditions. The emergence of this new class of professional, well-educated managers has brought with it many important benefits for less-developed nations. These managers are expected to make many useful contributions to their individual countries and to the world economy.

MNCs are not perfect organizations. They are run by people who, like others, are sometimes driven to excess. When the MNC transgresses sovereignty or breaks the law, it is the responsibility of the nation state to take punitive or remedial action. However, it does seem clear that MNCs do make the world economic system operate more efficiently, which should result in a higher standard of living for all people.

summary points

1. Corporate headquarters must play a key role in the international strategic planning process; otherwise, local subsidiaries and divisions may not be willing to put corporate objectives ahead of their own immediate profit goals.

2. The six steps of the international market planning process include establishing objectives, analyzing the environment, planning the marketing strategies, structuring the organization to achieve objectives, implementing operational market plans, and controlling the marketing program.

3. Expropriation of corporate assets without reimbursement is the most extreme manifestation of political risk, at least as far as private firms are concerned.

4. Other forms of political risk are exchange controls, import restrictions, tax controls, price controls, and labor problems.

5. In the long run, the best policy for firms operating abroad is not to get overly involved with host country governments.

6. The elements of the marketing strategy most affected by the culture of the host country are product positioning, distribution policy, and communication policy.

7. Two economic factors affecting international marketing are the level of economic development of the host nation and inflation.

8. The major advantages to the MNC of standardizing the market strategy across nations are production efficiencies, advertising efficiencies, and the fact that good ideas developed for one national market can be applied to another.

9. The cultural, political, and economic differences among nations, however, may make it all but impossible to develop a standardized market strategy.

10. Several approaches are available for entering foreign markets: indirect exporting via domestic organizations or export management companies, direct exporting, establishing a local marketing subsidiary, licensing arrangements, joint ventures, and total ownership.

11. Three specific events responsible for the rise of the multinational corporation after World War II were the establishment of the World Bank and the International Monetary Fund and the negotiation of the General Agreement on Tariffs and Trade.

12. Regarding the ethical legitimacy of "grease" payments, bribes, and other expediting services to foreign nationals, the best advice for the MNC is not to get involved in any financial arrangements not entered into its accounting records.

13. Despite the many criticisms of their business practices, MNCs have probably contributed significantly to a lessening of tariffs, to a reduction in international tensions, and to the development and dissemination of management expertise around the world.

questions
for
discussion

1. How does strategic planning for international markets differ from strategic planning for domestic markets?
2. How important is the problem of expropriation to most international firms? What other types of political risk does the firm face abroad?
3. Analyze the key uncontrollable environmental variables that the firm must consider when trading internationally.
4. What criteria should the firm use in determining whether or not to standardize its international marketing strategies?
5. What is the difference between a buying proposal and a creative presentation?
6. What are the managerial implications of a standardized marketing strategy?
7. What indirect export alternatives are available to the marketing executive? Explain the key differences between the alternatives.
8. What is the difference between direct exporting, reliance on local market subsidiaries, and licensing as ways of entering foreign markets?
9. What are some of the reasons why a firm might select a joint venture approach over total ownership as a way of selling its products in foreign markets?
10. What is a multinational corporation? How does an MNC differ from a firm that simply exports a significant percentage of its manufacturing output?
11. Do you think that MNCs will be more or less powerful in ten years than they are today?
12. Analyze Galbraith's argument for MNCs. Is this argument strong enough to counter the traditional criticisms of MNCs?

cases
part 7

case 18
metropolitan life
insurance

The question was raised by Metropolitan Life Insurance Company's top management as to whether the firm should expand its insurance offering to include property and casualty lines of insurance coverage. Many insurance companies offered "all-under-one-roof" insurance coverage to their clientele, and Metropolitan Life executives believed this approach would more fully serve its existing policyholders and attract new ones.

Metropolitan Life Insurance Company is the second largest life insurance company in the world with respect to volume of insurance in force. Company headquarters are in New York City.

Metropolitan Life is one of the few insurance companies that operates in all states, the District of Columbia, Puerto Rico, and all provinces of Canada. The company writes practically all types of life insurance as well as group accident and sickness insurance, including disability, hospital, and surgical expense and individual and group comprehensive or major medical expense insurance.

The company sells its insurance policies exclusively through its own sales representatives and encourages its representatives to build on a bond of trust with their policyholders. Except in rare circumstances, Metropolitan Life representatives are not permitted to sell insurance for other insurance companies. In con-

Metropolitan Life Insurance case is reprinted from Roger A. Kerin and Robert A. Peterson, *Strategic Marketing Problems: Cases and Comments.* © 1978 by Allyn and Bacon, Inc., Boston. Reprinted with permission.

trast, most property and casualty companies depend entirely on brokers or independent agents for their business.

Property and Casualty Insurance

In fact, property and casualty insurance represents a wide variety of different types of insurance coverage. Property insurance itself falls into two classifications. The first indemnifies insureds in the event of a loss to their own property, the second class undertakes to pay damages for which the insured is legally liable, and is known as "liability insurance." Fire insurance and multiple-line insurance such as homeowners insurance policies are the major types of property coverages. "Casualty insurance" is a broad term that generally refers to coverage for loss or damage arising from an accident. Automobile insurance is by far the most important type of casualty insurance.

Marketing, distribution, or delivery systems for selling property and casualty insurance fall into two categories: (1) the independent agency system and (2) the exclusive agency system. The independent agency system is one where an independent insurance agent represents between five and 20 insurance companies and can place a prospective insured with any one of them. The independent agent sells on a commission or fee basis. Under the exclusive agency system, an agent represents only one company, as is often the case in the life insurance industry. Occasionally, an agent will represent more than one insurer, providing the insurers are under common management. State Farm and Allstate are two of the largest companies providing automobile insurance that use the exclusive agency system.

Marketing of Life and Property-Casualty Insurance

It is a generally accepted belief in the life insurance industry that the average person buying life insurance buys from a particular individual and not necessarily from a particular company. This occurs because many people seem to think that there is little difference between the policies offered by insurance companies. Rather, buyers of life insurance place a great deal of emphasis on the way they feel about the agent who talks to them.

The feeling buyers have about life insurance does not carry over into the property-casualty insurance area. Here, buyers are trying to protect themselves against a loss that they believe could very likely happen within a short period of time. What buyers are primarily interested in is whether or not the insurance company will pay off when insureds sustain a loss that they believe they are insured against.

Research on property and casualty insurance purchase behavior indicates that about two out of three buyers have had automobile insurance with two or more companies, and less than one half have been insured by their current insurance company for six years or less. In the broader area of personal insurance, two out of three policyholders have two or more agents. However, about one half of policyholders would like to buy all of their insurance from one agent.

The vast majority of the firms which now handle both the property and casualty lines and the life insurance lines first began in the property-casualty area. Usually, these were auto insurance lines that expanded into the homeowners and related markets. The agents here were more "order-takers" than representatives, because customers already had decided on insurance as the instrument that would best protect them against loss, or because the law (state or federal) required that insurance be obtained if they wished to engage in certain activities.

The reason that most property and casualty companies expanded into the life insurance field was to give their policyholders an "all-under-the-same-roof" insurance service. This philosophy is expressed in the themes of two major companies that took this route: "Like a good neighbor, State Farm is there," and "You're in goods hands with Allstate." Both themes assure prospects that they can leave all insurance problems and financial planning with one company and one agent.

One reason why some independent agents do not sell property and casualty insurance and life insurance offered by the same company to one customer is the underwriting requirements for property-casualty insurance. When a company tries to sell life insurance to a client who will not fall into their property-casualty underwriting classification, there could be trouble. An example of what can happen is summed up in an irate policyholder's remark, "What do you mean you can't insure (auto) my 18-year-old son? You've got his life insurance!"

1. Do you feel that Metropolitan should enter the property and casualty business? Analyze carefully both the advantages and disadvantages of such a decision.
2. Assuming Metropolitan does decide to enter the property and casualty market, what type of marketing strategy should they utilize? Be specific in your approach to this question.

---

case 19
itt

India's Ministry of Communication has decided "to bring to an end foreign collaboration with the International Standard Electronic Corp. (ISEC)," which is an ITT subsidiary. This move is particularly surprising because ITT holds a mere 12.75 percent share and not a majority or even substantial interest in Indian Telephone Industries (ITI).

ITT's involvement in India dates back to 1964, when it won a World Bank tender to supply 47,000 lines of telephone switching for India's communications system and to render technical assistance in setting up an Indian factory that would produce 100,000 lines of the same equipment annually. A technical team of senior Indian officials had previously toured various countries extensively to examine all available technology. Upon its recommendation, the so-called pentaconta crossbar was selected for manufacture in India.

While negotiating details of the technology transfer, ITT was invited to take an equity interest in ITI, the government-owned telephone equipment manufacturing plant located in Bangalore. ITT accepted the offer, acquiring a 12.75 percent share of ITI. About $500,000 of this equity investment consisted of know-how, and the rest — some $750,000 — of cash. A seven-year licensing agreement was concluded between ITI and ITT's Belgian subsidiary, Bell Telephone Manufacturing Co. ITT was given one seat on the ITI board of directors, but was not involved in the firm's management.

Soon after ITI's crossbar section started production in 1967, a number of problems arose. Although the plant was licensed and equipped to manufacture 100,000 lines per year, output ranged between 40 percent and 60 percent of capacity. More important, technical difficulties began to develop in telephone exchanges equipped with crossbars. At this point, ITT's minority equity position became an apparent disadvantage. Having supplied the technology and training and having taken an equity part in ITI, the foreign collaborator became an easy scapegoat.

ITT case is reprinted with permission from *Business Asia* (June 15, 1973), pp. 186–187.

ITT feels that its critics are overlooking the following facts: (1) in accordance with ITT's obligations, the entire technology and know-how has been transferred to the Indian partners; (2) some 6.4 million ITT pentaconta crossbar lines have been operating satisfactorily around the world; (3) the entire production, installation, and maintenance process is in Indian hands; and (4) ITT cannot interfere in any activity unless requested to do so.

Upon World Bank suggestion, in fact, help from ITT was requested in order to increase the output of the Bangalore plant. Consequently, from October, 1971, to March, 1972, an ITT production expert worked in the factory and, during this time, increased the output rate to the full 100,000 lines per annum, proving — in ITT's view — that the machinery supplied is appropriate and its full capacity can be utilized with the proper supervision and management. To show goodwill, ITT offered to extend the licensing agreement by two years after its expiration in May, 1971, but forego any royalty or other payments. Moreover, the company agreed to eliminate the original agreement's provision that no other technology could be used while the contract was in force.

ITT's management feels that the continuing problems with the crossbar production and functioning are probably due to the following reasons: (1) India's telephone authority often changes the ordering pattern, thus hampering peak production; (2) import licenses for urgently required raw materials and components are frequently delayed or difficult to obtain; (3) in their anxiety to substitute as many locally manufactured products as possible for imports, ITI incorporates inferior domestic materials and components in its equipment; (4) labor at the Bangalore factory requires better supervision; (5) equipment used in conjunction with the crossbar lines may be substandard, defective, and improperly maintained; (6) recommendations for environmental conditions for the crossbar exchanges — such as air conditioning and absence of dust — are not heeded; (7) installed exchanges are insufficient to cope with the traffic load; and (8) maintenance of the equipment is inadequate.

Regarding proper maintenance, ITT has trained large numbers of personnel overseas. Following up their whereabouts, however, the company found that most of these people, upon returning home, pointed to their qualifications as foreign-trained technicians, demanding and obtaining promotions and transfers to departments other than maintenance.

ITT's management feels it has more than complied with all its obligations but states that it stands ready to grant the government additional assistance within reason. The company is willing either to maintain its equity in ITI or — if New Delhi insists and can offer an adequate valuation and payment formula — to sell it.

1. Explain what is happening.
2. Suggest alternatives for ITT. Support your recommendations.

8

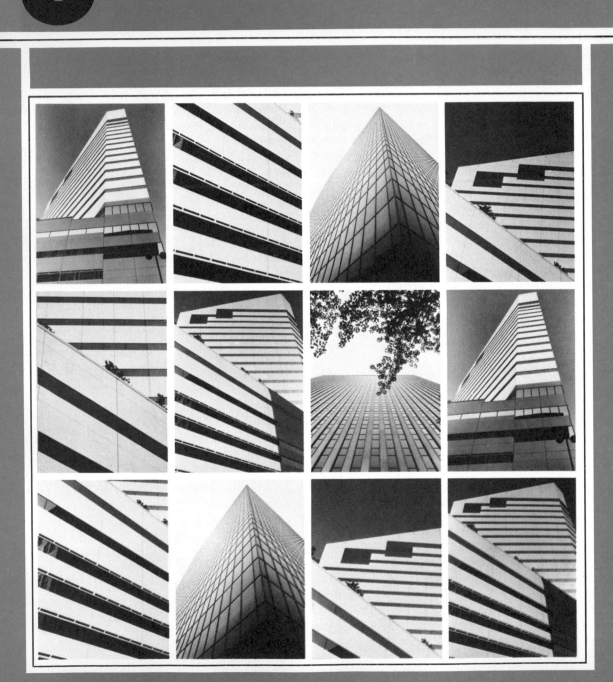

Marketing Planning

Marketing is a future-oriented activity and requires careful planning. Plans must be comprehensive and flexible in order to consider the many variables discussed throughout this text. But they must also be specific enough to permit measurement and control of performance.

Part 8 suggests ways in which firms can facilitate planning of marketing activities through organizational structure and the use of marketing information systems. The marketing audit is discussed as a valuable tool in monitoring and controlling the marketing effort.

Because marketing does require such farsightedness, Part 8 concludes with a look at the marketing trends of tomorrow, such as the increased use of marketing techniques by nonprofit organizations, being planned today.

20

Integrating the Marketing Effort

Unfortunately, many marketing executives are not as successful as they could be because they do not fully understand the importance of controlling their organizations properly. This lack of understanding often results from the fact that the executives have spent most of their professional lives performing specific marketing functions, such as running a distribution facility or designing advertising campaigns. Accordingly, when these individuals are thrust into the position of managing the marketing department, they are ill prepared to take a comprehensive view of marketing activities. To take such a view, the executive must know how the department should be organized, how marketing information and cost systems operate, and how marketing activities should be controlled.

THE MARKETING ORGANIZATION

We have analyzed a number of marketing functions that are critical to the success of the enterprise. There is no one best way to organize these functions. Let's look at four types of marketing organizations, the factors affecting the choice of an organizational framework, and the role of informal communications within the marketing department.

Types of Organizations

Three "pure" marketing organizational approaches plus a wide variety of mixed organization options are available to the firm. The pure types are functional, market, and product organizations. Each of these approaches as well as the combined market-product system is discussed below.

Functional Organization. For the relatively small firm or a large firm selling a limited line of products to one market, the functional approach is usually effective. Figure 20-1 depicts a functional organization suitable for either a con-

FIGURE 20-1 Functional Organization

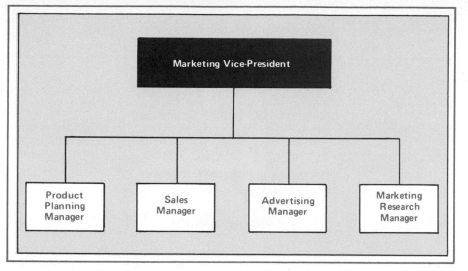

sumer goods firm or an industrial firm. The manager of each functional area, or specialty, reports directly to the marketing vice-president. In an industrial firm, the sales department might be in charge of both selling and servicing the product. In addition, product specialists from the engineering group might be available to assist the sales department when it makes sales calls for highly technical products.

One problem with the functional approach is that it tends to generate specialized subunits that may establish goals of their own that conflict with those of the marketing vice-president. This problem is made worse by the fact that the marketing vice-president is heavily outnumbered by the functional specialists. The proper amount of coordination can be achieved only if the marketing vice-president has direct staff assistance as well as a sufficiently strong personality to force the functional specialists to conform to the firm's overall marketing plan.[1]

Market Organization. The market organization approach is represented in Figure 20-2. Here, the firm organizes its marketing department on the basis of the markets that it services. In the example in Figure 20-2, market A might represent the consumer, market B the industrial market, and C the service market.

Under this approach, the responsibility for establishing the marketing strategy for the sale of the firm's products in each market rests with each market manager. If the market is large enough, the market manager may have the assistance of several functional specialists. The dotted lines in Figure 20-2 indicate that both the product planning manager and the marketing research manager communicate regularly with their staff counterparts, who report directly to the marketing vice-president. The purpose of this communication is to coordinate the efforts of the firm so that work is not duplicated between markets.

---

[1]Harper W. Boyd, Jr. and William F. Massy, *Marketing Management* (New York: Harcourt, Brace, Jovanovich, Inc., 1972), pp. 546–547.

FIGURE 20-2 Market Organization

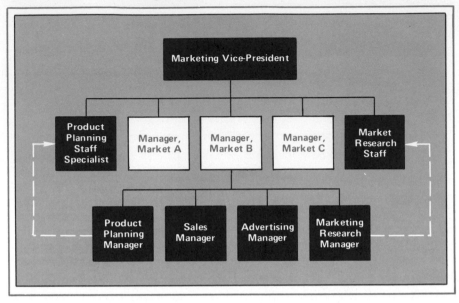

Product Organization. The product manager approach was discussed in some detail in Chapter 8. Under this approach, one individual is responsible for coordinating all aspects of a product's market strategy. This individual is held responsible for the success of the product but is not given much authority to see that it actually succeeds. Figure 20-3 illustrates the product manager system. Notice that the group product manager is on the same level as the managers of the classic marketing functions. Notice also that the product man-

FIGURE 20-3 Product Organization

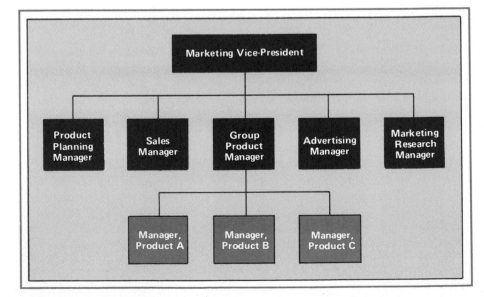

agers have no *formal* communication links between their groups and such vital functional areas as sales, advertising, and marketing research. Although it might appear for this reason that the product organization system cannot function effectively, it has worked very well for some large consumer product firms such as Procter & Gamble.

Combined Market-Product Organization. Depending on the precise needs of the firm, it is possible to create a hybrid organizational framework utilizing elements from the three pure approaches already discussed. The combined market-product approach depicted in Figure 20-4 has been utilized by several major firms. Here, as under the market organization approach, the firm first organizes its marketing effort according to its specified target markets. It then, however, adopts a rather traditional product manager system. As a result, not only do the basic functional specialists report to each market manager but a group product manager does as well.

The advantage of a combined market-product system is that it permits the firm to concentrate its efforts in terms of both its markets and its products, which in the long run may mean the more efficient delivery of the right products to the right customers. Unfortunately, the cost of such a system is quite high due to the many specialists required to coordinate all the people involved. In addition, this type of combined system is difficult to control; as a result, profit responsibility tends to be diffused among too many people.[2]

FIGURE 20-4 Combined Market-Product Organization

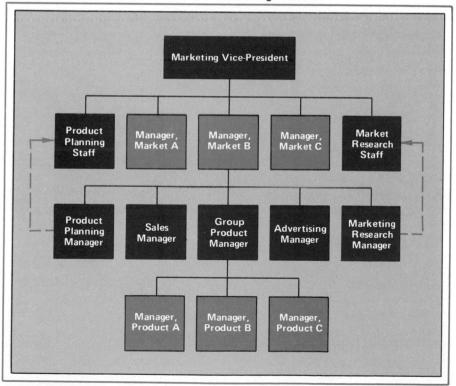

[2]*Ibid.*, p. 559.

Factors Influencing the Marketing Department's Organization

In organizing their marketing departments, most firms begin with the functional approach since it is the simplest to understand and implement. There are, however, several factors that may force the firm to adopt a more complex organization scheme.

Divergent Markets. When a firm serves several highly diverse markets, it may be most appropriate to structure the firm according to the market organization principle. As an example, a manufacturer of food refrigeration equipment may sell its products to restaurants, hospitals, and final consumers. These markets require slightly different products, but more to the point, they require dramatically different marketing strategies. In particular, each market may be serviced through a separate distribution channel; different media may be utilized to reach the buyers in each market; and the customers may purchase the various products for different reasons. As a result, it is essential that the firm recognizes the unique characteristics of each of its markets.

Width of the Product Line. A business with a large number of products may wish to utilize the product organization approach. The more products, the more difficult it is for the firm to manage each one effectively. Accordingly, many consumer product firms have adopted the product manager system. Even though all the firm's products may be aimed at the consumer market, the width of the overall product line often is such that a separate manager is needed for each product.

Top Management Philosophy. What effect does the management style and philosophy of the chief executive officer have on the organization of the marketing department? No business should be organized on the basis of the whims of any one person, even the chief executive officer, but it is a simple fact that the attitudes of top executives of the firm do play an important role in determining how the marketing department and the business as a whole are organized. As stated above, one major problem with the product manager approach is that product managers are held responsible for the product but do not have the authority to ensure that their plans are carried out. The reason that this approach has worked so well in firms such as Procter & Gamble is that top management has stood behind its product managers. In contrast, where the product organization has failed, top management usually has not given its full support.[3]

Importance of Informal Communications

What has been described above is the formal organizational structure of the marketing department. It is also important to realize, however, that there is always a great deal of *informal communication* among individuals not linked directly on an organization chart.

Figure 20-5 illustrates both the formal organizational structure of the marketing department as well as the one-way and two-way informal communica-

---

[3]Arnold Corbin, "Organization for Marketing," in Victor P. Buell, *Handbook of Modern Marketing* (New York: McGraw Hill Book Company, 1970), Section 8, pp. 6–7.

FIGURE 20-5 Formal and Informal Communications Within a Firm

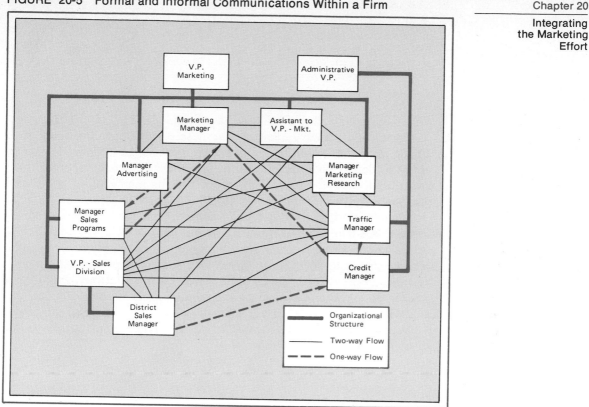

Source: R. Clifton Anderson and Edward W. Cundiff, "Patterns of Communication in Marketing Organizations," *Journal of Marketing* (July, 1965), p. 33.

tion networks among the marketing personnel of a large electronics firm. Note
that most of the firm's executives participate in regular horizontal communications. Although they are not required by the organizational structure to talk
with one another, they realize that if their firm is to prosper, they must be
willing to exchange useful information. For example, although the traffic manager reports directly to the administrative vice-president, the traffic manager
also has regular two-way communication with each of the senior marketing executives.[4]

THE MARKETING INFORMATION SYSTEM

A **marketing information system (MIS)** is the means by which the firm
coordinates the various marketing functions and integrates the activities of the
marketing department with those of the company as a whole. The purpose of
an MIS is to ensure that all information bearing on a decision is provided to the
decision maker in a timely and reliable fashion. Though MISs are not necessarily computerized, computerization has dramatically enhanced the collection
and dissemination of timely marketing information.

---

[4]R. Clifton Anderson and Edward W. Cundiff, "Patterns of Communication in Marketing
Organizations," *Journal of Marketing* (July, 1965), pp. 32–33.

Our discussion of market information systems begins with a comparison of MIS and marketing research. It then proceeds to an evaluation of some of the major information problems experienced by businesses, the various types of marketing information systems, and the procedure for implementing an MIS in an organizational setting.

How Does an MIS Differ from Marketing Research?

One reason why many businesses have found it difficult to establish effective marketing information systems is that these systems have been perceived as nothing more than sophisticated marketing research capabilities. Marketing research was defined in Chapter 6 as the systematic gathering, recording, and analyzing of all data about problems relating to the marketing of goods and services. Although this definition has been broadened by some businesses to also include the study of specific problems, it still does not encompass what is meant by an integrated marketing information system.

In reality, marketing research should be thought of as only one of several important inputs to an MIS. The problem with attempting to convert the marketing research department into an MIS department is that production data, information on transportation and warehouse availability, accounting data, and other key inputs tend to be left out. Marketing research, of course, can play a vital role, but it should not be asked to perform the integrating role of an effective marketing information system.

Why Does a Firm Need an MIS?

All enterprises disseminate information within their marketing departments. The real question, therefore, is not whether the firm needs an MIS but rather how sophisticated the system should be. The problem is well illustrated in a study by Albaum on the flow of information from salespeople to top marketing executives.[5] Albaum arranged to have six customers of a company pass on inaccurate marketing information to the company's salespeople. The information concerned new requirements for potential customers, the construction of a new factory, a competitor's new price structure, and the development of a potentially superior product by a competitor.

The results were staggering. Of the six salespeople given the information, only two passed it on to the other members of their organization — one within four days, although the information was grossly distorted, and the other not for two weeks. This study suggests the existence of three information problems within many firms:

1. **Information Disappearance.** Data are simply lost or not communicated to the right person. In the Albaum study, four salespeople did not even bother to inform their marketing departments of the information that they had been given.
2. **Information Delay.** Information is transmitted to other members in the organization but not in a timely fashion. The salesperson who took nearly two weeks

---

[5]Gerald S. Albaum, "Horizontal Information Flow: An Exploratory Study," *Journal of the Academy of Management* (March, 1964), pp. 21–33.

to transmit the information may have compromised the firm's competitive position.

3. **Information Distortion.** The information is communicated in a timely fashion but it is erroneous, distorted, or incomplete. In the case of such misinformation, the firm may be better off not receiving it at all.

Most business executives are aware that their firms can benefit from the elimination of information disappearance, information delay, and information distortion. However, the more sophisticated the marketing information system, the more money the business will have to invest in human resources and capital equipment. Therefore, an MIS investment decision should be approached like any other investment decision, that is, in terms of expected return on investment. In this way, the expected return on the MIS investment can be compared to the expected return from other investments within the firm.

Alternative Marketing Information Systems

From least to most sophisticated, the three basic types of marketing information systems are the control system, the planning system, and the research system.[6] Figure 20-6 summarizes some of the applications and potential benefits of each type of system.

Control System. The control system provides continuous monitoring of marketing activities. It permits the marketing executive to spot problems as well as new opportunities very quickly. An excellent example of a control system is the Schenley Instant Market Report (SIMR) system. This system gives Schenley executives current and past sales figures and inventory data by brand and package size for each of the firm's more than 400 distributors. Before the installation of the SIMR system, Schenley analysts had to spend several hours collecting this type of information; today, it is available via computer in less than one second.

Planning System. A planning system provides marketing executives not only with current data concerning sales or the inventory location of their products but also with the information needed to formulate marketing plans and to "replan" during the course of the planning cycle. General Foods and other manufacturers of baby food products, for example, are very interested in forecasting the impact on their markets of even minor changes in the number of babies born each year. At a more sophisticated level, planning systems can be utilized to simulate the impact of alternative marketing strategies on product sales.

Basic Research System. A basic research system is used to test decision rules and cause-and-effect hypotheses. This type of investigation helps the marketing executive learn more from the firm's past experiences. An example of basic research involving the use of a marketing information system would be an assessment of the impact on product sales of different types of advertisements (color vs. black and white, full page vs. half page, television vs. radio,

---

[6]Reprinted by permission of the *Harvard Business Review*. Adapted from "How to Build a Marketing Information System" by Donald F. Cox and Robert E. Good (May–June, 1967). Copyright © 1967 by the President and Fellows of Harvard College; all rights reserved. See also Stanley J. Pokempner, *Information Systems for Sales and Marketing Management* (New York: The Conference Board, 1973).

FIGURE 20-6 Applications and Benefits Possible with MIS Systems

	Typical Applications	Benefits	Examples
Control Systems	1. Control of marketing costs.	1. More timely computerized reports.	1. Undesirable cost trends are spotted more quickly so that corrective action may be taken sooner.
	2. Diagnosis of poor sales performance.	2. Flexible on-line retrieval of data.	2. Executives can ask supplementary questions of the computer to help pinpoint reasons for a sales decline and reach an action decision more quickly.
	3. Management of fashion goods.	3. Automatic spotting of problems and opportunities.	3. Fast-moving fashion items are reported daily for quick reorder, and slow-moving items are also reported for fast price reductions.
	4. Flexible promotion strategy.	4. Cheaper, more detailed, and more frequent reports.	4. On-going evaluation of a promotional campaign permits reallocation of funds to areas behind target.
Planning Systems	1. Forecasting.	1. Automatic translation of terms and classifications between departments.	1. Survey-based forecasts of demand for complex industrial goods can be automatically translated into parts requirements and production schedules.
	2. Promotional planning and corporate long-range planning.	2. Systematic testing of alternative promotional plans and compatibility testing of various divisional plans.	2. Complex simulation models both developed and operated with the help of data bank information can be used for promotional planning by product managers and for strategic planning by top management.
	3. Credit management.	3. Programmed executive decision rules can operate on data bank informations.	3. Credit decisions are automatically made as each order is processed.
	4. Purchasing.	4. Detailed sales-reporting permits automation of management decisions.	4. Computer automatically repurchases standard items on the basis of correlation of sales data with programmed decision rules.
Reseach Systems	1. Advertising strategy.	1. Additional manipulation of data is possible when stored for computers in an un-aggregated file.	1. Sales analysis is possible by new market segment breakdowns.
	2. Pricing strategy.	2. Improved storage and retrieval capability allows new types of data to be collected and used.	2. Systematic recording of information about past R&D contract bidding situations allows improved bidding strategies.
	3. Evaluation of advertising expenditures.	3. Well-designed data banks permit integration and comparison of different sets of data.	3. Advertising expenditures are compared to shipments by county to provide information about advertising effectiveness.
	4. Continuous experiments.	4. Comprehensive monitoring of input and performance variables yields information when changes are made.	4. Changes in promotional strategy by type of customer are matched with sales results on a continuous basis.

Source: Reprinted by permission of the *Harvard Business Review*. Adapted from "How to Build a Marketing Information System" by Donald F. Cox and Robert E. Good (May–June, 1967). Copyright © 1967 by the President and Fellows of Harvard College; all rights reserved.

broadcast vs. print). To date, much of this type of research has been performed in academic institutions. Unfortunately, because many companies have been unwilling to make current market data available to young scholars, this area of MIS has not moved forward as quickly as it might have. This problem is being partially alleviated as firms hire more and more highly trained research personnel.

Implementing the System

Once a firm makes the decision to implement a marketing information system, it must be prepared to go through several rather painful stages. Inevitably, some of the firm's executives will resist the implementation effort in the belief that the resulting system will be too complicated for them to understand. Also, during the start-up phase, data processing and handling mistakes are likely to occur. The first real step that the firm must take in the development of an MIS is a thorough evaluation of its current information system.

System Background Research. The implementation process begins with the establishment of an MIS evaluation committee, which has the responsibility of assessing the strengths and weaknesses of the firm's current MIS and of determining the type of system needed in the next three to five years and after five years. As Figure 20-7 indicates, this committee should be quite large since

FIGURE 20-7 MIS Evaluation Committee

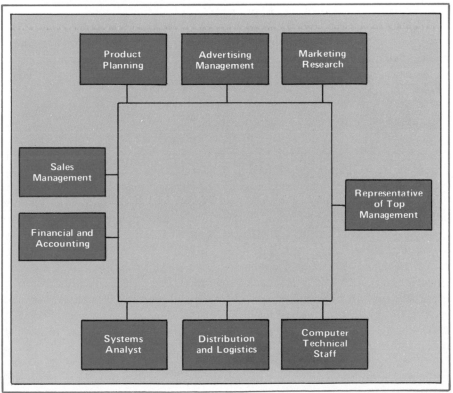

many different corporate points of view are relevant to the consideration of an improved MIS.

Top management should be very careful in selecting the members of the evaluation committee. For example, senior executives may be so busy operating their functional areas that they cannot spend sufficient time dealing with the MIS problems. In contrast, junior people may not have the experience necessary to make sound decisions. A compromise approach that has worked for several firms is to appoint senior executives to the committee, to provide them with a strong chairperson, and to give the chairperson the necessary staff support to bring proposals to the committee.

Information Coordinator. Once the system background research has been completed by the MIS committee and accepted by top management, someone in the organization must be given the responsibility of creating and implementing the new marketing information system. The chairperson of the system research committee is the logical person for such a position, known as the information coordinator. The information coordinator will need a permanent staff as well as the support of top management so that other people in the firm can be called on for short-term duty on the new system. The coordinator will also want to continue to have regular meetings with the original research committee in order to receive input from those most familiar with the information problem. This continuing interaction enables the committee members to see themselves as a part of the MIS implementation effort, thereby increasing the likelihood of its success.

We mentioned earlier that there would be costs associated with an MIS, just as with most business activities. The cost of all marketing functions must be analyzed and controlled. We now look at how this analysis and control can be undertaken.

CONTROL OF THE MARKETING EFFORT

A great deal of this text has been devoted to a discussion of planning the marketing effort. Planning has been understood as the development of marketing objectives and the determination of how best to meet these objectives. In contrast, **control** is the set of activities concerned with determining whether satisfactory progress is being made toward the achievement of the stated objectives. When proper control procedures exist, the firm is able to take timely action to improve its performance. This process of adjusting the marketing effort in response to changing conditions is critical for the success of the firm since very few such efforts proceed exactly according to plan. The discussion of marketing control begins with an examination of segmental analysis. We also look at an approach to analyzing the cost effectiveness of various marketing expenditures, two determinants of profitability, and the role of the marketing controller.

Segmental Analysis

Traditional accounting systems are designed to provide a financial account of the organization at any particular moment in time through the development of financial statements — primarily, the income statement and the balance sheet. When this approach is used to evaluate the success of a particular product or market segment, the firm usually stresses the net income derived from each product or segment. Unfortunately this approach involves the arbitrary assignment of overhead costs across the firm's product or market mix. Some of the overhead costs attached to a particular product, namely, the fixed cost element, would not simply disappear if the product were discontinued; instead, they would have to be reallocated to the firm's remaining products.

Contribution accounting, or **segmental analysis**, on the other hand, is based on variable cost-pricing, and can be used to evaluate profitability of products, sales territories, customers, or even salespeople.[7] As discussed in Chapter 13, a firm can produce and sell a product profitably in the short run only if its variable costs are less than its revenues. Accordingly, in order to match costs and revenues, segmental analysis involves the development of financial statements for each particular product, for example. In these statements all costs that can be functionally related to a product are allocated to it. Therefore, net sales minus costs indicate how much each product has contributed to overhead and profit. This information is vital for decisions relating to new product introduction and product abandonment.

Guiding Principles of Segmental Analysis. Four basic principles underlie the effective use of segmental analysis by the marketing decision maker — (1) profit contribution is the relevant measure; (2) future costs, rather than past costs, are considered; (3) opportunity costs must be considered; and (4) promotional expenditures must be allocated over time.[8]

Use Profit Contribution as the Relevant Measure. Only costs directly attributable to the product or market segment under analysis should be deducted from revenue. These are the costs that would be eliminated if the firm stopped production of the product or halted sales in the market territory under analysis. In reality, a hierarchy of cost attachment exists. For example, certain costs, such as the sales manager's salary, which cannot be allocated to each salesperson, may be allocated to each sales territory.

Use Future Costs, Not Past Costs. Whereas most accounting systems contain information about past events, segmental analysis is concerned with forecasting future events. Historical costs, therefore, are relevant only if they are indicative of future costs. Otherwise, these costs should be adjusted to reflect expected changes.

Include Opportunity Costs. When using segmental analysis, the firm should identify any opportunity costs resulting from the manufacture of the product or development of the market in question. Typically, the greatest opportunity cost is the cost of capital. It is an opportunity cost in the sense that this capital could have been used for some other purpose by the organization.

Allocate Promotional Expenditures Over Time. In accordance with the matching principle in accrual-based accounting, the cost of a promotional

---

[7]V. H. Kirpalani and Stanley S. Shapiro, "Financial Dimensions of Marketing Management," *Journal of Marketing* (July, 1973), pp. 40–41.

[8]W. J. E. Crissy, Paul Fischer, and Frank H. Mossman, "Segmental Analysis: Key to Marketing Profitability," *Business Topics* (Spring, 1973), p. 44.

effort should be matched with the revenues generated by that effort. The problem here is that the effects of a promotional campaign may last over time — in some cases, long after the completion of the campaign. Also, if the firm operates in more than one market, it may be necessary to allocate a share of these costs to each market. The matching problem is further compounded by the fact that the components of a well-designed promotional effort — advertising, personal selling, sales promotion — may have a synergistic effect upon one another, making it even more difficult to separate out the various costs involved.

Profitability Analysis. The American Accounting Association has designed a format for segmental analysis that is consistent with the above principles.[9] Table 20-1 illustrates the format applied to a sales territory. The analysis proceeds from variable to fixed costs. The first measure of the territory's profitabil-

TABLE 20-1   Budgeted Operation — Territory A

	Amount	Behavior
Revenues	$1,200,000	
Less: variable costs:		
Variable costs incurred within the segment	200,000	variable
Variable costs of products and services provided to the segment by other segments of the firm	120,000	variable
Cost of capital × current value of average traceable working capital	80,000	variable
Segment contribution margin	800,000	
Less: direct, programmed fixed costs incurred by or specifically for the segment	280,000	fixed
Segment controllable margin	520,000	
Less: specific long-run costs:		
User cost in current value of direct fixed assets of the segment based on estimated decline during period	150,000	primarily fixed, some portion may be variable with usage
Cost of capital × current value of average direct fixed capital	160,000	fixed
Net segment margin	$ 210,000	

Source: American Accounting Association, "Report of the Committee on Cost and Profitability Analysis for Marketing," supplement to *Accounting Review* (1972), p. 592.

[9]American Accounting Association, "Report of the Committee on Cost and Profitability Analysis for Marketing," supplement to *Accounting Review* (1972).

ity is segment contribution margin — segment revenue minus those costs that vary directly with the level of activity. Variable costs incurred within the segment might include production costs for the territory, inventory value, and ton-miles for freight. Also included in variable costs is an imputed interest charge to the segment for its specific and exclusive demands on working capital.

The second set of costs are subtracted to yield the segment controllable margin. These direct, programmed fixed costs are incurred either by or specifically for the segment but they do not vary with production. They are referred to as fixed, not because they are certain to occur, but because they have no direct relationship to any measure of segment activity. Advertising expenditures would fit within this cost category. Although advertising expenditures can be stopped at any time, they are fixed in the sense that they do not immediately vary with the number of units sold within the territory.

The net segment margin is the last figure calculated in segmental analysis. The costs deducted to arrive at the net segment margin are primarily fixed in amount and are nondiscretionary for the time in question. These charges are for costs incurred in previous periods but which benefit the current period. These deductions are not particularly relevant for short-term decision making but they are useful in a long-term analysis. They are, however, not the typical allocation of depreciation expenses. Rather they include a depreciation charge for assets based on the assets' expected decline in market value during the period in question as well as a charge for the capital the firm has invested in these assets. Again, these charges are only for assets directly used by the segment that is being analyzed. An example in a sales territory would be the anticipated depreciation and cost-of-capital charge on a sales representative's automobile.

Variance. The above procedure yields a **residual income** figure. Since this figure includes the opportunity cost of the capital required for the segment, it can be used to evaluate one segment against another. However, it is also useful for comparing budgeted expenses for territorial operations versus actual expenses. Table 20-2 shows a statement of operation for a territory along with the original budget and the resulting **variances**, which are obtained by subtracting budgeted expenses from actual expenses. Expenses in excess of the budget are referred to as *unfavorable variances*; those less than the budgeted amount are referred to as *favorable variances*. This procedure enables the analyst to identify any operating problems. In the example shown in Table 20-2, the difference of $20,000 in the net segment margin is the result of increases in several cost items.

Cost-Effectiveness Approach to Marketing Expenditures

Marketing executives are responsible for determining how much money should be spent on marketing campaigns as well as how these funds should be allocated among advertising, selling, and various special promotional efforts. In order to evaluate the value of extra marketing expenditures, the analyst needs to calculate a cost-effectiveness ratio for the campaign. The key measure of cost effectiveness is the additional profit attributable to incremental marketing expenditures.

TABLE 20-2 Statement of Operations — Territory A

	Budget	Actual	Variance*
Revenues	$1,200,000	$1,260,000	$60,000 F
Less: variable costs:			
Variable costs incurred within the segment	200,000	220,000	20,000 U
Variable costs of products and services provided to the segment by other segments of the firm	120,000	120,000	—
Cost of capital × current value of average traceable working capital	80,000	88,000	8,000 U
Segment contribution margin	$ 800,000	$ 832,000	$32,000 F
Less: direct, programmed fixed costs incurred by or specifically for the segment	280,000	325,000	45,000 U
Segment controllable margin	$ 520,000	$ 507,000	$13,000 U
Less: specific long-run costs:			
User cost in current value of direct fixed assets of the segment based on estimated decline during period	150,000	145,000	5,000 F
Cost of capital × current value of average direct fixed capital	160,000	172,000	12,000 U
Net segment margin	$ 210,000	$ 190,000	$20,000 U

*U = Unfavorable; F = Favorable.

Source: Adapted from William J. E. Crissy, Paul W. Fisher, and Frank H. Mossman, "Segmental Analysis: Key to Marketing Profitability," *MSU Business Topics* (Spring, 1973), p. 48. Reprinted by permission of the publisher, Division of Research, Graduate School of Business Administration, Michigan State University.

Calculating Profit Impact. To illustrate how cost-effectiveness ratios are calculated, assume a company is preparing a $10,000 advertising campaign that is expected to yield $80,000 in additional revenues. The marketing executive cannot make a decision on the merits of the campaign until its impact on the firm's profits is determined. Table 20-3 shows that the $80,000 in additional revenues involves $36,000 in additional variable costs. This $36,000 figure includes the cost of producing the additional units, as well as the increased inventory, distribution, and working capital expenditures. The firm must also deduct the cost of the advertising campaign itself, which is a programmed fixed expense because it is predetermined for the period in question. The result is a segment controllable margin of $34,000. In this case, the cost-effectiveness ratio is 3.4 — that is, each dollar invested in the advertising campaign generates 3.4 dollars of controllable margin for the firm.

TABLE 20-3 Financial Appraisal of Special Advertising

Additional sales revenue	$80,000
Less variable costs	36,000
Segment contribution margin	$44,000
Less programmed fixed expenses	10,000
Segment controllable margin	$34,000

$$\text{Cost-effectiveness ratio} = \frac{\text{segment controllable margin}}{\text{advertising outlay}}$$

$$\frac{\$34,000}{\$10,000} = 3.4$$

Allocating the Marketing Budget. The law of diminishing returns tells us that at some point increased marketing expenditures will not generate extra profits for the firm. For example, Table 20-4 shows that as the firm increases its expenditures on sales staff salaries and travel from $200,000 to $300,000, the controllable margin of the product in question jumps from $600,000 to $1,400,000. This $800,000 increase yields a cost-effectiveness ratio of 8 to 1. However, as more money is spent, the cost-effectiveness ratio of the extra expenditures declines until it reaches 0 at the $700,000 figure, at which point increased expenditures yield no additional profit. In short, there is no reason for this firm to spend more than $600,000 on sales staff salaries and travel. Based on data in Table 20-4 and assuming enough funds were available, the marketing executive is in a position to recommend a marketing budget of $1,420,000, made up of the following expenditures:

Sales staff expense	$ 600,000
Advertising expense	700,000
Special promotion expense	120,000
	$1,420,000

Now assume that the firm does not have $1,420,000 to allocate to marketing activities. In this case, the cost-effectiveness ratio is still a useful device for allocating whatever money is available. For example, if only $1,080,000 were available, the first step would be to allocate enough money to each marketing activity such that each reaches its peak-effectiveness ratio. The remaining money would then be allocated in increments by selecting the activity with the highest cost-effectiveness ratio until all of the funds were expended. If this procedure were followed with the data shown in Table 20-4, the manager would spend the $1,080,000 in the following manner:[10]

Advertising expense	$600,000
Sales staff expense	400,000
Special promotion expense	80,000
	$1,080,000

[10]A. V. Corr, "A Cost-Effectiveness Approach to Marketing Outlays," *Management Accounting* (January, 1976), pp. 33–36.

TABLE 20-4   Cost Effectiveness of Selling Activities

	Costs (000)	Controllable Margin (000)	Incremental Cost Effectiveness	
			Amount (000)	Ratio
Advertising				
	$ 100	$ 200	$ 0	—
	200	400	200	2
	300	800	400	4
	400	1,500	700	7
	500	2,400	900	9
	600	2,800	400	4
	700	2,900	100	1
	800	2,800	(100)	(1)
	900	2,600	(200)	(2)
Sales salaries and travel				
	$ 100	$ 200	$ 0	—
	200	600	400	4
	300	1,400	800	8
	400	1,900	500	5
	500	2,200	300	3
	600	2,300	100	1
	700	2,300	0	0
	800	2,300	0	0
	900	2,200	(100)	(1)
	1,000	2,100	(100)	(1)
Special promotions				
	$ 20	$ 140	$140	7
	40	240	100	5
	60	320	80	4
	80	400	80	4
	100	460	60	3
	120	480	20	1
	140	470	(10)	(.5)
	160	450	(20)	(1)

Source: A. V. Corr, "A Cost-Effectiveness Approach to Marketing Outlays," *Management Accounting* (January, 1976), p. 35.

Limitations. Although this approach is useful, it does have two limitations. First, it works best in stable industries where marketing analysts have a reasonably good understanding of the impact of various levels of marketing expenditures on sales. On the other hand, if a product is new, it may be difficult for even an experienced marketing manager to estimate cost-effectiveness ratios for selling, advertising, and special promotions.

The second limitation of this approach is that it assumes that selling, advertising, and special promotions expenditures are independent of one another, which, of course, is not so. A marketing program is a well-integrated set of expenditures on the activity area. Sales staff efforts, for example, are reinforced by effective advertising and special promotions. In the same way, advertising and sales promotion determine to some degree the success of the firm's sales force. Therefore, when determining how money should be spent, the analyst must never lose sight of the fact that each marketing activity is a part of a complete marketing program.

Determinants of Profitability

Profitability analysis of a firm's marketing effort enables the firm to adjust its marketing strategy in response to changing demand conditions. Thus, the firm is in a better position to meet its profit objectives.

What factors determine the firm's profitability? How important is each of these factors? A major study called "Profit Impact of Market Strategy" (PIMS) was undertaken to answer these questions. The study was based on data provided to the PIMS researchers by a large group of U.S. companies. Although 37 separate factors were shown to affect profits, two of the most important were found to be market share and product quality.[11]

Market Share. The PIMS study clearly shows the existence of a strong positive relationship between a firm's market share and its profitability. The market share categories shown in Table 20-5 have been constructed so that approximately one fifth of the sample is in each market share category. The average return on investment for firms with less than a 7 percent market share was only 9.6 percent; in contrast, the average ROI for businesses with more than 36 percent share of the market was 30.2 percent.

Why does market share seem to correlate with profitability? The answer may be experience: businesses with a large market share tend to have more operating experience and, as a result, lower total costs than do firms with smaller market shares. The PIMS data have documented this relationship by showing that businesses with a higher market share tend to have lower marketing-expenses-to-sales ratios. The market share data would also seem to suggest that it is better to be a major competitor in a small market than a small compet-

TABLE 20-5.   Relationship of Market Share to Profitability

Market Share	Return on Investment
Under 7%	9.6%
7–14	12.0
15–22	13.5
23–36	17.9
Over 36	30.2

Source: Adapted from Peter T. FitzRoy, *Analytical Methods for Marketing Management* (London: McGraw-Hill Book Co., Ltd., 1976), p. 324.

---

[11]Peter T. FitzRoy, *Analytical Methods for Marketing Management* (London: McGraw-Hill Book Company, 1976), pp. 323–325.

itor in a large market. This fact alone emphasizes the importance to the firm of choosing its market segments wisely.

Product Quality. The PIMS research defined products as of either superior, average, or inferior quality in relation to competitors' products. The PIMS data were very clear on the point that higher quality products are associated with higher return on investment. The correlation with ROI was even stronger when product quality was considered in conjunction with market share. As shown in Figure 20-8, firms selling inferior products and with less than 12 percent of the overall market for their products had a 4.5 percent average return on investment. At the other extreme, businesses with superior products and a market share greater than 26 percent had an average ROI of 28.3 percent.

FIGURE 20-8   Number of Businesses and ROI by Market Share and Product Quality

Product Quality	Market Share			Total No. of Businesses
	Under 12%	12%-26%	Over 26%	
Inferior	51* / 4.5**	58 / 11.0	35 / 19.5	144
Average	39 / 10.4	63 / 18.1	53 / 21.9	155
Superior	79 / 17.4	55 / 18.1	88 / 28.3	222
Total No. of Businesses	169	176	176	521

*No. of businesses.
**Average ROI.

From the above findings, it is clear that the enterprise must monitor carefully the quality and market share of its products in relation to its competitors' products. If either quality or market share begins to slip, it won't be long before profits also start to decline.

The Marketing Controller

Traditionally, relatively little real financial analysis has been performed in the marketing department. Any such analysis that has taken place in the marketing department has been performed by the accounting and financial analysts located in the controller's department. The responsibility of these analysts has usually been limited to checking expense accounts, monitoring adherence to budgets, and interpreting accounting reports. Although this information is useful to the firm, it is not the type of information needed by marketing executives in making decisions.

As a result, several major corporations — including DuPont, General Foods, Nestle, and Trans World Airlines — have created the position of marketing controller. Typically, the marketing controller reports directly to the chief marketing executive and is responsible for making accounting and financial data more serviceable for the marketing manager. The marketing controller meets with advertising agencies and suppliers of sales promotion materials as well as with all international marketing executives. The staff of the marketing controller administers all accounting data concerning media expenses, sales and distribution financial reports, as well as any other project utilizing financial data to make marketing decisions.[12]

THE MARKETING AUDIT

A **marketing audit** is defined as a "systematic, critical, and impartial review and appraisal of the total marketing operation: of the basic objectives and policies of the operation and the assumptions which underlie them as well as of the methods, procedures, personnel, and organization employed to implement the policies and achieve the objectives."[13] Most marketing executives would be insulted if they were told that they do not understand this definition and do not audit their operations. In fact, most would claim that they periodically monitor all aspects of the marketing department. The problem is that a marketing evaluation or even the sum of many such evaluations does not constitute a marketing audit.

An Evaluation Is Not an Audit

There are two reasons why most marketing evaluations are not true audits. First, most marketing evaluations are too limited in scope. For example, during a typical marketing evaluation, the management team might analyze the effectiveness of the sales force, the advertising program, or the product mix, but it would probably approach each of these elements of the evaluation separately and without an overall, coherent plan. In short, such an evaluation is not an integrated appraisal of all aspects of the marketing operation. The primary characteristic of a marketing audit, therefore, is that it is a comprehensive survey and analysis of the entire marketing function.

The second difference between a marketing evaluation and a marketing audit is that the evaluation is concerned primarily with performance evaluation, both of functions and of personnel, and not with the validity of the fundamen-

---

[12]Harold W. Fox, "The Marketing Controller as Planner," *Managerial Planning* (July/August, 1974), p. 33.

[13]Abe Scuchman, "The Marketing Audit: Its Nature, Purposes, and Problems," in Philip Kotler and Keith Cox, *Readings in Marketing Management* (Englewood Cliffs, N.J.: Prentice Hall, 1972), p. 375.

tal objectives of the marketing program. The marketing audit, on the other hand, not only involves performance evaluation but also an assessment of the size and nature of the various market segments, the firm's relative position with respect to each market segment, its short- and long-term objectives and capabilities in each market segment, as well as the effectiveness of current marketing tactics.

Prognosis, Not Merely Diagnosis

An audit is as much a search for opportunities as it is a search for problems. In other words, a marketing audit is concerned both with the past and the future, with both diagnosis and prognosis. Unfortunately, many executives are content only to search for and solve current problems rather than also to identify emerging issues that may cause problems or present opportunities for the firm in the future. Thus these executives are at a loss in making the necessary adjustments.

Sears provides a classic example of the kind of marketing farsightedness discussed above. In the early 1950s, top management at Sears became aware of the magnitude and implications for retailing of the movement of people from central cities to outlying suburban areas. Accordingly, Sears moved with its customers out to the suburbs. On the other hand, one of Sears' major competitors, Montgomery Ward, was slow in spotting this trend and in moving operations to the more profitable surburban areas. As a result, even today Sears still has a much larger share of the suburban business than Montgomery Ward. In more recent times, marketing audits have helped firms adjust to the changing shopping and working patterns of women, the shortage of petrochemical products, the high rates of inflation, as well as to emerging technology in their own industries.

When Should the Audit Take Place?

Many executives look upon a marketing audit as necessary only when the firm faces a major problem, such as dramatically deteriorating markets and profits. Unfortunately, in such a situation, it may be too late to perform a true audit; rather management must look for some immediate short-run cure rather than attempt to analyze fully the department's major problem. At this point, the prognosis is not a good one. Management may be successful in stimulating the department, but it is rarely able to devise a long-term solution when the immediate concern is keeping the product, or even the firm, alive.

Accordingly, the firm should perform periodic, comprehensive marketing audits even when the market effort appears to be proceeding successfully. When a product or marketing strategy is failing, the need for such an audit is apparent; when revenues are rolling in, however, the need may be less clear. The problem with success is that it tends to breed complacency and carelessness. For example, a successful executive can become deeply committed to existing policies and solutions which, as time goes by, may become outmoded and useless. Or success may make it difficult for the executive to consider new ideas and products objectively and carefully; instead, any changes are dismissed out of fear that they can only jeopardize current profits. In the long run, however, such adherence to the status quo leads to growing inefficiencies and an inability to develop new markets and to adapt to changing external events. The result will eventually show up on the bottom line of the income statement. The best way to protect against market share loss and declining profits is to perform periodic marketing audits.[14]

The Audit Process

An integrated marketing audit involves six basic steps. This process is outlined in Figure 20-9 and each of the six steps is discussed below.[15]

Step 1: Determine Corporate Strategy and Objectives. The marketing audit begins with a determination of the firm's overall corporate strategy. In many cases the corporate strategy is spelled out in an official corporate document. The elements of the strategy may include the firm's product mix, its potential market opportunities, the allocation of company personnel and financial resources, as well as specific sales, growth, and profit objectives.

If the enterprise does not have an official statement of strategy and objectives, the analyst typically assumes that the firm wishes to exploit its differential competitive advantages. These advantages might include research and development capability, the firm's image with its customers, low manufacturing costs, or a strong distribution network. Information about the firm's competitive advantages can be gathered by analyzing how the firm allocates its resources as well as by interviewing current customers and company officials.

Step 2: Identify Normative Marketing Objectives. The corporate strategy establishes guidelines for the operation of the marketing department, and other departments as well. The more clearly defined the strategy, the easier it is for the marketing department to formulate explicit, normative objectives for its operations. Firms with strong research and development strategies, such as IBM and Hewlett-Packard, require that their marketing departments provide a channel for the introduction of new products. In contrast, Singer, American Standard, and General Electric's appliance division have strategies centered on a highly developed network of independently owned dealers. The marketing departments of these companies emphasize the strength of their entire dealer structures. As a result, new products are often introduced simply to help dealers maintain their profitability.

Step 3: Determine Current Objectives. The marketing department's current emphasis and objectives may be different from the normative objectives that are required to carry out the firm's corporate strategy. The firm's current objectives can be determined by observing its behavior with respect to each of the major functional areas. Specifically, the marketing audit must include:

1. An analysis of the department's short- and long-term plans.
2. Interviews with top marketing executives.
3. Interviews with sales management personnel.

---

[14]*Ibid.*, pp. 373–379.

[15]Norman B. Judelson, "How to Evaluate the Company's Marketing Operations," in Victor P. Buell, *Handbook of Modern Marketing* (New York: McGraw-Hill Book Company, 1970), Section 10.

FIGURE 20-9 The Audit Process

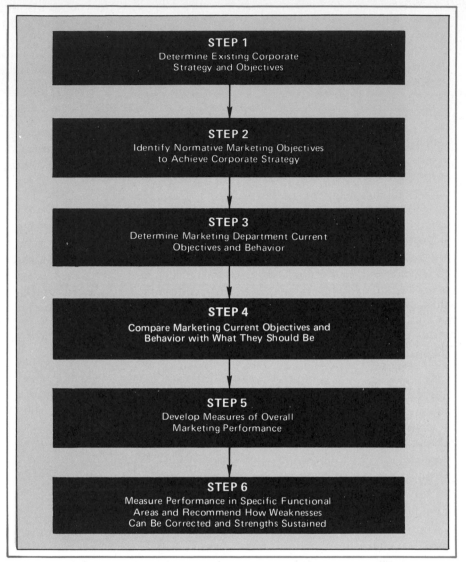

Source: Adapted from Norman B. Judelson, "How to Evaluate the Company's Marketing Operations," in Victor P. Buell, *Handbook of Modern Marketing* (New York: McGraw-
Hill Book Co., 1970), Section 10, p. 37.

4. Interviews with executives from general management as well as from other
functional areas within the firm.
5. Interviews with key customers.
6. An evaluation of the marketing department's expense statements.
7. An evaluation of the formal and informal structure of the marketing department.

Step 4: Compare Current and Normative Objectives. Comparing the
normative objectives of the marketing department with its current objectives is
a crucial step in the marketing audit. In some situations, the analyst may find
that the marketing department is placing its emphasis on products or markets

While many managers formally and systematically audit the activities of their firms, the vast majority of individuals do not audit themselves. As a regular practice, all of us should take a few hours to evaluate our success in meeting personal and career objectives as well as to look for new or alternate goals. The following steps, very much like the ones involved in a corporate audit, may help **you** conduct a self audit.

Determine Long-Term Strategy and Objectives. What do you and your family want out of your professional and personal lives? How much are you willing to sacrifice for your career? You'll have a much better chance of being satisfied in life if you take time to decide early just what you hope to accomplish.

Identify Normative Objectives. What explicit *short-range* objectives will help you accomplish your *long-term* goals? As an example, an individual with the long-term professional goal of becoming vice-president of marketing may first work toward the goal of becoming the firm's leading sales representative.

Determine Current Objectives. Is your *current* behavior in line with your normative objectives? To continue with the sales example, are you spending enough time developing new customers and selling new products? Are you selling your firm's most profitable products or just those that are the easiest to sell? Do your customers consider you pushy? Are you attentive to their needs?

Compare Current and Normative Objectives. Are you actually working toward your long-term objectives or are you doing things that will have relatively little impact on your future development?

Develop Measurement Criteria. Do you have a satisfactory way of measuring your progress? What yardstick(s) have you to measure your success? The scientist may measure success as a function of the number of articles published or prizes won, whereas the business executive may look more toward income and intrafirm status as indicators of professional development. Do you have a good family life, or have you sacrificed too much for career development?

Assess the Competition and Formulate Recommendations. How well have you done in comparison to others of approximately equal talent and training who entered the firm at roughly the same time you did? Are your long-term objectives and strategy still realistic? Should you modify them? Have you set your sights too low? If you have not been able to achieve your goals, perhaps you should modify them to bring your accomplishments and objectives more into congruence.

Most firms find self audits helpful, and conduct them at regular intervals. Shouldn't you?

Marketing & You

which have little or no long-term impact on the firm's success. When this situation occurs, the analyst often recommends that the audit be terminated so that full attention can be given to redefining the firm's objectives.

Step 5: Develop Measurement Criteria. Many yardsticks, or criteria, can be used to measure the success of the firm. But any measurement criteria chosen should measure explicitly that which defines the firm's success and should be relevant to the concerns of the industry as a whole. Figure 20-10 lists criteria, such as sales per outlet and sales per salesperson, that can be used for measuring market performance. The list could be customized to fit a particular firm or industrial category of firms.

FIGURE 20-10   Measures of Marketing Performance

Distribution	Sales Organization	Products
Sales by type of outlet	Sales per salesman	Number of new products introduced
Quality of outlets	Structure of sales organization	Evaluation of existing products
Number of outlets	Number of salesmen	Breadth of product line
Change in number of outlets	Salesperson's time allocation	Number of products discontinued
Sales per outlet	Salesperson capability	Estimated sales of new products

Growth and Profitability	Advertising and Sales Promotion	Pricing
Sales	Expenditures	Average realized price
Market penetration	Effectiveness	Price changes
Profits	Emphasis	
Return on investment		

Service and Sales Support	Marketing Research and Planning
Customer morale	Scope of staffing
Delivery time	Impact on company operations
Training	
Adjustments	
Technical service	

Source: Adapted from Norman B. Judelson, "How to Evaluate the Company's Marketing Operations," in Victor P. Buell, *Handbook of Modern Marketing* (New York: McGraw-Hill Book Co., 1970), Section 10, p. 39.

Step 6: Measure Firm Against Criteria and Formulate Recommendations. Once the appropriate measures of marketing performance have been selected, the analyst then evaluates the firm and the firm's leading competitors in terms of each of the criteria. Only competitors that perform consistently above the average for the industry should be included in the analysis. Information on competitors can be obtained from annual reports, competitors' catalogues, internal newsletters, interviews with the customers of competitors, various government sources, and special marketing research studies.

In this last step of the marketing audit, the analyst also formulates recommendations. If the problems are serious, the recommendations are forwarded to both top management and the chief marketing executive. Top management is apprised of the problems, and the chief marketing executive is given an opportunity to identify any errors in the report and to begin to make the needed strategy adjustments. In contrast, if the basic strategy of the department is found to be on target, the recommendations will be applicable primarily at the functional level within the marketing department. Here, the principal value of the marketing audit is that it enables the chief marketing executive to adjust department tactics in order to prevent major problems from arising in the future.

summary points

1. The three basic approaches to organizing the marketing effort are the functional approach, the market approach, and the product approach. A variety of "hybrid" organizational approaches also are available.

2. Three factors affecting the structure of the marketing department are (1) the number and diversity of markets served by the firm, (2) the width of the firm's product line, and (3) the managerial style and philosophy of top management.

3. Informal communications may be as important as formal communications in the exchange of internal, marketing-related information.

4. A marketing information system is the means by which the firm coordinates the various marketing functions and integrates the activities of the marketing department with those of the company as a whole.

5. Information disappearance, information delay, and information distortion are three communication-related problems commonly encountered in the marketing department.

6. The three basic types of marketing information systems are the control system, the planning system, and the research system.

7. Marketing control is defined as the set of activities concerned with determining whether the firm is making satisfactory progress toward the achievement of its stated marketing objectives.

8. Segmental analysis involves matching product cost to product revenues to determine product profitability.

9. The cost-effectiveness ratio is calculated by dividing the incremental contribution to profit and overhead by the incremental costs involved.

10. Two major determinants of product profitability are market share and product quality.

11. The marketing controller is responsible for managing all accounting data relating to media expenses, sales and distribution financial reports, and any other marketing project.

12. A marketing audit is a comprehensive survey and analysis of the entire marketing function. A market evaluation, on the other hand, is more limited in scope and concerned primarily with performance evaluation.

13. A marketing audit is both a search for problems and a search for opportunities.

14. An integrated, well-designed marketing audit involves six basic steps: (1) determine corporate strategy and objectives, (2) identify normative marketing objectives, (3) determine current objectives, (4) compare current and normative objectives, (5) develop measurement criteria, and (6) measure the firm against criteria and formulate recommendations.

1. Compare and contrast the functional, market, and product forms of organizations.
2. Do you feel that the combined market-product organization will displace the more traditional organizational schemes in the future?
3. Which type of market organization would firms such as the Coca-Cola Company and Exxon select? Explain.
4. What is the difference between marketing research and a marketing information system?
5. What can a firm expect to achieve with a fully developed marketing information system? How should the firm determine whether a sophisticated MIS is worthwhile or not?
6. How does segmental analysis differ from traditional accounting procedures?
7. How does the law of diminishing returns affect the way the firm allocates its marketing expenditures?
8. What are the major determinants of how profitable a product will be?
9. Why is a marketing evaluation not a marketing audit?
10. Analyze the marketing audit process. How would you modify this process?

Topics discussed in Chapter 21:

1. The marketing of nonprofit organizations.
2. Marketing practices in the 1980s.
3. The consumer education movement.
4. Marketing in periods of shortage.
5. The future of the marketing concept.
6. Why people study marketing.
7. Career opportunities for marketing majors.

21

Marketing and the Future

What role will marketing play in the 1980s? Will new analytical techniques substantially increase the productivity of the marketing sector of the U.S. economy? Has the ever-present possibility of product shortages forced marketing executives to consider abandoning the marketing concept? Does marketing represent a viable career alternative for you? Although there are no easy answers to any of these questions, we are now in a position at least to address them. We begin this last chapter by analyzing the recent application of the marketing concept to nonprofit institutions.

MARKETING FOR NONPROFIT ORGANIZATIONS

In the first chapter we said that the products and services of *nonprofit* as well as profit organizations must be marketed to the public. Simply doing something good or beautiful for society is not enough — the organization must also deliver the product or service to the people most in need of it. We now examine in greater detail how marketing can be of use to nonprofit institutions. The difference between advertising and marketing will be considered first.

Marketing and Advertising

Many people think that marketing is nothing more than advertising. Although this view is frequently encountered among the directors of nonprofit institutions new to marketing, it is found in other institutions as well. For example, as the managers of banks and savings and loan associations realized the need to compete for deposits, they began to adopt the marketing concept, or at least they thought they did. In reality, they merely invested heavily in promotional expenditures without first segmenting the market and determining the financial services most demanded by the public.

Unfortunately, the directors of many nonprofit organizations have also equated aggressive promotional schemes with marketing. Consider the following examples:

1. The admissions office at Northern Kentucky State University released more than 100 balloons filled with scholarship applications.

2. The admissions staff of one college passed out promotional frisbees to high school students vacationing in Fort Lauderdale, Florida.
3. Sunrise Hospital in Las Vegas ran an advertisement entitled "Introducing the Sunrise Cruise," which gave patients entering the hospital on a Friday or Saturday the opportunity to win a Mediterranean cruise for two.
4. St. Luke's Hospital in Phoenix introduced night bingo games for its patients — except for those with cardiac problems.[1]
5. The American Cancer Society initiates its yearly campaign in some communities with a church bell-ringing program followed by a parade led by local church and synagogue officials.

Although promotion certainly is important, marketing also involves examining the needs of the market, the external forces influencing the market, the

FIGURE 21-1   Issues in Market-Oriented Institutional Planning Facing Colleges and Universities

---

Market Analysis

1. What important trends are affecting higher education? (Environmental analysis.)
2. What is our primary market? (Market definition.)
3. What are the major market segments in this market? (Market segmentation.)
4. What are the needs of each market segment? (Need assessment.)
5. How much awareness, knowledge, interest, and desire is there in each market segment concerning our college? (Market awareness and attitude.)
6. How do key publics see us and our competitors? (Image analysis.)
7. How do potential students learn about our college and make decisions to apply and enroll? (Consumer behavior.)
8. How satisfied are current students? (Consumer satisfaction assessment.)

Resource Analysis

1. What are our major strengths and weaknesses in faculty, programs, facilities, etc.? (Strengths/weaknesses analysis.)
2. What opportunities are there to expand our financial resources? (Donor opportunity analysis.)

Mission Analysis

1. What business are we in? (Business mission.)
2. Who are our customers? (Customer definition.)
3. Which needs are we trying to satisfy? (Needs targeting.)
4. On which market segments do we want to focus? (Market targeting.)
5. Who are our major competitors? (Competitor identification.)
6. What competitive benefits do we want to offer to our target market? (Market positioning.)

Source: Philip Kotler, "Strategies for Introducing Marketing into Nonprofit Organizations," *Journal of Marketing* (January, 1979), p. 39.

---

[1]The above four examples are from Philip Kotler, "Strategies for Introducing Marketing into Nonprofit Organizations," *Journal of Marketing* (January, 1979), pp. 37–44.

purpose of the enterprise, the resources available to it, as well as the interaction of distribution, product and service, price, and communications decisions. On the other hand, when the decision maker leaps directly to promotional considerations, much of the potential impact of marketing is lost. Figure 21-1 presents a list of issues that the admissions director of a marketing-oriented college or university should consider before starting a recruiting campaign.

The Role of Competition

The cornerstone of marketing strategy for nonprofit institutions is the idea that they too operate in a competitive environment. Competition need not be destructive, as it occasionally is in the private sector, but it does still exist. Although most universities do not compete with one another for gift funds, they do compete with the American Cancer Society, the United Fund, the Salvation Army, and many other good causes. Even wealthy people have a limited amount of money that they can give away each year. As a result, nonprofit firms must differentiate their product from other good causes so as to be able to attract donations.

Many universities differentiate themselves from other worthy causes by giving the donor something in return for the donation. For example, donors of $10,000 or more to the University of Texas become members of the Chancellor Council, which meets three times a year to advise the chancellor of the university. Membership on the council gives the donor an opportunity to meet not only the chancellor but also other wealthy individuals who have contributed to the university. In much the same way, hospitals name rooms, wings, or even buildings after generous donors in order to recognize their contributions.

The Marketing Mix

As described in this text, the marketing manager has four decision areas: product, communications, pricing, and distribution. Each is discussed below in the context of nonprofit organizations.[2] It should be remembered, however, that marketing for nonprofit organizations involves the development of two strategies: one to solicit contributions from financial supporters and the other to encourage the public to use the organization's services. The profit-oriented firm, in contrast, needs to focus only on the buying public. To illustrate, local Goodwill organizations must first convince people to contribute unwanted household goods; they then must sell the repaired merchandise to needy families. Similarly, the American Cancer Society both solicits money for research and outpatient-care programs and encourages people to stop smoking and to have regular check-ups.

Product. As indicated above, a nonprofit organization has one product policy for contributors and another for users. With regard to the first, the organization relies primarily on such intangibles as personal satisfaction, pride, a feeling of belonging, and a ''warm feeling inside'' in order to encourage donations. Most

---

[2]Reprinted by permission of the *Harvard Business Review*. Adapted from ''Marketing for Nonprofit Organizations'' by Benson P. Shapiro (September–October, 1973). Copyright © 1973 by the President and Fellows of Harvard College; all rights reserved.

nonprofit organizations also remind donors that their gifts are tax deductible, thereby effectively reducing the cost of the contribution.

The product policy for service users also may be quite complex. If the objective is to provide warm lunches for the elderly or toys for children at Christmas, the policy is easily defined. The American Cancer Society, however, must assign priorities among the various types of cancer research and choose whether to emphasize detection or treatment. These priorities may vary from one part of the country to another, or from one year to the next.

Communications. Both advertising and personal selling are included in the communications program. The United Fund relies on television and newspaper advertising throughout the country in order to solicit donations for its programs. Other organizations target their communications based on market segmentation. Colleges and universities, for example, use direct mail campaigns to encourage alumni donations. The United Negro College Fund advertises in *Business Week* because readers of this magazine are wealthier and presumably more concerned about education than is society as a whole. Finally advertising is used to sell the product or service to potential users — the number of applicants to St. Joseph's College in Indiana increased by 40 percent after the school began to advertise in *Seventeen* magazine.[3]

Recall that personal selling is most effective when the audience is small and the message is complex. In personal selling, the message can be tailored specifically to appeal to specific segments — for example, to major donors to a charity or college fund. The United Fund raises more than 40 percent of its donations from less than 4 percent of its contributors — personal selling plays an important role in this effort. The most successful fund-raising programs of small colleges usually involve alumni telephoning their old college friends and asking them to contribute. These programs work because it is difficult to say no to an old friend, even though it may be easy to ignore an advertisement or direct mail solicitation.

Pricing. Pricing considerations can involve either money or the donation of time and energy. For example, the United Fund asks each person in a community to contribute 1 percent of pre-tax earnings to the fund. Certain welfare agencies charge their clients a percentage of the cost of the service to help defray expenses and to ensure that the recipient places a value on the service. In contrast, Alcoholics Anonymous charges a high but very different kind of price for its service. The alcoholic must first admit to a drinking problem in the presence of peers and then, if cured, volunteer time to help other individuals with their problem.

Distribution. At first glance, location decisions do not appear to be nearly as important as other marketing decisions for nonprofit organizations. At times, however, location decisions can be critical to the success of the organization. The Salvation Army, for example, positions its collectors at high-traffic shopping areas. The key to success for nonprofit clinics and neighborhood hospitals is to locate their outpatient facilities near the people who use them. Nearly 40

---

[3]Kotler, *op. cit.*, p. 38.

years ago, the California State College System began to establish campuses around that state in order to be within commuting distance for a majority of the population.

Ethics and Social Marketing

The marketing of nonprofit organizations would seem to involve at least three ethical considerations.[4] The first is cost: an aggressive marketing effort can add considerably to an organization's operating costs. However, if marketing contributes more to the organization than it costs, it would appear to be beneficial. Although there has not been much research in this area, a well-run campaign should be able to generate an amount of donations three to ten times in excess of its cost.

The second problem concerns the competitive aspects of nonprofit organizations. As mentioned earlier, nonprofit entities, to some extent, compete with one another. An organization without an active marketing program may find itself at a significant disadvantage in the competition for donations regardless of how much good it does for society. This problem is more difficult to solve than the first. One possible response is to encourage marketing specialists in the public and private sectors to contribute their services to these organizations.

The final ethical problem is the worthiness of the nonprofit organization's cause. Unfortunately, the best financed causes may be of the least benefit to society. For example, is it in the public interest for politicians to rely more and more on advertising specialists and pollsters? Should politicians speak their mind to the public, or should they tell voters what polls say voters want to hear? Using image studies, should candidates "reshape" their personalities to make them appear more decisive? These questions are difficult to answer, but they should be given some thought.

MARKETING IN THE 1980s

What will marketing be like in the decade of the eighties? Whatever the answer, marketing practices will certainly be shaped by new technologies, by what business people have learned about the marketplace, as well as by changing environmental factors beyond the control of the firm. Chapter 2 discussed the influence of the most important environmental variables on the marketing effort. These influences are summarized in Figure 21-2. Most, if not all, of these variables will affect the marketing executive in the 1980s. Three additional forces that need to be examined are the use of more analytical tools in marketing, the drive for more productivity, and the expanding role of government in the marketplace.

More Analytical Techniques

Marketing has long been considered more an art than a science. Traditionally, marketing was the province of people who knew how to get along well

---

[4]This section is based on Gene R. Laczniak, Robert F. Lusch, and Patrick E. Murphy, "Social Marketing: Its Ethical Dimensions," *Journal of Marketing* (Spring, 1979), pp. 29–36.

FIGURE 21-2   Summary of the Impact of Uncontrollable Environmental
Variables

Factor	Impact on Marketing
High rates of inflation	Emphasize the relationship between price and quality; consumers purchase lower quality products.
Slow economic growth	Sales increase will come from competition.
The energy crisis	More urban centers; new energy-efficient products.
The environmental movement	New markets for environmentally safe products; new morality for business.
Demographic shifts	New markets in Sunbelt and in medium-sized cities.
Consumer confidence	Purchase of expensive items will be postponed if confidence level is low.
Changing role of women	Higher family incomes for dual career families; more labor-saving products sold and shopping hours extended.
Consumerism	Consumers will be more knowledgeable about evaluation of products and of their rights as consumers.

with others. The marketing executive was often stereotyped as a back-slapping, cigar-smoking salesperson. If this image ever were true, it certainly isn't any longer. Modern marketing executives develop sophisticated programs for estimating sales under a variety of conditions. Today's marketing research analyst must be well trained in statistics, operations research, distribution, and product planning. To prove this to yourself, take a look at any recent issue of the *Journal of Marketing Research*. In all probability, it will feature articles dealing with such topics as conjoint measurement or the Schonemann and Wang Unfolding Model.[5] Although some of the techniques discussed in *JMR* may never be applied in business situations, many will prove invaluable.

How will marketing executives operate in the future? What will their offices look like? If current trends provide any indication, marketing executives will almost certainly have an interactive computer terminal for retrieving data on every aspect of the marketing program. At a moment's notice, they will be able to find out which products are selling and to whom. They will know which salespersons are meeting their quotas. They will have programs permitting them to estimate the impact of price, promotion, and distribution decisions on the performance of the product in the marketplace. To take advantage of such computer wizardry, the executive will simply need to know how to operate a terminal no more complicated than a typewriter; the programs will be written

---

[5]See, for example, *Journal of Marketing Research* (May, 1979).

by a computer specialist in a language, such as today's BASIC, that permits the executive to talk to the computer in plain English.

The Drive for Increased Productivity

Productivity is defined as the amount of output achieved for a given level of input. In business, we normally think of how much the firm can produce for every dollar it expends. In the 1980s marketing executives will be under a great deal of pressure to become more productive since marketing accounts for roughly 40 to 60 percent of the total costs of most companies. If U.S. firms are to stay competitive in world markets, they must learn to distribute their products more efficiently. In addition to the changes discussed in Chapter 17 that management science can be expected to bring to physical distribution, it is only reasonable to expect that dramatic changes will occur in the 1980s in advertising, retail merchandising, and personal selling.

Advertising. Many executives have long thought that they spend too much money on advertising. The problem with advertising expenditures is that it is difficult to measure their impact on productivity and thus to establish efficient advertising budgets. One approach to advertising budgeting, as discussed in Chapter 10, is to spend at least as much as the competition. When England banned all advertising of cigarette products, many industry experts predicted that cigarette sales would plummet. What happened, however, was that cigarette sales continued to climb at their historical growth rate, and the tobacco industry made more money than ever before. At least in this instance, most if

FIGURE 21-3 Advertising Effectiveness

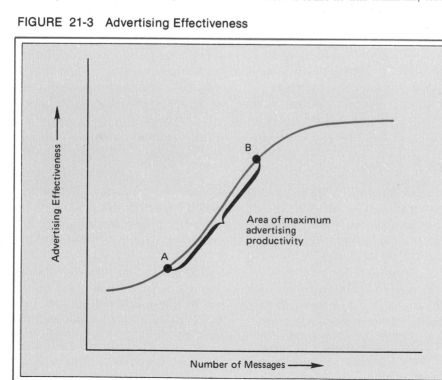

not all past advertising expenditures appear to have been wasted. The same thing happened in the United States during the early 1970s when tobacco firms were prohibited from advertising on television.

We don't mean to imply that all advertising is a waste of money, but rather that in some cases the cost of advertising is far greater than the return. According to most communications experts, advertising effectiveness can be visualized as an S-shaped curve, as shown in Figure 21-3. As the number of messages increases, the cumulative power and efficiency of advertising also increases. However, beyond a certain point (point B in Figure 21-3), advertising becomes relatively less productive. New advertising research techniques as well as access to sales and advertising data banks will make it possible for advertising executives to know when their advertising expenditures are no longer contributing to profits.

Retail Merchandising. At the retail level, we can expect to see the emergence of the superstore, that is, a store selling all the products currently sold in supermarkets plus other products purchased routinely by the family.[6] These other products may include pharmaceutical items, alcoholic beverages, hosiery, underwear, children's clothing, hardware items, books, records and hobby items, and lawn and garden products. The superstore, typically, will be located in a freestanding structure on the periphery of a regional shopping center. Unlike today's supermarkets, the superstore will offer such a large variety of products that it will not require satellite stores to attract customers. Finally, the superstore will be open long hours to serve the shopping needs of working men and women.

Superstores will develop for two reasons. First, during the 1970s operating profits as a percentage of net sales dropped in the supermarket industry from 1.97 percent to 0.92 percent, while average return on net worth declined from 14.4 percent to 8.88 percent. Attempting to increase profitability, food-chain operators will see the advantages of a more capital-intensive store — one requiring fewer operating personnel than the supermarkets of today. Second, superstores offer food-chain operators a way to differentiate themselves from their competitors. Small chain and independent supermarket operators will not be able to open superstores because of the difficulty of obtaining sufficient financing.

Personal Selling. In the years ahead, as management focuses increasingly on profits rather than on sales, salespeople will be under intense pressure to be productive. With today's accounting systems, a salesperson can be readily analyzed as an independent profit-and-loss center. This type of flexibility was not available a few years ago.

The most valuable asset of a salesperson is time. Improved scheduling as well as increased reliance on telephone selling will mean less time spent traveling from account to account. Many salespeople spend as much as a third of their day traveling. Reducing travel time by 50 percent could mean tremendous savings both for the firm and for its customers.

---

[6]This section is based on Walter J. Salmon, Robert D. Buzzell, and Stanton G. Cort, "Today the Shopping Center, Tomorrow the Superstore," *Harvard Business Review* (January–February, 1974), pp. 89–98.

The efficiency of salespeople will also increase as they are made more a part of the marketing team. Today, if a customer asks a salesperson when delivery will be made, the salesperson either guesses or says, "I'll check when I get back to the office." Tomorrow's salesperson, using a portable computer terminal, will simply call up the firm's computer in order to determine up-to-date inventory levels, transportation options, and expected delivery dates. Instant access to such data will permit the salesperson to serve customers more quickly and productively.

The Role of Government

As described in Chapter 3, federal and state governments have been playing an increasingly active role in the regulation of the marketplace and business activities in general. Although there has been some talk recently about the need to deregulate business, it is reasonable to assume that the marketplace will be even more tightly controlled by government at the end of the 1980s than it is today.

Why So Much Regulation?[7] The primary reason for increasing government intervention in the marketplace is simply that more and more of the nation's citizens want protection from industry abuses. People want manufacturing firms to stop polluting their air and streams and to eliminate health and safety hazards on the job. They want to be sure that the quoted interest rate on a new car purchase is the real interest rate. People also want to be guaranteed that they are buying products from firms that have met the test of the competitive marketplace and that are not engaged in collusion, price fixing, or any other practice in restraint of trade.

A second force behind government regulation is the growing sophistication of the natural and social sciences. Today's scientists are able to tell the public much more about the long-run implications of a firm's practices or products. We now know, for instance, that fluorocarbon propellants can have a negative impact on the earth's atmosphere. As a result, whether to use fluorocarbons is not merely a product design issue for Gillette's marketing department; it is an issue for society as a whole.

The final reason for more regulation in the 1980s is that many laws and regulatory agencies have stimulated real growth in the affected industries. One of the best examples is the U.S. banking industry. In the early 20th century, before there were any significant federal controls on banking practices, the industry was frequently characterized by abuse and uncertainty. These problems led to bank failures in 1929 and 1930 and to large losses for depositors. Since the Federal Reserve System and the Federal Deposit Insurance Corporation were established, however, not one customer has lost a single dollar deposited in a U.S. bank, and, on the average, banks themselves have become much more profitable. What this means for the 1980s is that the corporate beneficiaries of regulation may be less willing than commonly supposed to scrap the government rule-making machine.

---

[7]The following two sections are adapted by permission of the *Harvard Business Review* from "The Real Costs of Regulation" by Robert A. Leone (November–December, 1977). Copyright © 1977 by the President and Fellows of Harvard College; all rights reserved.

How Should the Firm Operate in a Regulated Environment? Will new management skills be needed in the 1980s to deal with increased regulation? The answer is yes. In the future, managers will need more political savvy than ever before. Rather than responding in a piecemeal fashion to each new regulatory problem, the firm will need to develop a well-coordinated, overall regulatory strategy. Such a strategy may mean concentrating the firm's legal and financial resources on winning one important battle and not contesting several, less critical regulatory issues.

The Weyerhaeuser Company has developed an unusual approach to regulation. The firm encourages its technical staff to deal directly and often with the technical staff of regulatory agencies. Weyerhaeuser believes that if staff members of regulatory agencies are well informed about industry concerns, they will be less likely to burden the paper industry with excessive regulation. The Weyerhaeuser approach is novel in that most firms view government regulatory agencies as the enemy. An unyielding adversary approach could cause major problems for some firms in the 1980s.

FIGURE 21-4 Marginal Cost Curve for Water Pollution Control in the Pulp and Paper Industry

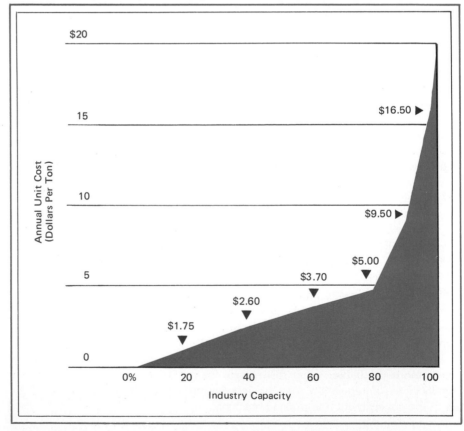

Source: Reprinted by permission of the *Harvard Business Review*. Excerpt from "The Real Costs of Regulation" by Robert A. Leone (November–December, 1977). Copyright © 1977 by the President and Fellows of Harvard College; all rights reserved.

In addition to possessing political savvy, marketing executives in the 1980s will need to realize that a regulation directed against their industry may affect each firm in the industry differently. As an illustration, the data in Figure 21-4 show the cost distribution necessary for the pulp and paper industry to comply with the 1983 federal water pollution regulation. Notice that almost 80 percent of industry capacity can be cleaned up relatively inexpensively, while to clean up the last 20 percent of production capacity businesses will have to spend a great deal more in order to operate efficiently. The high-cost firms will be forced to raise the price for their products beyond industry averages or to reduce profit margins to unexceptable low levels. Neither alternative is very attractive. The marketing departments of these firms will have to devise strategies for dealing with the regulation problem until they are able to build new plants with competitive cost structures.

THE CONSUMER EDUCATION MOVEMENT

The consumer education movement in the United States has grown a great deal since its beginnings in the early 1960s. Today, several major pieces of legislation provide consumers with information enabling them to make more intelligent decisions in the marketplace. The best known examples are the "Truth-in-Lending" and "Truth-in-Packaging" laws. Although these laws and others have made the market more efficient and equitable, several studies have shown that the consumer information provided is often misunderstood by the public.[8] Owing to the partial failure of these information laws, the consumer education movement in the 1970s was more concerned with showing consumers how to seek out and use currently available information than with providing new information. The following paragraphs describe the major sponsors of consumer education programs as well as the implications of consumer education for marketing in the 1980s.

Participants in the Consumer Education Movement

Over the years, the number of formal consumer education programs in the United States has increased rapidly.[9] Today, federal, state, and local governments as well as private nonprofit and profit institutions are all actively involved in the consumer education business. There is no reason to believe that any of these organizations will drop out of the consumer movement in the near future.

The Federal Government. The federal government sponsors a variety of programs in the consumer education area. Some agencies establish and run

---

[8]See George S. Day and William K. Brandt, "Consumer Research and the Evaluation of Information Disclosure Requirements: The Case of Truth in Lending," *Journal of Consumer Research* (June, 1974), p. 21; Jacob Jacoby, Donald E. Speller, and Carol A Kohn, "Brand Choice Behavior as a Function of Information Load," *Journal of Marketing Research* (February, 1974), p. 63.

[9]The following section is reprinted by permission of the *Harvard Business Review*. Adapted from "Consumer Education: Marketers Take Heed" by Paul N. Bloom and Mark J. Silver (January–February, 1976). Copyright © 1975 by the President and Fellows of Harvard College; all rights reserved.

programs while others merely fund local programs. The Office of Consumer Affairs (OCA) in the Department of Health, Education and Welfare distributes consumer education literature to elementary and secondary school teachers. OCA maintains a bibliography of consumer education material and a directory of programs in each state and also publishes *Consumer News*, a bimonthly newsletter with a large national circulation. Other federal agencies working in this area include the Office of Economic Opportunity, the Consumer Product Safety Commission, the Federal Trade Commission, and the Department of Agriculture.

State Governments. Many states, including Florida, Illinois, Wisconsin, and Texas, have initiated formal consumer training programs in the public school systems in order to promote intelligent buying practices. Typically, these programs provide teachers with consumer education information and encourage them to invite guest speakers into the classroom. As more and more education students minor in such fields as marketing and finance, high school teachers will become indispensable to the implementation of these programs.

Local Governments. Most locally operated programs are designed to fit a community's particular consumer education needs. For example, in Pueblo, Colorado, the All Indian Council operates a program to help Indians adjust to a money economy. Historically, Pueblo Indians, because of their high illiteracy rates, have been easy targets for unscrupulous businesses. This program has helped native Americans learn about credit, managing money, and their rights as consumers.

Private Enterprise. Nonprofit organizations, such as Consumers Union, the American Council on Consumer Interests, and the Council of Better Business Bureaus, provide the public with a considerable amount of consumer education information, including pamphlets, short filmstrips, and lists of guest speakers. In addition, *Consumer Survival Kit*, broadcast on nearly every U.S. public television station, has been effective in preparing consumers for the dangers awaiting them in the marketplace.

Several profit-oriented firms also actively encourage consumer education. JCPenney, for example, has one of the most advanced and diversified programs in this area. The company provides teachers with information on consumer issues and publishes two magazines on consumer education, *Forum* and *Insights to Consumerism*. JCPenney also maintains a large staff of home economists who travel from store to store presenting special consumer education programs for adults. Montgomery Ward offers a course on consumer education for teachers; its purpose is to increase the number of qualified teachers. Participating teachers receive graduate credit from nearby universities.

Who Should Be Responsible for Consumer Education?

The question of who *is* responsible for consumer education is easy to answer: the public school system backed primarily by federal and state grants. The question of who *should* be responsible is much more difficult to answer. It is our position that although public institutions must continue to take the lead in educating the public on consumer issues, private enterprise should play a much more active consumer education role in the 1980s than it has in the past.[10]

Private firms will become increasingly involved in consumer education for at least three reasons. First, and most simply, it is the right thing to do. The vast majority of business managers are honest people trying to provide the best products to their customers at a competitive price. To the extent that these people believe in the value of informed consumers, they will continue to develop consumer education materials for the public schools and to speak before groups of concerned adults. The second reason is that marketing executives are experts on the subject of how to deal with the marketplace. Many times, they are more effective than high school teachers at providing product purchase information and guidelines to the public. Honest business people stand to benefit if the public truly understands the real cost of credit, the proper use of short-term and long-term credit, why prices vary from store to store, the importance and cost of store services, and other issues.

The final reason for increased involvement in consumer education is economic self-interest: consumers will tend to patronize companies that appear to be on their side. Goodrich's recent advertisements on tire safety and Shell Oil's pamphlets on automobile safety and fuel efficiency are two excellent examples of consumer education programs that not only inform the public but also benefit the sponsoring firms. In effect, campaigns of this type tell the public that the sponsoring firm is truly interested in the customer's well-being. The result is a more positive public attitude toward the company, which, more often than not, leads to additional sales and profits. As more executives realize the power of such advertising campaigns, they will direct a greater percentage of their advertising budgets to consumer education.

How Will Consumer Education Change the Marketplace in the 1980s?

As a result of consumer education programs, the marketplace of the 1980s will be quite different from what it is today. The more educated members of society will be the first to feel the effect of these changes. It is unfortunate that the poor, elderly, and generally disadvantaged are usually the last to benefit from such social programs as consumer education. Special attention should be given to marketing these programs to the neglected members of society. In any case, the following behavioral changes will characterize the marketplace in the coming years:

1. Consumers will be more likely to let manufacturers know about their needs as well as about the success or failure of the manufacturers' products.
2. Consumers will seek out more information on price, quality, and service characteristics so as to make more intelligent product purchase decisions.
3. Consumers will purchase products from sellers who provide useful and reliable information about their products.
4. Consumers will be less likely to purchase products that are potentially harmful to themselves, their families, or to the environment.

[10]This section is drawn from James U. McNeal, "Consumer Education as a Competitive Strategy," *Business Horizons* (February, 1978), pp. 40 and 42.

If you had the opportunity, would **you** help in the consumer education movement? Perhaps you need to *make* the opportunity happen!

Many laws schools operate free legal clinics for the indigent in order to expose law students to real legal problems as well as to render a valuable service to the public. In colleges of business, accounting departments have also attempted to help the less fortunate, primarily by assisting in filling out tax returns.

As a marketing student, you too could perform a valuable social service by informing people about sound shopping procedures, the correct use of debt in buying durable goods, the advantages and potential problems of shopping at large stores, or how to deal with store management when a dispute arises between the customer and the store. With the assistance of law school students and faculty, you could also inform people of their rights as consumers and of the legal remedies for the resolution of grievances. Consider the following actions that you, as a marketing student, could take to educate the public about the marketplace.

Write and Distribute Pamphlets. Without too much difficulty, you could write a series of pamphlets dealing with specific marketing programs. The more specific the issue, the more practical the answer, and the more helpful the pamphlet.

Address High School Classes. Many high school teachers are unfamiliar with marketing problems. Marketing students could provide a great deal of useful information by regularly speaking to high school classes.

Sponsor Debates and Symposia. Although business students are trained to deal with the marketplace, most other students have never taken a marketing course. It would be relatively easy to sponsor debates and noncredit lectures concerning current problems in the marketplace.

Address Community Groups. Church groups, local PTAs, and other community organizations are potential forums for the discussion of marketing practices and consumer issues.

Cooperate with the Law School. If your university has a law school, it may be possible to sponsor programs jointly or to participate in their free clinics for the indigent. Law students could answer the legal questions, while marketing students could help clients become more productive consumers.

If you're interested in starting such a program, don't forget local business executives. Understanding that they have a responsibility to society, many of them are willing to offer advice as well as to get involved in the various work sessions you've scheduled with the public.

While you are helping others, the one to benefit most just may be you!

Marketing & You

5. Consumers will seek remedies when they are dissatisfied with a product or service.
6. Consumers will be more involved in debates about consumer issues at the local, state, and federal levels.[11]

None of these developments will hurt honest companies. The prosperous business manager of the 1980s will see the beneficial effects of consumer education and will adapt a business strategy in response to the new level of market sophistication.

MARKETING IN PERIODS OF SHORTAGE

Chapter 2 described at some length the causes and implications of the energy crisis. In the 1980s, spot and long-term product shortages will characterize not only the energy sector of our economy but other sectors as well. When the supply of a product or service falls behind the demand for it, shortages, either temporary or permanent, must be dealt with by marketing executives. They employ **demarketing**. Demarketing attempts to discourage customers from demanding large quantities of products that are in short supply.[12] Businesses operating in industries characterized by shortages will be required to make several significant modifications in their marketing strategies.[13]

Product Mix

One effect of shortages will be to force firms to take a long hard look at their product mix. As stated in Chapter 9, it is not easy for a firm to eliminate a failing product; top management frequently is unwilling to give up on a once successful product, and salespeople may hold to the belief that the product rounds out the firm's product line, even while admitting that it does not contribute much to overall company sales.

One unexpected benefit of shortages, then, is that they give the firm an opportunity to delete slow-moving, unprofitable products from the line. When raw materials are scarce, even the most ardent supporters of failing products will realize that the firm cannot afford to expend its limited resources on a losing effort. Therefore, it seems reasonable to conclude that material shortages will all but force firms to monitor product sales and profitability closely and to eliminate quickly those products that do not have a strong chance of success.

Customer Mix

There is an old saying in marketing that 80 percent of a firm's business comes from 20 percent of its customers. As there is a tendency in times of shortage to eliminate weak products, so too will there be a tendency to eliminate weak customers. In some cases, legal barriers will prevent firms from

---

[11]Bloom and Silver, loc. cit.

[12]Philip Kotler, *Marketing Management: Analysis, Planning, and Control* (3d edition: Englewood Cliffs, N.J.: Prentice-Hall, 1972), p. 11.

[13]The following three sections are adapted from Philip Kotler, "Marketing During Periods of Shortage," *Journal of Marketing* (July, 1974), pp. 20–27.

adopting this second strategy. As an example, the oil companies operate on a federally mandated allocation system whereby they must supply their retail customers a certain percentage of the gasoline made available to them in the one base year. The federal government changes the allocation percentage monthly depending on the availability of crude oil and gasoline.

A firm not prevented by legal constraints from dropping minor customers should consider establishing its own internal allocation system under which customers are classified according to their importance to the firm. The marketing department then can determine how much of each customer's preshortage order the firm will be able to fill.

For an allocation system to operate successfully, however, two considerations must be kept in mind. First, assigning a classification code to an account is to some extent a subjective decision. As a fundamental marketing decision, it should be made, or at least reviewed, by the chief marketing officer in combination with the salesperson who calls on the account. Also, once the decision is made, it should be reviewed periodically as the sales potential of the account changes. Second, the firm should inform each account immediately of the decision to establish an allocation system and of the likely impact of the decision on delivery levels. Most customers do keep current with events in the industry and understand that during a materials shortage the supplier may have no choice but to establish an allocation system. They will be more likely to accept the supply problem patiently if they feel they are being treated no worse than the supplier's other customers.

Advertising Strategy

When product shortages develop, the firm usually must modify its advertising strategy. The first response, typically, is to reduce the advertising budget — it doesn't make much sense to advertise a product that the firm does not have. An alternative to reducing the budget is to redirect advertising expenditures to products that are not in short supply. This strategy is particularly effective for new products, which can benefit greatly from the extra advertising dollars.

Another possible strategy is to use these budgeted dollars to explain to the buying public the reasons for the supply shortage, how long it can be expected to last, and how customers can use available supplies wisely. A good illustration has been Shell Oil's broadcast television campaign on fuel-saving driving habits. In its commercials Shell has explained why sudden starts and stops waste gasoline and why a well-tuned car is more fuel-efficient. If customers perceive commercials as genuinely helpful and informative, they will make an effort to keep doing business with the company.

IS THE MARKETING CONCEPT OBSOLETE?

This book is based on the philosophy that the long-term success of an enterprise depends on its ability to serve the needs of its customers. Rather than simply selling more and more products, the job of the marketing department is to determine the needs of the market and then to implement a strategy for delivering the product and/or service to the buyer profitably. This philosophy of business, commonly referred to as the marketing concept, has been adopted by most businesses. The question we must ask ourselves now is whether the actions of one or more large firms or continued long-term supply shortages signal the end of the marketing concept as a way of doing business.

An IBM Reversal?

IBM was not the first company to manufacture computers; however, it took the firm only a few years to capture 80 percent of the mainframe market, which today represents a 20 billion dollar market.[14] Although IBM has introduced many major technological breakthroughs, its success is largely a function of its marketing savvy and its understanding of the needs of the marketplace. Typically, the top executives at IBM have marketing backgrounds.

IBM introduced its first line of computers knowing that its customers were new to computers and understood little about what the technology could do for their business. As a result, IBM trained its sales representatives extensively in the service and data processing needs of its potential customers. In addition, IBM designed the customer's computer installation facility, redesigned the customer's data collection and reporting systems, trained the people who would operate the data processing equipment and later developed software packages to make the computer even more useful. Finally, IBM gave the customer the option of either purchasing or leasing the equipment.

This strategy of focusing on the needs of the market seemed to change when IBM introduced the Series/1 minicomputers. The sales force was dedicated to selling Series/1 machines and nothing else. No effort was made by IBM to train the Series/1 representatives in the special needs of potential customers. Also, IBM did not offer a lease option.

On the surface, it would appear that IBM abandoned the marketing concept, at least for the Series/1. In focusing on selling, however, IBM had not given up on the marketing concept, rather it was merely doing what the marketing concept required — adjusting to the ever-changing needs of the market and competitive conditions. When IBM first introduced the computer, the customer was totally dependent on the seller; the role of IBM, therefore, was to identify and then translate the needs of the market into specific pieces of hardware and related support services. In contrast, when IBM offered the Series/1 machine, the customer was quite familiar with minicomputers, as a result of years of exposure to the selling efforts of competing minicomputer firms, as well as with computers in general. In short, the buying public was no longer uneducated and uninformed; prospective customers simply did not need the total service package that IBM traditionally offered with its mainframe state-of-the-art computers.

In summary, IBM did not abandon the marketing concept with the Series/1 line of equipment; it merely recognized that the market for this relatively simple machine was such that selling, not total service packages, could most profitably drive the marketing effort. The key point of the IBM illustration is that the firm modified its marketing strategy in response to a change in the marketplace, and that such modifications should not be viewed unthinkingly as disillusionment with the marketing concept.

---

[14]This section is based on Theodore Levitt, "Marketing When Things Change," *Harvard Business Review* (November–December, 1977), pp. 108–110.

Shortages and the Marketing Concept

In the preceding section, we described how the firm modifies its marketing strategy in times of product shortages. We must now ask the question: Should the firm continue to be customer-oriented when it does not have enough merchandise to satisfy overall demand?

With a little imagination the firm can usually come up with a great many ways to serve its customers even during periods of shortage. For example, the sales representative, if sufficiently astute, may be able to suggest other products that will meet the needs of customers — products that the firm has in excess supply. The customer may not be able to operate as efficiently as in the past, but substitute products can make the difference between continuing or halting production. In addition, the customer-oriented sales representative can advise customers on a wide range of topics relating to their product or service requirements, including, in the case of industrial customers, other products they could manufacture and sell, inventory problems, and the effective use of reduced business hours. The salesperson can also keep the customer advised on delivery dates, price adjustments, and the supply outlook.[15]

These customer-oriented activities enable the firm to keep in touch with the changing needs of the market. The firm that anticipates customer needs is a step ahead in developing future product markets. Also, markets have a way of returning to equilibrium either through an increase in supply or a decrease in demand. When the product shortage is over, the firm will again have to compete for buyers' business. If the firm has treated its customers well during the shortages, it will have created a great deal of goodwill that it can draw upon when the supply situation improves.

THE MARKETING OF THE MARKETING MAJOR

Why study marketing? Beyond the fact that marketing courses may be required for graduation, we can identify several reasons why business students should consider taking advanced courses in marketing. We also examine entry-level positions available for marketing majors both inside and outside the field of marketing.

Why Study Marketing?

No one would argue with the assertion that people should study what interests them. Although it is wise to choose a subject of study based on career considerations, it is also important to bear in mind the value of a broad education, and the fact that many successful people change careers several times. Within that context, let's take a look at five reasons for studying marketing.

The Marketing Concept Has Caught On. As we have stated many times, more and more firms are adopting the marketing concept. It is important for all members of these firms to understand the role of marketing in defining the firm's mission. As an example, if the engineering group does not appreciate the

---

[15]Philip Kotler, "Marketing During Periods of Shortage" *Journal of Marketing* (July, 1974), pp. 26–27; see also A. B. Blankenship and John H. Holmes, "Will Shortages Bankrupt the Marketing Concept?" *Business Topics* (Spring, 1974), pp. 13–18.

fact that new product designs must be based on previously identified customer requirements, many new products will be technical but unmarketable master-pieces.

Marketing Combines Creativity and Science. Most successful marketing executives combine creativity with rigorous scientific analysis. There is no question that marketing is much more scientific today than it was ten or even five years ago. We now know more about buyer motivation and about how to determine whether a new product is likely to succeed in the marketplace. Although science continues to provide new techniques for solving marketing problems, marketing practitioners will always need to develop creative strategies in order to sell their products. In the marketing department, more than any other place in the organization, the individual is free to combine creativity with formal analysis.

Marketing Deals with Real-World Problems. Marketing often has been referred to as real-world economics. Although economics teaches us a great deal, its usefulness in decision situations is restricted by its limiting assumptions, such as that buyers are always interested in maximizing utility or that all firms are profit maximizers. In contrast, marketing problems are restricted not by artificial assumptions but by the analytic ingenuity and imagination of the decision makers themselves. Marketing managers can learn a great deal from past marketing successes and failures, but they also must be able to adapt to changing market conditions. People who enjoy working on problems that have no easy solutions will find marketing very exciting.

Marketing Has Applications Beyond Business. Marketing is important to any organization that operates in a competitive environment, whether a private firm, a political party, a church, or a charitable organization such as the United Way. If you're interested in politics, keep in mind that marketing research and positioning the candidate are central to the campaign process. If you're thinking about working for a church or charity, keep in mind that the provision of services meeting the needs of the public is central to the success of these organizations. Also, no matter how worthy the project, promotion can only help attract donors and service users.

Marketing Can Put You on a Fast Track to the Executive Suite. Many top-echelon corporate officers came up the ranks through the marketing department. As mentioned above, IBM traditionally recruits most of its senior-level executives from marketing. In fact, until 1977 only two of IBM's senior executives were non-marketers, and they were not a part of IBM's executive committee.[16] Typically, the more competitive the industry, the more likely top management will be made up of people with experience in the marketing department.

Maybe Marketing Isn't for You, or Maybe It Is

Like other areas of study, marketing is not for everyone. We can think of at least three reasons why some people should avoid careers in marketing.

_____

[16]Levitt, _loc. cit._

Marketing Managers Make Difficult Decisions. Marketing managers frequently make difficult decisions with only limited or incomplete information. A typical decision may involve committing millions of dollars to a promotion campaign without knowing for sure whether the product will achieve its sales goals or whether the competition is planning an aggressive promotional effort of its own. If making decisions under conditions of uncertainty bothers you, maybe you should think about a career in another field.

Marketing Executives Make Mistakes. All people make mistakes, but the mistakes of marketing people seem to be especially visible. When a salesperson blows a big sale, the sales manager and other members of the sales force know about it almost immediately. When the product manager's bright idea — paper shoes, linoleum pants, sliced popcorn, disco showerhead — bombs in the marketplace, everyone in the organization hears about it. No doubt about it, as a marketing manager, you will make mistakes. More than 50 percent of all new products never generate sufficient sales to justify their much heralded introduction to the marketplace. If you can't bear the thought of admitting to your friends and colleagues that you made a mistake, then a career in marketing isn't for you.

Marketing May Be Dangerous to Your Health. Marketing seems to involve a greater risk and greater return than such fields as public accounting, personnel management, or finance. Many marketing executives have been fired from $100,000-a-year positions. More often than not, they are hired by another firm at a substantial pay increase. The most famous recent example is Lee Iacocca, the man who introduced the Ford Mustang and long considered an automotive marketing genius. After rising to second in command at the Ford Motor Company, Iacocca was fired by Henry Ford II; in less than six months he was president of Chrysler Corporation.

In summary, marketing offers many exciting opportunities for people willing to operate under conditions of uncertainty. Also, the marketing executive travels frequently and, to a great extent, is his or her own boss. However, with high income and independence go the associated risks if things do not proceed according to plan. All too often, the people at the top are sacrificed because the entire department cannot be fired — not unlike baseball, where the owners fire coaches because they can't fire whole teams.

Opportunities for Marketing Majors

Several submajors can be found within the general category of marketing major. Figure 21-5 presents a list of college courses relevant to specific careers in marketing. The rest of this chapter looks at these submajors and the associated fields that you can enter directly from college.

Advertising. Most college graduates enter advertising by working at an advertising agency or in the advertising department of a business. In the latter case, job responsibilities include helping in the design of advertising campaigns, reviewing the advertising suggestions made by other people in the marketing

FIGURE 21-5 Selected Courses for Marketing Majors

Field of Concentration Within Marketing	Courses
Advertising and Sales Promotion	Buyer Behavior Advertising Statistics
International Marketing	Sociology Cultural Anthropology International Business and Finance International Accounting
Marketing Research	Buyer Behavior Statistics Computer Science Advertising
Physical Distribution — Logistics	Retailing Wholesaling Mathematical Modeling Systems Design Computer Science
Product Management	Buyer Behavior Advertising Marketing Management
Retailing and/or Wholesaling	Buyer Behavior Retailing Wholesaling
Personal Selling	Buyer Behavior Sales Management

department, and working with the advertising agencies that actually create the advertisements for the firm.

The person beginning a career at an advertising agency may work as an account executive or in the creative areas, such as illustration, photography, or copywriting. The account executive works on each client account on a regular basis in order to develop an appropriate advertising strategy. The creative people in the agency actually design the advertisements. Depending on the strengths of the people with which they do business, many advertising agency executives function almost as senior staff personnel for their clients. In these situations, they are involved in most marketing decisions — for example, whether to introduce a new product, or whether the firm should adopt a skimming or penetration pricing strategy.

International Marketing. As international trade grows in volume and importance, business firms will need to hire more and more international marketing specialists. In many ways, international marketing seems very glamorous — for example, the individual is able to travel overseas. However, most international firms now hire local people to run as much of the foreign operation as possible in order to strengthen their position in the host country. Accordingly, the U.S.-based international marketing specialist, despite an occasional overseas assignment to assist foreign managers, is likely to be involved with international operations as viewed from the home office.

Marketing Research. Men and women in marketing research organizations usually begin their careers by collecting and analyzing secondary market data. After gaining some experience, they may then conduct primary data research on such subjects as the type of products demanded by buyers in the future and the expected size of emerging markets or market segments.

Some firms believe that it is not a good investment to employ a large pool of market research personnel to conduct primary research studies. Instead, they let consulting firms such as Booz-Allen, McKinsey, or Arthur D. Little bid on the specific research projects. In these instances, the job of the marketing research people employed by the firm is to make recommendations as to the choice of a consultant and then to monitor the ensuing research and analysis.

Physical Distribution. Opportunities for marketing-trained people are especially numerous in physical distribution and logistics. With increasing frequency, new distribution system concepts are implemented in order to deliver the product to the consumer faster and at a lower cost. Whereas logistics was originally concerned only with reducing freight costs, today's physical distribution specialist looks at the entire distribution system to determine where savings can be realized without reducing the efficiency of the marketing department's sales efforts. Many young people begin careers in physical distribution as systems analysts concerned with the designing and upgrading of billing, transportation, and inventory control systems. These individuals must normally have some computer programming skills. Other individuals become involved in the management of a specific aspect of the physical distribution system, such as the operation of a warehouse or a fleet of trucks.

Product Management. Product managers are responsible for designing the entire marketing strategy for a product. As stated in Chapter 8, product managers are held accountable for product success but are rarely given the authority to manage or control the sales and advertising departments. As a result, product managers must be good at cajoling and compromising.

In most companies, product managers are thought to occupy very important positions. They typically begin their careers as assistant product managers, or they may transfer from sales or any other field of marketing. In addition to being persuasive, product managers must be familiar with all facets of marketing because it is their job to develop and approve the product's entire strategy, from functional design to the advertising campaign.

Retailing. Many marketing graduates are hired each year by retailing organizations as assistant buyers. Their responsibility is to help the buyer select the best available merchandise for their particular store. The buyer, together with the store promotion and sales personnel, then designs a merchandise selling strategy.

When the assistant buyer is promoted to buyer, frequently occurring within the employee's first few years at the store, he or she begins to travel to Dallas, Atlanta, New York, and other major trade markets in order to purchase merchandise. A great deal of the buyer's ultimate success, especially in buying fashion goods, depends on the individual's ability to spot trends in the market before buyers from competing stores do.

Personal Selling. Many college graduates begin their marketing careers in sales. Typically, these positions give the individual an opportunity to learn about the company and its products while calling on the firm's customers. These are not simply door-to-door selling jobs; rather the salesperson learns first-hand about the needs of the customer and about how to design a package of products and services to meet those needs.

Unfortunately, selling does not have as much status in the minds of most college graduates as do jobs in such fields as international marketing or marketing research. As a result, it is difficult to get young people to accept sales positions. However, once they spend some time selling, it is often difficult to talk them into managerial positions. The freedom of operation, the hours away from the office, meal allowances, compensation for automobile expenses, and sales performance bonuses make it hard for many people to leave selling and to accept even a sales management position.

Other Opportunities. Besides the traditional areas, many other opportunities are available to the marketing major. We will discuss only three — banking, management consulting, and nonprofit institutions.

In recent years, banks have become more aware of the importance of marketing; they must compete for deposits, loans, and related financial services with other banks as well as with saving and loans and insurance companies. As defining market segments and developing marketing plans have become increasingly important for financial institutions, the number of opportunities for marketing majors has grown dramatically.

For their part, management consulting firms hire marketing majors to work on special projects for their clients. Young people right out of college usually function as staff analysts before they are allowed to deal directly with the firm's clients. Most consulting firms charge a great deal of money for their services, and their clients would prefer consultants who have considerable industry experience in addition to sound academic training. Management consulting is exciting work; it gives the individual a chance to work with key decision makers in the client firm. One drawback, however, is that consultants are always just that — consultants. As such, they rarely experience the thrill of making the final decision since, by definition, the client can accept or reject their advice.

Marketing majors can work for any number of nonprofit enterprises. For example, their services are needed in almost any organization with a professional fund-raising program. They can help charity organizations position themselves in the mind of the public relative to other similar organizations. In addition, as previously mentioned, marketing-trained graduates have much to offer

FIGURE 21-6 Marketing People in Action

political candidates and parties. Lastly, marketing majors, to the extent that they are able to make reasoned decisions taking into account the needs of society, are of use to any government agency that must deal with the public.

Can you picture yourself in any of the snapshots of marketing people in action in Figure 21-6?

summary points

1. The marketing of nonprofit organizations involves more than just promotional decisions; the other elements of the market mix must be considered as well.

2. Since nonprofit institutions do compete with one another in their efforts to attract donations, the marketing concept can help the nonprofit firm differentiate its product from those of other good causes.

3. Nonprofit organizations must develop two marketing strategies: one directed to potential contributors and the other to potential users of the organization's product.

4. The marketing of nonprofit organizations involves at least three ethical questions: Is an aggressive marketing effort a misuse of operating funds that could be better spent in other ways? Are many good causes at a significant disadvantage in the race to attract donations because they cannot afford a marketing staff? Are many of the best financed causes the least beneficial to society?

5. Greater reliance on analytic techniques, the drive for more productivity, and the increasing intervention of the government in the marketplace will characterize marketing in the 1980s.

6. The consumer education movement in the 1970s was more concerned with showing consumers how to seek out and use available information than with providing new information.

7. Federal, state, and local governments as well as private nonprofit and profit organizations are involved in the consumer education movement.

8. Private firms will become increasingly involved in the consumer education business because it is the right thing to do and because they stand to benefit economically.

9. In the 1980s the average consumer will be better informed, more vocal, and less likely to put up with defective merchandise.

10. Materials shortages offer the firm a justification for deleting slow-moving items from the product line. It may also be necessary during shortages to quit serving weak customers and to modify advertising strategies.

11. Whatever the impact of shortages on the way the firm does business, shortages are not likely to render the marketing concept obsolete.

12. Why study marketing? Because most firms have adopted the marketing concept in one form or another. Because marketing combines creativity and objective analysis. Because marketing enables the practitioner to deal with real-world problems. Because the marketing concept can be extended to nonprofit and service-oriented organizations. Because marketing executives can move up to top ranks quickly in their firms.

13. The discipline of marketing can be broken down into seven concentrations: advertising, international business, marketing research, physical distribution, product management, retailing and wholesaling, and personal selling. Career opportunities for the marketing major exist in all these areas as well as in banking, management consulting, and nonprofit organizations.

questions for discussion

1. What does marketing have to offer nonprofit organizations?
2. How do nonprofit institutions compete with one another?
3. Is marketing for nonprofit organizations more complex than it is for profit-making firms? Explain your answer.
4. Will marketing be more of a science than an art in the 1980s?
5. What is meant by productivity? Will marketing be more productive in the 1980s than it has been in the past? Explain.
6. Many business executives distrust the federal government. Why? To what extent is this reaction justified?
7. How broadly based is the consumer education movement? Should private enterprise play a more active role in consumer education programs? In what ways?
8. Are there any risks in having private enterprise take the lead in consumer education programs? What are they and how might they be avoided?
9. What strategy or strategies should the firm adopt during periods of product shortages?
10. Will the marketing concept be a viable business philosophy in the 1980s?
11. Does marketing represent a meaningful career alternative for you? Analyze both the advantages and disadvantages of a career in marketing.
12. If you're thinking seriously about a career in marketing, in what area do you have the most interest? How do you plan to prepare for a career in this area?

cases
part 8
case 20
rocky mountain industrial cleaning corp.

Rocky Mountain Industrial Cleaning Corporation was founded in 1910 by Jess Totten. Initially the firm provided contract maintenance service for light industrial manufacturing firms, but is now no longer in the industrial cleaning business. Instead, it sells dishwashers and diswashing chemicals to restaurants, small businesses, and lodges. The equipment and chemicals it sells are not used in private homes, nor is the firm in a position to compete for the business of very large hospitals and large university dormitories.

The company's major competition comes first from the approach to cleaning dishes. Several major competitors of Rocky Mountain provide equipment that heats dishes to a very high temperature, thereby killing bacteria on the plates and sanitizing dishes. The other approach is to use a chemical to kill the bacteria without the use of very high heat. For many years the heat treatment was less expensive. Today, however, with the high cost of energy, the chemical process has a decided price advantage. In terms of the equipment itself, competition comes mostly from specialty houses such as Murphy Manufacturing Company of St. Louis. Major consumer product firms such as General Electric, Whirlpool, and Hotpoint do not manufacture this industrial equipment. Rocky Mountain is also responsible for installing and maintaining Murphy Manufacturing equipment in three states — Colorado, Utah, and Nevada.

Marketing Organization

Rocky Mountain's marketing department is directed by a vice president of marketing, to whom an advertising director and sales manager report directly. The firm does relatively little research, but what is done is conducted by an outside consultant at the University of Denver, who reports to the vice-president of marketing. Most of the staff marketing responsibilities are performed by the assistant to the vice-president of marketing and the marketing vice-president.

All Rocky Mountain products are sold by salespeople who are paid a salary plus a bonus for every new dishwasher system they sell. These salespeople are primarily high school graduates, although a few have some junior college experience. Rocky Mountain has a reputation for having technically competent salespeople who not only know chemicals but also are able to help with routine maintenance of dishwashers.

Current Sales

Sales of chemicals have grown at a relatively rapid rate during the last four years. Unit sales have increased an average of 7 percent per year during this period, and dollar sales have increased almost 17 percent per year. These figures reflect the fact that Rocky Mountain representatives have been able to take some customers away from other chemical distributors. Also, Rocky Mountain's representatives are able to instruct restaurant managers in the proper use of the chemicals. There is a tendency in this industry for restaurant managers to cut back a little bit on the chemicals, feeling that they don't need quite as much as recommended by the manufacturer. Rocky Mountain employees have been thoroughly trained to calculate the percentage of bacteria killed when the amount of chemicals used is reduced. Finally, the sales figure reflects the fact that sales of dishwashers have increased at approximately 1 percent per year.

In most years more than 90 percent of Rocky Mountain sales come from the sale of chemicals. Table 1 describes the financial data for Rocky Mountain's three territories.

TABLE 1   Financial Summary*

	Colorado	Utah	Nevada
Revenue	$900,000	$1,200,000	$600,000
Salespersons' salaries	135,000	32,000	40,000
Sales office expenditures	120,000	60,000	15,000
Depreciation on sales offices	15,000	9,000	12,000
Value of sales office	150,000	90,000	120,000
Advertising expenditures	130,000	25,000	30,000
Accounts receivable	90,000	100,000	25,000
Product demonstration	10,000	8,000	12,000
Corporate overhead	75,000	75,000	75,000

*Rocky Mountain uses 15 percent to calculate the cost of capital used in its organization.

Murphy's System 1000

Murphy Manufacturing Company has developed a new dishwashing system called System 1000. This system permits the restaurant to clean its dishes substantially quicker with less energy and less chemicals than do competitive products. The System 1000 is based on a combination of three different chemicals, a medium-temperature water, and a new water injection system. Murphy Manufacturing promotes the System 1000 as a substantial breakthrough for the commercial dishwasher business. It also has the potential of being modified to be used not only for restaurants but also for hospitals and other large institutions. While the System 1000 costs approximatley 20 percent more than most competitive products, a large institution should be able to break even on the added investment within the first two years of use because of the anticipated savings in chemicals and hot water.

Rocky Mountain has long felt that the best way to increase profitability was by selling more dishwashing systems. This would not only bring a substantial commission to the corporation, for its chemical products. To this end, Rocky Mountain sent three of its best salespeople and the sales manager to St. Louis for a three-day indoctrination program when the System 1000 was introduced five months ago. To date, Rocky Mountain has sold only two of the System 1000 units to restaurants and none to any other type of institution. It continues to sell a few of its traditional dishwashers as well.

The sales manager feels that one of the major problems has historically been that the sales representatives are not very effective at selling dishwashers. While these individuals are well trained and understand chemicals, they really do not understand the major advantages of various dishwashers, nor do they understand the financing problems and installation difficulties that are bound to concern the restaurant manager. To resolve this problem, the sales manager asked the sales representatives to attend Saturday sessions during which some of the intricacies of selling $60,000 dishwashing systems could be explained. The programs have dealt with professional selling, pricing strategies, an analysis of competition, and financial programs. While it is still a little early to judge the success or failure of this program, it does not appear to have generated a great deal of interest on the part of the salespeople. The underlying feeling of many of them is that they are being taken advantage of by being required to work on Saturday without special compensation.

The sales manager also feels that part of the problem is that there is no effective communication system to convey information from the field to the organization when new restaurants develop or when existing restuarants are considering installation of new dishwashing systems.

1. How profitable are the territories? Does the financial statement provide the data that Rocky Mountain needs to evaluate its marketing operation?
2. Should the firm reorganize itself to be more productive?
3. What type of information system should be created?

---

case 21
christian mission
home

The Christian Mission Home is a "home for unwed mothers" located near a large Southwestern metropolis. It is owned and supported by a religious denomination for the purposes of providing a residence for unmarried pregnant women and of serving as a licensed adoption agency.

The facility was built in 1968 to house up to 120 girls and provides modern living and recreational facilities. The Home attempts to provide an enjoyable atmosphere for young expectant mothers while they await the arrival of their babies.

The Home is open to young women from every background, but typically its clients come from the white, Protestant, middle class. The Home offers full maternity services to its clients, including food and lodging, prenatal and postnatal medical care for mother and child, and complete psychological counseling facilities. The fee for staying at the Home is $150 per month (plus medical expenses), but this covers only about 25 percent of actual costs; the difference is made up from adoption fees, government contracts, and contributions from churches. One notable feature of the fee schedule is that all of a woman's medical expenses and half of her housing are paid by the Home if she decides to release her baby for adoption after it is born.

The Situation in 1979

Given the recent changes in American attitudes toward extramarital sex, abortion, and women's liberation, the Home's current situation is not hard to imagine. The Home was operating at nearly full capacity as recently as 1971; however, by 1979 occupancy had fallen to only 20.7 pregnant residents per day. At the same time there has been a substantial increase in the number of couples seeking to adopt children through the auspices of the Home.

The Board of Directors of the Christian Mission Home is elected from members of the churches within the region of the country that the Home serves. Both lay people and clergy comprise the 65-member board. In 1978 the Home had gross revenues of $964,000 which came from the following sources: 45 percent, government agencies and contracts; 32 percent, adoptive and client fees; 16 percent, church contributions; and 7 percent, individual contributions. The Home's expenses that year were $923,795.

The Home has introduced a vocational training facility for physically handicapped adults. This has required some initial investment, but the program has been quite successful in its first two years of operation.

As a result of the development of the physical training center, the capacity for residents who are pregnant has been reduced to 40 girls. Nevertheless, the problem of the large number of requests from potential adoptive parents still persists. The home has recently initiated a number of activities to try to increase the number of women who choose to use the services of the Home.

One of these new ideas was based on the fact that parents who have previously adopted children tend to be extremely positive in their feelings about the value of the adoption alternative. The Home has been influential in getting past adoptive parents involved in speaking with counselors, guidance centers, and churches who have contact with unmarried pregnant women. These parents provide a vital link with local communities in explaining the services that the Home provides.

Assessment of Attitudes of Groups Served by the Home

Officials in the Home were convinced that most of the decline in occupancy was attributable to the increased use of abortion. The home commissioned a market researcher to attempt to assess attitudes of young women in the population usually served by the Home. A sample of over 300 young women was taken at two large high schools in a predominantly white, middle-class area of town and at a university whose student body was also largely white and middle class.

Three areas of interest were investigated: attitudes toward abortion, attitudes toward homes for unwed mothers, and attitudes toward adoption of children of unmarried mothers. In addition, the women were asked to select the agency they would most likely choose, if they were pregnant and unmarried, from the list of all such agencies listed in the phone book. Finally, the women were asked to rate their attitudes toward 10 hypothetical names of facilities for unwed mothers. No mention of the Christian Mission Home was made in the research.

The data indicated that the young women were relatively negative toward abortion and relatively positive toward homes for unwed mothers; at least three fourths responded that they disagreed or strongly disagreed with positive statements toward abortion, while only 17 percent expressed agreement with negative views toward homes. The women were also generally favorable toward the notion of adoption as an option for unmarried mothers. Only about one fourth of the women indicated negative feelings about adoption as an alternative. Also, somewhat to the surprise of the researchers, the Christian Mission Home was the agency most frequently listed as a choice for counseling in the case of problem pregnancy. Finally, a clear favorite emerged from the list of hypothetical names for a home for unwed mothers: The women chose "Regional Maternity Center" as the one most clearly conveying the services of the Home.

Cross-tabulation of responses indicated that the women most positive toward homes and negative toward abortion were those who were youngest, in high school, and who expressed a religious preference for one of the larger church denominations, particularly Catholic or Methodist.

To assess the attitudes of professionals who counsel pregnant women, interviews were conducted by two trained interviewers. Twenty-one counselors and gynecologists were contacted concerning their views on abortion, adoption, and homes for unwed mothers. Again, no mention of the Home was made. As was the case with the young women, the interviewees indicated that they were relatively unfavorable toward abortion, favorable toward adoption, and positive toward homes. Most counselors volunteered that they were "pro-choice"; that is, they emphasized that their practice was to discuss all possible alternatives with an unwed mother and encourage her to make her own decision in the light of her personal circumstances.

One of the interviewers was invited by one of the gynecologists she interviewed to be present at counseling sessions with two teenagers who had sought advice from the local Free Clinic. In both cases the interviewer noticed that the first thing that the doctor said after he had confirmed that the girls were pregnant was, "Do you want to terminate your pregnancy?" It was also noted that in both cases the girls had spontaneously mentioned that they had considered going to "a home," and in both cases the girls decided to have an abortion. In one case the girl had rejected the idea of a home when she learned that her parents would have to be told about it. Thus, it may be that a home for unwed mothers is an alternative that is frequently considered by pregnant girls but is rejected because of inconvenience or embarrassment.

The conclusion was drawn that both the young women in the community and the professionals who advised young unmarried women were generally not unfavorable to the adoption alternative advocated by the Home. Thus, it seems that young women and counselors are not *in principle* opposed to the adoption alternative or to homes; moreover, they may be *in principle* opposed to abortion. It is likely that the frequent choice of abortion in the case of a problem pregnancy results from an interaction between the high availability of abortion and the immediacy of a problem-pregnancy situation.

1. What market(s) is the home trying to serve?
2. How can the home most effectively communicate with its potential customers?
3. Design a marketing strategy for the home.

Glossary

advertising   Any paid form of nonpersonal presentation and promotion of ideas, goods, and services by an identified sponsor.

affirmative disclosure   Information about a product that may include facts about a deficiency or limitation.

agents   Intermediaries who facilitate buying and selling activities, but who do not take title to the products they ship, resell, or distribute.

arbitration   The process of negotiation whereby a third person acts as an impartial judge.

base stock   Inventory that is maintained to meet expected demand.

benefit segmentation   An assumption that markets can be defined on the basis of the benefits that people seek from the product.

brainstorming   Activity occurring when a small group of individuals with diverse backgrounds is brought together and asked to develop alternative problem-solving solutions.

brand   Name, term, sign, symbol, design, or combination of these which is intended to identify the goods or services of one seller or group of sellers so as to differentiate them from those of competitors.

break-even point   The number of units sold at which product revenues evenly match total product costs.

buying committee   A group of people, usually a buyer, merchandise manager, sales promotion manager, and store manager, that jointly decides the merits of buying new products or discontinuing the sale of existing products.

cash discounts   Price reductions intended to encourage buyers to pay their bills promptly.

cease and desist order   A ruling by the FTC requesting a firm to stop a specific business practice that it feels is an unfair method of competition.

census   A survey of the entire population.

centralized buying   Purchasing inventory on a company-wide basis.

chain stores   Two or more commonly owned outlets featuring centrally purchased merchandise.

channel of distribution   An organized network of agencies and institutions which, in combination, performs all the activities required to link producers with users and users with producers to accomplish the marketing task.

classical functionalism   A marketing approach that breaks the marketing task down into buying, selling, transporting, storing, standardizing and grading, financing, riskbearing, and collecting and disseminating marketing information without attempting to integrate the functions.

coercive reciprocity   One firm pressuring another to buy from it.

cognitive theory   Belief that habits are accrued by insights and thinking as well as by stimulus response.

commodity approach   Study of a vertical chain of distribution beginning with the producer and ending with the final consumer.

common carrier   Provides transportation services to any firm without discrimination.

communication   The process of making buyers aware of a product or service by means of personal selling and mass media promotional campaigns.

communication mix   The firm's combined promotional and public relations mix.

community shopping center   A shopping area that has a supermarket and/or pharmacy as well as a medium-sized department store.

competitive bid   A price quotation made in response to a public solicitation or a notice issued by a government agency.

concentrated marketing   A procedure whereby the firm aims at only a portion of the market, selecting one segment of the market and concentrating its efforts on that group.

consumer goods   Products produced for sale to individuals and families for personal consumption.

consumerism   A social movement whose objective is to increase the power of consumers relative to that of sellers.

consumer price index   A measure of the amount of inflation that exists in the economy at any point in time.

contribution margin   Revenue in excess of variable costs.

control   The set of activities concerned with determining whether satisfactory progress is being made toward the achievement of stated objectives.

convenience goods   Products that the consumer purchases frequently, immediately, and with a minimum of effort.

convenience stores   Retail stores for which the consumer, before a need for some product arises, possesses a preference map that indicates a willingness to buy from the most accessible store.

cooling-off rule   A rule by the FTC that a buyer can cancel the purchase of an item costing over $15 that has been purchased at home within 72 hours of the sale.

cooperative advertising   Retail advertising in which the cost is shared by the retailer and the manufacturer (or wholesaler) on a percentage basis.

cooperative chains   Chains organized by retailers to obtain a buying advantage through aggregated purchases that permit retailers to offer lower prices to consumers.

corporate planning officer   The individual in the firm that ensures that effective strategies are created.

corrective advertising   Advertising that is required by the FTC to remedy a false or deceptive statement about a product.

cost-oriented pricing   Pricing a product on the basis of its cost.

creative presentation   The method of communicating a buying proposal to the public.

cue   A weak stimulus in the environment that determines how an individual will react to a drive.

culture   A set of values, ideas, attitudes, and other symbols and objects created by people which shape human behavior.

cumulative quantity discount   A price discount for which the buyer may qualify based on the quantity of goods purchased over a period of time, often one year.

DAGMAR   (defining advertising goals for measured advertising results) An advertising approach that defines an advertising goal as a specific effect to be produced in a defined target audience over a given time period.

decentralized buying   A buying arrangement whereby each store or group of stores in a conglomerate makes its own purchase decisions.

decline   The final stage of product life cycle that is characterized by consumers beginning to switch to other products that come closer to meeting their changing needs.

demarketing   Attempts to discourage customers from demanding large quantities of products that are in short supply.

demographics   Population characteristics that provide easily understood and measurable data; usually related to income, social class, ethnic and racial backgrounds, age, and family life cycle.

derived demand   For industrial goods; is dependent on, or derived from, the ultimate demand for consumer goods into which the industrial goods are transformed.

developmental marketing   Process of converting latent demand into actual demand.

differential marketing   A marketing strategy of serving the whole market by designing different products and/or marketing programs for each segment within the market.

differential pricing   The sale of a product at price differentials that do not compare to differences in costs.

diffusion of innovation   A discussion of how products are adopted, who adopts them, and the attributes of innovations.

direct exporting   Exporting in which the manufacturer performs all the required tasks to export its products.

direct observation   A method of primary data collection where buyers' actions are observed in the marketplace.

distribution   the process and the institutions necessary for getting products from manufacturers to users.

divisibility   The degree to which a new product can be used on a small scale for purposes of evaluation by the buyer.

draw   A compensation method wherein a salesperson is given a specified level of income each month in spite of a sales drop.

drive   A strong internal stimulus impelling action.

early adopters   A new product adopter category that consists of people who are highly likely to purchase a new product close to its time of introduction.

early majority   A new product adopter category whose new product purchasing habits are deliberate.

economic man   A rational decision maker who evaluates the consequences of each variable in the purchase decision process, one at a time, in a stepwise manner.

economic order quantity   The amount of inventory that should be ordered at any one point in time.

economies of scale   As more products are produced or sold the firm is able to reduce its per item cost as fixed costs are spread over more units.

ego drive   The need to succeed that most successful salespeople possess.

elastic demand   A condition describing a situation when a reduction in price results in the sale of enough additional units to increase total revenue for that product.

elasticity   A term that describes the effects of price reductions or increases on total revenue for the product being sold.

empathy   The ability to see problems as the customer sees them.

environment   External variables over which the firm is unable to exercise control.

environmental scanning   The part of the strategic planning process that involves monitoring the environment to determine its impact on the firm's strategy.

exchange controls   The regulation of the movement of funds outside a country.

exclusive agreement   The seller, as a condition of the sale, forbids the buyer to purchase for resale the products of competitive sellers.

exclusive distribution   When a product is made available through one or only a few outlets in any trading area.

exempt carrier   Carriers that are not regulated in terms of what they charge their clients.

expected profit   The amount of profit that the supplier would receive on the average from a particular bid.

experience survey   A type of exploratory research in which knowledgeable people are asked about the problem under investigation.

exploratory research   Study to provide a tentative explanation of the issue in question.

export management company   An independent firm that provides most of the services of an in-house exporting department.

expropriation   When a host country takes the physical assets of a foreign company without providing compensation.

external secondary data   Previously generated data originating from outside the firm.

faltering demand   A situation in which the demand for a product has fallen off.

family brand   A description used when most of a firm's products bear the same name and are sold under that name.

family life cycle   A segmentation variable that combines the characteristics of age, marital status, and age of children.

financial resources   A firm's assets, excluding physical plant and inventories, that represent the purchasing power available to the firm to carry out its business.

fixed costs   Costs that do not vary with the level of production or sales.

flexible break-even analysis   Estimates of the total revenue for a product based on the expected sales volume for the product at varying prices.

FOB   (Free on Board) The seller loads the merchandise aboard a transportation vehicle, at which time the buyer takes title to the merchandise and has the responsibility for any transportation charges beyond loading.

FOB delivered   The manufacturer pays the entire cost of the delivery to the buyer.

focus group interview   A type of motivation research designed to uncover consumer motivation by convening a number of people and interviewing them as a group.

franchise   A contractual relationship under which the franchisor permits the franchisee to sell its products under a strict set of rules, to display the franchisor's sign, and to call upon the marketing and operating assistance of the franchisor; the franchisee pays the franchisor a fee.

freight-absorption pricing   When the delivery charge for a product to a customer is based on the delivery charges that the firm's competitor located closest to the buyer would charge.

frequency   The number of times an individual or household is exposed to an advertisement via a given medium.

Freudian psychoanalytic model   The belief that individuals are motivated by symbolic as well as economic functional concerns.

full demand   When current demand is equal to the firm's ability to supply the desired product.

full warranty   A condition in which the seller must assume a set of governmentally-mandated duties and responsibilities about the product.

functional organization   The organization structure in which each of the major marketing functions reports directly to the chief marketing officer.

general demarketing   An attempt to reduce overall demand for a product.

geographical control unit   A geographic area that the sales manager uses as a unit of analysis when assigning salespeople to territories.

hierarchy of needs   Maslow's theory that individuals rank need in terms of their importance.

horizontal price fixing   When two or more firms get together to establish a product's price.

human resources   Management and labor force, whose variables include experience, formal and informal training, and general abilities, employed by the firm

hypermarkets   A type of discount-generated merchandise store that sells groceries as well as most other products sold by department stores.

hygiene factors   Needs stemming from individuals' built-in drive to avoid pain; found in the job environment in company policy, administration, working conditions, and salary.

index of buying power   An objective way of forecasting sales relying on a territory's past retail sales, income, and percent of the population.

indirect channel   Distribution route using an intermediary, such as a wholesaler, in getting goods from the manufacturer to the retailer.

indirect exporting   The process of a firm selling its merchandise abroad without making special efforts on its own behalf; frequently entails achieving foreign sales through domestic operations or export management companies.

industrial goods   Products and services sold to commercial enterprises, governmental agencies, and nonprofit institutions for use in the production of their goods and services or for resale to other industrial customers.

inelastic demand   A condition describing a decrease in total revenue as a result of a decrease in price.

innocent reciprocity   An integrated buying and selling relationship between suppliers and customers without organized, coercive efforts; people doing business with their friends.

innovators   A new product adopter category that is eager to adopt new products and is characterized by an obsession with venturesomeness.

institutional approach   The study of specific marketing institutions.

intensive distribution   The level of distribution in which a product is made available to the public through as many retail outlets as possible.

internal secondary data   Previously generated data obtained from within the firm.

invited bid   A price quotation made by a single supplier or a small group of suppliers at the request of the procuring agency; usually occurs when state or local governments make reasonably small purchases.

joint ventures   The purchase of a percentage of a foreign business by a foreign company.

kinked demand curve   A description of the condition occurring when (1) price increases result in declining product revenues, assuming no change in competitive prices, and (2) price reductions do not increase revenues because competitors also lower their prices.

laboratory experiment   A type of primary data collection technique where the subjects participate in a controlled experiment.

laggards   The last people, among the new product adopter categories, to accept innovation.

late majority   A new product adopter category that views innovations from a cautious, skeptical perspective and acts out of economic necessity or unrelenting peer pressure in the purchase of new products.

latent demand   Demand state that exists when there is a significant, unmet need.

law of diminishing returns   The utility of each additional unit of the same product decreases as more units are consumed.

learning   The process by which a pattern of behavior is established or modified by means of a stimulus response or cognition mechanism; it does not include native response tendencies or temporary states such as fatigue.

licensing   An arrangement in which one firm, normally a manufacturer (licensor), gives another firm (licensee) the right to make and sell a product for a fee.

life-style segmentation   A segmentation technique that involves looking at the customer as a "whole" person rather than as a set of isolated parts.

list price   The established, publicly announced price for which the firm expects to sell a product.

loss leaders   Products sold below cost that the seller promotes to get people into the store.

macromarketing   The role of the marketing system in distributing goods and services to society.

maintenance marketing   The job of the marketing executive when full demand exists.

Management by Objectives (MBO)   A situation in which managers and personnel jointly identify performance goals and strategies for reaching these goals, using the agreed-upon objectives to grade performance.

managerial marketing   An approach to marketing that integrates the marketing functions into a coordinated effort.

marginal utility   The added satisfaction obtained from buying another unit of a given product.

markdown   A reduction from the original price.

market development   The first stage of the life of a successful product.

market-grid concept   A marketing approach focusing on the needs of consumers, not on the product; views the market as a matrix divided by relevant segmentation criteria, with each matrix cell representing a smaller, more homogeneous market.

marketing audit   A marketing review, both diagnostic and prognostic, concerned with both the past and the future.

marketing concept   The business philosophy that states that the firm must first identify needs in the marketplace and then provide a product to the market to meet those needs.

marketing information system (MIS)   The means by which the firm coordinates the various marketing functions and integrates the activities of the marketing department with those of the company as a whole through the collection of relevant data.

marketing mix   The four variables (price, product, distribution, and communication) that are available to the marketing executive to sell a product.

marketing research   Systematic gathering, recording, and analyzing of data about problems relating to the marketing of goods and services.

market organization   The organization structure which is based on market managers reporting directly to the chief marketing officer.

markup pricing   The practice of setting a price by adding a fixed percentage of the cost of the product.

maturity   The fourth stage in the product life cycle, which is characterized by a stable number of competitors, a large number of models, price stability, selective demand, greatly reduced margins, an extensive number of dealers, and low per-unit price.

merchant wholesalers   Wholesalers who take title and possession of the products as well as provide a complete line of services to their customers.

micromarketing   The process of formulating and implementing a product development, distribution, pricing, and communication strategy enabling the firm to earn a profit.

motivation   The drives, urges, wishes, or desires that initiate the sequence of events known as behavior.

motivators   Elements that contribute to satisfaction by fulfilling the need to grow psychologically.

need   A deprivation felt when physical or emotional balance, or homeostasis, is disturbed.

new product   A product that either performs a new function or provides a significant improvement over existing products.

new product committee   A committee consisting of the senior executives from the firm who evaluate new products.

new product department   A department with a small staff whose entire responsibility is to evaluate new products.

objectives   Specific statements about what a firm expects to accomplish with respect to specific products as a result of its strategy.

odd/even pricing   The belief that customers would rather pay an odd price than an even price for a product.

open to buy   An estimate that indicates how much should be purchased at any particular time of the month. (Formula: Open to buy = planned sales + planned reductions − current inventory − merchandise on order)

opinion survey   A polling of either a group of executives or the sales representatives as to their expectations regarding future sales.

opportunity cost   A cost that accrues to the organization because it fails to take some specific action.

overfull demand   The condition existing when demand is significantly greater than supply.

penetration pricing   Introducing a new product at a low price.

perception   The process by which individuals become aware of (through any of the five senses) and give meaning to their environment.

physical resources   Plant, equipment, and mineral resources.

planned purchases   How much the firm expects to purchase for a month (planned EOM + planned sales + planned reductions − planned BOM).

policies   Statements that restrict a firm's behavior.

population   All individuals who are part of a group under study.

positioning   Building readily identifiable images for a product.

post-purchase dissonance   The concern of consumers that the product selection choices they have made, especially when the product is expensive relative to their incomes, are not correct.

premiums   Nonmerchandise-related objects included in products' packages.

prestige pricing   The situation in which a higher price will attract more buyers to the product.

preticketing   Occurs when a vendor places a tag on each product, listing its price, manufacturer, size, identification number, and color.

price   What the seller feels a product is worth, in terms of money, to the buyer; frequently tied to the price of competing products in the marketplace.

price discrimination   When a product is sold to two firms at different prices.

price lining   The practice of pricing merchandise within traditional or market-determined price ranges.

price skimming   Introducing a new product at an artificially high price.

pricing objectives   The representation of the firm's overall pricing goals or targets.

pricing policies   The framework through which the firm translates its pricing objectives into actual market pricing tactics.

pricing tactics.   The determination of how the firm should establish its price.

primary data   Information collected by the researcher specifically for the problem under investigation.

primary demand stimulation   A situation taking place when the firm concentrates expenditures on persuading the public it should purchase the type of product in question; not concerned with whether customers actually buy its product.

private (dealer) brands   Brands created and owned by channel intermediaries.

private carrier   A transportation mode that is owned by the company that ships the product.

product   All factors that the consumer considers when making a purchase; a bundle of satisfactions or utilities to the purchaser

production orientation   The business philosophy that states that the firm focuses on selling the product, not on meeting the needs of the marketplace.

product item   An individual product or service.

productivity   The amount of output generated by a given amount of input.

product life cycle   A planning tool that illustrates the stages connected with profits, competition, sales, product design, communication, and distribution that all successful products undergo.

product line   A category or group of products.

product manager   An individual who is reponsible for designing a product strategy but does not have the authority to implement it.

product mix   The composite of all products offered for sale by a firm.

product organization   The organization structure that uses product managers as the key to developing strategies for the firm's products.

promotional discount   A price discount that is given to encourage the buyer to purchase a product that would not otherwise be purchased.

promotional mix   An element of the firm's external communication process that involves personal selling, sales promotion, and advertising.

psychological pricing   Pricing a product with the understanding that some non-economic forces affect buyers' reaction to products.

publicity   Any unpaid form of nonpersonal communication regarding a firm or its products or services.

public relations mix   Communicates the firm's corporate image through institutional advertising, publicity, and face-to-face communications, such as audiovisual presentations or company tours.

puffery   Innocent exaggerations used to sell a product.

purchasing agent   A professional buyer.

pure competition   An economic condition existing in a market when there are many manufacturers selling homogeneous products to many buyers with no government intervention; further, all products are sold at the prevailing market price, all buyers and sellers have perfect information, and both human and capital resources must be free to move to the location that yields the highest return on investment.

quantity discount   A discount granted on a product price because a large order has been placed.

random sample   When each person in the population has an equal chance of being selected as a part of the sample.

rapid growth   The life cycle stage in which sales rise faster than at any other point in a product's life cycle.

reach   The total audience a medium actually covers.

reciprocity   The use of purchasing power to obtain sales, coupled with the practice of preferring one's customers in purchasing.

reference group   A set of individuals that influences another individual when he or she makes a decision.

regional shopping centers   The largest type of shopping center; one having several major anchor department stores.

reinforcement   A positive and rewarding reaction to a response.

relative advantage   The degree to which a new product is perceived as superior to existing products.

remarketing   The stage involving a complete reexamination of the market to be served, the product's distinguishing features, and its marketing strategy.

resident buying office   An organization that facilitates the purchase and inventory planning decisions of retailers located in distant communities.

resources   The productive inputs used by the firm to manufacture its products.

response   The individual's reaction to a cue.

restraint of trade   Actions taken by two or more firms that are designed to restrict competition in the marketplace.

safety stock   Inventory that is maintained to meet unanticipated demand.

sales branch   A manufacturer-owned wholesaler who maintains inventory.

sales office   A manufacturer-owned wholesaler who does not maintain inventory.

sales promotion   Refers to displays, participation in trade shows or fairs, free samples, premiums, and contests.

sample   A group of people such that the results of surveying that group can be accurately generalized to the entire population.

scrambled merchandising   The practice of selling nonrelated lines of merchandise.

seasonal discounts   Discounts off a product's price because the product is sold during a specific season of the year.

secondary data   Information collected at an earlier time and for reasons other than solving the problem currently under investigation.

segmental analysis   An accounting system that attempts to match revenues with the costs that are directly associated with them.

segmentation   A demand-oriented approach that involves modifying the firm's product and/or marketing strategies to fit the needs of individual market groups rather than those of the aggregate market.

selective demand   Emphasizing those qualities of a particular product, service, or organization which are instrumental in developing awareness and favorable attitudes on the part of the general public.

selective demarketing   Limiting the demand of only certain segments (portions) of the market.

selective distribution   State occurring when a product is sold by a number of retailers but not by all the retailers in a community who could carry it.

selective perception   A situation occurring when only a few signals that are constantly seen are converted into messages.

services   Activities and benefits offered for sale.

shared monopoly   When two or more firms so dominate a market that other firms are unable to enter the market.

shopping goods   Items for which the potential customer normally examines factors such as quality, price, and style before making a purchase decision.

shopping stores   Stores for which consumers have not developed a complete preference map relative to the products they wish to buy, necessitating a search of these stores to construct a map prior to purchase.

social class   A rather permanent and homogeneous group of individuals who have similar behavior, interests, and life-styles.

sorting   The distribution channel function of buying in large quantities and rearranging them in suitable combinations for resale.

specialty goods   Products for which people are willing to make a special purchasing effort.

specialty stores   Stores for which, prior to need arousal, the consumer possesses a preference map that indicates a willingness to buy the item from this type of establishment even though it may not be the most accessible one.

stimulational marketing   The task of converting no demand to positive demand.

stock turnover   The number of times the average inventory for the firm is sold in one year.

storytelling   A type of motivation research where the subject is asked to respond to a visual or verbal stimulus.

straight commission   A compensation plan where the subject is asked to respond to a visual or verbal stimulus.

straight salary   A compensation plan in which a salesperson is paid the same amount of money regardless of how many units are sold.

strategic positioning   A market analysis best accomplished by looking at the long-term product/market attractiveness and competitive position of each market.

strategy   A set of plans, programs, and policies guiding managers in achieving their objectives.

stratified random sample   A research tool in which the population is broken down into strata, or subunits, from each of which a random sample is then selected.

subculture   A distinct cultural group existing as an identifiable segment within a larger culture.

subjective perception   The inability of individuals to perceive an object in the same way.

summative perception   The reception and recognition of messages as a cumulative effect of multiple signals.

survey   A systematic technique used to gather information by asking a group of people a series of questions.

test marketing   The process by which a firm makes a product available in a limited geographic area in order to determine the product's commercial viability.

time and place utility   Delivering a product or service at the right time and to the right place.

time-series analysis   The development of a sales forecast as a function of time rather than of any particular market variable.

trade advertising   Advertising that is directed at members of the channel of distribution.

traffic concept   The narrowest of three definitions of distribution wherein obtaining the best rates and routes is critical.

trademark   The legal grant to a seller giving such protection to a brand that it may not be used by anyone else.

transfer pricing   A pricing method used when corporations sell products from one of their divisions to another.

turbulence   The product life cycle stage in which the rate of sales increase for the product declines as new competitors begin to take sales away from the original manufacturer.

tying agreement   The situation occurring when a seller agrees to sell or lease a product to a customer on the condition that the customer also purchase other, often unwanted, merchandise.

undifferentiated marketing   Treating the market as an aggregate and focusing on what consumers have in common rather than on what makes them different.

undifferentiated products   When all competing products are basically the same.

uniform delivered pricing   Condition occurring when the seller charges all buyers the same delivery price regardless of their location.

unitary elasticity   A condition occurring when a change in price has no effect on total revenue.

vendor analysis   The method used to determine which vendors with which to do business.

vertical price fixing   When two or more firms in a distribution channel conspire to establish the price of a product.

venture management team   A collaboration of managers from the different functional areas of the enterprise who evaluate a new product idea and, if the product appears to have sufficient profit potential, carry it through to commercialization.

voluntary chain   A group organized by a wholesaler to combat large, integrated retailers.

want   The awareness of a need.

wholesalers   Intermediaries who perform certain marketing functions for their customers (usually retailers) and their suppliers (usually manufacturers).

ACKNOWLEDGMENTS

The following firms and individuals granted permission for the use of the listed photographs:

PART 1 p. 12: Richard Ustinich/THE IMAGE BANK; p. 14: © Freelance Photographers Guild, Pastner; p. 26: McDonald's Corporation; p. 38: Farmer Jack Supermarkets of Michigan; p. 38: © BLACK STAR, Bert Miller, 1979; p. 44: Trends & Associates, Inc. (a subsidiary of Beverage Management, Inc.); p. 67: The Bettmann Archive, Inc.; p. 76: Tim Kilby/UNIPHOTO.

PART 2 p. 135: Hazeltine Corporation.

PART 3 p. 242: TASS from SOVFOTO; p. 265: General Motors Corporation; p. 269: The Bettmann Archive, Inc.

PART 4 p. 284: Ford Motor Company and American Telephone & Telegraph Company; p. 310: Hanes Corporation; p. 337: ARA Services, Inc.

PART 5 p. 348: Photograph courtesy of NCR Corporation; p. 365: NW Ayer ABH International.

PART 6 p. 408: 3M Company (Transportation and Commercial Graphics Division) and White Advertising (a subsidiary of Whiteco Industries); p. 434: Westinghouse Electric Corporation; p. 442: Canteen Corporation; p. 457: Z.C.M. I., Salt Lake City (Ron Nelson, display director; Les Stewart, designer) courtesy of *Visual Merchandising*, Cincinnati, OH; p. 468: Broadway Plaza Management Services; p. 480: © Ernie Danek; p. 497: Philip Morris Incorporated; p. 499: Cary Wolinsky/STOCK BOSTON; p. 506: photograph courtesy of NCR Corporation; p. 509: Rapistan Incorporated.

PART 7 p. 520: The Coca-Cola Company; p. 529: American Airlines; p. 537: © Bohdan Hrynewych/STOCK BOSTON; p. 549: Sears, Roebuck and Co.; p. 555: McDonald's Corporation; p. 557: J. R. Holland/BLACK STAR.

PART 8 p. 572: © Environmental Communications, 1969; p. 624: The Charter Company and The Pillsbury Company

Name Index

Subject Index